SOUTH-WESTERN
Human Relations
2nd Edition

Marie Dalton, Ed.D.
San Jacinto College, Pasadena, TX

Dawn G. Hoyle
NASA–Johnson Space Center, Houston, TX

Marie W. Watts, SPHR
Marie W. Watts and Associates, Houston, TX

D0221850

VISIT US ON THE INTERNET
www.swep.com
www.thomsonlearning.com

South-Western
EDUCATIONAL PUBLISHING
Thomson Learning™

Australia • Canada • Denmark • Japan • Mexico • New Zealand • Philippines
Puerto Rico • Singapore • South Africa • Spain • United Kingdom • United States

Peter McBride: Business Unit Director
Eve Lewis: Team Leader/Executive Editor
Laurie Wendell: Project Manager
Alan Biondi, Cynthia Clampitt: Editors
Patricia Matthews Boies: Production Manager
Gordon Woodside: Manufacturing Coordinator
Mark Linton: Marketing Manager
Linda Wasserman: Marketing Coordinator
Lou Ann Thesing: Cover Design
IMBUE Design: Internal Design
Better Graphics: Composition

All photos copyright PhotoDisc Inc. 1997–'99 except where otherwise noted in the text.

All cartoons copyright Ted Goff.

ISBN: 0-538-72223-1

4 5 6 7 8 9 0 DC 05 04 03 02

Printed in the United States of America

For permission to use material from this text or product, contact us by
Web: www.thomsonrights.com
Phone: 1-800-730-2214
Fax: 1-800-730-2215

Table of Contents

CHAPTER 11 Leadership: *Styles and Skills of an Effective Leader*

CHAPTER 12 Appreciating Power: *Positioning and Politics*

CHAPTER 13 Change: *A Constant in an Inconstant World*

Preface

The world has changed, and a major theme today is connection—electronic, social, personal, intellectual, global. . . And that is the way learning should occur. Increasingly, learners want more than just an understanding of the concepts of human relations. They want to be able to apply the concepts through connections that are important in their daily lives. This edition of *Human Relations* connects you to the issues, challenges, and applications you will encounter in the twenty-first century.

The original intent of the book remains:
1. to provide some of the most intriguing and important aspects of human relations as seen in action in organizations and in personal lives;
2. to serve as basic study in business or social sciences; and
3. to form a solid foundation for further study, practice, and training in a variety of disciplines and industries.

This second edition contains over 30 percent new material representing new trends, additional concepts, and up-to-date connections communicated through the combined experience of three human relations professionals. A new chapter organization and design offer an accessible and practical format with dynamic new features.

FEATURES OF HUMAN RELATIONS 2nd EDITION

The following new features have been built into the second edition of *Human Relations*:

Features of *Human Relations*

- High impact *Connections* features on technology, global issues, ethics, SCANS skills, and diversity
- *Case Studies in the News* pulled from today's business headlines
- *Fast Chat* questions for review and discussion throughout each chapter
- *Chapter Projects* with workplace communication applications
- *QuickTips* success strategies from human relations and business professionals and others from a variety of fields
- New chapter organization that balances theory with more opportunities for skill building and application

---

REAL-WORLD PERSPECTIVE

Offering a dynamic real-world perspective to human relations, this book has more of the issues with which readers can connect:

- Diversity and global issues
- The impact of technology and the Internet
- Ethics and social responsibility
- Communication in the workplace
- Creative problem solving
- Personal and professional concerns in business today
- Customer service and teamwork
- Group dynamics and teambuilding
- Change dynamics
- Job search and career planning strategies
- Case studies from real workplaces

The book also has more applications for learners to build skills and solve problems, including:

- Hands-on activities and chapter projects
- Role playing and teambuilding activities
- Correlation to essential SCANS workplace competencies
- Extensive questions for review and self-assessment
- Workplace writing and communication in every chapter
- Internet and technology applications

TEXT ORGANIZATION

Chapter 1 is an introduction that motivates students by making clear why studying human relations is important. This chapter also provides an organizational and historical framework for the study of human relations.

Chapter 2 explains how our perception of people, events, and things can determine the nature of our relationships, while **Chapter 3** is a summary of current and past thinking about why people act as they do.

Chapter 4 suggests effective ways to solve problems and improve the quality of decisions. It also includes a lively discussion of creativity, its importance to organizational survival, and ways to foster it in ourselves and others. **Chapter 5** identifies organizational structures and discusses the strengths and weakness of the most common types of organizations.

Chapter 6, Group Dynamics, stresses the evolving importance of groups at work and explores aspects of group interaction. **Chapter 7** discusses the need for team concepts in the work environment and how teams can increase productivity. Several types of teams are presented as well as how to build an effective team. **Chapter 8** discusses the status of unions today.

Chapter 9 is a comprehensive study of communications. It covers various types of communication—verbal, nonverbal, written, and listening—and explores barriers that impede communication between people. **Chapter 10** presents a helpful, how-to-oriented approach to setting and achieving objectives. Its discussion of performance appraisal is unique in that it suggests ways that employees can make this a more pleasant, useful experience with growth opportunities for themselves and their supervisors.

Chapter 11 covers function and styles of leadership, while **Chapter 12** discusses sources and uses of power. It challenges readers to develop their own bases of power, and shows them how to do it.

Chapter 13 discusses change dynamics and includes a helpful section on coaching and counseling. Job-seeking skills are covered in **Chapter 14**, including how to look for a job, apply for it, and interview for it.

Chapter 15 presents a subject gaining renewed respect in today's depersonalized world, business etiquette. It emphasizes the important role that etiquette plays in our success today and presents guidelines regarding the current topics of office politics, networking, mentoring, and office romances.

Three chapters in particular challenge students to think for themselves by addressing contemporary topics. **Chapter 16** discusses ethics at work, **Chapter 17** substance abuse, and **Chapter 18** employee rights.

The last two chapters are additional strengths of the book. **Chapter 19** presents information for developing a personal wellness program, and **Chapter 20** includes updated projections for the twenty-first century and suggests ways of preparing for the changes it is bringing.

CHAPTER ORGANIZATION

This textbook was written to develop critical thinking and make connections with critical issues. To this end, each chapter is introduced with objectives that the reader should meet after studying the chapter.

Throughout the chapters are activities, experiential exercises, and "Fast Chats" calling for personal involvement. Since human relations means interaction among people, the more participative the class can become, the more students can learn from each activity.

SUPPLEMENTARY MATERIALS

Human Relations, 2nd Edition is supported by extensive tools that make teaching and training easier:

- Comprehensive Instructor's Manual with an explanation of the focus of each chapter, a chapter preview, presentation outline including suggested placement of exercises and applications, teaching-learning suggestions, key terms definitions, suggested responses to review questions, and suggested responses to discussion questions
- CNN videos on *Contemporary Career Issues* and *Diversity in the Workplace* to offer viewers an opportunity to analyze real human relations issues
- PowerPoint Presentation disk and Teaching Masters to be used with the supplementary activities
- Electronic Test Bank containing hundreds of questions for review and assessment

SkillSoft

Available through SkillSoft Corporation is a comprehensive library of web-based education products focused on a wide range of business and professional development skills such as management, leadership, communication, team building, and strategic planning. These SkillSoft courses provide self-paced training solutions—available in standalone CD-ROM or Web-based delivery that can be tailored to meet your Human Relations and Management needs.

For more information visit *www.skillsoft.com* or call Thomson Learning at 1-800-874-2383.

ACKNOWLEDGMENTS

Many people have contributed to the development of this text. The authors and publisher are grateful for the suggestions and contributions of the following reviewers on this edition and the first edition of *Human Relations*:

Mildred J. Blowen, Vice President, PTI, Inc., Houston, Texas
Susan Chin, formerly of DeVry Institute of Technology, Decatur, Georgia
Maxine Gross Christenson, Aims Community College, Greeley, Colorado
Rena R. Doering, Ph.D., San Antonio College, San Antonio, Texas
Lucy Guin, Directory of Education for Proprietary Schools, Houston, Texas
Charles R. Holloman, Augusta College, Augusta, Georgia
F. Stuart Keene, President, PTI, Inc., Houston, Texas
Richard C. Kogelman, Delta College, University Center, Michigan
Patricia Laidler, Massasoit Community College, Brockton, Massachusetts
Gloria McDonnell, Kingsborough Community College, Brooklyn, New York
Jean S. Nettelfield, St. Philips' College, San Antonio, Texas
Carol O'Grady, Tampa Technical Institute, Tampa, Florida
Marilyn Price, Kirkwood Community College, Cedar Rapids, Iowa
Carla Rich, Pensacola Junior College, Pensacola, Florida
Connie Roberts, Central Washington University, Ellensburg, Washington
Beverly Stitt, Southern Illinois University, Carbondale, Illinois
Peter B. Venuto, Ph.D., Bloomsburg University, Bloomsburg, Pennsylvania
Emily Volavka, Southern Ohio College, Fairfield, Ohio
Darlene Waite, Miami-Jacobs College of Business, Dayton, Ohio
Arlene White, Texas State Technical Institute, Waco, Texas
Rita Youngbauer, Pine Technical College, Pine City, Minnesota

We offer our gratitude to our past and present students who helped clarify our thinking of what a human relations book should be and to future students and instructors who use this book as a reference and learning aid. If this book makes your teaching-learning journey more pleasant, we would like to hear from you. Please contact us through South-Western Publishing if you have suggestions for how we might incorporate additional connections in future editions. Have a pleasant journey in getting to know yourselves and others!

Marie Dalton
Dawn Hoyle
Marie Watts

ABOUT THE AUTHORS

Marie Dalton, Ed.D.

Dr. Marie Dalton is Manager of Business Process Re-engineering for Continuing Education and Corporate Training for the San Jacinto College District in Houston, Texas. Her extensive professional experience includes positions as dean of continuing education, community college instructor, university professor, corporate trainer in the petrochemical and aerospace industries, and consultant to business and education in the areas of human relations, management, and communications. A successful author and popular speaker, Dr. Dalton has published four texts and numerous articles and has made dozens of presentations to international, national, state, and community groups.

Dawn G. Hoyle

Dawn G. Hoyle is a Human Relations Specialist and President of Hoyle and Associates. She has developed and conducted training seminars for major private industry and public sector organizations in the areas of communication, leadership, change dynamics, strategic planning, and time and stress management. Ms. Hoyle has also worked for 33 years with the NASA Johnson Space Center and is currently a Business Manager for the Office of the Comptroller matrixed to the Space Operations Management Office. She is also an Instructor in the Continuing Education Department at San Jacinto College, teaching courses on Human Behavior and Effective Supervision. She devotes her spare time to several programs for underprivileged youths and adult volunteer programs for improving job skills and literacy abilities.

Marie W. Watts,
SPHR

Marie Watts heads human relations activities in the Houston, Texas area for Petroleum Geo-Services, an international company that provides a variety of services for the oil exploration and production industry. Additionally, she is owner of her own human relations consulting firm, Marie W. Watts and Associates, that specializes in training in human relations skills, mediation, and discrimination investigations. Formerly with the Equal Employment Opportunity Commission, Ms. Watts investigated and supervised investigations of charges of discrimination in the workplace. From these activities, she developed a heightened awareness of how crucial human relations skills are to success in the workplace.

Human Relations:

The Key to Personal and Career Success

focus

Why are certain people successful? An article in *Small Business Monthly* (September 1998), which featured interviews with CEOs of the top 50 woman-owned businesses in Houston, helped answer this question.

When these 50 women, heads of companies ranging from aerospace to construction, were asked to share lessons they had learned as they climbed to the top in their different fields, almost half attributed success to good relations with others. The aspects of human relations they viewed as contributing to success included respecting others and having high ethical standards, treating other people "as you want to be treated," and listening to and appreciating customers. Other success factors named were having a positive attitude, empowering employees, communicating with customers and suppliers, dealing fairly with customers and employees, and always remembering those who "helped you reach your goals."

Based on the above news story, how do you think human relations skills can help business owners? How will human relations help you? What might you expect to learn in a study of human relations?

objectives

After studying this chapter, you should be able to:

1. *Explain the meaning of human relations.*

2. *Discuss the importance of human relations skills.*

3. *Trace the development of human relations in business.*

4. *Explain what factors influence human relations in organizations.*

5. *Identify how you can contribute to the objectives of an organization and how the study of human relations will help you succeed in your career.*

6. *Discuss some ways that technology is changing the world of work and affecting human relations.*

In This Chapter

What Is Human Relations?

1.1

You will find the study of human relations to be helpful and interesting—because it is about you and your interactions with others. Also, you will be able to use the material immediately. **Human relations** is the study of relationships among people. Your relationships can develop in organizational or personal settings and can be formal or informal, close or distant, conflicting or cooperating, one-on-one or within groups. Through this study you will learn skills that will help you achieve your personal and professional goals and help you contribute to organizational goals. Away from work your relations may include parents, siblings, children, spouses, and friends. On the job your relationships may be with subordinates, coworkers, supervisors or other superiors, or clients and customers.

Poor human relations skills can cost us.

"If I knew the secret of getting along with others, would I be sitting up here on a cold rock all by myself?"

Human relations, the study of relationships among people, will help you interact effectively with others.

Strengthening your human relations skills involves an understanding of your own psychology and that of others, the use of effective communication skills, and an appreciation for groups and their dynamics. The more you know about what motivates people and affects their morale, about setting goals and monitoring performance, and about how change can be managed, the stronger your human relations skills will be. Also key elements of good human relations skills are being aware of the sources and uses of power, gaining problem solving and decision making skills, and understanding creativity, team building, and legal and ethical considerations.

Quick tip . . . .

Dale Carnegie, in his 1936 book, *How to Win Friends and Influence People*, provided these guidelines, which are as valid today as they were then:

1. Show interest in others.
2. Smile.
3. Use people's names.
4. Listen carefully.
5. Talk about topics of interest to the other person.
6. Make the other person feel important.

CASE STUDIES IN THE NEWS

Time (June 28, 1999) reported that today's workers need soft skills even more than technical expertise.

Citing a study by staffing organization Select Appointments North America, the *Time* article showed listening, interpersonal skills and problem solving as both the most important and most lacking in employees.

Why do you think that listening, interpersonal skills and problem solving are so important in today's work environment? What kinds of problems do you think poor skills in these areas are likely to create?

1. What is human relations? How can human relations skills help you?

2. Give examples from your own experiences, movies or TV shows of successful human relations and of human relations gone wrong.

FastChat

1.2 Why Is Human Relations Important?

Learning
Objective 2

Discuss the importance of human relations.

The total person approach acknowledges that an organization employs the whole person, not just his or her job skills.

Organizations are concerned about the relationships among people because people are their most important resources. Increasingly, companies are adopting the **total person approach**, which takes into account employee needs and goals. Realizing that when they hire you, they are employing a whole person, not just your skills, they strive for win-win situations that allow the company and you to get what it and you want. Organizations know that they can be more productive and their employees more satisfied when effective human relations skills are used. Those companies that attempt to provide fair and just treatment for all employees and to fulfill both personal and organizational goals will normally be more successful than organizations that do not. They usually have less conflict, fewer errors in their products, less illness and absenteeism, lower employee turnover, and higher morale.

Effective human relations skills may be the greatest contributor to the success or failure of your career. According to the Carnegie Foundation, 85

TECHNOLOGY CONNECTION

Engineers, usually associated with hard skills and technology, are spending an increasing amount of time using "soft skills." A recent study by the National Society for Professional Engineers found that 75 percent of an engineer's time on the job is spent communicating via e-mail, over the telephone, by fax, and through reports, oral presentations, written proposals, conversations with team members, and meetings with clients. An engineer's communication skills are important in today's market. Communications and other soft skills, such as effective teamwork and strong leadership skills, are rising to the top of the priority lists of most employers once an engineer's technical skills are in place.

Houston Chronicle, "Focus on Engineering," December 6, 1998

Think of other jobs usually associated with technology. What are some of the human relations skills people in these jobs must use?

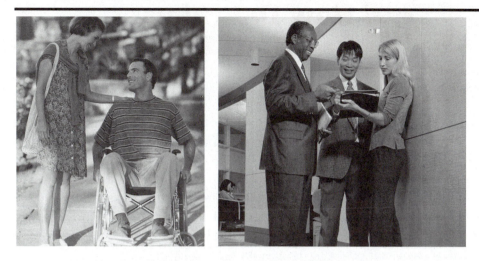

percent of the factors contributing to our job success are personal qualities, while technical knowledge contributes only 15 percent. The Harvard Bureau of Vocational Guidance reported that 66 percent of people fired from their jobs were fired because they did not get along with others while only 34 percent because of lack of technical knowledge. Additionally, in 1996 *The Wall Street Journal* reported that managers spend over 360 hours a year (the equivalent of nine workweeks) dealing with employee personality clashes.

The average worker will make three major career changes during his or her life. When you change careers, you may need different technical skills. However, because few people today work in isolation, all positions require similar human relations skills. People with these skills and the necessary technical skills will be in great demand.

Human relations skills are becoming increasingly important as our economy evolves. We are moving from an economy that produces goods to one that provides services, is information and technology based, and expects speed. This new economy requires that you and other employees communicate and interact effectively in complex situations.

1. Explain the statement, "Human relations skills may be the greatest contributor to your career success."

2. What is the relationship between human relations skills and technical skills as you progress in your career?

3. Think about the career you envision for yourself over the next 5–10 years and, in your own words, discuss how human relations skills will be important to you and to your employer.

*Fast*Chat

How Did Human Relations Develop?

To understand how organizations discovered the importance of human relations, we must look at the history of the United States economy and management practices. If you had lived here in the 1700s, you would have probably been a farmer or craftsperson living in a rural area. You would probably have grown your own food and made your own supplies. This era, known as the Agricultural Era, came to an end in 1782 with the invention of the steam engine. This machine revolutionized work by providing a cheap source of power to run factories.

During the 1800s the United States shifted into the Industrial Era, during which factories sprang up and towns grew. Had you lived during this period, your work might have shifted from the farm to a factory. Factory

The Information Age is characterized by rapidly expanding technology, increasingly large and complex organizations, and better informed employees.

managers realized that they needed to manage the behavior of their employees to increase productivity, and studies of management and worker relationships began. By the beginning of the 1900s, the United States had entered the most dynamic period ever in the history of work.

The invention of the computer in the 1950s ushered in another new age, called the **Information Age**. As you may have observed, this current age is characterized by rapidly expanding technology, increasingly large and complex organizations, and better-informed employees. The complexity of organizations and heightened expectations of employees have made human relations skills more important than ever. This importance will increase as world economies become more global and work forces more interactive. The Information Age will be discussed in Chapters 13 and 20.

The search for new management techniques began with a base in the social sciences—psychology, sociology, and anthropology. These studies deal with the institutions and functioning of society and how individuals interact as members of society. In studying human relations, we are concerned with why individuals and groups behave the way they do and how their interactions might be improved. These foundational disciplines are described in the following figure.

Armed with knowledge from these three disciplines, people began to study how to increase productivity at work. Their studies resulted in three different and distinct ways of treating employees, called classical, behavioral, and management science, each developing at a different time in American history.

Studies of management-worker relationships began during the Industrial Era.

Social Sciences Basic to Study of Human Relations		
Psychology	Of primary importance because it focuses on the behavior of individuals and why they act the way they do.	Industrial psychology looks specifically at motivation, leadership, decision making, and use of power within the organization.
Sociology	Centers on the interaction of two or more individuals and their relationships in group settings.	Important because we must all function in a variety of groups, and organizations consist of small groups.
Anthropology	Focuses on the origins and development of various cultures.	Increasingly important as society and work force become more multicultural and economy more global.

THE CLASSICAL SCHOOL
OF MANAGEMENT—1900 TO 1920s

The classical school of management focused on efficiency. Two branches of this school developed: **scientific management theory,** promoted by Frederick W. Taylor and Frank and Lillian Gilbreth, and **classical organization theory**, based on the work of Henri Fayol.

Frederick Taylor was an engineer and inventor who became known as the Father of Scientific Management. He had an inside understanding of industry, having begun his career as a laborer at the Midvale Steel Company, later becoming its chief engineer. He believed that management could be improved by thinking of it as a science-based art and that tasks could be scientifically analyzed to make them more efficient. For example, he discovered that changing the shape of a shovel resulted in more coal being moved with the same amount of effort.

His work during the late 1800s and early 1900s led to the idea of mass production, and his system influenced the develpment of every modern, industrialized nation. Though Taylor believed that maximum productivity could be achieved through cooperation of management and labor, some managers carried his system to extremes, and this caused resentment and the feeling that workers were being dehumanized.

Frank and Lillian Gilbreth, a husband-and-wife team, tried to measure and improve the motion of work. The Gilbreths used still and motion photography to identify the distinct steps required to do a task and then deleted the nonessential ones. The combination of the ideas of Taylor and the Gilbreths resulted in the famous "time and motion" studies that became a popular means of improving productivity.

As more studies were done, emphasis shifted from viewing the work itself to viewing the management of the organization as a whole. In 1916 Henri Fayol, a French industrialist, published his fourteen principles of management, which included division of work, authority, discipline, chain of command, and other concepts still used in management today. His belief was that management could be viewed holistically, with human relations, productivity, and the general administration of the organization being improved by applying basic principles.

THE BEHAVIORAL SCHOOL OF MANAGEMENT—
1940s TO 1950s

Managers continued to look for ways to improve productivity. Many were disenchanted with the authoritarian, task-oriented approach of the classical school, and by the late 1920s, the **behavioral school of management** had begun. Employees had started to unionize to protect their rights and to demand a more humane environment. The Depression, World War II, and post-war boom contributed to growing concern.

The behavioral school also had two branches, the first of which was the **human relations approach.** From the mid-'20s to the early '30s, Elton Mayo and his associates from Harvard Business School conducted research at Western Electric's Hawthorne plant near Chicago. These studies, which came to be known as the Hawthorne studies, considered how physical working conditions affect worker output.

Mayo is the "Father of Human Relations."

The researchers found that regardless of changes—such as heating, humidity, lighting, work hours, rest periods, and supervisory styles—productivity levels increased significantly. Finally, the researchers realized that productivity increased because the workers were receiving attention and felt that someone cared about them. This became known as the **Hawthorne effect,** the idea that the human element is more important to productivity than technical or physical aspects of the job. Mayo's work earned him recognition as the "Father of Human Relations" and provided discoveries that contributed to an understanding of human relations in organizations.

The Hawthorne effect: the human element is more important to productivity than technical or physical aspects of the job.

Mayo's Discoveries about Human Relations in Organizations

1. Attention given to people can change their productivity—the Hawthorne effect.
2. Employees have many needs beyond those satisfied by money.
3. Informal work groups can be very powerful within an organization, particularly through their ability to influence productivity levels.
4. The relationship between supervisors and employees is very important, affecting both quantity and quality of employee output. Good human relations is the key, not popularity.
5. Employees have many needs that are met away from the job. Therefore, managers cannot always control motivation.
6. Relations between coworkers affect their performance. These interactions allow employees to meet their social needs.

The second branch of the behavioral school was known as the **behavioral science approach**. In the mid- to late '50s, researchers began to use scientific methods to explore efficient management techniques. The studies included both workers and managers to get a total view of human behavior in the workplace. During this period, psychology, sociology, and anthropology first came into use as tools for understanding the organizational environment.

THE MANAGEMENT SCIENCE SCHOOL OF MANAGEMENT—1960s TO PRESENT

During World War II, both the British and the U.S. military needed to solve complex problems, such as coordinating massive troop movements and seeing that supplies arrived at appropriate places and in correct quantities. The military enlisted the help of mathematicians, physicists, and other scientists, leading to the **management science school.** The results were so successful that the techniques developed were later used by companies to solve complex business problems.

Two statistical models to help planning and control are PERT and CPM.

The computer made **statistical models** easier to use. Models are analytical tools that help managers to plan and control organizational activities. Examples of models developed during this period are the **Program Evaluation and Review Technique (PERT)** and the **Critical Path Method (CPM).**

PERT is frequently used when a major project to be finished by a deadline is made up of many separate activities or steps, each of which requires a certain amount of time to complete. Usually one activity must be completed before another can be started. A PERT chart assists in coordinating these activities. You could use PERT charts for projects ranging from planning a sales conference to building a new corporate headquarters and moving employees to it.

PERT Charts assist managers in coordinating activities.

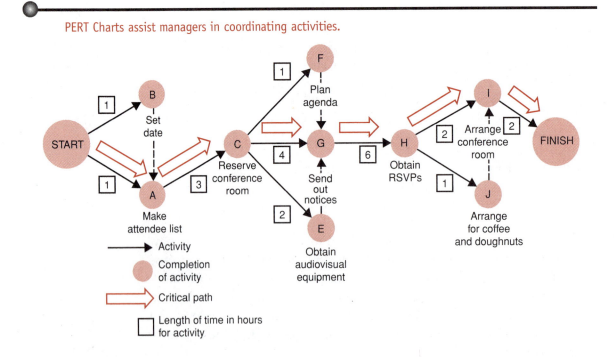

The critical path is the sequence of activities in a PERT chart requiring the longest time for completion. It will show the minimum time needed to complete a project.

Today computer models assist managers in making decisions. For instance, a model can predict how many units your company is likely to sell at a certain price. However, the computer is simply a tool. It is not infallible and cannot make decisions, and it does not reduce the need for effective human relations in the success of a project.

Quick tip . . . .

Typifying the human relations approach to high productivity, Gene Krantz, head of Missions Operations Directorate during some of NASA's most exciting space explorations, suggests that managers should use one or more of the following, every day and in every conversation, to get the most from their workers:

1. You did a good job.
2. What is your opinion?
3. I made a mistake.
4. Will you please . . .
5. Thank you.
6. We . . .

PRACTICES OF THE 2000s

Research continues for ways to improve productivity. Current theory revolves around worker involvement and information technology and emphasizes redefining the work and identifying new approaches. **Reengineering processes** involves eliminating unnecessary work, reducing cycle time, improving quality, and improving customer relations. **Process innovation** blends information technology and human resources management. Consider these examples. Thomas H. Davenport, author of *Process Innovation,* relates that, by changing processes to integrate technology, IBM reduced preparation time for quotes to buy or lease computers from seven days to one while preparing 10 times as many quotes. The Internal Revenue Service collected 33 percent more from delinquent taxpayers with only half the staff and one-third the branch offices.

The July/August 1999 issue of *Working Woman* suggests that when you're an unhappy customer, you can use the following "magic words" to win a fast and happy resolution:

"I'm not upset or angry at you—but I am very upset."	Acknowledge your anger while remaining detached, professional and nonaccusatory.
"What I want from you is . . ."	Remembering that this business transaction is a negotiation, think of a remedy that makes sense and say what you want.
"What would you do if you were in my shoes?"	Your goal is to break through the other person's shell and make him/her realize you are human also.

This advice can serve you well in any negotiation situation.

FastChat

1. Discuss examples from your own life of when you experienced the Hawthorne effect. This might have resulted from the attention of a coach, teacher, boss, parent, or other person.

2. Describe a project you have faced and how PERT or CPM or a computer model could have helped you. Sketch a simple PERT or CPM for your project.

3. Review Gene Krantz's advice above. Then review the "Focus" section at the beginning of this chapter. What do they have in common? How might you apply Gene Krantz's advice to your personal life?

Identify, organize, plan and allocate resources effectively.

What Factors Influence Human Relations in Organizations?

Organizations will continue to change dramatically during the 21st century if they want to remain successful. Characteristics of 21st century "cyber-corps" are shown in this table.

Explain what factors influence human relations in organizations.

Characteristics of 2lst Century Organizations

1. **Speed**—Things happen fast, calling for quick decisions.
2. **Turn-around time**—Actions and results must occur quickly.
3. **Uncertainty**—Change and uncertainty create problems and opportunity.
4. **Virtual corporation**—Staff and employees are not in one location.
5. **Unique capabilities**—An organization's unique abilities provide its competitive edge.
6. **Agility**—Flexibility is key.
7. **Knowledge infrastructure**—A base of knowledge is needed to capture, create, store, improve, clarify, disseminate and use information.
8. **Geographical Diversity**—Organizations are product specific and geographically diversified instead of geographically specific and product diversified.
9. **Learning**—The emphasis is on growing human potential as fast as technological potential.

James Martin. *Cybercorp*. New York: Amacom, 1996

An important part of using effective human relations in these cyber-corps, or in any other organization, is knowing how you fit into the overall organization. The quality and type of interaction among individuals and how it changes in organizations is influenced by many factors. They include goals, cultures, conflicts between groups, and outside influences.

GOALS OF ORGANIZATIONS

Being aware of the goals of organizations to which you belong (work, social, or civic) can help you understand why management makes the decisions or takes the actions that it does. Strong human relations skills can

Goals, cultures, conflicts, and outside forces can influence relationships in organizations.

help you function and contribute more effectively while your organization is trying to meet its goals and can help you adapt to and cope with changes.

Every organization has goals. A primary goal of any business is to make a profit. If a profit is not made, the business will fail.

Government and nonprofit organizations, while not seeking to make a profit, still have the goal of providing services. They must provide services that the public needs or wants at a price the public can afford. Since these organizations, like businesses, must remain within their budgets, government and other nonprofit organizations often practice the same management and cost-saving concepts that private enterprise uses.

Organizational culture: a mix of the beliefs and values of society, workers, and the organization's leaders and founders.

ORGANIZATIONAL CULTURE

Every organization has its own distinct culture. **Organizational culture** is a mix of the beliefs and values of society at large, the individuals who participate in the organization, and the organization's leaders and founders. The

CASE STUDIES IN THE NEWS

"New chief giving American a new personality" reads the title of an article by Terry Maxon in the November 29, 1998, *Houston Chronicle*. American Airlines had been hit with two employee strikes in less than four years and was facing the threat of unionization. Focusing on employee morale, American's new top executive, Donald J. Carty, put the issue of the company's "corporate culture" high on his agenda, with the goal of creating a culture where people like to come to work. He wanted to make the airline a kinder, gentler company without losing its competitive edge. Carty emphasized the "service profit chain," where happy employees attract happy customers who keep coming back. Asked what was wrong with the company, front-line managers to senior executives often responded that the company was too aggressive internally, creating an atmosphere in which fixing blame was more important than fixing problems. To help him change the culture, Mr. Carty named Thomas Kiernan, an executive known for his good people skills, to be senior vice president of human resources.

How might changing the corporate culture change the airline's goals and how it does business?

culture determines what goals the organization wants to accomplish and how it will go about accomplishing them.

Some organizations have strong values that are expressed. Here are some examples of expressed values with which you may be familiar.

Examples of Expressed Values

The Girl Scouts—"Do a good turn daily"
DuPont—"Better things for better living through chemistry"
Caterpillar—"Twenty-four hour parts and service anywhere in the world"
Sears, Roebuck—"Quality at a good price"
The Boy Scouts—"Be prepared"

Other cultural norms may not be as openly communicated but must be learned. Organizations, for instance, may have heroes—people with the beliefs, attitudes and behavior that the organization wishes to reinforce. These people with the "right stuff" are identified as individuals after whom members or employees should model themselves. Disney Productions, for example, reflected Walt Disney's values.

Most organizations develop some standards of behavior. These standards may include unwritten rules concerning appropriate clothing, formats for meetings, language standards for interpersonal communication, decision-making styles, and activities in which employees or members participate outside the organization. Some organizations have rituals and rites, such as awards programs, sales seminars, banquets, or the like.

Good human relations skills can help you learn the cultural norms of companies in which you work. Armed with this knowledge, you will cope more effectively with the expectations of the organization.

SPECIAL FUNCTIONS WITHIN THE BUSINESS ORGANIZATION

Organizations have formal structures that help them carry out their goals and objectives. Because one person cannot perform all functions of a large organization, duties are delegated to individuals or groups of individuals. You should understand that groups or departments must work together to avoid or reduce conflicting objectives.

The basic functions of most business organizations are shown in the following table along with some human relations skills needed in those jobs.

quick wit

"Ride the horse in the direction that it's going."

Werner Erhard

Function	Human Relations Skills Needed
Marketing & Sales	Understand the goals of the organization.
	Communicate with clients and customers.
	Coordinate work with others in the organization.
Production	Use teamwork to work together effectively to meet production and delivery deadlines and maintain quality. Use other skills such as motivation, goal setting, job performance, problem solving, and decision making.
Finance	Make decisions, listen and communicate effectively.
Human Resources	Handle confidential information and legal and ethical matters.
Accounting	Use effective oral and written communication.

Often each part of an organization has its own goals. For instance, the accounting department may be concerned with seeing that an accurate account of inventory is kept, while the production department is concerned with completing its work on time and cannot see the importance of filling out routine forms accurately. If you are to function effectively at work, you must recognize the needs of others in the organization and respect what they are trying to accomplish as a part of overall organizational goals. The development of sound human relations skills will help you.

OUTSIDE FORCES AT WORK

All organizations, profit and nonprofit, are vulnerable to their environments. If they do not adjust to a changing environment, they will lose jobs or go out of business. Human relations skills can assist you in adapting to and understanding these changes. The following table shows ten environments that may affect a business organization.

Ten Environments that May Affect a Business Organization

Environment	Cause	Possible Effect
Macro	Increased use of personal computers Shifts in interest rates Changing attitudes about work Concerns about the natural environment	Greater speed and communication More expensive business expansion Different work habits How/where work is conducted
Economic	Large strike or natural disaster General recession	Prices rise Postponement of luxury spending
Competitive	New business down the street	Lower prices
Legal-Political	An increase in taxes Road construction in front of a business Change in export regulations Political unrest in foreign countries	Limited funds for salaries and expansion Fewer customers and less sales Less foreign sales Less oil exploration and drilling
Socio-Cultural	Demographic shifts, aging baby boomers, changing ethnicity, patterns of literacy and shrinking middle class	Change in lifestyle and buying habits
Changing Technology	Widespread use of computers and the Internet	How business is done, how work and personal lives are organized, how people communicate and learn, patterns of residence, relationships, work, and leisure
Unexpected Disasters	Fire, tornado, earthquake Plane crashes, product tampering	Expense and anguish Deaths, injuries, litigation
Corporate Mergers	New merged organization	Laid off employees
Management Changes	Retirements and new managers	Change in philosophy and work methods
Global Economy	No economy stands alone	What happens in one economy affects the economy of other countries. Increased need to interact with people of many different nations with sensitivity to their customs, values, and attitudes.
	Goods produced less expensively in some countries Young, well-educated workers from undeveloped countries relocate to cities in developed nations ("brain drain").	Businesses move factories outside U.S. or have part of the work done overseas. Human relations challenges arise. Clashes may occur over relative importance of work and leisure, ethics, social responsibility, and copyrights.

GLOBAL CONNECTION

By the time Ivory Connection was almost ten years old, the upscale jewelry company in Houston was generating hundreds of thousands of dollars in annual revenue from the sale of elaborately carved ivory pieces. Then in 1988 the United States and other countries banned the import and sale of ivory pieces because overhunting was endangering the population of African and Indian elephants. The owner went on the offensive, changed the name of the company to Blanche Fine Jewelry, and expanded into gold, silver, and gemstone jewelry.

Houston Business Journal, November 6, 1998

What role did the legal-political environment play in this company's decisions?

The global economy may have a significant impact on organizations. Today's business person must be both aware of what is happening globally and flexible enough to adapt to changes as they occur.

To continue to compete globally, many organizations are merging. Such actions have the potential to affect thousands of people, many of whom are not directly involved with the merged organizations. For example, in late 1998 two large oil companies confirmed merger talks that would produce the world's largest nongovernmental oil company. Most energy experts concluded such a combination would be good for oil and gas production worldwide, thus benefiting consumers. The merger would eliminate duplicate facilities throughout the world and undoubtedly let go sizable numbers of their combined 123,000-person work force. However, other experts predicted that such a merger would squeeze out oil-service companies. The merger would result in less money being spent on companies that rent drilling rigs, evaluate rock, make drill bits and provide the whole array of products and services that make the oil field work. Additionally, experts predicted that if more consolidations occurred, they would create a wave of consolidation among oil companies, leading to further spending cuts. This example illustrates how a single change in one environment can have far-reaching effects on businesses and individuals.

ETHICS CONNECTION

A 1997 Microsoft survey pointed out the tremendous cost of software piracy. Nationwide, more than 130,000 jobs, representing $5.3 billion in wages and salaries, were lost in 1996 because of piracy, resulting in nearly $1 billion in lost tax revenue. The positions lost were not jobs that had been eliminated, but rather ones that were never created because of the financial losses. Hardest hit were development, marketing, and support. Additionally, some resellers went out of business because they could not compete with the low prices of illegal software. The purpose of the study was to show that software piracy hurts more than just the software industry.

Discuss examples of software piracy and the impact of these actions. How serious do you consider it to be if your friend borrows your software to load on his computer? a company pays for only one copy of a software package but loads it on 10 computers? or a store sells bootleg copies of software?

FastChat

1. Why should you understand the goal of organizations of which you are a part? Identify the goal of several organizations with which you are familiar.

2. What is organizational culture? Why do organizations differ in their norms or rituals? Describe the organizational culture of some organizations with which you are familiar.

3. Describe the various kinds of human relations skills that were needed in jobs you may have held.

4. Think of an organization that has undergone significant recent change. What created that change? How did the organization respond?

What Are Your Responsibilities?

If you join an organization with the attitude that your responsibility is to help the organization accomplish its goals, you are off to the right start. Having the necessary skills, understanding your objectives, accomplishing them as well as possible with the least expense and fuss, and making others' jobs easier by carrying your own weight are how you demonstrate that you have the right attitude. Human relations skills are essential. An employee or member who does not help the organization grow and prosper will not be a valued member of the team.

CONTRIBUTING TO THE ORGANIZATION

You can contribute to your organization by having a positive attitude and by performing your job or role well. Knowing your tasks, using effective human relations, and being polite and helpful to others are important. Ignoring or being rude to a customer may cause the shopper to go down the street to another business to trade. Peters and Waterman in their book, *In Search of Excellence*, point out that one key to business success is superior customer service. A study for the White House Office of Consumer Affairs found that 96 percent of unhappy customers never complain about discourtesy, but up to 91 percent never return. In addition, the average unhappy customer will tell at least 9 other people about the discourtesy, and 13 percent will tell more than 20 people.

Another way in which you can contribute to your organization is through effective communication. If you do not understand an assignment, you should ask for clarification. If you know that you will not meet a required deadline, let the person in charge know as soon as possible. At work, doing your tasks the way your supervisor wants, not the way you think it should be done, is vital. If your supervisor gives you instructions to do the assignment in the manner that you think best, which will probably happen once you have acquired experience and have demonstrated your responsibility, then you may do it your own way. Most organizations have room for honest discussion on the best way to approach a task. However, when your supervisor has made a decision following discussion, you should comply with these guidelines.

BEING FLEXIBLE

The growth of employment in small businesses and the restructuring of large organizations make flexibility more important than ever. Your positive attitude coupled with a willingness to follow orders, assist other workers, help with tasks not specifically assigned to you, or take on new tasks will make you a valued employee. And when decisions regarding layoffs or promotions are being made, employees with cooperative, helpful attitudes definitely have an edge over those who are inflexible and always complaining.

The willingness to retrain is another aspect of flexiblity. As technology changes, work changes, and employees are regularly expected to handle new and different jobs. Chip Bell, author of *Managers as Mentors*, said that in his work with corporations he found one interesting common thread among the "winningest" corporations: "Incessant learning. Nonstop learning. Daily learning. In fact, the ability to learn faster than the competition may be the only sustainable competitive advantage of the 21st century."

CASE STUDIES IN THE NEWS

In 1996, when AT&T decided to cut 40,000 of its 300,000 workers over the next three years, it used a novel approach which a company spokeswoman described as asking everybody out into a parking lot. Nearly all nonunion employees were given a standard two-page form on which to list their credentials. Senior executives used these forms in deciding which people had the valuable skills that made them worth inviting back into the building.

New York Times, **February 13, 1996**

What conclusions can you draw from this case study about the importance of "incessant learning" to both individuals and organizations?

According to *Worklife Visions*, by Jeffrey Hallett, 50 percent of the actual jobs performed in 1987 did not exist in 1967. The rate of change will increase, and by 2007 almost all work will be new. This means you will need to learn new skills at an increasing rate. Knowing how to learn will be as important as knowing what to learn. The following self assessment will help you determine your learning style, and thereby help you become a life-long learner.

PERSONAL NEEDS VERSUS ORGANIZATIONAL NEEDS

People work or belong to organizations for different reasons. Money, social relationships, power, prestige, status, and growth are only a few of the motives. Sometimes the needs and styles of the individual and the organization clash.

As an employee or member of an organization you must understand yourself and your own wants and needs and be aware of the written and unwritten rules of the organization. Often you must play a role. For instance, you may prefer to wear jeans, but if an employer's unwritten code calls for dressier clothing, then you should adapt to this standard. If you are unable or unwilling to meet organizational expectations, you may not thrive professionally in that particular environment and should probably consider finding a position or joining an organization that is more in line with your values.

Jobs today do not last forever. Technology comes and goes and businesses open and close. However, the skills of human relations can be used in any setting and can prove indispensable in helping you adapt to the changing world.

FastChat

1. Think of people you consider to be contributors to their organizations—work, church, civic, community or other. What contributions do you see them making? Describe their attitudes and behaviors.

2. Think about technological changes of the last 10 years and people you know who utilize technology in some way. In what topics or skills did they have to retrain—on their own, through on-the-job training, or in formal classes? What skills do you think you will need to learn or update in the near future?

3. How can you demonstrate your flexibility at school and/or work?

4. What do you hope to get out of working? Why should you be willing to continue learning and to retrain?

How Is Technology Affecting Human Relations?

Throughout this text, you will learn about the ways that technology is changing the world and how it is affecting people both at work and away from the job. As noted earlier in this chapter, the invention of the computer in the 1950s ushered in the Information Age. Many of the technological changes revolve around this invention. You can probably easily cite numerous ways in which computers have changed the way people live and do business. For example, skiers in Vail, Colorado, can rent waist packs with lightweight satellite equipment and sophisticated software for tracking their routes and speed (*Information Week*, March 23, 1998), and Sears, Roebuck & Co. is using a nationwide speech-recognition system that lets callers tell machines which departments they want or what items they are inquiring about (*Information Week*, April 5, 1998). As of 1998, cyberspace consists of 380 million Web pages and is doubling every five months. If you are not already involved with this technology, you no doubt soon will be among the growing numbers who work directly or indirectly with computers.

Computer and information networks have made possible the **virtual office,** allowing people in different ("remote") locations to communicate with each other through telecommunications, machines linked by

Learning
Objective 6

Discuss some ways that technology is changing the work world and affecting human relations.

The virtual office allows people in different locations to communicate with each other through telecommunications.

TECHNOLOGY CONNECTION

A recent Gallup poll of 40,000 Internet users found that users between the ages of 18 and 24 use the Internet for both recreational and practical reasons, while those between 35 and 54 use it for practical reasons only. Further, while 75 percent of the younger group use the Web for entertainment and 65 percent use it for news and information, only 45 percent of the older group use it for entertainment and 82 percent for news and information.

Directory World, May/June 1998.

If you are a Web user, for what specific purposes do you use it? If you do not currently use the Web, think of ways it might help you.

telephone lines. Various technologies have been developed to support telecommunications. These include fax machines, centralized voice mail, electronic mail, and teleconferencing. The term **telecommuters** was coined to describe people, frequently based at home, who use these technology networks to send and receive work and information to and from different locations, locations (such as offices) to which they would once have needed to commute.

Many companies offer the option of working at home to help employees with family responsibilities, to save office space, or for other reasons. Today over 20 million people are telecommuters. Businesses are experimenting with alternative workstyles, such as telecommuting, hoteling (sharing an office through reservations), and shorter work weeks. Yet many executives at companies offering workstyle options think that telecommuters do not advance as quickly on the career track as office-based executives. One consequence of telecommuting and virtual teams may be increased worker isolation. Without in-person interaction, workers' social skills can deteriorate.

Additionally, some companies worry about employee time on the Internet. About 55 percent of the executives polled by Robert Half International think their employees are spending too much time on the

TECHNOLOGY CONNECTION

Search engines are catalogs for finding information on the World Wide Web. To use them, you start by typing in key words that describe what you are looking for. This will get you a list of related sites, which you can then visit by clicking on their names. You probably will find that many are likely to not be relevant. To avoid this, narrow your request to a more focused topic. Some of the Web's current search engines are Yahoo (www.yahoo.com), Excite (www.excite.com), Lycos (www.lycos.com), HotBot (www.hotbot.com), Alta Vista (www.altavista.com), Metacrawler (www.matacrawler.com), KnowX (www.knowx.com), DejaNews (www.dejanews.com), and Scour.Net (www.scour.net).

1. *Briefly search each of the above search engines. What is the focus of each?*

2. *Search the Web to find a book that you would like to buy. Determine how much it will cost you. (Hint: WebMarket, www.webmarket.com lists places to buy books, electronics, clothing and other items on the Web. And Amazon.com, at www.amazon.com, is an online bookstore.)*

Internet. While the benefits for everything from market research to business communication still outweigh the negatives for the company, Max Messmer, chairman of Robert Half International, says it can be a distraction for some people.

TECHNOLOGY CONNECTION

The June 15, 1999, issue of *Inc. Technology* describes how four businesspeople use technology to stay productive while away from the office.

1. A self-employed consultant in cable-TV network architecture and related technologies says his laptop is his primary productivity tool when traveling.

2. The CEO of Sparks.com, an on-line retailer of print greeting cards based in San Francisco, carries a cell phone and a laptop. She uses the laptop to access When.com (*www.when.com*), a free Web-based calendar service; Hotmail (*www.hotmail.com*), Microsoft's free Web-based e-mail service, and the United Airlines Web site (*www.ual.com*).

3. The president of Marketing Services Group, a Bowling Green, Kentucky, company that acts as a manufacturer's representative to the industrial-catalog market, carries a cell phone and a CrossPad. A CrossPad is a standard-size paper tablet with a clipboard that stores his strokes electronically to record units sold and sales forecasts.

4. A sales representative and designer for $50-million Pacific Western and Pak West, based in Santa Ana, California, carries a numeric pager and a Clio (a Windows device that is slightly smaller than most laptops and has a stylus-sensitive display for making quick sketches).

Think of ways in which technology could make you more productive. Go to the Web addresses shown in the above discussion. How might the information or services provided in each help you?

1. What is the virtual office?

2. How might telecommuting affect human relations?

3. Do you know anyone who is telecommuting? What have been their reactions to it? What do they like or dislike about it?

FastChat

Key Terms

human relations
total person approach
Information Age
classical school of management
scientific management theory
classical organization theory
behavioral school of management
human relations approach
Hawthorne effect
behavioral science approach
management science school of management]
statistical models
Program Evaluation and Review Technique (PERT)
Critical Path Method (CPM)
reengineering processes
process innovation
organizational culture
virtual office
telecommuters

Chapter Summary

Human relations is the study of relationships among people. The major reason for studying human relations is to learn to interact more effectively with others, thereby becoming a more valued member within organizations and of society as a whole. All jobs and roles require some human relations skills.

The need for improved human relations in the workplace became obvious once workers moved from the farm to the factory. A knowledge of psychology, sociology, and anthropology was used to study human relations, especially as it related to the desire for increased productivity. Three schools of management came out of these studies: classical, behavioral, and management science. Today in the Information Age, with its large, complex organizations, better-informed employees, global economies, and emphasis on speed, the need for human relations skills is even greater.

Human relations in organizations can be influenced by such factors as goals, organizational culture, job function, and outside forces. Outside forces can include the economy, legal-political environment, socio-cultural environment, changing technology, unexpected disasters, corporate mergers and sales, management changes, and the global economy. Strong human relations skills can help you cope with these forces.

You have a responsibility to help employers or organizations accomplish their goals. You can contribute by having the necessary technical and human relations skills, communicating effectively, being flexible, retraining, and meeting organizational expectations. Solid human relations skills will also help you adapt to rapidly changing technology.

Review Questions

1. Explain the meaning of human relations.
2. Why is human relations important in our personal and work lives? What do you think would happen to a business that did not use effective human relations skills?
3. List the three schools of management and tell what they contributed to the study of organizations.
4. What is the purpose of an organization? What can cause changes in an organization? Explain how you can contribute to an organization.
5. How is technology changing the world of work and affecting human relations?

Discussion Questions

1. Identify some situations from home and work in which poor human relations skills were used. What happened? How could the situation have been improved?
2. Compare the three behavioral sciences (psychology, sociology, and anthropology). How do they differ? What does each contribute to the study of organizations?
3. Name the three schools of management theory and explain why they evolved.
4. Discuss the job skills needed in the Agriculture Era, the Industrial Era, and the Information Age. How are they different? How are they the same?
5. What changes are taking place in your community that affect local businesses? Identify the environment that causes the change.

Chapter Project

In the library or over the Internet find the 1995 *Fortune* magazine article, "Seven Habits of Highly Offensive People." With two or three classmates, interpret and discuss the article in light of what you have learned in this chapter. Together write a one-page summary and analysis that can be shared with the class. Format the report in an attractive, efficient, and effective informal memorandum style. It should include To, From, Date, and Subject at the top and side headings in the body. Give your recommendations and conclusions first, followed by the supporting evidence. You may use informal language such as first and second-person pronouns (we, you). One possible Internet address for your research is *www.fortune.com.*

Reading, listening, reasoning, allocating resources effectively, participating as a member of a team and contributing to group effort, understanding complex interrelationships.

Applications

In small groups analyze the following situations.

Chaos Is Cooking

Lauren is the production supervisor of a small company that manufactures specialty kitchen items. She has four employees. Juan is just out of high school. Ling Sao, in her early 40s and with the company 2 1/2 years, is absent frequently because she is taking care of her elderly mother. Mike, a 15-year employee, takes a lot of breaks. Kesia, the oldest employee, is the most productive.

Lauren is experiencing all sorts of problems: one of the machines is turning out bent pots, the workers frequently drop some of the lids when carrying them across the room to the packing machines, costly rush orders have to be placed for needed supplies, and production in general is not what it should be.

Lauren has been told by the company owner that she has six months to improve production or the company will be forced to close. The owner calls Lauren into the office and shuts the door.

1. What do you think the boss will tell Lauren?
2. Identify the problems that the owner needs to correct. Which management schools may provide ideas to assist the owner?
3. Identify the problems Lauren needs to correct. Which management schools may provide ideas to assist her in solving which problems?

Computer Crunch

Sam Keystone, the owner of a mid-sized computer manufacturing company, knows that proposed legislation to restrict exports to foreign countries will seriously affect his company. He is also concerned about the less expensive computer models some of his competitors are developing. And, of course, he lies awake at night wondering if he will read in tomorrow's paper that someone has developed a computer that totally revolutionizes the industry, making his models obsolete.

1. What environments are affecting Sam's company?
2. What changes might Sam have to make to stay in business?
3. What human relations skills will Sam's managers need to adapt to these changes? His employees?

Additional Readings and Resources

Dalton, Marie, Hoyle, Dawn, and Watts, Marie. *Human Relations.* Cincinnati: South-Western Publishing Company, 1992

Hammer, Michael, and James Champy. *Reengineering the Corporation.* New York: Harper Business, 1993.

Harrington, H. James. *Business Process Improvement.* New York: McGraw-Hill, Inc., 1991.

Leshin, Cynthia B. *Management on the World Wide Web.* Saddle River NJ: Prentice-Hall, 1997.

Ober, Scott. *Contemporary Business Communication.* New York: Houghton Mifflin Company, 1998.

http://www.ee.ed.ac.uk/gerard/Management/index.html—a series of articles on basic management skills from the IEE Engineering Management Journal, including teams/groups, presentation skills, time management, quality in teams, writing skills, delegation, managing people, oral communication, project planning and becoming a great manager.

http://www.lia.co.za/users/johannh/index. htm—deals with project management, TQM, reengineering, continuing improvement, benchmaking, productivity improvement and other related topics.

http://ls0020.fee.uva.nl/bpr—covers business process reengineering.

www.mcb.co.uk.hr/—HR Global network

www.shrm.org.hrmagazine—HR Magazine

www.providence.edu.mgt/resource/hr.html—human relations resources

Perception:

Different Views of the World

objectives

After studying this chapter, you should be able to:

1. *Explain why people may have different perceptions of the same events, objects, persons, or situations.*

2. *Use the Johari Window to analyze your relationships with others.*

3. *Explain the importance of a good self-image.*

4. *Recognize perceptual defense mechanisms, what can trigger them, and how they hinder our relationships.*

5. *Explain how perceptions can affect employee/supervisor relationships.*

One dark night, a ship spotted a light in its path. This is the transcript of the radio transmissions that followed (released by the Chief of Naval Operations 10/10/95).

Station #1 Please divert your course 15 degrees to the North to avoid a collision.

Station #2 Recommend you divert YOUR course 15 degrees to South to avoid a collision.

Station #1 This is the Captain of a US Navy ship. I say again, divert YOUR course.

Station #2 No. I say again, you divert YOUR course.

Station #1 THIS IS THE AIRCRAFT CARRIER ENTERPRISE, WE ARE A LARGE WARSHIP OF THE US NAVY. DIVERT YOUR COURSE NOW!

Station #2 This is the Puget Sound lighthouse. It's your call.
Round Top Register, **Winter 1998, p.26.**

Discuss a time when your perceptions conflicted with those of someone else. What happened? How was the issue resolved? Did you change your perceptions?

In This Chapter

What Is Perception?

Perception is an important element in human relations. It is the process by which you acquire mental images of your environment. Through it you organize, interpret, and give meaning to sensations or messages that you receive with your senses of sight, smell, touch, taste, and hearing. Many factors influence perception—culture, heredity, needs, peer pressures, interests, values, snap judgments, and expectations are only a few examples. These factors contribute, in varying degrees, to the way that you think and feel about people, situations, events, and objects. The following figure illustrates how perceptions can differ.

Awareness of factors in perception is vital to good human relations.

Is it a bunny or a duck?

The Rabbit/Duck illustration originated early in the Twentieth Century. The original artist is unknown. This version was created by Gabor Kiss for Scientific American *magazine. Used by permission.*

1. Would we be able to give meaning to messages without perception?

2. What is your perception of work?

3. Where did your perception originate?

2.2 What Influences Perception?

Learning
Objective   1

Explain why people may have different perceptions of the same events, objects, persons, or situations.

quick wit

Idealism is what precedes experience; cynicism is what follows.

David T. Wolf

People develop certain attitudes and tend to make decisions based on these attitudes. Some of the things that influence perceptions and contribute to attitudes are so much a part of us (culture, heredity, interests) that they are difficult to recognize. Others, such as peer pressure, needs, or conditions, might be easier to identify. We should, however, try to view each new problem or situation separately and objectively and base decisions on the facts.

Among the many factors which can influence perception are the **halo effect** and **reverse** or **tarnished halo effect**. When the halo effect is operating, we assume that if a person has one trait we view positively, all other traits must be positive. For instance, imagine that you are the owner of an office supplies store. Jane has been a bookkeeper for you for several years, doing an excellent job in the back office, so you promote her to manager. You soon realize to your dismay, however, that she is not an effective manager because she lacks the necessary people skills to meet the public and supervise other employees. You were probably influenced by the halo effect here.

Under the influence of the reverse halo effect, we allow one negative characteristic of a person to influence our whole impression negatively. That is, we consider one behavior or characteristic of a person to be "bad" and, therefore, view all other characteristics or behaviors of that person as bad. For example, you are operating under the reverse halo effect if you believe that people with poor handwriting are not intelligent or will not

Conditions and Characteristics Influence Perception	
Time and place	Employees sometimes erroneously assume that an order from a supervisor is not as important when it takes place in the hall as when it occurs in the boss's office.
Emotional state	We are more receptive to ideas when we are relaxed than when we are feeling nervous or tired.
Age	A building or room that you thought was large when you were a child may seem small once you are an adult.
Frequency	If your supervisor starts including you in weekly planning sessions, you may feel uneasy at first but become comfortable after a while.

perform well. Postpone judgment until you see how people function in a variety of situations.

Stress is another condition that distorts perception. When we are under stress, we are frequently unable to evaluate situations objectively. By learning to recognize situations that are stressful to you, you can make allowances for distortions that may cloud your perceptions.

Perceptions play an important role in the relationships we have with co-workers and supervisors.

"Of course we can do the impossible, in less time, and at a lower cost than our competition."

Many times when we lack information we fill in the void with negative thoughts.

1. Cite instances from your own experience when you or someone you know jumped to the wrong conclusion, expecting the worst, but discovered, once all the information was in, that your worries were unfounded.

2. How can you avoid situations where not having enough information draws you into negative thinking?

*Fast***Chat**

Perceptual awareness allows more self-control.

Being aware of your own perceptions and what influences them, as well as others' perceptions, is extremely important in today's workplace. With such awareness, you can withhold judgments until you have analyzed situations. Ask yourself why you are feeling the way you are, whether your feelings are justified, and whether you should act on those feelings. Perceiving situations accurately can prevent or resolve human relations problems in your personal life and at work. You may refrain from doing or saying things that could create difficulties.

Being aware of what may have influenced the perceptions of others can help you understand people and will help you be tolerant, even sympathetic. When you accept the fact that others have an equal right to their feelings or points of view, even if you do not agree with them, you can deal with situations better.

Open communication concerning feelings can be helpful in personal and work relationships. If people disclose their feelings to each other, they can develop better mutual understanding. Stronger relationships, built on honesty and openness, can help coworkers develop respect for each other's beliefs and opinions. Respect, in turn, can lead to fewer conflicts, greater job

GLOBAL CONNECTION

Conflicts continue worldwide between different ethnic, racial, and religious groups—Protestants and Catholics in Ireland, Jews and Palestinians in Israel, whites and blacks in South Africa, and ethnic Albanians and Serbs in Kosovo. Even in the United States, hate crimes occur, with the burning of African-American churches and random violence in the harassment of Jews, as well as other racial, religious, and ethnic groups.

1. *What role do perceptions play in the continuation of violence?*

2. *What changes might contribute to the elimination of these problems?*

3. *Do these types of problems spill over into work?*

satisfaction, and growth, resulting in higher morale. In addition, productivity may increase because ideas flow more easily.

Other people can learn about your perceptions when you practice **self-disclosure**, which means sharing honestly, but appropriately, your thoughts, feelings, opinions, and desires. Self-disclosure can increase the accuracy of your communication and may reduce stress because you no longer have to hide your feelings. Additionally, you can increase your self-awareness by being open to both positive and negative feedback. **Feedback** is information given back to a person that evaluates his or her actions or states what the receiver understood. For instance, someone may tell you, "I missed your point. You are speaking too softly for me." After evaluating their feedback, you may want to make changes within yourself. A theory that may help you understand the importance of open communication and feedback is the Johari Window.

Self-disclosure and feedback increase the accuracy of communications.

Perceptions can affect the accuracy of information.

---

1. What types of disclosures would facilitate a working relationship?

2. Who is responsible for verifying the accuracy of communication?

FastChat

The Johari Window helps us understand interactions.

Learning
Objective   2

Use the Johari Window to analyze your relationships with others.

The **Johari Window** is a model that helps us understand relationships and interactions among people. It is named for **Jo**seph Luft and **Har**ry Ingham who developed it.

Each of us has information within us of which we are aware and habits, attitudes, or talents of which we are not aware. Similarly, information about us or our habits, attitudes, or talents may or may not be known by others. Luft and Ingham combined these concepts to create four windowpanes, depicted in the following figure. These panes are called the arena or area of free activity, hidden or avoided area, blind area, and unknown area. The meanings of these terms are defined below.

USING THE WINDOW

The ideal Johari Window is one with a large arena and a small unknown area. To achieve this pattern, practice self-disclosure and be willing to accept and learn from feedback (negative or positive). At work, obvious ways in which you can do this include making suggestions and expressing opinions as appropriate and by being receptive to appraisals and suggestions made by your supervisor.

The Johari Window, a model of awareness

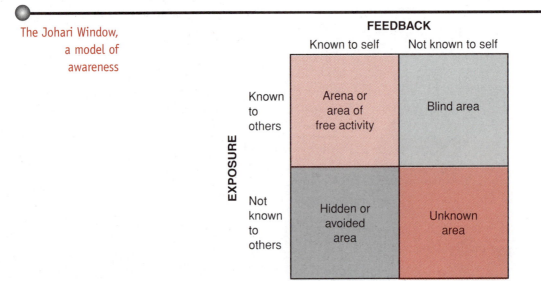

From Group Processes: An Introduction to Group Dynamics, Third Edition *by Joseph Luft. Copyright © 1984 by Joseph Luft. Reprinted by permission of Mayfield Publishing Company.*

Explanation of the Areas of the Johari Window

Arena	The arena contains information that you know about yourself and that others know about you. This pane will be bigger if you have effectively communicated your thoughts and ideas. It can include information about your job, preferred movies, disliked foods, and many other facts or feelings.
Hidden Area	The hidden area contains information that you know about yourself but do not divulge to others. The size of your hidden area suggests how trusting you are of those with whom you associate. Experiences, hopes, and dreams can be included in this window if you have not shared them with others.
Blind Area	The blind area is the section that represents what you do not know about yourself but what others do know about you. Blind areas can get in the way of interactions with others and can make people appear to have poor human relations skills. The size of this pane is an indication of how willing you are to listen to feedback about your behavior. Included in the blind area can be habits, attitudes prejudices, weaknesses, and strengths.
Unknown Area	The unknown area is the undiscovered or subconscious part of you. It contains information about you that neither you nor others know. This information can include unremembered experiences or undiscovered talents.

Your relationships away from work can also be improved by changing your arena. Ways to do that include accepting feedback from your family and friends about your actions and sharing your feelings and opinions in appropriate ways.

Disclosures, as described in the Johari Window, should be done carefully, particularly in the workplace. Telling too much about intimate matters or revealing personal information too soon can be harmful to careers. We all know people who blurt out their personal problems to almost everyone they meet. Such behavior is considered inappropriate in almost any setting, but especially so at work. Being critical under the guise of sharing your feelings can also hamper human relations. People who make rude or hurtful or inappropriate comments and excuse their behavior with "I'm just being honest about my feelings" have large blind areas.

Use great caution in sharing intimate information with people at work. Such information may detract from the professional image that you wish to create. Although all of us need people with whom we can share our confidences and problems, people away from work may be more appropriate choices for discussing intimate matters. Subjects shared only with caution

Self-disclosure must be done carefully and appropriately.

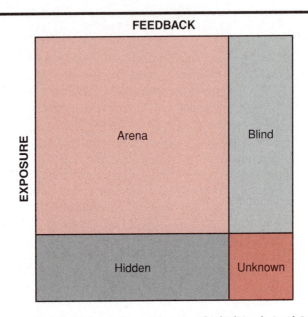

FEEDBACK

EXPOSURE

Arena

Blind

Hidden

Unknown

From Group Processes: An Introduction to Group Dynamics, Third Edition *by Joseph Luft. Copyright © 1984 by Joseph Luft. Reprinted by permission of Mayfield Publishing Company.*

include marital problems, financial difficulties, problems with children, many health-related matters, and opinions of coworkers. When deciding to disclose information, consider carefully the individuals with whom you will share information. What will their reaction be? Will they understand and be considerate of your feelings? Will they perceive what you have to tell them as a professional weakness that will inhibit your performance, or will they work with you to enhance your abilities? Is this the right point in your relationship to reveal such information?

If you determine that information can be shared, select an appropriate time and place for disclosures. Look for a time when the other person is most able to pay attention and distractions are least likely to occur. For instance, taking your supervisor's time to discuss a personal problem when the supervisor is working on a deadline project or has others waiting to be seen may create additional stress for the supervisor and hinder your communication.

FastChat

1. What topics are not appropriate for disclosure at work?

2. What should you do when someone discloses inappropriate information about themselves? Co-workers? Your boss?

How Do You Raise Self-Esteem?

Another aspect of perception important in human relations is how people feel about themselves, their **self-esteem**. Feeling good about ourselves is *the* key to success. All people, even those most confident and secure in their personal and professional lives, must work on their self-perceptions continually. We are never finished with this task.

Learning
O b j e c t i v e   3

Explain the importance of a good self-image.

Self-esteem takes time and practice.

Suggestions for Raising Self Esteem	
Love yourself	We can love and respect others only if we love and respect ourselves.
Believe in yourself	Realize that almost everyone is afraid to try new and different experiences. However, we must be willing to take reasonable risks to pursue our goals.
Analyze yourself	Know your strengths and weaknesses and set goals to overcome your weaknesses and enhance your strengths.
Forgive yourself and accept the fact that you are not perfect	Although we cannot change events of the past, we can learn from them and not make the same mistakes again.
Practice positive thinking	You will feel better about yourself and the world.

POSITIVE THINKING AND ITS IMPORTANCE

Positive thinking is looking on the bright side. People who think this way are called **optimists**, whereas people who always have a negative outlook are called **pessimists**. Research has shown that optimists are more successful than pessimists, and it is easy to see why. After all, few of us enjoy being around people who are always pessimistic. Then, too, people who are pessimistic probably give up in their endeavors too soon, not believing that positive results can occur. The difference between optimists and pessimists is demonstrated in the figure on page 40.

Three steps can be taken to develop positive thinking: (1) change your thought processes, (2) engage in positive self-talk, and (3) use visualization. Each step is discussed in the following sections.

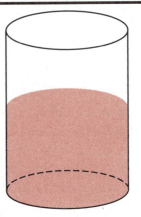

Is your glass (and your life) half-full or half-empty? Your perception reflects your degree of optimism or pessimism.

Change Your Thought Processes. Dr. David D. Burns, in his book, *Feeling Good,* describes thought processes that prevent us from thinking positively. One is seeing things in black-and-white categories, so that you consider your performance a total failure if it is not perfect. Another is exaggerating or minimizing the importance of your mistakes or someone else's achievements. Some other thought processes that interfere with positive thinking are over-generalizing so that you see every negative event as part of a failure pattern, disqualifying positive experiences as "not counting," and jumping to conclusions. Being aware of these processes and realizing when you are using them will help you begin to develop positive thinking patterns.

Engage in Positive Self-Talk. Positive **self-talk** involves making favorable statements to yourself. Statements such as "I can do that job," "I am a winner, " or "I performed well" can help you take control of your life. Taking time daily to say these things to yourself in front of a mirror will strengthen your positive self-image. Stephen Strasser, in *Working It Out—Sanity & Success in the Workplace,* points out that self-confidence, self-worth, self-direction, self-respect, self-dignity, and self-esteem are necessary before we can solve problems of job and career.

Reach positive thinking by changing thought processes and using positive self-talk and visualization.

Use Visualization. Taking time to practice **visualization**, or seeing yourself as a good, productive person, can also help you develop a positive attitude. Take time each day to picture yourself doing well. For example, if you have a test coming up, imagine yourself sitting at the desk, reading the questions, and writing the correct answers. Another example could be a project at work. If you are to make a presentation to your supervisor, visualize yourself successfully making the presentation and seeing your supervisor pleased.

Remember, however, that visualization does not take the place of hard work. If you have studied hard or prepared thoroughly and are rested and healthy, visualization can enhance your performance.

Elwood N. Chapman in his book, *Attitude—Your Most Priceless Possession*, says you can use the "flipside technique" to adjust your attitude. When a negative enters your life, immediately flip the problem over and look for whatever humor may exist on the other side.

· ·

Signals Give Clues to Your Attitude

Several attitudes and the signals they give off are described below. Some represent positive attitudes and others represent negative attitudes. Do these describe anyone you know? Can you add others to the list?

Attitude	Signals Given Off
Complaining	Nothing you do will make me happy.
Determined	Nothing can stop me.
Fearful	I worry about everything.
Rejecting	People don't like me.
Superior	I'm great at everything.
Inferior	I'm not good at anything.
Insecure	I'm not sure what I should say or do.
Arrogant	I'm pretty important.
Humble	We are all equally important.
Intimidating	I'll bully you.
Beligerent	Oh, yeah? Just try it.
Persevering	I'll keep trying until I make it.
Victimized	Poor me.
Optimistic	Things are going to be okay.
Pessimistic	Nothing works out right.
Enthusiastic	Okay, let's try it.
Caring	You are important to me.
Resilient	Nothing keeps me down for long.
Uncooperative	No, I'm not going to try anything new.
Confrontational	Make me.
Defensive	It's not my fault.

The School-to-Work Series "Attitude," by Career Solutions Training Group © 1996 South-Western Educational Publishing.

Take time each
day to visualize
yourself succeeding.

ALWAYS BEING POSITIVE IS DIFFICULT

All individuals face difficult periods in their lives. The "down" periods can be caused by stress from fatigue, tension, or illness. Other experiences, such as the death of a loved one, loss of a pet, loss of personal belongings through fire or natural disaster, divorce, robbery, moving, job loss, and retirement, also trigger stress. Even good things cause stress, if they involve major changes, deadlines, or lots of details (such as a wedding). When these events occur, we may have difficulty remaining positive. Stress can distort perception and our ability to identify truth or view matters realistically.

**The grieving
process affects
our outlook.**

Difficult events (even some that are positive, like leaving home and moving to a new state to start a new job) can trigger a natural grieving process that was first identified by the Swiss psychiatrist Elisabeth Kubler-Ross. She discovered five stages of grieving—denial, anger, bargaining, grieving, and acceptance. By understanding this process we can work through our grief and return to our positive perspective of life. Individuals

GLOBAL CONNECTION

Because of jet travel and modern communication and information technology, we now operate within a global, rather than regional, economy.

1. *How can differing perceptions cause problems working in a global economy?*
2. *Do you think that the world could eventually meld into one culture because of modern communication techniques? Why or why not?*

enter the stages of grieving at different times. Those persons who do not move through the stages or who stay at one stage too long may need professional help.

Check Out My Attitude

Evaluate your attitude by responding Yes or No to each statement.

1. I complain immediately when I don't like something	Yes	No
2. I can't stand do-gooders.	Yes	No
3. You had better not try to pull a fast one on me, or I'll get you back.	Yes	No
4. If you don't succeed the first time, give up because you'll embarrass yourself.	Yes	No
5. I think it's good to complain; then people know exactly how I feel.	Yes	No
6. Being positive most of the time is just too unrealistic.	Yes	No
7. If anything goes wrong, it ruins the rest of my day.	Yes	No
8. If I do a good job, nobody cares about the way I act.	Yes	No
9. Backing down makes you look weak	Yes	No
10. Few people understand what I go through.	Yes	No

If you responded Yes to one or two statements, you think negatively sometimes. If you responded Yes to at least five statements, you see the bad side too often. If you responded Yes to more than five statements, life must be tough for you. You need to learn coping behaviors.

The School-to-Work Series, "Attitude," by Career Solutions Training Group © 1996 South-Western Educational Publishing.

---

1. What events can cause people to grieve?

2. Have you ever seen someone stuck in a phase of grieving?

3. When you have a loss, should you allow yourself to grieve? Why or why not?

4. What difficulties can occur at work when someone is going through the grieving process?

*Fast*Chat

2.6 How Do You See Your Roles?

Conforming to expected roles can help us succeed.

Everyone has different **roles** to fill. Employee, parent, church member, student, volunteer, teacher, and friend are examples. Each role has its own acceptable behavior and dress. Realizing which role you are playing and behaving appropriately for that role is important. People feel more comfortable dealing with individuals who fit roles as the roles are perceived. For instance, we expect our auto mechanic to wear work clothes made to withstand oil and grease. A mechanic who is not dressed "appropriately" may be perceived as being unable to perform the tasks necessary to service cars. Parents expect public school teachers not to swear and frequently complain if swear words occur in classroom lectures, even though their children may hear these same words numerous times in a single evening of watching television.

Because of this phenomenon, be sensitive to the roles that you play and the perceptions and expectations that others have of you in those roles. Learn what the expected behaviors are and then conform to them when appropriate. Conforming to expectations of dress and behavior at work will help you do your job effectively, will enhance your image, and will help you move ahead professionally.

Some people feel more comfortable in one role than in another. For instance, a mother who is returning to school after 20 years will feel more

GLOBAL CONNECTION

Cultures perceive things differently. For instance, Americans see time as linear, with a beginning and end. Americans have sayings such as "a stitch in time saves nine." Many other cultures see time as circular; the seasons come and go and punctuality is not as important.

1. *What problems might this cause for individuals from other cultures who come to work in America? For Americans working abroad?*

2. *Should American companies operating overseas follow the customs of U.S. companies or of the country in which they are located?*

comfortable in her role of mother than in her role of student. The employee promoted to supervisor may feel ill at ease initially. Realize that being uncomfortable in a new role is natural. If you are aware of the behavior that the role requires and keep in mind that changing your behavior to conform to that role is expected and acceptable, you will handle transitions into new roles better.

Understanding our roles helps reduce conflict.

Sometimes roles are ambiguous. Most people feel awkward the first day on a new job or as a new member of a group because they are not sure what is expected of them. Again, this unease is natural. Learning a new role and developing confidence in it takes time.

Sometimes, too, roles can conflict. A father may need to be at work at the same time that his child's Scout meeting is being held. A mother may feel guilty about being at work and not at home with her children. Such conflict can cause anxiety. Recognizing the source of anxiety will help us cope with it.

We all play many different roles in life.

List your roles.

1. How do you behave differently in each of these roles?

2. How does your role at work differ from your role at home?

3. What might happen if you behaved at work as you do with friends?

*Fast***Chat**

Learning
Objective 4

Recognize perceptual defense mechanisms, what can trigger them, and how they hinder our relationships.

Perceptual defense mechanisms are used to cope with anxiety.

Everyone faces anxiety. Anxiety can be caused by a number of factors such as role conflict, ambiguity, or low self-esteem. To function satisfactorily, we need to feel adequate in our activities and acceptable to others. High feelings of acceptability can compensate for low feelings of adequacy. The weak student who is well liked because of a kind personality is an example. The reverse is also true: high feelings of adequacy can compensate for low feelings of acceptability. An example is the student who makes good grades but has no friends or social life. However, when both adequacy and acceptability are low, a person's overall feelings of worth suffer.

Individuals frequently cope with anxiety through the use of **perceptual defense mechanisms**. These mechanisms serve to protect our feelings of worth. Note that both positive and negative outcomes can result from the use of defense mechanisms. The trouble is that defense mechanisms may keep us from confronting the real problem. Some common defense mechanisms are explained on the following page.

While at work, be aware of the behavior of others. *Stop to think* before you *react*. Perhaps your supervisor has had a fight at home and now seems angry with everyone in the department. If you are aware that displacement is occurring, you will be less likely to take the gruffness personally. Taking a minute to think through interactions before responding can greatly improve your human relations skills.

FastChat

1. Examine your own thoughts and behaviors. Are you using defense mechanisms regularly? Which ones?

2. Does use of defense mechanisms cause you to avoid dealing with your problems?

3. Are there times when using these mechanisms is healthy?

4. Can you be more tolerant of others' behavior if you realize they are using defense mechanisms? Why or why not?

Perceptual Defense Mechanisms

Denial
Denying that anxiety exists
<u>Work example</u>: "I'm not worried about my upcoming performance appraisal." "I never become nervous before a presentation."
<u>Home example</u>: "Death doesn't frighten me." "I don't become nervous about tests."

Repression
Pushing stressful thoughts, worries, or emotions "out of mind"
<u>Work example</u>: The cashier who was robbed cannot remember the incident.
<u>Home example</u>: The child cannot remember being abused by a parent.

Rationalization
Explaining away unacceptable feelings, thoughts, or motives
<u>Work example</u>: "It's just as well that I did not get that promotion. I would not have been able to spend as much time as I want with my family."
<u>Home example</u>: "I know Joe didn't call me, but I am sure he likes me. He just had important things to do."

Regression
Returning to previous, less mature types of behavior
<u>Work example</u>: Ann's supervisor is reprimanding her for sloppy work. Ann starts to cry.
<u>Home example</u>: Mike wants to be waited on when he is sick, as he was as a child.

Scapegoating
Blaming another person or group for a problem
<u>Work example</u>: "It's the Personnel Department's fault. If they would hire better people, we wouldn't be in this mess."
<u>Home example</u>: "It's Billy's fault that I didn't get any of my chores done. He kept talking to me."

Projection
Attributing an unacceptable thought or feeling about yourself to others
<u>Work example</u>: The supervisor routinely comes in late and accuses employees who are on time of being late.
<u>Home example</u>: The husband accuses the wife of wanting a divorce when he is actually the one considering a separation.

Displacement
Finding safe, less threatening people or objects and venting frustration on them
<u>Work example that goes home</u>: An angry manager yells at a supervisor (who cannot yell back), the frustrated supervisor yells at an employee (who cannot yell back), the irritated employee yells at the spouse (who cannot or will not yell back), the furious spouse yells at their child (who cannot yell back), and the upset child kicks the dog.

Sublimation
Directing unacceptable impulses into socially acceptable channels
<u>Work example</u>: A person who is aggressive may make a career in the military or sports.
<u>Home example</u>: A suicidal person may take up a risky sport, such as sky diving.

Compensation
An attempt to relieve feelings of inadequacy or frustration by excelling in other areas
<u>Work example</u>: The employee who feels unappreciated by an immediate supervisor may take on tasks in other areas, such as committee or community projects, to experience success or receive positive feedback.
<u>Home example</u>: A physically handicapped person may become a computer expert to show that his or her mind is not impaired.

Perceptions play an important role in the relationship we have with supervisors and others above us. How you perceive superiors will determine how you act around them.

Feeling intimidated by authority figures with whom you have not had an opportunity to interact is quite natural. If you become so frightened by authority figures that you cannot communicate comfortably, look for opportunities to interact in casual ways. For instance, you might speak briefly in the hall or, if appropriate, stick your head in their doors for a quick "hello." This type of assertive behavior will help you see authority figures in a new light.

FEELING UNSURE OF AUTHORITY FIGURES

You may feel unsure of authority figures when a coworker is promoted over you or uncomfortable when you are promoted over coworkers. This type of change creates what psychologists call a loss of perceptual anchorages. An adjustment period is normal while everyone involved learns new roles and what each expects of the others in these roles.

Another time that can produce anxiety is when you get a new boss. You may miss the old boss and resent having to start from scratch in showing the new supervisor what you are capable of doing. You must remember that some time will be necessary for both of you to become comfortable with each other. Being ready with suggestions if asked and offering to help the new supervisor will encourage a good relationship. Keep an open mind and avoid prejudging the new boss.

VIEWING THE BOSS

The most effective way to view bosses is as humans with their own feelings and own jobs to do. They have their strengths and weaknesses, good days and bad days. Recognize this fact, and learn when to approach them. For instance, if you approach your supervisor about a trivial matter when she is in a hurry or has just arrived late to work because of a flat tire, you can probably expect a less-than-enthusiastic reception.

Also be sensitive to bosses' moods and viewpoints and do not challenge them in front of others or when they are not feeling well. Remember that bosses will appreciate tact and kindness just as much as you do.

Quick tip . . . .

Try this tactic in bringing a problem to your supervisor:
1. Define the current problem/situation as you see it.
2. State how you feel the situation should be and why.
3. Suggest a solution.
4. State specifically what you would like the supervisor to do.
5. Affirm your support and offer your assistance.

. . . .

MANAGING THE BOSS

Just as supervisors manage their staffs to meet goals and deadlines, you can manage your bosses to meet your own objectives. This behavior is called **upward management**. Upward management can result in better relationships, increased flexibility in assignments, and a greater understanding of how your work fits in with the overall organizational picture. As a result, you may be more committed to the job, have higher morale, and increase your productivity.

Managing your supervisor increases job satisfactions.

Walter St. John, in an article in *Personnel Journal*, pointed out that supervisors have the same concerns, fears, and anxieties as others. We can help ourselves by understanding and learning to cope with these fears:

1. Looking bad to the bosses or others and/or being criticized.
2. Not being respected or appreciated.
3. Appearing inadequate, perhaps because of outdated skills or sharp, aggressive subordinates.
4. Being rejected as a leader.

ETHICS CONNECTION

We are all confronted with situations requiring us to use ethical judgment every day. What is your obligation concerning the confidentiality of information revealed to you by others while at work? What if the individual reveals stealing money from the company? Taking company equipment or supplies? Falsifying a time sheet?

Tips for Managing Your Supervisor

1. Present your supervisor with suggestions for solving problems rather than just problems.
2. Keep your supervisor informed of the progress of your work so that those higher than your supervisor can be informed. No one likes surprises.
   (This will help lay the groundwork if you must ask for extra time or help later.)
3. Be honest about problems. Most supervisors will tolerate some mistakes as part of the learning process.
4. Be sensitive to the effect that you have on others and take responsibility for your own behavior.
5. Do not try to change your supervisors. Study their preferences and try to conform to them.
6. Try to make your supervisors look good. Build on their strengths and compensate for their weaknesses.
7. Be sure that your priorities are in agreement with your supervisor's and be aware of changing priorities.
8. Know your supervisor's goals and understand how you can help meet them.
9. Recognize that you can learn from criticism. Learn how to ask for specific information and feedback.
10. Try to see things from your supervisor's perspective. Supervisors may not always have the right perceptions, but they do have the power and do determine goals.

—*Government Executive*

1. Did you ever have difficulty viewing your boss as "human"? Why?

2. What is your current perception of authority? Where did it come from?

3. What can you do to see your boss as more human?

Summary

Perceptions differ greatly depending on a number of factors, including your upbringing, values, and culture. Recognizing and appreciating differences in perception is vital to your ability to function in the workplace. Others learn about our perceptions when we practice self-disclosure. We learn theirs by accepting feedback.

The Johari Window suggests that ideally we should have a large arena, the result of self-disclosure and openness to feedback. Positive self-esteem, an optimistic outlook on life, and an understanding of the roles people play in life are other important ingredients in a successful career. Positive thinking can be enhanced through changing our thought processes, engaging in positive self-talk, and using visualization.

Learning about the defense mechanisms that individuals use to cope with anxiety can help you deal more successfully with yourself and those around you. Defense mechanisms sometimes have positive outcomes, but they may prevent us from confronting the real problem.

Remember that the most effective way to view bosses is as humans and deal with them accordingly. Learn to manage them by using the concepts of upward management.

Key Terms

perception
halo effect
reverse halo effect
self-disclosure
feedback
Johari Window
self-esteem
optimists
pessimists
self-talk
visualization
roles
perceptual defense mechanisms
denial
repression
rationalization
regression
scapegoating
projection
displacement
sublimation
compensation
upward management

Review Questions

1. Explain why people have different perceptions of the same events, objects, persons, or situations.
2. Name the panes of the Johari Window and explain what they mean.
3. What is self-perception? Why is it important?
4. Name and explain the common perceptual defense mechanisms.
5. How can your perceptions of your supervisor affect the relationship you have?

Discussion Questions

1. Name three reasons why different people might view the same situation differently. Are these differences acceptable? Why or why not?
2. Draw the Johari Window of three people with whom you interact frequently at work or at school. Explain why you have drawn each pane a particular size, and describe examples of the person's behavior. How might they enlarge their arenas? What effect would enlarging their arenas have on them? On you?
3. What is your self-image at work? At home? Around friends? What can you do to improve it?
4. Describe an incident from home or work showing each of the defense mechanisms in operation.
5. Why is recognizing that supervisors are human important? How can you allow your supervisor to be "real"?
6. How would you describe an ideal worker? An ideal boss?

Listening, writing, reasoning.

Chapter Project

Invite a psychologist, social worker, or therapist to your class to discuss self-esteem. Write a plan on how you will raise your self-esteem or keep it high. The plan should include action items, target dates, and a maintenance plan.

Applications

In small groups analyze the following situations.

The Screaming Supervisor

Reading, listening, problem solving, leadership, participating as a member of a team

"You really messed this up!" Isaac yelled at Bobby and Maria. "I want it done right by noon or both of you are fired!" Isaac turned and stomped away.

"Oh, he makes me so angry!" Maria exclaimed under her breath. "What's been eating him? Nothing I've done has made him happy!"

"I heard he's split up with his wife," Bobby said. "They separated last weekend."

"That's true," said Ted, "but you two have really been doing a poor job lately. I don't blame Isaac for being upset."

1. Why do you think Isaac is behaving this way?
2. Is Isaac using a defense mechanism? If you think so, which one? Are Bobby and Maria using a defense mechanism? If so, which one?
3. What would be a more appropriate way for Isaac to deal with Bobby's and Maria's performances?
4. What would be an appropriate action for Bobby and Maria to take if they think that they are being unjustly criticized?

Viewpoint

"Don't ever take my tools again without asking," Ann growled at Dan as she stormed out of the room.

"I don't understand it," Dan said, turning to Sally. "I had ten brothers and sisters and I had nothing that was my own. We shared everything."

"Well, I understand," replied Sally. "My mother always taught me to ask permission before I borrowed anything."

Reading, listening, participating as a member of a team, working with diversity, problem solving

1. Which viewpoint is right?
2. Should Dan respect Ann's feelings?
3. Does Dan have to agree with Ann's feelings in order to respect them?

Additional Readings and Resources

Appellate, Gary. *Happiness—It's Your Choice*. Sherman Oaks, CA: Beginner Publishing, 1985.

Carter, Les, Frank Minirth and Paul Meier. *The Anger Workbook (Minirth-Meier Clinic Series)*. Nashville: Thomas Nelson, 1993.

Carter, Les, Frank Minirth (Contributor). *The Choosing to Forgive Workbook*. Nashville: Thomas Nelson, 1997.

Colgrove, Melba, Harold H. Bloomfield, and Peter McWilliams. *How to Survive the Loss of a Love*. New York: Bantam Books, 1993.

Harris, Thomas A. *I'm OK, You're OK*. New York: Avon Books, 1996.

Kubler-Ross, Elisabeth. *On Death and Dying*. New York: Collier Books, 1997.

Lee, John, and Bill Stott (Contributor). *Facing the Fire: Experiencing and Expressing Anger Appropriately*. New York: Bantam Doubleday Dell, 1995.

Lerner, Harriet Goldhor. *The Dance of Anger*. New York: Harper Collins, 1989.

Peck, M. Scott. *The Road Less Traveled*. New York: Simon and Schuster, 1998.

Rubin, Theodore Isaac. *The Angry Book*. New York: Touchstone Books, 1998.

Rubin, Theodore Isaac. *Compassion and Self-Hate: An Alternative to Despair*. New York: Touchstone Books, 1998.

Sheeny, Gail. *New Passages: Mapping Your Life Across Time*. New York: Ballantine, 1996.

Motivation:
Maximizing Productivity

focus

A Great Place To Work! The lead story in the August 25, 1997, issue of *Forbes* magazine illustrates how BMC Software motivates employees in today's work environment.

Every employee can get a free car wash, access to a bank and a dry cleaner on the premises, and almost all have their own private office. Prefer to work from home or on the weekends? BMC offers its employees a home computer and a telephone line for their free modem. How could they be making a profit with all these freebies? Well, the company earned $164 million on $563 million in revenues, and its stock has appreciated 36 fold since 1988.

The key to BMC's success is allowing employees to have a piece of the action. Employees who come up with successful new software ideas that make the company money are given 5 percent of the product's revenues. Since successful software products can generate a good deal of revenue, this package can add up to a lot of money. The plan certainly motivates employees to participate.

What are some of the motivating factors offered in places where you have worked? Do you think that money is the only motivator in the BMC situation?

After studying this chapter, you should be able to:

1. *Discuss why understanding motivation is important to organizations and individuals.*

2. *Trace the basic motivational behavior model from its point of origin through its completion.*

3. *Identify the two basic categories of individual needs.*

4. *Explain the differences between needs and wants.*

5. *Identify the major theorists and describe their contributions to the study of human motivation.*

6. *Discuss constructive versus destructive behaviors to fulfill needs.*

7. *Define the three motivational source fields in individuals.*

8. *Discuss motivational techniques that are increasingly important in motivating employees.*

3.1 What Is Motivation?

Learning
**Objectives 1
and 2**

*Discuss why
understanding
motivation is
important to
organizations and
individuals.
Trace the basic
motivational
behavior model
from its point of
origin through its
completion.*

Motivation is the emotional stimulus that causes us to act. The stimulus may be a need or a drive that energizes certain behaviors. At work, motivation is a combination of all factors in our working environment that lead to positive or negative efforts. If we understand what motivates us, we are more likely to achieve our personal and professional goals. Likewise, if organizations know how to motivate employees, they can increase productivity. This ability to boost production is increasingly important as United States organizations compete in the global market. While all companies make some effort to motivate employees, a growing number of organizations are introducing new strategies, including different compensation packages, as a means of motivating today's workers.

Quick tip.

"Success doesn't come to you . . . you go to it." Marva Collins

CASE STUDIES IN THE NEWS

Many organizations are phasing out or replacing traditional merit systems and are exploring other alternative systems of pay. The emphasis today is on pay for performance. For example, Fleetwood Enterprises, a California-based recreational vehicle and manufactured housing maker, relies on incentive pay to boost performance. Fleetwood's base pay is relatively low, but all its workers can and do earn production or incentive bonuses. Nucor Corp., a steel maker in Charlotte, NC, also places a strong emphasis on incentive pay. It hires production workers at a base rate of $10 to $12 per hour and offers production bonuses that can more than double that base pay rate. Both companies feel this appeals to entrepreneurial types.

The Wall Street Journal, April 9, 1998

How would you feel about working for one of these companies? What might be some disadvantages associated with these methods?

Predicting motivation is difficult. To understand what motivates someone, we must guess what physiological and psychological processes underlie behavior. For example, if Allen works much harder than Sid, we assume that Allen is more highly motivated than Sid to achieve some goal—perhaps a bonus, a promotion, or the prestige associated with being the top producer in the organization. Allen seemingly has a stronger need to work hard. However, unless Allen tells us why, we can only presume what his motivation or need may be.

Understanding motivation helps individuals and organizations.

Through studies of motivation and behavior, psychologists have generally concluded that all human behavior is goal-directed toward satisfying a felt need. The figure below illustrates a basic behavioral model with an unsatisfied need as the starting point in the process of motivation.

According to the model below, an unsatisfied need causes inner tension (physical or psychological). The individual engages in some action to reduce or relieve the tension. The individual wants to do something that will satisfy the perceived need. For example, a thirsty man needs water, is driven by his thirst, and is motivated to drink.

Human behavior is goal-directed toward need satisfaction.

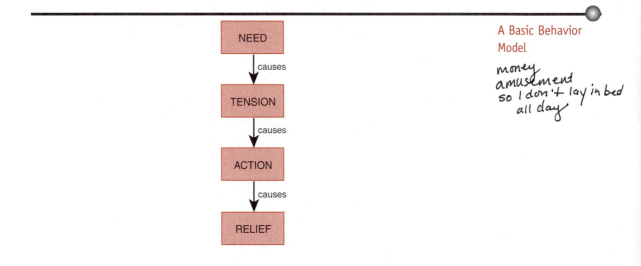

A Basic Behavior Model

money
amusement
so I don't lay in bed
all day

All humans have needs. They need to breathe, eat, drink, and rest. But these needs are only part of a much larger picture. People also need to be accepted, fulfilled, recognized, and appreciated. They need to dream, aspire, desire, acquire! Many are the motives of individuals and groups. Understanding the complexity of these motives or needs—our own as well as those of others—is essential in establishing and maintaining good human relations.

Our behavior is clearly motivated by needs, and yet we often do not understand the complexities and the subtleties of our motives and needs. How often have you done something and then asked yourself, "Why did I just do that?" or "What caused that?" Try a simple exercise to experience the full range of activities involved in the motivation. Think of something you "need" and your motive for that need. What will you do to satisfy that need? Could the action you take actually cause you to be dissatisfied? An awareness of these actions will help you understand your behavior.

Until basic needs are satisfied, other needs are of no importance.

"What's this on your resume about requiring food, water and sleep?"

FastChat

1. What is motivating you most today?

2. What actions might you take to satisfy the needs behind that motivation?

How Do Wants Differ from Needs?

People's wants may be very different from their needs, as in the following scenario.

Wimberley's New Car

Wimberley just graduated from college in June and is about to start her first big job. The new job is located almost 20 miles from her modest apartment, so she will need reliable transportation. As Wimberley shops for a car to satisfy this need, she finds one that greatly exceeds her budget allowance, but is what she calls her "dream machine."

Wimberley reasons, "I *want* one of these convertibles with the deluxe option package, but all I *need* is this economical gas-saver. I need safe transportation from point A to point B and that doesn't require deluxe extras. Besides, the economy car fits my budget, will be easy on gas, and I can afford the insurance, too."

Often we are conditioned to think that our "wants" are "needs," when, in fact, a need can be satisfied much more simply. We all have needs, which vary greatly in origin and occur in varying degrees of intensity. Needs fall into two categories—primary (physiological) or secondary (psychological).

Primary needs are the basic needs required to sustain life, such as food, water, air, sleep, and shelter (for individual survival) and sex/reproduction (for survival of societal group). Because these needs are so basic to survival, we can easily understand why and how a person's behavior is affected by them.

Secondary needs are psychological and are far more complex. They include the need for security, affiliation or love, respect, and autonomy. Secondary needs are a result of our values and beliefs. These needs are not identical in everyone, nor is the same value or priority placed on satisfying them.

Gary Applegate, in his book *Happiness, It's Your Choice*, states that we have eight secondary needs—security, faith, worth, freedom, belonging, fun, knowledge, and health. Everything else, according to Applegate, is a want. He suggests that wants can be seen as pathways to meeting our needs.

Primary needs are physiological and secondary needs are psychological.

1. What primary needs do you satisfy each day?

2. How are you satisfying your secondary needs?

*Fast*Chat

What Do the Theorists Say?

*Identify the major
theorists and
describe their
contributions to the
study of human
motivation.*

**Maslow,
Herzberg,
McClelland, and
Vroom explained
motivation in the
workplace.**

**Maslow
identified five
levels of needs.**

Many theories have been developed about motivation. Four of these theories apply to individual behaviors in the work setting. Abraham Maslow, Frederick Herzberg, David McClelland, and Victor Vroom have contributed the most to understanding motivation in the workplace.

MASLOW'S HIERARCHY OF NEEDS

Like many other psychologists, Maslow agreed that only a felt need motivates and that once a need is satisfied it ceases to motivate. However, he went on to identify a **hierarchy of needs**. The figure on page 61 illustrates Maslow's five need levels and briefly describes the needs associated with each level. The five levels are physiological needs, safety and security, social needs, esteem, and self-actualization.

Physiological Needs **Physiological needs** include our desire for food, sleep, water, shelter, and other satisfiers of physiological drives. These are our most basic needs and, until they are satisfied, other needs are of little or no importance. In the workplace, adequate air conditioning and heating, water fountains, cafeteria or snack machines, and other satisfactory working conditions are designed to meet some of these needs.

Safety and Security Needs Today **safety and security needs** are more often reflected in our need for economic and emotional security than for physical safety. Examples of how the safety need can be met in the workplace are safe working conditions, job security, periodic salary increases, adequate fringe benefits, or a union contract.

Social Needs **Social needs** center around our desires for love, affection, acceptance in society, and meaningful affiliation with others. These needs are often satisfied in the workplace by compatible friendships in the work group, quality supervision, and membership in professional associations or organizations. For most people, the need for satisfactory relations with others and a place in society is so important that its lack is often a cause of emotional problems and general maladjustment.

SELF-ACTUALIZATION

Personal Need to Maximize Potential (personal growth, full use of abilities, creative expression, challenging job, advanced professional achievement)

ESTEEM NEEDS

Personal Need to Feel Worthy (respect from self and others, meaningful work, increased responsibility, peer and supervisory recognition for work well done, merit pay increases or awards)

SOCIAL NEEDS

Personal Need for Belonging and Affiliation (friendships in the work group, quality supervision, membership in professional associations or organizations)

SAFETY/ SECURITY NEEDS

Psychological Need to Feel Free of Anxiety (economic and emotional security, safe working conditions, job security, periodic salary increases, adequate fringe benefits, union contract)

PHYSIOLOGICAL NEEDS

Basic Needs of the Body (food, sleep, water, shelter, others)

Esteem Needs   Often called the ego needs, **esteem needs** include our need for respect from self and others. Fulfilling these needs gives us a feeling of competence, control, and usefulness. In the workplace, these needs are generally met through meaningful work, increased responsibility, peer and supervisory recognition for work well done, and merit pay increases or awards. People whose esteem needs are not met often feel inferior and hopeless.

Self-Actualization Needs   **Self-actualization needs** refer to our desire to become everything of which we are capable, to reach our full potential. These needs include the desire to grow personally, to use our abilities to the greatest extent, and to engage in creative expression. In the workplace, these needs are most often met through a challenging job, the opportunity to be creative, and advanced professional achievement.

People actualize at different levels.

A common question asked about self-actualization is whether we ever fully actualize. The answer lies in the individual. People actualize at different levels. Some people, for example, are satisfied with a bachelor's degree from a local college, whereas others feel a need for a master's or doctoral degree from a prominent university. Some individuals reach their full potential at a simple job; others have a capacity far beyond that level. Some self-actualized individuals tend to be creative and will thrive on feedback. Satisfying this need level is, therefore, highly individualized.

Maslow believed that we generally satisfy these needs in a hierarchical order, fulfilling the lower-order needs first before moving on to the higher-order needs. However, he added that we can move up and down the hierarchy depending on the situation at hand. For example, in recent years many companies have merged, downsized, and streamlined to become more competitive in the global marketplace. With the mergers and down-

Individuals can move up and down the hierarchy of need levels.

TECHNOLOGY CONNECTION

From the age of 10, Lisa Lister envisioned a future in the fast-paced computing fields. Lisa had long been motivated toward a career in a technical field and began her quest by studying computer science at Stanford University. She soon had a successful career as a software designer in nearby Silicon Valley. Lisa loved her job and felt satisfied that her needs were fulfilled—for a while.

Today, she is a midwife in Mountain View, California, birthing babies rather than code. High-tech jobs such as the one Lisa left go begging for experienced female incumbents. Women are leaving or avoiding computer careers in droves. According to the Bureau of Labor Statistics, the proportion of women among U.S. computer professionals has fallen in recent years and the share of women in the academic pipeline has equally shrunk. A study at Carnegie Mellon concluded that the image of programming as a solitary, myopic fascination with obscure technical details is not without foundation in many industry jobs. And that image "is especially pernicious for discouraging and repelling women students" who want broader experiences. In Lisa's case, her motivations certainly took a dramatic turn toward new life interests and broader experiences.

Charles Piller, *Los Angeles Times*, August 1998

How do you feel about this report? Which of Maslow's need levels had Lisa satisfied at first and where on the needs hierarchy is she today?

sizing, jobs are often eliminated or greatly reduced in level of importance. Successful, often long-term employees who may have been operating at the esteem and self-actualization levels may suddenly be without a job. These people are compelled to return to the more basic levels of safety and security needs—they need work and an income. Most likely, these people will resume their natural progression through the need levels once the security of a paying job satisfies their lower-order needs.

Maslow's Hierarchy of Needs Theory was presented in 1954 in *Motivation and Personality*. This theory became an important building block in the understanding of human behavior, laying a foundation for the work of other theorists.

HERZBERG'S TWO-FACTOR THEORY OF MOTIVATION

In 1959, Frederick Herzberg presented his **two-factor theory of motivation**. After questioning over 200 accountants and engineers about what in their work led to extreme satisfaction or extreme dissatisfaction, Herzberg concluded that two sets of factors or conditions influence the behavior of individuals at work. He called the first set hygiene factors and the second set motivational factors.

Hygiene Factors   **Hygiene factors**, also known as maintenance factors, are necessary to maintain a reasonable level of satisfaction among employees. Included in the category of hygiene factors are company policies and procedures, working conditions and job security, salary and employee benefits, the quality of supervision, and relationships with supervisors, peers, and subordinates. Although the absence of these factors may cause considerable dissatisfaction among workers, their presence will not necessarily lead to motivation. Generally, these factors prevent employees from being unhappy in their jobs. However, happy employees are not necessarily motivated workers.

Motivational Factors   According to Herzberg, **motivational factors** build high levels of motivation and job satisfaction. These factors include achievement, advancement, recognition, responsibility, and the work itself. Another important finding in Herzberg's research was that highly motivated employees have a high tolerance for dissatisfaction arising from the absence of adequate maintenance factors. This fact probably has to do with employees' perceptions of motivational factors. A factor that motivates one individual may be perceived as a mere maintenance factor by another. The two-factor theory (see diagram, page 64) compares sets of satisfiers and dissatisfiers and their effects on job attitudes.

Herzberg's theory extended Maslow's ideas and made them more specifically applicable to the workplace. Additionally, it reinforced the concept

Herzberg defines two sets of factors in worker behavior.

Hygiene factors maintain satisfaction.

Motivational factors build motivation and job satisfaction.

Herzberg's Two-Factor Theory of Motivation

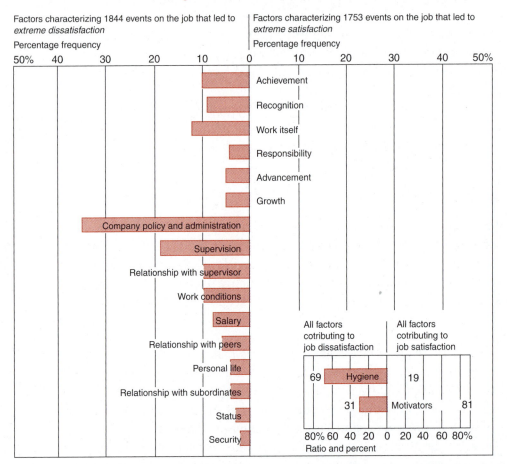

Reprinted by permission of Harvard Business Review. *An exhibit from* One More TIme: How Do You Motivate Employees? *by Frederick Herzberg,* Harvard Business Review Classic. *September/October 1987. Copyright © 1987 by the President and Fellows of Harvard College; all rights reserved.*

that while some factors tend to motivate employees, others have little to no effect on worker productivity. We tend to be motivated by what we are seeking rather than by what we already have. Maslow's hierarchy of needs theory is compared to Herzberg's two-factor theory in the following illustration.

Before we can successfully apply any motivational technique, we must assess the need level of the person concerned. Some people are both satisfied and motivated by hygiene factors, such as an adequate salary and comfortable working conditions. Others are only motivated by opportunities for additional responsibility or advancement to a higher-level position. This variation in need levels has been explored by other theorists with interesting results.

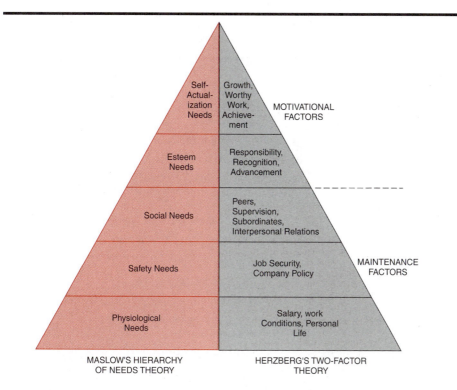

Self-Actualization Needs	Growth, Worthy Work, Achievement — MOTIVATIONAL FACTORS
Esteem Needs	Responsibility, Recognition, Advancement
Social Needs	Peers, Supervision, Subordinates, Interpersonal Relations
Safety Needs	Job Security, Company Policy — MAINTENANCE FACTORS
Physiological Needs	Salary, work Conditions, Personal Life

MASLOW'S HIERARCHY OF NEEDS THEORY — HERZBERG'S TWO-FACTOR THEORY

MCCLELLAND'S ACQUIRED NEEDS THEORY

In 1961 David McClelland developed a theory of motivation that says our needs are the result of our early personality development. Calling it the **acquired needs theory**, he wrote that through cultural exposure, people acquire a framework of three basic needs—achievement, power, and affiliation. McClelland's premise was that these three needs are the primary motives for behavior. His theory is outlined in the diagram on page 66.

Following McClelland's theory, if we recognize which of the needs is most important to others, we can create the right environment for them. For example, people with a high need for achievement have a natural tendency to become leaders or managers. Planning, setting objectives and goals, and controlling the methods of reaching those goals are a basic part of their work style.

People with a strong need for affiliation are less concerned with getting ahead than they are with developing close relationships and friendships with others at work. They tend to enjoy jobs that require a variety of interpersonal contacts.

People with a strong need for power naturally seek positions with a great deal of authority and influence. McClelland found that people who are considered highly successful tend to be motivated by the need for power.

McClelland says most people are motivated by achievement, affiliation, or power.

quick wit

"Just what you want to be, you will be in the end."

Justin Hayward, British Songwriter, Musician

quick wit
. . . .

"After climbing a great hill, one only finds that there are many more hills to climb."

. . . .
Nelson Mandela

McClelland's Acquired Needs Theory	
Individuals with a high need for:	Personality Trait Tendencies
Achievement	• Seek and assume responsibility • Take calculated risks • Set challenging but realistic goals • Develop plans to achieve goals • Seek and use feedback in their actions
Affiliation	• Seek and find friendly relationships • Are not overly concerned with "getting ahead" • Seek jobs that are "people intensive" • Require high degrees of interpersonal action
Power	• Seek positions of influence • Enjoy jobs with high degrees of authority and power • Are concerned with reaching top-level, decision-making positions • Need autonomy

McClelland's acquired needs theory provides additional insight into the kinds of needs and motives that drive individual behavior and strengthens our knowledge of how to influence the behavior of others. The theory also helps us determine our own motives and understand our behavior.

VROOM'S EXPECTANCY THEORY

Victor Vroom, another motivational theorist, took the basic ideas of Maslow, Herzberg, and McClelland one step further. His **expectancy theory** views motivation as a process of choices. According to this theory, you behave in certain ways because you expect certain results from that behavior. For example, you may perceive that if you study long and hard for an upcoming examination, you stand a strong chance of making an "A" in the course. If you have a need for the prestige or achievement inherent in making an "A," you will more than likely study long and hard, expecting to receive the high grade to fulfill your need.

According to Vroom, we are motivated by expected results of actions.

Vroom was careful to emphasize the importance of the individual's perceptions and assessments of organizational behavior. Not all workers in an organization place the same value on factors associated with job performance. What individual workers perceive as important is far more critical to their choices than what their supervisors view as important. This idea still intrigues researchers, and further work is being done in the area of the expectancy theory of motivation.

The opening story about BMC Software employees is an excellent example of Vroom's expectancy theory. The employees expect good bonuses based on their behavior and are, therefore, highly motivated to be productive in order to gain personally.

Although many other theories on motivation have been developed, these capture the main ideas. The most persistent theme in motivational theories is that all behavior is directed toward some goal to satisfy a need. If the action taken leads to positive outcomes, it will probably be repeated. If the action taken leads to negative results, the behavior will usually not be repeated. Understanding these basic concepts enables us to lead ourselves and others toward desired results.

quick wit

"I'm a great believer in luck, and I find the harder I work, the more I have of it."

Thomas Jefferson, American President

FastChat

1. What are the five levels of Maslow's Hierarchy of Needs?

2. What similarities exist between Maslow's and Herzberg's theories?

3. What three basic needs are the framework of McClelland's Acquired Needs Theory?

4. According to Vroom, what is the motivation for behavior?

Learning
**Objectives 6
and   7**

*Discuss constructive
versus destructive
behaviors to fulfill
needs. Define the
three motivational
source fields in
individuals.*

Knowledge of motivational theory can help us as individuals in a variety of ways. Understanding the difference between a want and a need, recognizing what motivates us, learning alternative ways to fulfill needs, and learning how to motivate others when we are in leadership situations can help us reach our personal and professional goals. Learning to recognize the difference between wants and needs can help us be satisfied with what we have. This lesson can also assist us in being patient and planning alternative ways to fulfill our needs and wants.

FINDING FULFILLMENT

The illustration below expands the behavior model discussed in the beginning of the chapter to show possible reactions. Here again an unsatisfied need creates tension and motivates a search for ways to relieve that tension. If the goal is achieved, the individual will usually engage in some form of constructive behavior. If the goal is not achieved, the individual has a choice of behaviors with positive or negative results.

A Basic Motivation Model

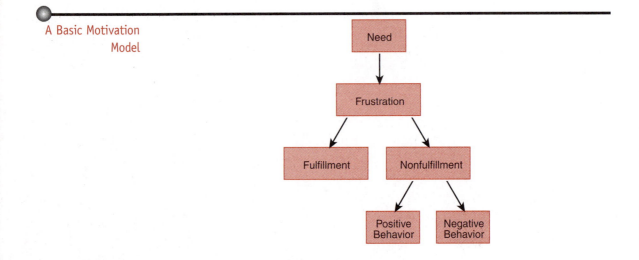

Recognizing possible outcomes and realizing that we have choices in our behavior can help turn difficult situations into positive ones. By avoiding negative behaviors, and by considering which behaviors might benefit you in the long run, you can often find the need fulfillment you desire. Two situations are described below. Determine the types of behaviors that may result from each of these real-world situations. Once you have identified the behaviors, discuss what would motivate you to react in such ways.

Motivation Theory Applications

As a student, you may really want an "A" on a term paper that took a great deal of time and effort to prepare. The high grade is needed to improve your overall semester grade for the class. Unbelievably, you get your paper back with a grade of "C" boldly appearing at the top of the page.

You can choose to react in the following ways:

POSITIVE	NEGATIVE
a. _____	_____
b. _____	_____
c. _____	_____
d. _____	_____

As an employee, you really want the supervisory position that is open in your work unit. You are very qualified to do the job and the extra money is needed to help with the expenses of a new baby. You have always been a team player and the boss seems to like you. Unbelievably, you get word on Friday that Jose was chosen for the position.

You can choose to react in the following ways:

POSITIVE	NEGATIVE
a. _____	_____
b. _____	_____
c. _____	_____
d. _____	_____

Note: Possible answers to these applications are available at the end of the chapter.

Reasoning, problem solving and decision making

From the exercise above, you can see that you can choose and apply positive behaviors that result in preferred future outcomes. From your discussions, you can also realize the negative effects that poor choices may have. Understanding why we act and react to any given situation can often help us avoid destructive behaviors that may limit future opportunities.

MOTIVATING OTHERS

Leaders must assess the motivation of followers.

Both at work and in our personal lives, we may be placed in positions of leadership and held responsible for accomplishing a goal. For example, you may be elected president of your local civic group or you may be selected for a supervisory job at work. In either of these two leadership roles, understanding motivation is important.

Leaders are frequently judged by the performance of their group. The output of followers usually depends on their motivation to do what they are asked to do. Performance and motivation are closely linked. Obviously, a large part of any leader's job is to assure maximum output of the group. This is not an easy task. Encouraging others to maximize their potential and contribute their enthusiasm and energies at peak levels requires a sound understanding of motivational concepts and techniques. When we are sensitive to what increases motivation and we understand the behavior of others, we are able to make the group more productive.

Although motivating followers is one function of the leader, the leader cannot do it alone. Because the decision to move comes from within us, we have a shared responsibility whether we are the leader or the follower. A leader, however, can influence a person's level of motivation.

Through psychological research, three **motivational source fields** have been identified that are believed to influence individual behavior. The diagram below illustrates the fields and their degrees of influence.

quick wit

. . . .

"Never confuse movement with action".

. . . .

Ernest Hemingway, Author

A leader works to assure maximum output from the group.

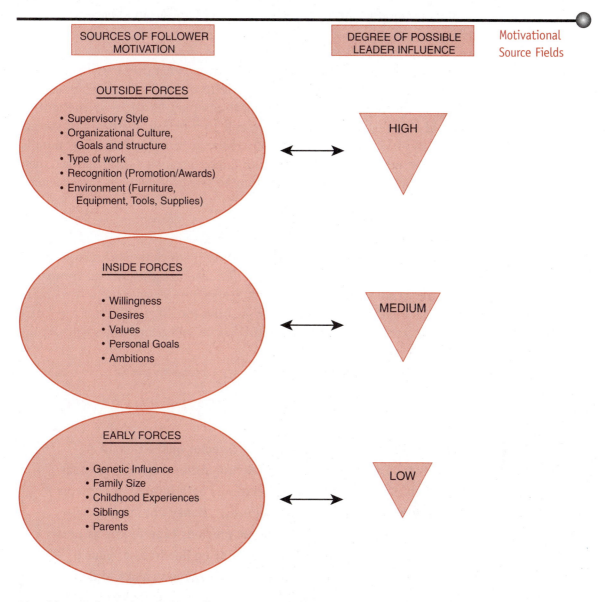

**SOURCES OF FOLLOWER
MOTIVATION**

**DEGREE OF POSSIBLE
LEADER INFLUENCE**

OUTSIDE FORCES

• Supervisory Style
• Organizational Culture,
  Goals and structure
• Type of work
• Recognition (Promotion/Awards)
• Environment (Furniture,
  Equipment, Tools, Supplies)

HIGH

INSIDE FORCES

• Willingness
• Desires
• Values
• Personal Goals
• Ambitions

MEDIUM

EARLY FORCES

• Genetic Influence
• Family Size
• Childhood Experiences
• Siblings
• Parents

LOW

Adapted from Joseph L. Massie and John Douglas, Managing—A Contemporary Introduction *(Englewood Cliffs, NJ: Prentice-Hall, Inc., 1985)*

Outside forces offer the greatest opportunity for influencing motivation. A few of these tools are praise, variation of the work task, and financial rewards. Praise involves positive reinforcement for tasks that are completed properly. Task variation can occur through enlargement or enrichment of a job, assignment to special task forces, or rotation through different work assignments.

Financial rewards, which include pay raises, bonuses, and stock options, are the most misunderstood of the outside motivators. Our society is increasingly materialistic, and we are constantly bombarded by advertising

**Outside
motivators
include money,
praise, and
changing the
task.**

telling us what we need. According to Peter Drucker in *Management: Tasks, Responsibilities, Practices*, we are driven to want so much that our income is never large enough to satisfy our needs. For some people, especially knowledge workers (people who earn their living by what they know rather than from what they produce), money is a form of feedback, equating to their value to the organization. If organizations paid us what we thought we should be paid, they would not be able to function. We begin to see pay raises and bonuses as a "right" rather than a "privilege" and become discontented with our salaries and, ultimately, our jobs. Organizations, then, cannot rely on financial rewards alone to satisfy employees. Other outside motivators must be used.

As testimony to the effectiveness of titles as motivators, Lee Svete, Director of Career Services at Colgate University in New York, has noticed employers dressing up the titles of the jobs for which they are recruiting college students. Instead of advertising for sales representatives, companies will advertise their "management leadership development program." Rather than getting 10 resumes for the sales job, they get 90 for the "management leadership" offer. Apparently, some college graduates will sacrifice

CASE STUDIES IN THE NEWS

Jack Roseman is currently the Associate Director of the Donald M. Jones Center for Entrepreneurship and distinguished Adjunct Professor for the Graduate School of Industrial Relations, both located at Carnegie Mellon University in Pittsburgh, PA. He believes, "Money doesn't buy loyalty—titles do!" He formed this opinion from his previous experiences as president of a growing computer service company employing hundreds of young, eager college graduates. He was able to save the company thousands of dollars by manipulating titles. He offered potential sales staffers a choice between the titles "sales manager" or "salesman" with the latter having an extra $2000 in salary definition. Nearly everyone took the title "Sales Manager" with the lower pay. Go figure!

Claudia Coates, *Associated Press*,
July 1998

Why do you think these sales people opted for the title over money? How might the sales people have countered the company's offer?

money for a title and the hope of future promotion. This seems to support the belief that money is not always a motivator.

Inside forces are less easily manipulated. Consider, for example, the company that wants its employees to learn a certain computer software program. Offering training on it may increase a worker's motivation. If the new ability promotes some personal goal, the worker will want to excel in its application. Influencing people's motivation through the areas of early forces is virtually

Methods For Enhancing Motivation

1. *Sell, don't tell.* Selling a course of action by explaining the benefits and the reasons for doing it is more likely to persuade employees to act than simply ordering "do it."
2. *Let your followers make their own decisions.* Employees must feel some control and authority over their own jobs.
3. *Delegate, don't dump.* Delegating only unpleasant tasks is called dumping and is considered an abuse of power. When delegating, give challenges that will develop a subordinate's abilities—and delegate authority with the responsibility
4. *Set goals with your followers.* Regular goal setting improves performance. Define subordinates' work in terms of goals and objectives.
5. *Listen to your followers and let them know that you are listening.* Schedule regular meetings to let them express what is on their minds. Followers tend to work harder if they feel that you care.
6. *Follow through.* Effective leaders take action to make their promises happen and keep their followers informed on what is happening.
7. *Don't change course midstream.* Followers need continuity. Be consistent.
8. *Build in a monitoring system.* Check with your group daily. You should be aware of possible problems to prevent disruption to the work environment. Encourage employees to report problems without being asked.
9. *Give criticism gracefully.* Reprimanding or ridiculing followers in public can cause problems. If criticism must be given, it should be done in private and in a constructive manner.
10. *Have a plan for employees' future.* People who cannot envision career growth will probably leave. People are more likely to work hard if they see a possibility of growth in their jobs.
11. *Avoid hasty judgments about work style.* Individuals will handle tasks differently than you expect. Allow the freedom of personal choice as long as the task is completed in an acceptable manner.
12. *Use rewards and incentives.* Use praise immediately when a task is well done. Praise is an important method of motivating some individuals.
13. *Encourage camaraderie and friendship.* A team atmosphere can be created by allowing employees time to socialize in the workplace. Given a chance to be sociable, employees can form essential networks and expand their means of being creative and productive.

impossible. These forces were established early in life and are firmly fixed within value and belief systems.

Understanding the motivation sources available gives the leader a framework to develop steps that may energize followers. Albert Bernstein and Sydney Rozen conducted research on successful methods that today's corporate leaders use to create environments that will motivate employees. They concluded that the steps shown on page 73 can enhance motivation. You may recognize some of these methods and choose to apply them in your role as a leader at work and elsewhere.

Effective leaders develop an atmosphere conducive to motivation.

CASE STUDIES IN THE NEWS

Radio station Oldies 94.5 FM has a monthly Friday staff luncheon to make the workplace less stressful. Planned and financed by the station manager, lunch is catered, door prizes are awarded, and free massages and shoe shines are given to employees. A feeling of camaraderie permeates the room. Employees enjoy each other and laud each other's accomplishments.

The manager's employees say she makes everyone feel special. She shows her employees respect and brings a new way of working to the airways. She is very approachable and open to new ideas and is always available to help solve problems. She goes out of her way to find out what motivates her employees.

L.M. Sixel, *Houston Magazine*, November 1998

Which of the motivation theories you have learned apply to this situation? How would you feel about working at this company? What would motivate you?

FastChat

1. What forces offer the greatest opportunity for influencing motivation? the least?

2. What methods other than payment can be used to reward employees?

How Are Motivators Changing?

Managers and supervisors are recognizing a significant change in what motivates employees in today's workplace. The assumptions that money alone will motivate and that the workplace is of prime importance in workers' lives are no longer valid. The changes have come about because the "baby boomers"—and now their children, the "Generation Xers"—entered the work force with far different values and expectations than did their parents and grandparents.

Baby boomers, for example, were more motivated by work that provided a sense of identity—interesting and challenging work, recognition and appreciation for a job well done, more participation in decision making, and more leisure time. Demands for a more flexible work environment grew more prominent. Employers responded by devoting more time to the development of their employees through training, job enrichment, and job enlargement. Rotating jobs and increasing responsibilities of existing jobs were also used as means of motivating baby boomers.

Learning
Objective   8

Discuss motivational techniques that are increasingly important to motivating employees.

Today's employees are motivated by new factors.

THE NEXT GENERATION

The real challenge is in motivating the next generation, the so-called "Generation X." GenXers have a very "untraditional" mindset when compared to their "baby boomer" parents. The boomers were at least familiar with a structured work environment and an established reporting process through a chain of command, they demonstrated good interpersonal skills, and they had reasonable written and oral communication skills.

Outspoken GenXers tend to have a confident attitude, and statistically, may be weaker in written and oral skills than the boomer generation. Sometimes described as cynical about the future and unwilling to conform, GenXers are known to jump from job to job if the work bores them or is not fun. But, put them behind a computer and hang on to your hat! Generation X workers are quick thinkers and risk-takers, want immediate gratification, and often have advanced technical skills. They are completely at ease cruising the information highway, using cyber tools for problem solving, and researching issues on the Internet.

Generation X is entrepreneurial. A 1995 *U.S. News and World Report* survey revealed that individuals in this age group are creating new businesses faster than all other age groups and maintaining successful start-up companies at a rate three times higher than any other age group. They want to control their destiny, make all the decisions, and keep all the money.

The success stories of Don Taylor and Edward Estipona described below and on page 77 illustrate the potential of GenXers operating in our fast-paced society. Other GenXers enter the general workforce and deliver a different challenge to supervisors who must manage to motivate them. These represent the cynical, non-conformist group.

Ralph Schomburg, a training leader and manager in the aerospace industry, has spent many hours learning what it takes to motivate GenXers. He believes we must take a look at the factors that influenced their values and belief systems. Unlike the baby boomer generation, many GenXers grew up with divorce, as latch-key kids, in struggling single-parent families, and as day-care youths. The threat of AIDS and other medical menaces, crooked politicians, pollution, and many other ecological concerns were looming large in their lives. He believes this group of workers places different priorities and values on traditional motivational tools and is more loyal to their personal careers than to "the company." The opposite diagram represents Schomburg's experienced view of GenX motivators.

TECHNOLOGY CONNECTION

Don Taylor, 25, found the perfect fit for himself in new technology. Taylor and three friends used their own money to start Welcome Net, a small advertising company that will soon expand from only California to the entire nation via the Internet. Taylor studied business for two years at a community college before starting his successful business. His employees say he pushes them to succeed the same way he pushed himself, and they consider him more of a mentor than a boss.

Steve Lamb, *Outpost Contributors*
August 1998

Do you think Don Taylor feels confident about the future? Why?

Motivating Generation X Workers

1. *MONEY:* Can be a strong motivating force. The desire for things and gadgets moves this group to work for reward. Money is a scoreboard, a measure, for their sense of accomplishment. Money also provides independence and identity.

2. *TRAINING:* This means of increasing their skills and abilities is important to GenXers. It makes them more marketable and mobile—and appeals to their need for self-fulfillment.

3. *FEEDBACK:* The need to know how they're doing is strong. Providing positive (or negative) feedback helps them gauge the next move to make.

4. *REWARDS:* Traditional "Employee of the Month" recognition won't work, but hand them free theater tickets, ball game passes, or dinner tickets immediately following good behavior, and you'll have a winner.

CASE STUDIES IN THE NEWS

A recent college graduate with no experience, Edward Estipona was caught in the middle of a recession, unlikely to land the great advertising job he sought. Jobs were hard to come by—so Edward created his own. Working out of a 12-foot by 8-foot back bedroom in his parents house, he started Envision—his own advertising and marketing firm. Less than six months later, he moved into his own offices with a partner, six employees, and a thriving business boasting 55 clients. He says, "Advertising is changing so fast with the Internet and multi-media methods, you've got to move with it. You have to deliver fast, quality service at competitive costs." Envision received the 1998 American Advertising Award for best new company. Edward's no-limitations philosophy is, "Do something you like. If you're not having fun, get a new job!"

Natalie Burke, *Outpost Contributors*
October 1998

Does Edward fit the typical description of the Generation X worker? How do you think he managed to become such a success in such a short period of time?

NEW METHODS FOR MOTIVATING WORKERS

To motivate workers of today and tomorrow, leaders will need to use a variety of motivational methods. In order to develop interesting and challenging work, employers will need to devote more time to employee development in the form of education and training, job enrichment, and job enlargement. Employees will need continuous training to acquire new skills and knowledge. This training will include classroom as well as on-the-job training. Rotating jobs will continue to be another way to motivate employees. This additional experience and training will empower individuals with the tools needed for success.

Organizations will also need to help employees with career planning and changes. Beginning second, third, or fourth careers will become more common as individuals continue to search for absorbing work.

The old "Waytogo!" still works in motivating some individuals.

In one recent survey reported by Bernstein and Rozen, great disparity was found between what people say motivates them and what their companies are actually providing. For example, although 91 percent of the individuals in the survey stated that recognition for good work is important, only 54 percent felt that they were actually receiving appropriate recognition. This finding points out that the old "Waytogo!" still works and that today's managers often fall short by using "management by exception." Under this technique, the boss only says something to you when you do something wrong. One of the key success concepts of the *One Minute Manager* says that the fastest way to motivate individuals is by applying a little praise. In fact, the book's advice is to "catch them doing something right!" It stresses that praise should be specific, appropriate, and immediate.

Smart leaders have discovered that words of encouragement given to a person who has done an outstanding job pay real dividends. By contrast, an old adage states, "Label a man a loser and he'll start acting like one." These practices illustrate the self-fulfilling concept that people tend to act in accordance with their self-image. If they see themselves as successful, respected, and contributing members of the work force, their behavior is likely to reflect this perception.

A strong motivational factor influencing worker behavior today is the desire for more leisure time. Increasingly, employers are finding their workplaces deserted by 2:00 or 3:00 P.M. on Friday. Employees slip away for an early start on the weekend's activities. This practice obviously affects productivity through lost work time, but it can also have an effect on employee morale. Dedicated employees who stay on the job until closing time resent having to handle the work left by those who skip out.

Some methods used by organizations to cope with employees' desires for more leisure time include changing work shifts to four ten-hour work days and instituting more flexible work hours on Fridays to accommodate earlier arrival and departure times. Other employers are allowing individuals the freedom to choose which two days of the week they prefer as their "weekend." For example, employees may choose Sunday and Monday as their days off as opposed to the traditional weekend combination of Saturday and Sunday. For some employees, this choice satisfies a desire for leisure time that is less crowded and ends the "skip out early" syndrome.

One employer's innovative method of using the increased desire for leisure time to solve a different type of motivational problem was reported in *Inc.* magazine. Walter Riley, president and CEO of Guaranteed Overnight Delivery, devised a solution to stop accidents. Tired of the $400,000 a year that accidents were costing his company, he felt that he could reduce costs by instituting a new safety program. First he scrapped the pin, patch, plaque, and $50 driving record award system. He replaced it with a 35-foot-long motor coach for vacation use by drivers who worked one year without an accident. The accident rate dropped by 89 percent the first year that program went into effect. More and more of these innovative approaches to motivating the new age worker may be seen as we adjust to the changing needs of the work force.

*Fast*Chat

1. What challenges do employers face in motivating a new generation of workers?

2. What methods work well for motivating today's workforce?

Key Terms

motivation
primary needs
secondary needs
Maslow's hierarchy of needs
   theory
physiological needs
safety and security needs
social needs
esteem needs
self-actualization needs
Herzberg's two-factor theory
hygiene factors
motivational factors
McClelland's acquired needs
   theory
Vroom's expectancy theory
motivational source fields

Summary

The study of motivation is an ongoing attempt to understand a complex side of human behavior. From past studies, we know that a significant relationship exists between needs and motivation. Motivation is defined as the needs or drives within individuals that energize certain behaviors. Only a felt need motivates. Once that need is satisfied, it will no longer be a motivator.

Maslow developed a hierarchy of needs arranged in a specific order. He believed that individuals normally address these needs in a natural order, fulfilling lower-order needs first before moving on to higher-order needs. Herzberg was able to identify two categories of needs. He believed that hygiene factors are necessary to maintain satisfaction among employees, whereas motivational factors build high levels of motivation. McClelland's theory states that individuals acquire needs for achievement, affiliation, or power through cultural exposure during early personality development. Vroom believed that people behave in certain ways based on expected results from that behavior.

The most persistent theme in motivational theories is that all behavior is goal-directed toward satisfying some need. If an action leads to positive outcomes, it will probably be repeated. If it leads to negative results, the behavior will usually not be repeated. Needs vary in importance and intensity with each individual but generally fall into one of two basic categories, primary or secondary. Primary needs are basic to physical survival, and secondary are psychological. By understanding the difference between wants and needs, individuals can learn how to make constructive choices that do not damage careers while fulfilling needs.

Outside, inside, and early motivational source fields influence behavior, and leaders can influence motivation by working with the outside source fields. However, we must examine significant changes in factors that motivate workers. Interesting and challenging work, recognition and appreciation for work well done, being included in key decision making, and having more leisure time have replaced some of the traditional motivators such as money and job security.

Review Questions

1. Why is understanding motivation important to organizations and individuals?
2. What is the basic motivational behavior model from its point of origin through its completion?
3. Who are the major motivational theorists, and what are their contributions to the study of human motivation?
4. What are the two basic categories of individual needs?
5. What are the differences between needs and wants?
6. What are the possible constructive and destructive behaviors that individuals use to fulfill needs?
7. What are the three motivational source fields in individuals?
8. Which motivational techniques are becoming increasingly important to motivate employees today and in the future?

Discussion Questions

1. Describe a personal situation in which the basic motivational behavior model was evident. What was the need you felt you had to satisfy? What action did you take to relieve the tension?
2. Using the above situation, describe whether the action resulted in constructive or destructive behavior. How might you have handled it differently?
3. Identify several sets of your personal "wants" versus "needs." How do they differ? What other ways can you find to fulfill your needs?
4. Identify a situation in which you were able to apply one or more of the motivational source fields to influence the behavior of a coworker. Which source did you use, and why was it effective?
5. Discuss your personal position on the levels of Maslow's hierarchy of needs. Describe what self-actualization will mean to you.
6. What changes in your work environment indicate a shift in motivational techniques being used? Describe some of the methods. Describe how you might choose to motivate the new age worker.

Chapter Project

Using any one of the popular Internet Search Engines (Yahoo, HotBot, Excite, etc.), select a job search location. Browse through job listings to find one that would motivate you to apply for that job. Prepare a written report on how you selected your new job and what motivated you to choose that job field. Format your report in an attractive, interesting, and informative format. You might include a copy of the application, copies of your search pages, or other indicators of why you were motivated to make this choice.

Applications

In small groups, analyze the following situations.

Reading, reasoning, listening, participating as a member of a team and contributing to group efforts, understanding complex interrelationships.

The Case of Ron the R.I.P.

Rosa is the supervisor of a small group of resource analysts for a major research and development company. Three of the four analysts have been in her group for less than two years and are highly motivated by opportunities for career growth and promotions to higher salary levels. They have much to learn in their advancement toward a journeyman level position. Ron, the fourth analyst, has been with the company for 26 years. He is 52 years old, financially comfortable, and happily married with no children living at home. He and his wife travel frequently and enjoy an active social and leisure life.

Ron reached the journeyman level almost 15 years ago. Although his performance is satisfactory, he has become known as an R.I.P. (Retired in Place). He has openly stated to Rosa that he does not want any responsibility added to his current work load. He does not desire a promotion because that would put him into a stress-filled management position, and he has no aspirations to become a star performer. Ron steadily arrives at work on time, works his eight-hour shift with an appropriate lunch break each day, and leaves on time. He strictly avoids overtime hours. When occasional new assignments are added to Rosa's work group, Ron often suggests which of the other analysts is best suited to the task, indicating his obvious lack of interest in accepting the assignment.

Rosa has been unsuccessful in her attempts to force Ron to accept any additional work. Assignments made to Ron most often go unattended or result in incomplete products that require more time to redo. The other

analysts are beginning to resent Ron's passive attitude and feel that they are having to carry him by shouldering tasks that should be more evenly distributed among all office personnel.

1. According to Maslow's theory, at which need level is Ron operating?
2. At what level of Maslow's theory does Rosa wish Ron was operating?
3. How do you think the others in the group will eventually react if Ron's behavior does not change?
4. What do you think will happen to Ron if his behavior does not change?

The Times They Are A-Changing

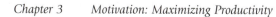

Reading, reasoning, participating as a team member and contributing to group efforts, and understanding complex interrelationships.

In his six years at Hoffman Manufacturing, David has always been preoccupied with plans for his days off and has been known to call in sick when his shift is due to face heavy periods of production. His supervisor, Carl, expects all employees to carry their load in the shop and to work overtime to meet production output schedules as required.

David's shift was nearly over when a lathe in the shop broke down, requiring a four-hour repair. Carl immediately called in a maintenance crew to make the repair and asked all production shift hands to work whatever hours it took to complete the day's order. David's reply was simply, "I have plans for this Fourth of July weekend, and I'm leaving." Carl was angry and took immediate steps to discipline David. He documented the case against David and found that the company policy requires a three-day suspension without pay as the usual disciplinary action.

When David returned to work and heard the news, his only request was, "Great, can I add the three days to a weekend period so I can plan for the extended time off?" Carl felt defeated but knew David's skilled experience was valuable to the company. He decided instead to try some different method to motivate David. Carl took the challenge of turning this negative situation into a positive one.

1. What motivates David?
2. Why do you think Carl's method of discipline was ineffective in this situation?
3. What will eventually happen to David if he continues to behave in this fashion and Carl continues to motivate him with suspensions?
4. What should Carl try?

Additional Readings and Resources

Bryant, Adam. "Looking for Purpose in a Paycheck," *New York Times*, Sunday, June 21, 1998.

Caudron, Shari. "Motivating Creative Employees Calls for New Strategies," *Personnel Journal*, May 1994, p. 105.

Jacobs, Karen. "The Real Thing", *The Wall Street Journal*, April 9, 1998.

Palmeri, Christopher. "Making the Grandkids Happy." *Forbes*, August 25, 1997.

Pillar, Charles. "Gender Gap Driving Women Out of Careers in Computing," *Los Angeles Times*, August 30, 1998.

Suval, John. "Teacher Shows a Lot of Class," *Houston Chronicle*, September 13, 1998.

Possible responses to "Motivation Theory Applications" page 69

As a student,

Positive	*Negative*
a. Ask the instructor why you received the grade.	Complain bitterly.
b. Study harder for the next test.	Cause a class disruption.
c. Learn the instructor's style of grading.	Drop the class.
d. Reflect on the learning experience.	Ignore the situation.
e. Analyze the failure (What could you have done better?)	Bad mouth the instructor.
f. Pay more attention in class.	

As an employee,

Positive	*Negative*
Take a class in supervision/management.	File a grievance over the selection.
a. Continue working as a team player.	Cause disharmony among staff.
b. Develop better rapport with supervisor.	Bad mouth Jose.
c. Volunteer to help train Jose.	Withdraw from office involvement.
d. Learn what the supervisor wants.	Do only what you are told from that point forward.
e. Improve your skills.	

Creative Problem Solving:
Making Good Decisions

focus

Johnson & Johnson is using a series of focused dialogues, called FrameworkS, to help infuse the $34 billion corporation with the energy of a small start-up company. Because innovation is crucial to J&J's business, FrameworkS first focused on the qualities highly innovative companies exhibit. They then catalogued J&J inventions by type of innovation: incremental improvement (Glow in the Dark Band-aids), substantial change that alters market demand with a new generation of products (Reach toothbrush), and transformational innovation that alters industry structure (disposable contact lens). From this has been developed a "tool kit" of actions line managers can take to infuse innovation into their organizations. FrameworkS's total dollar impact to J&J's bottom line is potentially large.

Continental, **March 1999**

How important do you think creativity is in successful organizations? What is the relationship between problem solving and decision making?

objectives

After studying this chapter, you should be able to:

1. *Define a problem and list the steps in problem solving.*

2. *Discuss various tools that can be used in decision making, including decision trees, cost-benefit analyses, ABC analyses, PERT charts, and quality circles.*

3. *Discuss the role of creativity in problem solving and list the basic steps in the creative process.*

4. *Name the sources of creativity in organizations and describe ways to encourage creativity and to get new ideas through organizations.*

5. *Discuss the blocks to creativity and how to overcome them.*

6. *Identify ways that you can improve your creativity.*

In This Chapter

What Is a Problem and What Are the Steps in Problem Solving?

Define a problem and list the steps in problem solving.

A popular definition of a problem is a puzzle looking for an answer. Whether the problem is an organizational one or a personal one, it can be defined as a disturbance or unsettled matter that requires a solution if the organization or person is to function effectively. Problems become evident when expected results are compared to actual results. The gap is the problem that needs solving. Determining that solution involves decision making.

Problems may be of three types, as shown here:

Three Types of Problems

Types of Problems	Examples
1. Occurring now and must be addressed now.	• The economy is forcing the XYZ Company to lay off several employees. • You have returned to school, requiring that you allocate part of your budget to school expenses.
2. Expected in the future and plans must be made for dealing with them when they do occur.	• The ABC Company has a deadline of May 1 to complete a project and is now behind schedule. • You have a major paper due in two weeks and have not started writing it.
3. Foreseen for the future but so serious that action must be taken immediately to prevent their developing.	• Earnings projected for a company reveal that it will be unable to meet its payroll by the middle of the last quarter. • The term paper that you have not yet started and that is due next week is a minimum requirement to pass the course.

Once a problem has been identified, specific steps should be taken to solve it. Decision making is an important part of the problem-solving process. Deciding which solution to choose is always necessary.

HOW ARE PROBLEMS SOLVED?

Regardless of your position in an organization, you are or will be faced with problems and the need to make decisions. Your personal life also requires problem solving and decision making. Human relations, if they are effective, can prevent or help solve problems. If they are not effective, they can create problems of their own. For this reason, problem-solving skills are considered an important part of human relations.

Problem solving and decision making are related. Effective decisions must be made if problems are to be solved satisfactorily. Identifying a problem and its possible solutions is important, but the process is incomplete until we decide which option(s) to implement.

Numerous ways exist for making decisions, some more effective than others. You should understand and be able to use a systematic approach to problem solving so that you do not have to rely on generalizations, snap judgments, or intuition. The following process can help you attain personal and career success.

A helpful maxim says that "A problem well defined is a problem half solved." Instead of saying, "We are behind schedule," say, "We have only two weeks in which to complete this project." Collect and analyze all information pertinent to the problem—people, processes, materials, equipment, or other matters. Although you do not want to overwhelm yourself with information, try to uncover all relevant objective data.

Brainstorming is a group problem-solving technique that involves spontaneous contribution of ideas in a nonjudgmental environment. It is freewheeling and fun.

PROBLEM SOLVING EXAMPLE

In looking at information related to a project that is behind schedule, you might find that absenteeism has been high, materials have been late in arriving, and the new computer system used on the project has had start-up difficulties. Consider what factors caused the gap between the expected and actual results. In this example, try to imagine the impact of each change— the absenteeism, late materials, and new computer system.

Steps in Problem Solving

1. Identify the problem, defining it clearly and specifically.

Be objective. See the situation as it actually is, not as you think it is. Don't let emotions color your perception. Quantify the problem if possible. Examine all facets of the issue and identify the source of the problem. Collect relevant data. List possible causes. Select most likely cause(s).

2. Generate ideas; use brainstorming to develop as many alternative solutions as possible for removing the causes of problems.

Brainstorming is a group problem-solving technique that involves the spontaneous contribution of ideas from all members of the group. The goal is to generate as many ideas as possible— more ideas means better results. Reserve judgment—no ideas should be eliminated initially. An idea that seems ridiculous may trigger a feasible idea in someone else. By throwing ideas back and forth and adding to them, members can form a plan. Brainstorming is a freewheeling, fun activity that encourages creativity.

3. Evaluate alternatives for practicality.

Analyze the implications of each alternative by evaluating the pros and cons. Rather than just saying that one solution is better than another, define "better." Develop criteria such as cost and speed. Consider the information gathered in Step 2 and possibly discuss the criteria with experts. Try to anticipate problems that some alternatives might create.

4. Select a solution.

Select your "best" solution. This step is the decision phase in the problem-solving process. Weigh all the chances of success against the risks of failure. The strengths of your solution should exceed its weaknesses. Develop a plan of action for carrying out your solution. What will be done, how, by whom, where, when, and at what cost?

5. Implement the solution.

Implement the idea by carrying out your "best" solution. Consider that you may have to alter your plans and be ready.

6. Evaluate results: follow up and modify actions when necessary.

Make sure that your actions accomplish your objectives by examining the situation carefully. If your goals are not being met, you may have to study the problem further and apply other alternatives.

Using a process of elimination, imagine what difference returning a changed factor to its original condition would make. If that does not solve the problem, keep checking. Would the project be on time if absenteeism had been at its usual rate, or if materials had arrived on time, or if the computer system had not been changed? After considering these options, you might decide that the most likely cause was the late materials.

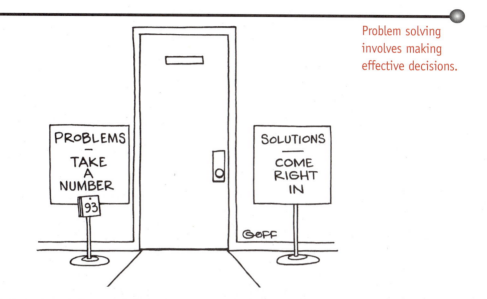

Problem solving involves making effective decisions.

TECHNOLOGY CONNECTION

An ad for Hewlett Packard introduced its e-services with a scenario of a daughter driving her parents' vintage Jaguar while they were out of town. A security chip in the car recognizes the daughter's key and engages a "soft limit" that won't allow the car to exceed 65 mph. When she immediately does, the car sends a signal to the parent three thousand miles away who speed dials the daughter to slow down, thereby heading off a potential problem. Hewlett Packard points out that businesses are using the Internet in ways that go far beyond today's websites and the next chapter of the Internet is about to be written.

Chip technology in this case has been applied in a creative way to prevent a potential problem. What other creative uses of this technology to solve problems can you envision?

In this example, what can you do to assure the timely arrival of materials in the future? You may, for instance, consider ordering earlier, or ordering from a different source, or even changing the design so that other materials can be substituted for the late ones.

Then anticipate the likely results of each alternative. You may discover that some alternatives create more problems than they solve: If you choose to substitute materials in our example, you may create design problems. Although ordering from another source seems reasonable, you may find that the second source is more expensive. You may decide that ordering earlier seems the best alternative, but you may not always have advance notice of the need.

The basic question is whether your projects are being completed on time using the specific plan for ordering supplies. If you are still running behind, you need to study the situation further and try other solutions.

Pitfalls in Problem Solving

When trying to solve a problem, be alert to pitfalls or problem areas. Common ones are the following:

- Over analyzing, which can lead to inaction.
- Not taking necessary action or acting too quickly.
- Erring in judgment or execution.
- Not having a backup plan.
- Not involving others in the problem-solving process.
- Perceiving the problem incorrectly.

Following the steps in the problem-solving process on page 88 can help you avoid these pitfalls.

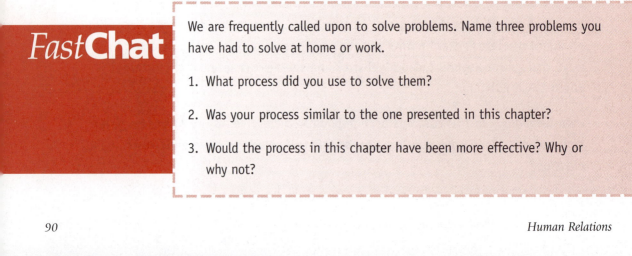

FastChat

We are frequently called upon to solve problems. Name three problems you have had to solve at home or work.

1. What process did you use to solve them?

2. Was your process similar to the one presented in this chapter?

3. Would the process in this chapter have been more effective? Why or why not?

TECHNOLOGY CONNECTION

Computers and other technologies are eliminating entire categories of jobs (such as telephone operators), but they are also constantly creating new jobs. They are also changing our work, particularly problem solving and decision making. An article in *Modern Maturity* pointed out that technology-savvy frontline personnel are now responsible for decisions formerly made by supervisors. Managers also have more control over their own work. Desktop PCs equipped with software that does everything from keeping appointments to formatting business letters and writing contracts have largely replaced personal secretaries. When people feel they have more control, they are usually more satisfied with their jobs.

Technology is also speeding up the rate at which decisions can be made. Sophisticated software used by NASA, for example, allows the agency to analyze numerous moving components of the Space Station simultaneously, thereby permitting decisions to be made more quickly and moving the project along faster.

On the other hand, computers permit the creation of so much data that even though most business people seek more information for decision making, they are drowning in a sea of data and detail. Additionally, a recent survey suggested that computers are eliciting rage in the workplace, or at least taking the brunt of it. The study found that 83 percent of corporate network administrators reported "abusive and violent behavior" by employees toward their computers—smashing monitors, throwing mice, kicking hard drives, and shattering screens. A follow-up study concluded that employees may be merely taking out the frustration they feel toward their bosses and work in general on their computers.

Technology is changing the way we make decisions.

1. *Overall, what do you see as the strengths and weaknesses of using technology in decision making?*
2. *Describe experiences you have had when technology enabled you to make a better decision. If, on the other hand, it actually hampered your problem solving, suggest what could have been done differently.*

**Learning
Objective   2**

*Discuss various
tools that can be
used in decision
making.*

**Decisions are
made when we
must choose
actions,
opportunities, or
solutions.**

**To make
decisions, use
decision trees,
cost-benefit
analyses, ABC
analyses, PERT
charts, or quality
circles.**

All organizations and people are faced with the need to make decisions. In fact, we make dozens of them daily—from what to wear to which e-mail to answer first.

Whenever we have more than one way of doing something, we must make a decision. Sometimes the decisions we must make include problem solving, as discussed earlier in this chapter. In such cases, we are trying to overcome the gap between expected and actual results. At other times, we must choose among a number of opportunities facing us. For example, at some point you considered whether to go to college, to go to work, or to combine the two. If you decided to go to college, you then had to consider your major field of study. You may have considered several occupations with different rewards such as travel, money, or flexibility.

Many people overlook opportunities for decisions, both personal and professional ones. Managers and individuals alike become comfortable with the status quo. We should, however, keep in mind the important point that *no decision is a decision*. By not making another choice, we have, in effect, decided to remain with the status quo. People sometimes fail to make conscious decisions because they fear change.

The decision tree illustrated in this figure shows various decision points and chance events that may occur in the growth of a company. Should additional employees be hired, should employees be asked to work overtime, or should the owner decide not to increase business?

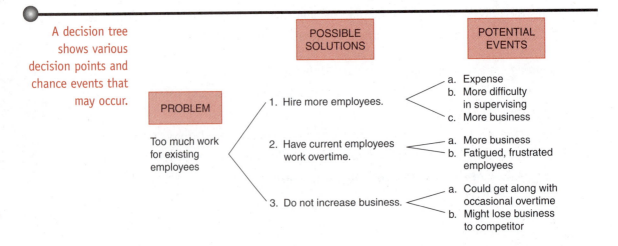

A decision tree shows various decision points and chance events that may occur.

PROBLEM	POSSIBLE SOLUTIONS	POTENTIAL EVENTS
Too much work for existing employees	1. Hire more employees.	a. Expense b. More difficulty in supervising c. More business
	2. Have current employees work overtime.	a. More business b. Fatigued, frustrated employees
	3. Do not increase business.	a. Could get along with occasional overtime b. Might lose business to competitor

Several well-known techniques or tools exist for helping us make personal and work-related decisions. What these tools are and how they might be used are outlined in the chart.

Decision-Making Tools

1. **Decision tree**—graphic depiction of how alternative solutions lead to various possibilities.

   Helps people and organizations see the implications that certain choices have for the future. Can be used formally by actually drawing them or informally in our heads.

2. **Cost-benefit analysis**—examination of the pros and cons of each proposed solution.

   A popular technique in the public sector, frequently used for evaluating proposals to provide a nonprofit service to the community, such as hospitals, playgrounds, or child-care facilities. Involves comparison of all costs against value of the service to the community.

3. **ABC analysis**—concentration of decisions where the potential for payoff is greatest.

   Involves concentration on the vital few items ("A" items), not the trivial many ("C" items). Example: In choosing a builder for your home or office, the quality of the construction would be considered an "A" item, paint color a "C" item, and brand of appliances probably a "B" item.

4. **PERT chart** (Program Evaluation and Review Technique chart)- a graphic technique for planning projects in which a great number of tasks must be coordinated.

   Shows the relationships between tasks and helps identify critical bottlenecks that may delay progress toward a project's completion. The critical path is the sequence of activities that must be done one after another and that requires the longest time for completion. (See Chapter 1 for examples and more detail.)

5. **Quality circle**—committee of 6 to 15 employees who meet regularly to examine and suggest solutions to common problems of quality.

   Widely used in Japan since the 1950s and in the United States during the '70s and '80s, quality circles are a form of participative management because employees provide input to key decisions.

Because you are faced with a multitude of decisions every day, you simply cannot devote much time, thought, or effort to all of them, nor should you want to do so. Economists point out that only a few problems or opportunities (considered vital) account for the greatest loss or gain. They call this fact the 20/80 syndrome, meaning that 20 percent of your problems will account for 80 percent of your losses or gains. It is the 20 percent to which you should attend. (In the ABC analysis identified above, this 20 percent would be the "A" items.)

In quality circles, the committee typically consists of volunteers from the same work area. They usually receive some training in group processes, problem solving including brainstorming, and statistical quality control. Statistical quality control is the use of statistics as tools. They are used in frequency distribution charts, quality control charts, and sampling tables. Computers, tools themselves, may be used to help with the statistical analyses.

Because quality circles focus on improvement of quality, problem-solving and decision-making techniques discussed throughout this chapter are used in them. Proponents of quality circles point out that as a member of a quality circle you are involved in challenging and fulfilling work; therefore, quality circles not only improve product quality and productivity, but they can also improve the quality of your work life.

Quality circles use problem-solving and decision-making techniques, including brainstorming.

SHOULD A GROUP DECIDE?

Whatever decision-making technique is being used, most work-related problems and many personal ones require that decisions be made by groups of people rather than by individuals alone. Such situations require strong human relations skills, skills that can be enhanced by a knowledge of group decision making.

In general, groups make better decisions than individuals because of the increased input and suggestions. However, there are pitfalls, such as wasting time and engaging in groupthink. The first step, then, is deciding whether a group should be used in making a decision. Factors to be considered are listed in the chart on the next page.

Group decision making seeks consensus, a solution all members can support.

Review the factors carefully. Notice that group decision making assumes that members are knowledgeable, will participate, can be creative in their solutions, and are likely to support what they help create. Human relations skills can help groups arrive at consensus decisions.

HOW DO GROUPS AGREE?

The goal of group problem solving is to reach **consensus**—to develop a solution with which all members can agree. Webster's defines consensus as "group solidarity in sentiment and belief" and "the judgment arrived at by most of those concerned." It does not mean that the final solution is the one each member thinks is the best one, but the solution is one that all members can at least support.

For a group to have the greatest likelihood of reaching consensus, certain guidelines should be followed. Consider the recommendations shown

Individual Versus Group Decision Making

Situational Factors Supportive of Individual Decision Making	Situational Factors Supportive of Group Decision Making
1. When time is short.	1. When creativity is needed.
2. When the decision is relatively unimportant.	2. When data for the solution rest within the group.
3. When the leader has all the data needed to make the decision.	3. When acceptance of a solution by group members is important.
4. When one or two group members are likely to dominate the discussion.	4. When understanding of a solution by group members is important.
5. When destructive conflict is likely to erupt among group members.	5. When the problem is complex or requires a broad range of knowledge for solution.
6. When people feel they attend too many meetings, don't feel they should be involved, or are pessimistic about the value of group meetings.	6. When the manager wants subordinates to feel part of a democratic process or wants to build their confidence.
7. When the relevant decision-making data are confidential and cannot be shared with all group members.	7. When more risk taking in considering solutions is needed.
8. When group members aren't capable or qualified to decide.	8. When better group member understanding of each other is desirable.
9. When the leader is dominant or intimidates group members.	9. When the group as a whole is ultimately responsible for the decision.
10. When the decision doesn't affect the group directly.	10. When the leader wants to get feedback on the validity of his ideas and opinions.

Lyle Sussman and Samuel D. Deep, COMEX: The Communication Experience in Human Relations *(Cincinnati: South-Western Publishing Co., 1984), 120. Used with permission.*

in the chart on the following page when you are working with a problem-solving group.

A healthy **"win-win" situation** occurs when both sides of an issue feel they have won. If one side runs roughshod over the other, the situation is considered to be a "win-lose" one. Aggressive, bullying people, in the long run, are not effective negotiators because other people are not likely to feel satisfied at the end of the negotiations. Because negotiation is a part of our

Recommendations for Group Problem Solving

1. State the idea or proposal in the clearest terms possible. Writing it on a chalkboard or flip chart will help.
2. Poll *each* member for opinions by asking, "What do you think of the idea (or proposal)?" Use an open-ended question such as this one rather than "do you agree?"
3. If everyone expresses positive opinions for the idea or proposal, you have total consensus.
4. If someone disagrees, ask why and ask for an alternative idea or proposal.
5. Restate any opposing ideas or proposals to ensure understanding.
6. Use problem-solving techniques to resolve the differences. For example:
   a. Find common ground and work toward another suitable alternative.
   b. Use a best-estimate approach to weigh alternatives, such as a decision tree or ABC analysis.
   c. Strive for a substantial agreement among group members and encourage willingness to try the idea or proposal for a limited time.
   d. Use negotiation that results in a "win-win" situation. **Negotiation** is discussion that leads to a decision acceptable to all.
7. Avoid forcing unanimity, voting, "averaging," "majority rule," or horse trading ("I'll do this if you do that"). Voting divides the group into a win-lose situation.
8. If one group member changes his or her mind, poll opinions from each member again.
9. If someone still disagrees, return to step 4.
10. If only one person, or a small subgroup, continues to disagree, get that person or group to give permission to try the idea or proposal for a limited time period. The permission might include the stipulation to test the counter idea or proposal if the first one fails to accomplish its objective.
11. If all parties now agree, consensus has been achieved.

daily lives, learning to negotiate properly will increase your effectiveness on the job and the satisfaction of everyone involved. Establishing a reputation of trust will also help you in negotiating. If you are seen as someone who can come through in a tight spot, keep your word, and never betray confidences, you are ahead in the process. Phrases such as "How do you think this idea would work?," "What are your feelings about. . . ?," and "Have you ever considered . . . ?" are helpful during negotiations. Other aspects of communication useful in negotiations are listening carefully, finding out what the other person wants, and watching that person's body language. Various tools can be used to improve the quality of decisions, including the use of group decision making.

GLOBAL CONNECTION

While effective organizational decision making is vital in today's global business environment, it can produce stress. Humor is a great way to deal with stress, and humorous buzzwords are constantly created to describe aspects of business. Some terms used today, identified and defined in the *Houston Business Journal*, are:

- *analysis paralysis*—The result of studying a problem in search of a perfect solution until everyone involved becomes stuck and unable to take any action until precisely the right course of action is identified (which may be never).

- *blamestorming*—Group discussion of why a particular project failed. (Often results in outplacement of the bozos who brainstormed the original concept.)

- *mousemilking*—Making a maximum amount of effort for a minimum possible benefit. You can milk a mouse, but is it really worth it?

- *scope creep*—This occurs when a project gets incrementally bigger and more sprawling after being imperceptible at first.

- *stratical*—Describes a project that is perceived as both strategic and tactical.

Think of other buzzwords you are currently hearing that deal with problem solving, decision making, or creativity.

1. *How do you think they originated?*
2. *What do they communicate about their subjects?*

List major activities you will face you in the next three days.

1. Label them as A, B, or C following definitions in this chapter. Explain your rating.

2. Can something rated a "C" become an "A" later? Why or why not?

*Fast*Chat

What Is Creativity?

As pointed out earlier, an important factor in problem solving is the need to be creative. In fact, creativity is so important in today's economy that many experts are suggesting that it is the only way for businesses to survive.

Creativity is a thinking process that solves a problem or achieves a goal in an original and useful way. Simply stated, it is the ability to come up with new and unique solutions to problems. A creative person has the ability to see practical relationships among things that are not similar and to combine elements into new patterns of association. Imagination, rather than genius, is a necessary ingredient. Research at Berkeley in the 1960s and 1970s showed that creative professionals were no different than others in intelligence. However, they had learned how to respond spontaneously to their intuitions and to investigate ideas that aroused their curiosity without immediately judging the ideas too harshly.

Learning
Objective 3

Discuss the role of creativity in problem solving and list the basic steps in the creative process.

Creativity comes in many forms. Devising a more effective office procedure is a worthwhile example.

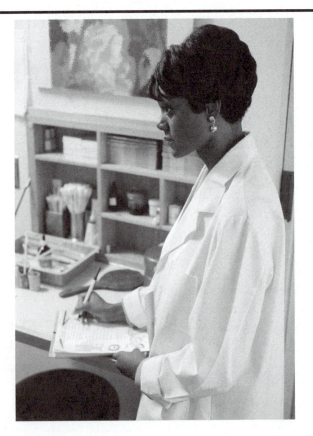

We all have the potential for creativity. Some people simply develop their potential more than others. Cultivating the vivid imagination that we have as children allows creativity to occur later in life. If we listen to Maslow's advice that creating a first-rate cake is better than creating a second-rate poem, we may be less judgmental of ourselves and others.

Creative people have been found to have several characteristics and traits in common, as summarized in this figure. Of course, not all creative people will possess all of these traits, and some of the traits or characteristics may be found in other people.

Innovation, the end product of creative activity, is vital to the success of organizations and individuals today. Businesses must be able to respond quickly to today's changing world in order to stay competitive. Failing to change and develop new products or techniques will eventually lead to the deterioration of a company.

quick wit

"Everything that can be invented has been invented."

—Charles H. Duell, Commissioner, U.S. Office of Patents, 1899.

Characteristics and Traits of Creative People

Creative people:
1. Can make "leaps of reasoning" from one fact to a seemingly unrelated fact and build a bridge of logic across the two.
2. Ask seemingly naive questions that frequently begin with "Why . . ."
3. Were nurtured to be creative by their social and educational environment rather than being born creative or intelligent.
4. May be of any age. Many of the most creative people in the computer industry today are in their 20s and 30s.
5. May be of either sex but probably have less rigid male and female role identification.
6. View nature as fundamentally orderly.
7. Engage in divergent rather than convergent thinking first. They use divergent thinking to search for answers in many directions and convergent thinking to make choices based on analysis, reason, and experience.
8. May appear highly sensitive, self-centered, and unconventional with chaotic lives and an unconventional morality. Because they are inner-directed, they do not worry about the approval of society.
9. May be "loners" with few close friends.
10. Tend to be introspective, open to new experiences, less emotionally stable, spontaneous, compulsive problem seekers, anxious, with an inner maturity.
11. On the job, may prefer ideas and things to people, have a high regard for intellectual interests, a high level of resourcefulness, high tolerance for ambiguity, be less concerned about job security, not enjoy detail or routine, and be persistent.

Innovation cannot take place without creativity. Many business experts point out that the ability to come up with new ideas and make them work is, for most companies, the only way to stay alive today. Companies are, therefore, interested in learning more about creativity, how to identify it, and how to foster it. For this reason, employees who develop their own creativity skills and produce more and better ideas for their organizations will become more valuable members of the workforce.

WHAT ARE THE STAGES IN CREATIVITY?

The stages of creativity are perception, incubation, inspiration, and verification.

Although the creative process is still somewhat mysterious, researchers have identified four stages. They are perception, incubation, inspiration, and verification. The **perception** stage requires that we view matters differently than others do. Sometimes it simply involves looking for relationships; at other times it means questioning accepted answers.

Incubation is the most mysterious part of the creative process. Numerous people have compared this stage to a bird sitting quietly on a nest of eggs waiting for them to hatch. Although not much action can be observed, much is happening below the surface. So it is with the innovator. This person may be mentally reviewing many ideas and much information, even in dreams. This stage can range in length from a few hours to many years.

Several major concerns are now in the incubation stage at many companies and in the minds of many people. They include how to deal with the European Common Market, how to solve food and water shortages, how to find new sources of fuel, how to develop effective mass transit systems, and how to market United States goods in changing global economies.

The **inspiration** stage is the flashing light bulb that cartoonists like to use. We usually experience inspiration as an "a-ha" feeling. This breakthrough to conscious thought lasts for only a few moments, but it is the result of lengthy thought. Its occurrence is unpredictable and can come at totally unexpected times.

The last stage of the creative process is **verification.** Thomas Edison once said, "Creation is 1 percent inspiration and 99 percent perspiration." Once an idea comes to us, we must begin the hard work of verifying it—that is, testing it, evaluating it, revising it, retesting it, and reevaluating it if necessary. Productivity is the ability to make new and unique solutions effective. This stage often requires working closely with others and, hence, having finely tuned human relations skills.

GLOBAL CONNECTION

Changing world markets and economies are literally forcing companies and individuals to expand beyond the limits of what they previously thought they could accomplish, to constantly learn new ways of working. A lifelong career now means lifelong learning:

- "The qualities that once nearly guaranteed lifelong employment—hard work, reliability, loyalty, master of a discrete set of skills—are often no longer enough."   —Radcliffe Public Policy Institute
- "The will to succeed is important. But, the will to prepare is even more important."   —Bobby Knight
- "If I had six hours to chop down a tree, I would spend the first four hours sharpening the ax."   —Abraham Lincoln
- "Learning is what most adults will do for a living in the 21st century."
                                                                        —Perelman

- "Tell me what you learned last and I'll tell you who you are."

                                                                    —Kevin Marler

Lifelong learning is crucial to survival in the global workplace.
1. *What do you think is the connection between learning and problem solving? Between learning and creativity?*
2. *What have you learned last? Of what are you proudest that you learned? How will what you have learned help you in your personal and professional lives?*
3. *What plans do you have for continuing your learning?*

Creativity requires "thinking out of the box."

1. Is this hard to do? Why or why not?

2. Is doing things the way they have always been done easier than finding new ways? Why or why not?

3. Why is getting others to try something different frequently difficult?

FastChat

What Are the Sources of Creativity and How Can It Be Encouraged?

Name the sources of creativity in organizations and describe ways to encourage creativity and to get new ideas through organizations.

Organizations should listen to their customers, clients, and employees, who can identify drawbacks to products and point out needs for new products or services. Ideas can then be developed based on these findings. For example, 3M inventor Richard Drew noticed that painters on automobile assembly lines had a hard time keeping the borders straight on two-tone cars, so he invented masking tape. Thomas Edison invented wax paper because he became tired of chocolates sticking to the tissue paper in which they were wrapped.

Executives at many organizations today believe that their companies must be more than lean and fast to create a successful future. They must transform their industries by reinventing themselves. Hamel and Prahalad in *Competing for the Future* say that industry transformers:

1. change the rules of engagement in an industry (like Charles Schwab in the brokerage business),
2. redraw the industry boundaries (as Time Warner is with "edutainment"), and
3. create new industries (as Apple did with personal computers).

The authors suggest that to imagine and create the future, managers need to unlearn the past, develop foresight, create a strategic architecture that helps identify core competencies needed for market leadership, create stretch goals that inspire, and preempt competitors.

As a worker in an organization, you may be more familiar with the processes involved in the performance of your job than anyone else. Therefore, you are in a good position to be able to identify creative approaches. What should you do if you think of what appears to be a better procedure or better product? Knowing how to successfully present ideas and get others to act on them is a crucial skill for creative individuals.

New ideas are not usually immediately embraced in a company. They must be cultivated and supported from conception to implementation. The idea must have a champion, someone who is willing to speak up for it and to commit to it. Being a champion of an idea takes enthusiasm and the willingness to take risks. After all, the idea may prove to be fruitless. The champion, who may be you or someone else such as your supervisor, must put together a team to develop the idea. Few ideas and projects are implemented by one person alone. Working as part of a creative team will not only require creativity, but it will also require well-developed skills in human relations, including problem solving, decision making, and communication.

If you are trying to get an idea through an organization, be prepared to persist. Even the most successful projects have their down sides when the going is tough and participants become discouraged. As the champion of an idea or as a member of a team developing an idea, you should be emotionally prepared for these periods. Having supportive family, friends, or coworkers can help tremendously.

Getting an idea accepted takes human relations skills.

Ideas must be sold to others. Effective communication and networking skills will help the champion develop a coalition and gather others who are willing to support the idea. You or the person serving as the champion must then work to maintain their support.

The above discussion points out the importance of effective human relations skills and explodes the myth that creative people work alone and, therefore, do not need people skills. Creative people have a much better chance of bringing their ideas to fruition if they are able to work effectively with others.

A strong trait in people with effective human relations skills is the willingness to share credit. When a creative group project or idea is successful, the person in charge must be sure to share the credit. While patents and copyrights exist to protect individuals' creations, taking individual credit for a group project is an excellent way to ensure that no further successful group projects will be completed. Learning and sharing information can contribute to a creative atmosphere.

HOW CAN SUPERVISORS STIMULATE CREATIVITY?

Wren and Greenwood in *Management Innovators* suggest that managers can learn a lot by knowing the history of business. Events in today's telecommunication industry are echoes of long-ago events in the telegraph industry. Sam Walton's retailing innovations at WalMart parallel Richard Sears' earlier innovations at Sears, Roebuck.

quick wit

"History doesn't repeat itself, but sometimes it rhymes"

—Mark Twain

If you are a supervisor in an organization, you have a responsibility to stimulate creativity among your employees. Several methods for accomplishing this are

- suspending judgment,
- tolerating a reasonable amount of failure,
- supervising carefully,
- offering constructive criticism, and
- tolerating some different behavior.

The National Institute of Business Management has pointed out that managers skilled in stimulating creativity among workers make it to the top faster than anybody else. They have overcome several common myths about creativity. Being aware of the myths shown here can help you move up in your organization.

Myths about Corporate Creativity

MYTHS	FACTS
1. Creativity is only important in the arts.	Creativity is essential to any organization's success, and managers skilled in tapping their employees' creativity rise faster in the organization.
2. Only a small number of people are creative.	Actually, most people can be creative. Companies should learn to spot creative ideas and use public recognition and money as incentives.
3. Creativity is intangible and uncontrollable.	Although people cannot be made to produce brilliant ideas on demand, an innovative spirit can be nurtured.
4. Creative thinking is needed only in the creative fields of an organization, such as research and product development.	Innovation can occur in policies, processes, and techniques as well as people's activities and behaviors. Additionally, innovation in one area can set off a creative chain reaction throughout the organization.
5. Creative thinking is play, not work.	Intensive thought about innovative problem-solving strategies can be draining. Companies should convey the message that creative work will be rewarded.
6. Creative thinking is risky and leads to unnecessary change.	Creativity is necessary for companies to survive today.

Adapted from "How to Harness Creativity, " in Personal Report for the Executive (New York: National Institute of Business Management, July 1, 1989), 2.

Human Relations

Supervisors interested in stimulating creativity must be sure that they suspend critical judgment during brainstorming sessions. They should also make sure that employees understand they are not responsible for any "crazy" comments they might make during the session.

Supervisors must also stress that failure will be tolerated. Failure is a natural part of innovation and risk taking. As individuals and as employees, if we never fail, we are probably setting goals that are too "safe" (which will be discussed at greater length later in the chapter on goal setting). Many companies stifle creativity because they do not tolerate a certain amount of failure or reward those persons who develop creative ideas. Employees then become afraid to present a project or product that might not be successful.

Quick tip

"He who is not courageous enough to take risks will accomplish nothing in life."

—Muhammad Ali

Supervising creative people takes some practice. Creative individuals find breaking, stretching, or overlooking rules to be natural. For this reason they must be supervised carefully. Goals and timetables need to be set for them while they work at their own pace. If your supervisor does this to you, view it as an attempt to help you succeed professionally, not hinder you.

Creative people also need quiet time to allow their unconscious mind to work. Supervisors should help ensure that such times are available.

Feedback in the form of constructive criticism, praise, and evaluation must be given even if the project is indefinite or long postponed. As pointed out in the discussion of Maslow's hierarchy of needs, creativity falls under the heading of self-actualization needs and is associated with a desire for personal growth and opportunities to use abilities to the fullest. Feedback is an important part of the process of fulfilling this need.

Finally, creative people can be eccentrics, and others in the company may become impatient with their progress or be bothered by their behavior. Creativity is not always a visible process. The person who is staring out the window with feet on the desk may indeed be working very hard. At times a supervisor may need to defend creative individuals, protect them from harm, and nurture them in the corporate political environment.

Nine Supervisory Steps Toward a Creative Workplace

1. Help people see the purpose of what they do.
2. Expect a lot.
3. Tell employees what you expect, not how to do it.
4. Realize that people are different.
5. Be really available.
6. Get the word out in 24 hours or less.
7. Provide the proper tools.
8. Say thanks.
9. Have fun.

Adapted from *Houston Chronicle*, April 11, 1999

TECHNOLOGY CONNECTION

Making a success of small new start-up businesses requires creativity—and particularly when the business in a virtual company. William R. Pope points out that the life of a virtual company happens on e-mail and suggests that employees check their e-mail at least twice a day. He also cautions that if e-mail becomes too disruptive, productivity can be threatened.

Inc. Tech, 1999, No. 3

1. How can e-mail become "too disruptive" for creativity and productivity?

2. Why is frequent checking of e-mail important in a virtual business?

*Fast*Chat

Creativity in the workplace is extremely important today.

1. Where do you think businesses today can gain creative ideas?

2. How might you be a champion for a new idea?

3. If you were a supervisor in an organization with which you are familiar, what might you do to encourage your employees to work creatively?

What Are Blocks to Creativity?

Creativity can be developed and nurtured. It can also be hampered in a variety of ways. Blocks to creativity include thought processes, emotional blocks, cultural blocks, and environmental blocks.

Learning
Objective   5

Discuss the blocks to creativity and how to overcome them.

Quick tip ....

"Knowing is not enough, we must apply. Willing is not enough, we must do."

—Goethe

1. *What do you think Goethe meant by this statement?*
2. *How does it apply to your life and work? to problem solving and decision making? to creativity?*

Reading, creative thinking

THOUGHT PROCESSES

To stimulate creativity, we must learn to modify our problem-solving habits and develop new ways of thinking that enhance creativity. The first block to overcome is the inability to isolate the real source of a problem. People often stereotype a dilemma and see only what they expect to see. To overcome this limit, develop the habit of taking a "big picture" perspective. Look at every angle and take a wide view of the dilemma.

Sometimes we become overloaded with information and cannot recall familiar information because our minds are cluttered with trivia that we are unable to clear away. This clutter can interfere with our creativity. Changing our activities can frequently help us overcome this block. For example, if you have been working in your office, you might go to the library for a short period; or you might temporarily put the problem out of your mind only to have the solution come to you when you are out walking that evening.

Failing to use all of our senses is an additional way that thought processes block creativity. Using sight, sound, smell, taste, and touch as inputs into the creative process can help. Many people, for example, find that watching playful kittens or happy children stimulates their creativity. Others are inspired by the sights, sounds, and smells of nature.

Thought processes that block creativity can be overcome.

We must become aware of emotional blocks to creativity.

quick wit

"There is the risk you cannot afford to take, and there is the risk you cannot afford not to take."

—Peter Drucker

EMOTIONAL BLOCKS

Fear of taking a risk or making a mistake is one of the biggest emotional blocks to creativity. Not all ideas are successful, and the creative individual must be willing to risk negative outcomes. We should, therefore, refrain from letting others (or ourselves) engender such fear in us. If fear is a problem for you, you may benefit from reading the section on attitudes that bring success and confidence, in the chapter on goal setting.

Being overly critical will also kill creativity. Most people would rather judge an idea than generate one. Many ideas die because they are judged too early, before they have been fully developed. Review the steps in the creative process and recall that generation of ideas and evaluation of them are two different parts of the process.

The ability to tolerate ambiguity is essential in the creative process. When something is ambiguous, it can be understood in two or more possible ways. That is precisely what you want in creativity. If you are able to look at a problem in a different way, you are closer to coming up with a novel solution. Black and white, either/or thinking is a communication barrier. If such thinking impedes communication, it will certainly inhibit creativity. Most people have an overriding desire for order and predictability, but the creative process is a "messy" one. New ideas or projects are not orderly or predictable, and people working on them can become frustrated if they cannot tolerate ambiguity. Being aware of this emotional block may help you overcome it.

If we are to be creative, we must **unlock our unconscious minds.** When we are tense or preoccupied, we are unable to be creative. Relaxation and the ability to "sleep on it" are helpful. Many excellent ideas have been conceived on the golf course, in the shower, on the way to work, or during routine chores.

Another emotional block is **fear of change.** Some people find tradition more comfortable. Because creativity by its nature is newness and change, we should develop a positive attitude toward change if we wish to be more creative. Engaging in new activities, sports, or hobbies can help our creativity.

Egos, too, can be the source of emotional blocks to creativity. People who feel that they can never be wrong and will not back down or who will not support an idea presented by another person even when it is a good one stifle creativity. Be careful of such behaviors in yourself.

Finally, some people are unable to **distinguish fantasy from reality.** The creative individual needs to be able to distinguish what is feasible from what is not. Remember that an important step in the problem-solving process is the evaluation of ideas for practicality.

CULTURAL BLOCKS

Some cultural taboos stand in the way of creativity. As noted above, the creative process is not always visible, and time spent gazing out the window may seem wasteful and might make an individual appear lazy. Playing is seen as an activity for children only, not for adults, and pleasure is considered unproductive and inefficient. To be creative we must rid ourselves of such notions and allow our minds to float in a random fashion sometimes, to see figures in clouds. Of course, this only works if you have done the real work first of filling your mind with ideas and information with which your mind can build and create when you do let it float.

Cultural blocks to creativity include taboos against daydreaming, intuition, and humor.

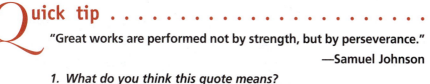

Q**uick tip** . . . .
"Great works are performed not by strength, but by perseverance."
—Samuel Johnson

1. *What do you think this quote means?*
2. *Describe some examples of "great works" that resulted from perseverance?*
3. *How might these examples apply to your life and work?*

Other cultural biases lock out the use of intuition and qualitative judgment in favor of logic, reason, numbers, and practicality. Reality, however, dictates that a balance be maintained between these two sets of forces. Another cultural block is the idea that problem solving must always be a serious business. Humor not only relieves stress, it can also unlock creativity.

Other studies have suggested that laughter enhances creativity because it frees up the child-like part of us. It also can help to strengthen team relationships. And, if used appropriately, humor can deflect anger and reduce tension.

ENVIRONMENTAL BLOCKS

Supervisors and subordinates can set up environmental blocks to creativity.

A lack of trust and cooperation among colleagues can short-circuit creativity. Group interactions are particularly vulnerable when members of rival groups are thrown together to resolve a problem. Autocratic bosses and those who provide little or no feedback can also hinder creativity. They may value their own ideas and not support those of subordinates, blocking contribution to the brainstorming process.

In some situations, groups become merely a rubber stamp and approve ideas without exploring them. This block may happen for two reasons. Sometimes people are afraid to speak up and present opposing views. At other times they fear jeopardizing harmony, so they make a decision that satisfies both sides but that is not the most practical or realistic.

CASE STUDIES IN THE NEWS

A recent study by two Toronto psychologists suggests that they have pinpointed the part of our brain largely responsible for our ability to understand a punch line and turn it into a hearty laugh. (Its publication in the journal *Brain* on April Fool's Day was, they said, merely a happy coincidence.) This study and others point to the right side of the brain as being the place where jokes are understood, where information from throughout the brain and emotional response are integrated. Studies of gender differences show women are more likely to enjoy jokes involving longer narratives, personal information, and memories. Men are more likely to enjoy slapstick.

—*Houston Chronicle*, April 1, 1999.

GLOBAL CONNECTION

A sense of humor in the global environment can place many potentially stressful problems in proper perspective, as shown by these communications found in Roger E. Axtell's book, *Do's and Taboos of Humo(u)r Around the World*. After all, one form of communication understood wherever we travel is the smile.

- "In Belgium, General Motors used a tag line, 'Body by Fisher,' but when that was translated into Flemish, it was said, 'Corpse by Fisher.' "
- "In China, Kentucky Fried Chicken's famous slogan 'finger-lickin' good' came out as 'eat your fingers off.' "
- "When Braniff Airlines translated a slogan about its luxurious upholstery ("Fly in leather") into Spanish, it came out as 'Fly naked.' "
- An American traveler in England asked an Englishman how Thanksgiving is celebrated in Britain. The Englishman with a smile dryly responded, "I suppose you could say in Britain we celebrate Thanksgiving on the Fourth of July."
- A traveler called the front desk at an Indonesian hotel to request a wakeup call and was told to use the alarm clock. Upon asking what happens if it didn't work, the traveler was told by the desk clerk, "Just call me."
- A detour sign in Japan: "Stop: Drive sideways."

Review the blocks to creativity.

1. Does your work environment block or encourage creativity?

2. What are specific elements in your work environment that influence creativity positively or negatively?

FastChat

4.6 How Can You Improve Your Creativity?

Learning
O b j e c t i v e   6

Identify ways that you can improve your creativity.

Ways to improve your creative ability, suggested by Jimmy Calano and Jeff Salzman in *Working Woman* and Eugene Raudsepp in *Nation's Business*, include the following:

Ways to Improve Your Creativity

1. Believe that you have the ability to be creative.
2. Listen to your hunches, particularly while relaxed.
3. Keep track of your ideas by writing down your insights and thoughts. Keep a pad near your bed, in your car, and in your pocket or purse on which to record your ideas as they occur.
4. Learn about things outside of your specialty to keep your thinking fresh.
5. Avoid rigid set patterns of doing things. Change your rhythms. Draw your problems instead of writing them down. Change your scene or environment by taking a trip or walking. Try a different route to work occasionally.
6. Observe similarities, differences, and unique features in things, whether they are situations, processes, or ideas.
7. Engage in an activity at which you are not an expert and that puts you outside of your comfort zone, such as tennis or playing a musical instrument.
8. Engage in hobbies, especially those involving your hands. Keep your brain trim by playing games and doing puzzles and exercises.
9. Take the other side occasionally in order to challenge and scrutinize your own beliefs.
10. Have a sense of humor and learn to laugh easily. Humor helps put you and your problems into perspective and relieves tension, allowing you to be more creative.
11. Adopt a risk-taking attitude. Nothing is more fatal to creativity than fear of failure or resistance to change.
12. Think positive! Believe that a solution is possible and that you will find it.
13. Turn your ideas into action; follow through. Use positive reinforcement with yourself and reward yourself as a payoff for completing a project.

GLOBAL CONNECTION

In "Managing Generation X," Kathy Simmons observes that worldwide, a new generation has come of age and started working during the most profound changes in our economy since the Industrial Generation. These workers, termed Generation Xers, are uniquely suited for the new high-tech, high speed, global knowledge-driven economy.

To tap the strengths and creativity of these young workers, managers must respect their unique characteristics. Managers should recognize Gen Xers' comfort with and desire for a fast pace, high levels of stimulation and change, impatience to see results, and readiness to demonstrate their chameleon-like adaptability skills, says Ms. Simmons.

The Rotarian, September 1999

1. *Why are Generation X workers so well-suited for a new high-tech economy?*

2. *How can managers develop the creativity of these young workers?*

FastChat

Reread the suggestions for improving your creativity.

1. How many of these ways have you used in your creative processes? Which suggestions do you follow routinely? Which ones are you most comfortable in using?

2. Which suggestions could you start practicing now?

3. How do you think your performance would change if you were to begin practicing these suggestions? (Be specific—don't simply say, "I'd be more creative.")

Key Terms

problem
brainstorming
decision tree
cost-benefit analysis
ABC analysis
PERT chart
quality circle
consensus
negotiation
"win-win" situation
creativity
innovation
perception
incubation
inspiration
verification

Summary

Problems are disturbances or unsettled matters that require solutions if organizations or individuals are to function effectively. Problems become evident when expected results are compared to actual results. They can best be solved by following specific steps beginning with defining the problem and ending with following up and modifying when necessary.

Decisions are needed when we must make choices among actions, opportunities, or solutions. There are several well-known techniques or tools that can be effective for making personal and work decisions. Decision making may be done by individuals or by groups. The goal of group problem solving is to develop a solution with which all members can agree. Negotiation, discussion that leads to a decision acceptable to all, is important. To be an effective negotiator, you should try for win-win solutions.

An important factor in problem solving is creativity, the ability to come up with new and unique solutions. We all have the potential for creativity, but it must be nurtured and developed. Innovation, the end product of creative activity, is vital to the success of organizations and individuals today.

Creativity involves four steps: perception, incubation, inspiration, and verification. Creative ideas can come from many sources. An employee trying to get a new idea through an organization should be prepared to persist, develop a coalition, sell the idea, work as part of a team, and share credit.

Supervisors wishing to stimulate creativity among their workers must be aware of the myths about corporate creativity. Blocks to creativity include thought processes, emotional blocks, cultural blocks, and environmental blocks. You can take several steps to develop your own creativity, starting with believing that you can be creative. Thinking positively helps, and following through is essential.

Review Questions

1. What is a problem and what are the steps in problem solving?
2. Define decision tree, ABC analysis, cost-benefit analysis, PERT chart, and quality circle.
3. What is the role of creativity in problem solving and what are the basic steps in the creative process?
4. What are the sources of creativity in organizations and what are ways to encourage creativity and to get new ideas through organizations.
5. What are the blocks to creativity? Give some examples. How can they be overcome?
6. How can you improve your creativity?

Discussion Questions

1. Think of a problem with which you were recently confronted. Apply the problem-solving process to it. Would you take the same action now that you did at the time? (Remember that no decision is a decision!) Share the answer with the class.
2. Think of two problems that you are currently facing. Apply a decision tree to one and ABC analysis to the other.
3. Think of a time when you came up with what you considered to be a novel solution to a problem. Think back carefully to the process you used. Try to identify the four basic steps in your creative process. Share this experience with the class.
4. If you are currently working or have worked, think about your organization. What is the level of creativity in it? What steps is the organization or your supervisor taking to stimulate creativity? What are you doing to develop your own creative ability?
5. Review the different blocks to creativity. Name examples of each kind and consider them in relation to yourself. Are they blocks to your own creativity? (Try to be objective!) If not, good for you. If so, identify what you can do to overcome each block.

Chapter Project

An interesting place on the world wide web to explore creativity is the *Creativity Web (http://www.ozemail.com.au/~caveman/Creative/)*. Go to it and find the Technique called "Attribute Listing," a way to help people examine an issue or product from all different angles to see if they can find a way to improve it. In a group choose a product you know well, break down its component parts and then consider how each part could be made better so that the resulting product is a more innovative one. Then think about products or services that you consider truly creative. In your group discuss how you think the companies that invented these ideas came up with them.

Read, listen, speak, think creatively, make decisions, solve problems, reason, participate as a member of a team to contribute to group effort, exercise leadership, negotiate, and work with diversity.

Applications

In small groups, analyze the following situations.

20/80 Syndrome

Paige, the head of the continuing education program at the local community college, finds that summer is the best time for her to develop new programs and courses. In looking at her "to do" list for this summer, she sees so many projects that she cannot possibly do all of them. In reviewing the list she finds the following:

1. *Courses for professional groups.* Some professional groups are required to complete state-mandated continuing education hours each year in order to remain licensed or certified. The state expects community colleges to provide such training, and Paige is interested in offering courses if they will have satisfactory enrollments. These groups include real estate sales people, Certified Public Accountants, and insurance agents.

Paige has tried to provide some courses for CPAs in the past, enrollments were low, yet she knows that other community colleges are experiencing high enrollments. One of these colleges said that it set up an advisory committee made up of members of the local CPA society. The advisory committee recommends courses, helps find instructors, and assists in publicizing the courses. Paige thinks that perhaps she should set up an advisory committee before offering additional courses for CPAs.

Paige has not yet offered courses for insurance agents, but she knows of a college nearby that does. That school reports low enrollments. Paige is uncertain whether she should try courses in this area, set up an advisory committee, or even devote effort to it.

2. *Other new courses and programs.* Paige also has several other programs and course possibilities on her list. They include classes for senior citizens and a "fear-of-flying" course for white-knuckle flyers. Other colleges report great success in targeting classes to local citizens over 55 years of age. Paige does not know of any colleges that offer the flying course or

even who would teach it for her (her college does have a pilot training program). She is also considering a dental assistant program and a gerontology program. Her community has several medical complexes in it, and students would probably be able to do internships in them.

3. *Business/industry contracts.* Paige would also like to devote some time to developing additional training contracts with businesses and industries in the community. She has been successful in building up a good working relationship with a number of companies around her college and would like to do more. Such contracts develop good will in the community, bring in additional money to the college, and provide jobs for teachers. Besides, Paige enjoys setting them up.

Although Paige can ask some of the other people at the college for input, she has to do most of the work herself designing and marketing courses and programs. As Paige looks at her list of potential projects, she grows both excited and frustrated. She enjoys creating new programs and courses, but she also knows that she will not be able to do all of this work in two and one-half months.

1. Apply ABC analysis to Paige's dilemma. Categorize each task, label it A, B, or C, and explain your reasoning.
2. Based on your ABC analysis, what recommendation would you make to Paige about her priorities for the summer?

HELP! HELP!

Two years ago Daniel started a roofing business. Most of his customers are homeowners and small businesses. His business has been so successful that six months ago he hired an employee to help him. He was lucky enough then to find someone who was experienced and fast.

Last month Daniel hired a second person when he found that work was stacking up and deadlines were not being met. The second employee is not experienced but is eager to learn and, in fact, seems to be a quick study. However, because of all the rush projects, Daniel has not had much time to train him and, hence, has to give him the less complex jobs.

Daniel is beginning to feel overwhelmed. One of his saws has been acting up for the last two weeks, resulting in some downtime. He and his employees frequently run out of needed supplies in the middle of a job. Another common problem is realizing that a job calls for a particular roofing material, and the local supplier does not keep it in stock. Daniel is dismayed to find that even though he has an additional person on the payroll, deadlines are still not being met and jobs are backing up. In fact, some

Read, listen, speak, think creatively, make decisions, solve problems, reason, participate as a member of a team to contribute to group effort, exercise leadership, negotiate, and work with diversity.

projects have even been put aside and not bid until the customer called once or twice causing much embarrassment. Daniel feels that he cannot blame anybody in particular, as whoever is free is the one who takes requests from customers, orders supplies, and moves on to the next project.

1. Imagine that you are a consultant hired by Daniel to try to bring order to his business. Using the problem-solving process described in this chapter, summarize your conversation with Daniel. Be specific.
   a. What do you think is the real problem? What information are you using to determine it?
   b. What do you think are the possible causes of the problem? Again, what information are you using?
2. Based on the conversation with Daniel and the application of the problem-solving process, what advice would you give him? Be specific.
   a. How practical are the ideas you have generated?
   b. What alternatives for removing the causes of the problem would you suggest? What are the implications of each alternative.
   c. What would you recommend as the most likely solution to Daniel's problem? Next most likely?
   d. Write an action plan for solving Daniel's business problem. Be sure to explain how the plan should be implemented and followed up.

Additional Resources

http://www.phlip.marist.ed/dessler/news/mlpo1117.htm
Helpful management stories in the news
http://www.ozemail.com.au/~caveman/Creative/index.html
Interesting resources for developing creativity
Bennis, Warren. *Why Leaders Can't Lead.* San Francisco: Jossey-Bass Publishers, 1990. (Part Three: "Parts of the Problem"; Part Four: "Parts of the Solution."
Chun, J. "Theory of Creativity." *Entrepreneur,* October 1997.
Lancaster, H. "Getting Yourself in a Frame of Mind to be Creative." *Wall Street Journal,* September 16, 1997.
Nanus, Burt. *The Leader's Edge—The Seven Keys to Leadership in a Turbulent World.* New York: Contemporary Books, 1989. (Chapter 7, "Creative Leadership.")
Pope, William R. Virtual Manager Size Matters." *Inc. Tech* 1999, No. 3, p. 31.
Simmons, Kathy. "Managing Generation X." *The Rotarian* September 1999, p. 8

Working within the Organization:
Structure and Climate

focus

What precisely is an organization? It used to be about buildings. About departments. About fat payrolls. Now . . . it seems that it's not.

Buildings are tumbling. Boundaries are vanishing. Temps . . . are coming. Where "you" start and where "I" stop are no longer clear.

The short and the long of it: Organizations, as we have known them for hundreds of years, are disappearing. Literally.

Tom Peters, *The Circle of Innovation*

What changes in organizational structure have occurred since the early 1900's? Why have these changes occurred? What changes do you expect to happen in the future?

objectives

After studying this chapter, you should be able to:

1. *Explain the purpose and importance of organizational structure.*

2. *Discuss the hierarchical pyramid and identify its roots.*

3. *Describe the ways power is distributed within the chain of command.*

4. *Understand the concept of span of control.*

5. *Define formal communication and identify the directions in which it can flow.*

6. *Discuss informal communication and the dangers of the grapevine.*

7. *Recognize the various types of organizational structures used by businesses today.*

8. *Identify corporate life cycles, reasons they exist, and how they affect organizational structure.*

In This Chapter

Structure divides and delegates responsibility.

Structure is the relationship among parts. In the case of a business or other organization, structure helps the organization divide its work and delegate tasks. Without structure, you and other employees do not know what your jobs are or who is responsible for what, resulting in frustration, low morale, conflict, and other human relations problems. An effective structure also helps people avoid duplication of work and delays that can happen when work must be reviewed by numerous layers of management.

There is no correct way to structure an organization. Notwithstanding, organizational structure will affect productivity, quality, employee morale, customer satisfaction, and, ultimately, the success of the entire business. For these reasons many organizations study their structure on an ongoing basis and make changes to boost efficiency. Increasingly companies are experimenting with radical new ideas concerning structure, attempting to flatten and decentralize control in order to spark innovation and allow a more rapid response to changing market demands.

The chain of command directs the flow of authority and information.

Regardless of which organizations you are involved in, an understanding of organizational structure will help you function well within them. Additionally, such knowledge will help you understand and adjust to organizational changes. The heart of organizational structure is the chain of command, of which you should be aware and to which you should be sensitive.

FastChat

Describe the structures of a variety of organizations: your job, your school, a volunteer organization.

1. How do they differ?

2. How would they operate without structure?

What Is the Chain of Command?

Organizational structure originally developed around the chain of command. The **chain of command** is the direction in which authority is exercised and policies and other information are communicated to lower levels. Authority begins at the top, and each level gives commands, delegates authority, and passes information to lower levels. Information and requests going up the line follow the chain upward. The idea of the chain of command developed in the military and is prevalent in today's organizations. It forms the classic **pyramidal hierarchy**, illustrated here.

You should respect the chain of command and exercise great caution in skipping levels. Such respect and caution will reduce the potential for human relations problems. One of the few occasions when you can safely ignore the chain is in emergencies or when time is crucial and your immediate supervisor is not present.

Learning
Objective 2

Discuss the hierarchical pyramid and identify its roots.

The business chain of command can be compared to that of the military.

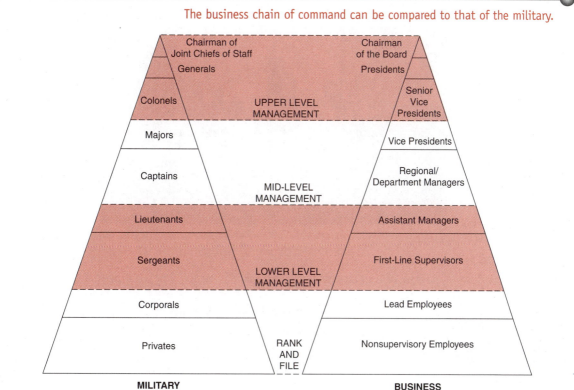

MILITARY		BUSINESS
Chairman of Joint Chiefs of Staff		Chairman of the Board
Generals		Presidents
Colonels	UPPER LEVEL MANAGEMENT	Senior Vice Presidents
Majors		Vice Presidents
Captains	MID-LEVEL MANAGEMENT	Regional/ Department Managers
Lieutenants		Assistant Managers
Sergeants	LOWER LEVEL MANAGEMENT	First-Line Supervisors
Corporals		Lead Employees
Privates	RANK AND FILE	Nonsupervisory Employees

CASE STUDIES IN THE NEWS

General Electric's aircraft-engine assembly facility in Durham, North Carolina, employs 170-plus people. There is, however, only one boss. Everyone reports to her. The workers are divided into 9 teams and are given only the date their engine needs to come off the assembly line. The workers decide who does what work as well as how to balance training, vacations, and overtime. There is no time clock and the boss sits in an open cubicle that is located on the factory floor.

1. *How is this structure different from the classic pyramidal hierarchy?*

2. *What skills do the workers in this structure need that they would not need in a traditional pyramidal hierarchy?*

3. *Which structure would you rather work in—a flattened structure or a pyramid structure?*

Organizational structure allows companies to divide work and delegate tasks.

FastChat

Think of a company or organization in which you have been a part.

1. Describe the chain of command. How would the organization have functioned without the chain of command?

2. Do you think the chain of command will disappear? Why or why not?

Who Has Authority?

As organizations grow in size and complexity, their heads find that making all decisions becomes increasingly difficult. For instance, if you were the president of a company with ten thousand employees, you could not possibly make every decision necessary in a day and supervise all your employees. Authority to make these decisions must be delegated to lower levels.

Two forms of authority distribution are common. When authority is closely held by those high up in the organization and these people are responsible for making all major decisions, the organization is said to be **centralized**. When important decisions are made at a lower level, authority is **decentralized**.

Centralization and decentralization have their positive and negative sides. A centralized purchasing function, for instance, can ensure that quality of supplies remains constant among locations. Additionally, buyers of large quantities frequently receive discounts.

A drawback to centralization is that decision making can sometimes be slow. Reporting through several layers of managers instead of making the decision immediately and acting on it at the lower level can take time.

Sometimes decentralization faces problems from weak managers. These individuals may not have the maturity or expertise to make effective decisions.

Learning
Objective 3

Describe ways power is distributed within the chain of command.

Authority is distributed because organization heads usually cannot make all decisions.

quick wit

How do you induce innovation? Simple: Decentralize! What's the problem with decentralization? It almost never works.

Tom Peters

Many companies today are trying to decentralize.

1. What does this mean for the people in the middle management positions?

2. Can you expect as many promotions moving up in an organization as your parents did? Why or why not?

FastChat

How Many Employees to One Supervisor?

The number of employees that can be supervised effectively by one person generally ranges between 12 and 21. More can be successfully supervised at one time if the employees are capable of working independently and their tasks are very similar. However, the higher up in the organization you go, the more complex jobs become, and the fewer people you can supervise.

The number of people that an individual can supervise is called the **span of control**. The span may be either tall or flat, as shown below. Not having the appropriate span of control can sometimes result in behavioral or performance problems. Employees may feel unnoticed—good performance may be unrewarded and poor performance may go uncorrected.

Span of control can be tall or flat.

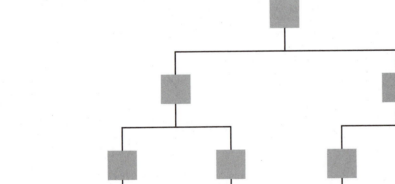

TALL STRUCTURE
(Narrow Span of Control)

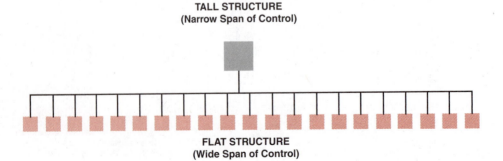

FLAT STRUCTURE
(Wide Span of Control)

A way that you can broaden your span is by delegating authority to others within your group. Broadening the span can lessen red tape and increase morale. Individuals allowed to perform higher-level tasks feel increased job satisfaction. One way that span of control could be expanded might involve using "lead" employees to oversee the work of others. These could be senior level individuals who would continue to perform their work but who would also monitor the performance of others. While lead people generally would not have authority to discipline or appraise performance, they would be given authority to direct work and give orders.

If you are to make your delegation of authority successful, you must communicate fully. The person receiving the authority must understand the new role and be willing to act accordingly. Likewise, the other employees must be informed of what is expected of them and of the person receiving the authority. Without this communication, serious human relations problems can develop. If you are the one being given such authority, ask your supervisor whether coworkers are aware of your new responsibilities. If they are not, suggest that your supervisor inform them. If that does not happen, you should probably communicate this information to your coworkers as early as possible in your new role.

FastChat

Organizations today are attempting to flatten their spans of control in order to bring products to the market place more quickly and improve service. This has increased the need for supervisors to delegate, though they often have little experience in delegating and sometimes find it difficult.

1. Why do people have trouble delegating authority?

2. How do you feel when you are not in control of something but responsible for it?

3. What can you do to get your supervisor to trust you with delegated tasks?

How Does Communication Follow Structure?

Communication flows upward, downward, or horizontally.

Formal communication, communication that flows up or down the formal organizational structure, is controlled by the chain of command. Organizational communication varies in the direction it flows, whether it is one-way or two-way, and in its chance of distortion.

DIRECTION AND DISTORTIONS OF COMMUNICATION FLOW

In any organization communication will flow downward, upward, or horizontally (sideways). **Downward communication** is communication that begins at higher levels of the organization and flows downward. Typical forms of downward communication are meetings, memoranda, policy statements, newsletters, manuals, handbooks, telephone conversations, and electronic mail.

Downward communication can become distorted for a variety of reasons. Long messages not in writing tend to be forgotten or misinterpreted. Furthermore, sometimes so many messages are received that a communication overload results. For example, the employee receiving 20 e-mails a day may fail to read all of them carefully. (Communication—how to make it effective and avoid problems—will be discussed in greater depth in Chapter 9.)

Various tools can be used to communicate formally within an organization.

Upward communication consists of messages that begin in the lower levels of the organization and go to higher levels. Upward communication can be in the form of memos, grievances (presented formally or informally), meetings, attitude surveys, or suggestion systems.

Upward communication can also become distorted. Frequently, subordinates who must deliver unpleasant messages misrepresent situations that they are communicating for fear the receiver may "kill the messenger who delivers the bad news."

Quick tip . . . .

When you must talk about a problem that no one wants to talk about, remember the following:

1. Spend time identifying the problem. Explore your motivation for bringing up the issue. Imagine how others will react.
2. Work to overcome your fear of presenting the problem. Use visualization (Chapter 2) to assist.
3. Be direct but tactful. Give the listener time to react.
4. Stay with the message. Continue to seek support for your point of view.

Michael Warshaw , Fast Company.

TECHNOLOGY CONNECTION

The Virtual Technology Laboratory of the University of Houston uses computers to turn data into three-dimensional images that respond to the viewer's action. The three-dimensional display, facilitated by a head-mounted viewing device (goggles or helmet) allows the computer to track hand, eye, or body motions as a user interacts with the images being viewed.

Scientists, doctors, and engineers will no longer have to be physically at a location in order to interact. They can consult with each other from the far corners of the globe and feel like they are working side by side. The possibilities are endless. Training, examination of data, and education can be carried on using this new virtual reality.

1. *What are the ramifications of this technology for organizational structures?*

2. *In what ways could this technology be used for examining data? In training? In education?*

Horizontal communication occurs between individuals at the same level in an organization. These messages can be in the form of telephone conversations, memos, meetings, informal gatherings, or electronic mail. These communications, too, can suffer from distortions whenever messages are not clear, perceptions differ, or attitudes get in the way.

ONE-WAY AND TWO-WAY COMMUNICATION

Communication within organizations is either one-way or two-way. **One-way communication** takes place with no feedback from the receiver. Some examples are memos or videotaped lectures. Although one-way communication can present problems, it is used frequently because it is quick, easy to generate, and orderly. Can you imagine the president of a corporation of thousands of employees attempting to communicate a new benefits program using two-way communication? In addition, one-way communication is less threatening for the sender because no one is present to give negative feedback.

Two-way communication is communication in which feedback is received. Although two-way communication is slower and less orderly than one-way communication, in general it is more accurate. The receiver of the message is able to provide feedback, and the sender is able to evaluate whether the message has been correctly interpreted.

ETHICS CONNECTION

Because they are human, bosses are not perfect. Some will be better than others, but you may encounter unethical behavior.

1. *Under what circumstances should you bypass your supervisor to report problems or unethical activities?*
2. *Should you try to work out things between yourself and your supervisor first?*
3. *Who else can you talk to besides your supervisor's boss?*

FastChat

Think of an organization of which you have been a member.

1. How was communication handled? Was it one-way or two-way?

2. How could communication have been improved?

How Else Does Information Flow?

5.6

Learning
Objective 6

*Discuss informal
communication and
the dangers of the
grapevine.*

Informal communication is another type of communication that occurs in organizations. This form of communication, the most common type, can either help or hinder an organization's efforts. If you discuss a new company policy with someone in another department, you would be using informal communication. Informal communication does not follow the formal channels of communication but travels through a channel often called the **grapevine**. The grapevine is an informal, person-to-person means of circulating information or gossip. It serves several functions for both employees and management. Many managers have learned to respect and even use the grapevine because of its speed. However, because of its unreliability, it must be used with caution. As an employee or organization member, you can satisfy some of your social needs through the grapevine, clarify formal orders, and use it as a release for your feelings and concerns. When employees feel that upward communication will be threatening, blocked, or ineffective, they frequently turn to the grapevine.

**Use the informal
grapevine with
care.**

The problem with grapevines is that often messages are distorted, exaggerated, partial, or even totally wrong. Grapevines are the primary means

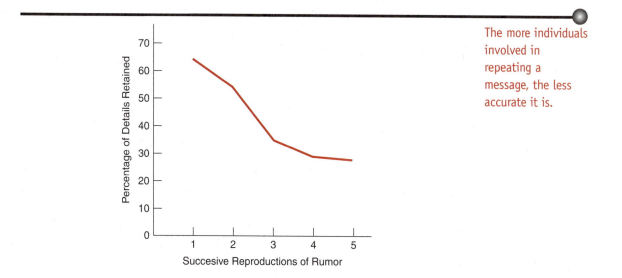

**The more individuals
involved in
repeating a
message, the less
accurate it is.**

"Successive Reproductions of Rumor" from Gordon W. Allport and Lee Postman, The Psychology of Rumor. *Copyright © 1947, 1975 by Henry Holt and Co., Inc. Used by permission.*

for transmitting rumors. Also, the chance of misinterpretation increases with the number of individuals through whom the messages pass, as shown on the previous page. Because downward communication is sometimes ambiguous and upward communication is often nonexistent, rumors too often occur. Such situations are fertile soil for problems in human relations. Grapevines exist in every organization, and you should understand how grapevines work and respect their potential, both good and bad. Be careful that you do not contribute incorrect or inappropriate information to the grapevine. Information can easily be introduced into the grapevine or garbled once it is in, but correcting it is almost impossible. Probably the best rule of thumb for good human relations is to ask yourself the question, "Does this need to be said?" The most valuable asset in human relations is common sense!

Communications authors Barry L. Reece and Rhonda Brandt have developed the following guidelines and cautions concerning grapevines. Understanding the grapevine can keep you out of trouble.

1. No one can hide from the grapevine, even though it may know only part of the truth. Our reputations are created by the grapevine and are hard to change. Be careful about what information about you makes its way into the grapevine. Watch what you tell others about yourself, choose carefully those with whom you share information, and use discretion in your behavior.

2. The message (gossip) of the grapevine tends to be negative. People who consistently communicate negative information about others ultimately become distrusted or shut out. Exercise discretion about information you contribute to the grapevine. Would you want others to know what you said?

3. Several grapevine networks operate in every organization. Each one is composed of people who have common experiences and concerns. In a particular network, usually only a few people pass on most of the information, and that is usually downward or horizontally. Do you want to be labeled one of these people?

4. The role you play in the grapevine will reflect your ethics, decision-making skills, and maturity. Mature people anticipate the consequences of their actions and words. Think about the image that you create of yourself before you participate in grapevine communication.

CASE STUDIES IN THE NEWS

Telecommuting centers in Lancaster and Santa Clarita, CA, which soared in popularity after the Northridge earthquake, are holding their own, but the centers' backers are questioning their long-term future because of changing work patterns in Southern California. These centers came into vogue when there was a rigorous state regulation requiring employers of over 100 workers to have a transportation plan encouraging employees to car pool or take the bus or train to work. A number of centers are making it but are not completely booked.

Furthermore, employers never liked the idea of paying rent on extra facilities without a demonstrable advantage and worried about employees working without supervision.

Los Angeles Times, Valley Edition, December 8, 1998

1. Why are more people not using telecommuting centers?

2. What are the benefits of interacting face to face with your coworkers rather than via e-mail, telephone, or fax?

3. Do you like to work alone? Why or why not?

The grapevine exists in all organizations.

*Fast*Chat

1. What problems can occur if organizations do not formally release information and most of the information comes through the grapevine?

2. Can you name a time when you heard information through the grapevine? Was the information accurate? Inaccurate?

What Other Structures Exist?

A variety of new organizational structures developed as organizations became larger and more complex. The basic pyramidal hierarchy was no longer meeting organizational needs. However, no one specific type of organizational structure is best. The most efficient structure depends on the size of the organization, whether it provides a service or produces a product, and the number of different products or services involved.

The formal structure can be organized by function (what each department does), by geographic area, by customer, or by product. Large, complex organizations may use a variety of these structures, depending on their needs. The figures that follow represent the various ways of organizing. Developing an organizational structure is a complicated process and is a whole study in itself.

Complex organizations have developed other structures to enhance organizational effectiveness. Some use a line and staff structure, others use a matrix structure, and still others mix the two.

LINE AND STAFF STRUCTURE

Line employees are directly involved in production activities. The **staff** employees support line employees through advice and counsel on a variety of subjects in their areas of expertise. This support may be in the form of legal, safety, personnel, or computer assistance or may involve maintenance of equipment or facilities.

Example of a function-oriented organizational structure

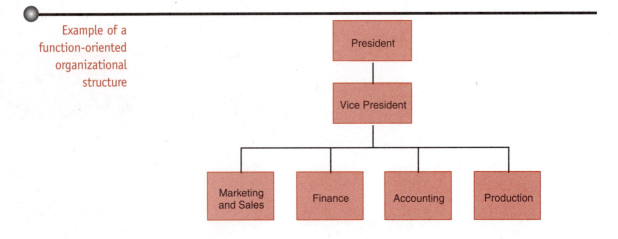

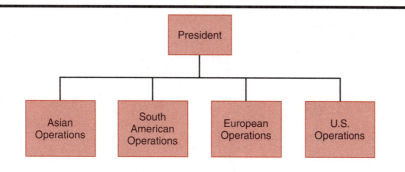

Example of a
geographical
organizational
structure

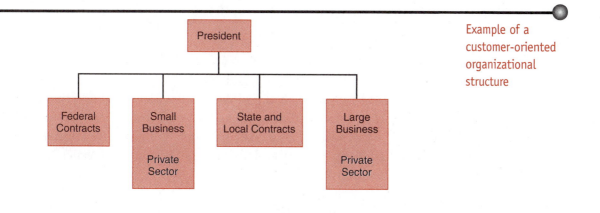

Example of a
customer-oriented
organizational
structure

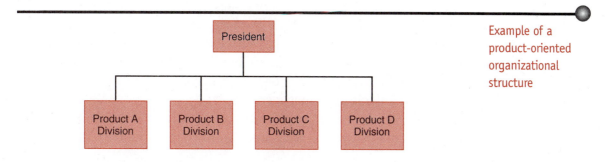

Example of a
product-oriented
organizational
structure

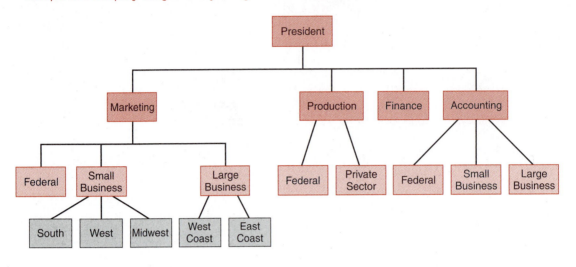

Many problems can arise from line and staff relationships. One common problem is that staff members usually have no authority to force line employees to cooperate. Staff people must frequently rely on their skills of persuasion to convince line workers that staff instructions should be followed. For this reason some staff members are given **functional authority**—the authority to make decisions in their area of expertise and to overrule line decisions.

MATRIX STRUCTURE

Matrix structures are frequently used by organizations that do many projects. Therefore, the matrix structure is sometimes called project structure. A **matrix structure** uses groups of people with expertise in their individual areas who are temporarily assigned full or part time to a project from other parts of the organization. The project has its own supervisor and can last a few weeks or a few years. For instance, an engineering firm may pull together a group of engineers to oversee the design and construction of a new plant and dissolve the group as soon as the plant is finished. The employees then return to their original supervisors, and the plant continues operation under its own management.

Some companies utilize the matrix structure to develop products or operate in markets where decisions need to be made quickly. These groups

GLOBAL CONNECTION

are given power to make decisions to speed their work, and they may be assigned experts on a number of fronts.

Matrix structures can cause difficulty. The individual assigned to head the temporary team may have no formal authority or control over the rest of the group. Power struggles may erupt.

If you find yourself in this type of situation, the best approach is to discuss it with the person who delegated the project to you and ask for formal authority. Someone higher in the chain of command than the participants should instruct them to cooperate and emphasize that they will be appraised on their participation and performance.

Everyone has a
place in the
organization.

Company Organizational Chart
(for this week)

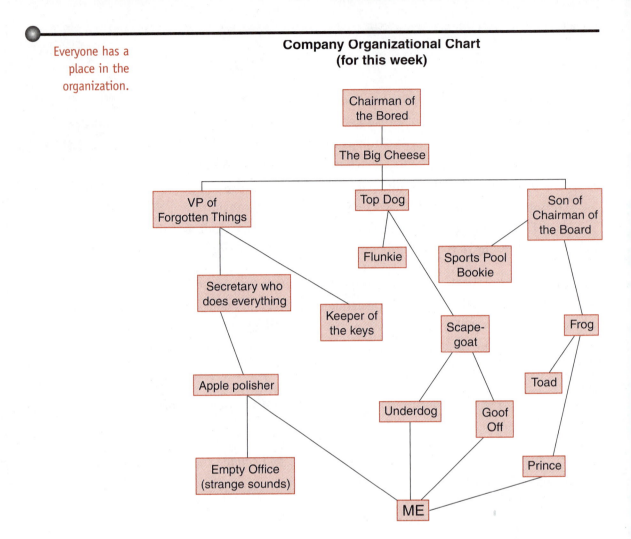

FastChat

Globalization and modern technology will cause organizations to experiment with structure.

1. What structures have you been exposed to?

2. Have you ever had two supervisors? How did you handle it?

Why Does Structure Change?

Organizations change for many reasons. New technology brings fresh products and makes old ones obsolete, new markets open and old markets fade away, and competition or the lack of it increases or decreases demand. All of these changes may call for a change in organizational structure. The economic downturn period of the 1980s saw United States companies adopting new manufacturing practices to remain competitive. Often they changed to a flatter organizational structure that gave employees more responsibility. The new management structures are less military and emphasize a greater team effort.

Another reason organizations change, according to Joseph L. Massie and John Douglas in *Managing—A Contemporary Introduction*, is that they go through **life cycles**, as shown below. After birth or start-up comes growth. The next stage is stabilization. After that the organization begins to slow down. Then it either closes or it revitalizes.

This concept can be illustrated by many companies that once produced only black-and-white televisions for sale in the United States. At first television was a new idea, and the technology was expensive. Sales were low because customers were unfamiliar with television, sets were costly, and few broadcasting stations existed. As the production of televisions increased, the price of production dropped and more stations were established. Then sales rose and television manufacturing companies grew to handle the demand. Soon the majority of households in the United States had a black-and-white television and the demand stabilized. Technology began to change, however, and color television was developed. Sales of companies

Learning
Objective 8

Identify corporate life cycles, reasons they exist, and how they affect organizational structure.

Structures change as companies go through life cycles.

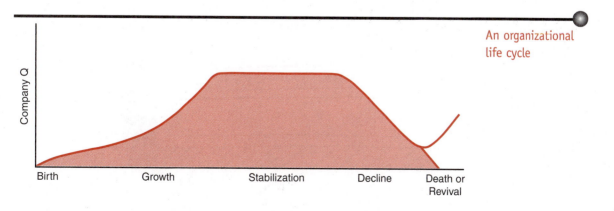

An organizational life cycle

Birth   Growth   Stabilization   Decline   Death or Revival

producing only black-and-white televisions began to drop. These companies then had two choices. Either they could reduce their production to match demand (taking a risk that they might go out of business) or they could revitalize. Revitalization could mean manufacturing color televisions or locating new markets in countries just beginning to use black-and-white television.

*Fast*Chat

Throughout civilization products have had life cycles.

1. Name products that have completed a life cycle.

2. What products that we have now will soon be on the downswing of their life cycles?

In many organizations, the customer has the greatest authority.

Summary

Structure is the relationship among parts. Organizations require structure to arrange their workload and allow smooth operations. Organizational structure originally developed around the chain of command, the direction in which authority and communication are utilized within the organization. The classic business structure, the pyramidal hierarchy, developed from the chain of command.

Authority in an organization can be either centralized or decentralized. Each choice has advantages and disadvantages. Then, too, an organization must consider the most effective span of control for its particular situation. The span of control indicates how many employees a supervisor manages.

Communication in an organization can be either formal or informal. Formal communication can travel upward, downward, or horizontally and can be either one-way or two-way. Each type of communication and flow has its positive and negative aspects. Informal communication ranges from conversations between employees to rumors that travel through the grapevine.

Organizational structure can take many forms besides the classical pyramidal hierarchy. Work can be organized according to function, geography, customer, product, or a mixture of these. Some structures, such as the matrix structure, while offering advantages, are complex and can cause difficulties for the employees involved. Organizational structures often change as organizations go through life cycles and tailor structures to meet their current needs. Understanding how organizations function and why structural changes are needed can help us in the organization.

Key Terms

chain of command
pyramidal hierarchy
centralized management
decentralized management
span of control
formal communication
downward communication
upward communication
horizontal communication
one-way communication
two-way communication
informal communication
grapevine
line and staff structure
functional authority
matrix structure
life cycles

Review Questions

1. What is the purpose of organizational structure, and why is it important?
2. What is the hierarchical pyramid, and where are its roots?
3. How is power assigned in an organization? How many employees can be supervised effectively at one time?
4. What is formal communication, and in which directions can it flow?
5. What factors decrease the effectiveness of formal communication?
6. What is informal communication, and what are the dangers of the grapevine?
7. Describe the types of structures used by businesses today.
8. What complex organizational structures exist? What problems arise from their use?
9. What is the corporate life cycle, and why does it exist?

Discussion Questions

1. Describe an organization that restructured of which you are or have been a member. What were the results? Is restructuring always the best step?
2. Have you ever received an inaccurate message through the grapevine? What happened as a result of this misinformation?
3. Should all firms attempt to decentralize authority? Why or why not?
4. Identify a company in your community and describe where you believe it is in its life cycle.
5. Why are we usually more willing to accept authority of those above us than those at our level or below?
6. Think of several organizations with which you are familiar through experience or the news. What organizational structure does each have?

Chapter Project

Search the Internet or your public library for the works of Henry Mintzberg. One Web site is the Business Open Learning Archive (BOLA) at http://sol.brunel.ac.uk/~jarvis/bola/competence/index.html. Find the definitions of his five types of organizations:

1. Simple structure
2. Machine bureaucracy
3. Divisionalized form

4. Professional bureaucracy
5. Adhocracy

Answer the following questions about each type:

1. What are the pros and cons of each of these structures?
2. Can you name organizations today with these types of structure?
3. Define your ideal organizational structure.

Applications

Reading, writing, technology, understanding complex relationships

In small groups analyze the following situations.

Nowhere to Run, Nowhere to Hide

Jacob sat at his desk staring out the window. He did not know what to do. Yesterday his boss, Carla, had told him to fire Lisa immediately for having one too many complaints. A patient complained about how Lisa had treated him. Carla's boss, the Director of Nursing, was furious and had threatened to demote Carla.

However, when Jacob spoke with Janet, the human resources specialist, she voiced concern. Janet did not think that Jacob had followed the company's progressive discipline policy and said that Lisa should be given a final warning before being fired. Janet cautioned Jacob that terminating Lisa without following company policy might result in a grievance from the union and a charge of discrimination filed with the Equal Employment Opportunity Commission.

Jacob reported this concern to Carla, who exclaimed, "I don't care what those human resources people say. We just can't let lazy, incompetent people continue to work here! I want Lisa fired immediately, and I want anyone else who makes another mistake fired, too."

Reading, listening, visualizing, problem solving, understanding complex relationships

1. What type of organizational structure is being used in this scenario?
2. What problem has the structure caused?
3. Could this problem have been avoided if Janet had been given functional authority? How?
4. Whose orders should Jacob follow? Why?

Order from Chaos

Lester's company is growing rapidly, and problems have emerged. He has a T-shirt factory on the outskirts of town and two sales outlets. The T-shirt factory makes 20 varieties of shirts with different logos. A special division does

Reading, listening, visualizing, problem solving, understanding complex relationships, integrity and honesty

custom orders for sports teams and corporations. The factory employs 61 individuals, and each outlet has 20 employees.

However, matters are getting out of hand. Supplies are late, paychecks are not coming out on time, and employees at the second outlet are sneaking off early after Lester leaves the shop. Yesterday, because Lester forgot to pay the bills, the electricity was turned off at the first outlet, and he had to close for the day until power was restored.

Currently, Lester has a plant manager to oversee production in the plant and two lead store clerks, one in each store. Lester takes care of ordering supplies, paying bills, writing paychecks, and hiring personnel. He makes all major decisions at the outlets and most of the decisions at the plant.

1. Does Lester need to restructure his organization? If so, how?
2. Should he add more layers of management? Why or why not?
3. Should management decisions be decentralized? Why or why not? In which areas should he add management?
4. What would be an appropriate span of control in the outlets? In the factory?

Additional Readings and Resources

Carr, David K. Henry Johansson (Contributor). *Best Practices in Reengineering*. New York: McGraw Hill, 1995.

Champy, James. *Reengineering Management*. New York: Harper Business, 1995.

Hammer, Michael and James Champy. *Reengineering the Corporation*. New York: Harper Business, 1994.

http://sol.brunel.ac.uk/~jarvis/bola/competence/index.html   Business Open Learning Archive Web site

http://www.semitechglobal.com   Corporate website for Semi-Tech (Global)

Peters, Tom, *The Circle of Innovation*. New York: Knopf, 1997.

Group Dynamics:
The Advantages of Working with Others

c h a p t e r

6

o b j e c t i v e s

After studying this chapter, you should be able to:

1. *Discuss the characteristics of a group.*

2. *Explain the importance of studying groups.*

3. *Explain the reasons people join groups.*

4. *Distinguish among types of formal groups.*

5. *Discuss the different types of leaders.*

6. *Discuss how groups mature and factors that influence their effectiveness.*

7. *Identify the pitfalls of groups and discuss various group roles.*

8. *Discuss the importance of groups in the future.*

focus

Anita's alarm goes off at 6:00 A.M. She quickly dresses for work and goes downstairs for breakfast with her family and her dog Fiesta. A horn blast beckons her to the carpool van already loaded with her fellow workers. Anita is a Manager at NASA's Johnson Space Center. She has a full day and evening ahead.

FRIDAY, AUGUST 19	
9:00 A.M. Division Staff Meeting	1:00 P.M. Window's 2000 Training class
10:00 A.M. Contractor Status Meeting	3:00 P.M. Fact finding for cost proposal
12:00 noon Lunch-Ralph	5:00 P.M. Journal entries and call backs
	6:00 P.M. Aerobics class at gym

After work, another meeting begins at 7:00 P.M. Anita is Chairperson for the National Management Association Conference scheduled for later in the year. Committee reports of current and planned activities are expected with limited time to cover the topics. After the meeting, Anita plans to join friends for dinner and a birthday celebration. What a day!

How many groups did Anita interact with after the 6:00 A.M. alarm? What types of human relations skills will be most important for her throughout the day?

In This Chapter

What Is a Group?

We interact in many groups daily.

Groups satisfy individual needs.

From the time we wake up each morning, we are involved in and influenced by group interactions. Individuals may act on their own, but their behavior has in some way been influenced by the values, attitudes, and perceptions formed from previous group interactions. Anita's busy schedule, discussed in the Focus above, brought her in touch with many small and large groups through the day, ranging from personal to professional. Her experiences represent the wide range of group activities that many people with today's busy life styles encounter. Increased encounters with groups make the understanding of group dynamics an important part of effective human relations.

A **group** consists of two or more individuals who are aware of one another, interact with one another, and perceive themselves to be a group. Group members usually interact on a regular basis and have a shared desire to attain common goals. Group interaction most often occurs face-to-face. Increasingly, however, groups are becoming geographically dispersed, relying on a variety of modern communications media to interact. This reliance on technology can create barriers to effective interactions but can also be used to facilitate communication.

Groups take many forms and evolve from many sources. However, all groups have a common thread—the purpose of satisfying needs—be they organizational needs or individual needs. Members of a group tend to receive some degree of satisfaction from their association or they will drop out of the group. For example, a dissatisfied member of a work group may ask for a transfer to some other department or simply resign to find another job. If a professional football player spends too much time on the side lines during a season, he may trade to another team or, as a free agent, negotiate a move.

A group can be as small as Anita's family at breakfast or as large as a U.S. Marine Corps battalion. The ability to function effectively in any group setting is important. The focus of this chapter will be on the expected behaviors and problems you may encounter when dealing with groups.

FastChat

1. Discuss the variety of group settings Anita encountered throughout the day.

2. What new forms of communications media are being used in group interactions today?

Why Are Groups Important to the Workplace?

The formation of groups in the workplace is natural. Groups tend to form whenever people are located close together and see and talk to one another on a frequent basis. They are then able to share ideas, opinions, and feelings and to pursue similar activities.

Work groups influence the overall behavior and performance of individuals in the workplace. The figure below illustrates the relation of behavior and morale to performance and productivity. As can be seen, the behavior of a work group does influence productivity. A positively motivated group can increase productivity. Unfortunately, a negative group can construct roadblocks to an organization's success.

Learning
Objective 2

Explain the importance of studying groups.

Groups influence behavior and performance at work.

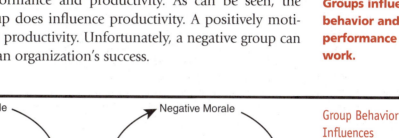

Group Behavior Influences Productivity.

This fact was first substantiated during the late 1920s when the Hawthorne experiments studied several work groups to determine the physical effects of lighting on the productivity of workers in the Hawthorne Plant of Western Electric. Two groups were observed. One experienced various changes in lighting. The other, a control group, experienced no lighting changes. The production in both groups rose because the contact and concern of the individuals doing the observations increased morale, and morale, in turn, increased productivity. The experiment further revealed that the plant workers had definite group norms related to work output, preferred channels of communication, acceptable behavior among group members, and roles for each member.

The Hawthorne Studies provided insight into group behaviors.

Other studies done from the 1930s to the 1950s left little doubt about the importance of group dynamics in the workplace. Harold Leavitt, an expert on groups, summarized why groups are important and should be taken seriously as shown in the following box:

Importance of Work Groups

1. Small groups satisfy needs within individuals and are good for them.
2. Groups can promote creativity and innovation and solve problems.
3. Groups can make better decisions, in many instances, than individuals.
4. Group decisions are more willingly carried out because group members are committed to the decisions.
5. Group members can frequently control and discipline their members more effectively than the formal disciplinary system can.
6. Small groups lessen the impersonality of large organizations, allowing better communication and a sense of belonging.
7. Groups are a natural part of an organization. They cannot be prevented.

For these reasons many organizations and companies use team concepts, participative management, and group decision making when appropriate. Additionally, today's work force members expect a greater voice in decisions that affect them.

CASE STUDIES IN THE NEWS

In search of ways to boost the productivity of the Xerox field service reps, an anthropologist was assigned to travel with a group of them to observe how they actually did their jobs. The anthropologist reported that the reps made it a point to spend time not with customers but with each other. They gathered in common areas, hung around the coffee pot, and swapped stories from their field experiences. Knowledge transfers were taking place through informal conversations in informal settings—not through formal "business process." To speed corporate efficiency, tech reps were given two-way radio headsets with a designated radio frequency over which they could communicate, identify problems, and share new solutions.

John Brown and Estee Solomon Gray
***Fast Company Magazine*, November 1995**

FastChat

1. Why did **both** groups in the Hawthorne Plant improve their productivity?

2. How have groups affected you at work or school?

Why Are Groups Important to Individuals?

6.3

The reasons that we join groups vary depending on our needs and which needs are strongest at any given time. Studies in the area of need satisfaction have identified the four most common reasons for joining groups as social connection, power, self-esteem, and goal accomplishment. Groups are important to both organizations and individuals.

Reasons That Individuals Join Groups

Social Connection (Affiliation)
Groups can provide us with a sense of belonging and reduce our feelings of aloneness. Being a member of a social group gives us an opportunity to share ideas or to exchange information, making us feel needed and increasing our sense of worth. People tend to feel a stronger sense of affiliation when they join a group on a voluntary basis than when they are assigned to a group.

Power (Security)
The fact that there is power in numbers is no secret. Groups may give us the confidence and courage to speak out and make certain requests. This sense of power and security can also provide us with the confidence to tackle difficult tasks by removing the feeling of facing the task alone.

Self-Esteem (Ego)
People frequently join groups for self-esteem or ego satisfaction. Membership in some groups can raise our sense of being "somebody." This is especially true if the group is a prestigious one (known for its power, unique skills, social status, or innovative and profitable ideas). Few people want to be "outsiders."

Goal Accomplishment (Strategy)
Joining a group may enable us to accomplish goals more easily because we can learn skills and acquire knowledge from other members of the group. Individual members may either have their own goals and objectives or simply agree with the goals desired by other members of the group.

---

1. Make a list of three groups to which you belong (such as a volunteer group, a sports team, a professional organization, a church group). Which of the four reasons prompted you to join each group?

2. How were your needs met?

FastChat

What Types of Groups Exist?

Learning
Objective 4

Distinguish among types of formal groups.

Two basic types of groups exist. The **primary group** consists of family members and close friends, whereas the **secondary group** is made up of work groups and social groups. This chapter focuses on the secondary groups that are essential to workplace operations and evident in our social surroundings.

Within the secondary group category are two types of groups, the formal group and the informal group. Both group types are important in the workplace. Although they may support similar organizational goals, they may also satisfy different needs.

quick wit

The moment we break faith with one another, the sea engulfs us and the light goes out.

James Baldwin

THE FORMAL GROUP

The **formal group** is generally designated by the organization to fulfill specific tasks or accomplish certain organizational objectives. Group members may have similar or complementary skills, responsibilities, or goals clearly related to the organizational purpose. Positions within the formal group are officially identified, usually "assigned" to individuals, and meant to provide order and predictability in the organization.

Formal groups are found in the workplace.

Two kinds of formal groups exist. The first is the **functional group,** which is made up of managers and subordinates assigned to certain positions in the organizational hierarchy performing the same tasks. If you have ever held a job and reported to a supervisor, you have been a member of a functional group. Group positions or assignments in functional groups are usually permanent and serve as the skeleton of the organizational structure.

The second kind of formal group is the **task group,** which is formed for a specific reason with members drawn from various parts of the organization to accomplish a specific purpose. Also known as cross functional, this group consists of individuals who may represent two or more different functional specialty areas. For example, in a hospital, a cross functional group is most commonly used in a trauma center's emergency room when specialties from various medical disciplines are required.

Another common example of a task group is the **committee.** Committees may be formed to develop procedures, solve problems, form recommendations for decision making, or exchange ideas and information. Committees may be considered ongoing or ad hoc.

The formal group is officially set up for a task or objective.

GLOBAL CONNECTION

British Airways recently brought together a group of experts in moving and reclaiming merchandise to create a new and innovative means of handling baggage. The group was given five general criteria to include in their task assignment. The criteria included: a. claim baggage within 20 minutes of arrival time, b. decrease "human handling" of baggage, and c. increase customer satisfaction. The group generated 62 things the company could do to improve their baggage handling. Some ideas were rejected, but many of the ideas were implemented. Today British Airways has one of the most efficient baggage handling systems in the world. In fact, the results were so successful that the company has begun to use the innovative group method to help attack other productivity-related problems throughout its operations. Overall, it has experienced a 67 percent increase in productivity that has enabled British Airways to maintain its reputation as the best international airline in the world.

M. Wylie, *Manage Magazine,* Fall 1998

What other companies could make good use of groups to improve operations or productivity? How would this method work in that environment?

Ongoing committees are relatively permanent groups that address organizational issues on a standing or continuous basis. Examples might include plant safety committees, employee promotion boards, or the local Rodeo and Livestock Show committees.

Ad hoc committees, on the other hand, have a limited life, serving only a one-time purpose, and disband after accomplishing that purpose. Examples of an ad hoc committee might include the Warren Commission formed to investigate the assassination of President Kennedy, a committee formed to create a new corporate logo, or a committee gathered to plan a celebration for the birth of the supervisor's first child.

INFORMAL GROUPS

Informal groups are formed by individuals to satisfy personal needs.

In addition to formal groups, informal groups may exist in the organizational setting. Unless you are a loner, you, no doubt, are a member of one or more informal groups at work. **Informal groups** are created by the group members themselves because the formal group seldom satisfies all of their individual needs. They form spontaneously when members with similar interests get together voluntarily. Although the informal group does not appear on the formal organization chart, it does have a powerful influence on members' behavior. Informal groups exist in all organizations and do not necessarily indicate that the formal group is inadequate or ineffective.

Informal groups may be peer groups that form because members have common interests, such as politics, recreational preferences, or religion.

Groups may form to share a common interest.

Human Relations

Types of Groups

Formal	Informal
Has recognized authority.	Has little or no authority.
Has a mission or direction.	May have a mission.
Has organized structure.	Has no organizational legitimacy.
Has organizational legitimacy.	Is considered a shadow organization.

Peer groups also form to satisfy members' needs for informal job training, to provide them opportunity for status, or to help them gain information concerning the organization.

Group Identity Quiz

Identify each group as a:

A. Primary Group
B. Secondary Group
C. Formal Group
D. Functional Group
E. Task Group
F. Informal Group
G. Ongoing Committee
H. Ad hoc Committee

_____ Independent council members
_____ Company softball team
_____ UN members meeting on current issues
_____ High school friends planning a reunion
_____ Workers setting new safety policies
_____ Firefighters on a ladder truck
_____ Office workers planning a conference
_____ Doctors and nurses in a trauma center

The various peer groups are not mutually exclusive and do overlap at times. While working in an organization, you can have relationships on both personal and professional levels that fulfill your needs within the organization. Furthermore, the wider your circle of acquaintances is, the easier time you will have fulfilling your needs.

1. Discuss the purpose of an informal group in which you have participated.

2. Identify a committee on which you have served and determine if it was ongoing or ad hoc.

FastChat

Who Leads a Group?

Within any group there may be two leaders—a formal leader and an informal leader. The **formal leader** is the one who is officially given authority over other group members, such as a supervisor or a team captain.

Dr. Warren Bennis writes in his book, *The Secrets of Great Groups*, ". . . the problems we face are too complex to be solved by any one person or any one discipline. Our only chance is to bring people together from a variety of backgrounds and disciplines . . . in common purpose. The genius of Great Groups is that they get remarkable people—strong individual achievers—to work together to get results."

Dr. Bennis believes that *group leaders of these Great Groups vary widely in style and personality*. Some are facilitators and some are doers, but all take on any role necessary for the group to achieve its overall goal. Effective group leaders will understand the chemistry of the group and the dynamics of the work and help provide direction and meaning.

The **informal leader** is the person within the group who is able to influence other group members because of age, knowledge, technical skills, social skills, personality, or physical strength. This leader is also known as the **emergent leader** because he or she will emerge without formal appointment but can exert more influence than the formal leader.

The formal leader must be able to recognize the informal leader, determine that person's purposes and goals, and deal with them. If the formal and informal leaders have different objectives, conflict will arise.

Learning
Objective 5

Discuss the different types of group leaders.

Identifying the formal and informal leaders is important.

quick wit
. . . .

None of us is as smart as all of us.

. . . .
Dr. Warren Bennis

Types of Group Leaders	
Formal	**Informal**
Is the boss.	Is a recognizable force.
Is appointed to the position.	Is unofficially designated.
Has legitimate power.	Emerges because of being
Is officially designated.	—respected, likable, knowledgeable,
Has authority with responsibility.	technically competent, a senior team
Has a mission.	member, strong physically, older

FastChat

1. Think of a good leader and discuss why this person is so effective.

2. Have you been aware of an informal leader within a formal group? How did this situation develop and how did it affect the group?

How Do Groups Develop?

A group is considered mature when its members help each other and address problems that impede its work. Initially, group members go through a "feeling out" stage, learning what each has to contribute and how to interact with one another. As they continue to work together, they become more comfortable with the group effort, performance improves, and eventually the group becomes a highly effective work team. Typically, a group will pass through four stages of group development: forming, storming, norming, and performing.

Learning
Objective 6

Discuss how groups mature and the factors that influence group effectiveness.

Groups mature through several growth stages.

The four stages of group development are forming, storming, norming, and performing.

Stages of Group Development

1. **Forming:** Individuals begin to identify what the group goals are and how their own goals may fit with the group. They decide how much time, energy, and effort they wish to commit to the group, and become acquainted with other group members. Everyone behaves politely and seldom takes strong stands at this stage.

2. **Storming:** Members may engage in constructive conflicts and disagreements. Individuals may question the group's direction and progress. Some will resist task assignments or attempt power plays to gain control. Some may display frustration with group's activities. Others become stronger through listening and handling challenges and complaints. Members earn how to effectively deal with disagreements and settle in with better balance and clear direction. Real progress occurs.

3. **Norming:** Group members pursue responsibilities and work toward group goals. The group works as a whole to resolve problems, establish action plans, and focus on getting things done. Individuals develop negotiation skills, deal with ambiguity, cooperate, and communicate effectively.

4. **Performing:** Individuals actively help each other complete assignments and tasks. Group members develop a sense of trust and commitment at both individual and group levels. Members acknowledge cooperation and performance, value learning, and imagine future objectives. The group is willing to accept creativity that may lead toward greater productivity. Not all groups reach this stage.

Group effectiveness depends on behavior of individuals, synergy, cohesiveness, norms, size, status of members, and the task.

Groups are in a constant state of change. Some of the changing factors in group effectiveness are behavior of members, synergy (combined action or operation) of the group, its degree of cohesiveness, group norms that evolve, size of the group, status of group members, and nature of the task to be accomplished by the group.

BEHAVIOR OF INDIVIDUALS

The behavior of individuals is in a constant state of fluctuation. As people begin to perceive things differently, they may alter their behavior within the group. Changes in behavior may occur for a number of reasons, such as the influence of family, peers, continued education, or acquisition of new skills. These behavior changes may have a positive or negative effect on the group. For example, you may once have been a member of a group of friends that socialized together every weekend. As individual members became involved in personal relationships, other friendships, or work or school responsibilities, the group grew smaller or broke up.

The group can also cause individuals to behave differently while they are within the group setting. Some people, for instance, behave one way in a one-on-one situation and completely differently in a group atmosphere.

TECHNOLOGY CONNECTION

Often, people in groups simply do not speak their minds. The problem may be a dominant personality intimidating the rest of the group or an ineffective leader who does not invite participation. Most often it is simply that people do not feel secure enough to voice personal opinions—a lack of trust. A powerful technique for promoting candor has been developed through technology applications. The computer-based tool enables people to express opinions and evaluate alternatives without having to divulge their identities. Developed for the military, private industries are using the software with groups who work together all the time. Anonymity changes the social protocols and people tend to say things differently and more freely.

Eric Matson, *Fast Company*, April 1996

Think about when you were in a large group. How did people act when asked questions? Did anyone raise a hand and offer answers or opinions right away?

SYNERGISM

Synergism is the cooperative interaction of two or more independent elements or individuals to create an effect which is different from that which they would attain separately. More simply stated, it means that, with synergism, the whole is greater than the sum of its parts. Groups can take advantage of synergism to develop better ideas and make superior decisions through the process of brainstorming. As discussed in Chapter 4, **brainstorming** involves generating ideas freely in a group, without judging the ideas at first. The group then selects the best ideas and forms a plan of action. These decisions are generally more effective because group members have a greater pool of ideas from which to draw. Studies have shown that decisions made by groups generally produce better results. The collective creativity of the group increases the number of alternative solutions generated, and group consensus assures commitment from individual group members. The effort is more likely to became a self-fulfilling prophecy.

Brainstorming relies on synergism to develop better ideas.

Brainstorming can help groups develop better ideas and make superior decisions.

Additionally, our involvement as group members in the decision-making process enhances our feelings of worth (as contributors) and of belonging to the group (as members). These are but a few of the benefits of using groups when making decisions.

Cohesiveness

Another of the factors influencing a group's behavior is cohesiveness. **Cohesiveness** is the degree to which group members are of one mind and act as

The more individuals are similar, the greater the cohesiveness.

one body. In general, the more cohesive a group is, the more effective it is, and, as the group becomes more successful, it becomes even more inseparable. This effect occurs because cohesive group members stick together, supporting and encouraging one another. Also, this support helps reduce stress for group members, leading to greater job satisfaction.

Group cohesiveness develops through a number of factors, one of which is group size. Smaller groups tend to be more cohesive because they can readily communicate and exchange ideas, goals, and purposes.

Similarity of the individuals in a group is also a factor in cohesiveness. The more individuals have similar values, backgrounds, and ages, the more cohesive they tend to be. Sometimes groups become more cohesive because of outside pressures. The "It's you and me against the world!" attitude draws members together to support and assist each other.

Group Norms

Norms determine group behavior.

The development of group norms is another of the factors that influences group effectiveness. **Group norms** are shared values about the kinds of behaviors that are acceptable or unacceptable to the group. These norms are standards of behavior that each member is expected to follow—similar to rules that apply to team members. Group norms develop slowly over time and usually relate to those matters of most importance to the group as a whole. Expected conformity to these norms applies only to our behavior and does not affect our private thoughts and feelings.

Nonconformity, or **deviance,** from group norms may provoke obvious displays of displeasure, ranging from rejection to physical violence or vicious harassment. Of course, if the group in question is a business and the deviance involves breaking company rules, the signs of displeasure may be

CASE STUDIES IN THE NEWS

Phil Jackson's job as head coach of the Chicago Bulls may have appeared easy. After all, he had one of the greatest players of all time as part of his group. However, he knew that for the Bulls to be truly successful, they had to perform as a cohesive group. One player could not be the whole team. Each member of the team was important to the effort and each player had to play a key role. He wanted to change the "me" to "we."

Tony Berken, *Strive*, February 1999

formal and might include poor reviews, docked pay, reprimands, and even getting fired. However, in smaller groups, displeasure is more likely to take the form of more informal sanctions.

The following list represents a few of the more common types of informal **sanctions,** actions taken to force compliance with established norms. Each is considered in the context of a work group of four secretaries, of whom only one, James, smokes. The suggestions from the other three secretaries that he not smoke in the office have fallen on deaf ears.

Deviance from group norms may provoke sanctions from rejection to violence.

Common sanctions provoked by deviance

1. *Ostracism* (cold-shoulder treatment). The nonsmokers have quit inviting James to lunch with them and do not include him in their coffee breaks and informal discussions.

2. *Verbal criticisms.* The nonsmokers frequently make critical comments to James about his clothes smelling like cigarettes, about ashes on his desk, and about the time he wastes lighting and puffing cigarettes.

3. *Open ridicule.* The nonsmokers have started imitating James, both in front of him and behind his back, blowing exaggerated smoke rings in the air and brushing imaginary ashes off the fronts of their shirts.

4. *Malicious gossip.* The nonsmokers begin gossiping about James' actions both on and off the job.

5. *Harassment.* The nonsmokers begin to save the pleasant tasks for themselves, giving James the most undesirable jobs to do.

6. *Intimidation.* The nonsmokers threaten to make sure that appropriate persons know about James' real or fictitious sloppy work.

The type of sanction taken may depend on how important group members perceive the violated norm to be. Some norms are considered more important than others. **Critical norms** are considered essential to the survival and effectiveness of the group as a whole. The sanctions for violating critical norms can be severe, with physical violence sometimes used in extreme cases. Personal safety and career success may depend on an individual's ability to operate within the established acceptable group norms.

Other norms are considered **peripheral norms** because they are not perceived as damaging to the group and its members. The sanctions for violating these norms are less severe than those for critical norms but can be just as meaningful.

We learn about group norms in various ways. In formal groups, we learn norms through formal orientation programs, classroom training, and on-the-job training. In informal groups we grasp group norms through conversations with other group members and observation of their behavior.

Often group norms enhance group effectiveness. For instance, the group may ostracize or criticize members who fail to do their fair share of the work or fail to behave in a way that is constructive on the job. These individuals are considered "social loafers" and will be punished if they do not pull their weight within the group. The individuals may react to this unpleasant treatment by increasing their productivity or in some way changing their behavior.

Unfortunately, group norms sometimes prevent members from working toward the goals of the organization. For instance, an assembly line worker may not work as fast as possible because the others at work would reject him. In this case, the sanctions and rewards of the informal group are stronger than those of the formal organization.

If you become the target of group sanctions, evaluate your situation carefully. Are the sanctions being applied because you have not followed group norms meant to increase organizational effectiveness? If so, determine why you are behaving the way you are and how you can change your behavior so that you contribute to the effectiveness of the group.

If you determine that the sanctions being applied are counterproductive to the organization and your career, you have several choices. You can conform to the group norms (which may jeopardize your career), attempt through persuasion and the use of effective communication skills to persuade group members to change the norms, tolerate the sanctions, or ask for a transfer to another area that would limit your interaction with the group. After all, norms are simply meant to keep a group functioning as a system instead of a collection of individuals.

Group Size

The size of a group will also influence its effectiveness. Studies have shown that the preferred group size for maximum effectiveness in problem solving and decision making is five or seven members. Groups of any larger size begin to experience problems with communication and coordination. Groups with even numbers of members may have greater difficulty in obtaining a majority opinion if members are equally divided in their opinions. Having no person to act as tie-breaker can cause increased tensions. The uneven-numbered group size offers an easy solution to this problem. The chart on page 159 identifies the characteristics of group interaction in certain group sizes.

Characteristics of Group Sizes

Fewer than five	More than seven
• Fewer people to share task responsibilities.	• Fewer opportunities to participate.
• More personal discussion.	• Members feel inhibited.
• More participation.	• Domination by aggressive members.
• Increased tension among group members.	• Tendency for "cliques" to form.
• Greater sense of satisfaction.	• More diverse opinions shared.
• Greater cohesion.	• Greater likelihood of absenteeism and turnover.
	• Coordination of activities more difficult.
	• Less cohesion.
	• Team effect lost.
	• Individual identities tend to be retained.

STATUS OF GROUP MEMBERS

The status of group members can also influence group effectiveness. What gives a person status may vary from group to group. In some groups, higher social class and economic success may confer higher status. In these groups, members who are financially successful, come from "good" families, or have college degrees may have more status. They may be given more respect, and other group members may pay more attention to them. People in white collar jobs are often viewed as having higher status than those in blue collar positions. Similarly, salaried workers may be seen as having higher status than those paid by the hour.

Clothing and cars can also make a difference in how much status people are perceived to have. In some groups, individuals who dress fashionably in expensive clothes and drive costly cars are perceived as having higher status. In other groups, the reverse may be true; expensive clothing and cars would be considered showy.

Physical appearance is another factor that can influence perception of status. Some studies have suggested that people who are overweight may be

Success, education, possessions, and physical appearance are factors that can contribute to a person's status within a group.

viewed negatively. Individuals who are tall are sometimes seen as being more competent and powerful.

Status at work is conveyed in a variety of ways. For instance, those in higher-status positions may have an office with a window, a larger or corner office, reserved parking, and nicer office furniture and decorations. Executives may even have special dining rooms separate from other employees or have memberships in private clubs. Groups whose members have high status are more effective because they are able to get things done.

NATURE OF THE TASK

The last of the factors influencing group effectiveness is the nature of the task itself. When a decision is required on a subject that is simple and uncomplicated, a highly homogeneous group whose members have similar backgrounds and compatible beliefs may be best.

When the task is complex and difficult, group members should be of dissimilar backgrounds and drawn from a variety of sources. This makeup will ensure diversity of ideas, foster creativity among the members, and result in a wider selection of alternatives from which to choose a solution.

*Fast*Chat

1. Does a sports team go through the four stages of group development? Using the Chicago Bulls as an example, discuss how they may have made the transitions.

2. What types of sanctions have you seen administered in group situations?

What Are the Pitfalls of Group Decision Making?

Three factors may negatively influence group decision making. They are wasting time, groupthink, and role ambiguity.

WASTING TIME

The group decision-making process is time consuming. If it is not handled correctly, it can waste time and cause costly delays, indecisiveness, and diluted answers. For this reason, groups must be handled with skill.

Not all situations lend themselves to group decision making. For example, an emergency situation such as a fire is hardly the time to call the office staff together for ideas on how the fire should be extinguished or who will call 911. The fire chief, barking out orders, gets the job done more effectively. Or perhaps the decision is such an easy one that it needs only a quick fix. For situations like this, making the decision yourself is certainly acceptable.

Learning
Objective   7

Identify the pitfalls of groups and discuss various group roles.

Wasting time, groupthink, and role ambiguity worsen group decisions.

Groups should not make emergency or small decisions.

If it is not handled correctly, the group decision-making process can waste time and cause costly delays.

"To insure that we keep this meeting under thirty minutes, I'll just set this timer."

However, if the situation lends itself to group decision making, using a group process is the preferred method. For example, if office policy is to be revised and enough time remains to seek office staff opinions, you would do well to apply the participative approach.

GROUPTHINK

Irving Janis identified the phenomenon of **groupthink** and defined it as "the process of deriving negative results from group decision-making efforts as a result of in-group pressures." Through groupthink, a group may be led to a conclusion without fully exploring or even considering creative alternatives.

For example, a supervisor may call a meeting of subordinates to determine how a new office procedure is to be implemented and start the meeting with the statement, "I believe the best way for us to do this is to . . . , don't you agree?" The pressure to accept the leader's approach and to retain group cohesion results in a "rubber stamp" of what may appear as a predetermined conclusion. The supervisor may even interpret the group's silence as a resounding and unanimous acceptance of the "proposed" approach rather than an attempt at retaining group cohesion.

All of us are influenced by our peers, especially those with more status or greater expertise. We should, however, try to avoid falling victim to groupthink.

ROLE AMBIGUITY

Roles of individual members are readily apparent when the group is a formal one with certain positions identified. This formal identification helps to define the role an individual is expected to play. However, in informal groups, these roles may not be as clearly designated. Expected behavior may never be stated or in any way formalized. **Role ambiguity** occurs when individuals are uncertain about what role they are to fill or what is expected of them. All of us experience some initial feelings of role ambiguity when we join new groups. The following chart on group member roles defines several of the roles most frequently expected in group situations.

Group Member Roles

Information Seeker: Asks for facts, feelings, suggestions, and ideas about the group's concern.

Information Giver: Gives information about the group's concerns, stating facts and feelings; gives ideas and makes suggestions.

Coordinator: Pulls all the group ideas and suggestions together and recommends a decision or conclusion for the group to consider.

Gatekeeper: Keeps communication channels open; facilitates participation.

Harmonizer: Reduces tension and reconciles differences.

Observer: Provides feedback on the group's progress; remains neutral and uninvolved in the process.

Follower: Goes along with the group; offers no resistance to suggestions or ideas.

Blocker: Resists any suggestions or ideas of the group; acts negatively toward group purpose and members.

Avoider: Resists interacting with group members; keeps apart from interaction.

Dominator: Forces opinions, ideas, and desires on the other group members; manipulates group behavior by asserting status or authority, using flattery, interrupting others, or other aggressive and obnoxious measures.

You may recognize some of these roles from groups in which you have been involved. You may recognize roles that you have played in group interactions. Many of the roles are important in making the group highly effective and productive. Some, however, can be destructive and should be managed by the group leader, a facilitator, or the other members themselves.

FastChat

1. Have you experienced "groupthink?" Give an example and discuss how it may have been prevented.

2. What other pitfalls in group interactions have you experienced?

3. Which of the group member roles have you played in group interactions? Which are you most comfortable performing?

6.8 Will Groups Remain Important in the Future?

Learning
Objective 8

Discuss importance of groups in the future.

In a world that is faster, harder, leaner, more downsized, merged, and streamlined than ever before, you might expect the demands of the work environment to curb the appetite for groups and team interactions. In reality, the opposite is true. People will naturally band together to increase their effectiveness. Group interaction will become more important and the ability to work well in groups will be a vital part of your career success. Indeed, competing in the "knowledge era" environment will require continual shifts from traditional thinking about the way we work.

GLOBAL CONNECTION

We are seeing trends toward distributed global groups. International teamwork is one of the key components of the new networked organizations. People will learn to work in globally dispersed virtual groups. A new or different set of skills must be applied when dealing with people and problems across multiple time zones, of different cultural backgrounds, with possible language differences, and from different countries. Schools and training facilities will help individuals prepare for this transition to an interdependent global village.

quick wit

Many hands make light work.

John Heygood

One of the expected trends will be an increased shift in the types of groups toward a new approach called Communities of Practice (COPS). Considered the critical stepping stone for a knowledge-based company, COPS are small groups of peers who have worked together over a period of time, have a common sense of purpose, and a strong need to know what each other group member knows. They are not a team, not a task force, and probably not identified as an official or authorized group. Chapter 20 will provide specific examples of how COPS are already being used by many companies as part of their re-engineering for survival.

Although the systems, methods, and tools used in group interactions may be different, groups will remain a vital part of our environment.

TECHNOLOGY CONNECTION

Further proof of the growing importance of groups is the computer software being developed for use by groups. Sometimes called "groupware," the technologies have a definite focus on improving the shortcomings of traditional group interactions. Specifically, these computer aids are designed to improve meeting capabilities, distributed global group interactions, and COPS operations. The technologies borrow from artificial intelligence, group psychology, organizational theory, linguistics, and other disciplines. The software simplifies problems encountered by groups trying to work in long-distance, multicultural settings.

1. Have you seen any of these new methods being used in your school or place of work?

2. How can you prepare to meet these challenges in our ever-changing environment?

*Fast*Chat

Key Terms

group
primary groups
secondary groups
formal group
functional group
task group
committee
ongoing committee
ad hoc committee
informal group
formal leader
informal leader
emergent leader
synergism
brainstorming
cohesiveness
group norms
deviance
sanctions
critical norms
peripheral norms
groupthink
role ambiguity

Summary

We all interact with a variety of groups on a day-to-day basis. Organizations encourage groups because they increase productivity and effective decision making. Individuals join groups because they fulfill needs such as power, affiliation, self-esteem, and goal accomplishment.

Secondary groups can be formal groups, which the organization creates for certain purposes, or informal ones, which spontaneously develop because individuals work close to one another. Each group may have two leaders, a formal and an informal (emergent) one. Groups go through various stages on their way to maturity, and many groups never reach the fully mature stage.

Groups are influenced by many factors that can affect their productivity, such as behavior of individuals, synergism, group cohesiveness, group norms, group size, status of members, and nature of the task. Although groups do, in general, make better decisions than individuals, pitfalls occur. Groups can be time wasters, give in to groupthink, and produce role ambiguity. Small decisions and emergency decisions are best left to individuals. Groups will continue to be a vital part of our collective environments.

Review Questions

1. What is a group?
2. What is the importance of studying group dynamics?
3. Why do people join groups?
4. What are the two types of formal groups?
5. Why is it important to recognize the informal or emergent leader in a group?
6. Name the five stages through which groups can evolve as they mature.
7. What are the factors that influence group effectiveness?
8. What are the pitfalls of group decision making? Explain.
9. What roles are open in a group setting?
10. Why is it important today at work to use groups in the decision-making process?

Discussion Questions

1. Examine the opening Focus scenario and identify the various types of groups Anita encounters.
2. Think of a group to which you belong, such as a social club, church group, civic group, or work group.
   a. What type of group is it?
   b. Who is the formal leader?
   c. Is there an informal or emergent leader? Who is it?
   d. Why is this individual recognized as the emergent leader?
   e. What was the reason that you became a member of this group?
   f. What level of maturity does this group have?
3. Give some examples of group norms and describe the groups to which they belong. How might these norms be violated? What would happen if the norms were violated?
4. Discuss the benefits to the formal group leader of identifying the informal leader. Explore the possible negative effects of not identifying this individual.
5. Identify the important roles in group dynamics. Which of these roles do you most often play?

Chapter Project

Choose a movie that you feel demonstrates aspects of large and small group interactions discussed in this chapter. Choose the movie carefully. Be certain that it illustrates a variety of group characteristics. An example might be *Saving Private Ryan*, a war film with groups ranging from squadrons to close personal friendships. While you watch the film, take notes about the different types of groups, types of interactions, leadership styles, types of role playing, and any other factors you may recognize relevant to this chapter material. Prepare a written description of these findings. This is not an invitation to play movie critic. *Do not critique the movie*. Whether or not you liked it is not important. Instead, describe the group and its peculiarities. Be prepared to discuss your findings in a small group.

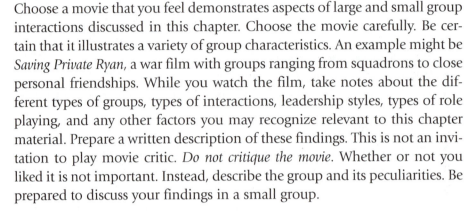

Applications

In small groups analyze the following situations.

Reading, creative thinking, problem solving, decision making, reasoning, sociability, team membership, and negotiation.

Who's The Boss?

Robert had just been promoted into his first supervisory position. Initially, a high degree of camaraderie existed among the eight office members. The lead analyst, Sandy, had a long-standing record of good performance, knowledge of the program requirements, and loyalty to the organization. Sandy had become a guiding force to the junior analysts, offering advice on certain topics and showing them the established office procedures of the job.

Robert seemed somewhat uneasy with the guidance being given by Sandy. He frequently challenged her decisions and questioned the approaches that she recommended to the junior analysts. Obviously he did not trust Sandy. Rather than relying on her knowledge and experience, Robert set out to gain absolute control and change the general office operations.

It didn't take long for the junior analysts to get the picture. After all, they did not want to do a job twice—the way Sandy suggested and then again the way Robert would require it.

Eventually, Sandy was left alone and was seldom made to feel a part of the group. The other analysts still went to lunch but seldom invited her. The feeling of being an "outcast" was a painful one to her.

After several months of seeing the situation deteriorate further, more distance coming between her and the other office members, and feeling out of place, Sandy asked to be moved to some other office within the company. After all, her own work reputation and career safety were being threatened.

1. Into what type of group was Robert promoted—formal or informal. What type of leader was he—formal or informal?
2. Was there an informal or emergent leader in the group? What made this person a leader?
3. What factors influenced this group's effectiveness?
4. What could Robert have done differently to minimize the group's disharmony? What could Sandy have done to assure continued group cohesiveness?

The Explosive Commission

The recent explosion at the chemical plant was the worst disaster in the company's twenty-year history, killing five workers. A committee of seven people was immediately formed to study the causes of the accident and prescribe protective measures to eliminate any future occurrence. The committee members were carefully selected from a wide cross section of appropriate representatives. Ralph Windham was brought in from the company's corporate headquarters to head the committee. He had 47 years of chemical plant experience and had often been used as a troubleshooter in hazardous cases. Derek Soong, the plant manager, had been personally involved in a similar accident with a different company. He was considered the expert in chemical plant accident investigation and would bring a great deal of experience to the committee's activities. Derek was to be the local company representative. The plant's local legal representative, Carol Harnett, would be a member, and, of course, the president of the local union, Tom Filbert, would be representing the employees.

Reading, creative thinking, problem solving, decision making, reasoning, sociability, team membership, and negotiation.

Great consideration was given to including other members of the community. The chief surgeon of the local hospital, Dr. Shardar Kahn, was appointed because of the enormous involvement of rescue teams and medical attendants. The mayor, Sharon Wilson, and Larry Brown from the Chamber of Commerce would represent the community and its members.

After an extensive investigation, the committee's final report was issued almost nine months after the date of the accident. The report cleared the company of any wrongdoing. From the beginning Ralph Windham's influence on the results was obvious. After all, he was the senior member, the chair, and a highly respected person throughout the chemical industry for his expertise and knowledge. Other members appeared to have voiced little or no opinion, and the recommendation showed obvious bias toward corporate reasoning. The industry and community members winced with anger and astonishment that the final outcome was not more representative of all members' interests and fairer in its summation and recommendation.

1. What three factors most heavily influenced the formation and selection of the committee?
2. Which factor undermined the committee, and why did it happen? How might this outcome have been prevented?

Additional Readings and Resources

Andrews, Katherine Zoe, "Cross-Functional Teams: Are They Always the Right Move?" *Harvard Business Review*, November/December 1995, pp. 12–13.

Beck, John and Neil Yeager, "Moving Beyond Team Myths," *Training and Development Journal*, March 1996, pp. 51–55.

Bennis, Warren, *"The Secrets of Great Groups,"* The Drucker Foundation and Jossey-Bass Publishers, *Winter* 1997, pp 29–33.

Burns, Greg, "The Secrets of Team Facilitation," *Training and Development*, June 1995, p.49.

Chaudron, David, "How to Improve Cross-functional Teams," *HR Focus*, August 1995, pp. 1–5.

Coleman, Gary D. and Eileen M. VanAken. "Applying Small Group Dynamics to Improve Action Team Performance." *Employment Relations Today*, Autumn 1991, p. 349.

Raney, Joyce and Mark Deck, "Making Teams Work: Lessons from the Leaders in New Product Development," *Planning Review*, August 1995, pp. 6–13.

Roberts, Paul, "Group Genius," *Fast Company*, October 1997, p. 202.

Teamwork:

Becoming a Team Player

focus

In September 1996, Intuit, the innovative software company that created Quicken, found its stock dropping fast. There were doubts, both inside and outside Intuit, about its future as an innovator and leader. The solution? Intuit management drew on the expertise of more than 70 people from a variety of functions and levels within Intuit to reinvent the company. The team led Intuit into the Internet with a new product, Quicken-Mortgage. By 1998, Intuit shares had almost tripled in price from what they were when Wall Street doubted the company's prospects.

Fast Company, **October 1998**

Why do you believe the leaders of Intuit put a team together rather than assigning one person to the task of inventing a new product? Why would Intuit want to use people in a variety of ranks? A variety of functions?

objectives

After studying this chapter, you should be able to:

1. *Define a team.*

2. *Understand the concept of teambuilding.*

3. *Identify the types of teams in use today.*

4. *Name the elements necessary to build an effective team.*

5. *Discuss some of the benefits and drawbacks of team membership.*

6. *Know when the team approach is appropriate.*

7. *Describe what you can do to be an effective team member.*

8. *Explain the difference between conflict and competition and discuss why they both can be healthy for an organization.*

9. *Understand the causes of conflict.*

10. *Describe common conflict resolution techniques.*

In This Chapter

7.1 What Is a Team?

Learning Objective 1

Define a team.

Throughout your life, you will be a member of many different teams, some limited to a business environment, some related to other areas of your life. Webster defines a **team** as "a number of persons associated together in work or activity." This could mean anything from a product development team at work to the group of people with whom you plan a charity fund-raiser, as well as less formal teams.

We commonly think of a team as a group of individuals doing the same thing, such as playing basketball or hockey. In today's work environment, however, teams may include representatives from a variety of disciplines, departments, or even different lines of business, who come together to achieve common goals and objectives that will enhance all their varied areas. An example is the cooperation and combined efforts in the Amish community when a family needs a new home. Carpenters, painters, bricklayers, roofers, and finishers come together to achieve a common goal, and the house is raised in just one day.

Teamwork, the combined effort of several disciplines for maximum effectiveness in achieving common goals, is important to individuals and

CASE STUDIES IN THE NEWS

Employers are working to create a climate that fosters creativity and productivity. Workers like bright colors, better lighting, high ceilings, and friendly places for meetings and casual conversation, and office architects are working to meet their needs. CompuServ headquarters, for instance, has a redesigned company cafeteria that also serves as a meeting place and employee lounge.

The Columbus Dispatch, **September 27, 1999**

1. *Describe a work environment with which you are familiar.*

2. *Was it conducive to team work? Why or why not?*

3. *In what type of environment would you like to work?*

organizations because it can increase productivity. For example, companies are increasingly using teams to speed up the cycle time in product development and get a better product out to the customers faster. This is done by assembling a team of marketing, design engineering, quality, and manufacturing people to attack the problem from the beginning. The old process involved having one group do the design, hand it off to the manufacturing team, and then forward the work to the quality crew. The final step was to have marketing people decide how to sell or market the final product. This process is slow and costly. With the team concept, product designs and quality are greatly improved, and total product cycle time is reduced.

Teamwork is a key to improved quality, productivity, and efficiency.

Read the Quick Wit by Eileen Hudson.

1. What can you do to ensure that you continue to learn throughout your career?

2. Many times people refuse to do tasks saying, "It's not my job." Is this attitude acceptable in today's workplace? Why or why not?

FastChat

What Is Teambuilding?

quick wit

*"You can get
anything you want
out of life if you
just help enough
other people get
what they want."*

—Zig Ziglar

Effective teamwork doesn't just happen. It evolves through the deliberate efforts of team members working to strengthen the group's purpose. For this reason many organizations have begun a conscientious effort to develop competent teams through teambuilding. **Teambuilding** is a series of activities designed to help work groups solve problems, accomplish work goals, and function more effectively through teamwork. Constructive teambuilding requires that each team participant accept the team goals and objectives and take ownership of the results. In this way, a high degree of cohesion develops within the group, and the open environment improves the quality of problem solving and decision making. **Synergism** (as you will remember from Chapter 6) involves cooperative action to achieve an effect that is greater than the sum of the individual effects.

The team concept, which involves the application of teambuilding and teams bonding together for effective teamwork, is a generic term used to describe the workings of teams in achieving common goals and objectives, with all their human relations complexities. The concept is not new to the work environment.

CASE STUDIES IN THE NEWS

Signicast Corporation, an investment-castings service that makes precise metal parts following customers' blueprints (such as kickstands for a Harley-Davidson motorcycle), built a state-of-the-art automated plant in Hartford, Wisconsin. The basic requirements for new hires are a high school diploma, a good work ethic, a team orientation, good trainability, good communication skills, and a willingness to do varied jobs over a 12-hour shift.

If you were being interviewed for a position at Signicast and were asked your definition of teamwork, what would you say? What experience have you had working in teams? How willing are you to do various jobs?

Quick Tip

Try this activity to build trust among team members:

1. One team member puts on a blindfold.
2. Another team member and a spotter lead the team member through an obstacle maze, taking care not to allow the blindfolded member to hit one of the barriers.
3. Each member takes a turn wearing the blindfold and leading the individual.

After the exercise, discuss what happened by examining the following:

1. How did you feel when you were blindfolded and had to depend on others to take care of you?
2. Are you able to accept losing control and trusting others on the job?
3. What, as team members, can you do to develop trust?

1. Which concepts of group dynamics from Chapter 6 are elements of successful team building? Unsuccessful?

2. Is it your responsibility in teamwork to achieve synergism? What could you do to make this happen?

FastChat

7.3 How Has the Team Concept Grown?

Learning
Objective   3

Identify the types of teams in use today.

Problem-solving and special purpose teams evolved into the self-managing teams of today.

quick wit

"You cannot build character and courage by taking away a man's initiative and independence. You cannot help men permanently by doing for them what they should be doing for themselves."

—Abraham Lincoln

Teams have been used since people began to perform complex tasks. The early Egyptians, for instance, used large teams to construct the pyramids. Major corporations in the United States began experimenting with team concepts on a small scale as early as the 1920s and 1930s with the introduction of problem-solving teams. **Problem-solving teams** generally consisted of 5 to 12 volunteers from different areas of a department who met once or twice a week to discuss ways of improving quality, efficiency, or work conditions. Initially they had no power to implement ideas, which limited their effectiveness. However, more widespread use of this team concept blossomed in the late 1970s based on Japanese quality circles, discussed in Chapter 4.

Special-purpose teams evolved in the early to mid-1980s. Worker and union representatives collaborated to improve quality and productivity. These teams introduced work reforms and new technology and actually met with suppliers and customers, linking various disciplines and separate functions. Special-purpose teams are frequently used today in unionized organizations.

The most common team in the modern work environment is the **self-managing team.** These teams usually consist of 5 to 15 employees who produce an entire product in a truly entrepreneurial sense. This approach fundamentally changes how work is organized and gives employees control over their own destinies. Organizational hierarchies are flattened by eliminating tiers of middle management and supervision. The use of self-managing teams usually increases productivity and substantially improves quality in the end product or service.

The number, types, and function of teams has steadily grown. Teams have become an integral part of the operation of any large organization that hopes to remain competitive in today's marketplace. While there is still room for innovation and individual genius, processes and business alike have become increasingly complex, so input from individuals with a wide range of expertise is vital for organizations today.

The use of teams involving diverse employee resources is necessary for the United States to remain competitive in a global marketplace. Companies are having to revamp ways of doing business to include more team efforts in order to cope with the rapidly changing economic environment. Studies indicate that work-team systems that allow workers real participation in decision making produce better quality products, improve quality teams, *functional teams*, cross-functional teams, DESIGN TEAMS, customer support teams, **work teams**, rank-and-file teams, *project teams*, planning teams, COMMITTEES, task forces, advisory teams, steering groups, action teams, **flat teams**, **hierarchical teams**, *leader-led teams*, leader-less teams, TEAMS AS SMALL *as two people* and as large **as 20,000 people**

efficiency, increase productivity, and yield more satisfied employees. Workers who are a part of a team find their jobs more rewarding and stimulating than the usual fragmented or production-line job. Additionally, today's workers are demanding a say in decisions that affect their work environment and want greater responsibility. Building productive teams is, therefore, becoming increasingly important in today's organizations.

The team concept is ever more important in an increasingly competitive global market.

TECHNOLOGY CONNECTION

Teams, particularly those whose members are not situated in the same location, need to establish e-mail protocol. Cornelius Grove, of Cornelius Grove and Associates, offers the following areas for consideration:

Topics: *Which are appropriate for e-mail? Which need to be handled in person or over the telephone? What about jokes? Profanity?*

Urgency: *What do the terms ASAP or urgent mean?*

Frequency: *How frequently should members use e-mail?*

Participation: *Does every team member need to see every e-mail?*

Showing respect: *How can team members demonstrate respect?*

Time of day: *Should there be a blackout period when e-mails are not sent or received?*

Teamwork Lessons from Geese

Fact	Lesson
1. As each goose flaps its wings it creates an "uplift" for the birds that follow. By flying in a "V" formation, the whole flock adds 71% greater flying range than if each bird flew alone.	1. People who share a common direction and sense of company can get where they are going quicker and easier because they are traveling on the thrust of one another.
2. When a goose falls out of formation, it suddenly feels the drag and resistence of flying alone. It quickly moves back into formation to take advantage of the lifting power of the bird immediately in front of it.	2. If we have as much sense as a goose, we stay in formation with those headed where we want to go. We are willing to accept their help and give our help to others.
3. When the lead goose tires, it rotates back into the formation and another goose flies to the point position.	3. It pays to take turns, doing the hard tasks and sharing leadership. As with geese, people are interdependent on each other's skills, capabilities and unique arrangements of gifts, talents or resources.
4. The geese flying in formation honk to encourage those up front to keep up their speed.	4. We need to make sure our honking is encouraging. In groups, where there is encouragement, the production is much greater. The power of encouragement (to stand by one's heart or core values and encourage the heart and core of others) is the quality of honking we seek.
5. When a goose gets sick, wounded, or shot down, two geese drop out of formation and follow it down to help and protect it. They stay with it until it dies or is able to fly again. Then, they launch out with another formation or catch up with the flock.	5. If we have as much sense as geese, we will stand by each other in difficult times as well as when we are strong.

—Based on the work of Milton Olson

FastChat

Review the various teams identified in *The World Abounds with Teams*, p. 177.

1. Pick four or five teams from the list and suggest the type of task or problem you think that type of team might handle.

2. Can you identify three types of teams in which you have been a member?

How Do You Build an Effective Team?

When people cooperate in a true team effort, powerful results are achieved. Several key ingredients are necessary to assure the kind of synergism that a competent team can produce. The box on the next page labeled "Elements Needed to Build an Effective Team" lists those ingredients.

Studies have shown that employees like participating in group or team activities and appreciate opportunities to contribute their ideas and knowledge toward improving operations. Increasing an employee's sense of responsibility translates directly into greater job satisfaction and loyalty.

Working as a team requires new management methods. It does not mean that the formal leader never leads. Today's formal leader must learn to allow others to assume a guiding role when appropriate. These responsibilities are listed below:

Learning
Objective 4

Name the elements necessary to build an effective team.

Formal team leaders must be willing to share control.

Responsibilities of a Team Leader

1. Assign the right people to the right task.
2. Make expectations clear.
3. Encourage participation by nudging, assisting, helping, and answering questions.
4. See the big picture.
5. Plan.
6. Involve "rookie" employees in the team to bring a fresh outlook or approach.
7. Provide encouragement, motivation, and spirit.
8. Administer rewards for performance, including positive reinforcement and acknowledgement of contributions.
9. Remove road blocks and obstacles that keep the team from performing.
10. Teach, assist, and answer questions.
11. Keep things on track and moving forward.

The choice of leaders in a truly effective team is made by consensus, and the team will usually select the leader based on strengths. Decisions are based on logic and agreed to by team members rather than dictated by authority or position power. The ability to acknowledge others' leadership ability and let go is a sign of an effective formal leader.

Elements Needed To Build an Effective Team

Vision

To build an effective team, whether at work or elsewhere, you must have a clear idea of the team's purpose, where you want to go, and what you must do. Allowing the team to contribute to the planning and setting of specific goals promotes teamwork. Goals should be specific and result in a mission statement through which team members can clearly understand their purpose. For example, President John F. Kennedy provided NASA's team with a clear and compelling vision that demonstrated the power of purpose. By committing to "place a man on the moon by the end of the 1960s," President Kennedy inspired team members of the Apollo Program to achieve their mission. The clarity and conviction generated strategies and an execution that in fact achieved the goal in the prescribed time frame.

Interdependence

Clearly identifying each person's role is essential in reducing conflict and negative competitiveness. Once individuals are comfortable with their role and mission, true team identity can arise. Members will feel like teammates. Teammates will feel comfortable sharing and will come to rely on one another rather than operate as independent entities. The use of "we/us/our" terms becomes noticeable, replacing the typical "I/me/mine" individualistic view. This togetherness reflects a sense of ownership in what the team is doing and builds team spirit.

Leadership

The leadership role in a team is a critical and often difficult one. Certainly, a leader is needed, but it need not always be the formal, legitimate leader. Sharing the leadership role with other team members when appropriate serves to strengthen the team feeling. Today's formal leader must learn when to let go and allow others to lead. Of course, the formal leader has very real responsibilities to the group, as noted below.

Coordination

Given the dynamic conditions of the team approach, coordination of information is critical. All members need to keep up with new facts or changes in direction. Establishing effective communication lines is essential. Something as simple as notification of meeting times and places can play a key part in the process.

Sharing information is also vital. All team members should be informed of important events, from policy changes to new technologies to priority modifications. Team members should be encouraged to establish networks with other team members and other external sources. Maximum cooperation occurs when people know they will have to deal with each other again.

Adaptability

Keeping pace in the rapidly changing workplace requires adaptability and flexibility. People working shoulder-to-shoulder in teams can get things done much faster than individuals out to protect their own turf, or those who may be required to obtain dozens of approvals of higher-ups before they can proceed. Meeting the challenge of change can serve to inspire team responsiveness and heighten synergism.

IDENTIFYING EFFECTIVE TEAM MEMBERS

Encourage team members to contribute their strengths and expertise.

Selecting the best team members possible is crucial to building an effective team. If you are selecting team members, a cross-section of talents with each member representing expertise in a separate discipline is desirable. However, when drawing a team from an existing group, you may need to rely on the strengths of certain individuals and develop abilities in others. You may choose to cross-train or rotate employees to enhance their knowledge of operations. You should recognize valuable traits in individuals and encourage them to flourish. Additionally, the freedom to make mistakes allows growth through trial and error. The following box identifies characteristics of good team players whom you should enlist or develop.

Characteristics of a Good Team Player

A good team member generally:
- Thinks in "we/us/our" terms versus "I/me/mine."
- Is flexible.
- Is willing to share information, ideas, and recognition.
- Gets along well with others.
- Exhibits interest and enthusiasm.
- Remains loyal to team purpose and team members.

IMPORTANCE OF COMMUNICATION, NETWORKING, AND HUMAN RELATIONS SKILLS

Once team members understand their roles and mission, communication, networking, and other human relation skills become important. One of the key ingredients for any team effort is open communication. It enhances creativity and camaraderie among team members and adds to the bottom line of improved productivity.

Open communication and networking enhance the team's creativity.

In a study done by Arthur D. Little, Inc., a research and consulting firm, researchers found a common positive attribute in ten of the United States' most innovative companies. The key was an organizational style stressing easy communication and networking. Innovation increased when collaboration disrupted the hierarchical power flows. Successful corporations such as 3M, IBM, AT&T, and General Foods place emphasis on internal communications and networking with the belief that the enormous information base thus created fosters new ideas and stimulates innovation and creativity.

Because an effective team is able to communicate openly and is highly cohesive, good human relations skills are in constant use. To examine some of these aspects, you need only ask the following questions about your team and its members. Are we supportive of one another? Do we share appropriately how we feel about important things? Do we share information and ideas? Are we effective listeners? Do we handle confrontation or problems within the team fairly, resolving issues well? Developing these basic human relations skills can go a long way toward improving your team's overall output.

Egos can get in the way of teamwork.

"There are some egos in here gumming it up."

Review the ingredients needed to build an effective team. The development of these elements or ingredients takes time.

1. How does this conflict with our culture that lives by mottos such as "Just do it!"

2. If you were the team leader, would you be tempted to take steps to short circuit the teambuilding process? Why or why not?

Human Relations

How Does a Team Affect its Members?

Being on a team has advantages. Teamwork creates a cycle of positive dynamics, with each part reinforcing the others. This enables individual team members to reach high levels of performance. Teams are an effective way to stimulate participation and involvement. Most people have difficulty feeling a strong sense of identity with or loyalty to an organization when they think that their impact is minimal. As team members, they have

Learning
Objective   5

Discuss some of the benefits and drawbacks of team membership.

Teamwork strengthens ownership, involvement, and responsibility.

Benefits and Drawbacks of Teamwork

Benefits

- Increased commitment and ownership of goals
- Higher sustained effort toward goal accomplishment
- Improved self-confidence and sense of well being for team members
- Increased levels of team member motivation, enthusiasm, and job satisfaction
- Improved decision-making and problem-solving results
- Greater emotional support within team structure
- Greater endurance and energy levels from team members
- Greater reservoir of ideas and information
- Increased sharing of individual skills
- Increased productivity
- Improved quality and quantity output
- Improved loyalty to goals and objectives

Drawbacks

- Fear of individual anonymity
- Restricted opportunity for personal career advancement
- Loss of power and authority
- Need to be generalists versus specialists in career field
- Team commitments overshadow personal desires
- Current leadership not geared to team concepts
- Duplication of effort
- Time wasted in team interaction
- Conflict and infighting
- Diminished opportunity to stand out/obtain rewards

a sense of making real, direct, and appreciated contributions. This increased feeling of worth improves their commitment to the goals and objectives of the team and the organization. However, drawbacks do exist in the teamwork process. Because of these personal drawbacks, the team approach is not always welcome. Some individuals may refuse to participate or may even sabotage the team's effectiveness.

ETHICS CONNECTION

You are team supervisor and have just been called to the President's office and informed that your group has won an achievement award for the past year. A banquet will be held next month and the award will be presented. You are instructed to be at the banquet to accept the award.

1. Should you accept the award by yourself and take credit for the accomplishments? Why or why not?

2. Should those individuals who work for you be given any credit? If you give them credit, will it detract from your ability to get ahead at the company?

FastChat

The United States was founded and built both by rugged individualists and solid communities. Americans have sayings such as "if you want something done, do it yourself," and yet "united we stand" is also a vital concept in U.S. history.

1. How might the two different sides of the American mindset contribute to effective teamwork?

2. How might these attitudes make forming teams in America more difficult?

Do Teams Fit All Occasions?

For a teamwork approach to work, participants must buy into the premise that, in order to succeed, they must commit to helping those around them succeed and that all the team members will be held personally responsible for the outcome. This adjustment is difficult for most individuals. Part of the problem occurs because organizations are in transition. Current structures and operating styles do not lend themselves readily to the universal use of teamwork. However, in situations where team concepts can be used, the benefits are well worth the effort of implementation and adaptation. Teams inspire peak performance and confer a critical, competitive edge.

Douglas McGregor, a management theorist, identified key factors of what works and what doesn't in teams. In his book, *The Human Side of Enterprise*, McGregor described the most common characteristics of effective and ineffective teams. The figure on the next page lists the characteristics that McGregor identified for both effectiveness and ineffectiveness.

Learning
Objective   6

Know when the team approach is appropriate.

The team approach is not always the best strategy.

GLOBAL CONNECTION

Global teams bring special challenges. Members first need to understand each other's differences before they can effectively come together as a group. Then, too, they must recognize the role of language difficulties and manner of speaking. Additional time will be needed for team members to become comfortable with each other.

1. *What can you do to be better understood when speaking with others for whom English is a second language?*

2. *What types of difficulties can occur when speaking with others who are native English speakers but have different accents?*

McGregor's Team Effectiveness

Characterisitcs of Effective Teams

- The "atmosphere" is a working atmosphere that tends to be informal, comfortable, and relaxed. People are involved and interested.
- There is a lot of discussion in which virtually everyone participates, but it remains pertinent to the task.
- The task or objectives of the group is well understood and accepted by the members.
- The leader of the group does not dominate it, nor does the group defer unduly to her.
- Disagreements are not suppressed or overridden by premature group action.
- Where there are basic disagreements that cannot be resolved and action is necessary, it will be taken but with open caution and recognition that the action may be subject to later reconsideration.
- Members listen to each other.
- Most decisions are reached by a kind of consensus in which it is clear that everybody is in general agreement and willing to go along.
- Criticism is frequent, frank, constructive, and relatively comfortable.
- People are free in expressing their feelings as well as their ideas both on the problem and the group's operation.
- When action is taken, clear assignments are made and accepted.
- The group is self conscious about its own operation.

Characteristics of Ineffective Teams

- There is a climate of defensiveness or fear.
- There is unequal participation and uneven use of group resources.
- The group is dominated by the leader.
- Avoidance of differences or potential conflicts is common.
- The team produces uncreative alternatives to problems.
- There are warring cliques or subgroups and rigid or dysfunctional group norms and procedures.
- Communication is restricted.

From *The Human Side of Enterprise* by Douglas McGregor, copyright © 1960, The McGraw-Hill Companies. Reprinted by permission.

FastChat

Atmosphere is important in effective teams.

1. Describe your ideal team environment.

2. What can you do to help ensure a good work atmosphere?

Human Relations

How Can You Be an Effective Team Member?

7.7

When you are a member of a team you can help make the team effective and the experience pleasant if you remember certain suggestions:

1. Know your role and the team's goals. Be aware of your strengths and weaknesses and what you can contribute to the team.
2. Be a willing team player. At times you may be asked to perform tasks that you dislike or with which you disagree. Realize how performing these assignments will contribute to the group productivity and perform them willingly (unless you disagree on ethical or moral grounds).
3. Cooperate with other team members. Harmony is enhanced by using open communication and solid human relations skills.
4. Support other team members by giving them encouragement and assisting them when necessary with their tasks.
5. Share praise. Do not claim credit for yourself if a team effort was involved.
6. When conflict occurs, attempt to turn it into a positive experience.

Learning
Objective 7

Describe what you can do to be an effective team member.

An effective team member needs extensive human relations skills.

Give other team members encouragement and assist them with their tasks if necessary.

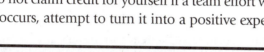

1. How can conflict be turned into a positive experience?

2. How can you turn mistakes into learning activities?

FastChat

Is Conflict Bad?

Introducing change sets the stage for conflict. Although conflict is often regarded as a barrier to teamwork, it is actually an essential part of the process. **Conflict** is defined as disagreement between individuals or groups about goals. It is inevitable. If no conflict occurs in a group, the group may actually be ineffective because members do not care about outcomes or make suggestions. Conflict does become a problem, however, when it is excessive, becomes disruptive, or causes a team to become dysfunctional.

Competition is a healthy struggle toward goal accomplishment without interference, even when the goals are incompatible. Competition can stimulate beneficial and creative ideas and methods by team members, whereas excessive conflict typically limits creativity.

Conflict can be healthy and positive if handled properly. Team members may be inspired or stimulated to resolve issues and reach new heights of creativity. Although too much conflict may be disruptive or destructive, too little conflict generally results in apathy or stagnation. A moderate amount of conflict controlled through resolution techniques can be of benefit to both the organization and the team members and can assure peak performance.

In Sections 7.9 and 7.10, some common causes of conflict will be discussed in addition to some common and effective methods of handling conflict situations.

quick wit

"Every difference of opinion is not a difference of principle."

—Thomas Jefferson

Fast Chat

Describe a time when you were in a group where conflict existed.

1. How was it handled?

2. Was it disruptive?

3. What could have been done differently?

What Causes Conflict?

Conflict can be experienced by any team member or by the team as a whole. Five causes are shown here:

Causes of Conflict

Incompatibility	Personality conflicts may arise within the team or even between two teams. Within the team, a conflict may occur between a supervisor and a subordinate or between any two or more team members. Between teams, ill feelings may exist for a variety of reasons. For example, plant operators may resent corporate engineers who design and implement changes that do not work well. The engineers may look down on the plant operators. Such conflict may create considerable trouble.
Organizational Reliance	In most organizations teams rely upon one another. For example, machine operators depend upon the maintenance crews to perform periodic maintenance on equipment. A production team may rely on the sales team to provide orders from customers to keep the production line in full operation. Conflict may arise between the teams if maintenance is slipshod or if sales orders force production into overtime to meet unrealistic schedules.
Goal Ambiguity	Team goals may differ from the goals of the organization. For example, the organization may want to hurry processes and jeopardize quality of product in order to get the job out and turn a profit. The work teams may want to take time to assure quality. The goals of the two groups clearly conflict.
Labor-Management Disputes	Labor and management have long had disagreements over work conditions, hours, and wages. However, the trouble often goes deeper. Conflicts may be based on roles that each feels necessary to portray. Management representatives may believe that "squaring off" with union representatives just prior to contract negotiations is necessary to set the stage. These situations are normal when the union and management have opposing views.
Unclear Roles	The uncertainty brought on by constant changes in roles and missions breeds conflict. These environmental changes cause instability among team members, and conflict will occur. Good communication among team members helps control this type of conflict.

Review the term "scapegoating" in Chapter 2.

1. Have you been in a team where one group or individual has used another as a scapegoat? Was this productive?

2. Did the groups/individuals have different goals?

FastChat

7.10 How Is Conflict Resolved?

Learning
Objective 10

*Describe common
conflict resolution
techniques.*

Conflict resolution is the active management of conflict through defining and solving issues between individuals, groups, or organizations. Given the fact that conflict is part of any team environment, understanding how to manage it is important. In a study conducted by Ronald J. Burke on methods of resolving conflict, five techniques proved to be the most common and effective ways of handling conflict:

Techniques for Handling Conflict

Avoidance	This technique involves totally refraining from confronting the conflict. Avoiding the situation can buy some time to learn additional facts surrounding the conflict or provide a "cooling off" period. It does not resolve the conflict but is often of immediate help.
Smoothing	Accommodating the differences between the two parties, smoothing plays down strong issues and concentrates on mutual interests. Negative issues are seldom even discussed.
Compromising	This technique does address the issue but seldom resolves it to the complete satisfaction of both parties. There is no clear winner or loser.
Forcing	Forcing results when two groups reach an impasse and allow an authoritative figure to choose one preference rather than work toward a mutually agreeable solution. This is considered a win-lose situation.
Confrontation	Although it sounds like a negative approach, confrontation is actually the most positive. It can create a win-win situation. Openly exchanging information and actively working through the differences assures that some agreeable resolution is reached.

These techniques give you some choices for dealing with conflict. The critical message when confronted with confusion or disagreements among team members is to be alert and aware that the conflict exists, look for the causes, understand the reasons as much as possible, and then meet the conflict head on to bring it to resolution.

FastChat

Recall a recent conflict that you experienced.

1. Which of these methods did you use to resolve the conflict?
2. Was this effective?
3. Would some other method have been more effective?

SUMMARY

Organizations use teamwork because it increases productivity. This concept was used in corporations as early as the 1920s, but it has become increasingly important in recent years as employees demand more direct involvement and companies strive to gain a competitive edge in the ever-changing marketplace.

Five basic ingredients must be present for a team to be effective. The team must have a vision, feel interdependence, have good leadership, use effective means of coordination, and have a high degree of adaptability.

Although a formal leader will be present in most teams, leadership is commonly shared without fear of loss of power. Good team members can be selected or developed and can be coached to share responsibility in achieving the team's goals and mission.

Effective networking systems and open communication are both required for maximum team effectiveness. The benefits derived from the use of teams outweigh the drawbacks and point to the usefulness of teamwork when increased productivity and improved quality are desirable. Occasionally, the team approach is not the best method to use, but these occasions are dwindling as companies seek new ways to meet the challenge of the future.

Competition among teams and team members can stimulate creative ideas and methods for accomplishing goals. Conflict, an active ingredient in the team process, can be healthy and positive. Conflict may also be disruptive or destructive. Excessive conflict typically limits creativity and should be properly managed. Major sources of conflict include incompatibility, organizational reliance, goal ambiguity, labor-management disputes, and unclear roles. However, the five common techniques of conflict resolution (avoidance, smoothing, compromising, forcing, and confrontation) can bring positive results.

KEY TERMS

team
teamwork
teambuilding
synergism
problem-solving teams
special-purpose teams
self-managing teams
conflict
competition
conflict resolution
avoidance
smoothing
compromising
forcing
confrontation

Review Questions

1. Why are team concepts necessary in today's work environment and why are they successful?
2. How do effective teams increase productivity?
3. What are the elements needed in building an effective team?
4. Why are communication and networking important ingredients in teambuilding?
5. What are some of the benefits and drawbacks of team membership?
6. What can you do to become an effective team member?
7. What is the difference between conflict and competition? Why can they both be healthy for an organization?
8. What are the most common techniques in conflict resolution?

Discussion Questions

1. You are responsible for building a team to improve quality and productivity in your work unit. Outline your approach and describe your reasoning.
2. Describe a conflict that you have experienced within a team setting. Identify the causes and discuss what conflict resolution techniques might have been used.
3. Identify a problem within your community. If you were the formal leader assigned to correct the problem, what types of individuals would you choose for your team? How would you approach the task of team formation?
4. Think of a team with which you have been involved recently. Identify the disciplines or areas of expertise that were represented in the team. How did they serve the team's purpose?
5. Identify tasks in your work or volunteer organization setting that are more efficiently performed by teams than by individuals.

visualizing, problem solving, sociability, participating as a member of the team

Chapter Project

Musical Chairs Exercise

Equipment Needed: music that can be turned on and off, chairs (one less than the number of participants)

Play the traditional musical chairs (this works best with a small group). Then replay the game with the following variation: Instead of removing players who lose their seat, remaining players assist individuals without chairs by helping them stay "on" chairs. (The goal is to end up with one chair and no one with their feet on the floor.)

1. Describe how the different games feel.
2. How did the second version simulate the team experience?
3. In which environment would you prefer to work?

Applications

In small groups, analyze the following scenarios.

The Magic at Magill Manufacturing

Anna Magill took over as chief executive officer at Magill Manufacturing after her father retired from running the business for 32 years. Magill Manufacturing was a keystone company in Lisbon, Ohio, and provided jobs to a large number of the citizens in the community. She took great pride in continuing the family business but knew that she would run the operation differently than her father had.

problem solving, reasoning, listening, speaking, reading, decision making

After only a short period of time in her new position, Anna realized the company was suffering from symptoms of high absenteeism, chronic tardiness, and low morale. Frequent complaints had been filed, employee attitudes were poor, and a general discontent existed among workers. Management was viewed as coercive, with "little dictators" running isolated kingdoms throughout the company. Employees felt that managers gave little support to their ideas or suggestions. Working at Magill Manufacturing had become a way to draw a paycheck and little more. These conditions were reflected in slumping productivity and declining quality of the products.

Anna knew that she needed to act quickly if she were going to turn this situation around. She felt a strong commitment to improving the quality of product, increasing productivity, and creating company loyalty. Her course was clearly charted.

1. How can Anna use team concepts to improve conditions at Magill Manufacturing?
2. What positive changes might be expected from the use of teams in the problem-solving process?
3. Do you think that the employees will respond to the new methods? Why or why not?

problem solving, reasoning, listening, speaking, reading, decision making

The Left-Handed Pressure Valve

The engineering office issued design drawings for the installation of a pressure valve in the plant. The design had been developed by the corporate engineers without consulting the users of the valve. Reviewing the design drawings, the operations people noticed problems with the design. They said nothing, however, because the engineers had not asked for their input.

The operators waited until the valve had been fabricated and installed before they told the engineers why the valve would not work. Indignantly they demonstrated that the valve could only be accessed from the left side and could not even be seen if approached from the right side. The entire operation had to be returned to the drawing board and redesigned, refabricated, and reinstalled incorporating the suggestions made by the operators.

1. What was the relationship between the two team groups? How effective was the approach taken by the engineers?
2. What did this conflict cost the company?
3. What techniques might have been employed to prevent the conflict in the first place? How might future conflict be prevented?

Additional Readings and Resources

Hunter, Dale; Anne Bailey; and Bill Taylor. *The Zen of Groups.* Tucson: Fisher Books, 1995.

Moran, Linda; Ed Musselwhite, and John H. Zenger. *Keeping Teams on Track.* Chicago: Irwin Professional Publishing, 1996.

Newstrom, John and Edward Scannell. *The Big Book of Team Building Games.* New York: McGraw Hill, 1998.

Quick, Thomas L. *Successful Team Building.* New York: American Management Association, 1992.

Robbins, Harvey and Michael Finley. *Why Teams Don't Work.* Princeton: Peterson's/Pacesetter Books, 1995.

Unions:

Organized Labor Today

focus

Until a few years ago, U S. workers at a General Motors (GM) plant in Flint, Michigan, made instrument panels, and a plant in Saginaw, Michigan, produced steering wheels for GM cars and trucks. Car radio production for Delco was done in Kokomo, Indiana, and windshield wipers for those same cars and trucks were made in Buffalo, New York. Today, GM has more than 50 final assembly parts plants in Mexico employing some 72,000 Mexican workers. In fact, GM's Delphi Automotive Services is Mexico's largest private employer.

GM says that transferring production south has enabled it to substantially cut costs to compete more effectively against Ford, Chrysler, and Japanese auto makers. The financial advantages of producing parts in Mexico are substantial. A 90 percent savings on labor costs allows GM to lower its auto prices and become competitive in today's global market.

Sam Dillon, *NY Times,* **June 28, 1998**

What other companies, making what products, have moved portions of their operations to other countries? What might happen to bring these operations back to the US?

After studying this chapter, you should be able to:

1. *Explain the differences between unions and employee associations.*

2. *Identify methods companies used to prevent union formation prior to passage of the Wagner Act.*

3. *Discuss the key federal legislation to establish and govern labor-management activities.*

4. *Discuss the steps involved in a typical grievance procedure.*

5. *Explain the key differences between mediation and arbitration.*

6. *Discuss whether unions are strengthening or weakening in today's work force.*

In This Chapter

What Is a Union?

Learning
Objective   1

*Explain the
differences between
unions and
employee
associations.*

**A union bargains
on behalf of
members for
improved
conditions of
employment.**

quick wit

*In union there is
strength.*

Aesop

A **union** is a group or association of workers who collectively bargain with employers to improve working conditions and to protect employees from unfair or arbitrary treatment by management. The working conditions in question are usually hours, wages, and benefits. For several reasons, many unions today are struggling to stay alive. In many areas, wages and working conditions are good, and workers don't want to pay often high union dues when they don't see benefits, or they don't like the way that unions spend forced dues. Another reason is the change from a labor-intensive work force to a service-industry work force.

Yet another factor is the moving of jobs overseas, since American companies are now often owned by multi-national corporations whose primary allegiance is to stockholders rather than to specific countries. In many countries, labor costs are lower and strikes are less likely.

The United Auto Workers (UAW) have cause for concern when they see jobs being relocated from the old traditional heavily unionized plants in the U.S. to the new plants in Mexico. Many of the Mexican plants have no unions and those that do are represented by the Confederation of Mexican Workers, which works with the Mexican Government to avoid strikes.

This relocation of jobs was the primary focus of the recent UAW strikes against General Motors. Union members at the Flint Metal Center stamping plant and the Delphi East parts plant in Michigan called for a strike to

GLOBAL CONNECTION

General Motors has been moving its final assembly plant activities to Mexico for the last 20 years to take advantage of lower labor costs, excellent Mexican management practices, and a dedicated Mexican work force. This south-of-the-border trend has a far greater importance in that it raises basic questions about our current national labor practices and the direction of future union activities.

Sam Dillon, *New York Times*, November 1998

What countries besides Mexico can you think of that now do work that was once done in the U.S.? What are the benefits and costs of such moves?

prevent the transfer of more job responsibilities to Mexico. The union picket lines caused the world's largest auto maker to shut down 27 of its 29 North American assembly plants and idled nearly 200,000 workers. The 54-day strikes were the costliest labor battle for GM in 30 years, with estimated losses of more than $75 million a day and total estimated loss of nearly $2.5 billion in profits.

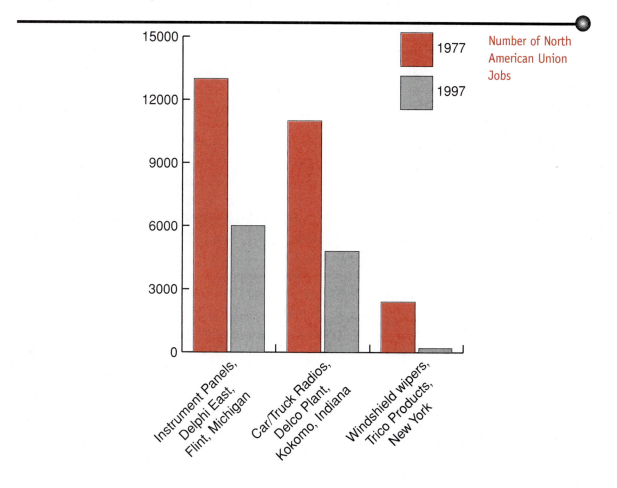

STRIKES

When representatives of a union and management are unable to reach agreement, union members may use a technique known as a strike to improve their bargaining position with a company's management. A **strike** is the refusal to work under the current conditions until some agreement can be reached toward the desired improvements.

Management may respond to a strike by hiring all new employees to replace the strikers. In the 1980s, President Ronald Reagan fired air traffic controllers (who were striking illegally) and had them permanently replaced under presidential executive order (a penalty that was specified in the contracts to which the controllers had agreed). By doing so he brought on a new era of labor-management relations in which replacing striking workers became legally permissible. However, in the 1990s, President Clinton, opposing that practice, signed Executive Order 12954, which directed federal agencies to refrain from buying goods or services from companies that permanently replaced striking workers.

Both union members and companies may lose valuable income during strikes.

Strikes can be costly for both the union members and management. Union members usually suffer income losses during the strike period. Although the union provides compensation benefits from union dues paid by members during nonstrike periods, income is considerably less than normal wages. For example, striking workers in the UAW strike against GM earned only $150 a week, so long as they spent at least four hours carrying signs on the picket line. Union members will often take some other full- or part-time job to supplement their income until the strike is settled.

Companies also suffer income or profit losses during a strike. Often the company is forced to operate with a skeleton crew of managers and nonstrikers who may not be fully trained and able to keep productivity levels constant with prestrike levels. A strike at an AC Delco plant that lasted only five days ended up costing GM $180 million dollars when the plant came to a full standstill from lack of expertise to operate the assembly lines. Unions do have the power to greatly affect the operations of any organization. Of course, while a major corporation may survive a strike, some companies may never recover, and jobs disappear. The use of that power is not always beneficial.

EMPLOYEE ASSOCIATIONS

Unions and employee associations perform virtually the same functions.

Today little distinction exists between unions and **employee associations.** Historically, employee associations were made up of group members from the white-collar and professional sectors of the work force, such as teachers, nurses, public sector employees, doctors, lawyers, and clerical workers. These individuals seldom engaged in collective bargaining activities, and a key distinction for some associations was the denial of the right to strike. Many federal and state employees, for instance, took an oath of employment that stated they would not strike against the government. However, because most employee associations have evolved to function much the same as unions, the U. S. Department of Labor no longer makes a distinction between the two.

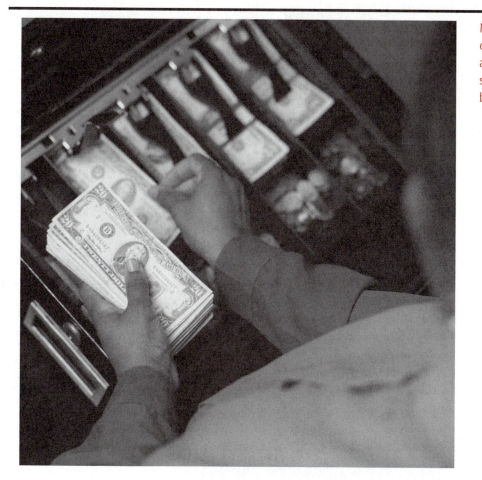

Many retail occupations, such as cashier and sacker, are covered by union contracts.

1. Discuss a strike currently in the news.

2. Would you join a union? Why or why not?

3. What is the difference between a union and an employee association?

8.2 How Did the Labor Movement Begin?

Early attempts to unionize were marred by conflict and controversy.

Prior to the 1930s, working conditions for many of America's workers ranged from unpleasant to truly awful. Early in the Industrial Era, factories were little more than sweatshops, exploiting the worker with long hours, unsafe work conditions and low wages, and even using child labor, as factories sprang up and the demand for goods exploded. Management emphasis was placed on the scientific approach popularized by Frederick W. Taylor (as discussed in Chapter 1). However, while Taylor's ideal was to make work efficient for the benefit of both management and labor, many adopted only the concept of maximizing productivity output, and workers' needs were ignored. Employers showed little concern for human relations and workers had no voice in influencing their work environment.

Attempts by workers to unionize were resisted by management and routinely brought before the courts, which customarily ruled against labor union activities. Companies habitually used injunctions to halt strikes and boycotts to inhibit union activity. Other anti-union techniques used by management included firing labor agitators, blacklisting, yellow dog contracts, and lockouts.

Children were exploited in the early Industrial Era.

Credit: CORBIS

Management Anti-Union Tactics	
Labor Agitators	Influential persons capable of rallying workers toward unionizing.
Blacklists	Names of labor agitators and other persons known to be sympathetic to unionizing efforts.
Yellow-dog Contract	Condition of employment that required would-be employees to sign a statement that they would not start or join a union.
Lockouts	Company management locked the factory doors and shut down operations.

Labor agitators, once identified by company management, were immediately fired and their names placed on a black list. Company managers would pass these lists of potential troublemakers around to assure that union organizers were denied employment. The threat of unemployment had the desired result of discouraging active support for the labor movement. When workers made demands for improved conditions or threatened early forms of strikes, company management could simply impose a lockout. Because companies could economically outlast the now unemployed worker, it was another effective means of discouraging union activities. The Yellow-dog Contract was also used until it was outlawed by the **Norris-LaGuardia Act of 1932** as a softening of anti-union attitudes began in the early 1930s. Sometimes even brutal and blatantly illegal methods were used by management of some shops to stop pro-union activities of employees.

However, mounting public and congressional disfavor of these activities gave rise to the trend toward legalizing unions. Further federal legislation would drastically change the labor movement and form the basis for union activities as we know them today.

An historic agreement by labor, human rights, and industry leaders was announced by President Clinton in 1997 after many months of publicity about the exploitation of workers making name brand apparel in the U.S. and abroad. Disney was accused of contracting with a Haitian company that pays its workers only 28 cents an hour to make Mickey Mouse pajamas. NIKE Shoes came under fire for allegations that its Asian factory employees are forced to work 60-hour weeks, are paid $2.20 per day, and are sometimes physically beaten. Television Co-host Kathie Lee Gifford was targeted with allegations that her clothing line, sold in Walmart stores, was made by underpaid teenagers working 20-hour workdays in Honduran sweatshops.

Designer and celebrity companies are working to change the image of manufacturing methods.

ETHICS CONNECTION

In a White House press release dated April 14 1997, President Clinton announced an historic agreement by labor, human rights, and industry leaders to help improve working conditions in United States garment and footwear companies and their overseas contractors. Clinton challenged the apparel industry to take steps to assure that company products are made in compliance with acceptable labor standards and to inform consumers that the products they buy are not made under exploitative conditions. President Clinton acknowledged that some of the shoes and clothing bought in America are manufactured under unacceptable working conditions in factories both here and abroad.

Wendy S. Ross, White House Press Release, 1997

Why do you think the federal government took a role in this agreement? Who will police the activities?

Guess moved over a thousand jobs to Mexico where workers earn about $30 a week. This move came on the heels of Los Angeles garment workers' demands that Guess end illegal sweatshop conditions in their local clothing factories. Similar public and congressional disfavor of these types of practices may give rise to drastic improvements and changes needed in our current conditions.

FastChat

1. What methods were used to discourage or prevent unions?

2. What were the employment conditions in 1930s industrial America?

3. Do any of these conditions still exist today in the U.S?. In other countries?

4. How do lifestyles, employment levels, and cost of living in some of these other countries differ from those in the U.S.?

How Did Federal Law Affect the Labor Movement?

Several key pieces of congressional legislation laid the framework for the labor movement and the unionization rights of workers. The Wagner Act of 1935, the Taft-Hartley Act of 1947, and the Landrum-Griffin Act of 1959 are of primary interest.

THE WAGNER ACT

The right of employees to form unions and collectively bargain with management on employment issues was established in 1935 through passage of the National Labor Relation Act. More popularly known as the **Wagner Act,** this legislation ordered management to stop interfering with union organizing efforts and defined what constituted an unfair labor practice by management.

Learning
Objective 3

Discuss the key federal legislation to establish and govern labor-management activities.

The Wagner Act legitimized labor unions.

The NLRB remains active in policing labor-management activities.

Practices that Developed from the Wagner Act

1. Management cannot fire or refuse to hire because individuals are union members.

2. Management cannot discriminate against a union member who files an unfair labor practice complaint or testifies before the National Labor Relations Board.

3. Management must bargain in good faith with a union and, once a union is elected, cannot recognize any other union.

4. Management can talk about the disadvantages of a union but cannot threaten, interrogate, or spy on individuals concerning union activities.

5. Management must allow union members to meet on their own personal time (such as lunch or breaks) to discuss union business but not on company time.

6. If employees strike for wages or working conditions, employers may hire replacements and are not obliged to rehire strikers unless so stated in the contract.

7. If employees strike over unfair labor practices (activities that violate the act), the employer must fire the replacements and take the strikers back when the strike ends.

The **National Labor Relations Board (NLRB)** was also established by the Wagner Act. The NLRB is a government agency responsible for enforcing the provisions of the Wagner Act. Regional offices throughout the U.S. are often called upon to help resolve disputes and to police strike activities for violations of federal legislation.

Because the Wagner Act was so sweepingly pro-union, unions gained enormous power and frequently called strikes to force desired improvements in work conditions. In 1946, 113 million workdays were lost in union strikes, causing a major shift in public opinion about unions. Many industries were paralyzed, which affected the general public and set the stage for more restrictive labor legislation.

THE TAFT-HARTLEY ACT

The Taft-Hartley Act, also known as the Labor Management Act of 1947, was a series of amendments to the Wagner Act. It imposed certain controls

CASE STUDIES IN THE NEWS

Five months into a strike by United Mine Workers (UMW), 98 camouflage-clad men and a minister seized the Pittston Coal Company plant in Virginia, forcing company guards into an office building. The intruders were able to occupy the plant for 21 days, successfully preventing the company from producing coal. For the first three days, nearly 2,000 sympathizers kept state troopers from entering the plant to free the guards and arrest the strikers. Eventually, a court order was issued to end the seizure of the property.

This strike became known as the most confrontational strike of the 1980s. The NLRB, which policed the strike activities for violations of federal legislation, issued more than 400 charges of unfair labor practices against both Pittston and the union. Nearly 3,000 miners and supporters were arrested for picket-line misconduct and violence. These charges constitute the largest number of charges ever levied by the NLRB in a single dispute.

John Hoerr, *Business Week*, Oct. 9, 1989

What might have been done to prevent the takeover? Why is this incident so important to labor law?

Human Relations

Key Provisions of the Taft-Hartley Act

1. Enables states to pass right-to-work laws (known as Section 14b).
2. Forbids discriminatory or excessive dues charging by unions of prospective employees.
3. Forbids makework practices that force employers to pay for services not rendered.
4. Invokes the "cooling-off period," which allows the President to request an 80-day freeze on any strike that threatens national health or safety.
5. Requires unions to bargain in good faith with management.
6. Requires 60-day notices to be given of any impending contract termination.
7. Forbids unions to use coercive means for recruiting members.
8. Allows employees to settle grievances informally with management.

on union organizing activities, internal union activities, and methods used by unions in collective bargaining attempts.

Several of these provisions are worth exploring because of their impact on union activities. For example, the closed shop was outlawed. A **closed shop** required a person to belong to a bargaining unit before being hired, and job loss was automatic if the person was expelled from the union for any reason (such as nonpayment of dues). This was eventually outlawed. In a **union shop,** the worker need not be a union member at the time of hiring, but is required to join the union within 60 to 90 days after employment. Unions shops are permitted by the Taft-Hartley Act. An **agency shop** requires workers to pay union membership dues whether or not they actually choose to join the union. This rule serves to protect the union from would-be free riders. **Free riders** are employees who received the same benefits as union members without paying dues.

The group represented by the union, those for whom the union negotiates, is called a **bargaining unit,** and it is in the union's interest to have as many paying members as possible. As part of most contract agreements, a company will deduct union dues directly from a worker's paycheck. This process is called a **checkoff** and guarantees that the union will always get its dues.

The Taft-Hartley Act also contains a provision that individual states may pass right-to-work laws. The **Right-To-Work Law** allows states to prohibit both the closed and the union shop contract agreements, giving the worker the choice of union membership without compromise.

One other federal law that had significant impact on labor activities was passed by Congress in 1959. Driven by reports of alleged corruption by union officials, extensive congressional investigations were held and

Closed, union, and agency shops protected the union's rights to membership dues.

Corruption and misuse of funds by some union officials led to the Landrum-Griffin Act.

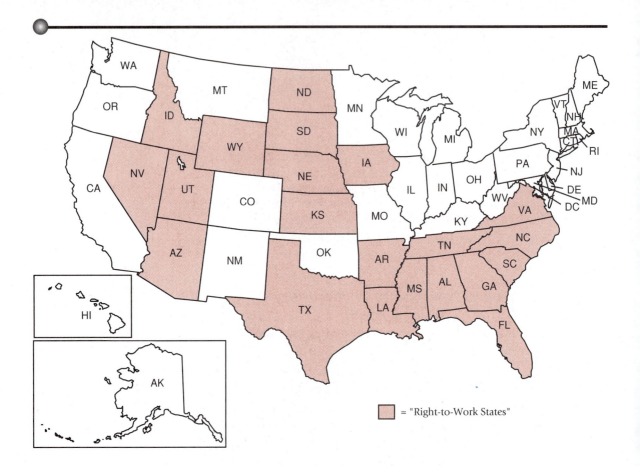

= "Right-to-Work States"

The Right-To-Work Law grants states the option of imposing union membership.

resulted in the passage of the Labor Management Reporting and Disclosure Act, also known as the **Landrum-Griffin Act.** This act requires unions and employers of union members to report certain matters to the Department of Labor. Unions must disclose the sources and disbursements of their funds, hold regularly scheduled elections of union officials by secret ballot, and restrict union officials from using union funds for personal means.

FastChat

1. Discuss two advantages of the Wagner Act.

2. What does the NLRB do?

3. What is the most important provision of the Taft-Hartley Act?

4. Why is the Landrum-Griffin Act important?

Whom Do Unions Represent?

8.4

In the early years, unions represented two major segments of the working population. The **craft unions** represented skilled workers, such as shoemakers, carpenters, and stonemasons, and were primarily concerned with training apprentices to be masters of their craft. The **American Federation of Labor (AFL)**, led by Samuel L. Gompers, was formed in 1886 of a small number of these craft unions.

The other workers represented by unions in the early years were industrial workers, who were unskilled or semiskilled, such as mine workers and steel makers. In 1936, this group of **industrial unions** formed the **Congress of Industrial Organizations (CIO)**, led by John L. Lewis.

Labor Union Statistics

General Membership Statistics:
In 1998, approximately 13.9 percent of the population belonged to a union.

Union Employees in Public Sector (federal, state, and local government employees)	6,500,000
Union Employees in Private Sector	9,700,000

Membership Within Major Occupational Groups:
Government workers have much higher unionization rate than their private sector counterparts (37.5 percent versus 9.5 percent).

Men are more likely to be union members than women, and blacks are more likely to be members than whites.

Among occupational groups, unionization rate is highest among workers in protective services (police, firemen).

Wage Differences:

Earnings of Union Members	Avg. $575/week
Earnings of Non-Union Members	Avg. $426/week

(The Bureau of Labor Statistics notes, however, that education has a greater impact than unionization on wages. Average weekly wages for workers 25 and above: with no high school diploma, $345/week; with a high school diploma; $489/week; with a college degree, $851/week.)

Source: Bureau of Labor Statistics

The two groups merged in 1955 to form the **AFL-CIO** as a show of strength to improve bargaining power. A few of the larger unions later withdrew to become independents. Examples include the Teamsters, Auto Workers, and Warehousemen. In the 1960s unions made significant gains in membership among government workers, white-collar professionals, and farm workers. Over the next 30 years, union membership grew in unlikely areas, and today, union members may be teachers, politics, police, fire fighters, professional athletes, grocery store workers, nurses, or clerical workers. Representation of these types of workers increased while the membership of the craft and industrial unions declined.

Today union membership is undergoing interesting shifts again. The auto workers, steel workers, and machinists are talking about forming a single union which comes on the heels of the merger of clothing and garment workers' unions. Merger talks between the two teachers' unions may bring about the nation's largest labor union ever. Even physicians' unions are gaining membership, largely due to the dilemmas of managed health care. Child care workers, phone workers and a host of other non-traditional categories are also increasing the numbers of unions in America.

*Fast*Chat

1. Which segments of the working population were represented by unions in the early years?

2. What groups experienced growth in the 1960s?

3. How is union membership changing today?

How Do Unions Work?

Unions come into existence in a precise way and their functioning involves specific processes.

FORMATION

Normally unions develop through an election. At least 50 percent of the employees in what is called a **bargaining unit** must vote to have the union represent them. The voting is monitored by the National Labor Relations Board. (Union members may also vote to decertify a union.)

Supervisors are considered part of management and are not allowed to vote or join the union. However, today's more aggressive union recruiting tactics include sending in a "union salt," to infiltrate nonunion companies. His/her job is to recruit employees by simply collecting signatures from a majority of the workers and asking management to go along voluntarily with recognizing the union. This tactic, know as "card signing," works surprisingly well but sidesteps the official election and recognition process regulated by the NLRB.

A **union steward** represents union members' interests and protects their rights on the job. Many times this person acts as a go-between, representing the union member to the company supervisor in settling disagreements. The steward is usually a senior employee elected by the union to act in this capacity. While many unions are large, national organizations with full-time staffs to negotiate key issues, most local unions have a **business agent** to administer their agreement, collect dues, recruit new members and perform other day-to-day activities. Sometimes local unions will do all their own negotiating and bargaining activities.

BARGAINING

Once a union has been elected to represent the workers, union representatives meet with company management representatives to establish a mutual agreement on hours, wages, and working conditions. This process of negotiation to reach a written agreement is called **collective bargaining.** Both union and management are expected to bargain in good faith to reach a mutually acceptable agreement. This written agreement is known as a **contract.** Once signed, the contract is legally binding to both parties. A contract usually covers a one- to three-year period. It then will be re-negotiated for

---

Learning
Objectives 4 and 5

Discuss the steps involved in a typical grievance procedure. Explain the key differences between mediation and arbitration.

Workers choose union representation by voting.

The union and management typically negotiate a contract for hours, wages, and working conditions agreeable to both parties.

---

renewal as is or with changes. The list below outlines the various topics most commonly addressed in collective bargaining.

Typical Collective Bargaining Topics			
Wages	**Hours**	**Working Conditions**	**General**
Wage rates	Shift hours	Employment requirements	Contract length
Shift-work rates	Lunch lengths	Work load/division	Grievance procedures
Overtime rates	Lunch times	Work rules/policies	Strike clause
Promotions	Break times	Safety rules/policies	Arbitration policy
Cost-of-living increases	Vacation days	Seniority policies	
Retirement plans	Sick days	Disciplinary policies	
Life and health insurance	Holidays	Firing policies	
Union dues payment			
Unemployment benefits			

By no means is the bargaining process a stagnant one. The contract is a written document often interpreted differently depending upon a reader's perception of the meaning. Disputes between a supervisor and a union worker over contract wording often result in what is called a **grievance.** Careful attention to the wording of the written contract can help reduce the frequency of these disputes; however, they are inevitable.

RESOLVING GRIEVANCES

Grievance procedures are clearly defined in the contract.

Ideally, disputes between workers and supervisors should be resolved informally, using effective human relations skills. However, if these first attempts fail, the dispute becomes part of a grievance system designed to handle these problems.

Most contracts have a specific **grievance procedure** written into the contract that carefully outlines the formal steps for resolving contract disputes. These procedures are not standardized in all contracts but follow a three- to seven-step process. Specific time limits are established for each of the steps to ensure timely processing of the dispute.

A formal grievance is usually filed in writing on a grievance form (see p. 212). At this point, the bargaining process officially begins, with each party responsible for presenting its position. As discussed in Chapter 7, such conflict can be healthy if good human relations skills are used to reach a solution that represents growth for both parties.

MEDIATION AND ARBITRATION

Contracts can include both mediation and arbitration as final steps in resolving conflicts. The two steps are quite different in their approaches and results.

Mediation brings both groups together under the influence of an unbiased third party who may skillfully guide the opposing parties toward new ideas or methods of resolution. This unbiased third party, known as a **mediator,** can only be summoned if both parties agree to try mediation. Upon agreement, a list of mediators is requested from the **Federal Mediation and Conciliation Service (FMCS)** or from state labor departments.

Mediators are usually highly skilled in the art of negotiation and conflict resolution techniques. They carefully pick the date, time, and location of the meeting and may restrict attendance for maximum effectiveness. Ground rules are quickly established, and both parties must commit to resolving the conflict. The mediator then helps develop alternative solutions in hopes that one will be mutually agreeable. If a solution is reached, it is written down and signed by both parties and the grievance is considered resolved. No further action is necessary.

Arbitration is a formal process similar to a legal court hearing. The sessions are led by an **arbitrator,** whose professional services are usually requested from the American Arbitration Association (AAA). During the hearing, both sides present their cases, call witnesses, and submit other supporting facts. The arbitrator is given a limited time to develop a written decision on the matter, which becomes legally binding on both parties. This is the key difference between mediation and arbitration. The final decision

Understanding the importance of effective negotiating skills and understanding and working within human systems.

A mediator leads informal sessions to resolve a deadlocked grievance.

An arbitrator's formal decision is legally biding to both parties.

GRIEVANCE

(FOR GRIEVANCES OVER INTERPRETATION OR APPLICATION OF THE NEGOTIATED AGREEMENT BETWEEN JSC AND LOCAL 2284, AFGE)

NAME OF EMPLOYEE		POSITION TITLE	
GRADE	ORGANIZATION CODE	EXTENSION	DATE INCIDENT OCCURRED
NAME OF SUPERVISOR WHO RECEIVED INFORMAL COMPLAINT OR GRIEVANCE		ORGANIZATION CODE	DATE INFORMAL GRIEVANCE PRESENTED TO SUPERVISOR

1. SPECIFIC PROVISION OF THE AGREEMENT WHICH IS AN ISSUE IN THE GRIEVANCE:

2. SPECIFIC REASONS SERVING AS THE BASIS FOR THE GRIEVANCE: *(Including how, when, and by whom it is alleged that the provision of the Agreement was misinterpreted or misapplied)*

3. RELIEF OR ADJUSTMENT REQUESTED:

4. NAME ADDRESS AND TELEPHONE NUMBER OF REPRESENTATIVE, IF ANY:

SIGNATURE OF EMPLOYEE	DATE
SIGNATURE OF REPRESENTATIVE, IF ANY _____ SIGNATURE OF UNION OFFICIAL (APPROVING REPRESENTATIVE _____	DATE _____ DATE _____
SIGNATURE OF SUPERVISOR ACKNOWLEDGING RECEIPT OF FORMAL GRIEVANCE	DATE

(USE REVERSE SIDE IF MORE SPACE IS NEEDED.)

JSC FORM 1347

NASA-JSC

CASE STUDIES IN THE NEWS

"Federal Mediators Fail to Revive Talks" read the headlines in an *Associated Press* news release on September 8, 1998. Federal mediators sent both sides in the Northwest Airlines pilots' strike home on Sunday to re-think their positions after "exploratory" talks produced no progress. Negotiators from Northwest and the Airline Pilots Association, the union representing the striking pilots, met separately over the weekend with federal mediators at a suburban Chicago hotel. A statement from the National Mediation Board chairwoman urged both sides to "redouble" their efforts to find common ground before discussions resume in Minneapolis on Tuesday.

Martha Irvine, Associated Press, 1998

What issues do you think might have been involved in the negotiations that would cause such a stalemate?

made by the arbitrator can only be challenged by taking the issue to public court, which is seldom done.

Arbitration can be a costly process. Arbitrators are paid a daily fee for their services plus expenses for travel, lodging, food, and other incidentals during the arbitration process. Most contracts require that this cost be split evenly between the union and management. Today costs can be a key factor in any decision unions make, with the diminishing numbers of members paying union dues. Because of the high costs involved, only grievances on issues of considerable importance are brought to arbitration.

FastChat

1. What is the difference between the steward and the agent?

2. Describe and discuss a grievance situation. Who would win?

3. What are the steps in a typical grievance procedure?

4. What does a mediator do?

5. Why/when would a situation require an arbitrator?

What Is the Status of Unions Today?

Learning
Objective   6

Discuss whether unions are strengthening or weakening in today's work force.

quick wit

* * * * * * * * * *

"*Problems can become opportunities when the right people come together.*"

* * * * * * * * * *

Robert Redford

Changes in America's work force have created special challenges for unions.

Social and legal changes have reduced union popularity.

Over the past few years, manufacturing jobs have moved offshore and overseas to cheaper labor markets, or they have disappeared completely because of advancing technologies. Many industries have and still are downsizing and merging to become more globally competitive. The vast majority of new jobs and businesses in America are in the service industries—an area particularly difficult for unions to recruit. Working America has changed. Unions are struggling to make the transition to the 21st century.

Unions have suffered through 40 years of membership declines, partly from the loss of industrial jobs and partly from general disinterest in or distaste for labor movement antics. The Bureau of Labor Statistics in 1998 revealed that only 13.9 percent of the total work force is affiliated with unions, down from 14.1 percent the preceding year. This erosion of union membership may come as a surprise to casual observers who repeatedly see media coverage of work conditions and business practices unfavorable to employees.

Factors contributing to the overall union membership declines in the past included the onset of social change and government intervention. The Equal Employment Opportunity Commission (EEOC), the Occupational Safety and Health Administration (OSHA), and the Employee Retirement Income Security Act (ERISA) took decisions on hiring, work conditions, and pension fund investing out of the hands of unions and management. Businesses have been forced to face lawyers and government specialists rather than unions on these issues.

Additionally, employer attitudes toward workers generally improved as evidenced by more participative management approaches in company activities. Workers have not felt the need to join unions. Quality circles and increased employee involvement programs have lessened the need for employee representation by union staff members to improve conditions. Clearly the purpose of unions as envisioned in the 1930s does not meet the requirements of our changing work environment.

Over the last 10 to 15 years, unions have had to re-think their tactics for organizing after not doing much active recruiting for several decades. Today unions are making a move into new territories and winning long-sought-after segments of the work force. Unionism in the United States is not dead.

CASE STUDIES IN THE NEWS

An Associated Press story dated 7/26/99 reported that workers in Vance, Alabama, are divided over the issue of whether or not to let the United Auto Workers union try to organize at the Mercedes-Benz assembly plant where they work. Workers were well paid and many saw no reason to have a union. One spokesman reported that management works hard to create a "positive, team-oriented environment," and feels little if anything is to be gained from a union. Pro-union workers disagreed. Though they stated that wages were not an issue because the pay was good, some felt that health issues and overtime could be improved and hoped that a union could make management uniform from department to department. The UAW was hoping to get enough people to sign union cards so that they could bypass a vote.

Based on what you know of the original purpose of unions (to end abuse and exploitation), what does this situation tell you about how unions have changed? Why do you think unions would be pursuing an organization where employees are highly paid, rather than seeking out poorer business where abuses might still occur?

ARE UNIONS WEAKENING?

Whether or not unions are weakening is a highly controversial question. Some labor analysts readily point out examples that support a downward trend in labor unions. Others, however, still feel that the need for unions is strong today, citing the recent surge in union strikes as evidence. Although greater labor-management cooperation has improved work conditions in most places, abuses can still be found.

In the past, unions were often viewed as outdated, costly, and ineffective. When economic downturns force employers to cut costs, wage and benefit increases promoted by unions are often the first things to go. And since unions have historically identified themselves almost entirely as a means to higher wages, these cuts weaken a union's ability to draw membership. Mergers and downsizing activities also render the union ineffective in saving jobs and creating better benefit packages for workers. Although unions recruited nearly 400,000 new members in 1998, overall union membership has declined. Recruiting gains have been outweighed and overshadowed by

San Antonio Squalor

At the Fechheimer uniform factory in San Antonio, workers say that until they started to organize a union, employees had to bring their own toilet paper and drinking water to work with them. Until the company recently moved to a new plant, the seamstresses were greeted each morning by the stench of dead rats and were covered in mosquitoes and other insects as they worked. The dead rats were all over the building including the restrooms. The 85 primarily Hispanic women workers were paid barely minimum wage, and virtually none of the employees had health insurance coverage. When threatened with unionization, company officials began talks of moving the plant to Mexico.

L.M. Sixel, *Houston Chronicle*, September 4, 1998

What should the employees do about this situation? What do you think the reporter who wrote the story should have done about these discoveries? The article states that the bad conditions existed "until the company moved to a new plant." Do you think this means conditions are better now? What other changes might workers still desire?

membership losses caused by layoffs, plant closings, and other factors. As American companies, many of which are now parts of multi-national corporations with management in several countries, have continued to streamline their corporate operations, unions have weakened in some labor sectors.

Unions may need new priorities to attract members.

Weakening trends have been especially noticeable in the private sector, with less than 10 percent of workers belonging to unions. Reluctance and indifference to union organizing efforts have also been experienced among the high-technology and information industry workers, and most home-based entrepreneurs do not feel the need for union representation. Additionally, many companies have broadened their use of participative management approaches and offer increased employee assistance programs, which further reduce the need for union representation.

Union efforts to curtail these declines include cooperating with businesses to improve and expand employee assistance program efforts. Finding new roles in teamwork plants is also helping unions change their image in the new work place. Industrial relations experts point to a new aggressiveness on the part of labor unions with a commitment of union leaders to pump money and manpower into organizing new members. Unions do not want to give up their power. To maintain it, unions may need to work closely with businesses in efforts to improve the country's overall competitive edge and maintain the U.S. market share.

ARE UNIONS STRENGTHENING?

Some labor analysts see several bright spots on the horizon for the strengthening of unions. The two major areas of hope are a perceived resurgence of support by union members and the successful attempts at unionizing new segments of the work force.

The future may hold surprises as unions struggle to recover from declines.

As management gets "leaner and meaner" through mergers, cutbacks, and downsizing, workers are unionizing in self-defense. A typical young man in today's work force actually earns less than his father realized at the same age in his career history (and pays far higher taxes, as well), and the young man's job and future are far less secure. The changing work force is seeking representation for new demands, such as adequate retirement plans, health benefits, federal support for child care, and more flexible work hours to address the needs of families with two working parents. If the unions can aggressively address these issues with employers and make gains, opinions about the worth of union representation could make a major swing.

Of course, since many of these issues now come under government regulation, unions have become more political, supporting candidates and lobbying Congress, rather than meeting with management on a local level. (And disagreement among union members over which candidates are supported with forced dues is another bone of contention in the union debate.)

Additionally, strong union member support for strikes has shown a renewed commitment to union activities. When United Parcel Services (UPS) workers recently combined strike efforts in a show of labor strength, they shut down a large segment of the nation's package and freight deliveries. This strike resulted in some small companies going out of business completely and had a serious impact on others' abilities to supply customer demands for their products. Many businesses were forced to rethink their methods of product delivery and receipt. Similar types of strikes at General Motors, Northwest Airlines, and AT&T have added to the show of strength that unions are perceiving as a positive sign of an upswing on the labor movement. (Of course, the question remains, how are the lost jobs, closed

Transportation strikes can affect many industries that rely on prompt deliveries.

businesses, and lost income ever regained, and how do these losses affect the economy as a whole.)

A relatively strong economy also makes workers want a greater share of the profit pie. Many workers are skeptical about working for companies with growing profits, lavish salaries, huge stock options for executives, and strong hiring and expansion plans but little in the way of wage, pension, and benefit increases for workers. For example, AT&T laid off 40,000 workers when its top executive was getting a $12 million dollar raise. Moves like this by corporate America help increase sympathy for unions in some sectors.

Still more evidence is in the shifting philosophies and strategies of unions to assure a rebirth of membership representation. Union plans are to be dynamic, innovative, and responsive to employee demands for the age-old improvements in work conditions, pay, and benefits. No longer do unions rise out of a core group within an industry, prompted by grievances. Today members are recruited by powerful, nation-wide organizations. New markets for membership are being successfully tapped by union organizers. The AFL-CIO is spending tens of millions of dollars to go after traditional and nontraditional areas. Working women, minorities, federal employees, agriculture workers, and construction workers will all receive the attention of the new labor movement.

Unions are trying to be more responsive to trends and seek membership in new markets.

For example, the AFL-CIO sponsored and coordinated a union summer event to employ 1200 interns across the country to work on organizing and social-justice issues. In 1996, $35 million dollars were spent on political campaigning and $30 million dollars were offered in matching funds to union locals that increased recruiting and membership activities. In 1998 union members were used to work phone banks to urge voters to the polls. An all-out effort is being made to become more visible and to convince the public of the benefits of unionization.

With dramatic changes in the way people work today, other new methods of organizing are being explored. Many people are temporaries, independent contractors, and other types of contingent laborers. In fact, the number of temporary workers has swelled more than fivefold since the mid 1980s. One of the new union efforts may be to create a new type of union hall for this new type of worker.

HIRING HALL MODEL

A union of temporary or independent employees could establish multi-employer relationships with multiple locations needing their services and expertise. The worker would report to the "hiring hall" in the morning, pick up a job/work assignment but remain independent of the employer. This would put the union back in control of the labor force. An analogy would be the old-time longshoremen's hiring hall before the industry was automated. What made them so powerful was the control the union had on that labor force. If a company needed a longshoreman, they could not get one anywhere else but at the hiring hall.

Modernized labor hiring halls may supply certain types of skills as required.

TECHNOLOGY CONNECTION

Unions are becoming increasingly more sophisticated in their approach to gaining new members. Evidence of these methods can be realized by surfing the extensive union sites on the Internet's World Wide Web. Prepared scripts for advertising, newsletter materials, videotapes, cartoons, logos, and up-to-date information spots are all available with the click of the mouse. These efforts provide local groups with polished »and professional advertising that is a draw to membership. To find these sites, use any of the variety of available search engines and enter key words for your particular area of interest—labor unions, AFL-CIO, UAW, union strikes, etc.

This is very similar to how a temporary employment agency operates today. For a significant segment of the short-term or temporary labor force, temporary agencies make contact with businesses and supply workers as needed. Many agencies also provide skills training and provide benefits of some sort. The next generation of labor unions may operate similarly but on a broader scale, acting as both temp agency and professional organization. With continued efforts by organizers to tap these new markets and apply shifts in bargaining strategies, unions could realize a strengthening in membership numbers.

SHOULD YOU JOIN A UNION?

If faced with becoming part of a union, you will need to consider both sides of the issue. Union supporters will tell you that you will have strength in numbers, your work and personal life will improve, and you will gain respect through membership. Office politics will be reduced, and your concerns will be heard, at least by the union. Of course, if it is a union shop, you will not be given a choice.

Opponents will tell you that you will be paying dues for rights you already have. They may point out that unions tend to establish strong work rules, making the workplace rigid and causing relationships between supervisors and workers to deteriorate. They may also note that the international union's highly paid officers control dues and how the money is spent, and that you will not be paid if they call a strike. Finally, it will be noted that the union often makes promises it is unable to deliver.

The decision will be yours alone.

FastChat

1. What changes or issues have contributed to union declines?

2. How would issues like forced dues or the political campaigning of unions affect your interest in joining a union?

3. What might cause you to join a union?

4. Report on or discuss any union activity going on in your home town.

5. Do you know of industries where workers are worse off because of union activities (lost jobs, closed businesses, etc.)?

6. Do you think a hiring hall model could work for you? How do you feel it would benefit you if you were an independent contractor or temporary worker?

Chapter Summary

A union is a group of workers who collectively bargain with employers for improved hours, wages, and working conditions. When unions first developed, they typically represented blue-collar craft and industrial workers. Employee associations represented the white-collar and public sectors.

Prior to the 1930s, working conditions were unfavorable for workers. Unions formed to improve the situation. The Wagner Act of 1935 was the first federal legislation that prohibited management from interfering with union activities. The Taft-Hartley Act was passed restoring some rights to management. The National Labor Relations Board was formed to police labor-management activities and enforce the provisions of federal legislation. The Landrum-Griffin Act, which was passed after fraud and corruption by some union officials was uncovered, required unions to report their financial activities and hold elections for new officers to reduce the risk of corruption in union ranks.

Collective bargaining between labor and management representatives results in a written agreement, known as a contract, which is binding on both parties. Disputes over interpretations of the contract are called grievances and are resolved through a grievance procedure. When a grievance is difficult to resolve, the matter is often taken to a mediator who assists in developing alternative solutions to the disputes. If this attempt is unsuccessful, the grievance is taken to arbitration and an arbitrator makes a ruling that is legally binding on both parties. The key difference between mediation and arbitration is the legal standing of the arbitrator's decision.

Unions have seen significant shifts in membership in recent years and a decline in representation. Labor analysts differ widely in opinion as to whether unions will revive and once again become an effective force in the workplace.

Key Terms

union
strike
employee association
labor agitator
blacklist
yellow-dog contract
lockout
Norris-LaGuardia Act
Wagner Act
National Labor Relations Board (NLRB)
Taft-Hartley Act
closed shop
union shop
agency shop
free rider
checkoff
right-to-work law
bargaining unit
Landrum-Griffin Act
craft union
American Federation of Labor (AFL)
industrial union
Congress of Industrial Organizations (CIO)
AFL-CIO
union steward
business agent
collective bargaining
contract
grievance
grievance procedure
mediation
mediator
Federal Mediation and Conciliation Service
arbitration
arbitrator

Review Questions

1. Discuss the differences between unions and employee associations.
2. What were some of the methods used by management to prevent unions from forming prior to the passage of the Wagner Act?
3. What are the three key federal acts that still govern labor-management activities?
4. Identify the sequence of steps in a grievance procedure.
5. What is the key difference between mediation and arbitration?
6. Discuss whether unions are growing stronger or weakening today.

Reading, reasoning, participating as a member of a team and contributing to group effort. Acquiring and evaluating information then interpreting and communicating information. Thinking creatively and visualizing result.

Discussion Questions

1. If your current work unit were voting for union representation, would you vote for or against it? Why?
2. If your current work is not union, have you noticed any effort on the part of your management to avoid unionization? What methods are being used and by whom?
3. Think of the hours, wages, and working conditions in your current place of employment. Which of them do you think would be worth negotiating for improvement?
4. Would you be willing to be a union steward? Why or why not?
5. Do you think unions have a positive image in your community? Why or why not?
6. Do you think that unions in your region are strengthening or weakening? Why?

Chapter Project

From materials found on various Internet sites about unions (for or against), prepare a brief "Union Newsletter" for your fellow employees. The newsletter should display creativity and originality in its formation. You may start by using any of the variety of search engines described in Chapter 1 and using such key words as *union*, or *right to work*, or even more specific key wording such as *union graphics*, depending upon the focus of your search. This project may be done individually or in small groups.

Applications

Individually or in small groups analyze the following situations.

The Master Mechanic

Pam was a member in good standing of the locally strong mechanics' union and had always been a good worker for the company. The union contract defined specific disciplinary actions for repeated or excessive absences from the job. The shop was small, and one person's absence caused work stoppages that crippled the work flow and created delays in finished products.

Pam's supervisor noticed a drastic change in her attendance over a recent two-week period. Almost every other day she was either late or absent. The supervisor began immediate disciplinary procedures according to the contract terms and conditions.

When he confronted Pam with his plans, she reacted in a hostile manner. "That's certainly not the way I read that part of the contract. How in the world could you be so unfair to me? You let Bill take off whenever he needs to. What's the difference here? I'm not going to take this lying down! You'll be hearing from my union steward!"

1. From the behaviors described, do you think that Pam will be willing to resolve this dispute informally? Why or why not?
2. Did Pam's supervisor respond appropriately to the situation? Should the situation have been handled differently?
3. What will the union steward do as his first steps of involvement in the process?

Reading, listening, interpreting and communicating information, participating as a member of a team and contributing to group effort, and understanding human systems.

The Banana's Really Ripe

Horace Lynch had seen his banana import/export company triple in size in just the five short years since he started the company. He had moved into the new warehouse location only a couple of years ago. Sure, he had been forced to cut some corners to afford the new place, and unfortunately he had not been able to give his employees a raise these past two years, but they did not really seem to mind. Frankly, they seldom mentioned it at all. He had also had to raise the air conditioning temperature by several degrees to reduce the electrical bills that were a real drain on his operating budget. Hardly any of the employees had mentioned much about it, and he had joked it off by suggesting they wear cooler clothes.

The only other action he had taken to be able to afford the move to the larger warehouse had to do with some of the unfair safety rules that the government agent had tried to force on him. Why did he have to provide

Reading, reasoning, participating as a member of a team and contributing to group effort, exercising leadership, and understanding complex interrelationships.

safety glasses for all his machinists when they had hardly ever had a serious accident? And the very idea that he should hang fire extinguishers near all possible flammable locations! Why couldn't the workers just call the fire department if something like that should happen? Horace had felt so strongly about these silly rules that he had made very clear to all his employees what would happen if they squawked about the possible safety hazards.

"If you don't like the conditions here, you can always go somewhere else. And if you complain to that government guy, I'll fire you on the spot and see to it that you are never hired in this line of work again!"

1. Is Horace in danger of his workers desiring union representation?
2. If the workers did gain union representation, what conditions ripe for improvement would be taken to the bargaining table?
3. If you were one of Horace's employees, how would you handle this situation?

Additional Readings and Resources

http://www.nilrr.org—National Institute for Labor Relations Research

http://www.nrtw.org—National Right to Work Foundation (non-profit organization; provides information to the public and free legal aid to employees whose human and civil rights have been violated by compulsory unionism abuses)

http://www.afl-cio.org Web site of the American Federation of Labor-Congress of Industrial Organizations (AFL-CIO)—provides current news about the AFL-CIO union.

http://www.sabra@nytimes.com—writer for the labor column for the *New York Times.*

http://www.UAW.com—provides current news about the United Auto Workers union.

Barrett, Katherine, "Kathie Lee Brings Attention to Sweatshops." CNNfn.COM May 31,1996.

www.snc.edu/socsci/chair/336/dave/.htm, "Current State of Labor Unions and Political Aspects of the NLRB."

http://www.unionist.com—provides variety of union news and information.

http://www.igc.org/igc/labornet—provides recent union news and information.

Communication:
The Essential Skill

focus

The increasing use of e-mail, voice mail, and faxes permits communication to occur more quickly and more frequently. However, that speed and frequency may mean less thought is put into the tone and meaning of messages, leading to potential problems in human relations and communication. Concern over these potential problems, as well as over problems that have already cropped up, has resulted in the creation of numerous instructional materials, in print and on the Internet, designed to assist people in "coping at work." In one such set of guidelines on the Internet, author Cheryl M. Hagen suggests that both the sender and the receiver have a responsibility to head off miscommunication and ill will, both electronically and in person.

What do you think are some of the potential human relations and communications problems that might result from reliance on e-mail, voice mail, and faxes? What advantage might face-to-face communication have over electronic communication?

objectives

After studying this chapter, you should be able to:

1. *Define communication and explain its role in human relations.*

2. *Discuss the communication process and the importance of feedback.*

3. *Identify barriers to communication and learn how listening skills can be improved.*

4. *List ways to improve your spoken communication.*

5. *Identify the qualities of strong written communication.*

6. *Discuss forms of nonverbal communication and why it is important.*

7. *Explain the importance of time, timing, context, and medium of a message.*

8. *Discuss two common forms of electronic communication.*

In This Chapter

What Is Communication and What Is Its Role in Human Relations?

Communication is the process by which we exchange information through a common system of symbols, signs, or behavior.

Communication is the process by which we exchange information through a common system of symbols, signs, or behavior. This process sends messages from one person to another. Symbols can be written or spoken words; signs can be shapes and colors; and behavior can be any nonverbal communication, such as body movements or facial expressions.

Listening, speaking, writing, and reading are the four basic skills that we use in communicating. Of these skills, the first two are the most frequently used, but unfortunately, they are the two in which we receive the least training. However, any communication skill can be sharpened, either through experience (which can sometimes be a tough teacher) or through training.

WHY IS COMMUNICATION IMPORTANT?

We are rapidly becoming an information society. Every technological advance seems to bring us into contact with more people. We communicate by phone, letter, e-mail, and in person with people at home, at work, and everywhere in between. We spend 70 to 80 percent of our waking hours communicating in one way or another—10 to 11 hours of each day. Strong communication skills are becoming an asset in all aspects of life.

Communication is the most important element of human relations. Being able to interact effectively with people around you at work will enhance your work experience—and theirs. The more sensitive and knowledgeable you are about communication, the stronger your human relations skills will be.

Quick Tip . . . .

Doris Lee McCoy in the book *Megatraits* identified good communication skills as being one of the traits possessed by great leaders that helped them obtain positions of power and recognition. Great leaders who did not already have effective communication skills made an effort to develop them. McCoy notes that creating good ideas is not enough. We must know how to explain our ideas to other people.

. . . .

Examples of the role communication plays in effective human relations are shown below:

Effective Human Relations

Away from Work	At Work
1. The wife who explains to her husband that she is bothered by the clothes he leaves lying on the floor and offers alternatives rather than yelling at him.	1. The employee who asks the boss for clarification of a written work order rather than do a job incorrectly and cause a problem.
2. The father who asks his child about a broken lamp and gives the child a chance to explain rather than yelling, blaming, and punishing immediately.	2. The boss who calls employees together to discuss a major company change rather than letting them hear it as gossip or sending it in a memo.
3. The neighbor who calls and asks nicely that the stereo be turned down the first time that it is bothersome rather than immediately calling the police.	3. The employee who waits for the "right time" to ask the boss for a change in schedule, not when the boss has just arrived late after being snarled in a traffic jam.

*Fast*Chat

1. What is communication? Why is effective communication so important?

2. Which of the four basic communication skills do you use and enjoy the most? Why?

3. What have you seen in the movies or on TV that you consider to be effective communication? What made it effective?

What Is the Communication Process and Why Is Feedback Important?

Learning
Objective 2

Discuss the communication process and the importance of feedback.

COMMUNICATION FLOW

As discussed in Chapter 5, in any organization communication will flow upward, downward, or horizontally (sideways). In each instance, the communication process includes three elements: the **sender,** who transmits (sends) the message; the **receiver,** to whom the message is sent; and the **message,** the content of the communication, which may be verbal (either spoken or written), such as questions and responses, or nonverbal, such as nodding, smiling, or frowning. In addition, communication can be one-way (such as a speech or bulletin) or two-way (such as a conversation or correspondence).

To be effective, a message must be understood by the receiver. Whether you are the sender or the receiver, you are responsible for determining that the correct message has been received. This is accomplished by using a process known as feedback.

Communication flows upward, downward, or horizontally in an organization.

Feedback is information given back to a sender that evaluates the message and states what the receiver understood. Because of the role feedback

ETHICS CONNECTION

The rise of telecommunicating coupled with the prevalence of cell phones is presenting ethical dilemmas for individuals and organizations. Is it OK to take unreported time off but use your cell phone to check your voice mail frequently so your boss and coworkers think you're working at home?

According to the September 1999 issue of *Home Office Computing*, whether this is good or bad depends on what your boss wants and how your productivity is measured.

What do you think about this behavior?

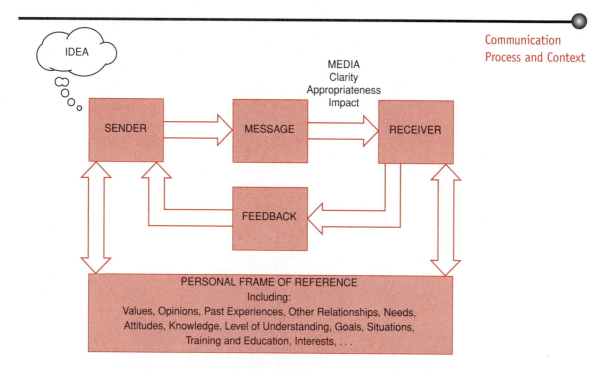

plays in clarifying communication, verifying understanding, and overcoming communication barriers (distortions and blockages), it is an extremely important part of the communication process. To be effective, feedback should be timely, often, and precise *(TOP)*.

Sender, receiver, and message are the three elements of the communication process.

COMMUNICATION PROCESS

The figure depicts the communication process and the relationship of feedback to the sender and the receiver.

The Importance of Feedback

Effective feedback can improve communication, save time, and reduce the possibility of errors and human relations problems. In face-to-face communication feedback can be fast, with both the listener and speaker continuously giving feedback to each other verbally and nonverbally. Examples of ways in which we do that include frowns, nods, verbal expressions of agreement or disagreement, questions, statements, and silence. (Silence can be a surprisingly powerful form of feedback, communicating power, uncertainty, agreement, or disapproval.)

As the sender of messages, you will want feedback from the person or persons for whom your messages are intended to help you determine whether your message has been received and interpreted correctly. Some possible ways for obtaining feedback are shown on the next page.

Feedback should be timely, often, and precise (TOP).

Ways of Obtaining Feedback

When Face to Face with the Receiver

1. Ask questions that determine whether the receiver has understood.

2. Ask the receiver to restate what you have said.

3. Watch for signs for understanding (such as nods) or confusion (such as frowns).

When Not Face to Face with the Receiver

1. If you have sent a memo or letter, request either a written answer to the memo or a written estimate of when the answer will be available.

2. If a written or oral answer is not received, follow up and check for compliance. (Repeat your request or see whether the action you requested has been taken.)

Ask questions and watch for signs of understanding to be sure your receiver has understood your message.

FastChat

1. How can you make sure that feedback occurs?

2. How does your frame of reference differ from that of your parents, peers, neighbors, teachers, or others? Why does it differ?

Human Relations

What are Barriers in Communication and How Can Listening Skills Be Improved?

9.3

Learning
Objective 3

Identify barriers to communication and learn how listening skills can be improved.

BARRIERS

Miscommunication can create serious problems in our personal lives and at work. Communications experts have identified a number of factors that can cause distortions and blocks in communication. Some of them lie in our senses, in word meanings, and in the emotions and attitudes of the sender and receiver. Others are role expectations, personality, appearance, prejudice, changes, poor organization of ideas, poor listening, and information overload. The chart on the next two pages describes some of the barriers to communication and how they can be overcome.

Listening

One of the most important elements—perhaps the most important—in strong human relations skills is the ability to listen. A study at Ohio State University found that 9 percent of our time is spent writing, 16 percent reading, 30 percent speaking, and a full 45 percent listening—yet listening is the least taught communication skill. Listening is vital at all levels of activity, but becomes more important as we move up in an organization. Authorities have identified seven barriers to listening:

Listening Barriers

1. Lack of interest in the subject or the speaker.
2. Outside noises, distractions, or fatigue.
3. Limited vocabulary of the sender or receiver or both.
4. Poor delivery of the message.
5. Thinking ahead to our responses or back to what the speaker said earlier; turning attention to other matters. (We speak at about 125–150 words per minute, but listen at 400–700 words per minute, so we usually listen in spurts, paying attention only about 60 seconds at a time.)
6. Lack of knowledge in the speaker or listener.
7. Prejudices; listening for what we want to hear.

Barriers in Communication

Barrier	Possible Problem	Potential Solution
1. Sensory organs	1. Poor eyesight or hearing can cause us to misunderstand or misinterpret. Or other noises or sights might distract, so full attention is not given to sending or receiving a message.	1. Periodic checkups can detect vision or hearing problems that hinder communication. If distracted, try to reduce the number of sights and sounds around you.
2. **Semantics** (study of meanings and changing meanings of words)	2. Words may have multiple meanings which can cause difficulty. The more abstract a term, the less likely people are to agree on meaning. Also, words change meaning, and new words are introduced.	2. Use feedback to ensure correct interpretation. Ask questions, such as "Do you mean . . .?"
3. Emotions	3. Our emotions can cause us to overreact to a message or prevent us from hearing all of it. Attitudes can cause us to have preconceived ideas that affect how we interpret what we hear.	3. Calm down before you send or receive messages. Have an open mind and withhold judgment until you have adequate information to evaluate the message.
4. Role expectations (how we expect ourselves and others to act on the basis of the roles played)	4. We may identify others too closely with their roles and discount what they say. Or we may not allow others to change their roles (such as a coworker who becomes a supervisor or a family member who has grown in maturity). People in positions of power may act superior to others or misuse their power.	4. Try to separate people from the roles they are playing, and recognize that roles change. Also, be sensitive to the effect that power may have on perception—especially if you are in a position of power. (For example, ask for compliance rather than making demands.)
5. Personality and appearance	5. Some messages are rejected because the personality or appearance of the sender is inappropriate (such as wearing ragged clothes on a job interview) or if the message itself is messy and full of errors.	5. Strive to make your behavior and appearance appropriate to the roles you play. Also, your correspondence should reflect the image you wish to present.

Human Relations

Barriers in Communication (continued)

Barrier	Possible Problem	Potential Solution
6. Prejudice	6. Sometimes, our opinions regarding the sender's race, religion, color, sex, national origin, age, or disability can alter our perception of the message. For example, someone might think a person "too old" to be creative.	6. Recognize the contribution different people can make. Try to evaluate communication on the basis of the message itself, not on preconceived ideas about the sender.
7. Changes	7. Failure to recognize changes can cause confusion and make more communication difficult. Sometimes we are so close to objects or people we don't notice changes. Other times changes occur too quickly, causing fear or mistrust.	7. Try to recognize that people, objects, and situations can change and interpret communication in that light.
8. Poor organization of ideas	8. We may present ideas (spoken or written) in such a disorderly fashion that listeners or readers find following difficult and lose interest. Also, credibility is lost when ideas are poorly organized.	8. Organize and revise correspondence and presentations so that they are clear and logical. If organization is a problem for you, consider classes or workshops in written and oral communications.
9. **Information overload** (More messages and stimuli coming at us than we can process successfully.)	9. Due to our busy society, increased communication, and hectic pace of life, too many messages and stimuli come at us at one time. When we become overloaded with information, we lose the ability to continue processing and remembering information, fail to listen carefully, and forget information. The result is a breakdown in communication.	9. Develop coping strategies for dealing with information, such as making notes and grouping activities (telephone calls, e-mail). Recognize overload, then work to relax, reduce noise, and focus. Getting enough rest and eating healthily are important, and delegating, saying no, getting an answering machine, and doing work before it builds up also help.
10. Poor listening	10. Most of us listen effectively to only about 25 percent of what we hear.	10. To listen effectively, determine what the speaker is saying and consider the speaker's emotions about the message.

To prevent the common difficulties and damaged relations caused by poor listening, we must want to improve and must engage in active listening. **Active listening** is a conscious effort to listen to both the verbal and nonverbal components of what someone is saying, without prejudging. Here are some steps to help you improve your listening skills.

How To Improve Listening Skills

1. Don't anticipate or plan rebuttals. Don't jump to conclusions. Keep your thoughts in the present.
2. Avoid prejudging the speaker. Be aware of your biases and prejudices.
3. Eliminate distractions by providing a quiet, private location for communication. Face the person speaking to you so that you can concentrate.
4. Ask for clarifications, restate important points by paraphrasing the speaker. Ask questions that make the other person go deeper, such as who, what, when, and where. (However, you should avoid the use of the word *why*. This word puts some people on the defensive.) Remain neutral and restate the person's viewpoint. Put the person's feelings into words.
5. Be ready to give feedback.
6. "Listen" to the nonverbal communication. It is through nonverbal communication that we can pick up the emotional message.
7. Avoid unnecessary note-taking. (Some may be necessary, as we forget one-third to one-half of what we hear within eight hours—but don't focus on your notes and risk missing what is being said.)
8. Listen for major ideas; don't try to remember everything.
9. Don't fake attention; it takes too much work and is distracting. (It's hard to disguise feigned interest.)

FastChat

1. Discuss barriers in communication that you may have observed or experienced. How might these barriers have been minimized?

2. Give examples from your own experience of when listening was blocked. What can be done to avoid the problem in the future?

How Can You Improve Your Spoken Communication?

9.4

Verbal communication is any message that we send or receive through the use of words, oral or written. Effective verbal communication requires good listening skills and an ability to use the written and spoken word. Vital aspects of spoken communication are outlined below.

Learning
Objective 4

List ways to improve your spoken communication.

Aspects of Spoken Communication	
Voice	Our voices should be pleasant and appropriate for the situation. Be aware of surroundings, and match tone and volume to situation. To learn how you sound to others, you may want to try recording yourself.
Word Choice	Correct grammar is important. We should develop an ability to use descriptive, specific verbs, adverbs, and adjectives. Slang should be used sparingly and carefully, so as not to confuse listeners.
"I" Phrases	Beginning communication with "I think," "I believe," "I feel," or "I don't understand" is much more effective than comments such as "You made me angry," or "You are wrong," or "You are confusing me," which can make people defensive.
Following Up	Follow up verbal directives or complex instructions in writing. Research has shown that immediately following a ten-minute lecture, college freshmen retain only 50 percent of it and forget half of that within 48 hours. Additionally, about 30 percent of a message is lost or distorted after passing through two people.
Willingness to Speak Up	Don't worry excessively about what others will think. The insight you offer may help others. Also, your participation may be encouraging to others. Ask precise questions, to show that you are paying attention and want to contribute.
Choosing the Right Level	We communicate on many levels, and need to pick the right level for the situation or relationship: conventional with strangers or casual acquaintances; exploratory when the communication is about facts or other people; participative when we start talking about ourselves, expressing ideas and feelings; and intimacy, the deepest level of communication, when we expose our intimate thoughts and feelings.
Keeping a Secret	Know when not to speak. Being discreet is extremely important in human relations. The importance of confidentiality in our work and personal relationships cannot be overemphasized.

In addition to working on the mechanics of good spoken communication (from grammar to voice control), we should remember other keys to good communication as shown here.

Suggestions for Improving Spoken Communication

1. Listen to the message in the words and the feelings.
2. Don't let your own ideas get in the way. Listen to what others are saying.
3. Know when to *just* listen. Sometimes one person may withdraw, and you will need to be patient and supportive and just wait.
4. Question assumptions. Appearances can be deceiving. Keep in mind that you are communicating with another distinctly individual human being who feels the need to like and be liked.
5. Tell the truth. You might never consider telling a "serious" or big lie, but even small white lies such as "I like it" (if untrue) or "I'll get back to you soon" (when you won't) can create hurt, confusion, and resentment.
6. Think before speaking. Ask yourself, "What do I want to communicate." The key to communication is truly understanding what must be communicated.
7. Now is the best time to get it correct. "I should have said" will never be enough.

ETHICS CONNECTION

When is it ethical to be a name dropper in your communication? When you are wooing a new client, *Success* magazine (January 1999) suggests that you learn the secretary's name. This helps develop a relationship with your clients' assistants and you can also drop the secretary's name into correspondence as a means of introduction.

How does this advice differ from what most people try to do when name dropping? Why might the wrong sort of name dropping backfire?

GLOBAL CONNECTION

As businesses become ever more global, more and more people are traveling extensively in their work. They are relying on technology to keep them connected. In one period alone, between January and August 1998, the number of PCs connected to the Internet in the U.S. increased by 35 percent, from 45 million to more than 60 million.

Some people are beginning to question the need to log on to e-mail at airports, from pay phones, from kiosks, etc. Are we attempting to stay connected simply because we can? Surely we are being weighed down by technology, and travel is becoming more complicated and stressful.

An article by Jeffrey L. Seglin, *Inc. Tech* 1999, No. 1, suggests that we rid ourselves of what we don't need, limit the number of times we check e-mail, and stay in touch by cell phone.

1. *What do you think about this advice?*

2. *Why do you think e-mail communication is gaining in use?*

FastChat

1. Reviewing the aspects of spoken communication, in which areas are your skills strongest? Explain.

2. Did any of the suggestions for improving communication surprise you? Which ones?

3. Think of a situation where having known this information might have made communication better. What happened, and how might you have improved it?

9.5 How Can You Improve Your Written Communication?

Learning
O b j e c t i v e   5

Identify the qualities of strong written communication.

The purpose of writing, like speech, is to communicate, not impress.

Good writing skills are essential to career success. Writing, the most durable form of communication, is used frequently, particularly at higher levels of an organization. The purpose of writing, like speech, is to communicate, not impress. Inexperienced writers sometimes think that they must change their personalities completely and write in a showy, unnatural manner. This is neither necessary nor desirable. Every written communication creates a mental image of the sender. Will your writing style cause you to be viewed as pompous and wordy, as disorganized and possibly unreliable, or as an intelligent, clear thinker with a sense of purpose? Here are some suggestions to help you make your writing a positive reflection of you.

Follow the KISS rule in writing: Keep it short and simple.

Suggestions for Improving Written Communication

What	How
1. Sentence length	1. Your average sentence length should be 17 words. (Means exist for analyzing the reading level of your writing, including several common word processing programs.)
2. Wordiness	2. Avoid thinking aloud on paper. Follow the KISS rule: "Keep It Short and Simple."
3. Organization	3. Think about what you want to communicate and the logical progression. Outlining and creating a rough draft can help you.
4. Appropriate style or tone for the intended audience	4. Know when writing should be formal and when informal writing would be effective.
5. Clearly stated purpose	5. Ask yourself, "Why am I writing this message" and then tell the reader.

GET TO THE POINT!

"Things are just horrible, but I don't know what I should do.
I have to decide is if I can go on like this, and if I can't go on,
should I end it all. I just don't know."
Shakespeare, Hamlet, Act II, Scene 1
Rough draft

"To be, or not to be,
that is the question . . ."
Final draft

In writing, you should follow the **4 C's of communication**: Writing should be complete, concise, correct, and conversational or clear. After you have written a memo or letter, check it against the suggestions given below.

Checklist for Written Communication

Criterion	Questions to Ask
1. Complete	1. Have I included all necessary facts and answered all questions?
2. Concise	2. Have I deleted unnecessarily long words? Is my message one page or less? Are my paragraphs short and easy? Is important information obvious?
3. Correct	3. Is my message accurate? Does it agree with company policy? Are the grammar, spelling and punctuation correct? Are corrections neat?
4. Clear	4. Is my writing easy to understand and friendly without being flowery? Have I avoided argumentative words or expressions?

Quick Tip . . . .

Human Relations Practices in Writing

1. Do not say anything in writing that you would not say in public.
2. Do not expect a written message to remain confidential.
3. Do not exaggerate.
4. Never criticize coworkers.
5. Wait 24 hours before sending anything written in anger.
6. Be courteous, brief, and specific.
7. At work follow the chain of command.

Working Woman, 1989

FastChat

1. Have you ever received a written message that was so badly written that you had difficulty understanding it? How might it have been improved?

2. How would you describe your own writing style? Which of the suggestions in this section do you think will help you improve your ability to communicate effectively in writing?

How Can You Use Nonverbal Communication?

Nonverbal communication—communication without words—has been mentioned several times in this chapter. **Nonverbal communication** is any meaning conveyed through body language, through the way the voice is used, and through the way people position themselves in relation to others. How something is said is frequently just as important as what is said. Tone of voice, facial expression, gestures, or haste may determine how we interpret the words used and may even overshadow them.

People with strong human relations skills are usually good at reading others' body language and in using nonverbal communication. Dr. Albert Mehrabian, an expert in nonverbal communication, says that nonverbal communication accounts for at least 93 percent of the impact of our communication and words only 7 percent. That 93 percent is made up of pace, pitch, and tone of voice (38 percent) and facial expressions (55 percent).

Understanding nonverbal communication is important, because people often show their feelings and attitudes by their actions rather than their words. When we appreciate others' thoughts and feelings, we can interact more effectively with them.

Learning
Objective 6

Discuss forms of nonverbal communication and why it is important.

Recognizing nonverbal communication is an important human relations skill.

Examples of Nonverbal Communication

Behavior at Work	Possible Message
1. The computer operator who averts her head or turns her body away when the supervisor leans over to explain a graph.	1. May mean she is uncomfortable with the closeness.
2. The employee who in a meeting rambles on in long, involved, unfinished sentences.	2. He may feel insecure.
3. The employee who engages in much unnecessary body, hand, or foot movement.	3. Can signal tension.
4. The employee who sits at the head of the conference table and participates.	4. May be signaling confidence and interest. (Environment, location, and seating can influence the kind of interaction that occurs.

Examples of Nonverbal Communication (continued)

Behavior Away from Work	Possible Message
1. The mother who puts her hands on her hips and looks sternly at her young daughter.	1. Wants the child to understand that she had better do as she is told.
2. The father who smiles as he tells his son that he is disappointed the boy left the house last night without permission.	2. A mixed message, with his words saying one thing and his body language saying another. When such a split occurs, we tend to believe the nonverbal communication. The message that the son will perceive is approval.

Some common means of communicating nonverbally are shown here. Be aware of them in yourself to make sure that you are conveying the message you wish to send. Noticing them in others will enhance your communication skills.

Common Means of Communicating Nonverbally

Nonverbal Transmitters	Examples
1. Posture while sitting and standing	1. A woman who sits in a chair with her legs wrapped around the chair legs, holding her head rigidly to one side, clasping her hands tightly or holding a clenched fist, is tense. Another tense person may be the man wandering about the room or continually moving his hands and feet, or twisting his head from side to side. Individuals in high-status positions usually display their status through relaxed positions, such a one arm in their laps and the other across the back of a chair; they keep their heads level and face forward. Those in lower-status positions keep their heads down and hands together or at their sides.
2. Facial expressions (must be considered in the total context of what is being said; some people do not show emotions on their faces)	2. Happiness, anger, surprise, disgust, and fear are displayed most often through facial expressions, particularly through the eyes and lower face. Smiling can detract from a serious message. (Women tend to smile more than men, which can create misunderstandings for them at work and in their personal relationships.)

Human Relations

Common Means of Communicating Nonverbally (continued)

Nonverbal Transmitters	Examples
3. Eye contact (direct and powerful form of nonverbal communication)	3. We generally use eye contact to signal a desire for communication, as when we try to make eye contact with a waiter in a restaurant. When we wish to avoid talking to someone, we look away and avoid eye contact as when our instructor asks a question we cannot answer or when we approach someone in the hall. A failure to make eye contact can indicate embarrassment, fear, or dishonesty.
4. Voice (pitch, clarity, breathiness, articulation, resonance, tempo, rhythm, and speech rate)	4. The voice can often tell us something about a speaker. For example, when people feel comfortable or secure, their voices tend to sound smooth and well modulated and their sentences are normal. A loud voice, fast rate of speech, and high pitch may express active emotions; while sadness, disgust, or boredom may be indicated by a quiet voice, low pitch, and slow rate of speech. A fast but not excessive rate is more persuasive and is viewed as more trustworthy and enthusiastic.
5. Body movements	5. Hand, arm, and body movements can reveal openness, suspicion, honesty, confidence, nervousness, or defensiveness.
6. Personal space (an invisible bubble around us, the size of which varies from culture to culture) Effective human relations skills demand that we respect others' personal space.	6. In general, people in the United States tend to have larger bubbles that people in other cultures. We will permit a smaller personal space when situations are comfortable or nonthreatening or we feel close psychologically. When our personal space is violated, we may react with embarrassment or move away to create distance. Common reactions to intrusions include turning our heads, placing an elbow between ourselves and the intruder, ignoring the intruder, or leaving the area.
7. Seating	7. High-status, dominant individuals tend to sit in the head table position and participate more than those who sit along the side. Conflict is more between people sitting across from each other than between people sitting next to each other.

The meanings of many movements are detailed on the next page. However, no clue should be considered in isolation. Always look for what other nonverbal transmitters may be saying and take all in the context of what is happening or being said.

Nonverbal Communication Clues

Clue	Possible Meanings or Interpretations
1. Shaking hands	Limp hand—person may be ill at ease or doesn't like to be touched. Firm handshake—confidence
2. Arms crossed on chest	Defensiveness or disagreement
3. Closed fists	Defensiveness or nervousness
4. Sitting with a leg over the arm of a chair	Defensiveness or indifference
5. Crossed legs	Defensiveness
6. Moving of the crossed leg in a slight kicking motion, drumming on table, tapping with feet, head in hand, or doodling	Boredom or impatience
7. Open hand with palms upward	Openness
8. Men unbuttoning their suit coats, and even taking them off	Openness, friendliness, or agreement
9. Hand to cheek gestures	Evaluation
10. Hand over heart, palms uplifted, looking the person in the eye when speaking, or touching gesture	Honesty
11. Short breaths, "tsking" sound, tightly clenched hands, wringing hands, or kicking the ground or an imaginary object	Frustration
12. Steepling (fingertips brought together), hands joined together behind the body, feet up on the desk, elevating oneself, or leaning back in a seated position with both hands supporting the head	Confidence
13. Clearing throat, "whewing" sound, whistling, smoking cigarettes, fidgeting in a chair, tugging at clothes while sitting, jiggling money in pockets, clenched fist, wringing hands, playing with pencils, notebooks, or eyeglasses	Nervousness
14. Avoiding eye contact, touching or rubbing the nose, or rubbing behind or beside the ear with the index finger when weighing an answer	Suspicion, secretiveness, or doubt

The National Institute of Business Management suggests that you can make your nonverbal communication work for you by the following means. Following these suggestions will make you a richer communicator.

Desired Result	How To Accomplish the Desired Result
1. Act confident.	1. Look people in the eye, stand straight, move quickly and with determination, speak loudly (within reason) and distinctly, and avoid nervous gestures.
2. Look efficient.	2. Dress well and keep a neat but not sterile office.
3. Get people to open up to you.	3. Lean forward when listening, look people in the eye, sit with arms and legs uncrossed, and nod occasionally. Smile, have a relaxed posture and movements, and shake hands in a firm but not overpowering way. Mirror the other person's posture or match the voice tempo of the other person to build rapport.
4. Be more effective on the telephone.	4. Explain the purpose of your call and indicate how long it will be. End calls gracefully, summarizing key points and thanking the other person, using a rising, upbeat tone of voice. Vary your tone, loudness, and speed. Using natural gestures, especially smiling, can help make your voice sound more natural and expressive.
5. Improve your speeches and presentations.	5. Be prepared. Practice in front of a mirror. Choose appropriate visuals, examples, anecdotes, and analogies. Keep your message short and simple. Look confident and calm, and your voice will relax. During the first half minute of your presentation, smile, walk confidently to the podium or front, establish eye contact by scanning the group, and say thank you to your introducer and audience. Begin with a humorous or light remark or just a friendly "Hello, how are you today?" to encourage the audience to participate, which takes the pressure off you.
	Vary your distances from sections of the audience to stop their talking or to get them to participate. Lean forward when asked a question and look at all people in the group. Draw in nonattentive or nonresponsive people by looking at them or asking them a question.
6. Appear more credible.	6. Avoid self-deprecating words or expressions such as "This may be a dumb idea" or tag questions such as "Don't you think?" Do not use expressions that hedge, such as "sort of" or "kind of" or excessive superlatives like "really, really great." Have notes to build confidence and add security in case you lose your train of thought. Be prepared with short answers if asked negative questions.

Quick Wit ·

"This 'telephone' has too many shortcomings to be seriously considered as a means of communication. The device is inherently of no value to us."

—Western Union internal memo, 1876.

"The wireless music box has no imaginable commercial value. Who would pay for a message sent to nobody in particular?"

—David Sarnoff's associates in response to his urgings for investment in the radio in the 1920s.

Where do you think communication technology is headed in the next 20 years?

· ·

When using nonverbal communication, certain cautions must be kept in mind:

1. Nonverbal communication must be considered in conjunction with the verbal message and the situation. If you try to interpret meaning from an isolated nonverbal cue, you may be wrong.
2. Nonverbal communication such as closeness or touching may be misinterpreted at work and may lead to charges of sexual harassment. Even an innocent pat on the back or hand on the arm can be mistaken for sexual interest. These gestures should be avoided in the workplace.
3. Recognize that nonverbal communication varies from culture to culture and that individuals from other cultures cannot be accurately assessed using the cues presented in this chapter.

1. What are some familiar nonverbal messages that you have seen?

2. Think of instances when you felt your personal space was being invaded. What did you do? Have you ever been made aware of having invaded someone else's bubble? What did the other person do?

*Fast*Chat

Several other factors can make a difference in the success or failure of your communication:

Time—The way you use time is important. Frequent tardiness will make you be viewed as disorganized and disrespectful. Using tardiness as a manipulative ploy to put yourself in a higher-status position will simply cause frustration and anger and will cost you respect. At work, tardiness may result in your being disciplined or even fired. Developing the habit of punctuality can enhance your human relations skills and professional image.

Timing—If you are to be effective in your communication, you must remember that at times everyone needs to be left alone or at least have fewer interruptions. Your supervisors may be tired, preoccupied, rushed, angry, or frustrated. If you force them to talk with you at those times, you should not be surprised or hurt if they seem disinterested.

Most employees feel that they do not have enough communication with their supervisors. Supervisors will not necessarily ask for communication, so you must use your own judgment in determining what to tell them and when. You should definitely keep your supervisor informed about matters for which your supervisor is held accountable and about upcoming proposals from you.

Context—**Context** refers to the conditions in which something occurs, which can throw light on its meaning. Being yelled at to "stop that machine" creates a different response if we are about to be injured than if we are in trouble or our boss is having a bad day. Hence, the context of a message must be considered along with its verbal and nonverbal components for accurate understanding.

Medium—The **medium** is the form in which a message is communicated. If you receive a registered letter from an attorney, it may create more anxiety than one through regular mail.

Humor—A healthy sense of humor can create a favorable long-term impression. People usually like people with whom they can share a laugh. However, most people are offended by distasteful jokes and lose respect for someone who is constantly clowning around.

A sense of humor can also help you get over some of the rough spots in life. Putting matters in proper perspective and not taking yourself too seriously becomes easier to accomplish. Some health experts have even suggested that humor can make us physically healthier and better problem solvers. Common sense must be your guide. When does humor become silly, sick, inappropriate, or counterproductive? When does it save the day?

Many factors can make a difference in the success or failure of your communication.

"How can I listen to you if you don't say the things I want to hear?"

FastChat

1. Can you think of a situation in which a message you received had a different emotional impact simply because of one of the factors in this section? Explain.

2. Can you think of a time when humor would have helped a situation? When it hurt a situation?

9.8 Electronic Communication

Learning
Objective 9

*Discuss two
common forms of
electronic
communication.*

Throughout this text you are confronted with the impact that technology is having on communication. An article in *U.S. News and World Report* (December 18, 1998) pointed out that, while innovation has always been a powerful force in American culture, what's dazzling today is the swift pace of recent innovations. A decade ago e-mail was exotic. Today it is so commonplace that when the Tom Hanks-Meg Ryan movie, *You've Got Mail*, was released, everyone understood the meaning. Shopping on the Internet increases daily. The result is that e-mail has become a common form of electronic communication.

Electronic communication allows data to be communicated by computers and other technology from one sender to one or more receivers. If you are not already using electronic communication, it's likely that you will be before too long—in both your personal and professional life—with e-mail and voice mail probably being the two you will use most.

Voice mail is a system that extends the capabilities of your telephone. While voice mail offers more options than the traditional answering machine, it also does the job of an answering machine, receiving and storing incoming messages for you. This is probably the most common application of voice mail that people use. It is also capable of responding to messages, or of transmitting messages by telephone to the voice mails of others. Voice mail capabilities differ and depend on the service provider.

TECHNOLOGY CONNECTION

Cynthia Lett, an etiquette trainer for the Lett Group, suggests that, if you get voice mail when calling someone back with a simple answer to that person's question, just leave your reply on the machine. Don't initiate the dreaded game of "telephone tag."

What are some frustrations you may have experienced with voice mail?

However, all allow messages to be received, to be sent to several locations, are easy to use, and do not require the sender to wait for the receipt. However, though the voice message received is nice, because you can hear the voice of the sender, voice mail utilizes conventional phone lines, and you must therefore pay phone costs.

Electronic mail or e-mail uses a computer, keyboard, and service provider to create messages and send them through electronic networks. The message appears in text rather than in voice. E-mail is a very popular form of communication and for good reasons: It is easy to use, allows time to compose, crosses the traditional lines of communication, is very fast, and can be sent to people who are not in their office. Also, users can send e-mail at times when a ringing phone would be unwelcome at the receiving end, and e-mail takes advantage of the Internet, so long distance phone charges are not incurred.

Quick Tip . . . .

Don't become abrupt or sloppy when composing e-mail messages. Use complete sentences. How would you like to see e-mail messages to you written?

—Hilka Kinkenbert, author of *At Ease . . . Professionally*

1. Name two forms of electronic communication.

2. What are some techniques you have used to make your communication more effective?

3. What do you think will be the impact of future communication technology on human relations?

*Fast*Chat

Key Terms

communication
sender
receiver
message
feedback
semantics
information overload
active listening
verbal communication
4 C's of communication
nonverbal communication
context
medium
voice mail
e-mail

Chapter Summary

Communication, the process by which we exchange information through a common system of symbols, signs, or behaviors, is very important today because we live in an information society and we must interact with a variety of people. Communication can flow up, down, or horizontally in an organization. It can also be one-way or two-way and includes three elements—the sender, the receiver, and the message. Feedback helps the receiver understand the message as the sender intended it.

Communication can be distorted or blocked because of barriers. Our verbal communication can be made a strong part of our human relations skills if we develop good listening skills and an ability to use the written and spoken word.

Nonverbal communication is any meaning conveyed through body language, the way the voice is used, and the way people position themselves in relation to others. It accounts for at least 93 percent of the impact of our communication.

Time, timing, context, medium, and humor contribute additional dimensions of meaning to messages and communicators. Electronic forms of communication are altering some of the ways we interact.

Review Questions

1. Define communication, its process, and its role in human relations.
2. Describe common communication barriers and strategies for overcoming them.
3. What is information overload? What are some effective ways of avoiding it?
4. How can listening skills be improved?
5. What are some guidelines to make your verbal messages and presentations more effective?
6. Why is an understanding of nonverbal communication important in organizations? What are the different components of nonverbal communication?
7. Name two common forms of electronic communication.

Discussion Questions

1. Think of five words that have either gone out of style or are no longer used and five words that have developed new meanings. Share them with your classmates.
2. Think of ways in which you have used nonverbal communication today, both as a sender and as a receiver. Share these instances with your classmates.
3. Think of instances in the news, in movies, or on TV in which communication has broken down. With your classmates analyze what created the breakdown and how it might have been avoided. How might the outcomes have been different if the breakdown had not occurred?

Chapter Project

In the library or over the Internet find the Cheryl Hagen article discussed in Focus at the beginning of this chapter or the January 1999 *Success* article, "99 Ways to Power Up Your New Year." In a small group of two or three classmates, write and prepare a 10-minute lesson, based on one of the articles, that can be delivered to your other classmates. Follow these steps: (1) Relate the article to the Electronic Communication section of this chapter. (2) Follow the suggestions for improving spoken communication given in this chapter. (3) Determine who will teach what. (4) Give the presentation.

Reading, using technology, writing, listening, speaking, thinking, self-management, allocating time, participating as a member of a team, and teaching others new skills.

Reading, thinking, writing, problem solving, participating as a member of a team.

(5) After the presentation, write a brief summary of your observations: (a) verbal and nonverbal communication in your team, (b) feedback you observed or heard during or after the presentation, and (c) problems in listening you may have observed in the team or during the presentation. Format the report in an attractive, efficient, and effective memorandum or e-mail to your instructor.

Applications

In small groups analyze the following situations.

The Medium Is the Message

Mac Delorian woke up excited. Today was going to be a big day for him. He finally had a chance to show management that he had some good ideas about how the company could be improved. Because of a new policy allowing employees to submit written suggestions for changes to top management, he planned to send a memo to the president for consideration. Having worked in the mailroom for three years, he had seen the great amount of time wasted by sorting and putting mail in individuals' boxes and then retrieving it and handing it to them at the front window. He thought that if each department were given a key to open its own box, much mailroom personnel time could be saved, speeding up distribution of mail and reducing the need for overtime.

Because of Mac's excitement last night, he forgot to set his alarm and woke up late. Knowing that the memo had to be received before the 8 A.M. managers meeting, he hurriedly prepared an e-mail instead and sent it without proofing it or asking someone else to read it for clarity or tact. After he sent it, he called the president's secretary to make sure she gave it to the president before the meeting. The e-mail the president received said, "Want to save a lot of money? Give everyone a key to the mail box so they can get their own mail and not waste so much of my time."

Mac eagerly waited for some response to his recommendation. Finally, he received a brief written memo thanking him for his suggestion and stating that, after consideration, management had decided not to make a change. He later learned that management did not consider his proposal because they did not understand it. They thought he was recommending that everyone, including managers, go to the window to retrieve his or her own mail rather than having office staff pick it up twice a day. Amazed, Mac said, "What? I told them what I thought would work. Why didn't they understand?"

1. What did happen? Why didn't the managers understand what Mac was recommending?
2. How could he have handled this situation better? Re-write Mac's message so that it is complete, concise, correct, and clear.

SCANS LINK

Reading, thinking, problem solving, participating as a member of a team.

Breakdown in Communication

It was the holiday season at Terry's Terrific Toys. The employees were exhausted and had been putting in twelve-hour days. Sleet was beginning to fall outside, which caused Anna Marie, the manager, to be late arriving. As she entered the store, she noticed that it was extremely crowded. Shoppers nudged each other in the aisles, fighting over the few remaining toys. The telephones were ringing, and cash register three was malfunctioning.

Suddenly Anna Marie heard loud voices arguing. As she moved closer, she saw the stock clerk, Samuel, and a well-dressed, attractive lady in her late 20s or early 30s. Both had raised their voices and were waving their hands excitedly.

"Buzz off!" Samuel yelled. "That Samuel," thought Anna Marie angrily. "He's always causing trouble."

Anna Marie ran up to Samuel and yelled, "You're fired! Out!" Samuel looked up at Anna Marie in surprise and began to protest. "You're fired!" yelled Anna Marie. "Yeah!" responded Samuel, equally as loud, as he stomped off. "And a Happy Holiday to you, too, Miss Scrooge."

A bit later Darrell, the assistant manager, came into the manager's booth where Anna Marie was filling out Samuel's termination papers.

"You know, Anna Marie, Samuel didn't start that. The woman yelled at him and demanded that he quit helping an elderly lady with two grandchildren. When he didn't, the younger lady came over and grabbed him by the arm and jerked him away. That's when Samuel told her to buzz off."

1. Identify all the communication barriers in this scenario. How should Anna Marie have handled the situation?
2. What communication skills should have been used by Samuel? by the customer? What do you think the outcome would have been if these skills had been used?

- AM didn't see the entire scenario
- The younger Lady could have been politer
- Samuel could have tried to stand up for himself
- he could have been politer

Additional Readings and Resources

Hall, E. T. *The Hidden Dimension*. Garden City, New York: Doubleday, 1965.

Hall, E. T. *The Silent Language*. Garden City, New York: Doubleday, 1966.

Martin, Phyllis. *Word Watcher's Handbook—A Dictionary of the Most Misused and Abused Words*. New York: St. Martin's Press, 1982.

Knapp, Mark L. *Nonverbal Communication in Human Interaction*. New York: Holt, Rinehart and Winston, Inc., 1972.

http://www.cohums.ohio-state.edu/english/facstf/kol/diverse.htm. (for editors and others interested in learning more about communication skills)

Goal Setting:

Steps to the Future

focus

In order to get what you want, it's very helpful to know what you want. If you don't know where you want to go, you probably won't get there.

—*The Portable Life 101*

Do you know what you want to do next week, next year, in 5 years, in 20 years?

What do you think are advantages of goal setting?

Why do many people and businesses fail to set goals?

After studying this chapter, you should be able to:

1. *Explain the importance of planning to people and to organizations.*

2. *Name and define three categories of organizational goals.*

3. *Discuss the characteristics and timing of goals.*

4. *Understand how goals are set and prioritized.*

5. *Describe Management by Objectives and name its benefits.*

6. *Grasp the importance of the performance appraisal and how it works.*

In This Chapter

The cartoon below typifies the way we all too often approach our desires or goals. We might want to accomplish certain things, but we do not think about the steps we must take. Being successful is almost never a matter of luck or fate; we must plan to increase our chances of being successful. Failure to plan is frequently described as taking an automobile trip to a strange place without a road map. You may reach your destination, but getting there will probably take longer and cost more. And you may never arrive.

Planning can increase our chances of success.

"Magnificent invention! Now, let's get the people in Marketing to figure out what it can do!"

Planning is important for organizations and individuals.

Planning is important for organizations and individuals (in both our personal and professional lives). Having specific goals gives us a better chance of making things happen and achieving success than if we just wait, watch things happen, wonder what happened, or criticize what happened. Goals provide direction and assist us in selecting strategies, communicating intentions, and evaluating effectiveness.

Planning is an attempt to prepare for and predict the future. It involves goals, programs, policies, rules, and procedures. Included are decisions about what resources to commit to future action. These resources can include time, money, supplies, material, and labor. Planning should be ongoing and flexible because goals will change as organizations and individuals grow or face new situations.

Saving to buy a home or car is an example of planning in personal life.

Psychologists suggest that lack of planning is a subconscious desire to create crises or even to fail. In our personal lives, lack of planning may make us feel more spontaneous and alive because of the temporary heightened emotion that results from scrambling to deal with unplanned events.

In an organization, managers may feel more important because they have immediate decisions to make. This kind of busyness is called "putting out brushfires." These are short-term "benefits" and ultimately are harmful.

WHY MUST ORGANIZATIONS PLAN?

Without planning, organizations have no sense of direction, and ultimately are not able to effectively manage resources. No planning or poor planning can result in crisis management (constantly putting out brushfires) and employee frustration. Managers spend their time on emergencies while employees are forced to move from one task to another as emergencies arise. Then, too, coping with change is more difficult without planning.

Planning is the difference between reactive management and proactive management. **Reactive management** is characterized by supervisors being caught off guard when problems arise and spending their time moving from one crisis to the next. (It is often called crisis management.) **Proactive management** involves looking ahead, anticipating problems, and determining solutions to potential problems before they develop. It may require goal setting by individuals.

TECHNOLOGY CONNECTION

Computers and cheap power have made it possible for companies to do extensive planning in the areas of just-in-time inventories, cost benefit analyses, and project planning. Companies can do "what if" scenarios to envision what might occur in the future.

1. Why do many companies not use these tools to plan into the future?

2. Change is increasing at an ever rapid pace. Is planning worth it?

3. Can you plan too much?

4. How important is it to be flexible with your plans?

Human Relations

HOW DO PEOPLE DIFFER IN PLANNING?

People generally fall into three broad categories when planning. Imagine three people playing a game of horseshoes. Here is how each would act if each were in a different category.

The underachiever will stand close to the target. **Underachievers** tend to set goals that are lower than their abilities. This is their way of protecting themselves from risk and anxiety. Because they seldom if ever push themselves, they do not achieve much.

The overachiever will stand so far back from the target that hitting it is almost impossible. **Overachievers** take on goals beyond their abilities. They are uncertain of what they can expect of themselves but cannot admit inadequacy. They lack self-confidence and reduce their anxiety by aiming beyond what they can achieve. Because their goals are unrealistic, they seldom achieve them or feel satisfied.

The realistic achiever will stand just far enough back to be challenged. **Realistic achievers** tend to have a positive self-image. They are usually successful in their endeavors because they set challenging but attainable goals. They, therefore, become high achievers.

Ten Characteristics of High Achievers

1. They like to control situations, and they take responsibility for their behavior.
2. They take reasonable risks.
3. They visualize their accomplishments in advance and allow their behavior to be determined by their goals for the future.
4. They tend to be driven and very focused on the job to be done.
5. They manage their time wisely and prioritize their work effectively.
6. They use effective communication techniques.
7. They value diversity and increase productivity through teamwork.
8. In negotiations, they are fair and seek solutions that are mutually beneficial.
9. They take time to renew themselves physically, spiritually, emotionally, mentally, and socially.
10. They like immediate feedback about their performance.

Consider the above traits in relation to yourself. Do you set moderate, attainable goals? Do you become involved in situations so that you may influence what is happening rather than just "going with the flow"? Are you receptive to feedback about your behavior and performance? Do you arrange your tasks to be free from interruptions? Do you allow yourself enough time? Do you persevere? If the answers to these questions are yes, you are probably already a realistic high achiever or well on your way to

being one. If the answers are no, analyze what you might do to increase your chances for success.

If procrastination is a problem for you, think about the pride you feel on accomplishing a task satisfactorily. Giving yourself credit for your accomplishments can provide "energy" for attempting other goals.

People procrastinate for a number of reasons. Some people procrastinate because they have an unrealistic view of successful people. They do not recognize the great amount of planning, organizing, and hard work required to make success seem "easy."

Other people procrastinate because they have poor coping skills or a low tolerance for disappointment. Instead of analyzing situations to determine alternative actions when complications occur or steps are blocked, they give up and do nothing.

Quick Wit

"Goals are as essential to success as air is to life."

—David Schwartz

Still others procrastinate as a way of rebelling against expectations, not recognizing the immaturity of such a response. A more effective approach

Human Relations

to handling expectations that we consider unfair or inappropriate for us would be to discuss the situation with the person who holds those expectations. Then we can decide for ourselves what is best and proceed accordingly. However, because many procrastinators lack assertiveness skills, they are uncomfortable addressing a difficult situation, hoping perhaps that the problem will go away. Lack of assertiveness can create additional delays or procrastination if people are reluctant to ask others for resources or help necessary to perform a task.

When you find yourself putting off work on a task or goal, a healthy approach will be for you to examine yourself closely to see why. Then decide what you want to do about the situation. If you feel overwhelmed, dividing a large task into several smaller ones may be the answer. Do not try to do everything at once. The best way to attack giant projects is to start with small steps and remember that the key to achievement is to think big but act *now*. A small success can motivate you to move on to the next step. Small, steady steps are the key.

Another factor that may help you overcome procrastination is the support of someone who believes in you, such as a friend, relative, or coworker. Developing supportive relationships takes effective human relations skills. (Procrastination will be discussed more thoroughly in Chapter 19.)

Think back to something that you planned lately.

1. Did the plans go as expected? Why or why not?

2. Did anything unforeseen happen?

3. Would your planning have been more effective if several people had been involved? Why or why not?

*Fast*Chat

10.2 What Kinds of Goals Exist?

Learning
Objective 2

Name and define three categories of organizational goals.

Organizational goals can be official, operative, or operational.

A **goal** is the objective, target, or end result expected from the completion of tasks, activities, or programs. In your personal life, your goals may include becoming a college graduate, a successful business person, or a respected community leader.

Much of what is written about goal setting in organizations can be applied to your personal goal setting. Two management authors, Ramon Aldag and Timothy Stearns, have identified three broad categories of goals in organizations: official goals, operative goals, and operational goals.

Official goals are developed by upper management, are formally stated, and may be published in annual reports or newsletters. They are usually the most abstract category of goals. They tend to be open-ended. That is, the goal itself may not include information about quantity, quality, or deadline. Official goals pertain to the overall mission of the organization. A common example in business today is "to provide excellent service."

Operative goals are those goals for which middle management is responsible. They concern the operating policies of the organization. These

CASE STUDIES IN THE NEWS

Despite the fact that companies continue to downsize, unemployment remains relatively low, because companies often need to fill empty positions in their new, restructured, and short-handed organizations. Many companies are obsessed with sustaining short-term profitability at the expense of long-term growth. Experts expect downsizing to continue at record levels.

1. *Why would companies lay off, then hire?*

2. *Is this wise planning? What pushes this trend?*

3. *What is the downside of downsizing?*

goals tend to be more specific than the abstract official goals. Operative goals usually include a mix of open-ended and close-ended goals. They are usually redefined on a yearly basis. Common examples of operative goals in business today are "to increase the company's share of the market" and "to hire more minorities."

Peter Drucker, a management expert, has identified eight types of operative goals. They are marketing, innovation, profitability, physical resources, financial resources, human resources, productivity, and social responsibility.

Operational goals are the responsibility of first-line supervisors and employees. They are statements of the expected results of the efforts of the various components of the organization. They include built-in standards of behavior, performance criteria, and completion time. They are concrete and close-ended.

An example of an operational goal is "to increase sales of XYZ chemical by 2002 by 20 percent over the current year by hiring and placing a marketing representative in the Far East." Another example is "to increase the proportion of Hispanic employees in the total work force of the company to one-fourth within three years by active recruiting and training." Notice that these two goals include specific dates for completion and specify how much.

Following the examples of goals in organizations, we can create specific goals in our personal lives. Here are two examples: "to complete an associate degree within two years by registering for and passing 15 credit hours each semester" and "to save $1,000 for a trip next summer by forgoing movies and eating out only once a month."

1. What sort of goals have you established for work, either regarding your own career or as part of your job? Into which category did these goals fall?

2. What are some other areas of life to which you might apply these concepts?

Fast**Chat**

Learning Objective 3

Discuss the characteristics and timing of goals.

Goals should be written, measurable, time specific, challenging, and participatory.

To be most helpful, goals, whether personal or organizational, should have the following characteristics:

Characteristics of Goals

1. Goals should be written. Writing increases understanding and commitment.
2. Goals should be measurable. For example, "I want to be more successful in school" is a vague goal because what constitutes success is not specified. Grade point average can be measured; therefore, a better way of expressing this goal would be "I will earn a GPA of 3.0 out of a possible 4.0." If goals are vague and uncertain, they will provide little guidance.
3. Goals should be specific as to time. Otherwise, they are not challenging. At the time specified, they can then be reviewed for correction or revision. Considering the goal above, we can make it time-specific by adding a deadline: "I will earn a GPA of 3.0 out of a possible 4.0 during the next academic year."
4. Goals should be challenging but attainable, to provide satisfaction and reduce frustration. Goals should be realistic, not wish lists, and should be reasonable expectations of what can be achieved over a given period of time.
5. In an organization, goals should involve participation. Participation increases commitment and communication and, hence, understanding and motivation. The most frequent participation is between the employee and supervisor.

Goals are not just a writing exercise to be put aside until the time comes to write goals for another period. They should be used personally and organizationally to monitor progress throughout the period. In organizations this monitoring may be as simple as observation by the employee and the supervisor or as formal as written progress reports. Such progress checks help identify change needed while time still remains. Progress checks must be planned for, and someone must be responsible for them. We should make frequent progress checks of goals in our personal lives as well, recognizing that we are responsible for our own checks and our own progress.

HOW FAR AHEAD ARE PLANS MADE?

As noted above, time is a key characteristic of planning. Plans can be long-range, mid-range, and short-range. The time involved will vary from level to

quick wit

"Whatever you can do, or dream you can, begin it. Boldness has genius, power and magic in it."

Goethe

level in an organization. For top management long-range plans may extend over several years, whereas for supervisors long-range plans may cover only several months. Short-range plans for supervisors may include today or this week, whereas for top management they may cover the current year. In the same way, mid-range plans, which fall between long-range and short-range plans, vary from level to level.

Individuals, too, have long-range, mid-range, and short-range plans. Sometimes we have difficulty completing our long-range plans because we grow tired, forget them, or allow short- or mid-range plans to interfere. Because long-range plans cover a greater period of time, situations and circumstances may change for us, making the long-range plans impractical. In this case, we may need to change them. Psychologists point out that change can be an indication of growth; therefore, a healthy approach for us is to review our plans from time to time to check our progress, modify our strategies if necessary, or perhaps discard the plan as no longer important or possible—and then set new goals.

Developing readily attainable short- or mid-range goals can actually help us accomplish long-range goals because they provide us with periodic feelings of accomplishment. For example, if your plans include a bachelors or masters degree, setting a short-range goal of satisfactorily completing each course in which you enroll or a mid-range goal of getting a two-year associate degree can help. Completion of each course and the two-year degree can provide satisfaction and motivation to continue. Patting ourselves on the back can be psychologically healthy, and completion of short- or mid-range goals provides opportunities to do so.

GLOBAL CONNECTION

The Japanese spend much more time planning projects than Americans. They get opinions and feedback as well as buy-in from all individuals concerned. The result is that they have fewer adjustments to make after plans are implemented. Americans spend much less time planning and much more time making adjustments after plans are implemented.

1. *Is the American way better? Why or why not?*

2. *Should Americans spend more time planning?*

3. *Why is it important to gain consensus from those involved?*

ETHICS CONNECTION

Attaining goals is a thrilling accomplishment. It makes you feel good inside.

1. *Should you attain your goals at the expense of others? Why or why not?*

2. *Should you embellish your accomplishments to obtain your dream job?*

3. *Should you "advertise" your accomplishments at work to supervisors and other superiors? Why or why not? In what appropriate ways can you make accomplishments that might affect your career known?*

Goals can become obsolete if we have achieved them. They can also become less important as we grow. Think of how your own goals have changed over the years. We can probably all recall various ways in which we answered the traditional question, "What do you want to be when you grow up?" At four years of age, we may have wanted to be a prince or princess, at six a dancer, at ten an astronaut, and in our teens a professional athlete. Somewhere along the line, we lost interest in some of these, decided we lacked the natural ability necessary for others, or found something else of appeal to us. Today we may have a different career goal in mind, one that probably combines dreams and practicality. Then after we have been working a while we may decide to set other career goals. Mid-career switches, for instance, are fairly common.

FastChat

1. Do you ever write your goals down? Why or why not?

2. Have any plans you've made possessed some or all of the characteristics listed above? Which ones?

3. Have you successfully reached a goal you set for yourself? What steps did you take to reach the goal? Were there intermediate steps (short-range or mid-range goals)?

How Are Goals Set and Prioritized?

WHICH GOALS COME FIRST?

Both organizations and individuals have multiple goals and priorities. We seldom have the luxury of pursuing one goal at a time. Aldag and Stearns have identified four techniques that managers in an organization can use to decide which goals to emphasize during periods of conflict. We can apply them to our personal goals and plans also. They include satisficing, sequential attention, preference ordering, and goal changes.

Satisficing. (Satisficing is a term created to define situations where one perfect and unique solution may not be possible. Satisficing refers to any group of solutions which offer good results under the circumstances.) When we are faced with numerous goals, we can reduce our stress by identifying a satisfactory rather than optimum level of performance for some of them. Some tasks just need to be done, and often there are several perfectly acceptable ways in which they might be performed. For example, in our lives, satisficing might consist of a quick job of house cleaning when we're pressed for time, rather than either sacrificing other goals (such as time with family) or doing nothing and letting it get steadily worse.

In many situations, perfection, or even excellence, may not be that important, and as a matter of fact can be costly or stressful. The desire for perfection can create havoc with goal accomplishment and people's lives if carried too far. Save your energy for the things that really do need to be as close to perfect as possible.

Sequential Attention. When we have multiple priorities, we may need to shift our attention from one goal to the next over periods of time. Successful working parents frequently adopt this tactic. Work priorities sometimes take precedence over family activities, and at other times the reverse is true. The main point is to keep the overall quality of performance in each area acceptable.

Preference Ordering. If we have several goals toward which we wish to work, we may need to rank them according to preference. For example, a company may decide to maximize profit over expansion for a period of time. Individuals may decide to save for a new car rather than take a trip this year.

Learning
Objective 4

Understand how goals are set and prioritized.

Prioritize goals by satisficing, sequential attention, preference ordering, and goal changes.

quick wit

"Whether you are successful at work depends not on how well you do all the tasks assigned, but on how well you choose which are the important tasks to do."

Charles McCloud

Goal Changes. As pointed out earlier, we may change goals because they become outdated or inappropriate, such as when we complete a degree or buy the car for which we have been saving. A well known example of goal-changing is the Foundation for Infantile Paralysis. Its original goal was to develop a vaccine for polio. Once the vaccine was developed, it changed its goal to conquering birth defects and became the March of Dimes.

HOW DO YOU SET PERSONAL GOALS?

The process for deciding where you want to go next with your life requires that you make a frequent, close examination of your preferences. Asking yourself specific questions can help you determine your priorities in life. Consider, for example, how important the Personal Preferences listed on the next page are to you.

Considering these questions objectively can help you in setting your personal goals. Notice that all of the measures of success require high levels of human relations skills.

Once you have examined yourself closely, you are ready to set your goals. Below are some guidelines to help you:

1. Remember to be realistic. If your goals are too high, you may lose confidence. In determining how high to set your goals, consider your own past performance and that of others. If your goals are too low, you will have no incentive or challenge to better yourself. Be careful that you do not underrate yourself. Finally, make your goals worthwhile.
2. Once you have determined your goals, openly commit yourself. Letting others know about them can help. Be sure to say specifically what it is you plan to accomplish, when, where, and how.
3. Your goals may have to be coordinated with other people. An examination of your professional and personal relationships is necessary.
4. Visualize success. Get a mental image of your goal and think when, not if.

Carefully applying the above guidelines can help you establish goals that are both meaningful and achievable. Such application must be an ongoing process to be effective.

WHAT ATTITUDES BRING SUCCESS?

Personalities have been characterized as Type A and Type B, based on a person's degree of aggressiveness and passiveness. Type A personalities are usually driven and aggressive, whereas Type B are patient and passive. Both have problems associated with them: Type A people may create stress-related health problems for themselves while Type B people may not be assertive enough.

quick wit
. . . .
"Our greatest need and most difficult achievement is to find meaning in our lives."

. . . .
Bruno Betelheim

Personal Preferences

1. **Affection.** If you are to have your need for affection met, you must obtain and share companionship and affection. Your goals must include other people. Are your other goals practical enough to accommodate others?

2. **Expertness.** If this is important to you, you must become an authority in some area and possess the human relations skills to communicate your expertise to others and have it received. What area? Do your human relations skills need developing?

3. **Independence.** Being independent may require time and at least some money. When will you have that time, and how will you obtain the necessary finances to be independent? Even more basic, what does being independent mean to you? Will it mean the same to others in your life?

4. **Leadership.** To be a leader, you must gain influence. Where? At work? In the community? How?

5. **Parenthood.** Parenthood requires a tremendous investment of time, finances, and physical and emotional energy. Can you afford that investment now? Later? How?

6. **Happiness, contentment.** What is your definition of these concepts? What will it take for you to achieve them? How? Without human relations skills, our lives can be in constant turmoil, which can prevent personal happiness and contentment.

7. **Prestige.** Prestige differs for different people. How will you measure it—by the house in which you live, the organization for which you work, or where you vacation? How will you acquire that house, gain employment at that company, or acquire the money and knowledge for that vacation?

8. **Security.** Security is important for many people but not for others. What kind of security do you need—financial or emotional? If financial security is part of your need, how much will it take and how will you acquire it? If emotional security is important to you, what does that mean—a supportive supervisor? A caring spouse? Concerned friends? What will you have to do to have that kind of relationship with your boss, spouse, or friends?

9. **Personal development.** Personal development can take the form of growth, hobbies, talents, or knowledge. It implies continuing to learn throughout your life. How will you feed this desire in yourself? Where can you find the necessary direction, guidance, and instruction?

10. **Wealth.** If money is important to you, how will you acquire it? How much will it take to satisfy you? How will you take care of it if you gain it? Human relations skills will be necessary to help you earn more and to keep others from begrudging you money for which you have worked hard.

11. **Service to others.** A sense of duty is important to many people and can make the difference in the quality of life in organizations, communities, and countries. If you desire to make such contributions to others, where and how would you like to use your energy and abilities?

Two psychologists, Robert Kriegel and Marilyn Harris Kriegel, suggest that all of us have the potential to perform as a Type C person. Type C behavior is versatile and adaptive. It enables us to perform at our peak and feel vital and full of energy. A Type C attitude combines commitment, confidence, and control.

Commitment. Identifying what you want, knowing your innermost desires, and translating them into action will result in harmony between what you do and what you want to do. The more committed you are to something, the less difficult it seems. Low commitment can make a task overwhelming. When Type C people look at a task, they see opportunities. Others see obstacles.

Confidence. Confidence in your own worth does not depend on others' moods, your looks, or other external factors. You may hate to fail, but you do not fear it, because you know that with risks come mistakes and failures, but also the possibility of learning and greater gain. Be alert to your own inner signals of fear. When you notice them, stop, take a few deep, slow breaths, hold each to the count of three, and exhale slowly. This practice can help put matters back into perspective. Doing a reality check can also help you manage your anxieties.

To do a reality check, measure and rate the difficulty, bring the past into the present, and imagine the worst.

Quick Tip

You can do a reality check to determine how serious a problem is.

1. **Measure the difficulty.** Rate it on a scale of 1 to 10. Measuring the difficulty may be as simple as writing it down.
2. **Bring the past into the present.** Think of similar situations and remember your successes. Analyze them: what were your actions, feelings, and thoughts that led you to success?
3. **Imagine the worst.** Ask yourself, "What is the worst that can happen if I fail in this endeavor? Will I die, lose my job, or lose my spouse?" Because the consequences are not usually that dire, such a reality check will immediately boost your confidence.
4. **Visualize yourself accomplishing your present goal.**

In doing your reality check, be careful of false confidence, which can lead to being unprepared. If the reality check shows the problem is indeed major, you can at least now concentrate on dealing with it rather than on your anxieties.

Control. Control is the third component of a Type C attitude. After doing a reality check, concentrate on what you can control to improve your performance and effectiveness. You can include your own thoughts, feelings, attitudes, and actions.

Robert Land, executive vice president of a large national human resources management consulting firm, pointed out that successful people are generally those who work to maintain control over their work environment and a myriad of unanticipated events. In other words, these people are proactive rather than reactive. He advises that we must be responsible for ourselves and our careers. We cannot expect our bosses to take charge of our careers, because bosses seldom have the time or interest to help us plan where we should be and how to get there.

One thing you can usually control is how you approach work. Employees must work to keep themselves employable. They need to accept change, learn to adapt, accept responsibility, and continue to develop. Also, bosses look favorably on employees who ease their burden and harshly on those who add to it. Ultimately, the most valuable subordinates are those who make their bosses look good. If you are now working, you can check your "progress pulse" to measure your career success by answering the questions below.

Check your "Progress Pulse" to measure career success.

To assess objectively whether your progress pulse is healthy, ask yourself these questions:

1. Have you had a formal or informal performance review within the last three months?
2. Have you asked your boss lately what you can do to help?
3. Do you know what your boss's goals and missions are?
4. Have you taken the initiative to do things your boss hasn't asked you to do?
5. Have you taken on any special projects within the last three months?
6. Have you been sought out recently for information or special advice?
7. Have you created some positive visibility for yourself?
8. Are you keeping notes on your recent accomplishments so you can give them to your boss before your next performance review?
9. Are you a team player and do you help your coworkers meet their goals?
10. Do people, especially your boss, like to work with you?
11. Do people ask you to meetings and copy you on memos?

(continued)

---

12. Have you aligned yourself with a confidential peer to get candid feedback on your performance and to determine how others perceive you?

13. Have you set down where you'd like to be in two to five years?

14. Do you know how your progress compares with others in your field at your age?

15. Are you aware of training or experience you'll need to advance to the next position?

16. Are you keeping a list of contacts in your field?

17. Have you been attending professional meetings?

18. Can you name an alternative field where you could transfer your skills if necessary?

19. Have you identified a mentor—someone to help you and to serve as a good role model?

*Fast*Chat

Many times in this fast paced society we cannot do everything well.

1. Can you name a time you had to attempt satisfaction rather than perfection?

2. In what situations might it be acceptable to do a satisfactory job rather than an excellent one? When might excellence be important?

3. Which personality type do you think you possess—A, B, or C? What would you need to do to become more like a Type C?

What Is Management by Objectives?

A variety of approaches and different degrees of formality are used in setting goals in organizations. One popular technique is **Management by Objectives**, originated by George Odiorne. This technique, sometimes abbreviated to MBO, is a method and philosophy of management that emphasizes self-determination. Its chief purpose is to improve employee motivation by having employees at all levels participate in setting their own goals.

Learning
Objective 5

Describe Management by Objectives and name its benefits.

FEATURES OF MBO

Proponents of MBO say that it helps increase motivation because of the involvement and commitment of the people participating in the process. It is characterized by three features:

MBO emphasizes self-determination for employees.

1. Employees participate in establishing the objectives and the criteria by which they will be judged. This step usually involves discussions between the supervisor and the employee. Employees should be aware of overall organizational and departmental goals. Then they can set individual goals that are valued by the organization.
2. Both the supervisor and the employee know what the employee is to accomplish. The employee knows what the supervisor expects and can work toward the correct goal. The supervisor, in turn, can guide the employee correctly if deviation should start occurring.
3. If the goal has been correctly written, it will contain specific descriptions of the end result desired (how much and by when). This feature will make evaluation of the employee's performance easier. Additionally, the employee will be more likely to agree with the appraisal, because the criteria were selected and agreed upon in advance.

BENEFITS OF MBO

The *George Odiorne Letter* summarizes several benefits to be gained from organizations using MBO:

1. Communicating job objectives helps people understand the purpose of their job, which increases the likelihood of success.

2. People today want to participate in decisions affecting them. Because MBO involves superior and subordinate in discussions about responsibilities and expected results, employees develop greater commitment.

3. MBO makes sense psychologically and may help motivation. Various studies have shown that high achievers are those who set goals, that goals have a powerful effect on behavior, that employees with clear goals achieve more than those without them, and that highly motivated people are those who achieve, especially goals to which they are committed. Odiorne points out that goal-centered people are more likely to be mentally healthy than are people driven by fear, intimidation, punishment, or hostility.

4. MBO can save time and money because people know for what tasks they are responsible and accountable.

5. Because individuals are exercising self-control under MBO, they can measure their own progress against the goals they helped create and adapt their behavior appropriately.

6. MBO allows people to present again their past creative ideas not previously accepted when they set their goals for a new period. This opportunity fosters creativity in organizations, considered vital for success today.

7. MBO makes performance appraisal more reasonable and compensation systems more rational. Because people are evaluated against goals and standards that they helped establish, appraisal becomes easier for both the supervisor and the employee.

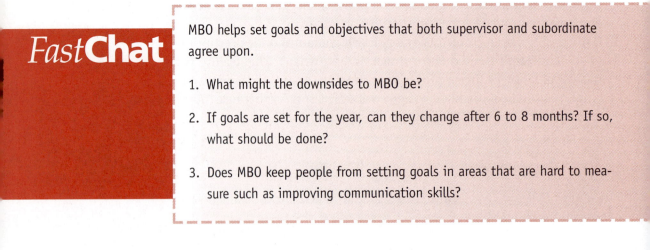

*Fast*Chat

MBO helps set goals and objectives that both supervisor and subordinate agree upon.

1. What might the downsides to MBO be?

2. If goals are set for the year, can they change after 6 to 8 months? If so, what should be done?

3. Does MBO keep people from setting goals in areas that are hard to measure such as improving communication skills?

Why Are Performance Appraisals Important and How Do They Work?

The **performance appraisal** is a measurement of how well an employee is doing on the job. Performance appraisals can be performed by supervisors rating their employees, employees rating their superiors, team members who rate each other, outsiders who rate employees, employees who rate themselves, or a combination of all these techniques. Because of the growing use of teams and a concern about customer feedback, the fastest growing types of appraisals are those that involve team members and sources outside the organization. The most common type of appraisals, however, are those done at least annually by an immediate supervisor.

Performance appraisal is a process that frequently both the employee and the supervisor dread. Being human, supervisors may fear that subordinates will not like them, that employees may do less work if the appraisal is a negative one, that employees may yell at them, or that friendships with subordinates may be jeopardized. At the same time, employees may wonder whether supervisors can be fair, doubt whether supervisors understand the subordinates' jobs, fear an average or below-average rating, or feel that a high rating may interfere with friendships with coworkers.

Learning
Objective 6

Grasp the importance of the performance appraisal and how it works.

Both supervisors and subordinates may dread appraisals.

CORBIS

Feedback is important. It lets us know what we are doing right and what behavior we need to change.

Organizations appraise employee performance for a number of reasons, as shown here:

Why Organizations Appraise Employee Performance

1. To encourage good job performance, to discourage unacceptable performance, and to correct inappropriate behavior that interferes with good performance

   If it is conducted correctly, the appraisal session can help communication. It can result in growth and increased motivation or at least a better understanding of what is expected of us.

2. To let us know how we are doing

   We want to know where we stand in the organization. Although we may dislike being judged, human beings need feedback, both negative and positive. Negative feedback allows us to make corrections in our behavior and performance, whereas positive feedback lets us know what is appreciated so that we will continue. (Psychologists say that we quit engaging in a certain behavior both if the behavior is punished and if it is ignored.) Feedback also assists us in making plans for personal improvement.

3. To give the organization information about employees that can be used in later career decisions, such as raises, promotions, demotions, transfers, and terminations.

   Appraisals can help move your career forward or help identify areas that need more work. They also help managers identify the need for training in individuals and in groups of employees.

If performance appraisals are to be effective, both the supervisor and the employee must prepare for them.

PREPARING YOURSELF

You can take several steps ahead of time and during the appraisal session to help make appraisal the positive process that it is supposed to be. These steps are listed in the box on the next page. Using a proactive, assertive approach is to your advantage.

Additionally, you can take three steps *during* the appraisal session to make the process effective and to help yourself. They are:

1. Go into the session willing to listen and participate. A defensive, closed mind will sabotage the session before it even starts. The appraisal is a good opportunity to share your career goals with your supervisor.

1. Make sure that you understand what is expected of you.

Effective supervisors will be preparing for the appraisal session throughout the entire appraisal period. They know what is expected of the employee, make sure the subordinate also knows, observe frequently, and tell you how you are performing. You also can prepare throughout the period. If you participated in the establishment of objectives for your job, you understand what is expected of you. If you did not, do not wait until the appraisal session to ask questions. Keep checking that your understanding of what you are to do is the same as your supervisor's understanding. You can also take the initiative and ask for feedback during the period. This way you will eliminate surprises in the appraisal session. Open communication with your supervisor is extremely important

2. Become familiar with the evaluation or appraisal instrument to be used.

Ideally, you should do this at the beginning of the appraisal period. Then, before your appraisal session, take the time to conduct a self-appraisal by completing the instrument as objectively as you can. This activity will help you remember accomplishments that you want to bring up if your supervisor overlooks them. It also can increase communication and understanding during the session. Identify areas that need improvement also.

2. If obstacles have been in the way of your performing satisfactorily, you should have made them known to your supervisor before now. However, if you have not, certainly share them at this time. Are you frequently late in completing a weekly report because the Sales Department is late in submitting figures to you? If so, let your supervisor know what you need to perform better.

3. Make sure that you understand what is expected of you at the conclusion of the appraisal session. For instance, should you continue as you have been, assume other responsibilities, or perform current responsibilities better?

Taking these steps will help you feel more in control of your life and can make the session more effective. Extremely important in each step of this process are strong human relations skills. The greater your skills and those of your supervisor, the better will be the outcome of an appraisal. This outcome, in turn, will benefit you, your supervisor, and the organization.

THE SUPERVISOR'S ROLE

Understanding the supervisor's role in appraisals can help you prepare

The effective supervisor will follow a number of steps in conducting the appraisal. Knowledge of these steps can enable you to use them to your advantage. The steps are:

1. The supervisor will schedule the appraisal in advance and ask the employee to think about achievements and areas for improvement to be discussed during the session. This step will allow the supervisor and employee time to prepare. Your objectivity and preparation can make a big difference in how smoothly the session runs and can enhance your supervisor's perception of you.

2. The supervisor will read the employee's personnel file and any other performance information available. If your file is open to you, you should review it periodically. This review will enable you to respond to negative information. If positive comments have been made or written about you that have not been put into the file, bring them to the evaluation session.

3. The supervisor will be prepared and will plan in advance what to say. Realizing that your supervisor is not treating you or the process lightly should make you feel more respected and, hence, more comfortable and receptive.

4. The supervisor will choose a quiet location for the session, free of interruptions, will allow plenty of time, and will give the employee opportunity to speak. If you know that the session will not be rushed, you can take the time to listen fully and communicate openly.

5. The supervisor will not usually discuss salary and performance in the same meeting. Recognizing that money should be discussed in a separate meeting frees you to concentrate on performance matters.

6. During the session, the supervisor will explain the purpose of the meeting, ask the employee's opinion, stay positive, discuss total performance, reach agreement on standards of performance, document the agreement, and get the employee's signature. If you accept these actions as part of the effective appraisal process, each step will seem less threatening to you.

APPRAISAL INSTRUMENTS

No one perfect technique or form has yet been designed for recording performance appraisals. You may be evaluated by a variety of means during your career. Numerous kinds of appraisal instruments exist. Some organizations have created their own forms, whereas others use commercially available ones. In general, the most common performance appraisal techniques fall into four broad categories. They are the narrative, category, comparative, and behavioral approach.

Narrative Approach The performance appraisals in this category include the essay and critical incident technique.

Essay Appraisal. Using the **essay appraisal** technique, the supervisor writes a paragraph or more about the employee's strengths and weaknesses, quantity and quality of work, current skills and knowledge, and potential value to the organization. The strength of this method lies in the fact that it probably gives a more complete picture of the employee. However, its use has several drawbacks. First, it takes longer to complete, and essay writing is more difficult. Secondly, it is likely to be more subjective than a graph. Finally, it makes comparison of employees almost impossible, because it has no scale. For these reasons it should be used only in appraising middle- and top-management employees.

Critical Incident. Using the **critical incident** technique, supervisors record in writing actual incidents in behavior that they observe in employees. The note or memo is then filed in the employee's personnel folder. Examples of negative incidents include tardiness, careless work, errors in judgment, and insubordination. Positive incidents may be completion of a project ahead of schedule, willingness to assist others, cooperation, or regular attendance at work. An obvious drawback to the critical incident method is that it is time-consuming. Its advantage is that it provides the organization with the necessary documentation for decisions about transfers, promotions, demotions, and terminations.

Category Approach These ratings include the graphic rating scale and the checklist.

Graphic Rating Scale. As you can see on the sample form that follows, a **graphic rating scale** lists the factors to be considered and terms to be used. Its strengths are that it is easy for the supervisor to complete and it helps make comparisons of employees easier. However, the categories and factors in the scale may overlap, making a thorough appraisal difficult. For example, individuals appraised with the sample form would almost automatically receive a high score in "effort" if they had been rated high in "quantity of work." Additionally, because descriptions are specified, the scale is rigid and does not give a complete picture of the employee. Because of its weaknesses, the graphic rating scale is often used in combination with the essay method.

Checklist. Supervisors check statements on a **checklist** to identify those that most represent the characteristics and performance of the employees. Different weights can be assigned to the statements, so they can be quantified. The problems with this method are that the words may have different meanings to different supervisors and that the supervisors can have difficulty explaining the appraisal if the weights assigned are not apparent.

Comparative Ranking Approach These appraisal techniques include ranking and forced distribution.

A Graphic Rating Scale Lists the Factors To Be Considered and Terms To Be Used in Appraising Employees

EMPLOYEE: _____

JOB TITLE: (GRADE) _____

DEPARTMENT: _____

DATE OF EMPLOYMENT _____

DATE OF EMPLOYMENT ON PRESENT JOB: _____

NUMBER OF MONTHS/YEARS ON PRESENT JOB: _____

PRESENT SALARY: $ _____

TO RATERS:

The value of this rating depends upon the impartiality and sound judgment you use when marking this form. Base your judgment of the employee in relation to others doing similar work, keeping in mind the duties and requirements of the job the employee occupies. Consider only one trait at a time. Do not let your rating of the employee on any one trait influence your rating on any other trait.

Place a check mark in the block on the scale below the expression that most nearly describes your opinion of the employee. You are requested to note any comments which you believe would furnish additional information concerning the employee's performance on his/her job or to record any significant observations made during the discussion in the space provided at the end of this form.

EFFORT: How well does he/she make use of his/her time? Consider his/her physical and mental application to his/her work, his/her energy and attentiveness.	☐ Wastes considerable time. Does only enough to get by.	☐ Keeps fairly busy. Allows idle conversation to keep him/her from work.	☐ Rarely unoccupied. Is energetic and attentive.	☐ Constantly applying himself/herself. Never seems to have an idle moment.
JOB KNOWLEDGE: How well has he/she acquired the knowledge of all elements comprising his/her job? Consider not only his/her own job's fundamentals, but also that of related work; his/her understanding of 'how and 'why' his/her work is done.	☐ Understands only the simpler or more routine phases of job.	☐ Is steadily acquiring the knowledge necessary to perform the more intricate job phases.	☐ Thoroughly knows most all phases of job.	☐ Has complete mastery of job. Remarkable understanding of all phases.
ACCURACY: How accurate is the employee in performing his/her duty? Consider the number of errors made—the orderliness and thoroughness of work produced.	☐ In need of improvement.	☐ Reasonably accurate.	☐ Very seldom makes a mistake.	☐ Exceptionally precise, orderly and thorough.
INITIATIVE: Is he/she eager and able to attack new problems, advance ideas, better improve his/her work? Consider his/her self-reliance. Aggressiveness—constructive thinking.	☐ Mildly progressive, but lacks certain abilities to go ahead on own.	☐ Possesses a normal amount of initiative.	☐ Usually self-sufficient in his/her work enterprise.	☐ A self starter, enjoys solving difficulties and originating better methods.

Category	☐	☐	☐	☐	☐
DEPENDABILITY: What are your feelings toward him/her when you are not at hand to give supervision? Consider his/her reliability in complying with standard procedures on his/her job following instructions and conducting self properly.	☐	☐ Needs occasional follow-up.	☐ Dependable.	☐ Is very dependable, needs little supervision.	☐ Completely trustworthy, can handle job without supervision.
JUDGMENT: How well does he/she display good common sense in his/her work? Consider how readily he/she grasps a situation and draws a correct conclusion, making best use of his/her experience and the facts at hand.	☐	☐ Apt to make hasty conclusions without due regard for consequences.	☐ Usually displays good common sense.	☐ Is levelheaded, able to draw sound conclusions.	☐ Displays superior discrimination in analyzing facts and coming up with the right answer.
QUANTITY OF WORK: How much work is he/she able to produce? Consider not only his/her regular daily output but also how promptly he/she dispatches those extra or rush assignments.	☐	☐ Pushed to maintain schedule. Sometimes needs help from others.	☐ Turns out satisfactory amount of work.	☐ Keeps well ahead in his/her work—on top of his/her job.	☐ Extremely rapid—'never seems to get enough to do.'
ATTITUDE TOWARD ASSOCIATES: How well does he/she get along and cooperate with others? Consider his/her relations with fellow workers, his/her supervisors, business contacts.	☐	☐ Frequently uncooperative. Too critical of others.	☐ Average ability to work with others.	☐ A good team worker.	☐ Very well liked and respected. An exceptional force for good morale.
ATTITUDE TOWARD WORK: What interest does he/she take in his/her job or line of work? Consider his/her eagerness to obtain more knowledge about his/her work—his/her enthusiasm in tackling difficulties—his/her pride in a job well done.	☐	☐ Mildly interested in some phases of job.	☐ Shows normal interest.	☐ Eagerness often displayed. Has pride in work.	☐ Extraordinary interest, wants to learn all about job and any related work.

COMMENTS:

RATING REVIEWED WITH EMPLOYEE: _____   SUPERVISOR: _____

EMPLOYEE'S SIGNATURE: _____   DATE: _____

Ranking. In the **ranking** method all the employees are listed from highest to lowest in performance. This can cause problems in that someone who is last in one group could be the top employee in another group. Also, quantifying the difference in how far apart the employees are from each other is difficult. For instance, there may not be much difference between #4 and #5 rated employees whereas there is a great deal of difference between #11 and #12.

Forced Distribution. Ratings of performance are distributed along a bell shaped curve in the **forced distribution** technique. The difficulties are that a supervisor using this system may resist placing employees in a very high or very low group. Further, small groups may not have a bell shaped distribution.

Behavioral Approach Appraisals These appraisals include the behaviorally anchored rating scale (BARS).

BARS. The **BARS** rating technique describes possible behaviors that the employee most often exhibits. The behaviors are then measured against a scale. For instance, a customer service representative taking orders may be rated from "used positive phrases to explain product" to "argued with customer about the suitability of the product requested." These scales take extensive time to develop and maintain, and scales must be developed for each different position.

In addition to these types of appraisals, in which supervisors rate subordinates, a recent rise has been seen in the use of 360 degree appraisals. The concept is that you receive feedback from a range of individuals around you—a 360 degree circle—including other employees, managers other than your immediate supervisor, and even customers. The intentions of the 360 appraisal are to find out how an employee interacts with others, avoid any chance of one person's bias either holding that employee back or advancing him or her too rapidly, and making sure that good human relations skills are being used with everyone around the employee, not just with a supervisor the employee is trying to impress.

*Fast*Chat

1. Have you ever been appraised at a job? What was it like? Did it worry you? Do you feel that you now would be better able to prepare for such an event?

2. In what ways do job appraisals differ from grades in school? In what ways are they similar?

3. What do you think makes creating an appraisal a difficult task for a supervisor?

Summary

Planning can benefit both people and organizations by improving the chances of success. Having goals gives us targets at which we can aim. Without planning, organizations tend to become reactive rather than proactive, creating frustration for employees.

Three broad categories of organizational goals are official, operative, and operational. They differ in how specific they are, what activities are included, and which level of management has responsibility for them.

To be most effective, goals should be written, measurable, specific, and challenging but attainable. In an organization, for the greatest understanding and motivation to occur, an individual's goals should be developed with participation of both the supervisor and the affected individual.

Goals differ in the time allowed for their completion. They can be long-range, mid-range, and short-range. When goals conflict, four techniques can be used to prioritize them: satisficing, sequential attention, preference ordering, and goal changes.

In setting personal goals, we should consider our priorities in life. They can include affection, expertness, independence, leadership, parenthood, happiness and contentment, prestige, security, personal development, wealth, and service. We should also apply four guidelines: (1) be realistic, (2) openly commit ourselves, (3) coordinate our goals with people important to us professionally and personally, and (4) visualize success. A Type C attitude that combines commitment, confidence, and control can improve our chances of personal success.

Management by Objectives is a method and philosophy of management used to formalize goal setting in organizations. The employee performance appraisal is a measurement of how well the employee is doing on the job. Although both the supervisor and employee may dread them, appraisals are necessary. Employees can take steps to make appraisal a beneficial experience. Numerous appraisal techniques exist.

Key Terms

planning
reactive management
proactive management
underachiever
overachiever
realistic achiever
goal
official goals
operative goals
operational goals
Management by Objectives (MBO)
performance appraisal
essay appraisal
critical incident
graphic rating scale
checklist
ranking
forced distribution
BARS

Review Questions

1. Explain how planning can benefit people and organizations.
2. What are the three categories of organizational goals? Whose responsibility is each category? What kinds of activities are included in each category?
3. Describe the characteristics of well formulated goals.
4. Define long-range, mid-range, and short-range goals.
5. Name and define the four techniques for prioritizing goals.
6. What is Management by Objectives? Name some of the reasons why an organization may use MBO. How would individuals within the organization benefit from its use?
7. What is employee performance appraisal? If it is so dreaded, why do organizations do it? How can employees help turn this process into a positive one?
8. Describe the common performance appraisal instruments.

Discussion Questions

1. Identify some situations in your personal life and, if you have held jobs, at work that developed because of a lack of planning. What happened? How could the situation have been improved?
2. When setting goals, do you see yourself as an underachiever, over-achiever, or realistic achiever? On what do you base your perception? Do you want to be in a different category? If so, what steps can you take? What steps are you willing to take?
3. Is procrastination a problem for you? Why or why not? If so, what has been the usual result of your procrastination? How might you work to eliminate this problem?
4. Write a goal that would be appropriate for a company with which you are familiar. Write a personal goal. Be sure that the goals are complete.
5. Briefly review your goals so far in life. Analyze why the goals have been accomplished or not. How has their status affected where you are today and your current goals?
6. Again considering situations in your personal life and at work, think about periods of conflicting goals. How was the conflict resolved? How might the four techniques for prioritizing goals described in this chapter have helped you?

Human Relations

7. Review the questions in the section of this chapter dealing with setting personal goals. Choose one long-range goal and develop a plan for accomplishing it. Then write three mid-range or short-range goals related to it.

8. After completing question 7, review the guidelines for setting goals. Examine your goals to see whether you have applied the guidelines for goal setting to them.

9. How can you apply the three components of Type C behavior to your accomplishment of the goals you wrote in question 7?

10. Think about a job that you have held. Did you make your boss's job harder or easier? How? Which approach would have been better for you in the long run? What, if anything, would you do differently today?

Writing, decision making, visualizing, self-management, responsibility, self-esteem

11. Have you ever worked in an organization that used MBO? If so, what was the process? What was the outcome of that process for the organization and those involved?

12. We have all received evaluations of our performance. We tested for a driver's license, tried out for sports, or completed tests. Think about specific times when you received appraisals, at work or at any other place. How did you react to the feedback? Were some of your reactions negative? Why? How did you use the feedback? Did feedback help you grow in some way? How?

Chapter Project

In a one-page essay, state where you wish to be in the year 2020 in the following areas: professional life, personal relationships, spiritual life, social life. Then, draw up a plan to get yourself from your current status to your desired state.

Applications

In small groups analyze the following:

You Can't Have It All At Once

Reasoning, participating as a member of a team, understanding interrelationships, decision making, problem solving, visualizing, time management

Sulynn is a part-time student at the local community college. She is afraid that she will once again have to drop her courses even though she wants an associate degree in management very much. Because Sulynn is a divorced mother with two children to support, she must work full time as a sales clerk in the nearby mall. Additionally, she feels she should serve as a room mother in her son's and daughter's schools each year. Having no help around the house, she also does all inside and outside maintenance and yard work. In fact, the appearance of her home is an area of special pride for her. Needless to say, all of this activity leaves little time for friendships.

Sulynn did not go to college immediately after graduating from high school and feels that she is falling even farther behind by going part time. For the last four semesters, she has tried to play "catch-up" by registering for three or four courses even though her counselor advised against such a heavy load. By the middle of each semester she felt so overwhelmed that she dropped all or most of her courses.

It is now Thanksgiving, and Sulynn once again recognizes that feeling of hopelessness.

1. What is wrong with Sulynn's plans?
2. What advice would you give her in setting long-range, mid-range, and short-range goals?
3. How might she prioritize her goals?

Reading, listening, reasoning, participating as a member of a team and contributing to group effort, exercising leadership, creative thinking, and acquiring and evaluating information.

MBO Gone Awry

Mike Aston is an engineer with a large oil and gas company. Four months ago he was asked to participate in the budgeting process for the next year. The corporate office cited use of MBO as the rationale for getting Mike's input. Willingly he spent hours in his office alone, carefully calculating costs for maintaining and operating several oil platforms in Indonesia for which his local office is responsible.

After many hours of hard work, he submitted his budget to his supervisor, Emily Rodriguez, who passed it on to the head of the Houston office, Ronald Wang.

One month after the process began, Mr. Wang gathered the budgets from the different departments in the Houston office and carried them to the corporate office in New York.

Six weeks later the corporate office issued the overall budget guidelines for the corporation. Mike was astonished to see no resemblance between the guidelines and the budget that he had submitted. Emily asked him to redo his budget to fit the parameters issued by the corporate office, which he did.

Exactly four months after beginning the process and after much frustration, Mike received approval of a budget for his next year's operations.

1. Is this application of MBO correct?
2. What happened to create the overly long time involved and the need to prepare a second budget?
3. What could Mike have done to make a more productive process? Emily? Ronald? The corporate office?

Additional Readings and Resources

Cairo, Jim. *Motivation and Goal Setting—How to Set and Achieve Goals and Inspire Others.* Franklin Lakes: Career Press, 1998.

Covey, Stephen R. *The 7 Habits of Highly Effective People.* New York: Fireside, 1989.

John-Roger and Peter McWilliams. *The Portable Life 101.* Los Angeles: Prelude Press, 1992.

Laabs, Jennifer. "Has Downsizing Missed Its Mark?" *Workforce*, April 1999, 31–38.

Maddux, Robert B. and Michael Crisp (editor). *Effective Performance Appraisals/A Practical Guide for More Productive and Positive Performance Appraisals.* Los Altos: Crisp Publications, 1993.

Mathis, Robert L. and John H. Jackson. *Human Resource Management.* Minneapolis/St. Paul: West Publishing Company, 1997.

McKinley, Karen. *Powerful Performance Appraisals: How to Set Expectations and Work Together to Improve Performance.* Franklin Lakes: Career Press, 1998.

Ziglar, Zig. *Goals: Setting and Achieving Them On Schedule.* (2 video cassettes) New York: Simon and Schuster, 1995.

Leadership:
Styles and Skills of an Effective Leader

focus

After studying this chapter, you should be able to:

1. *Define leadership and identify the difference between a leader and a manager.*

2. *Explain the importance of leadership skills in both our professional and personal lives.*

3. *Discuss the leadership theories that have developed throughout history.*

4. *Identify the three leadership styles.*

5. *Describe the skills required of leaders at different levels in an organization.*

6. *Name the methods of developing leadership skills.*

7. *Identify and discuss the basic elements of effective leadership.*

8. *Differentiate between transactional and transformational leadership, and describe the leaders of the next generation.*

Sidney Harman is the chairman of Harman International, maker of high-tech, high-quality audio systems with $1.4 billion dollars in annual sales. Harman is a maverick CEO who promotes long-term connections with his employees, rails against temps and layoffs, and has built his newest plant in the U.S. and not in a low-wage area overseas. Harman International's track record is a testament to his success. The company's JBL and Infinity Audio Systems are world class and world known. To keep workers a top priority of his managers, Harman insists that all executives spend time working on the production line every month. Harman also keeps regular employees on the payroll even when they are not strictly needed for production. In a program called OLE (Off Line Enterprises), regular workers are assigned to jobs that normally would be outsourced.

Hedrick Smith, *Management Video Program,* **1999**

Based on the above biographical information, what types of leadership skills does Sidney Harman exhibit? How does he apply human relations skills in his leadership style? Why do you think his company has been so successful?

In This Chapter

What Is Leadership?

According to Warren Bennis in *On Becoming a Leader*, three basic reasons explain why society and organizations need leaders and cannot function without them. First, leaders are responsible for the effectiveness of organizations. The success or failure of all organizations depends on the quality of their leaders. Second, leaders provide a guiding purpose, something greatly needed in today's world. Third, today's concerns about the integrity of our institutions emphasize the need for better leadership in religion, government, Wall Street, and business. The quality of leadership determines the quality of life in society and in organizations.

Learning
Objectives 1 and 2

Define leadership and identify the difference between a leader and a manager. Explain the importance of leadership skills in both our professional and personal lives.

Quick Tip

"One person can live on a desert island without leadership. Two people, if they are totally compatible, could probably get along and even progress. If there are three or more, someone has to take the lead. Otherwise, chaos erupts."

Warren Bennis

Often the terms "leadership" and "management" are used interchangeably. However, a distinct difference can be drawn between the two. A person can be a leader without being in a position of management or supervision. Likewise, a person can be a manager without being an effective leader. Several distinctions can be made between leadership and management.

Leadership is the process of influencing the activities of individuals or organized groups so that they follow and willingly do what the leader wants them to do. To be a leader you must deal directly with people, develop rapport with them, apply appropriate persuasion, inspire them, and thus influence them to cooperate in pursuing your goals and vision. Without followers, leaders do not exist.

Everyone has the capacity to develop and acquire leadership skills—it is a learned ability—and leaders are seen in many different activities, from politics to play. Not only must leaders be vocationally or professionally competent, but they must also establish and maintain positive relationships with their followers. Developing such skills will help you understand how people feel, what motivates them, and the best ways to influence

You do not have to be a manager to be a leader.

quick wit

"A leader has the vision and conviction that a dream can be achieved."

Ralph Lauren

them. If you ask successful leaders how they get people to help them achieve goals and visions, they will talk about human values, such as empathy, trust, mutual respect, and courage.

Management, on the other hand, is the use of resources, including human resources, to accomplish a goal. It can occur in many settings, but it is most frequently associated with a formal position within organizations and businesses. It may be nonbehavioral if it involves only nonhuman resources—but most managers manage people. A person can be a manager without being an effective leader. This person may lack the ability to inspire or influence others.

Influence is a key word in the definition of leadership. Managers can be leaders only if employees allow them to influence their attitudes and behaviors. **Influence** is our ability to change the attitude or behavior of an individual or group. This ability is the result of our power (discussed in Chapter 12), which can come from any number of sources. Leaders vary in their use of power sources. Even formal leaders on the same level often vary in their ability to influence others. Although they may have the same official title, for example, one may demonstrate greater knowledge or expertise.

Writers such as Bennis contrast leaders and managers, with leaders innovating, challenging the status quo, and "doing things right" and managers administering, accepting the status quo, and "doing right things." John Naisbitt and Patricia Aburdene in *Megatrends 2000* say that any well-trained person can be a manager, but that a leader is ". . . an individual who builds fellowship by ethical conduct and by creating an environment where the unique potential of one individual can be actualized."

CASE STUDIES IN THE NEWS

It's 7:00 a.m. on Christmas morning. I'm sitting on a Continental 737 trying to get to my family for what's left of a holiday season. From the front of the plane comes a hearty and jolly "Ho, Ho, Ho!" Looking up, I see a man in casual dress with a Santa hat shaking hands with a delighted cockpit crew and cabin attendants. "Thanks for your hard work all year long . . . and I really appreciate your working on Christmas Day!" The smiles on their faces sent the message of appreciation from that crew to Gordon Bethune, the President of Continental Airlines.

What are the possible reactions to this leader's actions?

Leadership is a skill that we all need to develop. To attain goals that we support, whether personal or organizational, we must be effective in directing and coordinating the work of others so that they want to work toward these same goals. For example, you may support a departmental goal of increasing sales by 15 percent by influencing your department members to sell more, whether or not you are their supervisor. A solid understanding of and a conscientious effort to acquire these abilities can enhance your career even if management is not your career objective.

Additionally, leadership skills are needed in situations away from work when we want to influence individuals or groups to work toward certain goals. You may, for example, want to start a Neighborhood Watch program to make your street safer. You might attend city board meetings and speak out, or go door to door and speak to your neighbors in order to influence them to get involved.

In understanding what leadership is, you should also understand what it is not. It is *not* a form of manipulation. Rather, it involves understanding your followers' motives and providing conditions so that their work-related needs are met while attaining your work goals.

EVOLVING ROLES FOR MANAGERS AND EXECUTIVES

Today, the many changes in organizations, employees, and the business environment in general have created the need for a different kind of manager—one who is a good leader. New management styles will encourage creativity, risk taking, healthy conflict, and learning from errors. Using cross-functional teams whenever possible, a more interactive leader will listen to the ideas of others and support the varied talents of team members. Good human relations skills, coupled with good technology skills, will be the solid foundation for both effective managers and effective leaders.

The diagram on the next page illustrates the levels of management in a typical organizational hierarchy. Though the new ideas about management will "flatten" the hierarchies in many organizations, this management hierarchy will likely survive to a certain degree. However, though management is confined to the upper levels, leadership can appear at any level.

Further changes may be ahead for business, and the roles of managers are certain to continue to evolve. In the opening chapter of *Effective Executive*, Peter Drucker makes the case that every "knowledge worker" in any organization has become, in effect, an executive. He says of this worker, "By virtue of his position or knowledge, he is responsible for a contribution that affects the capacity of the organization to perform and to obtain results." In defining effective executives as those who know where their time goes, focus on outward contributions, build on their strengths, and make effective decisions, Drucker makes it clear that future managers who succeed will need to know how to manage themselves as well as their employees.

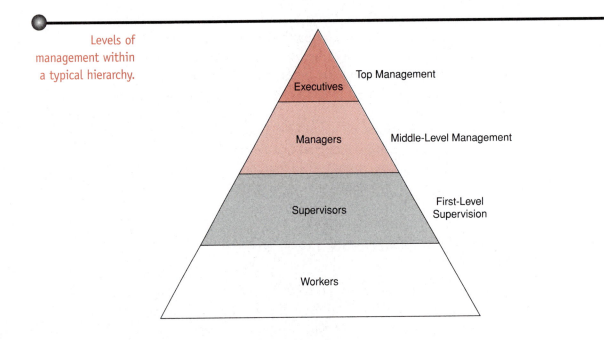

Levels of management within a typical hierarchy.

Top Management — Executives

Middle-Level Management — Managers

First-Level Supervision — Supervisors

Workers

*Fast***Chat**

1. Thinking of the opening Focus, state whether you think Sidney Harman is a leader or a manager. On what do you base your opinion?

2. Why do you think people skills are so vital to the success of a leader?

What Does Leadership Theory Say?

11.2

Ideas about leadership have changed significantly over the years. The **great man theory**, the first of these ideas to surface, was based on a belief that certain people are born to become leaders and will emerge in that role when their time comes. According to this theory, because of position, education, or mere exposure to other prominent leaders, these individuals develop a certain style or personality. Today we know that few leaders were born that way. Most people learn to be leaders through study, observation, and hard work. Modern theories of leadership fall into three broad categories—trait theories, behavioral theories, and situational theories. Each of these ideas has evolved with time and research; yet each remains in some way linked to its predecessor.

Learning
Objective 3

Discuss the leadership theories that have developed throughout history.

Leadership skill is acquired and developed.

TRAIT THEORIES

Wondering whether leaders have certain traits in common, researchers studied the physical, personality, and intelligence traits of prominent leaders in business, military, medical, and other fields. They looked at height, weight, personal appearance, and physique but found no conclusive results. They also looked at intelligence and at personality traits such as confidence, independence, and perception.

Lists of desirable traits were formed, giving weights to some believed to be more important than others. These lists were controversial at best and gave little recognition to the effects of the subordinates or the job itself on the success of the leader. The resulting confusion gave way to a belief that perhaps the success of leaders is based on their behavior rather than their traits. Several theories about leadership behavior then developed.

Trait theorists sought key physical, personality, and intelligence traits of known leaders.

BEHAVIORAL THEORIES

Theorists in this category believed that successful leaders can be identified by what they *do* rather than what traits they have. In an effort to identify certain behavioral patterns or "styles" of leadership, researchers measured typical leader behaviors such as amounts of control and authority, degrees of flexibility, concerns for goal or task accomplishment, and concerns for subordinates. Several well-known studies developed during this period are still used in identifying the styles of leaders.

Behavior theorists sought patterns or styles of behavior in leaders.

**Theory X
contends that
people are lazy
and dislike work.**

In his classic 1960 book, *The Human Side of Enterprise*, Douglas McGregor suggested that leaders treat followers according to the assumptions they hold about what motivates those followers. The traditional view, known as **Theory X**, exhibits a fairly dim view of workers' attitudes and motivation, while the second set of assumptions, **Theory Y**, takes a much more optimistic view of human nature.

McGregor's Theory X and Y

Theory X contends that people	Theory Y contends that
are lazy and unambitious	the expenditure of physical and mental effort in work is as natural as play or rest
have an inherent dislike of work, considering it necessary only for survival	people will direct themselves toward objectives if their efforts are rewarded
will avoid work if they can	most people are eager to work and have the capacity to accept, or even seek, responsibility as well as to use imagination, ingenuity, and creativity in solving problems
prefer to be directed, wanting to avoid responsibility	under the right circumstances, people derive much satisfaction from work and are capable of doing a good job

Leaders who hold Theory X assumptions believe that workers must be coerced, controlled, directed, and threatened to make them work, resulting in a leadership style that is strict and authoritarian.

**Theory Y
contends that
people are eager
to work and
capable of doing
a good job.**

**The Managerial
Grid plots a
leader's concern
for people and
for production.**

The Theory Y leader tends to be less directive and more supportive of subordinates' needs and uses a democratic or participative approach to leading others. McGregor thought that the ideal situation is to integrate the needs of employees with the needs of the organization. He believed that proper leadership helps employees set personal goals that are consistent with organizational goals.

Another of the well-known theories of this period is the two-dimensional **Managerial Grid®** developed by Robert Blake and Jane Mouton. A grid is used to plot the degree to which leaders show concern for people and concern for production (or getting the job done), with 1 being the least

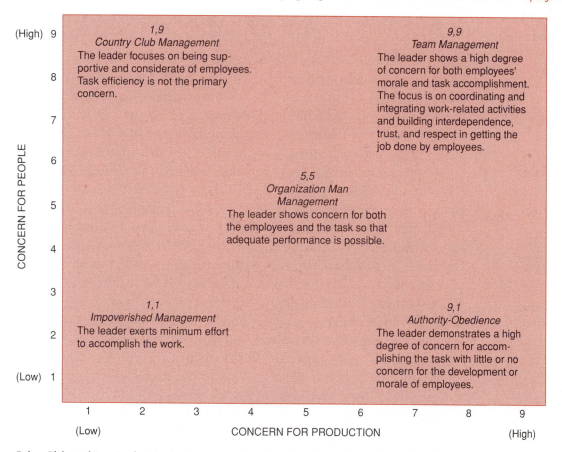

Blake and Mouton's Managerial Grid® identifies five specific leadership styles with varying degrees of concern for the tasks and the employees.

Robert Blake and Jane Srygley Mouton, *The Managerial Grid III: The Key to Leadership Excellence* (Houston: Gulf Publishing Company, 1985), 12. Reproduced by permission.

concern and 9 the highest concern. The diagram above illustrates the five specific leadership styles identified by Blake and Mouton.

This theory suggests that the 9,9 Team Management approach is the best leadership style because it results in maximum productivity and positive consequences. It is a goal-directed team approach. However, using a 9,9 leadership style in every situation is difficult. For example, in a conflict with an employee or any emergency job, the supervisor may need to use a 9,1 leadership style. The fluctuations in leader-follower situations, thus, gave rise to the next group of theories, which focus on the situation in which a leader is placed.

Blake and Mouton identified the 9,9 leadership style as the best.

SITUATIONAL OR CONTINGENCY THEORIES

Fiedler said a leader's success is affected by the leader-follower relationship, the task, and the leader's formal power.

As theorists continued their research of leadership styles, they realized that in most cases leaders need to adapt their styles to the situation at hand. One of the more important theories from this era was developed by Fred E. Fiedler in his 1967 book, *A Theory of Leadership Effectiveness*. Considerable research evidence supports Fiedler's belief that three important situational factors influence how much power and influence the leader has over the behavior of followers. These factors are the degree of confidence in and loyalty to the leader exhibited by the follower, the degree to which the task is routine or undefined, and the degree of formal or position power held by the leader. Fiedler suggested that some leaders function best in highly directive situations, whereas others are better suited to permissive situations. Therefore, organizations should consider each situation before assigning leaders because the same person may be effective in one situation but not in another.

An application of contingency theory is **situational leadership**, developed by Paul Hersey. Unlike The Managerial Grid® concept that stresses "one best way" to influence others, situational leadership says that leadership style must be adapted to fit the situation and varies with the "readiness" of subordinates. Readiness, according to this model, does not pertain to age or emotional stability but rather to a worker's desire to achieve, willingness to accept responsibility, ability and experience with the task, and confidence.

Situational leadership considers follower readiness, task behavior, and relationship behavior.

The diagram on the next page illustrates three dimensions of situational leadership. The bar across the bottom of the model describes the first dimension, **follower readiness**. Followers may be unwilling and unable, not able but willing, able but not willing, or willing and able to complete the task. The second dimension, **task behavior**, has to do with the extent to which a leader may or should be directive or "telling. " Does the leader closely supervise followers, telling them exactly what to do and when and how to do it, or does the leader allow a great deal of freedom in how followers accomplish the task? The third dimension of this model, **relationship behavior**, describes leader behavior with people, or the extent to which a leader is supportive of followers and engages in two-way communication with them.

Effective leaders adjust their leadership style to followers' task readiness.

Situational leadership suggests that leaders should vary their style as subordinates (either individually or as a group) develop and mature. When a task is new for followers, the leader must engage in many task-related behaviors to instruct them. Once followers begin learning the task, the leader reinforces them with supportive relationship behaviors (such as praise and encouragement) while still offering direction. After followers demonstrate that they are willing and able to perform the task, the leader should stop directing but still offer support and consideration. Finally,

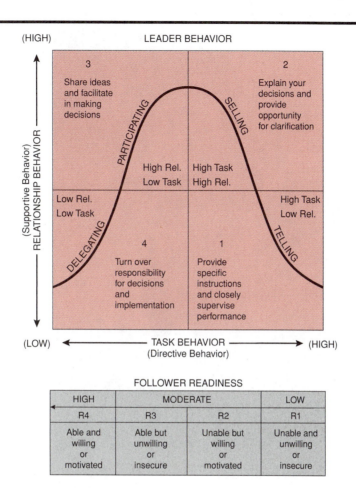

Situational leadership suggests varying the leadership style to match the different situations that leaders face.

when followers are high in readiness in a particular task, the leader reduces both task-related and relationship behaviors *in regard to that task.*

If followers assume additional new tasks, their readiness level may fall because they lack ability or confidence, and the leader must once again move through the cycle. For instance, if your office assistant is highly skilled in using a certain software package for building presentation charts and is suddenly given a new software version, that person's maturity level in preparing charts may decline. You will be required to return to the telling leadership style, providing training on the new software with close supervision until the assistant becomes skilled in its use and regains confidence. This approach allows leaders to handle various situations that occur in the workplace in a flexible manner.

quick wit

"Whether you think you can, or that you can't, you are usually right."

Henry Ford

Hersey believes that a leader who effectively matches style with followers' readiness motivates the followers and helps them move toward a higher level. You may have to change your leadership style to facilitate growth on the job, whether you are dealing with an individual or a group of employees. Groups may collectively go through the same changes in maturity as they progress through the forming, storming, and norming phases discussed in Chapter 6. Watching for behavior changes is the key to mastering this leadership application.

FastChat

1. Think of supervisors you may have had. Were they more Theory X or more Theory Y in their management style? Why do you categorize them as such?

2. What do you think is the most important feature of the situational leadership method of supervising? Why?

3. What situation can you think of that would require a change in the leadership style used? How would you react as the supervisor in that situation?

What Are Styles of Leadership?

11.3

A **leadership style** is a particular pattern of behavior exhibited by the leader. Most leaders have a style with which they are most comfortable and that they prefer to use. Studies of leadership behavior patterns have identified three traditional leadership styles. They are the autocratic, democratic, and free rein or laissez-faire styles. The **autocratic leadership** style is also described as authoritarian or directive. Leaders comfortable using this style usually show a high degree of concern for getting the job done. They are task-oriented and tend to provide close supervision, are highly directive, and are not at all comfortable with delegating their authority to others. A close match to this style is the Theory X leader and the 9,1 leader, described earlier in this chapter.

The **democratic leadership** style is often described as participative and is generally the style preferred by modern management and employees. These leaders tend to share authority with their employees, involving them in decision making and organizational planning. Democratic leaders show concern for their employees, especially in matters that directly affect them in the workplace. A close match to this style is the Theory Y leader and the 9,9 leader.

Typical of the democratic leader is the department manager who says to her work group, "The corporate office has set an overall goal of increasing production company-wide by 10 percent next year. I would like your thoughts about how much we can reasonably try for and how we might do that."

The **free rein or laissez-faire leadership** style is sometimes called the integrative style. These leaders allow employees more or less to lead themselves, offering advice or information when asked. Little effort is made by these leaders to either increase productivity or nurture employees. They may integrate the activities by handing out tasks and closing out assignments with a signature at job's end, but for the most part they are uninvolved with directing or controlling tasks or employees. This style can be effective if the task is highly routine or clearly defined and the employees are skilled and responsible in the performance of their duties. This leader is most commonly compared to the 1,1 leader of the Managerial Grid® theory.

An example of a person using the laissez-faire leadership style is one who hires good people, provides them with an arena to be as good as they

Learning
Objective 4

Identify the three traditional leadership styles.

The autocratic leader is highly directive.

The democratic leader encourages participation by followers.

The free rein leader allows followers to lead themselves.

quick wit

"The best of all rulers is but a shadowy presence to his subjects."

Lao Tzu

ETHICS CONNECTION

Henry Silverman, CEO of HFS, a franchising powerhouse, is a self-proclaimed authoritarian. At 58, he is a control freak, pure and simple. He wants to see and know everything! He grills his top deputies at three-hour monthly meetings and peppers them with daily faxes and phone calls.

Walter Forbes was CEO of CUC International, a membership club giant. His leadership style was considered by most to be that of a dreamy visionary. He spent his time out of the office trolling for acquisitions and hobnobbing with other famous CEOs like Bill Gates and Steve Forbes.

The merger of the two companies, to form Cendant, was consummated in late 1997 and surprisingly wound up as a landmark breach of faith case in the annals of Wall Street dealmaking. Under the misbegotten terms of the merger, Silverman was supposed to turn the business reins over to Forbes on January 1 of 2000, but it seems that he had no intentions of ever doing so.

Peter Elkind, *Fortune*, November 1998

Why do you think the breach of faith occurred? Given the difference in the two men's leadership styles, do you think the merger was wise in the first place?

Leaders should vary their style to fit the situation.

can be, and leaves them alone. Little direction is needed or provided and few decisions are made by this leader. In fields that are highly creative or primarily idea- or knowledge-driven, it is counter-productive to hire exceptionally creative or skilled individuals, pay them a huge annual salary, and then tell them what to do at every step. Scientists and doctors working on a research grant may respond quite well to this "uninvolved" type of leadership, as might software developers or creative directors.

Although leaders have a preferred style, they should vary their style to fit the various situations that arise in the workplace. Certain factors may influence a leader's preferred style, such as general disposition or personality, skill level or confidence, and perception of others. Failure to adjust to different situations can limit a leader's career.

CASE STUDIES IN THE NEWS

Do Marine Corps methods of focus, discipline, and teamwork apply to the banking industry? Hugh L. McColl, Jr. thinks they do. The mega-merger of his NationsBank and BankAmerica combined more than $570 billion in assets and some 200,000 employees. McColl is proud of the marine tradition of teamwork and believes that it is fundamental to his and the bank's success.

Says McColl, "I stay focused on my team. I try to get the very best people on the team, care about them, and see that they are rewarded for what they do. You have to lead from the front. The only way you can lead people is to demonstrate why they should follow you. Communication and motivation are two essential elements in building an effective, winning team."

Robert Deitz, *Spirit Magazine*, 1999

Do you share McColl's belief that discipline is an important part of making a team work in business? Based on the story, do you think you'd work well in this environment?

FastChat

1. Have you ever had the opportunity to use one of these leadership styles? Which one(s)? How did it work for work for you?

2. What problems, if any, could you envision with the use of the free rein leadership style?

3. What do you think were the leadership styles of the two CEOs in the Ethical Connection? What problems would you see with a proposed merger of those two companies?

11.4 What Are the Skills of a Leader?

Learning
Objective 5

Describe the skills required of leaders at different levels in an organization.

The leader's effectiveness may also depend on demonstrating an adequate level of skills. Fortunately, good leadership skills can be acquired or developed. Substantial research has identified three basic skills most beneficial to competent leaders. If you aspire to be a formal leader in an organization, you will need to pay particular attention to developing your technical, human relations, and conceptual skills, as discussed in Chapter 1. **Technical skills** are those skills required to perform a particular task. For example,

GLOBAL CONNECTION

There is only one Mickey Drexler! He transformed The Gap from a national retail chain into a recognizable global brand. Then came GapKids and now there's Gap-to-Go, which sports a list of basic Gap items from which you select and fax in your choices for delivery to your office or home by the end of the day. Don't forget Banana Republic—Drexler bought it and put Gap brands throughout. His Old Navy stores are "discount shopping with an attitude." His goal is to be everywhere, the Coca-Cola of the apparel business.

Drexler is driven. Work is his only hobby—and he knows the business! He frequently visits stores and looks at display racks and stacks, he checks out the threads, buttons, and the fabrics. He questions the sales staff about what customers are asking for and straightens a stack of khaki slacks while they answer. He talks to people in the store and in elevators and to employees in the stock rooms—always looking for fresh ideas and searching for ways to improve. He stays close to what makes the business work.

Nina Munk, *Fortune*, August 1998

Which leadership style does Drexler exhibit? Do you think there are disadvantages to having any organization of this size so much the "baby" of one person?

a first-line supervisor may need the knowledge and ability to step into the production line and assemble a part or tear down a mechanism to solve a problem or train employees on the process. Obviously, this skill is more important at levels of leadership closest to the actual work being done.

Conceptual skills are often referred to as administrative skills or "big picture" skills. The ability to think abstractly and to analyze problems becomes increasingly important as a person rises in the hierarchy to levels of top management. Planning and coordinating the overall activities of the organization and its personnel requires an ability to view the operations from a total perspective and anticipate as well as solve problems.

Human relations skills cut evenly across all levels of leadership in organizations. This ability to deal effectively with people includes effective communication, listening, empathy, inspiring and motivating, perceptiveness, and fair judgment when dealing with employees. Too often, the lack of this skill is the limiting factor in becoming a good leader.

These skills can be acquired or developed through various means as you progress along your career path. Common ways are exposure and observation, trial and-error experience, on-the-job training, and some forms of formal education. An important factor in your development as a leader will be your acceptance of the need for lifelong learning or continuing education. John Naisbitt and Patricia Aburdene, authors of *Re-inventing the Corporation*, point out that the constant change created by the new information society requires us to be lifelong learners. We must periodically upgrade our marketable skills

Competent leaders will develop their technical, human relations, and conceptual skills.

Lifelong learning will be an important factor in your development as a leader.

We must periodically upgrade our marketable skills and expand our knowledge, especially if we aspire to leadership.

John P. Kotter, the famed Harvard management professor, has written *Matsushita Leadership*, in which he chronicles the key events of Konosuke Matsushita's life. Kotter sets forth the lessons these events hold for corporations entering the 21st century. Matsushita came from humble beginnings, and with only 100 yen grew his business to $42 billion in revenues. He created thousands of jobs and a brand—Panasonic—known to millions of people around the globe.

The single biggest theme that runs through Matsushita's life is growth—as a human being, as a business person, as a leader. He was not highly educated, rich, charismatic, or well connected. Yet he became an entrepreneur, author, philanthropist, educator, social philosopher, and statesman. He kept learning and reinventing himself with the times. More than IQ, privilege, luck, personality, or dozens of other factors normally associated with great successes, Matsushita's quest for lifelong learning kept him out in front.

Cindy Kano, *Fortune*, March 1997

In what areas should learning occur as one grows? In what ways, in addition to formal classes, can we pursue the learning and development we need to stay marketable?

and expand our knowledge. We can no longer expect to get an education and be done with it—no education or skill will last a lifetime.

Coaching and mentoring by a senior person will also help you develop leadership skills. The way you function as a follower can also help or hurt your development as a leader. A valuable part of becoming a leader is being an effective follower, a role we all play throughout our lives.

FastChat

1. Which of the leadership skills do you think are easiest to obtain? Hardest? Why?

2. Why do you think lifelong learning will remain vital to success and achievement?

How Should You Follow?

11.5

Learning
Objective 6

*Name the methods
of developing
leadership skills.*

Lester Bittel and John Newstrom, in their book *What Every Supervisor Should Know*, point out that our personalities can determine under what kind of leader we perform best. You can either try to change your personality or seek out leaders who best complement your style. The suggestions below provide guidance on how you might choose a leader compatible with your personality or personal operating style.

Our personalities can determine our leadership needs.

Choosing Compatible Leaders

If you are an aggressive, cooperative person, you will probably do your best work under a democratic or free-rein leader. Your self-assertiveness will move you constructively in the right direction.

If you are an aggressive, hostile person, you will probably perform more effectively under an autocratic leader. Such a leader will help channel your feelings toward constructive ends.

If you are insecure, you will probably depend on your leaders for guidance. Such leaders should ideally be autocratic.

If you are an individualist who prefers to work alone and if you know your job well, you will probably perform most effectively under free-rein leadership.

Robert N. Waterman, Jr., author of *Adhocracy—The Power to Change*, suggests that followers can have a great influence on how successful a project is. Certainly, such success will reflect well on all members of the project, enhancing your image and potential as a leader. Additionally, working on a successful project is an excellent opportunity to observe effective leadership and build your skills for future use.

Learning these effective methods of good "followership" will certainly improve opportunities you may have for demonstrating your capabilities as a leader. Experience is the best teacher and provides excellent hands-on exposure to how projects operate.

quick wit

"There is the risk you cannot afford to take, and there is the risk you cannot afford not to take."

Peter Drucker

Leadership Learning

1. Try to understand any problems from top management's point of view. If you need more information to do so, ask for it.
2. Approach the project as an opportunity to learn and grow. After all, you will have a chance to hear various points of view, see different parts of the organization, interact with different people, and observe new skills.
3. Be committed to the project and show that commitment to your fellow team members.
4. If you believe that the project is doomed to failure, do not sit silently. Discuss this belief with your supervisor.

Our personalities can determine under what kind of leader we perform best.

1. Which of the types of leaders would you choose to best fit your personality and why?

2. How do you think project experience might be beneficial to you?

What Else Marks a Leader?

Aside from the skills described in the preceding paragraphs, certain other elements have proven critical to effective leadership. These elements include the satisfactory performance of the job functions, common behavioral characteristics, and certain attitudes and behaviors.

Learning
Objective 7

Identify and discuss the basic elements of effective leadership.

FUNCTIONAL ABILITIES

Early in the research on the basic functions of managing and leading, Luther Gulick, cited in Joseph Massie and John Douglas's management book, coined an acronym that has held through time as a quick reference. The letters in **PODSCORB** each represent a function basic to business leadership. They are **p**lanning, **o**rganizing, **d**irecting, **s**taffing, **c**oordinating, **r**eporting, and **b**udgeting. These elements are still needed despite the fact that they were first identified in the 1930s. Leaders and managers must be able to perform these key required tasks before they can motivate others and effectively operate in a business environment.

CHARACTERISTICS

A characteristic is a distinguishing feature or attribute that sets you apart from the norm. Studies that began during the behavioral sciences school of management development identified certain behaviors and abilities that were considered key elements. Successful leaders have consistently been labeled with the five characteristics shown in the box on page 310.

Motivating employees means getting commitment through the gentle art of persuasion and setting examples of excellence. Former CBS executive Barbara Corday, discussed by Bennis in *Working Woman*, says that empathy helps give leaders power. That power comes from the company's success and the leader's staff working well. In the same article, Bennis points out that followers' trust of the leader is essential to motivation. Leaders can develop trust by being steadfast in their goals, by "walking their talk" (living what they espouse), by being reliable and supportive, and by honoring their commitments and promises.

Leaders often find delegating the single most difficult thing to do. A mistake often made when delegating is giving the responsibility without the authority to get the job done. The steps to successful delegation are to select

Leadership Characteristics

Communicator

Leaders are able to express themselves well. Certainly this feature includes good oral and written communication skills but goes far beyond that. It means that they know who they are, what their strengths and weaknesses are, and how to use them to their full advantage. They also know what they want, why they want it, and how to get it. They set goals and achieve those goals by communicating to others what they want to gain support and cooperation.

Decision Maker

Leaders are comfortable making decisions. They are able to gather facts, organize information, and apply good judgment in their choice of action. The willingness to make a choice after considering all possible alternatives is essential. Depending upon the complexity of the decision to be made, decision-making models may be used. Most decisions are made independently, with the decision makers held fully responsible. They take risks that the decision is a good one.

Risk Taker

Effective leaders very often operate on instinct, go with their "gut feel", and are willing to try everything that may bring desired results. The willingness to take risks seems to set them apart from the crowd. Risk takers do not fear failure. They view it as a "temporary setback" or perhaps a "mid-course correction" and feel that failure today does not rule out success tomorrow. Some United States companies are deliberately making risk taking part of their corporate culture. Risk takers tend to be achievement-oriented, goal-directed, and self-confident. They are the great experimenters of life. The willingness to try new ideas often reaps great rewards for the individual and the company. Many experts have identified this characteristic as tantamount to being a successful leader.

Motivator

Leaders must be able to influence others to produce good results. In the climate of the 21st century, motivation of employees will lean away from the autocratic methods of the past toward the new style of inspiring and empowering employees. John P. Kotter, author of *The Leadership Factor,* says that leadership is "the process of moving people in some direction mostly through noncoercive means." A good leader recognizes that people are a key resource to the success of the organization, project, or vision.

Delegator

An effective leader delegates tasks to others to develop their skills and build a stronger team. **Delegation** means assigning tasks to subordinates and following up to ensure that they are completed properly and on time.

quick wit

"Well done is better than well said."

Ben Franklin

the person best qualified to perform the task, give good instructions and ask for feedback to assure understanding of the task directions. Then leave the person alone to complete the assignment. If you are the leader, follow up to assure completion but do not interfere with that individual's methods of getting the job done.

In an amusing analysis of the leadership style of Attila the Hun, author Wess Roberts describes Attila's rules on delegating. Roberts stresses that

GLOBAL CONNECTION

Society may be moving from an industrial economy to a knowledge economy, but the old business schools, like Harvard and Wharton, have not made the shift. They still have that golf-club culture. The founders of The KaosPilots, based in Denmark, hope to fill the void. Their 3-year leadership training program is designed to provide students the skills they need to succeed in rapidly changing and unpredictable business environments. Their approach develops administrative and technical skills useful in local, national, and global levels.

Nearly half of the curriculum focuses on developing each student's "inner pilot," using assertiveness training, stress prevention, group dynamics, risk-taking methods, and physical training to heighten their awareness levels. The other half offers students the chance to develop project management skills. The school is designed to merge theory and practice into "an intelligence ecology" and prepare students to navigate in chaotic systems and see risks as opportunities.

Dorte Hygum Sorensen, *Fast Company*, June 1996

What is your impression of the curriculum offered by this program? Do you think it is likely that more non-traditional programs will develop as the global economy continues to change?

"delegating demonstrates trust in your subordinates and helps build their skills and improves their loyalty." Specific rules that Attila applied are illustrated below.

Attila the Hun's Rules of Delegation

1. Never delegate responsibilities that require your direct attention.
2. Delegate to those people most able to fulfill the assignment, and grant them authority as well as responsibility.
3. Once you delegate a task, never interfere.
4. Do not give your Huns precise direction on how to accomplish their delegated assignments.

Warren Bennis, in *On Becoming a Leader*, adds that leaders seem to share some, if not all, of the characteristics in the chart that follows. In a related workbook, *Learning to Lead*, Bennis and Joan Goldsmith stress that these characteristics stand out as important for success and are deeply relevant for tomorrow's business environments.

Additional Leadership Characteristics	
A guiding vision	Leaders have a clear idea of what they want to do and the strength to persist.
Passion	Leaders love what they do and love doing it. Leaders who communicate passion give hope and inspiration to others
Integrity	The integrity of leaders has three components: self-knowledge, candor, and maturity. Leaders never lie to themselves, know their flaws and assets and deal with them, are honest in thought and action, and experience and grow through following.
Trust	Trust must be acquired. It is the product of a leader's ability with coworkers and followers.
Curiosity and daring	Leaders wonder about things, are willing to experiment and learn from adversity.

ATTITUDES AND BEHAVIORS

Attitudes and behaviors most commonly displayed by successful leaders are listed on the opposite page. Sometimes described as states of mind or feelings, attitudes play an important role in the workplace. Followers are affected by the example you set and will react to your enthusiasm and dedication. A showing of empathy for them is important and will gain you their respect. Each of these attitudes has a direct bearing on your success as a leader.

Attitudes reflect predispositions, mental states, emotions, expectations, and moods. Keeping attitudes positively focused will assure better leadership and strong followership. Displaying a sense of humor is also a method of maximizing good human relationships. That is not to say you need to be the village (or office) clown, but that you can express feelings and enjoy the workplace. Closely related to attitudes are courtesy and enthusiasm. Being courteous toward others and demonstrating civility can create a positive workplace setting. Your enthusiasm and show of positiveness go a long way toward inspiring and motivating people. This is an important part of being an effective leader.

Typical Attitudes and Behaviors of Effective Leaders

Positive-thinking

Dedicated with a sense of mission

Open-minded

Enthusiastic

Spontaneous

Courageous

Empathetic

Flexible

Responsible

Ethical with high character

Self-denying; willing to forgo self-indulgences, such as showing anger

Competent (both in leadership and technical skills)

Wise

Energetic

Considerate

Fair

1. Which of the characteristics discussed above do you feel are most important and why?

2. In which areas do your strengths lie, and in which areas do you think you need to develop?

3. How important do you think attitudes are and what impact do you think they can have on the work environment?

FastChat

What Is the Future of Leadership?

Differentiate between transactional and transformational leadership, and describe the leaders of the next generation.

According to Bernard M. Bass, a leadership researcher, leadership can be categorized in two ways—transactional and transformational. **Transactional leadership** encompasses the theories presented in this chapter and requires that leaders determine what followers need to achieve their own and organizational goals, classify those needs, and help followers gain confidence that they can reach their objectives. **Transformational leadership**, on the other hand, motivates followers to do more than they originally expected to do by raising the perceived value of the task, by getting them to transcend self-interest for the sake of the group goal, and by raising their need level to self-actualization.

Richard Boyd, another leadership theorist, suggests that today's business environment requires a variation of transformational leadership. He feels that leadership skills should include the following:

1. *Anticipatory skills*—the ability to foresee a constantly changing environment.
2. *Visioning skills*—the ability to induce people to take action that agrees with the leader's purposes or those of the organization.
3. *Value-congruence skills*—the ability to understand followers' economic, safety, psychological, spiritual, aesthetic, and physical needs in order to motivate them on the basis of shared motives, values, and goals.
4. *Empowerment skills*—the ability to share power.
5. *Self-understanding*—the ability to understand one's own needs and goals as well as those of followers.

Recurring themes seem to ripple through all the practices and prognostications of the leadership gurus. Since Michael Hammer and Steven Stanton pioneered the re-engineering movement for the '80s and '90s, the big theme has been repositioning and reposturing for the future. Indeed, little doubt remains that we all need to prepare in some way or another for the new millennium, the new work environment, the new workers, the new globalization, and the information revolution. There is no question that these clichés have real meaning. But what does all this have to do with leadership development?

The majority of new models still deal heavily with human relation skills. As technology advances, we will necessarily grow and improve those skills to remain a viable part of our environments—at work and at home. Some shifts in paradigms will occur, but on balance people are people and management is management.

Warren Bennis suggests that we are our own raw leadership material. We must "invent" ourselves by discovering our own native energies and desires and then find our own way to act on them. Numerous experts predict that the days of the "big bad boss" are gone. Bennis says that the next generation of leaders will be more intellectually aware, will be comfortable with and excited by ideas and information, and will anticipate and accept change, seeing it as an opportunity. These new leaders will share the following nine characteristics.

quick wit

"One doesn't get to the future first by letting someone else blaze the trail."

Gary Hamel

New Leader Characteristics

1. They will have a broad education, maintained through lifelong learning.
2. They will have boundless enthusiasm.
3. They will believe in people and teamwork.
4. They will be willing to take risks.
5. They will be devoted to long-term growth rather than short-term profit.
6. They will be committed to excellence.
7. They will be ready for change.
8. They will demonstrate virtue in their integrity, ethics, and respect for self and others.
9. They will be wise, giving followers a chance to look good.

The effective leader of the future will optimistically embrace change and will continue to do the most important task of helping others to perform to the highest of standards.

FastChat

1. What do you think is the most difficult task facing leaders in the 21st century?

2. How would you prepare for meeting the expected challenges facing future leaders?

3. Do you think the challenges will be much different than those faced by Matsushita when he led Matsushita Electric in the 1920s on the trail toward Panasonic in the 2000s?

Key Terms

leadership
management
influence
great man theory
Theory X and Y
Managerial
situational leadership
follower readiness
task behavior
relationship behavior
leadership style
autocratic leadership
democratic leadership
free-rein (laissez-faire)
   leadership
technical skills
conceptual skills
human relations skills
PODSCORB
delegation
transactional leadership
transformational leadership

Summary

Leaders, people who influence the behavior of others, may be found at all levels of the organizational hierarchy and in personal life. A person can be a leader and not be a manager and vice versa. Leadership has long been a subject of concern with considerable research to define its origin and identify those traits or behaviors in individuals that single them out to be leaders. From the great man theory, researchers moved into trait and behavioral theories and identified various means of recognizing and even developing leadership abilities. Some of the best-known theories are Theory X and Y, the Managerial Grid®, and situational leadership.

Several distinctive styles of leadership have also been identified. They are autocratic, democratic, and free rein. Most leaders have a preferred style but change their approach to fit the needs of the situation. An effective leader in an organization must be able to apply technical, conceptual, and human relations skills. These skills can be acquired or developed through exposure and observation, trial-and-error experience, on-the-job training, formal education and continuing education, coaching and mentoring, and effective following. Successful leaders will also display certain functional abilities, characteristics, and attitudes and behaviors known to be critical to effective leadership. Future leaders will be transformational, motivating their followers to transcend self-interest for the sake of the group goal by raising their need levels to self-actualization. Leadership experts predict that the next generation of leaders will possess characteristics that allow this transformation to happen.

Review Questions

1. Define leadership. What is the difference between a leader and a manager?
2. What is the importance of leadership skills to us at work at any level? In our personal lives?
3. Discuss the various leadership theories that have developed throughout history and name and define the three traditional leadership styles.
4. What are the three categories of skills required of leaders? How do they vary with the leader's level?
5. What are the methods of developing leadership skills? Why is lifelong learning now necessary?
6. Identify the basic elements of effective leadership. Name the functions, characteristics, and attitudes and behaviors of effective leaders.
7. How do transactional and transformational leadership differ? Which is expected to be more important in the future? What elements are part of it?

Discussion Questions

1. Think of a situation in which you have been involved and identify the leader's style. Was that style appropriate for the situation?
2. Describe the leadership style from a situational perspective that should be applied to you in your present job situation or in an organization to which you belong. Is that style being used? Why or why not?
3. Describe situations that call for each of the three traditional leadership styles. Discuss why that particular leadership style best fits that situation.
4. Cite examples from your experience of leaders you perceive to be transactional and transformational. What skills and special characteristics do they demonstrate?
5. Describe follower roles that you now have. How are your behaviors and attitudes in those roles helping you develop leadership skills?

Reading, reasoning, participating as a member of a team, contributing to group efforts, exercising leadership, and understanding complex interrelationships.

Chapter Project

Develop and design a brochure for a professional training course aimed at preparing employees to be effective leaders in the 21st century. Create a professional-looking product with serious content. Assume you will be the course leader. Outline and describe the topics you plan to cover, describe why these topics are important, and identify what the proposed benefits of this course will be for the participant. You may want to use the Internet as a source for some materials. Using any of the search engines, leadership topics will render many ideas for your brochure. Embellish this brochure with any other items of interest that add to its professional appeal. Make the reader want to take your course.

Applications

In small groups analyze the following situations.

Do We Want to Follow the Leader?

Andy ruled the production crew with an iron fist. He had come up through the rank and file and had many years of experience to his credit. His success was based on technical expertise. He had no formal education but knew more about the manufacturing processes involved than any young college graduate in the company. Although the people in the work unit respected his technical knowledge and abilities, they felt that he was a bit heavy-handed in his method of supervising the day-to-day operations. "He cracks the whip around here and closely supervises every move you make," said Ron, the lead technician. "He wants to be involved with every detail and won't let go of any responsibility. You would think that he doesn't trust us or that maybe he just doubts we would get the job done."

1. What leadership style is Andy using in this situation? *autocratic*
2. What assumptions has he made about his employees, and what typical behaviors of the leadership style is he demonstrating?
3. How do you think the workers feel about his leadership style? How would you feel?

What Caused the Boat to Sink?

The Administrative Office had a staff of seven seasoned employees running daily operations. As a service organization, they helped other company employees with questions about policies and procedures and processed all official paperwork on promotions, reassignments, health and life insurance, and many other administrative matters. Wilma, their supervisor for nine years, respected the knowledge and maturity of her employees and normally left them alone to do the job as they saw fit. When Wilma retired and moved away, Doris was hired from another company to replace her. On her first day as the new supervisor, Doris changed many of the internal office procedures to her way of doing business. She required that all incoming calls from company employees be directed to her. She became the single point of information for the office. She requested a daily prioritized list of activities from each of the staff members for approval by her. She then determined whether the priorities were in order or correct and revised them. Within six months, complaints became common, morale declined, and finally five of the original seven staff members resigned. Doris replaced those employees with members from her previous company's staff, and the operation began to run smoothly again.

Reading, reasoning, participating as a member of a team, contributing to group efforts, exercising leadership, and understanding complex interrelationships.

1. Using situational leadership, what would you assess the readiness level of the seven office staff members to be?
2. What leadership style had Wilma applied?
3. What leadership style did Doris apply in her new position as head of the Administrative Office?
4. Was Doris's leadership style the correct one to apply in this situation? If not, why not?
5. What might Doris have done to improve human relations in this example?

Additional Readings and Resources

Elkind, Peter. "A Merger Made in Hell." *Fortune*, November 1998, 134.

Deitz, Robert. "Bank On It." *Spirit*, Spring 1999, 26–32.

Kotter, John P. *Matsushita Leadership*. New York: Free Press, Simon & Schuster, 1997

Munk, Nina. "Gap Gets It." *Fortune*, August 1998.

Appreciating Power:

Positioning and Politics

focus

After studying this chapter, you should be able to:

1. *Define power and explain why developing power is necessary.*

2. *Identify and discuss the basic power sources available to you.*

3. *Name and discuss the three basic power personalities.*

4. *Identify and discuss techniques used in the planning and implementation of power positioning.*

5. *Discuss the importance of applying power politics.*

6. *Explain the ways that power symbols can be used for power positioning.*

7. *Discuss why empowering others is important.*

8. *Discuss the pitfalls of developing power.*

The once power-shy Oprah Winfrey says, "Power wasn't even a part of my vocabulary. I grew up dirt-poor in Mississippi and had the good fortune to hit it big with a job hosting a Chicago TV talk show. I didn't recognize the influence I could have." Now she does and she has defined it: "It's the ability to impact with purpose. Power is the privilege to influence." And she has made the most of her power applications—contracting with ABC to produce inspiring TV movies, cutting a feature-film deal with Disney, posing for magazine covers from *Fitness* to *Vogue*, and creating Oprah's Book Club. The book club has turned Winfrey into the publishing industry's fairy godmother. No one can know the true impact and influence of her on-air endorsements, but she has magically turned 20 sleepers into best-sellers—in some cases boosting sales by millions of copies.

Fortune Magazine, **October 1998**

How do you think Oprah was able to become such a powerful influence in our modern society? What do you think her sources of power have been? Do you think she will continue to be such an influential force?

In This Chapter

What Is Power?

Power is our ability to influence others to do what we want them to do. It involves changing the attitudes or behaviors of individuals or groups. Power is exercised by nonmanagement as well as management employees and by people in their personal lives.

Power gives us the means to accomplish tasks and can help us reach our goals. Many experts point out that people cannot succeed in organizations today without acquiring some power and learning how to use it. Also, an understanding of power can help you recognize when those around you are attempting to influence you through the exercise of power. The appropriate use of power can be a strong factor in how effective your human relations skills are.

A fine distinction exists between influence and power. Influence is the application of power through actions we take or examples we set that cause others to change their attitudes or behaviors. People must possess power from some source before they can influence the behavior of others. Patricia Sellers notes in her article, "The 50 Most Powerful Women in American Business," that power is shifting to people who aren't in traditional corporate America at all. For example, Oprah Winfrey's company, Harpo Entertainment, is small but her influence on culture and the way Americans think is enormous.

Too often the word "power" brings to mind negative images. Terms such as manipulation, control, domination, exploitation, corruption, and coercion are frequently associated with power. Because of the tarnished image of power, many individuals tend to shy away from learning about and practicing positive power.

Learning
O b j e c t i v e   1

Define power and explain why developing power is necessary.

Acquiring power and learning to use it are essential to accomplishing goals.

Power, sometimes seen as negative, is desirable when used appropriately.

Q uick Tip . . . .

"Professional excellence requires the knack of knowing how to make power dynamics work for us, instead of against us."

John P. Kotter

Power can be a healthy, desirable attribute when channeled appropriately. It is most effective when its use is not obvious. Positive uses of power include influence, leadership, control, authority, and direction. These strong behaviors are very necessary in both your personal and professional life.

"The Power 25: The Influence Merchants" is a list of the most power-ful and influential forces on Capitol Hill. Lobbyists are a permanent establishment in Washington, and Fortune's Power 25 is the undisputed "A" list. It is where some of the nation's most powerful people play an extraordinarily high-stakes game of persuasion, where backs are scratched, arms twisted, favors granted and redeemed. This is where the business of poli-tics really gets done. And for all the talk of money in politics, the greenback doesn't always rule. Many interest groups derive their clout from the size and commitment of their membership, not the net worth of their members.

Jeffrey H. Birnbaum, *Fortune*, December 1998

Why would a large and committed membership give an interest group more clout on Capitol Hill? What interest groups have you heard of, and about what are they trying to persuade politicians?

Acquiring some power and learning how to use it, then, is essential to your achievement of personal and organizational goals. An understanding of the sources of power available to you and techniques for drawing upon them will assist you in strengthening your power base.

FastChat

1. Why is power a necessary tool?

2. How have you had power exercised over you and how did you feel about it?

What Are the Sources of Power?

John French and Bertram Raven, two researchers on power, identified five basic power sources: reward, coercive, legitimate, expert, and referent. The first three sources are derived from our position within the organization; the last two are generated from our personal characteristics. Other theorists add derivative and passive power to the list.

REWARD POWER

Reward power is the ability to give something of material or personal value to others. The rewards may be in the form of promotions, bonuses, supplies and equipment, highly desirable job assignments, or reserved parking places. It may also take the form of valued information, praise for a job well done, or a desired position title. At home reward power may come in the form of an unexpected gift, an allowance, a night to eat out, or a trip to the movies.

Reward power is considered the most important source of power by French and Raven because it places the reward seeker almost totally at the mercy of the reward giver. Only by submitting to the desired behavior can the seeker hope to obtain the reward from the giver. The strength of this power source varies with the amount of rewards controlled by the giver. This power source can be held by a full range of individuals, from the corporate chief executive to the unit secretary who controls the distribution of supplies.

Learning
Objective   2

Identify and discuss the basic power sources available to you.

Developing or acquiring power sources is a necessary step in gaining power.

Quick Tip . . . .

"Power doesn't corrupt people, people corrupt power."
—William Gaddis

COERCIVE POWER

Coercive power is based on fear and punishment. Demotions, dismissals, reprimands, assignment of unpleasant tasks, and public embarrassment are examples of coercive power. This form of power can be directed toward superiors, coworkers, or subordinates. At home, coercive power comes in the form of spanking, scolding, grounding, or loss of privileges.

Coercive power can be used in a positive manner, such as in an emergency, to let others know that you mean business. When an employee's performance is slipping, being firm and pointing out the consequences of continued nonperformance can have a positive effect.

However, open use of coercive power is generally considered unacceptable in the work environment, and the user may risk retaliation, sabotage, or malicious obedience. Low morale may result, because coercive power is a negative motivator. This counterproductive use of power also places the user at great risk of being removed from any position of power. Because of its potential for harm, coercive power should be used with great caution.

LEGITIMATE POWER

Legitimate power is derived from formal rank or position within an organizational hierarchy. A company president holds greater legitimate power than a regional vice president, and a general department manager will hold more legitimate power than a first-line supervisor or a technician on the assembly line. This power source is dependent on the formal, established chain of command within the organization and the perceived authority of the individual in that position of power. Examples away from work include a team captain or a committee chairperson. These individuals are perceived to have an "appointed" power.

However, just because you are ranked higher in an organization does not mean that you hold total power over those under you. An example is the security guard who has the legitimate power to request the president of the company to present identification to enter a secured facility.

EXPERT POWER

While reward, coercive, and legitimate power are linked to position, expert and referent power are derived from personal characteristics.

Expert power develops when an individual possesses specialized skills, knowledge, or expertise. This power source is limited in that it is only useful when the knowledge is of value to the seeker. This power source is not dependent on appointed rank or position. It can be held by individuals ranging from the chief executive officer to the computer technician to the janitor. For instance, when the building heat is malfunctioning, employees will turn to the janitor rather than the company president, who may have no knowledge of machinery or equipment.

Expert power can also be found off the job. You may, for example, defer to a neighbor with extensive mechanical experience when dealing with an automobile that will not start or a dishwasher that does not work.

REFERENT POWER

Referent power is power based on respect or admiration for the individual. This respect or admiration may result from personal charisma and "likable" personal traits. Sports heroes, political leaders, and dynamic religious or business leaders can influence the behavior of others who have a desire to emulate their heroes' perceived success. Bill Clinton may have retained his legitimate power as President but may have lost his referent power with some of the public after the White House scandals erupted.

DERIVATIVE AND PASSIVE POWER

Derivative power comes from close association with a powerful person. We are all familiar with signs and symbols of people using this power technique. Name dropping and use of the "good old boy" system are examples of using derivative power to gain advantages.

Derivative and passive power are not strong or reliable power sources, and tend to damage the credibility of those who rely on them.

Passive power, the last of the power sources, stems from a display of helplessness. A child often uses this power source effectively on a parent to gain attention or solicit help with some undesirable task. Unfortunately, we sometimes see this same technique carried into adulthood and used in the workplace. For example, an employee will act incapable in order to gain help in accomplishing a task or to escape it altogether. A simple statement that says, "I cannot possibly manage this all by myself and, besides, you are so much better at this sort of thing than I am," will often subtly but powerfully gain the desired results.

Derivative and passive power sources are not dependable in the long haul. They tend to damage the image and credibility of the user. Recognizing that these power sources exist and avoiding their use will aid you in developing more desirable power sources. Being knowledgeable will additionally help you avoid being the pawn that gets duped in the game of passive power.

1. Which of these power sources do you think apply to you?

2. Which of these power sources do you think are more important than others?

3. Who might represent examples of some of these power sources?

*Fast*Chat

Can You Combine Sources of Power?

Learning
Objective   3

Name and discuss the basic power sources available to you.

The power sources are highly linked. They tend to occur in combinations, as the following example illustrates. As you read the example, note the various sources of power that are used and how they are linked.

Power Source Linking

Thomas, the head of the accounting department, glared down at the junior accountant sitting in the chair beside him. He was angry at his antics and felt that he had to show him he could not get away with foolishness that reflected badly on the company. Thomas's brow was furrowed, reflecting a scowl. When he spoke, it was in low-toned, slow phrases that revealed his anger. He was the department chief with full authority to administer the punishment due for the embarrassment caused the company and to delay any promotion until the junior accountant's behavior matured.

Thomas has legitimate power given to him through his position in the organization. Additionally, he is exercising coercive power through his intimidating body language and threats of consequences.

Another example of power source linking would be the prominent sports figure Michael Jordan. He has expert power because he possesses special skills and expertise in the sport of basketball and has referent power because he is admired and respected for his ball-handling and point-scoring abilities. He also had legitimate power as the ranking, or senior member of the team and acquired the position of Most Valuable Player (MVP) on several occasions.

With some individuals we don't have to guess or be told which power sources they use or possess. The names or faces of certain individuals are easily recognized because of the impact they've had on us or on our world. We immediately acknowledge and can often easily identify the power sources of people such as those pictured on the next page.

The type of behavior response from individuals will vary in different situations depending upon what the receiver perceives the power source of the sender to be. For example, individuals with a high degree of expert power are usually admired and respected and, therefore, have a high degree of ref-

quick wit

"Life is full of obstacle illusions."

Grant Frazier

What are the power sources for these individuals?

CORBIS/Mitchell Gerber

CORBIS/Reuters Newsmedia Inc.

CORBIS/Reuters Newsmedia Inc.

CORBIS/AFP

Oprah Winfrey   **Bill Gates**   **Tiger Woods**   **Fidel Castro**

erent power. Similarly, individuals with a high degree of legitimate power may wield strong reward and coercive power over others.

Many combinations of power can be developed. A particularly powerful combination to acquire is expert, legitimate, and reward power sources. Obviously, the more power sources you acquire, the stronger your influence will be in the work environment and on a personal level.

Our ability to use these power sources individually or in combination relies heavily on the perception of those involved. They must believe that our power source is genuine. Kotter, as summarized by James Stoner and R. Edward Freeman in *Management*, suggests that, in order to develop the perception in others that you are truly powerful, you must use your power sources wisely and appropriately. Recognize what sources you do not have and avoid their use. Using undeveloped sources or abusing your power sources weakens your credibility and strips you of what power you do have. Understand the risks and benefits of using each of your power sources and develop your skills accordingly.

You must use your power sources wisely and appropriately.

FastChat

1. How were the power sources of the individuals pictured above developed? How are these power sources linked?

2. Which of the power sources do you think link in your personal activities?

3. Have you ever seen or heard about someone who used linked power sources unwisely and in appropriately? What was the outcome?

12.4 What Is Your Power Personality?

Some theorists believe that power is based on personal characteristics.

Some behavioral theorists believe that a person's use of power is based more on personal characteristics, charisma, and acquired personality traits than on other factors. These traits vary in intensity in different people, resulting in three basic power personalities: the power-shy, the power-positive, and the power-compulsive.

Power-shy individuals tend to avoid being placed in positions that require overt use of power. They quickly sidestep or totally shun responsibility and leadership, feeling extremely uncomfortable with decision making and influencing or controlling the behavior of others. Power-shy individuals make excellent followers and will usually excel in positions that require them to operate independently and rely on individual skills and abilities. You may recognize why Oprah Winfrey was once considered a power-shy individual.

On the other hand, **power-positive** people genuinely enjoy accepting responsibility and thrive on the use of power. Highly power-motivated, these individuals enjoy controlling situations and directing and influencing the behavior of others. They express strong views and opinions and are usually risk takers and adventurers. Power-positive individuals can be valuable resources when placed in leadership roles requiring the described qualities. How do you think Ms. Winfrey's success in her field helped her transform from being a power-shy to a power-positive person? Only when the need or desire for power becomes compulsive and is a driving force directing all actions toward selfish goals does it take on negative overtones.

Power-compulsive individuals have a lust for power and are seldom satisfied with the amount of power they have. These individuals constantly seek increased levels of control and influence over others and have a strong need to display power plays for personal gain in all situations. This use of power is destructive and intimidating, seldom benefiting the organization or the individual.

Fortunately, the need and desire for power does vary greatly in individuals. The power-shy and power-positive personalities are both needed in the work environment to create balance. We acquire power in varying amounts, from different sources, and at different times in life. How we choose to use it reflects our positive or negative motives.

The short self-inventory presented below will rate your power personality. Does the need for power control you, or do you constructively use the power that you have for growth and advancement? As in any self-test, you must be honest in your responses to get a true reflection of yourself. You may also want to have your spouse, close friend, or coworker answer the questions about you. Seeing yourself as others see you is an excellent method of gaining insight.

INSTRUCTIONS: Answer each question with 2 (often true), 1 (sometimes true), or 0 (seldom or never true). The scoring interpretation appears below.

1. "Get the last word in" is my motto. 1
2. It is important to me to "wear the pants" in my family. 1
3. It disturbs me when things are disorganized. 2
4. It angers me when somebody tries to take advantage of me. 2
5. When I entertain, it is important that plans go smoothly. 1
6. For my leisure time, I usually plan things/activities well in advance. 0
7. People who don't behave the way I expect really irritate me. 2
8. Nothing angers me more than people trying to dominate me. 2
9. In my position, I feel it is demeaning to do subordinate tasks. 1
10. I always conceal my true feelings. 1
11. I do not tolerate my child publicly displaying poor manners or bad behavior. 1
12. In a public or business meeting, I make certain my viewpoint is known. 0
13. I cannot tolerate others humiliating me. 2

14. I would turn down a tempting job offer with another firm if the position had less prestige and power than my current one. 1
15. I agree with Michael Korda's quote about the workplace, "Without power we're merely cogs in a meaningless machine." 2
16. I feel good when I can make others perform menial tasks for me. 0
17. To show others "who's the boss," I will sometimes humiliate them undeservingly. 0
18. When people get "out of line" at work, it really irritates me. 1
19. I never allow other people to push me around. 1
20. Inconveniencing others, forcing them to adhere to my schedule, or keeping others waiting provides me with a certain degree of enjoyment. 1
21. It angers or depresses me when a rival at work upstages me. 0
22. I will feel like a failure if I do not achieve my targeted key executive position in my company. 0

16

1, 2, 4, 8, 9, 12,
13-17, 19-22

卌 卌 ////
(14)

SCORING INTERPRETATION:

Control Scale   Total the scores for your answers 3, 5, 6, 7, 10, 11, and 18. Your total score reflects the degree to which you seek or need control and order in situations.

卌
///

(8)

Total Score of:		
	0–3	Little to no need
	4–6	Moderate need
	7 or more	High, compulsive need

A high score in the control scale means you seek consistency and prefer predictability. You need or desire the security of certainty. You seldom "go with the flow" or allow yourself the freedom of spontaneity. You prefer rigid control. Learn to be more flexible. Decrease your need for control by enjoying your emotions. Allow your feelings to surface.

Power Scale   Total the scores for your answers to questions 1, 2, 4, 8, 9, 12, 13, 14, 15, 16, 17, 19, 20, 21, and 22. Your total score indicates the degree to which you have a need for or seek power.

Total score of: 0–6   Little to no need
                  7–14   Moderate need
                  15 or more   High, compulsive need

A high score on the power scale means your need for power may be excessive and may require some self-evaluation of your motives. In your interpersonal actions with others, examine your behavior to better understand the origins of your power compulsion. What did you do, and what were the effects of your actions? Why did you feel the need for power in that situation? Did your dominance decrease your overall effectiveness? Compulsive power needs can be destructive to the development or use of good human relations skills. Plan and implement change in your behavior to lessen a strong compulsive drive for power if necessary.

Adapted from Robert Meier, "Power—Do You Lust for It?" Success, May 1984.

FastChat

1. If you are power-shy, how might you change that power personality?

2. Was your score on the Power Personality Test what you expected and are you comfortable with the results? How will you use this information?

How Do You Develop Power?

Building power is a complex process and seldom comes without planning and careful execution. Some individuals may operate from a totally subconscious level in their quest for power, whereas others consciously and methodically plan their steps to the top. Building and maintaining a strong power base usually requires a thorough understanding of power positioning, power politics, and power symbols.

Learning
**Objective 5
and 6**

Discuss the importance of applying power politics. Explain the ways that power symbols can be used for power positioning.

CASE STUDIES IN THE NEWS

One of the most powerful women in American business today is Carly Fiorina, CEO and President of Hewlett Packard. Carly Fiorina's chance of becoming this woman seemed almost nonexistent early in her career. She majored in medieval history and philosophy, she was impractical and unfocused. In law school she was restless and dropped out her first year. Job to job—receptionist, teacher—she floated. Finally, she went to AT&T as a sales rep and refused to join the savings plan because she just knew she would not stay past two years.

Today, Fiorina is a star in the computer industry. Fortune magazine dubbed her the most powerful woman in America for two consecutive years. Earning $100 million a year for her skills in marketing and customer relations, Florina is comfortable with power. She grew up with a "sense of no limits," and her mother taught her "the power of positive attitude."

Cora Daniels, *Fortune*, October 1998

What power sources do you think Carly Fiorina possesses? What do you think her power personality is?

POWER POSITIONING

Power positioning is the conscientious use of techniques designed to position yourself for maximum personal growth or gain. Achieving success is sometimes attributed to luck or being at the right place at the right time. (How often have you heard the cliché, "It's not *what you* know, but *who you* know"?) However, you can apply specific techniques of power positioning that do not rely on luck or influential others.

Developing power requires planning and careful execution.

Some 20 years of research by behavioral scientists have resulted in the identification of major techniques that strongly influence the degree of personal power that we attain. The techniques, shown on the next page, should be cultivated in your quest for power, as they will greatly enhance your chances for success.

Seldom are individuals fully proficient in all these techniques. Self-assessment is an important first step in identifying which technique needs attention and which already is fully developed in you. Effective power positioning requires skillful planning and careful implementation.

POWER POLITICS

In his book *Unlimited Power*, Anthony Robbins says, "The meeting of preparation with opportunity generates the offspring we call luck." Success is not an accident, and **power politics** allows us to develop opportunities for success.

Not all decisions for promotion and rewards are made on the bases of merit, fair play, rationality, or even ethics. The only defense you may have against unfair practices is becoming politically astute. This means developing an awareness of power politics, understanding how it works, and applying those techniques with which you are most comfortable.

A first step in this process is to determine how politically inclined you are. The checklist on the page 334 is a quick self-test that will give you some insight into your political inclination. It is an abbreviated version of the Organizational Politics Scale developed by Andrew J. DuBrin in *Winning with Office Politics*. DuBrin's complete test consists of 100 comprehensive questions that provide an in-depth index of an individual's political tendencies. He places the scores in five categories that illustrate a person's identity as a politician. The shortened test version above may help you determine where you would fall in the category scale.

Techniques to Strengthen Your Personal Power

1. Be goal-oriented. — Know what power sources you have and how you plan to strengthen them

2. Learn to take risks. — Show that you are willing to take action and make decisions. (Risk taking is discussed in Chapter 11.)

3. Look for ways to become visible. — Volunteer for special projects and other activities that expose your strengths and capabilities.

4. Acquire positions of authority and knowledge. — Controlling resources and information strengthens power.

5. Develop communication skills, including the ability to negotiate. — These skills are crucial in learning to persuade and influence others.

6. Learn to make decisions. — Think through issues on which you wish to take a stand. Taking a stand just for the sake of winning and being right can backfire in the long run.

7. Develop commitment. — Show through your determination and will power that you are committed to your cause. Display that inner drive that shows you are dedicated to excellence.

8. Network. — Learn to call on individuals inside and outside your organization who can help you accomplish your goals. They can be superiors, subordinates, or colleagues. Discover how to ask for and return favors that will help you build your coalition.

9. Learn how to be a team player. — Help others reach their goals and objectives. Do not be afraid to delegate authority to others. Display a cooperative attitude.

10. Create a following. — Be sensitive to the feelings of others and be careful not to abuse your power. Establishing a reputation for being credible, reliable, and ethical will draw others to your side.

11. Select a mentor. — Choose a successful person with whom you can develop rapport to give you advice and guidance. Having a mentor with political savvy is advisable.

12. Develop confidence. — Sharpen public speaking and other communication skills that will enhance your positive self-image. Portray a professional impression through appropriate dress. (Confidence is discussed in Chapter 10.)

13. Develop advanced skills. — Become an authority by developing and maintaining advanced skills in some area that is perceived as important to others.

14. Understand your organization — Be knowledgeable in the philosophy, politics, communication channels, and structures of your organization. Discover where the power lies and how it is used.

15. Anticipate resistance. — Realize that others may resent your use of power or view you as a threat to their own goals. Develop an information feedback system that lets you know how others perceive you. Then deal positively with the situation.

How Political Are You?

Directions: Answer each question "mostly agree" or "mostly disagree," even if it is difficult for you to decide which alternative best describes your opinion.

1. Only a fool would correct a boss's mistakes.
2. If you have certain confidential information, release it to your advantage.
3. I would be careful not to hire a subordinate with more formal education than myself.
4. If you do somebody a favor, remember to cash in on it.
5. Given the opportunity, I would cultivate friendships with power people.
6. I like the idea of saying nice things about a rival in order to get that person transferred from my department.
7. Why not take credit for someone else's work? They would do the same to you.
8. Given the chance, I would offer to help my boss build some shelves for his or her den.
9. I laugh heartily at my boss's jokes, even when they are not funny.
10. I would be sure to attend a company picnic even if I had the chance to do something I enjoyed more that day.
11. If I knew an executive in my company was stealing money, I would use that against him or her in asking for favors.
12. I would first find out my boss's political preferences before discussing politics with him or her.
13. I think using memos to zap somebody for his or her mistakes is a good idea (especially when you want to show that person up).
14. If I wanted something done by a coworker, I would be willing to say "If you don't get this done, our boss might be very unhappy."
15. I would invite my boss to a party at my house, even if I didn't like him or her.
16. When I'm in a position to, I would have lunch with the "right people" at least twice a week.
17. Richard M. Nixon's bugging the Democratic Headquarters would have been a clever idea if he hadn't been caught.
18. Power for its own sake is one of life's most precious commodities.
19. Having a high school named after you would be an incredible thrill.
20. Reading about job politics is as much fun as reading an adventure story.

Interpretation of Scores. Each statement you check "mostly agree" is worth one point toward your political orientation score. If you score 16 or over, it suggests that you have a strong inclination toward playing politics. A high score of this nature would also suggest that you have strong needs for power. Scores of 5 or less would suggest that you are not inclined toward political maneuvering and that you are not strongly power-driven.

Andrew J. DuBrin, *Human Relations: A Job-Oriented Approach*, 4th ed. (Englewood Cliffs, NJ: Prentice-Hall, 1988), 273–274.

DuBrin's Five Power Categories

1. Machiavellian	A power-hungry, power-grabbing individual. Often ruthless, devious, and power-crazed. Will try to succeed at any cost to others.
2. Company Politician	A shrewd maneuverer and politico. Most successful individuals fall into this category. Company politicians desire power, but it is not an all-consuming preoccupation. Will do whatever is necessary to address their cause except deliberately defame or injure others.
3. Survivalist	Practices enough power politics to take advantage of good opportunities. Not concerned about making obvious political blunders and will stay out of trouble with others of higher rank than self.
4. Straight Arrow	Not particularly perceived as a politician, nor seen as a person intent on committing political suicide. Fundamentally believes that most people are honest, hardworking, and trustworthy. Favorite career advancement strategy is to display job competence and may neglect other important career-advancement strategies.
5. Innocent Lamb	Believes fully that good people are rewarded for their efforts and will rise to the top. Remains focused on the tasks at hand, hoping that hard work will be rewarded.

Obviously, some individuals are well suited to applying whatever methods and techniques will advance them toward their goals. The Machiavellian and Innocent Lamb types are extremes to avoid, but falling somewhere in the middle of these categories may prove valuable in power politics.

Organizational politics are unavoidable. The political implications of your actions, and the actions of others, must be taken into consideration whenever operating within an organization, be it large or small. Playing power politics can be negative or positive. Negative methods are manipulative, coercive, exploitative, and destructive. Positive methods are used to achieve common goals, empower others, build cooperation, develop effective personal contacts, and gain credibility and leadership.

Office politics are unavoidable and must be played like any game.

The Political Power Checklist itemized in the box below provides a quick reference to methods that you may use to become politically powerful. It can be used to check your progress or map your strategies.

Political Power Checklist

Use this checklist to assess your progress in building a power base.

X	Do you have a mentor?
Y	Are you sought out for advice or information?
X	Are your achievements visible?
X	Do you present your major accomplishments at performance appraisal time?
Y	Have you set your mid- and long-range goals?
N	Are you tracking (and remaining ahead of) your competition?
N	Are you paying attention to power dynamics?
N	Do you attempt to influence others?
Y	Do you get credit and recognition for your ideas?
N	Are you developing and increasing your power sources?
N	Do people like to work with you?

POWER SYMBOLS

Power symbols come in the form of physical traits and personality characteristics as well as external physical factors, such as clothes or cars. Power symbols are everywhere. We turn on the soap operas and watch as the rich, handsome tycoon and his ex-model wife, who is draped in minks, are driven in their Rolls to a romantic weekend on their 80-foot yacht. We then pick up the paper only to see that another corporation has built an even larger building designed by a popular architect.

Power symbols influence perceptions.

Do individuals acquire these power symbols after they obtain power? Do some persons with little power use them to portray the illusion of power? If you do not have power, will use of power symbols speed your ability to obtain it? The answers are unclear. One thing is certain, however—our perceptions are influenced by these symbols. Understanding power symbols will help us decide how we wish to use them and recognize their use by others.

Traits and Characteristics Do some characteristics identify the potential of an individual to hold power over others? High achievers are generally perceived as powerful, and their traits have been associated with power. These individuals are seen as self-confident, ambitious, dominant, attractive, selfish, ruthless, decisive, strong-willed, determined, accomplished, and goal-directed.

Whether individuals start with these traits or acquire them is undetermined. However, most theorists believe that they are learned abilities nurtured from infancy. Individuals gain these strengths through exposure and experience and cultivate them because of benefits that they derive from their use. The desire for some of these traits is no doubt strengthened through the constant reinforcement by the media that these are the dynamic traits of success and power.

Some studies have supported the idea that some physical traits make a more powerful impression. For example, people do make a mental connection between height and power, reported Wayne Hensley, a scientist who has done research on whether height provides any real advantage. He

CORBIS/Wally McNamee

Could height have helped Clinton win his position twice?

found through a survey of some 243 executives that 90 percent of them were taller than the average 5-foot-9-inch male. He also found through a sampling of male university professors that the taller the teacher, the higher the academic ranking. Full professors averaged a two-or-more-inch advantage. The same pattern held true in his research on the last 21 presidential elections. The taller candidate was chosen to be our nation's chief executive in 17 of the 21 elections.

Additionally, some studies have shown that specific nonverbal behavior patterns differ between high- and low-power individuals. These behaviors deal with direct eye contact, facial expression, body gestures, and body positioning. For example, a less powerful person is more likely to *be* touched, whereas the more powerful person is far more likely to *do* the touching.

External Physical Factors   Clothing is an external physical factor that may send power signals. The famous adage "Clothes do not the man make" does not hold completely true. Certainly, the idea of "dressing for success" has

GLOBAL CONNECTION

Helayne Spivak is the worldwide creative director of Ammirati Puris Lintas, a global advertising firm. She considers her appearance an extension of her business. "Clothes are advertising, and I dress to fit the culture of my clients." Ernie Grunfeld, born in Romania from humble beginnings, is now the president and general manager of the New York Knicks. "Even though we didn't have much, my father always wore a well-fitting suit or sports coat and tie. He taught me to take pride in the way I look." The president of Canada's leading magazine company, Francois Beaubien favors double-breasted suits and richly patterned suspenders, ties, and vests. "You can win the race in jeans," he says, "but your opponents in suits start with a 100-yard lead on you."

Esther Wachs Book, *Fortune*, November 1998

Why do you think clothing and appearance make a difference in business? Think of several different styles of dress and appearance; what messages are sent by each?

merit. Personal appearance does seem to carry importance in most cases. The way we dress, from hair style down to shoes, is believed to make a statement about the degree of power we either hold or seek. For some, personal appearance can make desired impressions while others disavow the need for all the fuss.

The examples below illustrate a variety of business environments in which stylish appearance makes a perceived difference. Entrepreneurs in custom-fitted suits, board members in the "corporate uniform," and power brokers in the "right kind of suit" understand the psychological advantages gained from dressing for the part.

On the other hand, we all know many examples of less rigid appearance requirements. To some, not only the style but the very nature of executive power has changed. Some attribute the different visions of appropriate dress for success to an "East Coast-West Coast" phenomenon. The West Coast's Silicon Valley originated the "dress-down" or "casual" Friday for winding down a busy business week. The following case illustrates how many of today's powerful people have lowered the once-rigid standards for power symbols.

In some cases, powerful people will enjoy large zones of personal space. For example, the corporate CEO may be seated behind a large, executive-style desk issuing orders to a subordinate standing on the opposite side of the desk. A less powerful person will usually make an appointment and

CASE STUDIES IN THE NEWS

The office of Andy Grove, CEO of Intel, is a cubicle whose walls are shorter than his 5-foot-8 body. America's most powerful banker rides the subway from Citicorp's Manhattan headquarters to its offices in Queens. Bill Gates sports polo shirts and khakis and is known to "peck out his own E-mail." America's most powerful chicken-plucker, Donald Tyson, showed up in the office in the same brown uniform his workers wore, with "Don" embroidered above the shirt pocket. You may find Steve Jobs, Apple's CEO, totally barefoot in his office—eating granola doused in apple juice for breakfast.

Jeffrey Pfeffer, *Managing With Power*, 1996

wait to be ushered in by invitation to see the power holder, whereas the more powerful person is far more likely to walk right into the smaller office area of a subordinate and be given immediate recognition and respect. Although these cues are subtle, they do leave the impression that an individual is powerful.

Which of these two women is most likely the boss? What external factors are sending power signals?

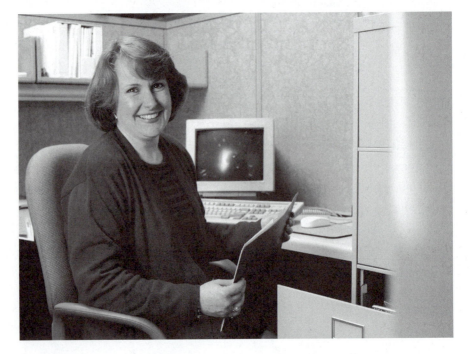

On the other hand, some feel that the "power office" is passé. Robert Tillman, CEO of Lowe's Cos., the giant discount retailer, sets the modern example. He turned down an office on Executive Row at the front of the building. He chose a windowless office smack in the middle of the building instead, saying, "The ideal office layout would be senior executives in the center, with operating areas fanning out from it." It seems to be an idea that has caught on in other arenas. Jim Hackett, CEO at Steelcase, gave up a two-room suite with a marble fountain for a nearly phone-booth-size office. He feels, "People don't need to see me in a big fancy office to know that I'm the CEO."

Thoughts today about what is appropriate seem to move in extremes from one end of a continuum to the other. This is attributable in part to the rise of the baby boomer, who has moved away from tradition in many areas, and to the dramatic changes in business itself, as technology of the Information Age continues to alter the way we do work. The 21st century will continue to transform our work and personal environments.

Some believe that the kind of car they choose to drive and the size and location of their homes give the appearance of status and power. These silent symbols say, "I have arrived!" For those who are truly successful, the cars may be a suitable way to display the success of the company, and the

TECHNOLOGY CONNECTION

Owens-Corning has left its 28-story building, the second-tallest in Toledo, Ohio, for a spanking-new three-story edifice a few blocks away. CEO Glen Hiner tells why: "People referred to management as "the 28th floor." It had a stigma to it. It was restrictive. In the new building the leadership is in the middle of the second floor—the middle of the middle—accessible by all." The building does boast state-of-the-art technology connections. The latest electronic communication tools are available to all employees.

Thomas Stewart, *Fast Company*, January 1997

How do you think the change in the location of the executive offices will affect the attitudes of employees? How might it affect the attitudes of the executives who were moved?

house may be needed for entertaining, but many get into trouble trying to buy the image without the success, which can lead to financial problems, rather than power.

Regardless of how the world changes, the power person will always acquire benefits. As an individual rises to a position of power, certain symbols will set that person apart from others. Today power symbols provided by organizations may include a company car, a cell phone, a beeper, a personal secretary, and a large corner office. In the future, benefits might be a dedicated data line, more powerful computer, or access to newer technology. These extras, or perks, are seldom enjoyed by the mail room clerk who holds a considerably less powerful position.

*Fast*Chat

1. How do you feel about power symbols? Are they necessary or useful in some ways?

2. Do you agree with the "casual Friday" concept for corporate settings? What effect do you think this idea has had on the work environment?

3. Were you surprised or comfortable with your power category based on DuBrin's political assessment instrument? How will you use this to your advantage?

Why Is Empowerment of Others Important?

Empowerment became a trendy management catch phrase in the nineties. This trend is carrying right into the 21st century. As organizations continue to flatten, decision making is being pushed to lower levels in organizations. The need for a leaner and meaner operation naturally requires passing the power to those most qualified to make the right decision. **Empowerment** is allowing others to make decisions and have influence in desired outcomes. It involves not only delegation of tasks, but assigning the appropriate authority and supplying the necessary information and training with the task, so that the individual has considerable likelihood of being successful. It is the giving of power to others, helping them to develop their own power sources. The ability to empower others is a sign of an accomplished leader.

Kenneth Blanchard is a world-renowned consultant and author of several books, including *The 3-Keys to Empowerment: Release the Power Within People for Astonishing Results*. The title speaks to his strong support of

Learning
Objective 7

Discuss why empowering others is important.

Empowerment is allowing others to make decisions and influence others.

CASE STUDIES IN THE NEWS

"Power is all about empowerment." The former police commissioner of New York City, William J. Bratton, makes no pretense about having held vast power in his formal position. But the key to his success during his 2-year tenure was not in the power he held, but in the power he handed out. "I gave away a lot of my power, but I held those to whom I gave it highly accountable for it," confesses Bratton. He had a simple, 3-step approach that seemed to work for him: 1) define the goal, 2) find who in the organization could have the greatest impact on reaching that goal, and 3) hand the power to achieve the goal to that person or persons. "You must be willing to share the information and knowledge necessary for others to make good decisions."

Rajiv M. Rao, *Fortune*, January 1999

Have you areas in your life where you feel that, if you were given the authority, you would be able to successfully reach a goal?

empowering others. He feels you must start by sharing information with others, allowing others the autonomy to use that information. You must flatten the decision-making process and push the freedom to do that down to the lowest levels at which a competent decision can be made. If these steps are taken, you may expect to get remarkable results from subordinates.

Blanchard points out that many people will be uncomfortable with this newly acquired power, but given the opportunity to use their power and the freedom to make mistakes, they will mature in confidence. This approach is a winning approach for all involved. Blanchard states, "The rewards include more tuned-in employees, less turnover, and ultimately, a wealth of brainpower and expertise from which to draw." With the trend toward larger, global businesses, empowerment may become an increasingly important element of successful human relations and effective business.

Knowledge work, with its reliance on project teams and cross-functional collaboration, is naturally resistant to the old forms of authoritarian leadership. Relinquishing power and giving it away will be a method of survival. Companies cannot be fast or global unless people in the field are empowered to make judgment calls and make decisions in a timely manner.

Frances Hesselbein, the woman who modernized the Girl Scouts of America, shares her opinions on empowerment in *WorkingSmart*, a monthly publication of the National Institute of Business Managers. "The concept of empowerment requires some adjustments in traditional thinking. Authoritarian managers and leaders who view empowerment as a threat to their personal power are missing the point. In fact, the more power you give away, the more power you have." The important thing is to increase productivity and competitiveness in the new "leaner meaner" organizations.

One final testament in behalf of empowerment comes from Warren Bennis in his workbook, *Learning to Lead*. He feels that in organizations with effective leaders, empowerment is widely evident. The organizations are successful and its leaders are fulfilled. He states that, "In organizations where leaders lead through empowerment, people feel significant, learning and competence matter, people feel part of a community, and work is exciting." Individuals are motivated through identification with a worthwhile group and feel they make important contributions.

FastChat

1. How do you think empowerment differs from delegation, or does it?

2. Is empowerment a trendy phase or a real asset in leadership?

3. What other benefits do you think might come from empowering others?

What Pitfalls Should You Avoid?

The more power you are able to exert, the more easily you will accomplish your goals. With each goal accomplishment, some degree of additional power is gained that enhances further accomplishments. Each cycle increases the ability to go beyond the previous level.

A number of behaviors, however, can block the development of power. Individuals who are so eager to be liked that they bend over backwards to please others will find the development of power difficult. Being eager to please includes being unwilling to face a conflict for fear of offending others or refusing to take some action that will displease others.

On the other side of the coin, being aggressive and coming on too strong at inappropriate times can reduce your power. Refusing to share power by being unwilling to delegate is also viewed negatively.

In an executive coaching session, consultant Bob Cuddy recommends methods of using power more effectively. He advises participants to force themselves to speak for no more than two minutes in any meeting. Other people have many good ideas and thoughts that should be heard.

Learning
Objective   8

Discuss the pitfalls of developing power.

Wise use of power allows you to become even more powerful.

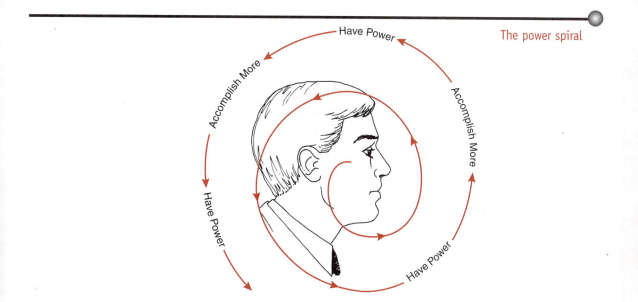

The power spiral

CASE STUDIES IN THE NEWS

Power is in many ways a game of appearances, and when you say less than necessary, you inevitably appear greater and more powerful than you are. Your silence will make other people uncomfortable. Humans are machines of interpretation and explanation; they have to know what you are thinking. When you carefully control what you reveal, they cannot pierce your intentions or your meaning. Your short answers and silences will put them on the defensive, and they will ponder your every word. This extra attention will only add to your power.

Success Magazine, **October 1998**

Why do you think silence makes people uncomfortable? Have you ever had an experience where you knew you said too much? How do you think you can get better at judging when to speak and when to be silent?

A major pitfall of power gaming is overconfidence or arrogance. It is easy to get carried away with the exhilaration that power can bring. Care should be taken to guard against becoming too fond of our own abilities and basking too long in the glow of the spotlight. Remembering that others may know how to play the power game would indicate a certain amount of wisdom and maturity. A truly powerful person has the ability to recruit allies and harness resources to accomplish a mission or goal. Power use is most effective when it is an exercise of strength that enables you to achieve your goals and objectives without harm or damage to others and least effective when it is abused for selfish, personal gain.

*Fast*Chat

1. What are some means of reducing your power? How would you safeguard against this happening?

2. In meetings you have attended, who did the most talking? Was the speaker perceived to be more or less powerful?

3. How can you guard against becoming arrogant or self-centered?

Human Relations

Summary

Power is the ability to influence others to do what we want them to do. Despite its sometimes negative image, experts agree that the acquisition and appropriate use of power is necessary for individuals at all levels of an organization if they are to accomplish goals and objectives.

Many sources of power are available and need to be cultivated for maximum effectiveness. These sources include reward, coercive, legitimate, expert, and referent power. Derivative and passive power are sources best left uncultivated. In addition to these power sources, research has defined three basic power personalities, the power-shy, the power-positive, and the power-compulsive.

Developing power is not a matter of luck. It must be planned. Part of this planning and development involves a thorough understanding and respect for power positioning, power politics, and power symbols. Empowering others is also a method of acquiring power and can be beneficial for all parties involved. Crucial to power development is avoiding the power pitfalls and ensuring that you have used power in a positive manner.

Key Terms

power
reward power
coercive power
legitimate power
expert power
referent power
derivative power
passive power
power-shy
power-positive
power-compulsive
power positioning
power politics
power symbols
empowerment

Review Questions

1. What is power, and why is developing power necessary?
2. Which basic power sources are available to you?
3. What are the three basic power personalities?
4. What techniques can you use in the planning and implementation of power positioning?
5. Why is applying power politics important?
6. How are power symbols used for power positioning?
7. Why is empowering others important?
8. What are the pitfalls in developing power?

Discussion Questions

1. Think of individuals who are powerful or have power over you. Which power sources do they possess? Which ones are most effective?
2. Review the power sources available to you. What is your strongest source, and which is your weakest? Do you have linkages?
3. Do you effectively plan the use of your power to gain personal advantages? How and why?
4. Which of the power personalities best fits you? Are you comfortable with your assessment? Why or why not?
5. What power symbols do you possess? How do you use these symbols in your power building?
6. How many of the power techniques have you cultivated? How have they benefited your power positioning?
7. Do you agree that playing power politics is an unavoidable means of assuring personal and professional success? Why or why not?

Chapter Project

As a group, collectively pool your resources and decide on a prominent person from somewhere in your community whom you may invite to speak to your class on how they became successful. This person should hold a reasonably powerful position. Based on the chapter topics, prepare a written report on how you believe this individual became and remains powerful. Describe traits, characteristics, power plays, etc.

Applications

In small groups, analyze the following situations

Linda Loophole, The Legal Eagle

Working in teams, thinking creatively, and reasoning

Linda is the best lawyer the firm has. All the junior associates admire her abilities and pattern their courtroom style after hers. She has been at the business longer than most of them have been living. She is known to be persuasive and shrewd. Just her physical presence in a courtroom demands attention. Her nearly 6-feet-tall, slender frame displays her immaculate and expensive clothing to its maximum flair. She really has it together. Linda knows exactly when to exert her strengths and when to let others have their opinions heard.

Everyone is aware of how she has used every legitimate method available to her to reach the pinnacle of success that seems rightfully hers. She was mentored by the firm's founder, gained high visibility by landing two highly controversial cases early in her career, and outpaced most of her peers with little effort.

1. What power sources has Linda developed during her years with the law firm? How are they linked?
2. What power symbols does Linda use to add to her power positioning?
3. What power techniques has she used to aid her in becoming a success?
4. Do you think that Linda used power politics to acquire her status as the best lawyer in the firm? If so, why do you think that?

The Case of the Coercive Commander

Dave Hanks was a retired naval commander who had done a tour in private industry to round out his retirement income. Then came the call to serve his government again. He took the post as a favor to an old Navy buddy who needed help bringing about change at his agency. He was a tall, physically fit individual, an easy fit to the leadership position. As Director of the Technology Commercialization effort, Dave had a small staff of highly skilled, competent individuals, all of whom had many years of experience in the public sector. They were an easy-going, cohesive group with many accomplishments to their credit.

When Dave first arrived, the winds of war began to blow. Wielding his power like a baseball bat, he began systematically "squeezing out" employees he felt had outlived their importance to his organization or just didn't fit the "new culture." He tried to run the office like a private industry business, railing against the bureaucracy of government operations. His demands were often unreasonable. His orders sometimes bordered on unethical practices in government work. He constantly "reminded" people of his connections to his buddy, the Agency Director, and alluded to his power base being indestructible. Stress levels grew to unmanageable heights among the employees.

Those that could retired. Others sought reassignments to any other part of the Agency to escape the constant badgering and belittling. Accusations of fraud and abuse of government funds were leveled at him. A few employees filed claims of sexual harassment and mental cruelty. Complaints were made to appropriate sources, but nothing was done to change his behavior. A 150 percent turnover in staff occurred, but no one could please the coercive commander.

1. What power sources did Dave use?
2. Why did the agency employees fear him?
3. What might Dave have done differently?
4. What do you think the agency authorities should have done?

Additional Readings and Resources

Fisher, Anne. "How Can I Prevail Over Poisonous Office Politics?" *Fortune*, June 1999.

Greene, Robert and Joost Elffers. *48 Laws of Power*. Viking Press, 1998.

Sellers, Patricia. "The 50 Most Powerful Women in American Business." *Fortune*, October 1998.

Weil, Elizabeth. "Power Camp." *Fast Company*, August 1997.

Change:

A Constant in an Inconstant World

focus

Experience and research tell us that organizations that are doing well are making more changes . . . more in number and in size, or significance of change. A few examples of changes being made include:

General Electric initiated a quality change program that boosted its earnings by nearly 15 percent in 1996 and 1997.

Procter & Gamble came up with "Breakthrough Efficiencies" that in 1998 cut $1 billion in operating costs by simplifying and standardizing processes. They promised the same for 1999.

So what's the message for you? For your firm? Maybe it is to keep changing, keep raising the bar, keep pointing to those firms recognized for excellence. Once change was the exception and not the rule. Today change is the rule!

Dutch Holland and Bill Nash, *The Management Edge,* **1999**

Think of other businesses that have made changes recently. What do you think brought about these changes? What effect did the changes have?

In This Chapter

After studying this chapter, you should be able to:

1. *Describe significant factors that are changing in today's workplace.*

2. *Identify who usually recommends and implements organizational changes.*

3. *Explain several effective methods of planning and implementing change.*

4. *Understand common reasons for resistance to change and how to overcome that resistance.*

5. *Describe the role leaders have in facilitating change.*

6. *Explain what is meant by the term "coaching."*

7. *Explain what is meant by the term "counseling."*

8. *Discuss the need for Employee Assistance Programs in change processes.*

13.1 Where Are Changes Occurring?

Learning Objective 1

Describe significant factors that are changing in today's workplace.

Companies strive to become globally competitive.

Change is a basic condition of today's work world. In recent decades, the number and speed of changes have escalated. Perhaps the Industrial Revolution is the last time conditions changed as rapidly. Thousands of the world's largest corporations have undergone some form of restructuring around the globe. In addition to internal changes, such as reorganizations, the merger explosion has caused dramatic changes in the corporate world. The British Petroleum takeover of Amoco Oil, the merger of America's Chrysler Corporation with Germany's Daimler-Benz, the Exxon and Mobil Oil merger, and major co-minglings in the banking and telecommunications industries all represent the diversity of the multinational business activities prevalent today. Even the government has felt the need for streamlining its ranks.

TECHNOLOGY CONNECTION

Major technology innovations have brought changes to Wall Street—the linking of computers to the Internet has given the world immediate and direct access to greater information and knowledge. This has brought about precedent-setting mega-mergers in business and industry. The British Telecommunications takeover of MCI was the largest ever foreign takeover of a U.S. corporation. Media giant Time Warner swallowed Turner Broadcasting Systems in a $7.5 billion dollar deal. Bell Atlantic and NYNEX are eating European communications companies like popcorn. Not to be outdone, the banking industry revealed the merger of Chase Manhattan with Chemical Bank in a $13 billion dollar deal.

U.S. News and World Report, April 1997

What changes will you personally experience from these major mergers? What changes do the company employees experience? Do you think these large mergers will continue and, if so, what will be the eventual outcomes?

Millions of jobs have been eliminated throughout the world. The buzz words "merger," "takeover," "buyout," and "downsizing" have become real to a multitude of workers and cause anxiety for many more. The illustration below reflects the reality of corporate downsizing in the U.S. during the last decade. This trend is expected to continue well into the new millennium as companies strive to become more competitive in the global business environment.

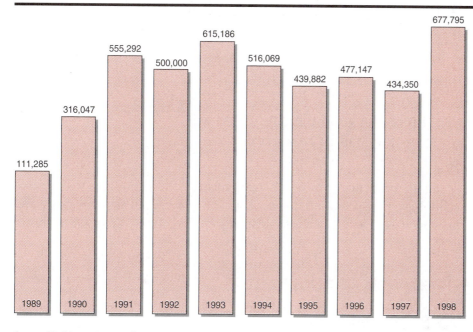

111,285 — 1989
316,047 — 1990
555,292 — 1991
500,000 — 1992
615,186 — 1993
516,069 — 1994
439,882 — 1995
477,147 — 1996
434,350 — 1997
677,795 — 1998

1998 was a year of downsizing, when employers nationwide cut more workers than in any year of the decade.

Source: Challenger Gray & Christmas

Although change is necessary to avoid stagnation, it can be difficult. People are often unwilling to step out of their comfort zones or abandon routines to which they have grown accustomed and which they see no reason to change. However, in today's complex environment, the premium is on adaptability. No person or company will function long or well without deliberate and intelligent planning for change. A planned change is a method of helping people develop appropriate behaviors for adapting to new methods while remaining effective and creative. The key to an organization making a positive transition is getting people involved in and committed to the change in the beginning. Then employees are more likely to view change as an opportunity rather than a threat. The application of sound human relations skills will make adapting easier during any transition.

No person or company will function long or well without deliberate and intelligent planning for change.

Technology is one of the main forces affecting the work world.

"I miss the good old days when we only had to *read* email."

Change is rapid in the economy, science/technology, the work force, management styles, and work itself.

Areas experiencing rapid changes include the economy, science and technology, transportation, the general work force, management styles, and the work itself. Each area has far-reaching effects on the others. We are bom-

CASE STUDIES IN THE NEWS

CASE STUDIES IN THE NEWS

Changes in the corporate landscape of America are common. A $59.3 billion dollar merger between Nations Bank and BankAmerica Corporation in April 1998 created the largest bank in America. Weaving the two together will eliminate 8000 jobs and bring greater efficiencies to banking capabilities.

Jim Zarolli, *National Public Radio*, New York, 1998

What other effects do you see these giant mergers having, both for employees and customers or consumers? The flip side of the merger trend is the explosion in the number of new small businesses and independent contractors. How do you think these trends balance each other?

barded daily with these changing elements in our environment. The illustration below provides a graphic view of the many forces working to change our work world.

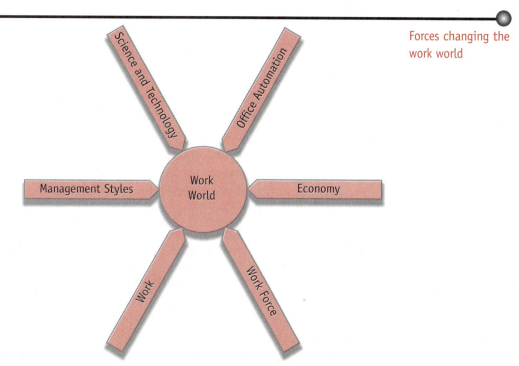

Forces changing the work world

Science and Technology

Office Automation

Management Styles

Work World

Economy

Work

Work Force

GLOBAL CONNECTION

The use of a single currency, the Euro, by all eleven countries of Europe's Economic and Monetary Union (EMU) will bring basic and irreversible changes to how Europe is governed and how it deals with foreign friends and competitors. The Euro was introduced on January 1, 1999, and is scheduled to make its physical appearance on January 1, 2002, to replace all other forms of currency in the EMU countries. This switch to a single currency will draw together almost 290 million Europeans in an economic and political colossus to rival the United States.

James O. Jackson, *Time Magazine*, May 11, 1998

What impact might this European union have on international trade? What impact might it have on U.S. business?

ECONOMY

As we continue the globalization of business activities, more opportunities for growth are being realized. The opening of the eastern and western European markets in the early 1990s caused an explosion in free trade and created a vast array of entrepreneurial opportunities. Today goods, services, people, and capital move across national borders in Europe as easily as we cross state borders in the United States, which will have a major impact on the world market.

The North American Free Trade Agreement (NAFTA) was another international economic decision that opened trade and employment opportunities between countries. Signed into effect on January 1, 1994, NAFTA's main objective was to promote fair competition, increased investments, and enhanced trade cooperation between the U.S., Mexico, and Canada. These types of trade agreements continue to shrink the world in which we live.

SCIENCE AND TECHNOLOGY

Advanced space exploration and experimentation are resulting in new scientific discoveries about our universe and continues to add new technologies to our lives. New research in medicine and nutrition science contributes to improving our health and well-being. Technological advancements are increasing as we share our knowledge and experience

GLOBAL CONNECTION

For 20 years, the Milton Bradley Wood Products Co. produced wooden letter tiles and racks for the popular board game Scrabble® in Fairfax, Vermont. These tiles and racks are now being made by a Hong Kong company in Shanghai, China. Hasbro, the owner of the game, has closed five of its toy and game manufacturing plants around the world and moved them to the Asian Continent. The moves are expected to save the company $350 million before taxes within five years.

Associated Press Release, February 1999

What factors might motivate companies to move business to other countries? How might these savings benefit stock holders, employees, or communities? Who might these changes hurt?

through joint ventures with other nations. As we continue to move from the Industrial Era to the Knowledge Era, we have a greater need for computer competencies and other higher level skills. These requirements are driving the need for a more capable, adaptable and educated workforce. The need for life-long learning in areas of science and technology affects everyone from the farmer to Wall Street stockbroker.

TRANSPORTATION

While nothing as dramatic as going from horse-drawn carriages to cars is happening these days, transportation continues to be one of the forces changing our lives. The crush of commuter traffic has become so bad in urban areas that alternatives are being pursued, from mass transit to telecommuting. The need for efficiencies and speed in business has put great pressure on transportation companies to move more products swiftly and economically, with bigger trucks and fewer drivers taking on the increased work.

WORK FORCE

Numerous changes are occurring in the work force. The "baby boomers," the "Gen-Xers," and the "Millenniums" have all brought their sets of values

CASE STUDIES IN THE NEWS

The U.S. Department of Labor established a means for identifying skills and competencies necessary for the workplace. A report developed by the Secretary's Commission on Achieving Necessary Skills (SCANS) identified certain skills and personal qualities needed for solid job performances in jobs at all skill levels. Schools and educators across America have incorporated these recommendations into curriculums and texts. Systems information skills (interpreting and communicating computer-derived data), technology skills (applying, maintaining, and troubleshooting technology tools), and interpersonal skills (working on and leading team efforts and working well with diverse cultures) were among the strongest skills advocated.

U.S. Dept. of Labor, Govt. Printing Office, 1992

How can you use this information to help yourself become a more potentially valuable employee? What other skills do you think might be valuable?

and beliefs into the workplace, requiring different methods of leadership, motivation, and other human relations skills. Workers in the twenty-first century feel less strongly about long-term employment security than did previous generations, realizing that these tumultuous times create uncertainties. The hopes are for career development opportunities, training and retraining, and opportunities for job and knowledge improvements. The general work force is aging, but retirements are fewer. Overall, there are fewer qualified workers to replace those who do leave the work force. Continued immigration to the United States is affecting the ethnic diversities of the work force. Considering the variety of changes foreseen in the workplace, the workers who are most likely to succeed are flexible and adaptable to changing conditions.

MANAGEMENT STYLES

Peter Drucker, author of *The New Realities*, predicted that "in so-called knowledge-based companies, hierarchies will give way to something resembling a symphony orchestra with dozens or even hundreds of specialists reporting directly to the conductor/CEO." He was right. The age of the standard pyramidal hierarchy is fast passing. Organizational structures are becoming more open and fluid, able to adapt quickly. Power is becoming increasingly decentralized, and the use of matrix-style structures is allowing organizations to adjust more readily.

Leadership is becoming more team-oriented and participatory. Managers are delegating more tasks to the lowest level possible and empowering others with greater responsibility. Because of this, managers increasingly appreciate characteristics such as speed, flexibility, risk-taking, and decisiveness in employees.

WORK ITSELF

The evolution from Industrial Era to Information Age is moving us from an emphasis on manual to mental labor. Work continues to shift from industrial manufacturing and production to information and knowledge-based goods and services. Increased global competitiveness is forcing U.S. employers to achieve productivity with fewer and better-educated workers with different skills. Characteristic of the new skills required is the ability to interpret information using more abstract and creative methods. Within the general labor force critical skills are becoming scarcer. Companies are already realizing a gap between basic skills and the highly technical skills required to operate their rapidly advancing equipment.

The need for improved quality of product or service continues to be a force shaping the way work is performed. In the new global economy,

The 42-year-old President of Heinz USA is a real-life practitioner of the new, more participatory management style. He walks the walk, wandering the halls of Heinz's Pittsburgh headquarters chatting up janitors and hobnobbing with employees on the cafeteria lunch line. Rather than shouting orders, he relies on everyone to contribute to the success of the company. He has also seen management approaches evolve to suit flatter organizations. "When I first joined corporate America, the person in the corner office was a big guy with a loud bark and a very nasty bite. Now, everything has changed. You have to be more like an NBA coach, warm and motivating."

Justin Martin, *Fortune Magazine*, June 1996

Does the new management style seem to be more work than the old? Explain. What benefits to the company would motivate managers to change management styles?

employees compete in a much broader field. Work performance is taking on a new shape, with decisions being pushed to the lowest level possible in increasingly horizontal organizational structures.

An equal number of more personal changes will influence the immediate work setting. Organizations are examining work patterns and looking for alternatives to the traditional workplace. In 1998, Cornell University's International Workplace Studies Program (IWSP) focused its research on "Changes in the Workplace." The IWSP teams explored innovative approaches to planning, designing, and managing the workplace. Leading-edge ideas such as satellite offices, telework centers, home-based telework, and collaborative team environments were examined. The team discovered that most organizations are changing workplace environments to reduce costs, emphasize ergonomic safety, and improve productivity.

Advances in communications systems will continue to provide innovative access to offices, information, and individuals globally. E-mail allows access to hundreds of co-workers worldwide in minutes rather than days, and e-mail seems to be just the beginning of a revolution in how information flows and people are managed. Rapid advancements in technology in all areas of communication will continue to change the

quick wit

"Everybody thinks of changing humanity and nobody thinks of changing himself."

Leo Tolstoy

CASE STUDIES IN THE NEWS

Research led by Frank Becker at Cornell's International Workplace Studies Program (IWSP) indicates the most productive work setting is in the home environment with less interruptions and better concentration. The biggest drawbacks are the difficulty with professional and social communication efforts and the different management applications required to effectively supervise telecommuting. However, trends indicate that business and industry will continue to change to accommodate mobile work patterns and develop an infrastructure to support these changing work style methods.

W. R. Simms and J. Rappaport, Cornell University Press, 1999

How could current technologies contribute to overcoming the communication problems created by telecommuting? Discuss the pros and cons for the employee of working at an office and at home. What are the pros and cons for the employer?

Tomorrow's offices cannot be created without designing physical, social, technical, and organizational systems that are in harmony.

workplace. Andrew S. Grove, in his revised edition of *High Output Management*, states that "to operate effectively in the new environment, you have only two options: Adapt or die."

While CEO at Intel Corp., Grove warned company employees, "The new environments dictate two rules: First, everything is happening faster—second, anything that can be done will be done, if not by you, then by someone else, somewhere in the world. These changes lead to a less gentle and far less predictable workplace." Clearly one message for survival in the future is to focus on continual self improvement.

The emerging organizational environment is characterized by three principal trends: intense global competition, rapid technological advancements, and continuing turbulence and uncertainty. The reality of the changing world around us highlights the need for understanding change dynamics.

TECHNOLOGY CONNECTION

Some companies are providing team workplace environments—shared Internet sites for distance learning and international work force collaboration. These locations on the Internet provide a place for virtual offices to communicate. Important information is posted on bulletin boards, electronic post-it notes are left, calendars and schedules are shared, and "share files" are established. Electronic, real-time whiteboards download to individual PCs, and employee chat rooms are provided for meeting efficiencies. Remote teams can work together or leave information for later pickup, additions, or changes. The workplace is changing to embrace globalization.

Franklin Becker, *Workplace by Design*, 1998

With which of these technologies are you already familiar? What are some of the benefits of these technological applications? What are some of the drawbacks?

FastChat

1. In what ways do you think you will be affected by any of the future changes described above?

2. How have changes in science and technology already touched your life? Give examples.

Learning
Objective   2

Identify who usually recommends and implements organizational changes.

Professional planners, outside consultants, special task forces, and top executives plan most change.

Methods for implementing change are unilateral, participative, or delegated.

Recommendations for change in organizations originate from a variety of sources. These sources include professional planners and outside consultants who may be hired and brought into an organization to define methods and techniques for increasing effectiveness. Additionally, special task forces or teams may be formed of representatives from within the organization to participate in streamlining operations. CEOs and other top-level managers are also the initiators of change within an organization. Changes are usually carried out by mid-level and first-line managers using unilateral, participative, and delegated methods.

With the **unilateral method,** employees have little or no input in the process. Supervisors dictate the change—what it is, when and how it will be accomplished, and who will be involved. Employees merely follow the directives. In the **participative method,** employee groups are used in the problem-solving and decision-making processes that precede change implementation. Both the supervisors and the employees share in bringing about the change.

In the **delegated method,** employees are given the responsibility and authority to effect the change. They diagnose, analyze, and select the best method for implementation. This method is used most when employees are closest to the situation that needs changing. It is being used more frequently as organizations push decision making further down into the ranks, so knowing how to plan change is an increasingly valuable skill, even at lower levels. You may find the steps below useful in implementing changes.

To better understand how organizations bring about change, study companies with successful track records using the methods discussed here.

Personal Guide for Effective Change Planning

* Establish consistent goals—consider present and future conditions.
* Have vision—foresee the future and raise expectations of those involved.
* Have a "big picture" outlook—take a broad view of change effects.
* Make your intentions known—communicate openly for change acceptance.
* Know your options—develop alternative plans.
* Time your change—introduce processes carefully for least resistance.
* Be flexible—adapt or modify process if necessary.

CASE STUDIES IN THE NEWS

When Chrysler wanted to improve its public image, it undertook cultural change on a grand scale. The CEO wanted Chrysler to become the technology and quality leader in cars and trucks. This was a clear, globally applicable vision called "Customer One." This change was done with the same people working in different ways. Everyone was involved. Teams were set up throughout the organization's massive structure to harness the best ideas and creativity.

Designers were sent out to photograph the interiors of about 200 competitors' pickup trucks to see where cups, maps, etc. were being stored. Assembly line workers met with engineers *before* production started. Shop mechanics provided *real-life* maintenance suggestions. The teams even called in customers and suppliers to solicit ideas and suggestions on the front end of the changes. Sixty percent of the 4600 ideas were used and resulted in $235 million dollars worth of production savings. One team leader proudly admitted, "We succeeded because the groups and individuals knew exactly what we're trying to do. We had commitment from the top to the bottom."

David A. Zatz, *The OD Pages*

The obvious benefit was production savings, but in what ways does participation like this benefit employees? Why would employees feel good about the company's success?

FastChat

1. Think about ways in which you may have participated in change activities in a work or personal group situation. What method do you think was used in that process?

2. How do you think different workers deal with the varied changes occurring in the workplace?

The goals in managing change are to anticipate the need for change and to bring the change about effectively. The most common methods for achieving these results include strategic planning, organizational development, job redesign, and force field analysis.

STRATEGIC PLANNING

**Because changes
in any
environment are
continual,
planning must be
ongoing and
flexible.**

The essence of planning is designing a desired future and identifying ways to bring it about. Plans must be designed to fit the unique characteristics of each organization. **Strategic planning** is the systematic setting of organizational goals, defining strategies and policies to achieve them, and developing detailed plans to ensure that the strategies are implemented—always taking into account the unique character of the organization. The process helps determine what is to be done, when and how it is to be done, who is going to do it, and what is to be done with the results. Because changes in any organization's environment are continual, strategic planning must be ongoing and flexible.

Strategic planning is not simply forecasting based on trends, nor is it a set of plans that can be carved in stone to be used day after day. This type of planning for change is more a thought process than a prescribed set of procedures and techniques. A formal strategic planning system links three major types of plans: (1) strategic plans, (2) medium-range programs, and (3) short-range budgets and operating plans. The diagram on page 365, illustrates the information flow and steps in a typical strategic planning process.

In the initial steps, consideration is given to the concerns of outside and inside interests and how they may be affected by the planned goal. For example, as a manager you may ask how the local community will react to the proposed building site for a new factory near the downtown area. Will this expansion please the stockholders by increasing profits and better serving our customers? Will it generate revenue to pay our creditors and increase orders to our suppliers? Will Joe Chang agree to leave his current foreman job to manage and operate the new facility? What has our past performance capability been in the area of pipe manufacturing, and how will the new factory change that performance? Can we forecast with reasonable

PHASE A
Initial Thinking and Strategy Development

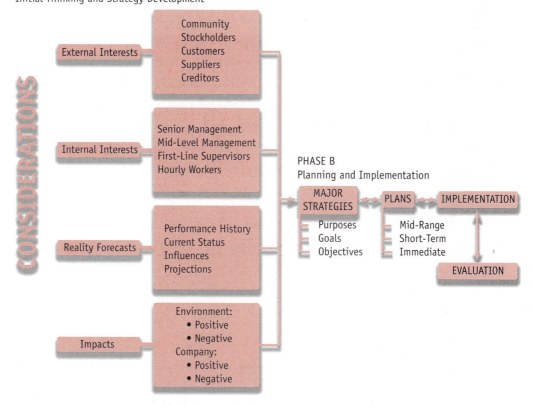

accuracy the outcome of making this major investment? What effects over-all will this plan for expansion have on the environment and the company? Careful thinking is needed to initiate strategic planning.

Once all the questions are favorably answered, the next step is to design a master strategy for implementation. The purpose and objective are clearly defined and policies are established. Then medium- and short-range steps are developed and the plan begins to take shape. With a step-by-step program plan in place, implementation can begin. The land may be purchased and cleared, building specifications drawn to scale, and contractors hired to build the facility. As construction begins, each phase is carefully reviewed and evaluated to assure maximum efficiency upon completion.

The thought process continues throughout the year that building the facility takes. If new facts arise, changes may be made to accommodate them. No plan is absolute. It may best be described as a fluid or dynamic process that allows change to occur as warranted.

Catherine Hapka was recently profiled by *Fortune Magazine* as one of six new CEOs under age 50. Her job with US West Communications puts her in charge of providing phone service to 25 million customers in 14 states. She says her job is ". . . getting us ready for brutal competition." Her track record includes stints with General Electric, a Schlitz Brewery, and McKinsey & Company. While at General Electric, she was required to put in a requisite two years in its strategic planning area before being named General Manager of the $150 million Special Health Products unit.

Amy Kovar, *Tomorrow's CEO's*

Why do you think GE required the two years in strategic planning before promoting Hapka? How could these skills be carried to other jobs?

ORGANIZATIONAL DEVELOPMENT (OD)

Organizational development (OD) is a planned change process for meeting organizational needs through employee participation and management involvement on a continuing basis. It is similar to strategic planning in concept but not in practice. OD is a holistic approach, involving the entire organization—its people, structures, culture, policies and procedures, and purpose. Undergirding OD is the belief that any planned change process must continuously adapt to the ever-changing environment.

Because OD is strongly rooted in human relations management theories, it involves a number of methods to identify degrees of concern for people as well as tasks. Methods might include sensitivity training, team building exercises, and goal setting activities to bring about the desired changes in both the employee and the organization. Other methods used in the OD change process include survey and feedback techniques, confrontation meetings, and teambuilding exercises. These methods involve a high degree of participation by employees and management to improve organizational effectiveness.

When speaking of OD, buzzwords such as total quality management (TQM) and benchmarking come to mind. Each of these methods is a new means of accomplishing an old goal—effectively implementing change in

OD methods involve a high degree of participation by employees and management to improve organizational effectiveness.

organizations. Each has roots in OD, and many high-powered companies are still using these techniques to deal with changing business environments.

TQM focuses on involving employees in continuous process improvements to keep the organization on the cutting edge. TQM has its roots in the theories of the American statistician and educator, Dr. W. Edwards Deming, who became interested in methods of achieving better quality control in the 1930s. Deming's ideas were put to the test in the 1950s, when Japanese business leaders invited him to teach quality control, as they tried to rebuild after WW II. In addition to statistical analysis of production as it related to quality, Deming advocated involving employees at all levels in the pursuit of quality. In the 1980s, American companies began to adopt Deming's ideas to compete more effectively against foreign manufacturers. Today, employee involvement in improving quality has become the vanguard of progressive companies.

Benchmarking is a method that involves comparing the company's practices—among internal divisions, against those of outside competitors, or both—to determine which are the best. For example, Johnson & Johnson compared financial report filing in its internal branches and discovered ways to streamline the processes. Xerox matched prices and procedures with a Japanese competitor and improved its bottom line. This method involves employees in the analysis of information, taking action, and reviewing the results for effectiveness.

Instrumental in bringing about any of these change processes is the change agent. Also known as an OD practitioner, the **change agent's** powerful role is to diagnose problems, provide feedback, help develop strategies, or recommend interventions to benefit the organization as a whole. The challenge is to develop a creative, innovative organization that easily adapts in an ever-changing world, yet remains competitive. To foster such flexibility, employees must be made to feel part of a team. Change should be perceived as an opportunity for growth among team members as they accept new challenges and learn new skills.

Actions of a Change Agent

- Be open, honest about why the change is happening.
- Encourage participation, solicit feelings.
- Allow negative comments but not negative actions.
- Explain benefits of change.
- Involve others in initiation/implementation phases.
- Acknowledge loss of old method.

CASE STUDIES IN THE NEWS

Gerhard Schulmeyer, the new CEO of German-based computer giant Siemens Nixdorf (SNI), launched Europe's most ambitious corporate overhaul. A cultural transformation of this scale would demand drastic intervention. Schulmeyer hired Mark Maletz, a veteran change agent with experience at Xerox, American Airlines, and Citicorp, to invent a school for change, training a cadre of change agents who could, like a virus, infect the host company. He drafted the young and the restless within SNI, hard-charging business people from the field who cared about the company's future. They were trained in the art of change and then injected back into the stiff, slow-moving, hierarchical SNI culture—with the promise that they'd make a difference. They did!

Charles Fishman, *Fast Company*, April 1997

What advantages do you think there would be in having a number of change agents trained by the same person? How do you think these change agents could help the CEO reach his goals?

Quick Tip . . . .

"Creating change, managing it, mastering it, and surviving it is the agenda for anyone in business who aims to make a difference."

Mark Maletz

JOB REDESIGN

Job redesign changes the makeup of an employee's tasks.

Job redesign is a method of bringing about gradual, low-risk changes in an organization by changing tasks performed by individuals. Job redesign means changing the makeup of tasks to make them more interesting and challenging for the employee. The goal is to relieve boredom, create interest, and obtain a more satisfied and productive worker. The most common methods used in job redesign are job enrichment, job enlargement, and job rotation.

REENGINEERING

Reengineering takes redesign to the next level: instead of simply redefining jobs, whole divisions or corporations are retooled. Michael Hammer and James Champy, in their landmark *Reengineering the Corporation*, defined **reengineering** as the fundamental rethinking and redesign of business processes to achieve dramatic improvements in critical, contemporary measures of performance, such as cost, quality, service, and speed. Organizations around the world have been implementing this form of change with dramatic results. Microsoft, General Electric, General Motors, IBM, Intel, Levi Strauss, Germany's Siemens, Brazil's Semco, and the U.S. Government are only a few of those who have undertaken some form of reengineering.

Quick Tip

"You can't expect people to change if you don't give them the tools. We can create opportunities for people to change, but we cannot change them. People have a personal responsibility to get involved and change themselves."

Thomas M. Kasten

Common Redesign Methods

Job enrichment	Builds greater responsibility and interest into task assignments. Means adding tasks that encourage and motivate employees. Also known as vertical loading or adding tasks of increased responsibility. Excellent means of bringing about positive change within an organization.
Job enlargement	Known as horizontal loading, increases the complexity of a job by adding similar tasks to those already being performed. May not motivate employees, but may appeal to their higher-order needs.
Job rotation	The shifting of employees from one job to another in hopes of reducing boredom and stimulating renewed interest in job performance. The content of a particular job is not affected. May also be used to prepare an individual for permanent assignment to a higher-level position.

FORCE FIELD ANALYSIS

Force field analysis is a technique used to analyze the complexities of the change and identify the forces that must be altered. This useful tool, developed by Kurt Lewin, views any situation in which change is to be made as a dynamic balance of forces working in opposite directions.

The forces that move the situation in the direction of the anticipated change are called driving forces. The opposite forces, those which tend to keep the situation from moving in the direction of the anticipated change, are called restraining forces. These two sets of forces working against each other create a dynamic equilibrium or a balance that can be disturbed at any moment by altering either the driving or restraining forces.

Quick Tip ·

"There is at least one point in the history of any company when you have to change dramatically to rise to the next performance level. Miss that moment and you start to decline."

Andy Grove, Intel CEO

· ·

A change agent who uses force field analysis to determine how those opposing forces operate in an organization can predict the consequences of altering either set of forces or can alter the forces to create the desired change. The forces may include people, tasks, technology, equipment, or the organization's basic structure.

Planning for change is important to ensure a smooth transition with the least resistance possible. Each situation should be analyzed to anticipate the consequences of the change process.

FastChat

1. Describe a situation in which you may have been a change agent helping to bring about change.

2. What changes have you seen occur in the government that may have been a result of reengineering efforts.

3. How do you think the dramatic changes at Levi Strauss may have affected you? How would you have felt about having to re-apply for a job at a company in which you already had a job?

CASE STUDIES IN THE NEWS

Levi Strauss & Co. has a uniquely progressive business culture. Led by CEO Thomas M. Kasten, it recently undertook what has been hailed as the most dramatic change program in American business. Kasten and a team of hundreds, drawn from the middle ranks of the company, became a flying wedge of change. Occupying the third floor of the Levi's headquarters in San Francisco, the team hatched a plan to totally redesign the company: new business processes, systems, and facilities.

Thousands of jobs were invented by the team—complete with formal job descriptions, qualifications, and titles, and a new staffing process through which current employees were asked to apply for the jobs. The team became change agents dealing with everything from fear to resistance and anger. Employees had to ask themselves, "Where can I best add value to this company?" and often it was not in the job they had been doing or the job they thought they liked the best.

Finance people went to Production, General Managers became Customer Relations Specialists, and people in Hungary went to Japan. Implementing this total change, Levi created a "handbook" for building the company of the future. Kasten believes you have to be a catalyst, not a controller, and must turn over the process to the people. "That's how you generate commitment to make it happen."

David Sheff, *Fast Company*, 1996

What do you think would be the most difficult part of a change this great?

13.4 Why Do People Resist Change?

Learning
Objective 5

*"Understand
common reasons for
resistance to change
and how to
overcome that
resistance*

People are naturally resistant to change, both in their personal and their work lives. Their feelings create barriers to effective change. Understanding how people feel about change can help us remove the barriers and ensure an easier change process.

Four Common Reasons for Resistance to Change	
Fear of the unknown	When situations remain constant, we know what to expect, how to respond, and how things fit together. We have stability, security, and predictability. Change presents us with an unknown and uncertain situation. This disorganization of the familiar often arouses anxiety, fear, and stress.
Fear of power loss	Often our power and status are so tied to the existing situation that any change means a potential personal loss. The change may "cost" us too much.
Fear of economic loss	We may feel threatened by loss of income due to reductions in salary or cuts in benefits or possibly the ultimate loss of our jobs.
Conflict of interest	Traditions, standards, values, or norms of a person or a group may be threatened by the change. Social affiliations may also be jeopardized.

Resistance often provides clues for the prevention of failure.

Resistance to change can result in some benefits. For example, initiators of change may put more thought into clarifying the purpose of the recommended change and identifying the desired results. The fear of the unknown may lead people to examine possible consequences, both immediate and long-range, with more care. When we find a poor flow of information, we can improve communication systems, a vital link to effective change implementation. Resistance often provides clues for the prevention of failure. The following suggestions might help you when facing change.

Suggestions for Dealing with Change

1. Remember that change is inevitable and that fear of change is normal.

2. Analyze the reasons that you want to resist the change. What fears do you have? What behaviors will you have to adjust in order to effect the change?

3. Search for the positives. How will the changes constructively affect your work?

4. Seek assistance if you are having difficulty adjusting to the changes. A supervisor or a more experienced employee can help.

5. Learn how to learn. The most important skill to acquire for the future is learning to keep abilities fresh and desirable in the job market.

Open communication about any change process is critical in making smooth transitions. Keeping people informed about each step and telling them how it will affect them helps to garner commitment and assure that change is embraced.

FastChat

1. What are some of the most common fears individuals may experience? Have you ever been in one of these situations? How did you deal with it?

2. What positive things would you find in a situation like the one described about the GSA?

How Do Leaders Facilitate Change?

Learning
Objective 5

Describe the role leaders have in facilitating change.

Leaders have an opportunity to facilitate change processes.

Creating a climate conducive to change is an important step in change management. When change is needed, leaders are called upon to act as change agents to facilitate the process. (Conversely, those who are able to act as change agents are more likely to attain positions of leadership.) If you are in a position of leadership at work or in other situations, organizational or personal, and are asked to implement change, the following seven-step process may help you.

Steps in the Change Process

1. *Conduct present state assessment (PSA).*	Diagnose the present situation. "Where am I now, and what are the current conditions?" Examine why you need to change.
2. *Conduct future state assessment (FSA).*	Determine the desired results. "Where do I want to be, and how will the conditions change?" Visualize the desired results.
3. *Generate alternatives.*	Identify the possible approaches through use of "What if . . . " questions. Consider the probable outcomes and reactions. Who will be involved and how will they be affected?
4. *Select one alterntive.*	Make a selection from the alternative solutions. Decide which method will best achieve the desired results.
5. *Implement the change.*	Put a plan in motion to assure that the change occurs. Alter whatever conditions are necessary or introduce the change method.
6. *Evaluate the change.*	Allow time for implementation and acceptance; carefully evaluate the results to see whether you have achieved the desired outcome
7. *Modify the change.*	Modify as required. You may make only a minor revision or repeat the entire process with a different alternative.

Modifying or changing an alternative is appropriate if the expected results are not achieved or if they prove undesirable. However, too frequent changes make us appear indecisive. Use of these steps in your change process may reduce the negative effects on people involved.

As mentioned earlier, communication is an important factor in facilitating change. It helps get more people involved in the process. The more individuals feel involved, the more likely you will be able to keep change moving in the right direction. Communication can also contribute to the ongoing evaluation of both the process and the results. The following suggestions can help individuals adjust to change.

Facilitating Changes

Discuss the change.	Communicate early in the process with those who will be affected. Educate them in how, why, and when the change will occur.
Invite participation.	Ask people who will be affected by the change to take part in the formulation of the change. Involvement will create "ownership" and commitment to the success of the change.
Be open and honest.	Share facts and information with those who will be affected. Stick to the facts and avoid what you "hope" or "think."
Accent the positives.	Stress the benefits. In the work environment, increased pay, fringe benefits, lighter work load, elimination of hectic deadlines, or more flexible work hours may be some of the positive outcomes expected of the change. Although individuals are interested in how the change will affect them, they are even more interested in what benefits it will bring them.
Do not downgrade past methods.	A mistake often made when introducing change is to tear down old or existing methods. If you imply that the old or existing method is inadequate, individuals may resent the implication that they have not been doing an adequate job using that method.
Follow up on the process.	Frequently resistance to change is shadowed or hidden, only to surface later. Follow up to see whether individuals are having problems accepting it or implementing it, and provide help.
Allow time for adjustments.	Changing long-standing habits can take time. Give individuals a chance to adjust to the change. Be prepared to make adjustments if you hit a snag in the process.

Applying these methods will help those involved accept change. The box on page 376 illustrates the stages of acceptance individuals must go through.

You may want to try additional human relations approaches when introducing change. For example, you may try the change first on a small scale. Begin the process with some small segment of the whole group to be affected. Other individuals will see the advantages and importance of the change. Their uncertainties will be reduced. A similar approach calls for

quick wit

. . . .

"Man is a creature of hope and invention, both of which belie the idea that things cannot be changed."

. . . .

Tom Clancy in
Debt of Honor

Stages in Acceptance of Change	
Recognition:	Individual must recognize need for change.
Choice:	Individual must decide change is beneficial and act to make it happen.
Plan:	Individual must think through the change process to develop a specific approach.
Support:	Individual must seek understanding and assistance of others to help implement plan.

special timing. Before you begin, find allies who will be supportive of your ideas. This way you may ease the general resistance.

Finally, you can use special human relations skills to facilitate change. Unwelcome change often results in low morale or motivation, apathy, uncertainty, instability, frustration, and symptoms of stress. Even change that is welcomed can cause some of these symptoms. These behavior changes are hardly the ones hoped for in reaching your change objectives. Additionally, changes that tend toward restructuring, compressing, or reducing the work force may result in a mismatch of skills and jobs. In this case, you may notice performance problems and a decrease in productivity while change is being implemented.

Coaching and counseling skills often help you implement change.

The most effective means of dealing with behavioral problems, performance and productivity problems, and employee training and development concerns brought on by change is through coaching and counseling employees. Open communication, which is stressed in these methods, is always a good way to cope with problems.

*Fast*Chat

1. How would you tell valued workers they are losing their jobs because of "reengineering" the organization?

2. What recurring themes do you see in effectively bringing about change?

What Is Meant by the Term Coaching?

Coaching is a method of employee development that closely resembles on-the-job training. Typically, a skilled and experienced employee, usually of high-ranking status within the organization, is assigned to develop or train a junior employee with lesser skills and abilities. A coach may help identify career paths, help define career goals and objectives, explain the organization's culture and established norms, or simply share expertise for skills development. Immediate and ongoing feedback is provided. A popular form of coaching is known as **mentoring**.

A **mentor** is usually a manager with political savvy and an interest in helping employees achieve both career goals and the objectives of the organization. Many corporations are recognizing the benefits of establishing formal mentoring programs. Some companies are providing mentors to help new employees rapidly enter the corporate culture. A mentor and protégé are often matched on the basis of backgrounds and interests.

Learning
Objective   6

Explain what is meant by the term "coaching."

Coaching by a senior-level employee is a good employee development method.

GLOBAL CONNECTION

Fidelis Umeh, President and CEO of SEI Information Technology, is proud of the growth and success of his small business. He attributes much of the success to his mentoring program designed to meet the special needs of some of computer science graduates recruited from his native Nigeria. The mentoring process addresses social as well as professional issues. "We want them to work side-by-side with some people who can really bring them up to speed and help them feel that they are part of the community."

"Program Spotlights," *HR Magazine Focus,* **April 1998**

What questions, issues, or difficulties might an employee have who was new not only to the job but to the culture as well? How would a mentor be able to help?

If you are not assigned a mentor, you should attempt to find one either within your organization or within your profession. A mentor is often selected on the basis of being a kindred soul. You can best achieve the close rapport necessary in this relationship when the ethics, values, and operating styles of both participants mesh. A foundation of mutual respect must exist. A mentor will listen to you empathetically, suspend judgment, probe for your concerns, and offer specific suggestions regarding training and development opportunities. The selection of a mentor can be a wise investment in career planning and development.

While having a mentor is not a requisite to getting ahead, it can make adjustment to the company swifter and the learning curve easier—and it makes it more likely that your skills and accomplishments will be noticed. Many companies have begun to realize the benefits to both the company and the employee by providing this "nurturing" relationship.

ETHICS CONNECTION

Ford Motor Company provides new employees with a mentor to help them learn the ropes. Each person is matched with someone whose background is similar, perhaps because they grew up in the same city or state, or went to the same school. The mentor may be from one of their employee resources groups for African Americans, Hispanics, or Asians, or perhaps they share a particular educational discipline. The mentor usually has many years of experience from which the new employee may benefit.

"Working Smart," *Executive Strategies*, 1999

Do you think you'd like to have a mentor if you were new to a company? In what ways do you think you could benefit from working with a mentor? How do you think a formal mentor program might compare to the informal approach?

FastChat

1. If you have a mentor, how has that person helped you most?

2. If you are a mentor, what benefits have you realized?

Human Relations

What Is Counseling?

In most organizations, **counseling** is a technique used to assist employees with problems affecting performance on the job. These problems may be personal or work-related. Employee problems may result in unacceptable quality and quantity of work, absenteeism, and low morale, which cost companies millions of dollars.

Learning
O b j e c t i v e   7

Explain what is meant by the term "counseling."

In an article published in *Manage*, Lin Grensing reports on a six-year study that found 18.7 percent of all adults in the United States suffer from at least one mental health disorder (which can include anything from anxiety to depression to more disabling problems) during an average six-month period. Not only can problems of this nature affect an individual's performance, but the behavior of these individuals affects employees who are in contact with them. Of course, the problem may not be related to any "disorder," but rather to such situations as personality conflicts, being overwhelmed by the job, or uncertainty engendered by company changes.

Counseling is generally used to assist employees with performance problems.

If the problems are not easily resolved, the intervention of a counselor may be needed. A **counselor** may be a supervisor or a trained professional capable of dealing with a wide variety of employee problems.

Once a counselor identifies the problem and documents the specifics to

Basic Types of Counseling Methods

Directive counseling	The counselor listens to the individual's problem, allows emotional release, determines an action plan, and advises the person on what needs to be done.
Nondirective counseling	Requires the individual being counseled to participate more actively. Through a technique known as reflective listening, the counselor will mirror feelings and statements back to the person and allow the person to freely define the problem, develop solutions, and choose an appropriate plan of action.
Cooperative counseling	This method is a mutual problem-solving effort. Both parties explore and solve the issues. This process may be more time consuming because of the sharing of ideas and experiences and the evaluation of suggested approaches. The person with the problem is expected to develop the ultimate solution to increase ownership and commitment.

be addressed, a counseling session may be scheduled. During the counseling interview with the employee, any of the three basic types of counseling methods may be used—directive, nondirective, or cooperative.

Some supervisors find counseling a difficult part of the human relations skills required in leadership positions. They prefer to have a professional staff counselor take the responsibility. An alternative solution would be to make a referral of the employee to an employee assistance program.

CASE STUDIES IN THE NEWS

One crucial characteristic of CEOs recently identified as fast track leaders in America was that they "know how to coach and inspire people." Catherine Hapka, one of the six, believes in a management style she calls "existential leadership." She says, "I try to involve workers in big ideas that matter to the survival of the company rather than just the small processes. I have learned to be more of a coach and less of a supervisor." Making your employees winners will make you one too.

Justin Martin, *Fortune Magazine*, 1996

Have you ever worked with anyone—a teacher, leader, coach—whom you would describe as inspiring? What about that person's approach inspired you? Did you feel better prepared to take on the expected task when working with this individual?

FastChat

1. Which of these counseling methods would you be most comfortable using and why?

2. What are some situations that would lend themselves to using each of the methods?

What Are Employee Assistance Programs?

Employee assistance programs (EAPs) are formal programs designed to aid employees with personal problems, such as substance abuse, serious depression, overwhelming stress, family tensions, or psychological problems, that affect their job performance and/or disrupt their lives. These personal problems often result in undesirable behaviors at work, such as absences, errors, tardiness, decreased productivity, accidents, or an inability to operate equipment safely. Problems are generally identified by the immediate supervisor. In some companies the supervisor is expected to take immediate action. In most companies, employees have the option of seeking confidential help before a problem affects their jobs or is even noticed by coworkers. Sometimes the rate or type of change in a company creates the problems, and stress is a growing issue.

Most companies have specific guidelines for handling situations where employees' problems have started to affect their work. The supervisor is usually required to document incidences of unsatisfactory behavior or performance, counsel the employee on performance expectations, and reach an agreement with the employee on a specific time for improvement of performance. If appreciable improvement is not shown within the time limit, a supervisor is expected to refer the employee to the EAP for assignment to a qualified professional counselor.

Whether an employee seeks help or is referred by an employer, the counselor to whom he or she is assigned will recommend whatever treatment is required to aid the employee in coping with personal problems. The problem may be marital strife, financial troubles, substance abuse, parenting problems, care for aging parents, difficulty balancing life and work, or adjusting to foreign surroundings.

Employees are guaranteed confidentiality when entering an employee assistance program. In most cases, the employee begins to handle the problem and job performance improves. In fact, these programs have been so successful that EAPs have virtually exploded, with almost every major U.S. corporation now offering assistance to its employees.

Any planned change must give as much attention to the emotional or psychological dimensions as to the practical and informational aspects of the change process. The most important condition for effective change management is the certainty that the climate is conducive to the change being introduced, implemented, and accepted.

Learning
Objective 8

Understand why employee assistance programs are important in change environments.

quick wit

"The difference between a mountain and a molehill is your perspective."

Al Neuharth

GLOBAL CONNECTION

Comparing top Fortune 500 companies operating globally, researchers identified significant similarities in their international management policies and practices. Senior international human resources directors in 32 of the 50 "best-in-class" companies were interviewed and all agreed that ". . . change is an overriding factor in the global marketplace and requirements for global relocations will demand innovation."

Sixty-six percent of those interviewed expect the number of international assignments within their companies to increase and plan to expand their employee assistance programs, placing increased emphasis on their expatriate support projects. These leading-edge companies realize that dealing with "soft issues" is as integral to the success of an employee assignment as administering their payroll, pensions, and other benefits.

Rita Bennet and Heidi O'Gorman, *HR Magazine Focus*, April 1998

What kind of support do you imagine employees would need if they were suddenly transferred to a foreign country? How might an EAP help them adjust to their surroundings?

*Fast*Chat

1. What types of employee assistance programs do you think are most used in today's "techno-stress" work environment?

2. Do you think that people are more comfortable seeking help these days? Explain.

13

Summary

Change is a basic condition of today's work world. Changes will continue to be a way of life as we move into the twenty-first century. Areas experiencing rapid change include the economy, science and technology, the general work force, management styles, and work itself. The organizational environment of the future can be described as intensely competitive, technologically advanced, and filled with turbulence and uncertainty. Because change can be difficult for employees, organizations must use sound human relations skills to facilitate necessary changes.

Recommendations for change originate from professional planners, special task forces, CEOs, and other top-level executives. However, the change is usually carried out by mid-level and first-line managers. Unilateral, participative, and delegated methods are used in effecting change. The most common methods of planning for change include strategic planning, force field analysis, and various organizational development strategies such as benchmarking, redesign, and reengineering.

Reasons for resistance to change include a fear of the unknown, a fear of power loss, a fear of economic loss, and a conflict of interest. The steps involved in the change process include a present state assessment, a future state assessment, generation of alternatives, selection of one alternative, implementation, evaluation, and modification, if required. Several methods of overcoming resistance to change may be applied. Coaching and counseling skills are used to help individuals cope with uncertainties of change. Coaching and mentoring are methods of developing employees to their maximum potential. Counseling is a method of assisting employees with personal problems affecting their performance. The most common methods of counseling are directive, nondirective, and cooperative. Employee assistance programs are formal programs provided to help employees with their personal problems that may be effecting their performance.

Key Terms

unilateral method
participative method
delegated method
strategic planning
organizational development
change agent
benchmarking
job redesign
job enrichment
job enlargement
job rotation
reengineering
force field analysis
coaching
mentoring
mentor
counseling
counselor
directive counseling
nondirective counseling
cooperative counseling
employee assistance program (EAP)

Review Questions

1. Discuss the significant factors that are changing in today's workplace.
2. Who usually recommends and implements organizational changes?
3. Discuss several methods used in bringing about change.
4. What are the most common reasons for resisting change and how might you overcome them?
5. Explain why coaching and counseling are needed in the change process.

Discussion Questions

1. Which of the major factors changing in today's workplace are affecting you personally? How?
2. What changes in your immediate work environment have you resisted over the past year? Discuss why and explain what action you took to adjust.
3. Think of the last major change that was introduced in your organization. Was the method used to effect that change unilateral, participative, or delegated? Describe how you were involved.
4. Think about several mergers or takeovers that were mentioned in this chapter or ones with which you may be familiar. How do you think these changes may be affecting you personally?

Chapter Project

Do you have a mentor? If so, prepare a brief, one-page written description of why you selected that individual as a mentor for your career. If not, think of someone in your organization whom you might select and describe why you would choose that person. Be specific about the advantages you feel might result from this alliance. What skills and information might you exchange? Using the Internet, you may choose to investigate companies in which you have an interest to see whether they have programs that assist new employees to more easily enter that organization. You may find one that interests you and want to apply.

As we become more globally involved, understanding the extent to which we will be affected by change becomes more important to our success and well-being. Using a personal computer, locate http://www.euen.co.uk/ You can learn about the European Union from this site. Think about how this information may affect you in your current environment. Be prepared to discuss the ramifications of Europe's changing economy in small groups in class.

Applications

In small groups, analyze the following situations.

Would Somebody Help Me, Please?

Marc Tross had been a faithful worker for the Whitaker Transportation Corporation for nearly 20 years. His work record was outstanding with few absences to mar his attendance record and no lateness. He was considered a pillar of dependability and highly respected for the expertise he had developed over the years about the transportation industry.

"I don't understand what's going on with Marc's performance lately," remarked Chauncey, his first-line supervisor. "He has begun to come in late and take excessively long lunch breaks, and he slips out before quitting time. I've spoken with him about the changes in his behavior, but he seems unwilling to admit that he has changed or to commit to correcting the problem."

"Have you documented the circumstances and followed the usual procedures?" asked Patrice, the trained counselor from Human Resources. "Yes, but I don't know what my next step should be," replied Chauncey. "I am not comfortable with this situation."

1. From the behaviors described, what do you think is the problem?
2. Do you think Chauncey has taken the appropriate steps to help his employee in this situation?
3. What do you think Chauncey should do next? Why?

Where Will All the People Go?

"This new office system will revolutionize your department's operations, increase productivity, and reduce your overhead costs. You can't beat it, and if you plan to stay competitive in this market, you must adopt this system." Darla knew that she needed to make the decision soon on converting her department to this new system, but it would mean a reduction in her office staff of nearly 60 percent. Then the department would have a period of lost productivity while employees were trained to use the new equipment and adjusted to the changes. Many factors needed to be considered.

Reasoning, creatively thinking, visualizing, participating as a member of a team and contributing to group efforts, and understanding complex interrelationships.

Reading, listening, speaking, reasoning, problem solving, participating as a member of a team, negotiating, and exercising leadership skills.

1. What methods should Darla consider using to implement the new system in her department?
2. Is there any evidence that Darla's management had planned for this change in technology and prepared for implementation?
3. What will be some of the typical responses to the implementation of the new system, and how will Darla react to the concerns of her employees?

Additional Readings and Resources

Fishman, Charles, "Change." *Fast Company.* April 1997.

Http//IWSP.Human.Cornell.EDU/Research.HTML. March 1999

Jackson, James O. "The One-Way Bridge." *Time*, May 11, 1998

Moulier, Phillipe. "Europe's New Challenge to the Almighty Dollar." *U.S. News & World Report*, January 11, 1999.

Sheff, David, "Levi's Changes Everything." *Fast Company*, June 1996.

Skarke, Gary, and Linda Wilson. *The Art and Science of Change.* Holland & Davis, Inc., 1997.

Wildavsky, Ben. "Not Happy After NAFTA?" *U.S. News & World Report*, January 25, 1999.

Zarolli, Jim. "All Things Considered." National Public Radio, New York,. November 1998.

Zatz, David A. "Harnessing the Power of Cultural Change." *The OD Papers*, February 1994.

The Job Search:

Getting the Job You Want

focus

A typical job hunt:

NO NO NO NO NO NO NO NO NO NO NO NO NO NO NO
NO NO NO NO NO NO NO NO NO NO NO NO NO NO NO
NO NO NO NO NO NO NO NO NO YES

Tom Jackson, *Guerrilla Tactics in the Job Market*

Describe a time when you looked for a job. What did the word "no" do to your self confidence? How did you overcome this?

In This Chapter

After studying this chapter, you should be able to:

1. *Explain the importance of strong job-seeking skills.*

2. *Define your ideal job.*

3. *Identify potential obstacles to job hunting and learn how to overcome them.*

4. *Explain how to learn about occupations.*

5. *Write a solid résumé.*

6. *Research and find companies in which you want to work.*

7. *Realistically evaluate job prospects.*

8. *Identify methods of locating a job opening.*

9 *Explain the appropriate behavior for a job interview.*

10. *Identify ways to handle job search stress.*

11. *Respond to job offers.*

12. *Explain how to cope with starting and ending jobs.*

Why Are Job-Seeking Skills Necessary?

Job-seeking skills are those skills that assist you in finding employment. They include the ability to determine the type of position that will satisfy your needs, to locate available positions, to obtain interviews for those positions, and to land the job.

Everyone who wants to work searches for a job at least once. However, your first job search is usually not the only one. Some people lose jobs because of layoffs, terminations, or downsizing. Others simply want to find positions that are more suitable, with working conditions, location, wages, or job duties that more nearly match their needs or interests.

Strong job-seeking skills are necessary because finding a job is one of the most difficult tasks you'll ever face. It is full of frustration and rejection. Although there are sources of help and guidance, most aspects of a job search are things you must do on your own and for yourself.

For these reasons a carefully organized, well-executed job search is vital if you are to obtain the best possible job in the shortest amount of time. To begin the search, develop a profile of the type of position you would like to have.

A job search can be full of scrutiny and rejection.

Human Relations

CASE STUDIES IN THE NEWS

Workforce, a magazine for human resource professionals, cites the following job interview incidents reported by readers:

1. A candidate said she was no longer living at the address on her résumé because her home had been taken over by aliens.

2. One applicant brought his lunch to an interview because it was scheduled during his lunch time.

3. Although an offer was never made, a candidate for a receptionist opening showed up and sat at the receptionist desk.

4. A job candidate searched through the interviewer's desk when the interviewer briefly stepped out of the room.

5. An applicant for a management position was so inebriated when he arrived for his interview that he could not stand up straight.

6. An applicant came for an interview wearing an ear on a chain around his neck.

7. A CEO went to the candidates' homes to conduct his interviews. He would ask the spouse why he should hire the applicant.

1. *If you were the recruiter, would you recommend these individuals for a position?*

2. *How would you feel if the interviewer came to your home?*

The Bureau of labor Statistics estimates that the average person in the U.S. holds 6 to 8 different jobs from the age of 18 to 32.

1. Why do you believe so many jobs are held by people in this age range?

2. What are the pros and cons of holding so many jobs in the time period?

3. Do you think the number decreases after age 32? Why or why not?

*Fast*Chat

The first step in determining the perfect job for you is to review your previous activities—paid work, volunteer work, professional organizations joined, and educational courses taken. What things did you do well? What courses did you enjoy? Which activities did you like best? Richard Bolles, in his book *What Color Is Your Parachute?*, identifies three primary areas of skill—people, data, and things. Identifying where your greatest skills lie can help direct you, help you determine what kind of work would most fit your skills. Bolles suggests that you ask yourself the following questions to help analyze into which areas your skills fall.

Identifying Skills

People	Do you communicate effectively orally and in writing, and do you get along with others? Do you know how to handle, motivate, organize, direct, persuade, and coach others? Are these activities enjoyable to you?
Data	Are you able to gather, compile, interpret, analyze, and problem solve around data (mathematical or other)? Do you enjoy these types of activities?
Things	Do you competently operate machines, equipment, or tools? Do you like these activities?

Analyzing your skills shows the types of jobs you would like and the skills you can market.

After identifying those skills, determine how you might use them on the job. This process will assist you in identifying the type of job for which you are best suited as well as recognizing what skills you can market to your prospective employers.

The Transferable Skills Worksheet below will help you determine how the skills you've identified might transfer into a work situation.

Values are another important area to explore. What is important to you? Respect? Helping others? Having freedom of expression? Caring for the environment? Someone who values helping others, for instance, may be happier as a social worker or teacher than as an accountant.

Environmental preference is another factor to consider. Would you rather work inside or outside? Alone or with others? In a structured or

Skills I Have	How and Where I Used These Skills	How I Can Use These Skills on the Job
People	Organize a 10K race open to all runners in the city for a charitable organization	Can organize, coordinate, & direct—can delegate responsibility. Follow up to see that everything is in order
Data	Prepared weekly sales report when I worked for X, Y, Z Corporation	Collect, analyze, & prepare data in usable format
Things	Responsible for maintenance on photocopy machine—adding paper, clearing paper jams, & replacing toner—for the church	Understand office equipment & can perform routine maintenance duties

Enter Your Own Information Here

People		
Data		
Things		

unstructured environment? In a large or small organization? Pay requirements are an additional consideration. How much do you actually need to earn? Also, do you have any physical or mental disabilities that would prevent you from performing certain jobs?

Answering these questions will help determine the types of jobs for which you will be most suited. This activity is particularly helpful for the individual beginning a first career or seeking a career change. Complete your self analysis by becoming aware of your personal strengths and potential obstacles to overcome.

According to a year-long study from McKinsey and Company, the most important corporate resource over the next twenty years will be talent: smart, sophisticated business people who are technologically literate, globally astute, and operationally agile. Talent has become more important than capital, strategy, or research and development. People are the prime source of competitive advantage.

1. *What are you doing to enrich what you have to offer a company?*

2. *Why has talent become such a vital resource for corporations?*

*Fast*Chat

Spend a few minutes listing your values.

1. Why is it important to consider your values when looking for a job?

2. What happens if your values are not in alignment with those of your position?

3. Can you name a time when you have been in this situation? How did you handle the situation? What was the outcome?

What Are Your Strengths and Obstacles?

Become aware of the strengths you do have. Intelligence, punctuality, trustworthiness, sense of humor, patience, and loyalty are but a few of the personal characteristics that are valued by a company. The Personal Strengths and Potential Obstacles Analysis shows you a way to chart both these strengths and potential obstacles to employment.

Ask friends and family members to help you identify strengths (you may have some you don't even realize you have). Discuss work experience that others have had to help you identify how strengths fit into various situations. If you want more help identifying your strengths, especially as they apply to business, numerous books and assessment tools have been developed. Ask business associates, school counselors, or a librarian for suggestions on titles that might help.

Learning
Objective   3

Identify potential obstacles to job hunting and learn how to overcome them.

Analyzing your strengths and potential obstacles shows your realistic prospects.

Personal Strengths and Potential Obstacles Analysis

Personal strengths	How these strengths can be valuable to an employer
Type 65 words/minute, completed computer courses + know Word and Excel.	I can use my skills + knowledge to turn out work quickly with a minimum of training time for the company.
Potential obstacles	How potential obstacles can be turned into an asset
Have been out of job market for 4 years.	I'm mature, know what I want, performed volunteer work while being out of the job market.
Have 3 young children.	I am a responsible adult.

What are your own strengths and obstacles?

Many applicants have obstacles to overcome. However, with careful thought and preparation, liabilities can be turned into assets. Review the following list and determine whether you have any of these concerns.

Obstacles to Overcome

You have been convicted of a crime.
You are older.
You are unable to relocate.
You have been away from the job market for a long time.
You are young and have no work experience.
You were fired from your previous job.
You were not born in the United States.
You have too much education.
You have too little education.
You have a physical disability.
You have a mental disability.
You are a minority.
You are a woman.
You have no experience in the industry for which you have applied.
You have changed jobs frequently.

Being older, for instance, can be turned into an asset. You have maturity and poise and understand the nature of work. Develop a positive attitude and work on presenting your obstacles to employers in a positive light. Of course, you can work to remove some obstacles: gain more education, improve your skills, or gain experience—even if it's through volunteer work.

Once you have honestly evaluated yourself, you are ready to identify occupations that interest you. However, be realistic and do not set yourself up for disappointment by setting inappropriate goals (applying for a job that requires travel, for example, if you are unable to travel). Most obstacles can be overcome or turned to advantage if you are honest and open and have strengths and skills that you can offer to an employer.

FastChat

Review the Obstacles to Overcome box.

1. What obstacles do you have?

2. How are you going to present them as assets?

3. Is there anything you could do to change an obstacle?

Human Relations

How Can You Learn About Occupations?

The Internet, local library, and your school career counseling center are the best places to start learning about careers. Many books, magazines, and journals concerning careers describe what different occupations entail. The librarian or career counselor can direct you to this information.

Several references, in particular, are extremely helpful. The *Occupational Outlook Handbook, Occupational Outlook Handbook for College Graduates, Occupational Outlook Quarterly,* and *The Job Outlook in Brief* from the U. S. Bureau of Labor Statistics are good starting places for your search. The *Occupational Outlook Handbook,* for instance, lists major occupations and explains what the future of those careers looks like, the nature of the work, earnings, working conditions, and usual training required.

O*Net is the Department of labor's Employment and Training Occupational Information Network. Located at http://www.DOLETA.gov, it identifies job skills requirements for various occupations.

If you are still unsure, try an informational interview. Start with your teachers. If you know that they are familiar with a profession in which you are interested, ask to discuss it with them. Perhaps they know people currently employed in this profession who would be willing to talk with you about what their jobs are like.

Learning
Objective   4

Explain how you learn about occupations.

Information on careers may be obtained through the Internet, library, or interviews.

CASE STUDIES IN THE NEWS

Each year, nearly one million small businesses are started in the U.S. Some fail, of course, but enough succeed that small businesses are now adding millions of jobs to the economy, while the Fortune 500 companies are actually cutting jobs.

Cynthia Clampitt, *Vital Times,* May 1995

What might be some of the advantages of working for a smaller company rather than a large corporation? Disadvantages? What kinds of small businesses do you see starting up in your area?

Friends and neighbors are another source of informational interviews. Ask if they know someone who does the type of work in which you are interested. Also, you can call a company and ask for an informational interview. Ask the receptionist for the name of an individual who holds a position in the area in which you are interested. For instance, if you are curious about jobs in accounting, you may ask the name and correct title of the accounting manager. Then, armed with that information, either call or write that individual and ask for an appointment.

When calling, explain that you are interested in learning more about the individual's occupation and ask for an appointment at a time that would be convenient. If you were referred by someone else, mention that individual's name as your referral source. Be prepared with some questions to ask, such as what tasks are performed, what entry-level positions lead to the individual's position, and what salary you could expect. Do not stay too long. Be sure to thank the individual speaking with you. Then, when you have decided on a career area, you are ready to develop a résumé.

FastChat

Determine a job in which you are interested.

1. How would you obtain an informational interview?

2. What questions would you ask?

3. Go to the Web site http://www.DOLETA.gov and review the job skills requirements given for an occupation that interests you. How do your current skills fit? What can you do to further develop these skills?

What Goes into Your Résumé?

A **résumé** is a sales tool designed to assist you in obtaining an interview. It provides a prospective employer with a brief summary of your skills, education, and job experience. The résumé does not get you a job. However, a poorly written résumé that does not identify your skills and abilities, contains typographical errors, and is unattractive will not get you an interview.

Here are some tips and guidelines to keep in mind while you're developing your résumé:

Learning
Objective 5

Write a solid résumé.

A résumé's sole function is to get you a job interview.

Résumé Writing Tips

1. Limit the résumé to one page unless you have extensive work experience.

2. Target your résumé to specific employers. With word processing software, you can easily customize résumés that fit the job or company for which you are applying.

3. Do not enclose a photograph or list your marital status, number of children, height, weight, or race. This information may disqualify you from the interview. Religion, too, should not be listed, unless it's specifically related to or required for the job.

4. List extracurricular activities or hobbies if they are relevant to the position for which you are applying, or highlight skills that could be useful in that position.

5. Use action verbs such as earned, planned, wrote, achieved, and completed when describing your accomplishments.

6. Avoid the use of "I."

7. Expect to complete several rough drafts. Ask someone else to read your draft critically, reviewing for clarity, spelling errors, and format.

8. Be sure that your résumé is pleasing to the eye. A well laid out résumé with white areas and one-inch margins will be easier to read.

9. A résumé that has been printed on a laser printer and then photocopied on a higher grade paper of at least 20 pounds is a relatively inexpensive alternative to a professional résumé.

10. Use white or light-colored $8\frac{1}{2}$-by-11-inch paper when printing your résumé.

Hundreds of large companies are using text-searching or artificial-intelligence software to track résumés. These systems use optical scanners to input résumés or accept résumé files transmitted through e-mail or a Web site. They then search for skills that match a job description.

1. *Why are companies beginning to scan résumés?*

2. *What do you think are the benefits of using software to make these searches—to the employer and to the employee? What are the disadvantages?*

As more companies use scanners and accept résumé files over the Internet, formatting your résumé in such a way that it can be easily read by the software will become increasingly important. Your résumé must be clean and free of stray marks that a scanner might pick up. The Quick Tip lists the most important considerations for making your document compatible with this technology.

Quick Tip

Use the following guidelines for making your résumé scannable and/or cyber-ready:

Use words in your résumé on which companies will perform key searches.

Study current job listings for popular key words, especially ones appropriate to the field in which you're interested.

Put these key words in your summary, which should be coherent and well worded.

Use nouns rather than verbs.

Use type fonts such as Helvetica or Courier at 12 points or larger.

Print the résumé in letter quality, or transmit it as an ASCII or text-only file.

Do not use underline, bold, bullets, italic, or graphics.

Avoid folding or creasing a printed résumé.

Use white or off-white rather than colored paper.

FORMATS

Endless formats exist for resumes. The two basic forms are chronological and functional. The **chronological résumé**, which is illustrated on page 400, is the most common résumé style. It lists experience in reverse chronological order, identifying the most recent employment first. This format is good when an individual has a continuous work history with progressively more responsible positions. However, it may not be helpful for those who have gaps in their employment or are attempting to return to the job market after a prolonged absence such as caring for a family.

The **functional résumé** emphasizes special skills that can be transferred to other areas, making it useful for individuals reentering the job market or changing careers. Also those with little work experience, extensive volunteer experience, or frequent job changes can benefit from this format. An example of a functional résumé is shown on page 401.

Résumés can also be developed that incorporate both chronological and functional forms. These are called **hybrid résumés**. This style of résumé is illustrated on page 402.

ETHICS CONNECTION

Embellishing accomplishments, or even lying about qualifications on résumés, is perhaps not as common as you think, but it does occur. Experts estimate that from 10–30 percent of job applicants lie on résumés.

1. *How could this practice damage an individual's career?*

2. *How might this hurt companies?*

3. *How would you feel if you lost a job for which you were qualified to someone who lied?*

4. *How would you feel if you hired someone and found out that person had lied? What might you do?*

James W. Adams
278 Maple Street
Cowpens, SC 29682
803-555-1234

JOB OBJECTIVE

Entry-level sales position leading to opportunities for advancement to supervisory position and broad opportunities for utilizing communications skills.

EXPERIENCE

1997-2000 Sales clerk in Montgomery Crawford Hardware Store after school. Responsible for entire store when owner was away.

1997-1999 Summers; counselor and lifeguard at Camp Sequoia for boys.

1994-1997 Miller's Grocery Store; clerk, delivery and stock attendant on Saturdays and during summer.

EDUCATION

Associate degree, Spartanburg Junior College, 2000
Specialized in marketing and communications
Grade point average: 3.2 (A=4.0)
Diploma, Spartanburg County High School, 1997 (Upper third of class)

ACTIVITIES

High school varsity letters in football, basketball, and track.

President, Methodist Youth Fellowship,
Grace Methodist Church, Cowpens, SC.

Member of the Debating Club and French Club,
Spartanburg County High School.

REFERENCES

References are available upon request.

Janet D. Hernandez
114 West 23rd Street
Nashville, TN 46302
615-555-1708

JOB OBJECTIVE
Secretarial or office assistant position.

SPECIAL SKILLS
Developed high capabilities in operating computers and utilizing several word processing software packages, including Microsoft Word and WordPerfect.

Capable of utilizing spreadsheet software packages, such as Excel and Lotus 1-2-3.

Trained in office procedures, including telephone etiquette and reception techniques.

EXPERIENCE
Prepare, edit, and publish weekly college newspaper.

Assistant editor of high school newspaper, The Scribbler, at West End High School.

Word processed theses, themes, and other papers for Vanderbilt University students during the summer.

EDUCATION
Candidate for computer job skills certificate, Nashville College, Sept. 2002. GPA: 3.7 (A=4.0).

Diploma, West End High School, Nashville, TN, 2000.

REFERENCES
References are available upon request.

Pauline R. Jackson
10 New England Ridge Road #5
Washington, WV 26181
304-555-1234

JOB OBJECTIVE
Laboratory technician in hospital, doctor's office, or medical laboratory.

ACCOMPLISHMENTS
Performed x-rays, various laboratory tests, assisted patients, and aided the physician in minor in-office surgical procedures.

Processed blood and performed other advanced laboratory tests in state medical laboratory.

EMPLOYMENT HISTORY
Office Assistant
Dr. Mortimer Smith, Charleston, WV
1997-2002

Laboratory Technician
West Virginia State Laboratory, Charleston, WV
1995-1997

Office Assistant
Dr. Cynthia Raddock, Morgantown, WV
1992-1994

EDUCATION
West Virginia University
B.S. degree, General Science, 1992.

West Virginia University Parkersburg campus Laboratory Techniques course, 1999.

REFERENCES
References available upon request.

REFERENCES

References are individuals who can vouch for your work performance and your character. They include former bosses, coworkers, teachers, and fellow professionals or neighbors who know you socially. Family members are not considered good references, as most employers do not view them as unbiased. Offer references such as former employers and teachers who can attest to your performance first. Only if you are asked for character references should you provide the names of others.

Never use individuals' names for a reference without obtaining permission. Tell them about your job search plans and the type of work you are seeking. Be sure that you have their complete mailing addresses, daytime telephone numbers, and the correct spelling of their names. Between three and five references is the usual number.

Be sure to express appreciation to references for being willing to assist you in your job search. Call them after an interview to let them know that they can expect a telephone call from your prospective employer.

Tips for Filling Out a Job Application Form

In addition to having an up-to-date résumé, be prepared to fill out job application forms:

- Follow all directions carefully.
- Write neatly in black ink, type, or word process an application.
- Answer all the questions.
- Make sure each answer is correct and well phrased.
- Make sure your application is free from typing, spelling, grammar, and punctuation errors.
- Use complete and accurate addresses in the references section.
- Be sure the completed form is attractive, neat, and clean.
- Sign and date the application.

---

1. Which of the résumé formats do you think would work best in your situation? Why?

2. What sorts of questions do you think employers would ask your references?

FastChat

14.6 What Companies Are Out There?

Learning
O b j e c t i v e   6

Research and find companies in which you want to work.

Before deciding which organizations will be the focus of your job search, you must make some decisions concerning the locations in which you are willing to work. In what area of the country do you want to work? Are you willing to relocate? How far are you willing to drive to a job? What areas of town are inaccessible to you?

Organizations in your area can be identified through library resources. Some of the available resources are:

- Local business directories, such as the Chamber of Commerce directory
- Company reports, such as annual reports and *10K* reports
- *Encyclopedia of Associations*
- *Standard and Poor's Register*
- *Dun and Bradstreet Million Dollar Directory*
- *Thomas Register of American Manufacturers*
- *Value Line*

Library resources can help target specific companies for your job search.

Local libraries contain information specific to your community. Ask the librarian for assistance in locating this information.

These resources can tell you where organizations are located and other information about them. This information will be useful during the interviewing phase. At this point a realistic look at the job market is in order.

GLOBAL CONNECTION

New jobs can be anywhere in the world. The global applicant needs to take into consideration the cost-of-living differences, moving costs, and the characteristics of a new city when considering a job offer.

1. *How can you find this information?*

2. *Visit http://www.homefair.com. Locate another city in which you are interested. What do you find attractive about the city? What is the difference in the cost of living between your current location and the new city?*

Additional information can be found online at the following sites:

- Security and Exchange
  Commission: http://www.sec.gov/edgarhp.htm
- Career Magazine   http://www.careermag.com
- Career Mosaic   http://www.careermosaic.com
- Career Resources   http://www.rpi.edu/dept/cdc/homepage.html
- The Catapult   http://www.jobweb.org/catapult/catapult.htm

When you land an interview, be prepared to state how you can benefit the company.

"I have a plan to make this company the greatest in the world, starting with the position you have open in the mail room."

*Fast*Chat

Imagine that you have just landed an interview:

1. Is it important to know something about the company before you interview? Why or why not?

2. What sort of information might be useful?

3. What information might you be able to find locally that is not available from national resources?

14.7 What Can You Realistically Expect?

Learning
Objective **7**

Know how to realistically evaluate job prospects.

Evaluation of the companies and the economic realities of your region gives you realistic expectations.

After reviewing what you would like in a job, what skills you have, and what types of companies exist, you can realistically evaluate what type of job you will be able to obtain. Using an assessment tool, like the Job Parameters chart, can help you evaluate your prospects.

Take into consideration your local economy. If the unemployment rate is high and layoffs are occurring, you may have to accept a position that is not quite what you want in terms of job duties and pay. (But don't worry—statistics show that, no matter where you are in your career, you will probably change jobs again at some point. So make the best of whatever jobs there are, and do whatever you can—on-the-job training, education, extra responsibilities—to prepare for your next job, which may be closer to your ideal.)

With these realities in mind, locating the jobs can actually begin.

Quick Tip

The Americans with Disabilities Act requires that employers make "modifications or adjustments to a job application process that enable a qualified applicant with a disability to be considered for the position such qualified applicant desires. . ."

An employer may have to provide a number of possible reasonable accommodations in connection with the application process. These may include:

- making existing facilities accessible,

- changing tests or hiring practices, or

- providing qualified readers or interpreters.

If you are a qualified individual with a disability and find you need an accommodation during the application process, you should immediately advise the organization's representative. You can find out more about reasonable accommodation by visiting the Equal Employment Opportunity Commission's web site at http://www.eeoc.gov.

JOB PARAMETERS

	Ideal	Realistic
Salary	$ 32,000 a year	$ 27,000 a year
Location	Los Angeles	L.A., Sacramento, San Francisco
Hours	9–5	7AM–7PM any time between these hours
People (Groups) Young, Old, Individual	work by self	groups near my age
Outdoors/Indoors	outdoors	in + out
Size of Company	below 50	any size
Dress Code/Supervision	no dress code minimal supervision	willing to conform to moderate dress code + more close supervision

We would all like a "perfect" job.

1. What factors restrict us in obtaining our ideal job?

2. How much does the economy affect this?

3. What can we do to improve the chances of landing our ideal job?

Fast Chat

Where Are the Jobs?

Learning
Objective 8

*Identify methods of
locating a job
opening.*

You must take a number of approaches to find an open position. Networking, the Internet, the direct approach, newspaper want ads, hot lines, private employment agencies, public employment agencies, temporary agencies, job fairs, summer jobs and internships, and school placement centers are all ways in which individuals find jobs.

NETWORKING

Networking is one of the most effective methods of looking for a job opening. Sixty to seventy percent of jobs are found through networking. It involves telling people you know that you are looking for a job and asking them to contact you if they hear of any openings. These people include teachers, former employers, friends, parents of friends, former coworkers, and contacts in professional organizations. Ask these acquaintances to inquire on your behalf. Having a friend within the organization you are targeting deliver your résumé and recommend you for a position will dramatically increase the odds of receiving an interview.

The informational interview mentioned previously can also be used in networking. Ask individuals with whom you speak to refer you to others who may know about jobs and to call you if they have any openings at their firm.

THE INTERNET

The Internet is becoming an increasingly important way to search. You can check web sites for individual companies to learn about job openings with an employer in which you might be interested. You could visit some of the many sites that maintain lists of job openings; the list of Internet sites on the next page can get you started, but new sites keep popping up. And don't forget to check the web site of your local newspaper.

DIRECT APPROACH

The direct approach to a company is another extremely effective method of locating an opening. Many large organizations have human resources departments that post all job openings and accept applications for employment on a regular basis. Before going to the company, call human resources to determine when the company takes applications and where jobs are posted. Going to a company unannounced is not recommended.

Another approach is to call the company, asking for the name of the individual who supervises the department in which you wish to work. For instance, you can call and ask for the name of the data processing manager and the correct company address, explaining that you are developing a mailing list. Then, send a target letter to that individual, giving your qualifications and asking for an interview. A sample of a target letter is illustrated on the next page. This letter should be modified to fit the qualities you have that may interest this particular employer. Follow up by telephone and ask for an interview. If you are told that the company has no openings, ask if you can call back later or if the official knows of any other job openings. Express thanks, and always be polite and professional.

NEWSPAPER WANT ADS

The want ads of the newspaper contain many positions. However, the newspaper is probably the least effective way to find a job. The competition is fierce for the positions advertised. Scan the ads and answer only those advertisements for which you are qualified. Never depend totally on the newspaper to identify positions.

HOT LINES

Many large employers, such as hospitals, universities, corporations, and governmental entities, have 24-hour telephone hot lines that run a recording of open positions. These lines can be checked at your convenience. Develop a list of these numbers and check them weekly. Also, if you belong to any professional organizations, see if they have job hot lines or Internet sites.

quick wit

"Work is of two kinds: first, altering the position of matter at or near the earth's surface relative to other matter; second, telling other people to do so."

Bertrand Russell

489 Longren Circle
Rancho Palos Verde, CA 90274
714-555-2645

August 28, 2000

Ms. Darnelle Johnson, Data Processing Manager
Springboard Products, Inc.
836 Spring Oaks Avenue
Los Angeles, CA 90047

Dear Ms. Johnson:

I recently obtained an associate degree in data processing. My willingness to work hard and my ability to cooperate with others, along with this degree, will make me a valuable member of your data processing staff. To further highlight my accomplishments, I have attached a copy of my résumé.

I would appreciate an opportunity to discuss my skills and abilities with you. I will call in a few days to schedule a mutually convenient time for us to meet.

Sincerely,

Lucinda Colton

Lucinda Colton

PRIVATE EMPLOYMENT AGENCIES

Private employment agencies have jobs for those with skills and a proven track record. However, carefully check to see what your financial obligations to the agency may be. Some require you to pay a fee for the job you obtain through them. Other jobs are fee paid. This term means that the employer, rather than the employee, will pay the fee.

PUBLIC EMPLOYMENT AGENCIES

Public employment agencies operate in each state. Visit your state employment commission and find out how its services operate and what positions are available. Many organizations with government contracts are required to place job openings with the state employment commissions, and federal and other government openings can be obtained through these agencies as well.

TEMPORARY AGENCIES

Individuals working with temporary agencies frequently find permanent employment through a long-term temporary job assignment. Finding a job in this manner can be beneficial because you have a chance to learn about the company and the people in it prior to accepting permanent employment. If you do not wish to stay there, you simply ask for a new assignment.

JOB FAIRS

In some regions, Job Fairs are held to introduce companies to potential employees. Local firms will often offer on-site interviews or will at the very least accept résumés from interested searchers. These fairs can give you an opportunity to meet Human Resources representatives from several companies at the same time. Dress well and take lots of copies of your résumé—plus a calendar, so you can write down any interviews you schedule.

SUMMER JOBS AND INTERNSHIPS

Summer jobs and internships are an excellent way to find a full-time position. After seeing the part-timer's skills and capabilities, companies will often offer full-time employment.

SCHOOL PLACEMENT OFFICE

Do not overlook your school placement office. Assistance in interviewing, job leads, and moral support can be obtained through the center. Recruiters frequently come to campus and interview students through the office.

The most efficient way to obtain a job interview is to take advantage of as many job search methods as possible. This will allow you to quickly locate more positions and generate more interviews. These interviews must happen before hiring occurs.

Review the different ways to seek job openings.

1. Why is networking so effective?

2. What can you do to ensure that you have a large network?

FastChat

How Do You Handle an Interview?

Learning
O b j e c t i v e   9

Explain the appropriate behavior for a job interview.

An **interview** is a process by which the prospective employer learns more about you and evaluates whether you are the best qualified candidate for the position. As the interviewee, you have the responsibility to sell yourself, allowing the interviewer to see exactly what you are capable of doing for the company. In addition, the interview is a time when you can evaluate the company and learn more about the position that is available.

The interview, which obtains the job, requires practice and planning.

PREPARING YOURSELF

A number of steps can be taken to prepare for the interview. The first is to be prepared to answer questions that the interviewer might pose. Examples of the types of questions an interviewer might ask you are shown

At an interview you learn about the company and the company learns about you.

below. Extensive time should be spent in developing honest, thoughtful answers. Prepare a two-minute summary of yourself in response to the "tell me about yourself" question. Study potential weaknesses and learn how to present them in a positive light. For instance, if you are younger and have little work experience, present yourself as eager, energetic, and willing to work hard. Remember, interviewers will not believe that individuals have no weaknesses and appreciate frank answers to their questions. In addition, study the Questions to Ask the Interviewer. These are samples of the kinds of questions you will want answered about the company and the position.

Questions an Interviewer Might Ask

Tell me about yourself.

What are your strengths?

What are your weaknesses?

Why should I hire you?

What are you looking for in a job?

Why did you leave (or why do you want to leave) your current job?

Why do you want to work for this company?

What are your long-term career objectives?

What are your short-term career objectives?

How long would you stay with us?

What do you know about this organization?

What do you find most appealing in a job? Least appealing?

How would you describe your personality?

What interests you most about this job? Least?

What don't you do well?

What did you think of your last boss?

What would be an ideal job for you?

When an offer to interview is extended, be sure that you verify the correct time, date, location, and the name of the person with whom you will be speaking. Then research as much information about the company as possible. You might go to the library or Internet, call a friend who is employed there, or read the annual report or *10K* report. Be sure that you know how to find the location; if necessary, make a trial run on the day before the interview.

Be prepared for the interview to take one of several forms—directed, nondirected, group interview, board interview, or stress interview. A directed interview has specific predetermined questions, whereas a nondirected interview is less structured, involving more frank and open discussion. At a group interview several candidates are interviewed at one time by one or more interviewers. At a board interview one candidate is interviewed by more than one individual at the same time.

The stress interview may take place in any of these formats. This type of interview is designed to test an individual's reactions to uncomfortable situations. (Don't worry—this is only likely to happen if you are applying for a job where grace under pressure is vital.) The candidate may be subjected to verbal attacks, silence, or rapid questioning. Not allowing yourself to become flustered and remaining calm will earn you passing marks in this type of interview.

Sometimes you can expect a series of interviews. A representative from the human resources department may perform a screening interview to be sure that you meet the general job qualifications and then refer you to the department with the opening. The supervisor will then interview you. Sometimes you may interview with several individuals in management with whom you would be working.

SALARY QUESTIONS

Know ahead of time the least amount of money you require. This amount will most likely be quite different from what you would like. Knowing what the local market generally pays for that position is also important. This information can be found through library or Internet research or by asking individuals in similar positions or counselors at your school placement

Suggestions for Successful Interviews

1. Be on your best behavior from the time you drive onto company property. Many a job applicant has unknowingly run into the interviewer in the hallway, parking lot, or rest room.

2. Arrive a few minutes early.

3. Dress appropriately for the position, as if you were working there. Clothes that are revealing are unacceptable. If you feel you can wear the outfit to a party or a picnic, it is unsatisfactory for the interview. Be sure that your clothing is clean and wrinkle-free. Polish your shoes. Do not wear too much jewelry, perfume, or makeup. A watch, small to medium earrings for women only (men should not wear earrings), and one ring is considered appropriate. Do not wear large chains, ankle bracelets, or other heavy jewelry. Dressing conservatively is a good idea.

4. Be physically clean, with combed hair, clean nails, fresh breath, and deodorant.

5. Do not smoke or chew gum.

6. Smile and be pleasant. If offered a hand, make sure your handshake is firm.

7. Use eye contact but do not stare. Review the oral communication skills presented in Chapter 9 and make extensive use of them.

8. Remember that the first few minutes of the interview develop the all important first impression. Small talk can be expected.

9. Explain how your qualifications make you the best candidate for the position. Use the knowledge you developed earlier about your skills to explain how you have used them in the past and how you will use them to the benefit of the company.

10. Never speak badly about a previous employer. Interviewers fear you will one day speak badly about their organization.

11. If you must, explain any negative work experiences in an unemotional manner, emphasizing how this experience makes you a better employee.

12. Remain enthusiastic even if you feel that this position may not be for you. Ask for the position. Ask the interviewer when the decision will be made and whether you may call to inquire about the decision.

13. Be prepared to take pre-employment tests, such as a word-processing or proofreading test. Ask several questions about the job or the company.

center. With a bottom line in mind, you can decide whether a particular job is worth a lower salary because it offers a chance for rapid advancement or is in an industry that you are eager to enter.

Do not bring up salary first. If the interviewer asks what salary you had in mind, you may try something such as, "I'm fairly open. Do you have a salary range for this position?" Once you know the range, you can better handle negotiations.

Sometimes, if the salary is lower than you can comfortably handle and is on the low side for your skills, abilities, and the market, you may want to decline the position. Refusing is particularly important if you feel you would not be happy with yourself if you accepted the position.

INAPPROPRIATE QUESTIONS

At times you may be interviewed by an inexperienced interviewer and asked questions that are inappropriate. Some of the inappropriate questions—and the ways in which the topics can be appropriately addressed or questioned—are shown in the box below.

Inappropriate Interview Questions

Topic	Inappropriate	Appropriate
Age	How old are you?	Are you at least 18?
Marital status	Are you married? Divorced? Single?	The job requires frequent overtime. Are you able to meet this requirement?
Children	Do you have children? If so, how many?	(Same as above)
Criminal record	Have you ever been arrested?	Have you ever been convicted?
National origin	Where were you born? Are you a citizen?	Not appropriate. New hires must provide proof of ability to work in the United States within three days of hire.
Religion	What religion are you?	Not appropriate.
Disability	What is your handicap?	Are you able to perform the essential functions of this job with or without a reasonable accomodation?

Inappropriate questions usually indicate that you have an inexperienced interviewer—but they may also indicate discrimination, which is why they are illegal in most states. If these questions were used during an employment interview and you feel that they were the basis for the company's failing to hire you, contact your state fair employment commission or the Equal Employment Opportunity Commission. Remember, however, that most interviewers are not professional interviewers; they are likely to be unaware of the law, and probably do not intend to discriminate.

Being faced with one of these questions poses a dilemma. If you refuse to answer or if you tell the interviewer that the question is illegal, you may diminish your chances for employment because the interviewer may feel you have something to hide. Also, you may embarrass the interviewer or cause discomfort. On the other hand, answering it may decrease your chances for employment. An employer who learns that you are a single parent with four preschool children may not hire you for fear that you will be absent frequently.

Be prepared with an answer in the event you are asked any of these questions. For instance, a good response when faced with the question of how many children you have would be, "You need not worry about my family. I have made arrangements and I do not let my personal obligations interfere with my work."

H. Anthony Medley, in his book, *Sweaty Palms: The Neglected Art of Being Interviewed*, suggests that if the response will not hurt you, give an answer. Examples of replies that are safe would be "no" if you have never been arrested or "Catholic" if you are interviewing for a position at a Catholic school. However, he says that if the reply will hurt you, try to avoid answering it in a joking manner. If the interviewer persists, say that you thought he was joking because that question is not a permitted pre-employment inquiry. You could also explain that you would be happy to answer the question if the interviewer will tell you how the question pertains to your ability to perform the job.

FOLLOW UP

Immediately after the interview, write a thank you letter to the individual with whom you interviewed. Express your appreciation for the interview, discuss your interest in the job, add any facts or points you may have omitted from the interview, and ask for the job. The sample thank you letter below shows how formal the letter should be, and how short it can be. This is another opportunity to make a good impression, so be sure the letter is neat and without errors.

Keeping progress charts will help you measure your job search progress. Count the applications placed, resumes mailed, and follow-up telephone calls made each week. Also, develop an interview chart that will help you keep track of interviews and follow-ups. Samples of these charts are on pages 418 and 419.

128 Daisy Trail Lane
Edmond, OK 73013
405-555-5432

September 20, 2000

Mr. Sam Hathaway, Accounting Manager
Von Rheen Enterprises
611 Cutler Lane
Edmond, OK 73018

Dear Mr. Hathaway:

Thank you for the opportunity to interview for the accounts payable position.
Attention to detail and ability to follow instructions will allow me to do an excellent
job for you as accounts payable clerk. I look forward to hearing from you on
September 26.

Sincerely,

Michael Ottero

Michael Ottero

Sample interview
chart

Company/ Offical Name	Date Interviewed	Thank You Note Sent	Followup Date	Analysis	Offer/ No Offer
1. SPIDEX INC. Frank Turner President	3/26	Yes	4/4	good company would like to work there	no offer
2. ART INC. Lois Frazier	4/8	Yes	4/10	salary not what I want	no offer
3. The Ray Company Lou Smith Vice President	4/4	Yes	4/12	good company, liked job and people	offer $27,000/yr
4.					

	Applications	Resumes Mailed	Followups/ Phone Calls	Interviews	Thank You Notes
Week 1	ⅡⅡⅡ Ⅰ	///	////	//	//
Week 2	ⅡⅡⅡ ///	ⅡⅡⅡ	ⅡⅡⅡ //	/	/
Week 4					
Week 5					
Week 6					
Week 7					
Week 8					
Week 9					
Week 10					

Review the inappropriate questions.

1. Have you ever been asked one in an interview?

2. How did you handle it?

3. What were the consequences of your answer?

4. Could you have handled it in another way?

FastChat

14.10 How Do You Handle the Job Search Stress?

Learning Objective 10

Identify ways to handle job search stress.

Seeking employment is one of the most stressful activities ever. Rejection abounds, and we hear more "no's" than "yes's." Picking up the telephone or writing a letter or going to fill out an application that may lead to rejection takes an unusual amount of self-confidence when we are feeling good about ourselves. Having lost a job or being unsure of our ability to do a first job plays on our self-doubt, making the task even more difficult.

The rejection itself is not the only part of the job search that is stressful. Driving to new locations for interviews, meeting with unfamiliar people, waiting for telephone calls or letters, and worrying about finances all increase the tension. Learning how to cope with these strains is of the utmost importance for a smooth job search.

To ease job seeking anxiety, construct a less stressful environment.

Arranging your environment is a first step in coping with job search stress. Statistics show that people who join a job search club or group find jobs more quickly than those who work alone. You can share your distress concerning rejection and receive support from others in the job search group. Ask your school counselor or inquire at your state employment commission concerning job groups. Or, start a group with a friend who is also searching for a job or search for a group on the Internet. Meet regularly for discussions and practice interviews.

Discuss job search problems with your family. Explain to them how rejection feels. Be sure family members understand how to answer the telephone and take accurate messages. If you do not have an answering machine, provide an alternate number of someone who has a machine or who is available to take messages.

Approach job seeking as a job. Work at least six hours a day on your job search—doing research, writing letters, making telephone calls, and completing applications. Spend some time each day exercising and doing pleasurable activities such as a hobby or volunteer work with others less fortunate. These types of activities will help you manage the stress.

The fear of rejection is the main reason job searches are unsuccessful. This fear can be countered by keeping a positive attitude and concentrating on the adage "Nothing ventured, nothing gained."

FastChat

1. Why do you think individuals in job search groups find jobs faster?
2. What kind of support can you get from a group?

How Do You Handle Job Offers?

Job offers can be made by telephone, letter, or in person. If the job, the organization, the location, and the salary are right, accept the job immediately. Be sure to inquire when you are to start, where and to whom you should report, and what time you should arrive.

Many times, however, you may want to think about a job offer. You may have another offer that you expect to materialize, or you may need to discuss the offer with your family or friends before accepting. Asking for 24 to 48 hours to allow for a decision is acceptable, with a maximum of 72 hours. Be sure that you have asked the company representative if a decision-making period is permissible and set a time when you will get back with the representative.

If you decide to reject a job offer, do so professionally. Practice your reasons for refusing the job ahead of time. Avoid reasons such as a personality conflict with the new boss or an offer of more money from your old company. Acceptable excuses are:

"I want very much to work for the company but feel the position offered does not fit with my career objectives."

"At present, I am unable to relocate, but I expect to be able to do so in several years."

"Your offer is excellent, but the opportunity for promotion does not seem to be as great as I need to meet my career objectives."

After declining a job offer, you should write a thank you letter. You may want, at a later date, to work for this company and should leave the door open for future employment.

Imagine you have just received a job offer.

1. What reasons may you have for wanting to think about the job offer?

2. Why is it important to decline a job offer gracefully?

*Fast*Chat

How Do Jobs Begin and End?

The first week on the job can be a frightening affair. Although we are excited to have the position, we have much to learn, everything from people's names to where the restroom is. These adjustments can be stressful even though we looked forward to beginning the new job. Be patient with yourself and with the job. Give yourself time to get adjusted before you make any judgments concerning your new position.

At the opposite end of the spectrum is leaving. Jobs are not forever. Individuals may become bored and find no opportunity for growth. Companies lay off workers because of economic conditions, mergers, or buyouts. Sometimes people are terminated because of ethical misconduct, poor work performance, or personal chemistry that is not right. Whatever the cause, almost everyone leaves a job for one reason or another.

The first day on the job can be an exciting and stressful experience.

How To Keep a Job

Be on time for work/from breaks/meetings/turning in assignments.

Call in if you are going to be tardy or absent.

Try your best.

Anticipate problems and needs of management.

Show a positive attitude.

Avoid back stabbing, office gossip, and spreading rumors.

Follow the rules.

Look for opportunities to serve customers and help coworkers.

Avoid the impulse to criticize your boss or company.

Volunteer for training and new assignments.

William T. Simmons, Legal Counsel to Commissioner Ron Lehman, Texas Workforce Commission

Warning signs of impending termination abound. If you begin to recognize some of them, it may be time to take action. The signs are listed below:

Jobs do not last forever, and knowing when and how to leave is a must.

Warning Signs

1. You hate your job and spend more time thinking about what you will do after work than at work. You find getting out of bed in the morning difficult. These attitudes tend to show at work, and others on the job realize how you feel about your job.

2. You lose your voice. Your ideas and opinions are not listened to and others around you pull back and quit communicating with you, perhaps because they realize your job is in danger. You see others being promoted around you as you stay in the same position.

3. The economy is working against you. You begin to hear about layoffs because of a recession or a potential takeover.

4. You're not personally productive, which appears in the form of missed objectives, poorly managed time, or confused priorities.

5. You fail to change. You feel unwilling to adapt and learn new skills and ways of doing things.

If you see the handwriting on the wall and feel you will soon be terminated, or if you feel ready for a job change, decisions must be made. Just how bad is the job? Can you hang in there until you find another position? How will you support yourself if you resign? Can you draw unemployment if you resign? Will the company pay severance pay if you resign?

Finding another job is usually easier while you still have one. In fact, approximately one-third of all job seekers are looking for another position while employed. Never use company time to conduct your job search. Do research in the evenings or on weekends and schedule telephone calls on breaks and interviews during your lunch period. Many times prospective employers will agree to see you late in the evening or even on Saturdays.

If you decide to resign, even if you have a new job, give two weeks' notice of your resignation. This length of notice is standard and proper. Your new employer usually will allow you time to give notice. Sometimes a company may ask you to leave immediately once your resignation is submitted, especially if you deal with trade or strategy secrets or if they feel that your immediate removal is in the best interests of the other employees.

No one is ever totally prepared for termination from a job. However, if you have been reading the warning signs and suspect it is a possibility, start preparing yourself. Expect to feel anger, shame, fear, sadness, and self-pity. Try to control these emotions during the termination interview and remain as professional as possible.

During the termination interview, find out what benefits, if any, the company may give you. Ask, if you think you will need it, for a reference that is positive or at least neutral. If you feel too out of control to discuss benefits, ask if you can return the next day to do so.

Be aware of the unemployment laws in your state. Some states will not pay unemployment if you resign but will if you are terminated. If you are asked to resign rather than be terminated, this may be important.

Never burn your bridges. Throwing a tantrum while being terminated, threatening to kill someone, destroying computer files, tearing up documents, or smashing furniture may make you feel better temporarily but will

Checklist for Making a Successful Job and Career Change

- Keep yourself on the cutting edge of the workforce by continuing your education.
- Before changing jobs or careers, determine whether your discontent is job-based or career-based.
- Consider the pros and cons of staying in your current job before making a change. Avoid quitting until you've secured another job.
- Change to a new career if it's realistically available and meets your needs.
- Always resign professionally and courteously.
- In relocating, consider the impact on your loved ones, values and interests, costs involved, and impact on your career goals.
- Research a new community before moving, and build a new support network immediately on arriving.

hurt you in the long run. You may need a reference or want to return to the company under different circumstances.

Do not be surprised if your supervisor or a member of security escorts you to your work area to remove articles. This procedure is standard practice in a number of companies because of terminated employees who have destroyed company property.

Many employees, after being terminated, react with disbelief. Some are relieved to be out of an uncomfortable situation, whereas others turn to violence or drinking. Many experience a combination of these reactions. Whatever your reaction, you can expect to grieve because of the loss of a job.

Quick Tip

There is life after being fired! Should it happen to you, remember the following do's and don't's:

- Do try to have a calm conversation with your supervisor to clarify the reason for your termination.
- Don't make things worse by verbally (or physically) attacking your supervisor or co-workers.
- Don't focus on how unfairly you were treated.
- Do analyze objectively what you may have learned from this experience.
- Do reestablish and rebuild your support system and contact network.
- Do review your job search materials, update your résumé, and develop new skills.
- Do use the term "laid off" rather than "fired" when asked about your past job experience.
- Do remember that many people who have lost their jobs in the past have gone on to enjoy successful new jobs and careers. This is the beginning of new opportunities.

Leaving a job with dignity is important.

1. Have you or someone you know left a job by "burning bridges"? What were the consequences?

2. How can you begin to prepare if you feel you will soon be terminated?

FastChat

Key Terms

job-seeking skills
résumé
chronological résumé
functional résumé
hybrid résumé
reference
networking
interview

Summary

Job-seeking skills, which help us in finding employment, are important. Finding a job is one of the most difficult tasks we face. The job search is often filled with frustration and rejection.

Before we can begin a job search, we must determine the type of positions that interest us and identify which skills we have to offer an employer. The library and Internet are good sources of information about different organizations that can use our talents.

The résumé is a device that enables us to obtain an interview; however, it does not land us a job. A poorly done résumé, with typographical errors, can prevent us from being interviewed. Various formats of the résumé are available, including chronological, functional, and hybrid resumes. Above all, a résumé should be factual.

Many approaches are necessary to locate available jobs. These approaches include networking, the Internet, the direct approach, newspaper want ads, hot lines, private employment agencies, public employment agencies, temporary agencies, job fairs, summer jobs and internships, and the school placement office. A variety of strategies must be utilized in order to secure interviews.

Interviewing is an art in itself, and preparation is the key to a successful interview. The interview can come in several forms—directed, nondirected, group interview, board interview, or stress interview.

The job search can be stressful. We hear many more "no's" than "yes's." Discussing the situation with our family, joining others who are job seeking, getting regular exercise, and working at the job search at least six hours a day will help manage stress.

Once a job is obtained, we can expect a stressful first week. We should give ourselves time for transition to the new position. Leaving a job can be just as stressful. We should learn the warning signs of impending termination and be prepared to leave our jobs gracefully, without burning bridges.

Review Questions

1. Why are strong job-seeking skills important?
2. How can you figure out an ideal job for your skills and abilities?
3. What are the obstacles to job hunting, and how can you overcome them?
4. What resources for information on organizations and careers are available?
5. What goes into a solid résumé?
6. Where can you locate job openings?
7. What behavior is appropriate for a job interview?
8. How can you handle the stress of the job search?
9. What are the early warning signs of impending termination?
10. How can you cope with the termination process?

Discussion Questions

1. Have you ever looked for a job? Describe your job search and discuss the feelings associated with it.
2. Have you ever been terminated from a job? What happened? Could you have better handled the termination interview?
3. What is the economic situation in your community? Are jobs plentiful or scarce? What adjustments will you need to make in your search because of the economy?
4. What are your strengths? How can you market these strengths to potential employers?
5. What are your potential obstacles? How will you overcome them?

Chapter Project

Develop a résumé for both online and regular use. (You might want to check some of the Internet job search sites to learn how online résumés might differ in format from regular résumés.) Use the form of your choice. Share it with your classmates for critiquing.

Applications

In small groups analyze the following:

Graduation Blues

"I've had it," Joshua's father, Alex, remarked to his wife, Selma. "That boy has just been sitting around the house since he graduated. I don't even think he's picked up the newspaper to look for a job. At this rate we'll be supporting him until he's 40. I wonder, what can we do to get him interested in looking for a job?"

"You know," Selma said thoughtfully, "at first he really tried. He did look in the want ads and applied for a few jobs. I remember he even had one interview. He was upset when he returned from the interview, but he never said what happened. After that he seemed to lose interest in looking for work."

"Well, I don't care. If he doesn't take some action soon, I will," muttered Alex.

1. What do you think happened that caused Joshua to stop looking for a job?
2. What do you think he could do to get his job search back on track?
3. What other methods of job search should he employ?
4. What types of environmental controls does Joshua need to establish?

Nine O'clock Nightmare

Cindy breezed in for her 9 A.M. interview five minutes late. She always liked to attract attention and keep people waiting. As she told Darin, Mr. Lightfoot's assistant, that she was here for the interview, she began to pull out her hairbrush and lipstick to freshen up a bit. Just as she was tucking everything away in her purse, Mr. Lightfoot walked out. He did a double take as he stared at Cindy. She had on a low-cut spaghetti strap dress that was bright red and yellow.

Mr. Lightfoot escorted Cindy into his office. She dropped into the chair and exclaimed, "The traffic was awful! It really got my nerves jangled. I've just gotta have a cigarette." She opened her purse and lit up. "Want one?" she asked.

Mr. Lightfoot proceeded to interview Cindy. She told him how good a typist she was and how much she wanted to work for the company.

Mr. Lightfoot walked her to the door and, as she left, turned to Darin and said, "Well, what do you think?"

"Seems like a real flake to me, Mr. Lightfoot. I wouldn't hire her if I were you. I see nothing but trouble."

"Darin, I think you're right. She does type 90 words a minute and has mastered several software programs, but I don't think she would fit in here. Call the woman I interviewed yesterday—Carlita—and offer her the job."

1. What interview rules did Cindy break?
2. What should Cindy have done during the interview?
3. Are skills always the most important factor?
4. What do you think would have happened if Cindy had been hired?

Additional Readings and Resources

Chartrand, Sabra. "Finding a Few Tips For Salary Negotiation." New York Times on the Web. July 20, 1997.

Dawson, Kenneth M. and Sheryl N. Dawson. *Job Search The Total System*. New York: John Wiley and Sons, 1996.

"Don't Call Us: Tales from the Recruiting Front." *Workforce*, June 1999, 42.

Green, Susan D. and Melanie C.L. Martel. *The Ultimate Job Hunter's Guidebook*. New York: Houghton Mifflin Company, 1998.

Http://www.EEOC.gov

Jandt, Fred E. and Mary B. Nemnich. *Using the Internet and World Wide Web in Your Job Search*. Indianapolis: JIST Works, Inc., 1997.

Kennedy, Joyce Lain. *Job Interviews for Dummies*. Foster City, Ca.: IDG Books Worldwide, Inc, 1996.

Levitt, Julie Griffin. *Your Career: How To Make It Happen*. Cincinnati, OH: South-Western Educational Publishing, 2000.

O'Brien, Jack. *The Complete Job Search Organizer How to Get a Job Fast*. Washington, D.C.: Kiplinger Washington Editors Inc., 1996.

After studying this chapter, you should be able to:

1. *Understand etiquette and protocol.*

2. *List five reasons knowledge of etiquette is important today.*

3. *Understand how important appearance is to your success.*

4. *Use basic table manners in socially acceptable ways.*

5. *Introduce and meet people with confidence.*

6. *Use good judgment in face-to-face interactions.*

7. *Understand cross-cultural etiquette.*

8. *Use socially appropriate behavior to develop effective customer relations.*

9. *Use correspondence and communication technology in appropriate ways.*

10. *Use networking, mentoring, and office politics sensibly.*

11. *Differentiate among behavior types.*

Workplace Expectations:

Business Etiquette

focus

Bennie Smith, managing partner of Newcomer-Smith Memorial Chapel and Crematory in Kansas, knows just how distracting and inappropriate a ringing phone can be in some places. At a recent graveside service, a phone rang. The person answered the call as if at home. It was very annoying to those trying to listen to the minister's message. This was not the first time the ring of a phone pierced the presence of those in reverence to the dead. Last week, inside the chapel the minister had to stop the services and ask an attendee to step outside to finish a cell phone call. Smith feels it will only be a short while before signs and messages will be printed asking people to be sensitive to the grieving families by turning off communication devices.

Robert A. Cronkleton, *Knight Ridder News*

How do you think this should have been handled? What would you have done in this situation? Have you ever been in a situation—perhaps at a movie or concert, if not a funeral—where someone's ringing phone and/or cell phone conversation was a serious annoyance?

In This Chapter

What Is Etiquette?

With the popularity of voice mail, fax machines, cell telephones, video phones, pagers, home computers, e-mail, caller-ID, and other communication conveniences, the electronic age has indeed arrived—and along with it a whole new set of etiquette problems. The following incidents portray only a few of the blunders we are encountering.

Learning
Objective 1

Understand the difference between etiquette and protocol.

Examples of Etiquette Errors

A world-renowned actor in a Broadway play stopped the production to address a member of the audience misusing a cell phone and received an ovation from the crowd.

When a pager went off in a business conference, the executive did not excuse himself to a more private place to return the call. He carried on a lengthy cell phone conversation disrupting the other conference participants.

The head of an executive recruiting firm accidentally faxed a résumé of a promising executive to the firm where he was currently working instead of to the one trying to hire him.

A newspaper columnist received a 12-page fax that contained only about two lines of information useful to her.

Practically every week another article appears in the newspaper or in a popular journal about the growing importance of business etiquette. **Etiquette**, according to Webster's, is "the forms required by good breeding or prescribed by authority to be observed in social or official life." In simple words, when we use correct etiquette, we act appropriately in social and business situations. Etiquette is the oil that prevents friction in business and social settings.

Articles report that people are signing up for etiquette classes in record numbers, that businesses are sending their employees to etiquette classes, and that business schools are incorporating etiquette lectures and classes into their programs. This renewed interest in manners has been too long in coming. We can trace the breakdown of polite society back to the 1960s and 1970s when dress codes faded, permissiveness was the norm, Viet Nam protesters carried the banner of rebellion, and "flower children" were followed

Etiquette is acting appropriately in social and business situations.

by "latchkey kids." The traditional household meal time relaxed—or disappeared. Good manners were mocked and etiquette was viewed as being old-fashioned and out-dated.

Companies now view business etiquette, often called corporate etiquette, as a way of giving them a competitive edge in winning and retaining a solid market share. Knowledge of the finer points of good manners can help build long-term relationships among employees and with customers and clients. Chip Ricketts, in an article in the *Dallas Business Journal*, reports that people skills account for about 85 percent of a person's success and technical skills only 15 percent. Therefore, social skills are increasingly important. Often the ability to engage in small talk over dinner or in small groups, listen effectively, and make introductions—all in a natural and sincere way—is a part of corporate protocol and a part of many company's marketing strategies.

Etiquette provides us with a code of behavior in different settings, much as rule books provide us with a set of directions for playing golf, tennis, bridge, and other games. If we know the rules, we can play the game better and enjoy it more. When we walk into a situation and are sure that we know how to handle ourselves, our self-confidence will be obvious to others.

CASE STUDIES IN THE NEWS

Well, this is certainly welcome! According to a news report, "charm schools" are becoming popular all across the fruited plain. Adults are apparently flocking to these schools in droves, paying good money to learn good manners. Businesses are getting in on the act—sending their employees for lessons on how to dress, carry themselves, present business cards, and shake hands properly. One woman who teaches etiquette at corporate seminars in Chicago says her business has more than doubled in the past three years.

Rush Limbaugh, *The Limbaugh Letter,* 1999

Why do you think so few people know etiquette today? What topics besides those listed do you think might be included in one of these courses?

Tim Janisch, a human resource executive in the banking industry, says of etiquette training, "It's money well spent. A lot of our younger employees will be well-equipped with book knowledge, sales skills and computer skills, but what we find they lack is social grace—and the reality is that it does still matter." He has sent over 60 people to etiquette classes. Jeff Garton, director of staffing and placement at Kraft Foods added, "Initially, workers are not enthusiastic about taking etiquette classes, but eventually they are won over. It just does wonders for your self esteem to do the right thing, the right way."

Protocol is that part of etiquette dealing with behavior in business, diplomatic, or military situations. It is used in determining matters such as displaying the flag of this country, seating people at formal dinners, determining the sequence for introducing people, and using formal titles correctly. Protocol is designed to simplify meetings. It answers questions and everybody accepts it. At affairs of state, protocol rules unambiguously answer questions about the order in which dignitaries will arrive, how and what flags will be flown, and if or how world leaders will be saluted.

Protocol involves rules for business, diplomatic, or military etiquette.

Quick Tip . . . .

"Preparation for a global market requires sensitivity to cultural, gender and generation differences. Since the rules of international business protocol are constantly evolving, it is just as important to keep abreast of the protocols of doing business as it is to keep pace with technology."

Jonathan Siskin, CNN

. . . .

As our world becomes increasingly global, understanding the effects of good manners and protocol in all cultures becomes increasingly important. Gloria Petersen runs seminars in the Washington, D.C. area and stresses, "You never get a second chance to make a first impression." She believes ". . . the way we dress and present ourselves plays a powerful role in other people's perception of us. Dressing establishes one's credibility in today's business arena."

Protocol issues abound now that women are such a strong part of corporate America. In social situations, women do not rise when a man enters the room. But in business situations, staff members—both men and women—to show respect stand up when a superior enters the room. Who initiates a handshake these days? Socially, it is still the woman. But in business protocol, it does not matter. Possibly the host would offer a hand first, male or female. All of this, however, may be completely different in another country.

Rules, then, are an important component of etiquette, but they are not the only one. Knowledge of etiquette rules alone will not strengthen your human relations skills. You must use two other components: courtesy and good taste. When you act with courtesy, you are combining kindness and politeness. An unkind act is never a courteous one, no matter how correct it may be, and impolite acts are neither courteous nor correct. Several etiquette experts point out that being courteous involves the following behaviors.

Behaving Courteously Means:

Considering others, even in little ways.

Respecting and encouraging accomplishments in others.

Being thoughtful of others.

Being democratic in our relations with others.

Saying "thank you" with sincerity.

Using a friendly voice.

Good taste is concerned with the suitability or fitness of actions, objects, and other things. An important part of good taste is the ability to recognize good proportions, orderliness, symmetry, quality, and beauty.

FastChat

1. Have you ever had a "good manners" class or discussed etiquette in school? How was it helpful to you?

2. Have you ever been in a situation where you felt uncertain about what to do or how to act? How did you feel? How did you overcome the feelings of uncertainty?

Human Relations

Why Is Etiquette Important Today?

Marilyn Pincus, author of *Mastering Business Etiquette and Protocol*, points out that mastering business etiquette is important to any person who wants to attain and maintain success in today's rapidly changing, fast-paced business world. Lack of knowledge of protocol can cause embarrassment and misunderstanding. Pincus and other writers on etiquette emphasize that etiquette is more important than ever today and give several reasons.

Learning
Objective   2

List five reasons a knowledge of etiquette is more important today than ever before.

Mastering business etiquette is important to any person who wants to be successful.

Why Etiquette Skills Are Important

1. High-tech tools and toys are being used by more people in more places today. The development of high technology all too often results in our being treated impersonally and our treating others that way. This situation leaves us desiring human sensitivity, a need that can be at least partially met through socially correct interpersonal behaviors.

2. The growth of the global economy and our own diverse population requires that we interact with people of all cultures. If we are to be successful in our dealings, we must be careful not to offend people of other cultures by violating their communication or behavioral norms.

3. Because of the influx of women, minorities, and the handicapped into the workplace, old behavioral rules are being reexamined and new ones created. Some of these behaviors are being determined legally; others fall outside of the legal domain and are less specific.

4. During the 1960s and early 1970s "doing your own thing" became the norm and children were not taught etiquette, resulting in a generation of business people who may feel awkward and ill at ease in social and official situations.

5. Because work is being increasingly restructured to include teams and group decision making, people must get along with each other. Studying etiquette can improve our ability to do that.

Quick Tip

"Every action done in company ought to be with some sign of respect to those that are present."

—George Washington

Knowledge of etiquette, then, is a key ingredient in human relations and in business and personal success. Such knowledge can help you feel comfortable because you know what to do and can do it with grace, style, and ease. Work situations that call for effective etiquette include relationships with coworkers, with managers above you, with people below you in the hierarchy, with customers and clients, and with the general public where you are seen as representing your organization. Away from work you will enhance your chances for satisfactory relationships with people if your behavior says that you respect them.

Appropriate behavior depends on where you are, when, and with whom.

An important point needs to be made about etiquette: what is appropriate will depend to a certain extent on where, when, and with whom the interaction occurs. Behavior considered appropriate with one group or individual may be considered offensive with someone else. Think, for example, about the different perceptions of the handshake around the world, as discussed in Chapter 9. Often, etiquette will come down to learning a person's preferences, then respecting them.

Because etiquette depends on timing and setting, you must develop good judgment and a sensitivity to people around you. This awareness will give you the best chance of success in your relationships, in business situations such as negotiations and sales, in leadership positions, and in any situation requiring cooperation and teamwork.

The remainder of this chapter will discuss etiquette as a typical worker might use it on a normal workday. Etiquette starts with dressing for work in the morning and carries through work activities such as writing and using the telephone and other forms of communication technology. It also applies to meeting people, introducing people, having lunch, networking, mentoring, and participating in office politics. Imagine yourself in these situations and apply the suggestions to your own life.

Fast**Chat**

1. What other reasons for good etiquette can you imagine?

2. Which one of these reasons do you think is most important and why?

Why Is Appearance a Form of Etiquette?

Experts point out that we form our impressions of people in the first few seconds we see them and that initial impressions can be difficult to change. Because of this, we need to be aware of what impression our own appearance makes. Consider what you wore to work or class today and your overall appearance, which includes hygiene. When dressing this morning, did you consider whether the statement your clothes would make would be the one you want to make? Did you ask yourself whether your appearance would indicate that you fit in with the environment in which you function?

If etiquette pertains to appropriate behaviors, certainly it must be extended to include appropriate dress, hygiene, and grooming. Inappropriate dress suggests a lack of respect for the situation and the people involved. People who take their careers seriously know that image is important. You will be a poor representative for your company if your appearance is making a statement that does not agree with the image of the company.

Learning
O b j e c t i v e   3

Understand how important appearance is to your success.

Quick Tip

"The first impression is the most lasting, most significant mark you can make. If you don't act professionally or dress accordingly, the chances are good that a potential employer won't give you a second glance."

Lyn Vallillee, President of Etiquette Etcetera Inc.

Additionally, our clothing and accessories can help us feel better about ourselves, which can in turn make us feel more comfortable interacting with others. If we can forget about our appearance because we are satisfied with it, we are free to concentrate on the other person.

This, then, is the most important rule of dress for work: dress appropriately for your organization. Some organizations—insurance companies, for example—are conservative in nature, and expect their employees to dress accordingly. Organizations that stress creativity, such as advertising firms, expect that their employees will reflect that creativity to a certain extent and will tolerate less conservative dress, though good taste is still expected.

Sexy clothes in most kinds of jobs are never considered to be in good taste. Neither are strong colognes, flashy jewelry, dirty or messy hair, or extreme hairdos and makeup. Clothes and shoes do not have to be expensive, but they should fit well and be clean.

Many experts still suggest following the adage "Dress for the position to which you aspire." Also important is consistency in dress. People will not be viewed as stable employees who know where they are going if they dress professionally one day and inappropriately the next.

The moment people look at us they begin to form an opinion about our education and economic level, our social position, and our success level. Casual, dress-down Fridays does not mean sloppy weekend wear.

CASE STUDIES IN THE NEWS

To everyone's surprise, I was picked over two senior managers to head the marketing department of my company. After I arrived at headquarters, I went to lunch with the CEO and two senior vice presidents. During the meal, the CEO told me the reason I had been promoted was that I had made a remark (almost 3 years ago) about the dangers of going casual. I believed that ". . . casual might gradually turn into sloppy unless we were careful."

The CEO had decided to conduct a study within the company. Headquarters reps visiting the field sites were asked for several months to report on how the people were dressing. My prediction had come true. The top managers saw this as a crisis because some of those people dealt with clients on a regular basis and were fired for reflecting poorly on our company. Management's solution was to bring in the one who had predicted that casual dress could create an image problem and let him work on the problem. That would be me, the new Director of Marketing.

John T. Malloy, *Dress for Success, 1998*

Why do you think people might get sloppy in their appearance, even though it affects their jobs?

"Courtesy, up 25%. Effort, up 25%. Quality, up 25%. Customer retention, up 250%."

FastChat

1. Does your place of business have a dress code? How do you feel about that?

2. Why do you think appearance is so important to success?

3. Have you ever had a bad first impression of someone? What was it about the person that created the bad impression? Did the impression last?

Practically everyone shares meals with others at some time as a part of the workday. Whether you are eating in the company cafeteria with coworkers or attending a business luncheon outside the company, you can make these times more relaxed and enjoyable by understanding certain basic rules of etiquette. In general, the following rules should be used in any setting.

Correct table manners make business luncheons more relaxed and enjoyable.

If you think good table manners are outmoded or, worse yet, overrated, think again. Laurin Caldridge, a talk show host, frequently hears stories about job candidates disqualified from competition when the top brass witnesses their uncouth behavior over dinner. Among all the new etiquette classes being offered, Silicone Valley's " Workshoppe" is billed as "Etiquette Training for Geeks." A retired marketing director and fashion model take a small group to dinner in one of the Valley's premier restaurants and offer them the ". . . opportunity to hone your job skills and enhance your career." Between courses, blunders get pointed out to the rest of the group for lively discussion. Participants are coached on every part of the meal, from the bread to the bathroom break. They have standing reservations at the restaurant once a week for the next year and have contracts with the likes of Netscape, AT&T, Motorola, and Loyola University.

Basic Table Manners

1. To keep people from bumping into each other, sit down from the left side of the chair when possible.

2. In general, wait until all people at the table are seated and have their food before beginning to eat. The company cafeteria, where people are on different schedules, may be an exception. Another exception may be when you are served a dish that will lose its flavor if cooled or warmed.

3. Place your napkin in your lap as soon as you are seated, and sit with both feet on the floor.

4. Avoid playing with your silverware or food.

5. Keep the hand not holding the fork in your lap (unless you need to use a knife). Do not place your elbows on the table while eating or lean on the table to eat. Remember to sit straight but not rigid throughout the meal.

6. Never reach for food or condiments across the table. Ask the person nearest the item you want to "please pass the . . . ." Bowls are passed to the right.

7. Do not smack or slurp while eating or talk with your mouth full.

8. Do not groom at the table. If women need to add lipstick or men or women need to smooth wind-blown hair, they should go elsewhere to do so.

9. When finished eating, lay your silver in your plate placed in a 5:20 position and your napkin on the table to the left of the plate. Do not shove your plate away from you or comment about how full you are.

10. Cocktails before or after dinner may be appropriate in a social setting, but alcohol is best avoided at work-related meals.

---

1. How many of these rules of the road have you missed on occasion? Which one was news to you?

2. How effective do you think the "Workshoppe" approach is for teaching etiquette? Would you enjoy a class of that sort?

FastChat

15.5 How Should You Handle Introductions?

Learning
Objective 5

Learn to introduce and meet people with confidence.

We are constantly meeting new people in our jobs and at times must introduce people to each other. The latter situation is more likely to create anxiety. You can reduce your anxiety, be more comfortable, and create a gracious atmosphere if you remember the overriding goals of putting people at ease and showing them proper respect.

Introductions should put people at ease and show them respect.

General Rules for Making Introductions

1. Introduce younger people or people lower on the organizational hierarchy to older people (those appearing to be 15 years older) and superiors. Address the older person or person higher on the hierarchy first: "Dr. Rutherford, I would like you to meet Rhonda Elliott, the new associate in our office."

2. Introduce a man to a woman if they are about the same age and on the same level of the hierarchy: "Ms. Salinas, I would like you to meet Mr. Freedman."

3. If you forget the name of someone you are introducing, as we all do occasionally, be honest and ask people to introduce themselves to each other, as follows, "My mind is not giving me names today. Will you please introduce yourselves."

If you are the one being introduced and your name is mispronounced, you may give the correct pronunciation when acknowledging the person to whom you are introduced. For example, if your name is Dalton and you are introduced as Dawson, you may correct this mistake simply by saying, "Sam Dalton. I'm glad to meet you." If no one introduces you in a group, you may handle the situation graciously by smiling and saying something like, "I'm Danielle Muster from accounting."

The handshake, a common part of introductions, should be firm but not hand-breaking. It may include one or two gentle pumps and should be accompanied with a smile, eye contact, slight forward lean, and a short phrase such as, "I am happy to meet you." When you shake hands with someone, make it brief by releasing the hand after the pumps.

GLOBAL CONNECTION

The corporate handshake versus the hug-and-kiss greetings have become a bit blurred these days. It may have to do with a more relaxed society or more likely how we are more of a global culture than ever before. Some of the controversy stems from having more women in the workplace, some of it's just a trendy European thing (a kiss on both cheeks), and some may be attributed to the New Agey hug-as-therapy thing—you know, the importance of touch in a computer culture. The problems arise when both parties meeting are not in agreement about which way it should be. With sexual harassment cases as prevalent as they are, coworkers can not afford to take liberties. When in doubt, go for the handshake.

—Glynis Costin, *Talk of Los Angeles,* May 1997

Have you ever been in a situation where greeting was awkward, as you tried to decide between a hug and a handshake? Do you think that, in business situations, most people are more comfortable with a handshake? Why?

Although in some social situations people routinely kiss or hug when meeting each other, such behavior is totally out of place in a United States business setting. You should not put an arm around coworkers of either sex, place a hand on their shoulder, or touch them in any way. However, if you are involved in international business circles, following the norm for that culture is appropriate.

1. What types of greetings have you observed that are different than what you use?

2. What situations do you think would permit the hug and kiss as a greeting?

FastChat

What Is Male-Female Etiquette at Work?

Use good judgment in face-to-face interactions, including male/female situations and office romance.

quick wit

. . . .

"In this world, there are two kinds of class— first class and no class. You must develop the first or you will have to live with the second."

. . . .

William Thourlby

Once you know someone's preferences in business protocol, you should comply with them.

The women's movement and the influx of women into the work world have created confusion and uncertainty for many men and women. If you are male, you may wonder whether you should open doors for women at work, help them take off their coats, or automatically pay for business lunches shared with a woman. If you are female, you may wonder whether you are insulting men if you open the door yourself or acting improperly if you let men help you remove your coat. Marilyn Pincus suggests the "offer and refusal technique" and the "understanding strategy" as simple ways of eliminating this dilemma. The **"understanding strategy"** suggests that once you know someone's preferences regarding business protocol, you should comply with them. The **"offer and refusal technique"** suggests that men continue to offer the kind of manners they were taught and that women accept those gestures they consider proper in the setting and graciously decline those they would rather not have.

Helpful Guidelines for Dealing with Doors and Coats

. . . .

When approaching a door, the woman can slow her pace and let the man open it. If she reaches the door first, she can open it for him. If a man reaches around her to open it, she can, if she prefers, say, "Thank you. I have it."

If it appears likely that an individual of either sex is going to have difficulty with a door—because they are carrying packages, are on crutches, or for similar reasons—try to get to the door and open it before it becomes a problem, regardless of whether you're male or female. However, even in these situations, be prepared to back off if the person objects.

If a man tries to help a woman when she is removing her coat, she can either accept his assistance or simply say, "Thank you. I can handle it myself."

In business lunches, the person who is hosting the meeting should simply reach for the bill without comment. Servers still sometimes give the bill to males without asking. This mistake can be avoided by discreetly indicating on arrival to whom the check is to be presented.

Business travel involving men and women is becoming more common but still poses some potentially awkward situations. Meetings should probably be held in public rooms or only in suites with a sitting room.

Holding a door for a colleague is polite. Today's woman may also choose to open doors for men.

An additional guideline that should not have to be pointed out pertains to the use of words like "Honey," "Dear," or "Sweetheart." Although these terms have been more commonly used by men when talking to women, their use is inappropriate and demeaning to either sex in the workplace.

Judith Martin, known as Miss Manners, suggests that comments such as "Gee, you look adorable," to a woman about to make a business presentation are inappropriate because they imply the woman is a social creature and not a serious worker. She advises that men err on the side of caution lest such comments be interpreted as sexual harassment.

Terms such as "Honey," "Dear," and "Sweetheart" should never be used at work.

Be wary of developing personal or social relationships off the job with your supervisors or subordinates. Such relationships can prove to be harmful to you, your subordinate, or your supervisor for two reasons. First, they may convey inappropriate appearances. Also, problems may develop because of the potential resentment that other employees may feel.

WHAT ABOUT OFFICE ROMANCES?

Currently more than 50 percent of the work force is female. Women are continuing to enter career fields that have traditionally been held by males and vice versa. A growing proportion of our population is single and feels that the workplace is a good and safe place to meet potential dates. Romances, then, are inevitable. Also inevitable is that others will learn of the relationship. Any employee contemplating an office romance should consider the potential for trouble.

A romantic relationship at work has pitfalls.

The situation of a boss and subordinate dating is a particularly difficult one. If you are the boss and are initiating the moves, be cautious. Your subordinate may not be interested in becoming romantically involved and may complain of sexual harassment. Even if your subordinate is willing, the relationship could cause havoc in the organization. Even if the boss acts appropriately, subordinates may not take the same view of the situation. Morale may suffer and productivity decline. Dating among coworkers takes on some of the same risks.

If the relationship breaks up, other problems may develop. For the boss, the danger exists that the other party may now allege sexual harassment as a motive for revenge. For the subordinate, the danger is that the boss may retaliate through poor performance appraisals and less favorable job assignments. Additionally, former lovers may not be able to function productively when they see each other daily. Communication and cooperation may be hampered, causing office productivity to decline.

Some companies have policies stating that no fraternization may take place among employees. Others have rules stating that relatives or spouses cannot work under the same supervisor or supervise one another. Be aware of the policies where you work before considering a relationship.

If you are a supervisor and one of your subordinates is involved in an office romance, your best approach is to ignore it unless the romance causes problems or decreases productivity of the parties involved. If the relationship is causing performance difficulties, the participants should be counseled. The counseling should be done in an objective fashion, with an emphasis on productivity. Moral judgments concerning the relationship should not enter into the conversation. Most companies take a dim view of supervisor-subordinate relationships because of the conflict of interest. If you are a supervisor, you should refrain from such associations.

*Fast*Chat

1. Which do you think is easier to use-the "understanding strategy" or the "offer and refusal technique"? Why?

2. If your boss and a co-worker were involved, how would you feel? How would you handle it?

What Is Cross-Cultural Etiquette?

Quick Tip . . . .

"It is the mark of a cultured man that he is aware of the fact that equality is an ethical and not a biological principle."

—Ashley Montagu

Learning
Objective   7

Understand the importance of cross-cultural etiquette in the global community

With the growing numbers of international mergers, multi-national takeovers, and international trade reforms, business people are recognizing the need to learn how to work effectively both abroad and at home with foreigners. Short courses on cross-cultural work relationships and workshops on international business etiquette are springing up all over. Anne Fisher, business advice columnist for *Fortune* magazine, suggests that if you anticipate a foreign assignment, taking a vacation there for exposure would be a smart move. She says, "Doing your homework, on Asian customs and more, can help you avoid breaches of etiquette when you finally do get to work there." Most importantly she strongly suggests that wherever you go, become an expert in that country's language, markets, and political situation.

Some common stereotypes concern Japanese business practices. For example, many people have heard that American managers in Japanese firms have no real power, the Japanese punish initiative, the Japanese insist that management be by consensus or else, and the Japanese do not respect women employees. Americans experienced in working with the Japanese suggest that the stereotypes are not valid. Numerous authorities point out that experience with other cultures, even if only through travel, is helpful in working with foreign business people. Such experience is likely to give a person greater tolerance—even admiration—for ways unlike those at home.

Female engineers in particular have no trouble fitting in among the Chinese. Nattalia Lea, who runs a petroleum-industry consulting firm based in Canada with clients in Indonesia, says, "About half of all Chinese engineers are women, and many of the embassy commerce officials with whom we have to negotiate are both engineers and female. No one thinks twice about my being a woman."

Tolerance and acceptance is necessary when working with people of other cultures.

International business assignments have their pitfalls. Donald McBride, who has worked abroad for 32 years, warns to keep a sharp eye for cultural variances and learn to be tolerant of different standards of behavior. What is considered sexual harassment in the U.S., for instance, may not raise an eyebrow in other cultures. Also, pantsuits, no matter how dressy, are not acceptable business attire in Japan, especially not in serious negotiation settings. The many cultural sensitivities required in today's business arena make fertile ground for business etiquette and protocol schooling.

If you are called upon to work with people from another country, as you probably will be, certain guidelines may help you.

International Work Guidelines

1. Learn as much as you can about the nonverbal communication and customs of the other culture. Numerous organizations offer such classes, books and articles are available, and people familiar with the culture can be helpful. This aspect of communication is a ripe area for misunderstandings. For example, the Japanese almost always bow when exchanging their business cards. In Arab nations, a man will hold another man's hand a long time when they meet. Additionally, business transactions almost always take longer outside the United States. Knowing these cultural differences, you will not be caught off guard.

2. Learn some of the other language. Even a little knowledge will demonstrate that you are trying to meet people of other countries half way rather than insisting that everyone know your native language. Several language schools offer "crash courses" for the business traveler emphasizing frequently used terms and phrases that will get you through a day. By using a beginning like this, you are communicating that you do not necessarily expect others to know English. Also, it can help you get around when you're overseas. (Your business contact may speak English, but does the taxi driver?)

3. Talk to someone knowledgeable about the culture before offering gifts, inquiring about family members, or beginning business discussions. Norms for these behaviors vary from culture to culture, and the pace at which discussions flow from personal to business differs. The Japanese, for example, frequently give gifts, whereas western European business people generally do not.

4. Being courteous and sincere can help you over the rough spots.

As our world continues to shrink and international borders become more blurred, special attention must be given to our cultural IQ's. The self-quiz on page 450 will introduce you to multi-cultural terms dealing with just "hats." Test your cultural IQ.

GLOBAL CONNECTION

John Graham, who teaches marketing and international business at the University of California at Irvine, reports " . . . in interviews with Japanese executives we find that many of them would much rather work with a woman than a man." Many American men's conversational styles tend toward competitiveness, even aggressiveness, and can get in the way of a free-flowing exchange of information. By contrast, the negotiating styles of their female counterparts, emphasizing interpersonal warmth and willingness to listen and to compromise, are much less disconcerting.

—Carol Hymowitz, *Wall Street Journal,* December 1998

Which of the skills appreciated by the Japanese can be developed? Discuss how this might be accomplished.

1. How many different cultures do you encounter in a normal day? How do they influence your life?

2. If you were given a choice to take an overseas assignment, where would you choose and why?

3. What would you do to prepare for your international assignment?

FastChat

Hat Trick

1. The traditional clothing of an Arabic man includes a *thoub* (robe), as well as a head scarf and black braided cord called:

   A. A *bisht*, or *mishlah* B. A *ghutra* and *igaal* C. A *bourgha* and *abaya*

2. Wide-brimmed sombreros have been keeping the sun off Latin Americans for centuries. True or false: The classic sombrero is kept in place with a strap beneath the chin.

3. Popularized by King Edward VII of England, this felt hat has a high crown with a deep crease across the middle, similar to the fedora. It is a:

   A. Bowler B. Deerstalker C. Homburg

4. Originating in Scotland, the tam-o'-shanter is a larger version of the beret. True or false: Except for size, there is no difference between the tam-o'-shanter and the beret.

5. The Stetson was designed in 1865 as the quintessential cowboy hat of the American West. For years, Stetsons were manufactured in which city?

   A. Austin, Texas B. Denver C. Philadelphia

6. The Dutch *hoofdijzer* (head iron) and oorijzer (ear iron) styles added metal to headgear. True or false: These hats were designed to protect men in battle.

7. This flat cloth hat was ubiquitous in France between the 1920s and the 1950s, and is still worn by French soldiers. Which is it?

   A. Beret B. Fedora C. Toque

8. For much of this century, upper-class Englishmen wore bowler hats, called derbies in the U.S. True or false: This style is very similar to hats worn by women among the indigenous people of Peru.

9. Variations of the cowboy hat are found throughout the world. Can you match the following hats with their countries of origin?

   A. Bush hat 1. Australia
   B. Akubra hat 2. Canada
   C. Tilley hat 3. New Zealand

10. Closely associated with Spain, the mantilla is a lace veil or shawl worn over the head and shoulders. True or false: The mantilla is draped over a stiff, tiaralike frame called a *peineta*.

ANSWERS

1. B. The bisht, or mishlah, is a formal cloak; the bourgha and abaya are the robe and veil that some Arabic women wear.
2. True
3. C. Although popularized by an English king, it was named after its original manufacturer in Homburg, Germany.
4. False. The tam-o'-shanter usually has a pompom on its crown.
5. C
6. False. These were actually women's hats, with metal decorations under a linen cap.
7. A
8. True
9. A, 3; B, 1; C, 2
10. True

Human Relations

How Should You Treat the Public?

How employees treat customers and clients is a crucial factor in the success of a business. Poor service or bad treatment will lose a company customers. And it loses more than just the customer who was treated badly, because while a customer will seldom tell the company about the treatment, they do tell their friends and others. Effective customer relations, then, is an important part of an organization's marketing strategy.

If you come in contact with customers in person, by mail, or over the telephone, the most important guideline that you can remember is, "Do unto others as they would have you do unto them." The ways that employees should treat customers seem so obvious that mistreatment seems almost unthinkable, yet it occurs every day and drives customers away by the dozens. One rude employee can do untold damage to a business, whereas one helpful employee is worth thousands in marketing dollars.

The three situations shown on page 452, could have been improved if the employees had remembered these basic guidelines pertaining to customer relations. In reviewing these incidents, think how you would have felt if you had been the customer. If you are like most people, you would have been somewhat hurt or angered by the treatment. More than likely, you would have been reluctant to return.

Learning
Objective 8

Use socially appropriate behavior to develop effective customer relations.

Learning
Objective 9

Write correspondence and use the telephone and other communication technology in appropriate ways.

The best rule for customer relations is the new Golden Rule.

MANNERS IN CORRESPONDENCE AND ON THE TELEPHONE

As an employee of a company, you portray the image of that company each time you write someone or use the telephone for a business purpose. Effective human relations is just as important in correspondence and on the telephone as in person.

In writing, the tone of a message is important. Polite requests, such as "Please return both copies" sound much more pleasant than "Return both copies." Including a person's name on all correspondence rather than just a company or department name can help to make the receivers feel that they are dealing with real people, not just an impersonal organization.

Manners are as important in correspondence and on the phone as in person.

Examples of Customer Treatment

Poor Treatment	Correct Treatment
Incident 1. About five minutes before Arnold was to leave for the day to start a two-week vacation, a customer, Helen Williams, came in wanting to submit an application for credit. When Arnold was told that the customer was in the outer office, his loud response was, "Well, she had better hurry. I have things to do." When the supervisor said, "Shhhh," with a finger to her lips, Arnold replied, again loudly, "Oh, she didn't hear me."	*Incident 1.* Arnold should have either handled the application or have politely asked someone else to help her. No comments about his leaving should have been made in front of the customer.
Incident 2. Wanda has been taken off the telephone to free her for handling customers. However, when all of the other clerks are on the telephone or busy, the calls will roll over to her station. This chore displeases her so much that when she answers the phone, she is abrupt with her "Hello" and snaps out answers to the callers' questions.	*Incident 2.* Because callers do not know what a situation is in an office and have every right to expect the person answering to be ready to deal with their business, Wanda should treat each call with patience, respect, and consideration.
Incident 3. Ronald is busy waiting on a customer in the eyeglass shop when Angie walks in. He continues to help the customer with whom he was working, assuming that Angie can look around while she is waiting. After about five minutes of standing nearby and waiting for his attention without even getting a glance from the salesclerk, Angie leaves the shop.	*Incident 3.* Ronald should have acknowledged Angie as soon as she walked into the store. This he could have done with a friendly, "Hello. I'll be with you shortly. Would you like to look around in the meantime?"

Additionally, because everyone's time is at a premium, unnecessarily long messages are a form of waste and poor manners. To improve your writing, review the suggestions given in Chapter 9.

When you answer the phone, you represent the company. Therefore, your voice and manner should present a friendly and professional image. Right and wrong ways to handle telephone communications exist—ways that are tactful, courteous, and efficient, and ways that are abrupt and rude.

The suggestions on page 454 are from Southwestern Bell Telephone's *Telephone Manners*. They can help you present the best possible impression for your company and do an efficient job at the same time.

Good Customer Relations Guidelines

1. Never say anything *about* a customer that you would not say *to* the customer.
2. When serving a customer by phone or in person, give that person your full attention. Do not shuffle papers or try to do other work at the same time.
3. Every customer who walks into your place of business should be acknowledged immediately. Your manner should be pleasant and helpful. The customer should not be left unattended long.
4. Consider the role you play in your company's marketing strategy by dressing appropriately each day. Remember to exercise good hygiene by having clean clothes, hair, and teeth. Do not chew gum or eat in front of customers. Your demeanor should be professional. A ready smile, eye contact, correct posture, and smooth voice are helpful in client relations.
5. Remember to use "please," "thank you," "thank you for your interest in our company," and "please come again." Calling people by name is an easy way to make them feel important.
6. Never conduct personal telephone calls or carry on personal conversations in front of clients or customers.
7. If you must answer a phone while working with a customer who is with you, ask that person, "Will you excuse me please while I catch this call?" Remember to take care of the first customer first by asking the second whether he or she can hold or would like you to call back. Use the telephone guidelines presented in the next section.

You represent the company each time you answer the telephone at work. Your voice and attitude should present a friendly and professional image.

Tips on Telephone Manners

1. *Answer promptly*	Answer calls on the first ring, if possible, in a friendly, enthusiastic way.
2. *Answer correctly*	Speaking clearly and enthusiastically, say, "Good morning (or good afternoon)," and on an outside line, give your company name. On an inside line, use your first and last names in answering instead of the company name. Adding "May I help you?" is a courteous way of letting the caller know that you are immediately available and interested.
3. *If you are answering for someone else*	First identify the department, office, or area, and then identify yourself as a substitute for the expected person and add "May I help you?"
4. *Transfer calls only when necessary*	People may become irritated if their calls are switched from one person to another. Instead, put the caller on hold, get the information, and return to the line. If you cannot get the information, explain to the caller who can help, giving the name and number of that individual, then ask if you may transfer them to that number. Always ask first. Then indicate that you are transferring by saying, "I'll transfer your call now. One moment, please."
5. *When the caller asks for someone you do not know*	Use a courteous, gracious manner and a tactful reply, such as, "May I have that name again, please?" or "I'm sorry. I don't find that name on our list. Could you tell me in which department she works?"
6. *Calls on hold*	If you are going to be delayed in continuing a call, tell callers that you are going to put them on hold for a moment and then, before placing the instrument down, put it on hold.
7. *If you are delayed*	Do not leave callers on hold more than 30 seconds without returning to say that you have not forgotten them. If you must leave the telephone for more than a minute, offer to call back and state the approximate time when you will do so.
8. *If the requested party is busy*	Explain in a courteous manner that the person is unavailable and offer the caller the option of waiting on the line or being called back.
9. *If the party is out*	Project your company's image by stating that "Ms. McWright is out of the office until . . .." Ask callers whether someone else can help or would they like to leave their names and numbers.
10. *Taking messages*	Keep a message pad and pencil by your telephone. Request the information courteously, using a phrase such as, "May I have your name, please?" Correct spelling of names is important. Ask if you are unsure. Repeat the number to the caller to make sure that you have it right.
11. *Saying good-bye*	Continue your professional demeanor by thanking the party for calling and saying good-bye.

Another suggestion offered by Southwestern Bell is to cultivate a good telephone personality. Be alert, keep a smile in your voice, speak clearly and distinctly, and greet the caller pleasantly. Other ways to project a good telephone personality include using the caller's name, treating every call as important, being tactful, apologizing for errors or delays, taking time to be helpful, and saying "please," "thank you," and "you're welcome."

RULES FOR OTHER COMMUNICATION TECHNOLOGIES

We are drowning in a sea of communication. According to a recent study by Pitney Bowes, the average worker at a Fortune 1000 company sends and receives an astounding 178 messages during the course of a single day. Office workers are feeling overwhelmed by the flood of faxes, phone calls, e-mails, and other interruptions. Technology has made information readily available and communication easier across boundaries of time and space.

These reps are sent to "netiquette" school to learn the proper ways to handle e-mail and provided process improvement techniques. This cyber-world approach to improving communication and information overload is only the beginning of things to come.

In 1922, Emily Post called Americans to action with her first book on etiquette, stating "A knowledge of etiquette is essential to decent behavior." Nearly 80 years later, her great-granddaughter, Peggy Post, helped co-author

TECHNOLOGY CONNECTION

You come back from a week-long business trip and check your e-mail and—Oh my! There are hundreds of messages to answer. There's been an e-mail traffic jam while you were gone. You may need the help of the new electronic traffic cop to ease the congestion! A whole new job category has opened up to ease your pain: the Cyber Rep. All e-mail messages are routed through the Cyber Rep who is trained to winnow out the junk and redirect only the important stuff to the right parties.

—Sheree R. Curry, *Fortune*, May 1997

Have you ever found yourself overwhelmed by incoming information? How have you dealt with it?

the 75th anniversary edition of *Emily Post's Etiquette*. The impact of the current explosion of electronic communications is reflected in that fact that, in addition to traditional guidelines to good manners, this edition provides such useful tips as how to use wireless phones in business and social settings without incurring the wrath of family, friends and colleagues, and how to "behave" on the Internet and with other telecommunications forms.

As further evidence of the need for rules on the use of electronic devices, a survey done by Pacific Bell revealed that 60 percent of those surveyed said, " . . . they would rather visit the dentist than sit next to someone talking on a cell phone in a movie theater."

The few "netiquette" tips on page 457 may be helpful when you have questions about proper use of the Internet for business.

An area of major concern for companies is how e-mail documents are showing up in courtrooms offered as a legal documents. E-mail messaging may be a popular form of communication, but it is not a very private one and messages can be intercepted or in some way compromised. A good rule of thumb is, if you don't want your message to wind up in someone else's hands, don't send it by e-mail.

The increased use of many other communication technologies has brought a whole new set of etiquette problems, as shown in the chapter

TECHNOLOGY CONNECTION

With more than 74 million wireless subscribers today, and more than half of all Americans expected to have wireless phones by the year 2003, Peggy Post recently joined forces with Pacific Bell Wireless to increase awareness of the need for proper wireless etiquette. Post says wireless phones can provide a level of convenience and safety unmatched by any other form of communication. "With options such as Caller ID, Voice Mail, and vibrating batteries, it's easy to use a wireless phone and still be considerate of those around you. You can enjoy the benefits of wireless without being rude."

—Pacific Bell Network News Center, Pleasonton, CA, May 1999

Do you have a wireless phone? Were you aware that how and where you use it can be important?

Human Relations

opening anecdotes. Employees act inappropriately when they send personal messages over the company fax (no love notes or carry out orders, please!), leave one caller hanging to talk with the second one, spend excessive time on personal telephone calls, or violate confidentiality of information they receive through computer usage. The guidelines offered on page 458 can help you use this multitude of communication forms in ways that are less likely to cause problems-for you as well as for others.

quick wit

"No man who is in a hurry is quite civilized."

Will Durant

CASE STUDIES IN THE NEWS

In 1997 auto maker Daimler-Benz demonstrated a prototype car with Internet access, complete with a computer screen in the center of the dashboard. Companies are creating these devices because people want them, and more will be coming on the market. They can be very distracting. As the use of electronics devices in our automobiles increases, so does the need for caution. These new technologies have to be used responsibly.

—Steven Levingston, *Readers Digest,* November 1998

For what reasons can you imagine that someone in a car would need Internet access? Remembering how dangerous even cell phone use is while driving, what safety guidelines would you recommend for Internet use in cars?

Etiquette for Telecommunication Methods

1. **Fax etiquette.** Be careful, be considerate, and be brief. Fax machines, while convenient, can be the cause of endless irritation. Know your fax recipient. To prevent problems, call ahead to check for any ground rules and to notify your recipient that a fax is on its way. Sending unwanted or long correspondence can tie up the machine unnecessarily. Be certain you have the correct fax number. Don't walk away from the fax machine—wait (or, at very least, check back often), especially if you are using redial or multiple recipient features. (If you entered someone's home number, the machine won't hear the voice that answers, it will just keep calling back—which is a major annoyance.)

2. **Car phone etiquette.** Because the owner of a car phone pays for every call, that person may choose to limit the people to whom the number is given. Of great concern is the danger involved with using cell phones while driving. A 1998 study done by a group of researchers at the University of Toronto revealed that drivers talking on a cell phone were four times as likely to have an accident as those not on the phone. The AAA has stated unquestionably that cell phone use in automobiles contributes to crashes.

3. **Call waiting etiquette.** The call waiting feature on telephones signals us while we are on the line that another call is coming in. Except in emergencies, the first caller should receive our complete attention. Many etiquette writers consider call waiting to be a rude interruption and suggest that the accounting method of first in, first out be used. That is, do not ask the person with whom you are speaking to wait while you handle a second caller. Instead, once you have determined that no emergency exists, politely ask the second caller to call back or offer to return the call yourself, stating when you will be free.

4. **Answering machine etiquette.** Messages on answering machines should be clear and precise. Jokes and blaring music are distasteful in any setting and totally inappropriate on office telephones.

5. **Voice mail etiquette.** Some people feel this may be the most infuriating of the electronic devices because callers receive instructions from a computer. However, it is generally a very reliable way to leave and receive messages. The best advice on using voice mail is to leave a straightforward message about your reason for calling and the information you desire.

6. **Pager etiquette.** Remember to treat beepers in public like babies: when they make a noise, remove them immediately to another room. Noisy users of beepers can be politely asked to be quiet. Most theaters now require that pagers be turned off before performances. If it is vital that you stay in touch, get a silent, vibrating pager.

FastChat

1. What are some other forms of technology that you think will further advance our means of communicating?

2. How do you handle the overload of messaging occurring in your life?

3. What suggestions can you make that might be helpful to others?

Human Relations

How Should You Treat Associates?

15.9

Having "a friend in the business" can be helpful when you face a problem or need advice. **Networking** is a process whereby you can get moral support, career guidance, and important information in areas outside your expertise by developing contacts with people in your place of employment and in professional organizations. Networks can be used by members to exchange information, ideas, and occasional favors.

To be effective, you must use your networks appropriately. Members of a network will come to resent anyone who abuses the process, for example, by trying to solicit free advice from professionals such as doctors, lawyers, and accountants. You must also assist others in the network in turn. Needless to say, confidentiality is important, as it is in any relationship.

Networking contacts should not be abused.

A **mentor** is an experienced person who will give you objective career advice. Such a person can give you pointers, offer advice concerning sensitive situations, and help you avoid mistakes. A mentor can be someone inside or outside your organization but in your profession. Your choice of a mentor should be someone you respect. Therefore you should act in such a way that your mentor will admire both the way you behave and the way you handle your job. Do not abuse your mentor's time or position.

Respect your mentor's time and position.

Office politics are impossible to avoid but can be extremely sensitive. Discretion and courtesy should be your guidelines in participating in office politics. Participating in or even listening to gossip is not only ill-mannered, but it can also kill your career. When confronted with gossip, avoid the discussion by simply saying, "Oh, I never pay attention to things like that."

Should conflict develop between you and a coworker, kindness and graciousness may restore your relationship. If you did something that offended the other person, you need to apologize. If you do not know why the person is upset, ask in a concerned manner. Refrain from making critical comments. Your goal is a win-win resolution of the conflict.

Etiquette can help coworkers resolve conflicts.

---

1. What kinds of networking opportunities are available to you?

2. How can good manners help prevent conflict as well as resolve it?

FastChat

Learning Objective 11

Differentiate among passive, aggressive, and assertive behaviors.

How well you put etiquette into practice depends on your usual behavior. Three basic behaviors can be found in the workplace—passive, aggressive, and assertive. Understanding the different behaviors can assist you in becoming more effective on the job. Edward Charlesworth and Ronald Nathan, in *Stress Management*, define these behaviors.

PASSIVE BEHAVIOR

Individuals who consistently engage in **passive behavior** value themselves below others, do not appear self-confident when they speak, want to be liked and try to please others, and avoid unpleasant situations and confrontation. Their passivity shows, in part, through their nonverbal communication. Passive people may look down or to the side in order to avoid eye contact. They will also mumble and hesitate when speaking. Slumped shoulders and poor posture may round out this person's passive demeanor.

Failure to communicate wants and needs is also part of passive behavior. Others may become angry, especially when they sincerely want to know the passive person's desires or preferences. A common example is the group questioning passive individuals about their choice of restaurants. Frequently, even after repeated questioning, the only response from the passive person is, "I don't care. You decide."

Others often become irritated at passive individuals' manner and begin to view them as "pushovers," "nerds," or "wimps." This loss of respect may lead some people to attempt to take advantage of passive individuals by burdening them with excessive work or responsibilities. Passive individuals will say nothing, but inside them anger is building and eventually that anger must be confronted.

AGGRESSIVE BEHAVIOR

People who consistently engage in **aggressive behavior** value themselves above others and say what they feel or think at the expense of others in an attempt to get anger off their chests. They may attempt to dominate or humiliate, use threats and accusations, or try to show up others. They also frequently choose for others and speak with an air of superiority and in a voice that is demanding or rude. Their aggressive behavior includes nonverbal communication intended to intimidate or put down other people. It consists of glaring at others with an angry facial expression or using a voice that is sharp and curt, demanding, and rude. Aggressive individuals' stance makes them appear to be ready to fight, and their fists may be clenched.

Others, of course, are offended by this type of behavior. They may feel angry, defensive, or humiliated and may possibly want to strike back at the aggressor. Often aggressors get what they want but, by offending others, have trouble working with coworkers later.

Both of these behaviors—passive and aggressive—can damage your career. For instance, suppose that you are working on an important project for your supervisor and discover that your supervisor has made a huge mistake that will cost the company thousands of dollars unless corrected. If you are a passive person, you will not want to tell your supervisor about the mistake. You will be afraid of causing offense. What do you think will happen later, when your supervisor learns that you did not report the error? Is this the kind of person supervisors like to have on their teams?

If you are aggressive, you will not fare much better. You will tell your supervisor but will probably say something like, "Well, you really blew it this time." Such behavior will immediately make your supervisor defensive and unwilling to listen, even though you are right. The supervisor may look for something for which to reprimand you as a form of revenge.

ASSERTIVE BEHAVIOR

The situations above are better handled with **assertive behavior**. Assertive individuals are comfortable in using correct etiquette, feel that they are equal to others, and make their own choices. They also use "I" phrases and other effective communication techniques, appear calm and confident, and want to communicate and be respected. They have self-esteem and are respected by others.

Assertiveness requires that you speak clearly, calmly, and firmly. Maintain eye contact without staring. Have a relaxed facial expression with no evidence of tension in your body. Keep your shoulders back and your posture erect. This type of nonverbal communication is not intimidating but shows that you have confidence.

Assertive individuals are respected and valued by others and, therefore, often obtain what they want. Others do not feel offended or violated, and everyone's rights are respected. Even in situations that are not ideal or potentially annoying, the assertive person remains calm, pleasant, and in control. For example, if the assertive person needed to repeat a message because another person did not pay attention the first time, he or she would repeat the message with firmness and respect.

Learning to behave assertively takes patience and practice. The following steps can help you build assertive behavior skills.

quick wit

"The truth of the matter is that you always know the right thing to do. The hard part is doing it."

General H. Norman Schwarzkopf

Assertive individuals are comfortable in using correct etiquette and make their own choices.

Developing Assertive Behavior

1. Monitor your own behavior. Pay particular attention to your own responses—eye contact, gestures, body posture, facial expression, and voice tone and volume. Decide which behavior you usually exhibit.

2. Imagine situations at work and at home. What would have been the outcome if you had behaved differently? Practice how you would handle the situations assertively by saying the appropriate words aloud when you are alone. Practice nonverbal communication in front of a mirror.

3. Begin communication with "I" phrases. Opening a conversation with "I think" or "I feel" is particularly effective. Practice this phrasing and other communication techniques presented in Chapter 9.

4. Enlist a friend to help you practice assertive behavior. Role playing assertiveness with someone whose advice you trust and respect can be effective.

5. After you have practiced and are confident, try the new behavior on those around you.

6. If you need more help, consider enrolling in a short assertiveness training course. Your local community college and other groups probably offer one. Many people have benefited from such instruction.

7. If your lack of assertiveness results from negative feelings about yourself, professional counseling may help. Your school counselor is a good starting point in seeking assistance.

Remember that it will take some time for everyone (including you) to become comfortable with your behavior. If you are a passive person, those around you may be uncomfortable when you become assertive. Also, you may go overboard and become aggressive while trying to become comfortable with your new behavior. However, continued practice will help you become skilled and confident in dealing with other people.

*Fast*Chat

1. Among your acquaintances, can you think of individuals who fall into each of these categories? How could you identify their behavior types?

2. Which of the tips in this section do you think will be most helpful to you?

Summary

Etiquette, acting appropriately in social and business situations, is becoming ever more important in business. Etiquette involves following rules, using courtesy, and showing good taste. What is appropriate will depend to a certain extent on where, when, and with whom the interaction occurs.

Appearance is a form of etiquette because it communicates respect for the situation and the people involved. Dress should be appropriate for the situation. Following basic rules of table etiquette can make these times more relaxed and enjoyable and can also potentially improve your business opportunities. Etiquette is used when making introductions to put people at ease and to show them proper respect.

Male/female interactions at work are changing because of the influx of women into the work world. Following the "offer and refusal technique" and the "understanding strategy" can simplify uncertain business protocol that involves men and women. Comments that could be construed as sexual harassment are inappropriate. Personal and social relationships with supervisors and subordinates off the job are best avoided to eliminate potential harm to both parties. Office romances may be inevitable, but anyone contemplating one should be aware of the pitfalls.

Today's business person must be able to work effectively with people of other cultures. Through experience and travel, we can develop greater tolerance and acceptance of others. Studying the nonverbal communication of the other culture, knowing a little of the language, being sensitive to the norms of that culture, and using courtesy with sincerity will help.

Effective customer relations can make or break a business. The best rule to follow in working with clients in person, through correspondence, or on the telephone is the Golden Rule. Remember that to customers you are the company.

Key Terms

etiquette
protocol
understanding strategy
offer and refusal technique
networking
mentor
passive behavior
aggressive behavior
assertive behavior

The increased use of communication technology has brought with it a whole new set of etiquette problems. Exercise common sense in using faxes, cell phones, call waiting, voice mail, and pagers.

Networking and mentoring can help your professional development if you use your network appropriately and treat your mentor with respect. Discretion and courtesy should be your guidelines in participating in office politics.

Three types of behavior found in the workplace are passive, aggressive, and assertive. Assertive behavior will bring you the best results. You should, therefore, try to develop your assertive behavior skills by following the steps recommended in this chapter.

Review Questions

1. Define etiquette and protocol. What is the relationship between the two?
2. Why do many business experts believe that knowledge of etiquette is more important than ever today?
3. List three basic guidelines for table manners.
4. Name two points to be remembered in making introductions.
5. List at least one etiquette guideline for correct use of each communication technology discussed in this chapter.
6. How can you use networking, mentoring, and office politics to help, not hurt, your career?
7. Differentiate among aggressive, passive, and assertive behaviors and explain which is appropriate.

Discussion Questions

1. Think of times when someone showed poor manners. What part of etiquette was violated? How did the violation make you feel? How did you respond to it?
2. Name some examples of protocol in your daily life or work.
3. Assume that a friend has developed a crush on a coworker. What advice would you give your friend?
4. Name some instances of communication technology abuse of which you are aware through experience, the media, or friends. What are the correct behaviors?
5. Are you a member of a professional network? If so, describe it. How do you use it? How do you contribute to it?

Chapter Project

As a group, discuss the resources available to you for inviting a guest speaker in for a discussion of that individual's experiences, expertise, or general information on topics from the chapter. This person may be a representative from the local phone company to speak on telecommunications etiquette. Perhaps a classmate knows someone who may be involved in international travel who could share some valuable work experiences with the class. Invite a member of an ethnic group in to share the customs of his or her culture. In pairs, properly introduce one another to the speaker. Prepare written thank you notes to the speaker indicating your grasp of sound business etiquette.

Applications

In small groups analyze the following situations:

Hot times In Hamburger Heaven

"Yeah, what do you want?" Gary said gruffly to the lady on the other side of the counter at Hamburger Heaven.

"Well, I'm not sure yet," Mrs. Chang said, as she looked at her two small children, who were trying to make up their minds.

Gary rolled his eyes and frowned. He stamped around in a circle and said, "You ready now?" When Mrs. Chang shook her head, Gary slammed down the tray and went to check the French fries.

"What's wrong with him?" Mrs. Chang's son asked. "Did I do something wrong?"

"No, son," she said. "I'll tell you one thing. I don't like his attitude. You can bet our next meal will be down the street at Bea's Burgers. He has just spoiled my appetite."

Reading, listening, reasoning, participating as a member of a group, contributing to the group effort, and understanding complex interrelationships.

1. Was Gary displaying passive, aggressive, or assertive behavior?
2. How should Gary have behaved?
3. What has Gary cost his company?

Telephone Tales

Tom had just had a wonderful date, and he was busy telling his buddy, Carlos, about it on the phone. Things were slow in the plant, and Tom was bored with his bookkeeping job. As Tom was telling the story, the other line blinked. He picked up the phone and mumbled quickly, "Ashton Enterprises. May I help you?"

The caller on the other end of the line did not speak at first, and Tom said, "Hello, hello?" in an irritated fashion.

Mr. Zanigo said, "Oh, is this Ashton Enterprises?"

"Yeah, what do you need?" Tom said impatiently.

"Is Ms. Tate in?" asked Mr. Zanigo.

"Yeah, hang on," Tom replied. Tom then switched back to his friend. "Sorry about that, Carlos. I had to catch the other line. Let me tell you what a great dancer she is . . . ." When he went back to the caller's line ten minutes later, it was dead.

About two hours later Claudia Ashton, the president of Ashton Enterprises, called Tom into her office. "Tom," she said, "I'm going to have to let you go. My best client was trying to reach Ms. Tate and finally gave up in frustration. If we lose that contract, our business is ruined."

1. What telephone etiquette rules did Tom violate?
2. How should Tom have handled the telephone call?
3. What might Tom's behavior have cost the business?

Additional Readings and Resources

Baldrige, Letitia. *Letitia Baldrige's Complete Guide to Executive Manners*. New York: Rawson Associates, 1985.

http://www.getcustoms.com—visit Getting Through Customs. Deals with customs of over 60 countries.

http://www.protocolconsultants.com—provides protocol tips based on questions from reader audience.

Levingston, Steven. "Danger Beneath the Dash." *Reader's Digest*, November 1998

Martin, Judith (Miss Manners). *Guide for the Turn-of-the-Millennium*. New York: Pharos Books, 1989.

Post, Emily. *Emily Post's Etiquette—75th Anniversary Edition*. Harper Collins, New York, 1999.

Schonberg, Alan R. *169 Ways to Score Points With Your Boss*. New York: Contemporary Books, 1999.

Ethics at Work:
Your Attitude and Responsibilities

focus

"So far, about morals. I know only that what is moral is what you feel good after and what is immoral is what you feel bad after."

Ernest Hemingway

Is feeling good or bad "after" enough of a guide to ethical behavior in today's global environment? How do your feelings of what is good or bad differ from those of others?

In This Chapter

What Is Ethics?

We are faced with decisions every day that require drawing on our sense of what is right or wrong, good or bad, ethical or unethical. We make the ultimate choice from a set of values instilled early in life. The process of choosing can be complicated by many factors, so that we often find ourselves facing difficult situations with questions not easily answered.

Ethics, as defined by the *American Heritage Dictionary, is* "the study of the general nature of morals and of the specific moral choices to be made by individuals in their relationships with others; a set of moral principles or values." More simply stated, ethics is the study of what is good and right for people. Ethics involves not only telling right from wrong and good from evil, but doing what is right, good, and proper. To understand ethics, we must explore a few related terms.

One term frequently linked with ethics is **integrity**, which is the strict adherence to a code of behavior. The lack of integrity has become a critical issue in individual and business behaviors today, causing some of the very incidents discussed later in this chapter. Another term closely related to ethics is values. **Values** are principles, standards, or qualities you consider worthwhile or desirable. More specifically, your values are your beliefs about what is right or wrong, good or bad, and acceptable or unacceptable. These beliefs develop during your formative years and are heavily influenced by your family, friends, religion, schools, and the media. Values determine how we will behave in certain situations.

Values vary widely in our diverse society. In 1992 the Josephson Institute set out to determine whether a diverse group could agree on common core values. The 30 leaders they brought together from all walks of life agreed upon six values that make up the ground rules for decision making. These "Six Pillars of Character" are trustworthiness, respect, responsibility, fairness, caring, and citizenship. Along with these common values, each of us will have other things we value, as well, such as family, specific beliefs, honor, duty, etc. We demonstrate our values by how we interact with others and make decisions in our daily lives. Ethics brings our value systems into play.

Ethics is not only an individual issue but an organizational issue. We cannot avoid ethical issues in business any more than we can in other areas of our lives. Corporate culture influences decisions that affect not only not only the organization's employees, but its customers and the public in general.

Learning
O b j e c t i v e   1

Understand the differences among ethics, values, integrity, and social responsibility.

Integrity is strict adherence to a code of behavior.

quick wit

"Good people do not need laws to tell them to act responsibly, while bad people will find a way around the laws."

Plato

Human Relations

In the 1980s, a *Wall Street Journal* article called business ethics "an oxymoron, a contradiction in terms like jumbo shrimp." Many felt it was the bottom line that counted and nothing more. As long as businesses obeyed the law, their obligations were fulfilled.

Ford Motor Company learned the hard way that just obeying the law is not always good for business. In 1978 three young women were burned to death when the Pinto they were driving was struck from the rear and the gas tank burst into flames. Ford was indicted and tried on charges of criminal homicide. Company attorneys argued that the Pinto was in compliance with the law, even though safety changes needed would have cost only $11 per car. Ford had done a cost-benefit analysis comparing the benefits to society of Ford paying for burn deaths and injuries versus the costs of making the gas tank safer. The study determined that it would be less costly to pay for deaths and injuries. The jury ultimately returned a verdict of not guilty. Ford lost in the court of public opinion, however, and paid millions of dollars in civil suits.

Balancing the bottom line and ethics is now seen as a smart business move. This becomes even more important as companies try to gain a competitive advantage by empowering employees and pushing crucial decisions

CASE STUDIES IN THE NEWS

A Catholic nurse in Erie, Pennsylvania, was fired for refusing to hand out birth control pills or condoms to single men and women.

Many times our values differ from those of our employer.

1. *Do you believe the nurse had the right to refuse to perform legal activities that were against her values system? Why or why not?*

2. *Do you think it is ethical for an employer to assign duties that would conflict with an employee's beliefs? Why or why not?*

3. *Should the nurse have been fired? Why or why not?*

4. *Would you perform activities that are legal if ordered on your job even though they conflicted with your values? Why or why not? What other options might you have?*

down to individuals at lower levels of the organization. Companies must be able to trust that their employees are making ethical decisions. Two hundred thirty-three year old Barings PLC, England's oldest investment firm, was single-handedly toppled by a 28-year-old trader who made unethical decisions and took unjustifiable risks with other people's money.

Both individuals and corporations must deal with ethical issues on a day-to-day basis. James Stoner and R. Edward Freeman in their book *Management* describe four levels of ethical issues, which are mutually exclusive:

Levels of Ethical Issues

1. Societal issues — At the societal level questions deal with the basic institutions in a society. For example, are Chinese Communists ethically correct, when they imprison or kill those who disagree with them? Is it ethical for the US government to confer "Most Favored Nation" trade status on China, when human rights violations are common?

2. Stakeholders' issues — Stakeholders' issues pertain to appropriate treatment of and relationships with employees, suppliers, customers, shareholders, bondholders, and others. They deal with business policy, such as how much obligation a company has to notify its customers about the potential dangers of its products.

3. Internal policy issues — Questions of internal policy pertain to the relationship between a company and its employees at all levels. Examples are policies dealing with employee rights, due process, free speech, employee participation, and others.

4. Personal issues — Personal issues are the day-to-day questions that occur in every organization. They revolve around two basic questions: Do we have the right to treat other people as means to our ends? Can we avoid doing so?

At work, ethics concerns the ground rules on all four of these levels. Because most of our personal ground rules are already in place, making ethical decisions requires us to be critical of our own ground rules and to improve them. Occasionally situations in business result in applying a set of ground rules different from personal life. For instance, an organization may set ground rules that prohibit accepting gifts from vendors while you may feel that accepting the gift would not violate your personal standards.

What other common situations involve making the distinction between ethical and unethical actions? The following box describes some possible unethical behavior in personal and business settings.

Some Unethical Behaviors

Personal	Business
• Cheating on exams/tests	• Copying computer software
• Accepting credit for favors not performed	• Accepting gifts from subordinates
• Cheating on income tax reports	• Falsifying time/expense reports
• Betraying personal confidences	• Doing personal business on company time
• Keeping unauthorized materials/monies	• Taking company materials/supplies for personal use
• Violating minor traffic rules	• Polluting the environment with toxic waste

Unethical behaviors may lead people to financial gain or other benefits, but the consequences may range from a guilty conscience to a fine or prison term. Corporations may gain sizable market shares and higher profits but, if exposed, may be faced with large fines and serious penalties as well as decreased sales and a loss of confidence from customers and the general public. Ethics is a concern for both individuals and organizations.

Does It CLICK?

When faced with a tough decision, see if it CLICKS.

Consequences: What are the consequences if I do this? Who will benefit? Who will suffer?

Legal: Is it legal?

Image: Would I like to see this on the front page of the newspaper? Would I like to tell this to my kids?

Culture: Does this decision support or damage our organization's culture or values?

Knot: Does it cause a knot in my stomach?

Developed for Florida Power Corporation by Lee Gardenswartz, Ph.D., and Anita Rowe, Ph.D., of Gardenswartz & Rowe, Los Angeles, CA and Patricia Digh of Realwork, Washington, DC and reprinted by permission from Society for Human Resource Management *Mosaics* Diversity Newsletter.

Social
responsibility
plays a key role
in decisions
about pollution,
discrimination,
welfare, and the
well-being of
society.

SOCIAL RESPONSIBILITY

Social responsibility is the obligation we have to make choices or decisions that are beneficial to the whole of society. These types of decisions most commonly involve issues such as environmental pollution, welfare, inflation, discrimination, and homeless and hungry people. Corporate social responsibility may be viewed from one of three perspectives—classical, accountability, and public.

The **classical perspective** holds that businesses need not feel responsible for social issues and should concentrate on being profitable, as an economy based on strong businesses best serves society overall. This view suggests that ethics should have little influence on decisions and that profit is the bottom line. We need only consider the effects this approach could have on our environment if no concern were shown for air quality or water pollution.

Social responsibility
is the obligation to
make choices or
decisions that are
mutually beneficial
to the whole of
society.

The **accountability perspective** holds businesses accountable for their actions, with a responsibility to be fair and considerate in their business practices. This view requires sensitivity to environmental and social issues and prevents unethical decisions in such matters as toxic waste disposal and discrimination against minorities, women, aged, or handicapped workers.

The **public perspective** links businesses with the government and other groups to actively solve social and environmental problems. This view requires involvement by all parties in improving the general quality of life. Decisions are made with the goal of profit for the business but also with consideration of impact on pollution or unemployment.

From any of these perspectives, ethics plays a critical role in the decisions to be made. Should a company pollute the air or water because control devices are expensive to install and would reduce profits? Should the company install expensive pollution devices that may have a negative impact on the budget and cause employee layoffs, affecting local unemployment problems? Considering these questions makes more obvious the relationships of the terms mentioned in the chapter's beginning. Values, integrity, and ethics must all be exercised in situations involving social responsibility.

Recent events suggest a need for more ethical decision making.

With the obvious escalation in numbers of events in recent years, we are left wondering whether we are living in a mindless, valueless society on a path of destruction or whether we are victims of media hype. With the media now probing all areas of society, government, and business activities and focusing on negative ethics, individuals and organizations have a greater need to improve current ethical practices.

Unethical practices cut across all occupations.

CASE STUDIES IN THE NEWS

Unethical behavior has been with us since the beginning of time. From all appearances, however, the United States is currently suffering a crisis in ethics. Television news broadcasts and newspapers (beginning in the 1960s and mushrooming through the '80s and '90s) have been filled with reports of unethical business practices and unethical personal behaviors. Few professions or occupations are left unscathed. Corporate CEOs, bankers, doctors, lawyers, government officials, defense contractors, investment counselors, food and medicine manufacturers, and military employees are being indicted in unprecedented numbers for a variety of unethical activities.

Were these kinds of events happening in previous years but unnoticed because the ethical culture of those times was different? Do you believe that Americans have become less ethical? To what do you attribute the current trends in ethics?

The Homeless and Hungry • Greenhouse Effect • **ILLITERACY** • *Civil Rights* • **ILLEGAL ALIENS** • Child Abuse • **Violence at Work** • **HMO Cost Savings Practices** • **increased religious persecution** • Illegal campaign fund raising • Drive-by shootings • POLITICAL SCANDALS • *Elder abuse* • **foreign child labor** • hate crimes • VIOLENCE IN SCHOOLS • *Nuclear Power Safety* • **ENVIRONMENTAL POLLUTION AND DESTRUCTION** • *U.S. Involvement in Foreign Wars* • **AIDS** • **Insider Trading Scandals** • Illegal Drug Use by Athletes • SELLING MILITARY SECRETS • spouse abuse • *ethnic cleansing* • **gang activities**

Aside from the media keeping the subject in the forefront, the public seems to have reached the full span of the pendulum swing. Public opinion now reflects the sentiment, "We are fed up. Let's all play by the rules."

At the base of all these activities are human beings placed in positions of making ethical decisions. All bring their own set of standards, traditions, rules, and values, and all must struggle with deciding what is ethical.

*Fast*Chat

We hear reports of unethical behavior daily.

1. Name recent sports, business, or political leaders whose conduct has been exposed. What were the consequences?

2. Joseph de Maistre wrote in 1821 that "Every nation has the government it deserves." That is, leaders reflect something about those who put them in power. In view of this statement, what about American ethics was reflected in President Clinton's controversial behavior and subsequent trial for perjury and obstruction of justice? Think of other government leaders. What common attitudes are reflected by each?

How Do You Set Ethical Standards and Solve Ethical Dilemmas?

16.2

Learning
Objective 2

Describe some of the methods of determining ethical standards.

Methods have been developed to assist us in evaluating whether a decision is ethical. Five of these methods are described below.

Methods for Evaluating Ethical Decisions

1. Legality
Is your decision within the legal limits? Laws governing situations usually correct some previous misjudgment or define the boundaries of an activity. Some people believe that if a decision complies with current laws, it will by definition be ethically sound. Other people suggest that the demonstration of ethics begins where the law ends.

2. Personal morality
Personal commitment to uphold human rights and dignity will most always assure ethical choices. This method reflects personal integrity and moral sensitivity.

3. Enlightened self-interest
Some people argue that organizations should promote socially responsible behavior because it is good business. This idea, termed **enlightened self-interest,** suggests that organizations' and people's best interests are served by being genuinely concerned for others. The internal payoff for being socially responsible may be self-esteem. External payoffs may be higher profits and other measurable consequences.

4. Corporate or professional codes of ethics
Many organizations attempt to institutionalize ethical policies and decision making in a number of ways, such as ethics committees and training in ethics. One popular approach is adoption of a **code of ethics** that requires and prohibits specific practices. Although few companies actually display their codes, most will dismiss, demote, or reprimand employees who intentionally violate the codes. Codes may not actually change people's behaviors, but proponents argue that they do communicate to employees that the company is committed to its standards and is asking employees to adopt them. Codes of ethics are sometimes categorized in two ways: corporate, if they are for business organizations, and professional, if they are for a specific professional group. The National Management Association's Code of Ethics is in the box that follows. Following these types of standards when making your decisions will influence your choices in a positive manner.

5. Common practices
The means of ethical decision making known as common practices relies on the belief that "everyone else does it this way." This method is least likely to assure ethical choices. If others accept gifts from contract bidders, following their example does not make you right.

Legality,
personal
morality,
enlightened self-
interest, codes
of ethics, and
common
practices may
help you make
ethical decisions.

The National Management Association's Code of Ethics

I will recognize that all individuals inherently desire to practice their occupations to the best of their ability. I will assume that all individuals want to do their best.

I will maintain a broad and balanced outlook and will recognize value in the ideas and opinions of others.

I will be guided in all my activities by truth, accuracy, fair dealing and good taste.

I will keep informed on the latest developments in techniques, equipment and processes. I will recommend or initiate methods to increase productivity and efficiency.

I will support efforts to strengthen the management profession through training and ideation.

I will help my associates reach personal and professional fulfillment.

I will earn and carefully guard my reputation for good moral character and good citizenship.

I will promote the principles of our American Enterprise System to others, by highlighting its accomplishments and displaying confidence in its future.

I will recognize that leadership is a call to service.

The National Management Association
By permission of the National Management Association

Ethical dilemmas challenge us to make the right choice.

Relying on our value system to guide us in our decision making will most often result in ethically sound judgments. We may, however, experience conflicts with this method when we operate in an environment that does not share similar values. Operating in certain other ethnic cultures, for example, may create difficulties. What may be considered unethical in our culture may be perfectly acceptable in another. In some cultures, for example, expectations are that government officials will be given "gratuities" for services rendered. In the United States, this is considered not only unethical but illegal.

The Foreign Corrupt Policy Act of 1977 was passed to guard against such conflicts. This law requires United States companies to operate ethically in their worldwide business dealings, and the U. S. Justice Department polices activities of U.S. companies overseas to prevent unethical actions.

In addition, in order to deal with issues related to differences in values from one culture to the next, the Caus Round Table was formed. It has developed world standards to measure ethical behavior. The standards are based on two principals: the concept of human dignity and the Japanese doctrine of KYOSEI—the idea of living and working together for the common good to enable mutual prosperity.

SOLVING ETHICAL DILEMMAS

Ethical dilemmas, or conflicts in values, arise when our sense of values or social responsibility is questioned internally or challenged externally. "Examples of Personal and Business Ethical Dilemmas," on the next page, provides examples of situations that may be considered ethical dilemmas. These dilemmas are separated into personal situations and business situations. Do any of these dilemmas seem familiar? Think how you handled them or what ethical decision you might make.

The heart of ethical dilemmas is not whether you know what is right or wrong, but whether you will choose the right behavior. Individuals must decide whether they are willing to risk making a decision that challenges wrongdoing even though that decision may result in losing or not obtaining something desired. An example would be filling out your time sheet showing a few extra hours that you did not work because you want money to buy a new outfit. You feel that without the new clothes, you will not be able to impress your friends, which is very important to you. Obviously, the

GLOBAL CONNECTION

In Bangladesh many children younger than 14 (the age set by International standards as a reasonable working age) are significant contributors to family income. If underage children did not work in factories, they would probably be forced into other ways of earning money, such as prostitution or begging.

Assume you own an American company with a clothing factory in Bangladesh. On a recent visit you see children who appear to be under 14 working. When you question the plant manager, you find there are no birth certificates so he is unable to determine ages accurately.

1. *Would you fire all the children who appeared to be under 14? Why or why not?*

2. *If you did not terminate the children and the American public learned you worked underage children, how would you handle it?*

Examples of Personal and Business Ethical Dilemmas

Personal	Business
Should I pay at the checkout counter for the candy bar I ate while grocery shopping?	Should I turn in 8 hours time worked today even though I took 2 hours for Dave's retirement luncheon?
Should I tell the salesclerk that the item I am purchasing is mismarked with a lower price or consider it a lucky bargain and buy two?	Should I accept these basketball tickets from my contractors?
Should I call in sick today and enjoy the time off?	Should I pad my trip expense report to pick up a few extra dollars?
Should I turn in to lost and found the billfold I found in the ladies lounge?	Should I copy this new computer software to load onto my PC at home?
Should I cheat on my income tax?	Should I use the office copier to run copies of the recipe for the cake Jane brought in this morning for the office staff?
Should I tell the bank they have credited my account with extra amounts of money?	Should I type my term paper on the company's PC during duty hours because it is more convenient?
Should I admit I got the exam answers from another student?	Should I select my old basketball team member for the job opening or the most technically qualified applicant?
Should I take this book from the library without properly checking it out with the desk clerk?	Should I pressure my new employee for a date this weekend?
Should I completely stop at the red light even thought there is no one around for miles?	Should I pay my quarter for the coffee or just enjoy a free cup?
Should I take credit for this presentation even though I borrowed most of the materials from my neighbor?	Should I authorize the dumping of this waste material directly into the remote landfill site without proper hazardous waste handling and labeling?

ethical choice would be to report your time correctly and find some other way to save or earn the money for the outfit.

Responses to value conflicts are different for each individual. Some people may respond physically with ulcers, alcoholism, or mental disturbance. Others will show no symptoms and easily adjust their value to the new accepted norm.

If your boss asked you to bend the rules, how would you react? An article by Pat Amend suggests the following steps:

1. *Validate the conflict.* It may not be real. You may not have all the facts. Play dumb and ask questions in a nonthreatening way: "Are we allowed to do that in our work agreement?"

Human Relations

2. *Assess the risks involved.* How much are you personally willing to risk? Amend quotes Barbara Ley Toffler, author of *Tough Choices: Managers Talk Ethics*, as saying, "Everyone has to decide where the line is. You have to pick your cause." Doing a cost-benefit analysis to assess the possible harm versus the probable benefits of your choice may clearly guide your decision.

These steps may be useful in ethical decision making.

3. *Act on your decision.* Decide, and then proceed with tact. If you are willing to take the risk, you might mention that you are uncomfortable with what you have been asked to do. Rather than making accusations, give your boss a chance to save face or reverse the request.

4. *Get help in a troubled situation.* If the talk with your boss does not resolve the situation, seek help from a slightly senior-level manager you know and trust. Opposing decisions, policies, or practices within the organization that we consider to be detrimental or illegal is known as **whistleblowing**. It also can include publicizing such behavior to people outside the organization, which is a sensitive matter. Correcting detrimental or illegal situations may involve replanning, redesigning, and reworking and, hence, much time and money. For this reason, many managers choose to ignore these situations. If you go to someone above you, you should be subtle and not name names or point fingers. Approach this advisor with a general question, such as "Does the company usually do this?"

5. *Consider a change in jobs.* If your boss's ethics are in conflict with yours, you may choose to transfer or leave the company. The majority of business executives in the U.S. agree that in order to be ethical in business, you need the support of an ethical boss. Although individuals can behave ethically on their own, they may be "frozen out" by the boss. You may, therefore, adjust your ethics in order to survive professionally in this particular organization. Self-esteem begins to erode, and by age 50, you may not like yourself any more, but you may be reluctant to leave because you are locked into a high salary and comfortable benefits. You have become the organization.

Quick Tip

Various environmental laws provide protection from discharge or other discriminatory actions by employers in retaliation for the employee's good faith complaints about health and safety hazards in the work place. If you have a concern, contact the Employment Standards Administration Wage and Hour Division, or, if you are a public employee, your human resource office. Additional federal and state laws protect public employees who are whistleblowers.

Authors Kenneth Blanchard and Norman Vincent Peale provide a simple three-step approach to resolving ethical dilemmas. In their book, *The Power of Ethical Management*, they offer the following questions to be used in an ethics check of behavior:

1. Is it legal? Will you be violating any laws or company policies?
2. Is it balanced? Will your decision be fair to all parties concerned, and will it promote a win-win situation?
3. How will my decision make me feel about myself? Will I be proud of my choice? Will I feel good when my family reads about my decision in the local newspaper?

Blanchard and Peale think that ethical behavior is strongly related to self-esteem and that people who feel good about themselves are more able to make ethical decisions and withstand the pressures against those choices.

One other approach to ethical decision making, suggested by Stoner and Freeman, is a questioning process using common morality. Common morality is a set of ground rules covering ordinary ethical problems. These questions may help you when faced with ethical dilemmas:

Questions that May Help When You Are Faced with Ethical Dilemmas

Promise keeping	Am I keeping promises that I have made?
Nonmalevolence	Am I refraining from harming other human beings?
Mutual aid	Am I helping someone else if the cost is not too great for me to bear?
Respect for persons	Am I treating people as ends in themselves, rather than as mere means to my own ends? Am I taking them seriously, accepting their interests as legitimate, and regarding their desires as important?
Respect for property	Do I have the consent of others before using their property?

FastChat

1. Review the Methods for Evaluating Ethical Decisions at the beginning of this section. Think of stories in the news where problems resulted from unethical decisions. Applying which methods might have avoided these problems?

2. Review the questions above that may help you when you are faced with ethical dilemmas. Which have you dealt with lately? Using situations you feel comfortable revealing, discuss how you handled these questions.

How Are Companies Addressing Business Ethics?

16.3

Learning
O b j e c t i v e   4

Discuss how companies are addressing business ethics.

A recent survey of Fortune 500 companies indicated that organizations are taking steps to incorporate ethics and core values into their operations. Being socially responsible was listed more often than any other as the main reason for building ethics into the organization.

Specifically, companies are facing ethics problems by providing guidelines to their employees for dealing with vendors, competitors, and customers. Texas Instruments, for instance, begins its ethics guidance at the new employee orientation. They use stickers, posters, and wallet cards as well as written materials and an ethics briefing to reinforce the message.

Companies are working to improve their tarnished ethics.

ETHICS CONNECTION

Ethics at work is a serious concern. A poll of over 4,000 employees conducted by the Washington, D.C.-based Ethic Resource Center stated that nearly one third of the respondents reported they felt they had at some point been pressured to violate company policies in order to achieve business objectives. Additionally they had witnessed various forms of misconduct in the past year such as lying to supervisors (56%), lying on reports or falsifying records (41%), stealing and theft (35%), sexual harassment (35%), abusing drugs or alcohol (31%) and conflicts of interest (31%).

1. *Have you ever felt you were being pressured to violate company policies in order to achieve business objectives? If so, what did you do?*

2. *What do you think employees should do when they observe their coworkers lying to supervisors, lying on reports, stealing, engaging in sexual harassment, abusing drugs, or engaging in conflicts of interest?*

Hercules, Incorporated, a supplier of specialty chemicals and engineered polymers, has developed a detailed ethics policy, and the ethics statement was penned by the chairman himself. The ethics training at Hercules lasts about six to eight hours and covers ethics policy, the ethics brochure, and how to use the help line. Follow-up training is used to educate employees about legal issues.

J.P. Morgan & Company, the Wall Street banking firm, backs up its commitment to ethical behavior by evaluating each employee's commitment to the company's core values during the annual performance appraisal. The core values are repeated on the first page of the performance appraisal document.

Even the most detailed, well constructed ethics program will not be successful without commitment, communication, and mutual trust, with the tone set by top management. The key is the CEO. A strong code of ethics, written rules, and corporate procedures are important, but without strong

Commitment, communication, and mutual trust are the keys to a successful ethics program.

TECHNOLOGY CONNECTION

Technology brings with it the potential for a whole new range of unethical behavior. It is now possible to alter photographs and videos or to create viruses that will ruin thousands of computers. It is also possible to publicize information widely via the Internet—and not necessarily accurate information. "Urban legends" abound, such as the story of the man who attends a party and later wakes up in a bathtub of ice to find his kidney has been harvested.

1. How can you discover what is real and what has been altered?

2. Is it wise to take things we read or see on the Internet without questioning the source or the validity? Why or why not?

3. Do individuals who disseminate information over the Internet have an obligation to be truthful?

4. What steps can you take to protect yourself and others from untruthful, altered, or otherwise unethical material, both on the Internet and elsewhere (TV, book store, gossip, etc.)?

commitment and enforcement from senior management they are merely words on paper. Communicating expectations through continuous training programs may serve to build the mutual trust required in an effective ethics program.

Companies today try to prevent unethical behavior, such as stealing software.

FastChat

1. In what areas do you think companies can offer ethical guidance?

2. Sometimes people suggest that the government should establish more guidelines for behavior for individuals, both on the job and off. For what issues might government guidelines be helpful. At what point is government intervention a violation of human rights and freedom of choice?

16.4 What Is Your Responsibility Regarding Ethical Behavior at Work?

Learning
Objective 5

Understand your responsibility regarding ethical behavior at work.

You are ultimately responsible for your own behavior.

Behaving ethically and responsibly enhances your life, makes human interactions less stressful and more rewarding, and boosts self-esteem. Additionally, understanding ethics and behaving appropriately can make or break your career. Anyone working today needs to take the following measures:

1. *Know your own value system.* Explore with yourself your own value systems and beliefs. Understand the events in your childhood that shaped your values. If you feel that some areas are not fully developed, pursue ethical teachings to help you fill any gaps.

2. *Learn about and respect the value systems of others.* Remember that others grew up in different circumstances and may have developed a different set of values. Learn to respect those values.

3. *Learn about the ethics and the norms of your place of business.* If your business has a written ethics policy or guidelines, be sure you are familiar with them. If there is no written code, then ask questions to determine how management views certain behavior. For instance, before giving a gift to a supervisor, inquire of others around you if this is an accepted practice.

4. *When confronted with something that feels uncomfortable, take time to think.* Use some of the techniques suggested in this chapter in order to sort out how you wish to handle the situation. Make a list of your options and the pros and cons before you decide what to do.

5. *The decision must be your own.* Remember, in the end, you must live with whatever decision you make. You will reap the benefits or pay the consequences.

FastChat

Values development starts when you are young.

1. Which values are you most likely to learn at home? How might a home situation affect your values?

2. What values should be taught in school?

3. When do you believe training in business ethics should begin—high school? college? Why?

4. Do you feel that it would be better to change your values system or quit a job where your values differ from those of the company or your supervisors?

Summary

Ethics is the application in decision making of values learned in early years. These values are heavily influenced by our environment. Individuals and organizations may gain temporary benefits from unethical behavior, but in the long run, they reap problems. Personal ethics involves decisions outside work, whereas business ethics applies to work-related decisions. Beginning in the 1960s, unethical practices began to escalate, resulting in today's ethics crisis. Unethical practices have penetrated political, environmental, religious, military, business, and sports fields, affecting all of us. The topic of ethics is now receiving attention in hopes of reversing this trend. The five most common methods for determining appropriate ethical standards are following common practices, checking the legality of the action, considering enlightened self-interest, abiding by codes of ethics, and relying on personal morality.

Each person is faced with ethical dilemmas in everyday life situations. These dilemmas involve making decisions on issues that question our value system. Several steps guide ethical decision making: validate the conflict, assess risk, decide, get help, and, if necessary, change jobs.

To improve business practices, companies are issuing codes of ethics and ethical standards handbooks. Training programs are being used to reinforce company positions on ethical issues. Top management participates in these programs to emphasize their importance. In order to deal more effectively with ethical issues you need to know yourself and your values, know and respect the values of others, make an effort to learn your company's values, explore situations before acting, and then make the best decision you can.

Key Terms

ethics
integrity
values
social responsibility
classical perspective
accountability perspective
public perspective
enlightened self-interest
code of ethics
Foreign Corrupt Policy Act
KYOSEI
ethical dilemmas
whistleblowing

Review Questions

1. Explain the differences among ethics, values, integrity, and social responsibility.
2. Identify two recent events that have fostered the current emphasis on ethics.
3. What are some of the methods used in determining ethical standards?
4. What is meant by ethical dilemmas?
5. What methods can you use in dealing with ethical dilemmas?
6. What steps are companies taking to improve the standards of ethics within the companies?

Discussion Questions

1. From the illustration, "Events That Have Focused Attention on Ethical Issues" (page 474) select the three events that you think have had the most profound effect on ethics in business. Why did you pick those three events?
2. Review the figure "Examples of Personal and Business Ethical Dilemmas." Which of the dilemmas in the chart have you faced? Are some of them ones that you have not faced but have seen others deal with?
3. Does the company for which you work have a code of ethics or some other form of ethics program? Discuss that program and its effectiveness.
4. Name an ethical issue with which you are faced or expect to be faced. Make a list of the pros and cons each decision will bring.

Chapter Project

With your class divided into two groups, discuss a different side of the following ethical dilemmas. Choose one of the dilemmas and write a position paper in which you defend your decision.

1. The XYZ Company wants to build a new, modern facility on the outskirts of your town, which has been suffering economic difficulty for a long time, with high unemployment and low wages for the jobs that do exist. However, an environmental survey discovered that a rare bird that lives only in the area has its main nesting ground where the company wants to build the factory. If the factory is built there, the bird will most likely become extinct. The company has tax incentives from other cities who want the factory, but it prefers your site.

2. You are a high level manager in the Last Chance Corporation. You have been in talks with the management of your company and know that a large layoff is about to take place. You are aware that one of your employees is about to close on the purchase of a new house. Shortly after the close, he will be laid off. You have been told that everything is strictly confidential and you are not to tell anyone about the layoff.

3. You and your best friend work at a fast food restaurant. Your friend has been giving free meals to his girl friend who comes into the restaurant. Your friend feels that he doesn't get paid enough for what he does, and, since the company is so big, the meals will never be missed. You are behind the counter and the girl friend comes in. She expects you to give her a free meal. What should you do? Politely refuse to serve her? Report your friend? Break the rules and give your friend's girl friend a free meal?

Problem solving, reasoning, listening, speaking, writing, participating as a member of a team.

Applications

In small groups analyze the following:

All Money Is Green

Guy Walters is the chief executive officer of a major engineering firm. He has been appointed committee chairman for the High Speed Transportation System (HSTS). This group is expected to develop a viable method of transporting mass quantities of products safely and quickly to major distribution points around the world. Funding for this project has come from many companies interested in rapidly moving their products into global marketplaces. Guy feels strongly about making a success of this project and believes that it will greatly benefit the transportation industry, his company, and his personal career.

In a meeting with Shalonda Hall, his chief financial officer, Guy discovers that his budget is too limited to complete the project. Shalonda explains that they are confined by the company's policies to using the HSTS funds and that getting approval for additional funding will be difficult.

"We'll just have to bring the matter before the executive board and request additional funds before we can go on," explained Shalonda.

Guy responded to the news with, "I don't want to do that! You know how they feel about budget overruns. Why can't we just divert some of the leftover funds from other study programs to wrap up this thing? What's the big deal anyway? All money is green! We are all working toward the same

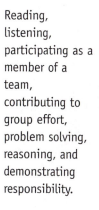

Reading, listening, participating as a member of a team, contributing to group effort, problem solving, reasoning, and demonstrating responsibility.

end—profits for the company. We're so near completion on this job that I don't want to slow the progress by begging for dollars. Go do some of that 'creative financing' for which you budget people are famous. They'll never know the difference!"

1. What is the ethical issue in this situation?
2. What does Guy mean by "all money is green"? Is he correct?
3. How should Shalonda respond to Guy's instructions?
4. How would you resolve the ethical dilemma Shalonda faces?

The Bootlegged Booty

John was to report to the office on Monday as the new supervisor. Alan was eager to make a good impression on his new boss and had heard John was fond of using his PC. As a special treat, Alan decided to load John's PC with all the bootlegged software that he had acquired over the last few years. He knew some of the applications would be needed by John as soon as he hit the door. Getting software orders through the regular channels took as much as six months and then only if you knew someone to pull strings for you. He felt that John would appreciate his outfitting the PC and he could make some points.

When John arrived on Monday and discovered that his PC was loaded with software that was not authorized, he immediately called his staff together for a meeting. He told them that he felt very strongly about the ethical issues in question in copying software and that he had asked the software specialists to unload the bootlegged copies from his machine. "I have also asked them to remove all illegal copies from your machines. We should be able to order whatever we need. That may take a while, but at least we'll be legal."

1. Why did Alan think that John would appreciate the added software?
2. Could Alan have handled this situation so that John would have felt more comfortable? How?
3. Do you think that John acted responsibly by ordering that all machines be legal, even though it might temporarily limit the working capability of his staff?
4. How might you have handled this dilemma?

Human Relations

Additional Readings and Resources

Batsell, Jake. "Corporate Ethics: The Great Divide?" *Seattle Times*, April 6, 1998.

"Be Cool! Cultivating a Cool Culture Gives HR a Staffing Boost." *Workforce*, April 1998, Vol. 77, No.4, pp. 50–61.

Digh, Patricia. "Doing the Right Thing Just Got Harder." *Mosiacs*, (Society for Human Resource Management), January/February, 1999, Vol 5, No. 1, pp. 1, 4, and 5.

Driscoll, Dawn Marie. W. Michael Hoffman, and Edward Perry. *The Ethical Edge; Tales of Organizations That Have Faced Moral Crises*. Media Masters, 1995.

Flynn, Gillian. "Make Employee Ethics Your Business." *Personnel Journal*, June, 1995, Vol. 74, No.6, pp. 30–41.

Hopkins, Willie. *Ethical Dimensions*. Sage Publications, 1997.

http://www.condor.depaul.edu/ethics/bizethics.html

http://www.eoa.org

http://www.ethics.org

http://josephsoninstitute.org/med/medintro.htm

Kidder, Rushworth M. *How Good People Make Tough Choices: Resolving the Dilemmas of Ethical Living*. New York: Simon and Schuster, 1995.

Madsen, Peter, and Jay M. Shafritz, eds. *Essentials of Business Ethics (A Collection of Articles by Top Social Thinkers)*. New York: Meridian (Penguin Books USA Inc.), 1990.

Naisbitt, John, and Patricia Aburdene. *Megatrends 2000*. New York: William Morrow and Company, Inc., 1990.

Pardue, Howard M. Ph.D., SPHR. "Ethics: A Human Resource Perspective." SHRM White Paper, December, 1998.

Solomon, Charlene Marmer. "Put Your Ethics to a Global Test." *Personnel Journal*, January 1996, Vol 75. No.1, pp. 66–74.

"Whistleblower Protection." SHRM White Paper. Excerpted from "Small Business Handbook: Laws, Regulations, and Technical Assistance Services," U.S. Department of Labor, 1993.

Substance Abuse:

The Multi-Million Dollar Problem

After studying this chapter, you should be able to:

1. *Define substance abuse and identify its costs to organizations.*

2. *Describe what organizations are doing to combat substance abuse.*

3. *Be aware of the pros and cons of drug testing.*

4. *Identify substances that may be abused and their effects.*

5. *Describe actions you can take if you are a substance abuser.*

6. *Explain the actions an employee can take when a coworker or supervisor is abusing substances.*

"It may seem harmless, but an employee who drinks too much champagne at a Sunday evening wedding, consumes a few too many beers during Monday Night Football, or has a drink at lunch could be costing your company money."

—National Institute on Alcohol and Alcohol Abuse and the Robert Wood Johnson Foundation

Are there ways that companies can discourage social drinking of employees away from work? What can companies do to help employees avoid or recover from substance abuse? What other groups can help discourage substance abuse, or assist in recovering from it?

What Is Substance Abuse?

Substance abuse is the misuse of alcohol, illegal drugs, or prescription drugs. It has become a great concern for organizations because of the millions of dollars lost each year through decreased productivity, absenteeism, theft, industrial accidents, and excessive benefits use. Estimates are that employee drug use costs United States businesses $60 billion to $100 billion or more annually.

The United States Department of Labor estimates that:

- Seventy-one percent of illegal drug users are employed.
- Alcoholism causes 500 million lost workdays each year.
- Drug and alcohol-related problems are one of the four top reasons for the rise in workplace violence.

Learning
Objective   1

Define substance abuse and identify its costs to organizations.

Substance abusers cost companies money.

CORBIS/Bettmann

Two train workers tested positive for drugs immediately following this 1987 railway collision that left 16 people dead and 175 injured.

- Of those who called the cocaine helpline, 75 percent reported using drugs on the job, 64 percent admitted drugs adversely affected their job performance, 44 percent sold drugs to other employees, and 18 percent had stolen from co-workers to support their drug habits.

A study conducted by the Institute for Health Policy, Brandeis University, found substance abuse to be the number one health problem in the country, resulting in more deaths, illnesses, and disabilities than any other preventable health condition.

Additionally, the Bureau of National Affairs reports substance abusers are:

- One-third less productive than non-drug-abusing employees.
- Three times more likely than other workers to be late or absent from the job.
- More than three times as likely to be injured or to injure a co-worker on the job, and five times more likely to be involved in an accident off the job.
- Five times more likely to file a worker's compensation claim.
- Seven times more likely to have a wage garnishment.
- Likely to take three times the average level of sick benefits.
- In addition, families of abusers are four times more likely than family members of non-drug-abusing employees to use medical or psychiatric benefits.

In short, substance abuse costs companies money. The federal government became so concerned that in 1988 it issued **Executive Order 12564**, which established a drug-free federal workplace and a drug testing program for federal employees.

The federal government also passed the **Federal Drug-Free Workplace Act** in 1988. This act requires federal contractors and grantees who receive more than $25,000 in government business to certify that they will maintain a drug-free workplace. These companies must:

1. establish and communicate to employees an anti-drug policy,
2. notify employees that compliance with this policy is a condition of employment,
3. establish a drug-awareness program that educates employees on the dangers of drugs and identifies assistance available to those with substance abuse problems, and
4. make a good-faith effort to maintain a drug-free workplace.

Additionally, the Drug-Free Workplace Act of 1998 has authorized $10 million in grants for technical assistance and services to small businesses that want to establish a drug-free workplace program.

Don't let substance abuse jeopardize safety in your workplace.

Sixty percent of employed drug users work for small companies.

1. Why do you think this is occurring?

2. Do you expect this will change any time in the future?

3. How would you recommend that this problem be handled by employers?

*Fast***Chat**

How Do Organizations Fight Abuse?

Organizations fight substance abuse by drug testing, employee assistance programs, and education.

Organizations are using a variety of techniques, such as drug testing, employee assistance programs, and employee education, in an effort to curtail substance abuse at work. Testing can be performed on potential employees as well as current employees.

Pre-employment drug testing requires job applicants to pass a urinalysis examination for drugs in their system prior to employment. Applicants who do not pass the examination or refuse to take the examination are not hired.

A growing number of organizations are also testing current employees for substance abuse. A variety of testing schedules is used, depending on the preference of the organization. One type of schedule is known as **expected interval testing**. Under this method, employees are informed ahead of time when testing will occur. It is then performed at the same time on a continuous basis. For example, the test may be scheduled for the first workday after each payday.

CASE STUDIES IN THE NEWS

In Michigan, a four-month operation at a brake manufacturer led to 72 terminations for drug abuse. Undercover operations are a last resort for companies to control serious substance abuse in the workplace. In order to set up the operation, the company needs the cooperation of the local police and a private investigation firm. The undercover agent assumes an identity and applies for a position. Then the agent gains the trust of coworkers and pretends to take drugs.

1. *Should companies run undercover sting operations for drug use? Why or why not?*

2. *If companies do not conduct undercover operations, how else might they eliminate substance abuse on the job?*

Random interval testing involves giving tests at random to a particular group of employees. For instance, all employees in the accounting department may be informed that they are to report immediately for a drug test. This testing is most often used for job categories involving public safety or security.

A third type of testing schedule is called **"for cause"** testing. Under this method, individual employees may be tested when they appear to exhibit signs of substance abuse, such as slurred speech or dilated pupils. Testing is sometimes done after industrial accidents or for reasonable cause.

Employees may also be expected to submit to **treatment follow-up testing**. This type of testing is used to monitor an employee's success in remaining drug free after being allowed to complete a substance abuse treatment program rather than be terminated.

Other organizations test only employees who are transferred or promoted or employees who are in critical positions. Examples of employees in critical positions are factory employees who work with dangerous equipment and airline pilots.

Company policies and procedures vary on what happens to an employee who fails or refuses to submit to a substance abuse test. Many companies require termination on the spot. Others may require mandatory enrollment in a substance abuse program. Generally, the policy will be more lenient for legal substances than illegal. Employees should be familiar with their company policy on this matter.

> **Organizations are testing employees for substance abuse.**

> **Companies take action against employees who abuse substances.**

Quick Tip

Just Say No.

—D.A.R.E.

Many companies reserve the right to search all areas and property over which the company maintains control without consent of the employee. On occasion organizations have been known to call local law enforcement agencies or use dogs trained to locate illegal substances in an effort to curtail substance abuse.

Other actions are being taken by employers, when policing employees seems excessive, in order to reduce substance abuse. Many firms are establishing employee assistance programs. These programs, which are discussed in detail in Chapter 13, provide short-term counseling to employees and assist them in obtaining appropriate treatment for substance abuse.

Companies are also establishing employee education programs concerning drug and alcohol addiction as part of their employee wellness programs. These programs are discussed in Chapter 19. Employee education includes alerting employees to the dangers of substance abuse and encouraging those who are abusing to seek treatment.

Drug Use Among U.S. Workers

Construction	17.3%
Construction Supervisors	17.2%
Food Preparation	16.3%
Waiter and Waitress	15.4%
General Laborers	13.1%

—Drug Abuse Prevention Network

FastChat

In general, the courts have upheld the rights of companies to test for drugs.

1. Should the company's right to a drug-free workplace override the right of an employee not to be subjected to an intrusive urinalysis test?

2. Should employees who fail a drug test be allowed to go to rehabilitation or be fired immediately?

Is Drug Testing Appropriate?

Learning
Objective   3

Be aware of the pros and cons of drug testing.

Although proponents of testing say drug testing saves companies money, opponents say that testing is intrusive, humiliating, and an invasion of privacy. Civil libertarians and other students of the U.S. Constitution see drug testing as a serious violation of Fourth Amendment rights, which protect us from unreasonable search and seizure. Employees who feel violated may suffer from low morale, which may lead to decreased productivity.

Random testing subjects many innocent employees to degrading urinalysis tests. The acquisition of the specimen, to ensure that it is not altered and that it belongs to the individual who is doing the test, must be observed. Blood tests, necessary to detect alcohol levels, can also be intrusive. Because random testing targets many individuals who are not abusers, the cost of testing is extremely high in proportion to the positive results uncovered. For example, Texas Instruments' testing of 1,000 employees cost $1 million—about $20,000 for each of the 49 positive test results. So if saving money is a prime motive for drug testing, it appears to have failed at that particular task.

Another concern is that the tests are not foolproof. Many legal substances, including poppy seeds, tonic water, cold medicine, and prescription drugs such as Tylenol Plus 3 (with codeine) can test positive. To ensure that false positives are not obtained, many companies use drug testing laboratories that meet the rigorous standards established by the National Institute on Drug Abuse (NIDA). These labs use a strict criterion for chain of custody of

Many people find drug testing intrusive, humiliating, and an invasion of employee rights.

TECHNOLOGY CONNECTION

Drug testing of the future may not involve use of urinalysis tests. Scientists are perfecting tests for drugs using saliva, sweat, and hair. Saliva will reveal drug usage in the last 12 to 24 hours while sweat patches can identify drug usage over a period of one to two weeks. Hair, on the other hand, can reveal historical drug use dating back 90 days or more. As the cost of these alternative testing procedures lowers and their use becomes accepted by the courts, they will be used more extensively.

specimens, a second test to confirm positives, as well as a Medical Review Officer who speaks with the individual providing the specimen and investigates the circumstances to determine whether a positive finding is warranted.

Drug test results can be positive long after the substance was used.

Opponents point out that drug tests do not measure the impairment present, nor do they reveal when the substance was consumed. As pointed out earlier, positive results can be obtained days after the drug has been used. Detection times vary depending on the drug taken, the frequency of use, and the amount of drug ingested. Mark Rothstein, Director of the Health Law and Policy Institute at the University of Houston, estimates that as many as 99 percent of those who test positive are casual marijuana users. Except for the truly dependent, some experts believe employees who use illegal drugs confine their use to evenings and weekends.

Approximate Time Limits within which Drugs Can Be Detected through Testing

Drug	Detection Time
Amphetamines	48 hours
Barbiturates	24 hours to 3 weeks
Cocaine	6 to 72 hours
Opiates	2 days
Methaqualone	14 days
Marijuana	3 to 20 days or more

These time periods can vary greatly, depending on the dosage, body weight, body composition, and many other factors.

Additionally, though drugs are certainly a serious problem, they are not the primary substance being abused in the U.S. Alcohol abuse is far more widespread and, purely by virtue of numbers of abusers, is more costly to businesses and more damaging to lives and families.

FastChat

Urinalysis tests are commonly used to test for drugs.

1. Should an individual be watched while a specimen is given? Why or why not?

2. What methods do individuals use to thwart drug tests?

3. Do you believe a blood test is intrusive? Why or why not?

What Substances Are Most Abused?

Understanding the short-term and long-term effects of substance abuse is important for several reasons. First, if you are abusing substances, or plan to, you should be aware of what you are doing to your body and how these chemicals will alter your ability to perform on the job—and may ruin your life. Then, too, knowing substance effects will help you detect substance abuse in those around you and will help you deal with them.

Commonly abused substances include alcohol, cocaine, and marijuana. Also abused are sedatives, tranquilizers, hallucinogens, and narcotics.

Alcohol is the most abused drug in the United States. A depressant, it slows down the activity of the brain and spinal cord and knocks out the control centers one by one. Although it may produce feelings of well-being, it can lead to sedation, intoxication, blackouts, unconsciousness, and death.

Heavy consumption of alcohol may cause immediate physical problems, such as inefficiency, low energy, weight loss, lethargy, sleeplessness, accidents, and memory loss. Emotionally, it can cause a person to feel jealous, sexually aroused, impotent, moody, easily angered, guilty, depressed, worthless, despondent, and suicidal.

Over a period of years, the effects of heavy drinking include malnutrition, brain damage, cancer, heart disease, liver damage, ulcers, gastritis, and birth defects in children whose mothers abused alcohol during pregnancy.

Cocaine is a stimulant derived from the coca leaf. It has been used in the United States for years and, prior to 1900, was an active ingredient in many soft drinks and patent medicines. Common feelings experienced by the person who has taken cocaine are hyperalertness, euphoria, and power. These feelings are short-lived, not over 30 minutes. For these reasons, cocaine is highly psychologically addictive, and individuals begin to want more and more the sensations they receive from cocaine.

Heavy use of cocaine can lead to weight loss, insomnia, and anxiety reactions. Paranoid thinking may also develop, as well as severe anxiety and depression when the effects of the drug wear off. Long-term use causes serious physical damage and can result in death. Because of its temporary effects, cocaine has become popular among professionals who are achievement-oriented and feel an obligation to be "up" constantly.

Learning
Objective 4

Identify substances that may be abused and their effects.

Commonly abused substances can be legal or illegal.

---

quick wit

"O, that men should put an enemy in their mouths to steal away their brains."

**William Shakespeare,
Othello**

Crack, the street name for a powerful form of cocaine, is smoked rather than sniffed through the nose or injected. Crack creates the same side effects as cocaine but is even more addictive.

The second most commonly abused substance in the U.S. is believed to be **marijuana.** Researchers are discovering that marijuana, the dried leaves and flowering tops of the distillate hemp plant, is a much more dangerous drug than was originally thought.

Marijuana produces relaxation, spontaneity (because of loss of inhibition), disorientation of spatial relationships, heightened (though not always accurate) sensory awareness, and hunger. It also causes immediate memory loss, impairment in thinking, and a loss of motivation. These effects can be particularly disruptive in the workplace. The heavy smoker is detached, cannot judge or concentrate, and is not motivated. Psychologically, heavy usage can cause "flashbacks" (viewing scenes from the past) and acute adverse reactions.

The physical effects of heavy marijuana usage are cause for concern. Regular marijuana use appears to cause lung and other types of cancer and respiratory diseases more rapidly than does cigarette smoking. In addition, it has an adverse effect on both the male and female hormonal balance and reproductive functions. THC, the active ingredient in marijuana, also possibly suppresses the immune system, leading to lower resistance to disease.

Sedatives (barbiturates) and **tranquilizers** include Seconal, Tuinal, Nembutal, Phenobarbital, Quaaludes, Glutethimide, Doriden, and Valium.

GLOBAL CONNECTION

Employees on overseas assignments need to be aware that the penalties for substance abuse in foreign countries can be vastly different—and usually far more severe—than those in the United States. Failure to respect the differences can result in jail time or worse.

1. *Should Americans working overseas be protected from foreign laws? Why or why not?*

2. *Where can you get information concerning views about alcohol and illegal drugs in other countries?*

Street names may be downers, ludes, barbs, yellow jackets, red devils, or blue devils. Methaqualone is also known as quaaludes, ludes, or sopers. Some of them are legal drugs that can be obtained with a prescription.

Sedatives and tranquilizers are depressants and can cause drowsiness, agitation, intellectual confusion, and physical impairment. Abusers may have slurred or emotional speech as well as poor body coordination. Overdoses can be characterized by difficulties in walking and speaking, constant uncontrolled eye movements, lethargy, and coma.

Amphetamines are synthetic nervous system stimulants. They have a number of street names, such as speed, ice, bennies, dexies, uppers, black beauties, meth, crystal, and pep pills. They are used to lose weight, stay awake, increase energy, and "get high." The physical effects are dilated pupils, rapid heartbeat, loss of appetite, anxiety, irritability, rapid speech, tremors, and destructive mood elevation.

Some drugs, called designer drugs, have been derived from amphetamines. Known by names such as ecstasy, eve, and rhapsody, they temporarily make people feel more alive and sensitive to people around them. However, research shows that these drugs destroy cells in the brain that produce dopamine, a vital nerve transmitter.

Inhalants are another category of abused substances. The practice of sniffing hydrocarbons contained in substances such as airplane glue, gasoline, cleaning fluid, and aerosols is prevalent among children 11 to 15 years old. Symptoms include restlessness, excitement, lack of coordination, confusion, and coma.

Long-term use of inhalants can cause damage to the brain, nerves, liver, and kidneys. Fatalities have occurred from suffocation caused when the abuser used a plastic bag to inhale the substance and lost consciousness.

Hallucinogens produce chemically induced hallucinations. The list of hallucinogens includes LSD (acid), mescaline, MDA, and PCP (or angel dust). The fact that these hallucinogens can create immediate emotional disturbances or cause flashbacks years later makes them particularly dangerous in the workplace. Symptoms include euphoria, loss of inhibition, agitation, confusion, stupor, and paranoia. Violent or bizarre reactions are not uncommon, and extreme doses can lead to convulsions, coma, or death. In addition, these drugs can reduce or eliminate inhibitions, potentially leading to dangerous, illegal, or lethal behaviors.

Narcotics include heroin, opium, morphine, dilaudid, and codeine. All are derivatives of the opium poppy. They can cause euphoria, sedation, nausea, vomiting, insensitivity to pain, watery eyes, and skin problems and infections. These drugs are physically addictive, and withdrawal causes painful physical symptoms. Death from overdoses is not uncommon.

quick wit
. . . .
Abstaining is favorable both to the head and the pocket.
. . . .
Horace Greeley

Many prescription and over-the-counter medications, such as cold remedies, can cause drowsiness, impairing an employee's ability to drive or operate machinery on the job. These drugs can also be abused. Employees operating equipment and taking medication should consult their supervisors.

We can readily see that abusing substances takes a toll on people's ability to perform as well as their physical and mental health. Those who are abusing substances need to seek help immediately.

*Fast*Chat

Many individuals believe marijuana should be legalized.

1. Do you believe it should be legalized? Why or why not?

2. If it were legalized, should employers be able to refuse to hire users, since it is likely to affect their performance?

3. Given the dangers and side-effects of marijuana and other drugs, would you want to work closely with someone who was using these substances? Why or why not?

What If You Are an Abuser?

If you are abusing substances, you need to take action before their use interferes with your current job, prevents you from obtaining a job, disrupts other major areas of your life, destroys your health, or kills you.

Substance Abuse Affects Many Life Areas.

Relationships
Individuals who abuse substances have difficulty maintaining healthy family relationships. Friends who do not abuse substances may avoid contact with the abuser, particularly at social functions, because the abuser often behaves in a fashion that causes embarrassment. Many substance abusers drop non-using friends in favor of those who also abuse substances.

Finances
Abusing substances is expensive, and an abuser may spend more than he or she earns to support the habit. In addition, the abuser may not pay attention to finances and may become careless with money.

Work
Performance may deteriorate, resulting in disciplinary action or termination. Friction with coworkers may become a problem as coworkers become irritated at the abuser for not doing a fair share of the work.

Health
Abusers develop health problems such as high blood pressure, deterioration of brain cells, depression, malnutrition, cancer, and cirrhosis of the liver.

Adapted from Robert B. Maddux and Lynda Voorhees, *Job Performance and Chemical Dependency*.

Check the telephone book for treatment and counseling centers. If you are employed and your company has an employee assistance program, use it. The program is designed to help employees with substance abuse and other personal problems. It is confidential and almost always free.

Many individuals are reluctant to use an employee assistance program for fear that their employer will learn they have a problem. Most plans ensure confidentiality and do not reveal to the employer which employees have used the services. Employers will eventually find out about substance abuse problems left untreated when performance declines.

Substance abusers need to seek help.

Seeking help is the first step in controlling a substance abuse problem.

Quick Tip . . . .

If you drink socially, take steps to ensure that your alcohol intake is under control and to keep it within responsible boundaries:

- Limit drinking to under one ounce of ethanol, the intoxicating ingredient in alcoholic beverages, on any day that you drink. (One-half ounce of ethanol equates to 12 ounces of beer, five ounces of wine, or one ounce of hard liquor.) Measure your alcohol when making your own drinks.

- Abstain completely from alcoholic beverages for at least two consecutive days each week.

- Drink slowly and intersperse alcoholic drinks with nonalcoholic drinks while at parties.

- Don't drink on an empty stomach.

- Don't medicate yourself with alcohol. It will only make you feel more depressed.

- Avoid social patterns that revolve around alcohol and associate with responsible drinkers or nondrinkers.

Human Relations

While some individuals are able to drink socially in moderation, others should not drink at all. Abstinence is usually the only way that recovering alcoholics and individuals from alcoholic families are able to prevent abusing substances. More information can be obtained from the National Council on Alcoholism, Alcoholics Anonymous, or other organizations that deal with alcohol abuse.

Do You Have a Problem with Alcohol?

1. Do you drink to relieve stress and escape problems?
2. Is it difficult to stop drinking once you start?
3. Are you, at times, unable to remember what was said or done while drinking?
4. Do you drink alone?
5. Do you find it necessary to drink larger quantities to obtain the same effect?
6. Is your drinking becoming a worry or concern to your family?
7. Is it necessary to have a drink to get over a hangover?
8. Is drinking interfering with your ability to perform your job?
9. Do you find yourself craving a drink at certain times of the day?
10. Does your personality change, causing you to become more moody, irritable, and harder to get along with while drinking?
11. Is your social life centered around activities that involve alcohol?
12. Has drinking become a daily necessity?

Yes answers to several of these questions may indicate a problem with alcohol.

If you do not take action to correct your substance abuse problem, most likely your supervisor will. Most organizations that operate drug testing programs have trained their supervisors to recognize behavior that signals substance abuse. These signs are listed in "How a 'Troubled Employee' Behaves," on page 506.

Many substance abusers deny having a problem and fail to realize that the problem is interfering with their work. Because of employee denial, organizations usually instruct their supervisors to do the following about suspected instances of substance abuse:

- Judge on performance only and do not accuse the employee of having a substance abuse problem.
- Do not accept excuses for prolonged poor work performance or absenteeism.

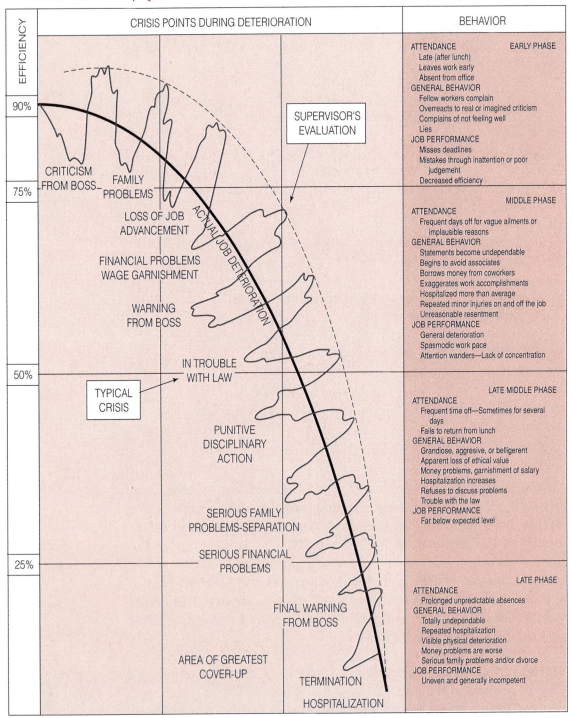

How a "Troubled Employee" Behaves

CRISIS POINTS DURING DETERIORATION	BEHAVIOR

EFFICIENCY

90%

CRITICISM FROM BOSS

FAMILY PROBLEMS

SUPERVISOR'S EVALUATION

75%

LOSS OF JOB ADVANCEMENT

ACTUAL JOB DETERIORATION

FINANCIAL PROBLEMS
WAGE GARNISHMENT

WARNING FROM BOSS

50%

IN TROUBLE WITH LAW

TYPICAL CRISIS

PUNITIVE DISCIPLINARY ACTION

SERIOUS FAMILY PROBLEMS-SEPARATION

25%

SERIOUS FINANCIAL PROBLEMS

FINAL WARNING FROM BOSS

AREA OF GREATEST COVER-UP

TERMINATION

HOSPITALIZATION

ATTENDANCE   EARLY PHASE
    Late (after lunch)
    Leaves work early
    Absent from office
GENERAL BEHAVIOR
    Fellow workers complain
    Overreacts to real or imagined criticism
    Complains of not feeling well
    Lies
JOB PERFORMANCE
    Misses deadlines
    Mistakes through inattention or poor
        judgement
    Decreased efficiency

                                       MIDDLE PHASE
ATTENDANCE
    Frequent days off for vague ailments or
        implausible reasons
GENERAL BEHAVIOR
    Statements become undependable
    Begins to avoid associates
    Borrows money from coworkers
    Exaggerates work accomplishments
    Hospitalized more than average
    Repeated minor injuries on and off the job
    Unreasonable resentment
JOB PERFORMANCE
    General deterioration
    Spasmodic work pace
    Attention wanders—Lack of concentration

                                  LATE MIDDLE PHASE
ATTENDANCE
    Frequent time off—Sometimes for several
        days
    Fails to return from lunch
GENERAL BEHAVIOR
    Grandiose, aggressive, or belligerent
    Apparent loss of ethical value
    Money problems, garnishment of salary
    Hospitalization increases
    Refuses to discuss problems
    Trouble with the law
JOB PERFORMANCE
    Far below expected level

                                        LATE PHASE
ATTENDANCE
    Prolonged unpredictable absences
GENERAL BEHAVIOR
    Totally undependable
    Repeated hospitalization
    Visible physical deterioration
    Money problems are worse
    Serious family problems and/or divorce
JOB PERFORMANCE
    Uneven and generally incompetent

Adapted from "How an Alcoholic Employee Behaves," © 1976 CompCare Publishers, Minneapolis, MN

Human Relations

- Document all poor performance.
- Assist employees in obtaining treatment if asked.
- Do not preach or moralize.
- Begin action up to and including discharge if the employee does not satisfactorily perform the job.

Employees with substance abuse problems should recognize that supervisors have support from higher management in taking these actions. Abusers should address their problem if they wish to remain employed.

Two federal laws can assist substance abusers in getting treatment and keeping their jobs. One is the **Americans with Disabilities Act** (ADA) and the other is the **Family Medical Leave Act** (FMLA). The Americans with Disabilities Act requires that employers with 15 or more employees give a reasonable accommodation to individuals with disabilities. Under the act, alcoholism is treated as a disability. However, employees who abuse alcohol may be disciplined and discharged when their alcohol use adversely affects job performance. Users of illegal drugs are not protected and can be discharged for drug use. Former drug addicts, however, are covered.

Individuals who voluntarily check themselves into a drug treatment center prior to being identified by the company as a substance abuser will most likely be protected by the act and be allowed a reasonable amount of time to pursue treatment.

The Family Medical Leave Act requires employers with 50 or more employees within a 75-mile radius to provide employees who have worked for the company at least 1250 hours in the past 12 months to provide 12 weeks of unpaid leave during a 12-month period for a serious health condition. Absence for treatment of substance abuse does qualify for FMLA leave.

As these laws and their interpretations rapidly change, anyone wanting protection for treatment under these laws or any state laws should check with the company's human resource department or obtain legal counsel.

Many employees refuse to use company-sponsored employee assistance programs for substance abuse or other problems.

1. Why do you think employees refuse to use company-sponsored assistance programs?

2. What other methods of treatment are available in your community?

3. Why is denial a problem when dealing with substance abuse?

FastChat

17.6 What If You Know an Abuser?

Learning
Objective   6

Explain the actions an employee can take when a coworker or supervisor is abusing substances.

Becoming aware that a coworker or supervisor is exhibiting the warning signs in "How a 'Troubled Employee' Behaves" presents a dilemma. If you allow such people to operate machinery or perform any activity that might injure them or others or destroy equipment or property and something actually happens, living with yourself will be difficult. If you report the individual to management, resentment will most likely result, causing future difficulties in working with this individual. Others in your work group may feel uncomfortable around you, feeling that you will report their activities to management.

Covering up for coworkers or supervisors by doing their work or making excuses for their tardiness or absence is called **enabling**. This behavior allows substance abusers to continue this conduct and to avoid confronting the problem. Enabling will keep peace in your work group. However, you will continue to perform extra work while the abuser carries on the pattern of missed hours and substandard performance. Resentment on your part will soon build.

Additionally, you may wish to assist the individual in trouble. You may give advice, preach, or moralize. This action generally does not help, because substance abusers typically deny that they have a problem. The more you attempt to help, the more resentful the substance abuser will become, frustrating both of you.

ETHICS CONNECTION

Employees who have drug habits may steal from employers.

1. **If you see a friend taking company property to support a drug habit, what would you do?**

2. **Would you report this same employee for stealing time? Why or why not?**

Dealing with substance-abusing coworkers and supervisors, then, requires human relations skills. Use tact and diplomacy, involving only those who need to know. Tell abusers that their behavior is making your working with them difficult. Point out a specific behavior, such as absence, that is causing you difficulty. Offer support by showing concern that they do not appear to be their old selves and asking what you can do to help. Be supportive if they decide to enter treatment.

Not allowing impaired employees to operate equipment, refusing to "enable" by covering for them, and not preaching or moralizing are the best ways to help yourself and your fellow employees. Both of you benefit: the abuser is forced into treatment quicker, and you won't be worried about potential disaster or feel that you're being used or taken advantage of.

Take action when a coworker abuses substances.

FastChat

Review the definition of "enable" in this chapter and the defense mechanism "denial" in Chapter 2.

1. Name some specific actions that are enabling.

2. Why does moralizing or advising an abuser to seek assistance normally not help?

Key Terms

substance abuse
Executive Order 12564
Federal Drug-Free Workplace Act
expected interval testing
random interval testing
"for cause" testing
treatment follow-up testing
alcohol
cocaine
marijuana
sedatives
amphetamines
tranquilizers
inhalants
hallucinogens
narcotics
Americans with Disabilities Act
Family Medical Leave Act
enabling

Summary

Organizations are concerned about substance abuse because abusers cost them money in the form of lost productivity, industrial accidents, and excessive use of benefits. Many companies are beginning to take action to control substance abuse by testing both prospective and current employees and by offering employee assistance programs and substance abuse education. A variety of testing schedules of current employees, such as expected interval testing, random testing, "for cause" testing, or treatment follow-up testing, are used to detect substance abuse.

Critics of drug testing point out that it is unconstitutional, humiliating, intrusive, and an invasion of privacy. False positives on tests are possible, and tests do not reveal when the drug was taken or the level of impairment. To reduce the chances of false positives, many companies follow testing procedures developed by the National Institute on Drug Abuse (NIDA).

Knowledge of the commonly abused substances can help you understand how, if you abuse or intend to abuse substances, you decrease your own productivity and threaten your health. Also, you can better recognize abuse in others and react appropriately. Commonly abused substances include alcohol, cocaine, marijuana, sedatives, tranquilizers, amphetamines, inhalants, hallucinogens, heroin, and prescription drugs. Individuals who are abusing substances need to take action to control their problem. If they do not, their supervisors may take action. Any employee confronted with a coworker who is abusing substances needs to take positive steps to handle the problem.

Review Questions

1. List the costs of substance abuse to organizations.
2. What are companies doing to combat substance abuse?
3. What three types of drug testing schedules do companies use?
4. What is the downside of drug testing?
5. What substances are commonly abused? What are their effects?
6. How does the substance abuser generally behave in the early, middle, and late phase of abuse?
7. What actions can an abuser of substances expect from a supervisor who has been trained to deal with substance abusers?
8. How can you handle a coworker who is abusing substances?

Discussion Questions

1. Review the effects of each of the major types of substances. Give examples of accidents or mistakes that the misuse of substances can cause on the job.
2. What difficulty would you have in handling a coworker and good friend who is abusing substances? What might happen to the coworker if you became an enabler, allowing him or her to continue in the abuse? What might happen to you? To others? To the company?
3. Should employers have the right to administer drug tests to employees? Why or why not?
4. What resources are available in your community to assist individuals in controlling substance abuse?
5. Study carefully the information in "How a 'Troubled Employee' Behaves." Have you ever been around individuals exhibiting some of these behaviors at work or at home? What happened to them? How did their behavior affect you? Others?

Chapter Project

Visit the web site for the Partnership for a Drug-Free America (www.drugfreeamerica.org). Research information presented concerning use of marijuana for medical treatment. In two groups—one supporting the pro position and one supporting the con position—make an opening statement and then debate the issue.

Applications

In small groups analyze the following:

Listening, speaking, reasoning, problem solving.

Opportunities Up in Smoke

Jane was excited. She was scheduled to start her new job Monday. It was a good feeling, after having worked so hard—two years in junior college and ten weeks of intensive searching for the perfect job. As she sat on the couch daydreaming about the new car she was going to buy, the phone rang. Suzette, the personnel officer who had interviewed her for the position, was on the telephone.

"I'm sorry, Jane," Suzette said, "but your drug test was positive. We can't hire you for the position."

Jane hung up and frantically called her boyfriend, Carl.

"It's not fair, " she sobbed. "I only smoked one joint at the party last week. I never dreamed it would show up on my test. That's just not fair!"

1. Was Jane's test fair? Should Jane have the right not to be tested? Should employers have the right to test her?
2. What could Jane's drug use cost the company in the future?
3. What did Jane's drug use cost her? What should Jane do in the future?

Problem solving, visualizing, reasoning, choosing an ethical course of action.

Liquid Lunches?

"Where's Harry? He was supposed to have returned from lunch an hour ago. He was going to give me the figures for the mid-year report. The report is due at 5 P.M. today," grumbled Albert.

"You know," said Yuki, "he's had many problems lately. He and his wife have separated. Give him a break."

"Yuki, it's more than that," replied Albert. "His lunches have gotten longer, and last week he didn't even come back after lunch. His work has gotten so bad that I don't know if I can cover for him any longer. If the boss finds out about this, she'll hit the ceiling."

1. What do you think may be happening to Harry?
2. What should Albert and Yuki do?
3. Are they helping Harry by covering for him?

Human Relations

Additional Readings and Resources

"Background Information: Workplace Substance Abuse." U.S. Department of Labor. (www.dol.gov/dol/asp/public/programs/drugs/backgrnd.htm)

Bahls, Jane Easter. "Dealing With Drugs: Keep it Legal." *HRM Magazine*, March 1998:106–116.

Bahls, Jane Easter. "Drugs in the Workplace." *HRM Magazine*, February 1998:81–87.

"Drug Use Among U.S. Workers." *Drug Abuse Prevention Network* newsletter. Volume 2, Issue 4, Winter, 1997, p. 2–4.

Friends of Recovery. *12 Steps: A Spiraul Journey (Tools for Recovery)*. New York: RLPI, 1994.

http://www.health.org/pubs/primer/drugtest.htm "Prevention Primer: Drug Testing in the Workplace."

http://www.usdoj.gov/dea Drug Enforcement Agency

http://www.dare-america.com Drug Abuse Resistance Education

http://www.nida.nih.gov National Institute of Drug Abuse

http://www.naadac.org National Association of Alcoholism and Drug Abuse Counselors

http://www.health.org National Clearinghouse of Drug and Alcohol Information

http://www.inhalants.org National Inhalant Prevention Coalition

http://www.well.com/user/woa Web of Addiction

Kuhn, Cynthia; Scott Swartzwelder; Wilkie Wilson; Jeremy Foster; and Leigh Heather Wilson. *Buzzed: The Straight Facts about the Most Used and Abused Drugs from Alcohol to Ecstasy*. New York: W.W. Norton and Company, 1998.

McGladrey & Pullen, LLP. *Mandated Benefits 1998 Compliance Guide*. New York: Panel Publishers, 1998.

National Institute on Alcohol Abuse and Alcoholism, No. 16 PH 315. April, 1992.

"New Developments in Drug Testing Technologies." *Drug Abuse Prevention Network* newsletter. Volume 2, Issue 4, Winter, 1997, p. 1.

"Substance Abuse Programs." The Bureau of National Affairs, Inc. Policy and Practice Series, 1999.

Thompson, Robert W. "Study Tallies Costs of Workers' Social and Problem Drinking." HR Online News, Society for Human Resource Management, 2/8/99.

Employee Rights:

Working Toward Mutual Respect

focus

After studying this chapter, you should be able to:

1. *Identify and discuss federal employment laws concerning discrimination, fair wages, and family and medical leave.*

2. *Explain how OSHA protects employees from safety and health hazards.*

3. *Name benefits available to employees and distinguish between those that are required and those that are optional.*

4. *Identify and discuss other employee rights at work.*

"Shoney's Inc." agreed to pay about 20,000 former and current employees a total of $18,000,000 to settle three class action disputes that alleged violations of the Fair Labor Standards Act. Managers and assistant managers were classified as exempt from overtime but treated as hourly employees.

BNA, Inc. *Bulletin to Management, April 1, 1999.*

What do you do if you think you are due overtime but not being paid? Where can you go to seek help?

In This Chapter

What Federal Laws Protect Workers?

Local, state, and federal laws regulate six aspects of employment. These regulations cover employment discrimination, family and medical leave, fair labor standards, employee safety and health, employee benefits, and miscellaneous employee rights. Both individuals and organizations need to understand these regulations.

Individuals should understand what their rights are and how to take appropriate action when those rights are violated. Sometimes employees assume they have rights on the job that they, in fact, do not. Problems may arise when employees act on these assumptions. The consequences can range from lost promotions or raises to disciplinary action or termination.

Organizations also need to be aware of, and respect, employee rights. Violating employee rights can lead to costly investigations by federal and/or state agencies. These investigations require the submission of paperwork and can disrupt the workplace by removing employees from the job to provide witness statements. In addition, employees may spend time discussing or worrying about the impending investigations rather than working. Violations may require payment of fines or back pay and reinstatement of employees. Payment for damages may be required as a result of a lawsuit. More important, employees whose rights are abused will be unhappy and less productive. Of course, ideally, we will treat people well and fairly because, not only is it a smart business tactic, it is the right thing to do.

Because laws in the area of employee rights change rapidly, both employees and organizations must keep track of changes. *Consult a lawyer for recent changes in legislation discussed in this chapter and for an explanation of state and local laws.*

EMPLOYMENT DISCRIMINATION

Abraham Lincoln abolished slavery on January 1, 1863, by signing the Emancipation Proclamation. However, the freed slaves continued to be deprived of their liberty and blocked in their pursuit of happiness through **discrimination**, or a difference in treatment based on a factor other than individual merit. A grassroots movement began in the 1950s, demanding that these inequities be corrected. As a result, several acts were passed to protect blacks and others against discrimination in the workplace.

Learning
Objective 1

Identify and discuss federal employment laws concerning discrimination, fair wages, and family medical leave.

quick wit

"[Our mission is] to protect the workers in their inalienable rights to a higher and better life; to protect them, not only as equals before the law, but also in their health, their homes, their firesides, their liberties as men, as workers, as citizens; to overcome and conquer prejudices and antagonism."

Samuel Gompers

Democracy arises
out of the notion
that those who are
equal in any respect
are equal in all
respects.

Aristotle

Federal law requires equal treatment of workers, regardless of color, religion, sex, race, age, or national origin.

Title VII of the Civil Rights Act of 1964, the Pregnancy Discrimination Act, the Equal Pay Act, the Age Discrimination in Employment Act, and the Americans with Disabilities Act were enacted to stop discrimination in the workplace. The **Equal Employment Opportunity Commission** (EEOC) is the federal agency responsible for enforcing these laws. These acts are briefly summarized below.

Title VII of the Civil Rights Act (1964) Title VII of the Civil Rights Act of 1964 prohibits discrimination by companies that have 15 or more employees. Discrimination based on race, color, religion, sex, or national origin is forbidden. All terms, conditions, and privileges are covered—hiring, placement, training, promotions, transfers, layoffs, compensation, and terminations. This act also prohibits sexual harassment.

ANYONE CAN DISCRIMINATE!

BIAS + INSTITUTIONAL POWER = DISCRIMINATION

Some employers attempted to get around Title VII by setting specific qualifications for a position. For instance, some police departments set height and weight requirements that effectively eliminated females from the position of officer. These practices were curbed by requiring a **bona fide occupational qualification** (BFOQ). The employer must show a legitimate business necessity for eliminating certain groups of individuals from a job. Requiring proof that restrictions are bona fide has limited the use of discriminatory occupational qualifications by employers. However, some restrictions have been found to be valid. For instance, a producer may hire only females for a female role in a movie. Legitimate age limitations may be placed on some occupations, such as airline pilot. The courts have ruled, however, that preferences, such as females for airline attendants, are not BFOQs.

Quick Tip

When determining whether you are being subjected to discrimination, remember the following:

- The law covers differences in treatment based on specific characteristics (such as race or gender). Adverse treatment because your boss "doesn't like you" or because you smoke is not covered by the law.

- Civil Rights laws do not promise good treatment or even fair treatment, only equal treatment. You can be treated badly yet still equally.
- A disability or pregnancy does not give you permission to be less productive than other individuals in the work place.
- Whether you have been sexually harassed depends on whether the behavior is "unwelcome." For example, you cannot complain about off-color jokes if you laugh at the jokes or join in telling them.

* *

Pregnancy Discrimination Act (1978)   The **Pregnancy Discrimination Act** is an amendment to the Civil Rights Act of 1964. An employer cannot refuse to hire a woman because of pregnancy as long as the woman is able to perform the job.

A pregnant woman may work as long as she is able to perform the job and may not be required to stay out a certain length of time after the baby is born. Federal law does not require that special considerations, such as light duty, be made for pregnant women. It does, however, require that pregnant women be treated the same as other employees who are temporarily disabled. If nonpregnant individuals are given light duty, pregnant individuals must be allowed the same privilege.

A company is required to hold a job open for a woman on maternity leave the same length of time that jobs are held open for other employees who are on sick leave or disability leave but are not pregnant. This law does not guarantee a position upon return from maternity leave. If the company routinely fills positions of individuals who are sick for other reasons, it may legally fill positions of women who are on maternity leave. Some states, such as California, require that a position be held open for a certain length of time after the start of maternity leave.

Equal Pay Act (1963)   The **Equal Pay Act** requires that men and women be paid the same for equivalent work. For instance, a male and female teacher with similar backgrounds and experience are to be paid equal salaries.

quick wit
* * * * * * * * * *

"We hold these truths to be self-evident, that all men and women are created equal."

* * * * * * * * * *

Elizabeth Cady Stanton

The inequities that the Equal Pay Act are designed to correct are not found as frequently in the workplace as they once were. However, a new issue, which revolves around the differences in salaries paid in traditionally female occupations versus salaries in traditionally male occupations, has emerged. This issue is known as **comparable worth**. For instance, a female-dominated position such as secretary that requires skills and responsibility may command lower wages than a male-dominated position such as janitor that requires fewer skills. This issue is expected to command more attention in the future.

Age Discrimination in Employment Act (1967) The **Age Discrimination in Employment Act** prohibits employers with 20 or more employees from discriminating based on age. The law covers individuals 40 years of age and older. As long as employees are able to perform their jobs, they cannot be forced to retire. However, an exception for highly paid corporate executives does exist.

Sexual Harassment Sexual harassment in the workplace is prohibited by the Civil Rights Act of 1964. **Sexual harassment** includes any *unwelcome* sexual advances, requests for sexual favors, or verbal or physical conduct of a sexual nature. Examples are telling sexually-oriented jokes, standing too close, touching and making physical contact, displaying sexually-oriented material, or making sexual comments about a person's body if these actions are unwelcome.

Either sex can commit sexual harassment. Men can harass women, and women can harass men. Additionally, men can harass men, and women can harass women. Harassment can be from a coworker, supervisor, an agent of the employer, or a nonemployee such as a repair person who comes on the company premises to perform work. Organizations are responsible for stopping the harassment from a coworker, nonemployee, or agent of an employer as soon as a management official becomes aware of the harassment. Furthermore, they are responsible for the harassment from a supervisor whether other management officials are aware of the harassment or not.

President Johnson signing The Civil Rights Act of 1964 into law.

CORBIS

The law requires that employers provide an atmosphere free of sexual harassment. However, employees must make it clear that the harassment is unwanted. The individual being harassed, for example, should tell the harasser in no uncertain terms that the comments or actions are not appreciated and to stop. If the harassment continues, the victim should report the harassment to a management official or the human resources department.

Employees must make clear that sexual harassment is unwelcome and report it immediately.

The Americans With Disabilities Act The **Americans with Disabilities Act** (ADA) prohibits discrimination against individuals who are disabled. Disabled individuals are those whose impairment (physical or mental) is severe enough to affect a major life activity. The individual with the disability must be able to perform the essential functions of the job, with or without reasonable accommodation. **Reasonable accommodation** is any action that assists the disabled employee without imposing undue hardship on the company. It may include making existing facilities accessible to individuals with disabilities; job restructuring; part-time or modified work schedules; reassignment to a vacant position; acquisition or modification of equipment or devices; appropriate adjustment or modifications of examinations, training materials or policies; the provision of qualified readers or interpreters; or similar accommodations for individuals with disabilities.

Civil Rights Act of 1991 **The Civil Rights Act of 1991** was passed in order to strengthen and improve Federal civil rights laws. The act provides for damages in cases of intentional employment discrimination. Among other changes, the Act reversed a number of Supreme Court cases that weakened Civil Rights legislation.

If you think you have been the victim of discrimination, you should attempt to settle difficulties within your organization before resorting to outside sources. If your company has a grievance or complaint procedure, use this process. If such a procedure is unavailable, approach your supervisor or a responsible individual in the human resources department. Explain your concerns and difficulties in a calm, clear manner, using the communication skills from Chapter 9. Listen carefully to the explanations of the company officials. External circumstances of which you are not aware may exist. Work with your organization in good faith, giving the company a chance to correct the problem. Such action on your part demonstrates a belief that a person, not the company, is the problem.

If the company will not take action, you should file a charge of discrimination with the Equal Employment Opportunity Commission or your state commission on equal employment. Employers, by law, cannot retaliate against individuals who have filed a charge of discrimination with the EEOC. However, companies can continue disciplinary action that is reasonable and expected and is administered to other employees not filing charges.

Trends in Employment Opportunity **Affirmative Action**, a practice originally designed to correct past discriminatory practices against minorities and women in the workplace by setting goals for hiring and upward mobility, has become increasingly controversial. Companies who do business

If companies do not take action, employees have the right to file charges.

quick wit

Injustice anywhere is a threat to justice everywhere.

Martin Luther King, Jr.

with the Federal government as well as many who do business with state and local entities are still required to develop and implement an affirmative action program. Currently the Supreme Court has ruled that these types of programs are constitutional only if they are "narrowly tailored" to remedy the lingering effects of past discrimination. However, the justices have not clearly defined how serious the effects must be to warrant favoring women and minorities in employment and contracting decisions. Increased dialog on this topic can be expected.

Valuing diversity advocates appreciating employee differences and the value they add to the company rather than ignoring differences and expecting everyone to think and act the same way. Because companies are beginning to realize that diverse workforces can be more productive than those that are not diverse, more emphasis in this area can be expected.

Lastly, current federal laws do not prohibit discrimination against gays and lesbians. Calls to prohibit this type of discrimination can be expected to increase in the future.

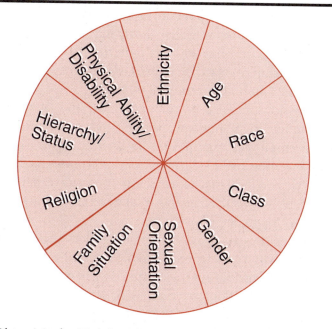

Key Dimensions of Workplace Diversity

Reprinted with permission from Workplace Diversity *by Katharine Esty, Richard Griffin, and Marcie Schorr Hirsch.* © 1995, Katharine Esty, Richard Griffin, and Marcie Schorr Hirsch. Published by Adams Media Corporation.

FAIR LABOR STANDARDS

As discussed in Chapter 1, the Industrial Revolution saw a major shift in the work force from farms to factories. Unfortunately, this rush to fill the rapidly multiplying factories with workers often meant that children and women were exploited. Young children worked the same hours as adults, sometimes 12 to 14 hours a day or all night, and often worked in unsafe conditions. They were paid less than adults, which tended to lower the adult wage. Women also were subjected to low wages and long hours of work. Public concern mounted, and states began to pass laws restricting child labor and providing a minimum livable wage.

The mass unemployment of the Great Depression of the 1930s brought a public outcry to regulate hours of work in order to allow more individuals to be employed. The result was the first national legislation to regulate working hours, wages, and child labor, which is known as the Fair Labor Standards Act.

The **Fair Labor Standards Act** of 1938, as amended in 1966, 1974, 1977, and 1985, sets the minimum wage, equal-pay, overtime, and child-labor standards for several types of employers and employees. These include employers engaged in interstate commerce or the production of goods for commerce and employees who are employed in enterprises engaged in commerce or the production of goods for commerce. Employers in retail and services whose sales volumes exceed a certain amount and agricultural workers are also covered. The minimum wage has slowly increased over the years. In 1981 it was set at $3.35 an hour and has risen to $5.15. A subminimum training wage allows employers to pay individuals under the age of twenty a training wage of $4.25 an hour for the first 90 days.

Overtime provisions require payment of time and one-half of the employee's regular rate for all hours worked in excess of 40 hours per week except for those employees exempted from overtime (see box on next page). This base rate must include incentive pay or bonuses received in that week. A workweek is considered to be seven consecutive days and may begin on any day of the week. State and local governments are allowed to pay compensatory time in lieu of overtime.

Individuals under 18 years of age are not allowed to work in hazardous occupations. Individuals 14 to 16 years old are allowed to work in industries other than manufacturing, but their duties cannot conflict with school. Exceptions to the age limitations are for newspaper carriers, farm workers, and wreath makers.

If you feel your rights to fair wages and hours have been violated, attempt to work it out with your employer first. If this attempt fails, contact the Wage and Hour Division of the Department of Labor.

Future Trends in Wage and Hour Issues concerning payment of overtime are developing as companies are forced to become more competitive in the workplace. Additionally, because of technology, work is becoming "virtual," enabling many employees to put in work hours away from the job.

Many organizations are finding that, even with requirements to pay overtime, working skilled employees more than forty hours a week is less expensive than hiring and training new workers. Also, employers, always anxious to reduce costs, want to able to offer compensatory time (time off for hours worked in lieu of pay), as state and local governments are allowed to do.

Furthermore, some professionals who are exempt from overtime are routinely putting in 70 to 80 hours a week. Many feel individuals working excessive hours are being exploited. Suggestions have been made to limit hours of work for everyone or to raise overtime pay to double pay.

Lastly, the idea of a livable minimum wage will continue to be an issue. Stories surface regularly of the working poor, who work 40 hours a week but earn so little that they are unable to afford decent housing or other basic necessities of life. Periods of inflation will further fuel this debate, as we search for a balance between the need for employers to remain competitive in the global economy and the need of the worker to survive.

FAMILY MEDICAL LEAVE

As the work force in the United States expanded with women, single mothers, and dual income families during the '60s through '80s, the need to balance

CASE STUDIES IN THE NEWS

Approximately two dozen cities in the United States have already passed "living wage" laws which typically require firms doing business with local government to pay higher-than-minimum wages. These laws are part of a large, growing campaign that could ignite a national debate about economic inequality and raising the U.S. minimum wage.

San Francisco lawmakers argue that anyone who works full time in a city-supported job should receive enough money to support a family without turning to charity.

1. *Do you think that the minimum wage provides a viable living in a large metropolitan area? Why or why not?*

2. *Who do you think makes up the majority of those earning minimum wage?*

3. *Do you think that jobs traditionally offered to minimum wage earners (mainly students or those with few skills) will disappear? Why or why not?*

4. *If companies are forced to pay more, what would be the effect on products you buy every day?*

work, health, and family responsibilities became more pressing. Many states began to pass laws designed to provide some sort of job-protected family or medical leave. Then, in 1993, the federal government addressed this need by passing the **Family Medical Leave Act (FMLA)**.

The FMLA provides that eligible employees be allowed up to 12 work-weeks of unpaid, job-protected leave within a 12-month period for

- The birth or adoption of a child
- The placement for foster care of a child under 18 if not disabled, or over 18 if child is incapable of self-care
- The care of a child, spouse, or parent with a serious health condition
- An employee's own serious health condition.

The leave can be taken consecutively or on an intermittent basis. Upon returning from leave, the employee, unless deemed to be a key employee, is entitled to return to the same position held before the leave or to a position that is equivalent in pay, benefits, privileges, and other terms and conditions of employment.

Eligibility Requirements for FMLA

To be eligible for a job-protected leave under FMLA, you must:

- Be an employee who has been employed for a total of at least 12 months by the employer on the date on which any FMLA leave is to commence
- Have been employed, on the date on which any FMLA leave is to commence, for at least 1,250 hours with the employer granting the leave during the previous 12-month period
- Be employed in any U.S. state, the District of Columbia, or any U.S. territory or possession
- Be an employee who is employed at a work site at which the employer employs more than 50 employees, within a 75 mile radius, measured by the shortest route using surface transportation

*Fast*Chat

The federal government has passed legislation that restricts who employers can hire and how much time off they need to give employees.

1. Should the government intrude on the decisions businesses make? Why or why not?

2. Are discrimination regulations still needed? Why or why not?

18.2 How Are Safety and Health Regulated?

Learning
O b j e c t i v e   2

Explain how OSHA protects employees from safety and health hazards.

Federal law requires employers to provide a safe work environment.

More than 14,000 workers were killed and over two million were injured in industrial accidents in 1970. Estimates suggested that 300,000 new cases of occupational disease were being discovered annually. These work-related injuries had steadily increased since the 1960s, and no end to this trend was seen. Although many companies were concerned with safety and taking action to provide their employees with a safe environment, these individual actions were not considered sufficient. The public demanded action, which came in the form of the Occupational Safety and Health Act.

The **Occupational Safety and Health Act** was passed in 1970 to "assure so far as possible every working man and woman in the nation safe and healthful working conditions and to preserve our human resources." The act sets health and safety standards for United States businesses. **Safety** standards address hazards that can result in a direct injury, such as broken bones and cuts. **Health** standards address the role of the work environment in the development of diseases and illnesses, such as asbestosis and black lung. (Black lung, or pneumoconiosis, is a disease coal miners acquire from breathing air filled with coal dust.) These types of diseases are known as occupational diseases.

The **Occupational Safety and Health Administration** (OSHA) was established as a federal agency to ensure that each employer provides a place of employment free of recognized hazards causing or likely to cause death or serious harm to employees. Almost all businesses that affect commerce (except government) are covered. However, only businesses with ten or more employers are required to keep records concerning occupational illnesses or injury.

OSHA establishes standards for safety and health in the workplace. These standards cover many facets of the work environment, such as training and safety procedures for operating hazardous machinery and equipment, instructions for handling dangerous chemicals, permitted noise levels, designation of protective equipment and clothing, and sanitation regulations.

In order to enforce the act, OSHA makes inspections of company sites. These visits may be unscheduled. Unscheduled visits may be in response to complaints of imminent danger or to deaths or catastrophes. Other visits are scheduled in advance. These visits can be prompted by a high injury rate

CORBIS

Companies are responsible for providing a safe work environment.

or a specific type of injury reported. Sometimes OSHA chooses a certain industry to monitor.

If violations are found during the visit, citations are issued. These citations must be posted in a public location in the workplace. In the case of gross violations, OSHA can secure a court order to close the facility. Failure to correct the infractions immediately can result in fines or jail sentences.

OSHA further requires that companies give employees access to certain information about the physical and health hazards of chemical substances produced, imported, or used in the workplace. This right-to-know regulation is known as **Hazard Communication Standard** (HCS).

Hazard Communication Standard (HCS) Requirements

- Establish a written hazard communication program to inform employees of the potential dangers of hazardous substances used or encountered in the workplace.

- Train employees to handle hazardous chemicals as well as emergency and first-aid procedures.

- Provide **Material Safety Data Sheets** (MSDS), which describe the chemical and the proper first aid treatment, and keep them where all employees have immediate access in an emergency.

- Place warning labels on all containers of potentially dangerous materials.

WORKING SAFELY

Every employee has a responsibility to follow OSHA and company rules concerning safety. If you work in an environment that requires goggles or a hard hat, your compliance with these regulations is extremely important. These measures may prevent your losing an eye or suffering a concussion. Even though workers' compensation helps support an employee who has been injured, payment in any amount can never make up for a lost hand or a damaged back. Specific tips for on-the-job safety are listed in Tips for Working Safely.

Tips for Working Safely

1. Observe all safety rules.

2. Wear personal protective equipment correctly.

3. Know how to operate all equipment properly. If you do not know, ask.

4. Check equipment before using to be sure it is in proper working condition.

5. Be alert for unsafe conditions.

6. Report any hazardous conditions or malfunctioning equipment immediately to your supervisor.

7. Do not participate in or condone horseplay while working in hazardous areas or while using equipment.

Accidents can be caused by incorrect lifting of equipment or supplies; careless operation of saws, lathes, or machinery with gears, pulleys, and belts; inattention while using hand tools; negligence while working with electricity; or falls on stairs, ladders, and scaffolds.

Office workers also need to be alert to safety. Time has been lost from injuries that occurred when file cabinets tipped over because too many drawers were opened at once. Falls on floors made slick by spilled coffee are another source of injury.

Those in the health care industry and those who deal with individuals in a variety of public settings need to follow guidelines on handling blood and other potentially infectious materials in order to minimize exposure risks to blood-borne pathogens such as hepatitis or human immunodeficiency virus (HIV).

OSHA also gives employees rights under the law. An employee may request an inspection and have a representative, such as a union member, accompany the inspector. Employees may talk to the inspector privately. In addition, regulations must be posted regarding employee rights under the act, and employees can have locations monitored for exposure to toxic or radioactive materials, have access to those records, and have a record of their own exposure.

Employees may have company medical examinations or other tests to determine whether their health is being affected by an exposure and have the results furnished to their personal doctors. Furthermore, employers may not retaliate against employees for exercising their rights under the Occupational Safety and Health Act.

If you ever feel unsafe on the job, you should discuss the problem immediately with your supervisor or the safety committee if your facility has an active one. Should you feel that the danger is life-threatening, you have the right, by law, to refuse to work. If the problem cannot be resolved by working through the company, you should, of course, contact OSHA.

FUTURE HEALTH AND SAFETY ISSUES

Health and safety will continue to be areas of concern for both employers and employees. Employers, faced with spiraling insurance and worker compensation premiums, will be searching for ways to reduce employment-related injuries and diseases, usually through the use of protective equipment and/or training in safe work habits. Furthermore, fit employees are more productive employees, adding incentives for organizations to provide a healthy work environment.

Of particular interest is developing an ergonomics standard to try to reduce the cumulative trauma disorders (repetitive stress injuries) that cost $15 to $20 billion annually in workers' compensation costs. Commonly reported are strained muscles, sprained joints, and carpal tunnel syndrome.

Some employees still work in unsafe environments.

1. Why do some employers fail to provide a safe working environment?

2. Why do some employees fail to work safely?

3. What is your responsibility when you see someone working unsafely or notice an unsafe working condition?

FastChat

What Benefits Are Available to Employees?

Learning
Objective   3

Name benefits available to employees and distinguish between those that are required and those that are optional.

Most employers must provide social security, unemployment compensation and workers' compensation.

Traditionally, care of those too infirm or too old to work was left to charitable organizations or to families. This method of caring for those unable to help themselves worked fairly well in an agrarian society where an extra mouth could be supported by planting another row of crops or raising extra livestock. However, urbanization and industrialization began to put a strain on the ability of individuals to care for extended families. Some organizations initiated benefit programs for their employees, but the majority of employees were left without assistance.

The Great Depression intensified the crisis, leaving a great many individuals without work and unable to provide the basics for themselves, much less for their dependents. As a result, legislation was enacted that required organizations to provide retirement benefits, benefits to those who became unemployed, and compensation to those injured on the job.

FEDERALLY MANDATED BENEFITS

Social Security   The **Social Security Act** was passed in 1935 and has been amended many times since. Social Security benefits include retirement insurance, survivor's insurance, disability insurance, and Medicare. These benefits are mandatory for approximately 95 percent of all United States workers. The benefits are summarized in the figure on the next page. Social Security was founded to replace a portion of earnings lost as a result of old age, disability, or death—not all lost wages.

Social Security is funded through payroll taxes. Effective January 1998, employees contribute 7.65 percent of their salary up to a $68,400 maximum. The company matches this contribution. Regardless of the number of companies for whom an employee works, benefits will accumulate in the employee's account. Anyone who is self-employed must pay both the employee's portion and the company match for this tax.

The Social Security program is administered by the Social Security Administration. You may contact the Administration to review your earnings statement to be sure that your earnings have been correctly recorded and to inquire about details of benefit programs.

Job Loss Compensation   **Unemployment compensation** was created by the Social Security Act of 1935 to assist those who became unemployed

Social Security Benefits

Who May Draw Retirement Benefits

1. Individuals who are fully insured and at least 62 years old.
2. Wife or husband of retiree if age 62 or older.
3. Wife or husband under age 62 if he or she is caring for retiree's child who is under age 16 or disabled.
4. Children of retiree if under 18 or disabled.
5. Divorced spouse if 62 or over and married ten years or more.

Who May Draw Disability

1. Individuals who have a physical or mental impairment that lasts or is expected to last one year or more or expected to end in death and who meet the requirements for being insured.
2. Dependents of the disabled individual.

Who May Draw Survivor's Benefits

1. Widow or widower at 60 (50 if disabled) or any age if caring for entitled children, under 16 or disabled, of a fully insured wage earner.
2. Divorced widow or widower if married over ten years or if caring for entitled child.

Who May Be Covered by Medicare

1. Insured individuals age 65 and over.
2. Disabled individuals who have been entitled to Social Security benefits 24 or more months.
3. Insured workers and their eligible family members who need dialysis or kidney transplant because of permanent kidney failure.

Consult your local Social Security office or the Social Security website (http://www.ssa.gov) for details concerning wage credits needed to be fully insured and specific requirements for drawing benefits.

until they could find another job. The federal government set up minimum standards for unemployment compensation, and the states developed their own standards around the minimums. For this reason the state agency governing unemployment compensation should be contacted concerning specific benefits and qualifications.

In most instances employees who quit voluntarily are unable to receive unemployment compensation. Employees also are denied benefits in most states if they have been discharged for misconduct. Misconduct is discussed in the figure on page 532.

Individuals receiving unemployment compensation must be actively seeking employment and must accept suitable employment when offered. States may interpret these terms differently; therefore, you should consult your local unemployment agency when you have specific questions.

What Is Misconduct?

Misconduct	Not Misconduct
Not performing work after having demonstrated ability to do the work.	Laid off due to lack of work.
Deliberate damage to equipment; willful failure to follow safety rules.	Incompetence, the genuine inability to do the work.
Unreasonable or excessive use of obscene language in violation of employer's rules.	Justified absences and tardiness.
Excessive and unjustified absences and tardiness; failure to inform supervisor.	Refusal to work in unsafe working conditions.
Lying; stealing; using equipment without permission of supervisor.	Significant changes in the hiring agreement.
Not obeying reasonable rules and following reasonable orders.	Not receiving payment for your work.
Unjustified assault on coworker or supervisor.	Quitting on your doctor's advice.
Spending too much time socializing at work after being told not to.	Medically verifiable illness, injury, disability, or pregnancy of claimant or claimant's minor child.
Refusal to work on the weekend unless it is for religious reasons covered under religious discrimination laws.	Quitting to care for a minor child if required for a documented medical reason.
	Failure to obey unreasonable rules and follow unreasonable orders.
	Justified assault on coworker; self-defense.
	Associating with coworkers or marrying coworker in violation of employer's rules.

The unemployment compensation system is funded through employer taxes. The amount of tax depends on the total wages and the number of former employees drawing unemployment compensation. For this reason employers have an incentive to keep undeserving former employees from drawing unemployment benefits.

Compensation for Injury on the Job Workers' compensation is a system that compensates individuals who have been physically or mentally injured on their jobs or who have developed an occupational disease. The compensation can include cash payments, reimbursement for medical costs, and, in some cases, the costs of rehabilitation for the employee or compensation for survivors of an employee killed on the job.

Employers are required either to purchase insurance to cover workers' compensation or to become self-insured, and state regulations vary on how they can acquire coverage. Employers do, however, have an incentive to reduce injuries, because injuries mean not only lost time from the job but higher premiums.

Each state has its own compensation laws. Federal employees are covered by the Federal Employees' Compensation Act, and federal coverage is extended to maritime workers on navigable waters of the United States. As with unemployment insurance, the state agency should be contacted for specific details.

Benefits Employers Voluntarily Offer

Employers typically offer a number of benefits voluntarily. They have found that attractive benefit packages help draw and keep qualified employees, allowing them to remain competitive in the workplace. The variety of benefits that may be offered by employers is listed in the figure on the next page. These benefits may be paid for in part or in full by the employer. An employer may give employees a choice of benefits so that they can design their own benefit packages. All benefits together, mandatory and optional, can average as much as 35 percent of salaries.

Voluntary plus mandatory benefits can amount to 35 percent of an employee's salary.

In 1974 the federal government enacted the Employee Retirement Income Security Act (ERISA). This act regulates benefit plans for health insurance, group life insurance, sick pay, long-term disability income, pension plans, profit sharing plans, thrift plans, and stock bonus plans. It sets legal standards around which employee benefit plans must be established and administered. In addition, ERISA requires that employees be given a summary plan description and have access to plan financial information. Plan termination insurance, which guarantees benefits if certain types of retirement plans terminate, is another provision of ERISA.

If you have questions concerning your benefits or options, consult your supervisor or the human resources department. The company will have literature or other information that will explain the benefits available in detail.

The Future of Benefits   Employee benefits will be a controversial topic in the twenty-first century. An aging work force will bring with it the need to revise Social Security regulations that specify how much work an employee is allowed to perform and still draw benefits. Funding can be expected to continue to be an issue because of the large number of individuals who will be drawing benefits. Currently the social security fund is solvent until the year 2034 if no tampering with the funds is allowed.

Voluntary Company Benefits

Financial Plans
Pension plans
Profit sharing
Thrift plans
Employee stock ownership plans
Individual retirement accounts

Insurance
Health—hospital, medical, dental,
   vision, prescription drug
Life insurance
Disability insurance

Payment for Time Not Worked
Vacation
Holidays
Sick leave

Other Benefits or Services
Housing or moving assistance
In-house health services
Flexible work hours
Parental leave
Child care programs
Social or recreational services
Educational assistance
Employee assistance plans
Legal services
Financial planning
Assistance or discounts on purchasing
   food or other goods
Credit unions
Medical savings accounts
Transportation services
Wellness programs
Concierge and personal benefits
   services

Already a crisis is brewing concerning medical benefits offered by employers. Many are hiring only part-time workers in an effort to avoid paying medical insurance premiums. Others are shifting the burden of rising premiums to employees. In a further effort to reduce medical costs, some insurance carriers are dropping the amount of coverage allowed on some claims, which leaves the employee paying an increasing share of medical bills. On the positive side, employers are offering more wellness programs as a way to reduce medical costs—which is better for both employees and the health care system.

*Fast*Chat

Most companies offer more benefits than are legally mandated.

1. Why do companies offer extra benefits?

2. Would you work for a company that did not offer vacation time? Why or why not?

What Are Other Employee Rights?

Learning
Objective 4

*Identify and discuss
other employee
rights at work.*

In general, our rights as employees differ from those we have away from the workplace. Understanding our rights as employees is crucial to functioning in the work world. Using sound communication and human relations skills is important as we attempt to work out problems on the job.

The rights of employees of governmental bodies and union members are usually better defined than those of other employees. The rights discussed in the following sections are controversial at this time. Many areas are gray and subject to change. Changes in rights evolve from court and arbitration decisions. At times, court cases can be inconsistent, with one court deciding for an issue while another court rules against it.

As an employee, you should be aware that standing on principle over some of the issues discussed below may result in termination. A court case may be needed and years may pass before the case comes to trial.

State and local law varies in the areas discussed below. *Consult a local legal expert for additional details in these areas of the law.*

**The principle of
employment at
will is eroding in
the United
States.**

Employment at Will   **Employment at will** means that an employee serves at the discretion of an employer and can be terminated at any time for any reason even if the employee is performing well. The employee also has the right to quit at any point. Presently the legality of this practice is in question, and the law is rapidly changing in this area. In general, most states support the concept of employment at will. However, employees who have contracts or implied contracts should consult an attorney, since recent decisions have favored employees in cases where "at will" statements in employee handbooks or on contracts have been unclear.

The exceptions to employment at will are individuals who assert their rights under certain federal legislation, such as the equal employment laws, Occupational Health and Safety Act, Fair Labor Standards Act, Vietnam Era Veterans Reemployment Act, Clean Air Act, and Federal Juror's Protection Law. These people cannot be terminated for exercising those rights.

Courts have also ruled that employees cannot be terminated for filing for workers' compensation benefits, obeying a subpoena, leaving for jury duty, refusing to participate in an employer's lobbying efforts, or reporting an employer's illegal acts.

Proof of Eligibility to Work The Immigration Reform and Control Act (IRCA) of 1986 bans employment of unauthorized aliens and requires employers to document the identity and authorization to work for all new employees. Employers are required, within three days of hire, to complete an employment eligibility verification form called an I-9 on all new employees. The documents that may be used for identification are listed in the figure below.

New employees must prove their identity and their authorization to work.

All individuals seeking employment should be sure that they have the correct documentation to provide proof of authorization to work in the United States. If you have any questions concerning your documentation, consult the Immigration and Naturalization Service.

Establishing Authorization to Work in the United States

List A Documents that Establish Identity and Employment Eligibility	List B Documents that Establish Identity	and	List C Documents that Establish Employment Eligibility
1. U.S. Passport (unexpired or expired)	1. Driver's license or ID card issued by a state or outlying possession of the United States provided it contains a photograph or information such as name, date of birth, sex, height, eye color, and address		1. U.S. social security card issued by the Social Security Administration (*other than a card stating it is not valid for employment*)
2. Certificate of U.S. Citizenship (*INS Form N-560 or N-561*)	2. ID card issued by federal, state, or local government agencies or entities provided it contains a photograph or information such as name, date of birth, sex, height, eye color, and address		2. Certification of Birth Abroad issued by the Department of State (*Form FS-545 or Form DS-1350*)
3. Certificate of Naturalization (*INS Form N-550 or N-570*)	3. School ID card with a photograph		3. Original or certified copy of a birth certificate issued by a state, county, municipal authority or outlying possession of the United States bearing an official seal
4. Unexpired foreign passport, with *I-551 stamp or* attached *INS Form I-94* indicating unexpired employment authorization	4. Voter's registration card		
5. Alien Registration Receipt Card with photograph (*INS Form I-151 or I-551*)	5. U.S. Military card or draft record		

Employees must provide either one document from List A OR one document from List B and C.
This list is an abbreviated list. Consult the Immigration and Naturalization Service for a list of alternative documents (http://www.ins.usdoj.gov).

Human Relations

Freedom of Speech Public employees, in general, cannot be terminated for speaking on matters of public concern. This right, however, can be limited if the speech interferes with the efficient operation of the government. They can be terminated for speaking on matters of personal interest.

Public employees are not allowed to campaign for people who will become their bosses. The Hatch Act was passed in 1940, limiting the political activity of federal civil servants. Many states and large cities have passed their own Hatch acts.

The rights of free speech for private employees vary from state to state. Some states offer broad protection, whereas others offer little or none. In general, individuals in high positions in a company have fewer rights than individuals at lower levels. The potential impact of statements coming from individuals in higher positions of authority or prestige is greater.

AIDS AIDS (acquired immunodeficiency syndrome) is one of the most serious health problems facing this country today. The disease destroys the body's ability to fight other diseases that eventually kill the AIDS victim. Though the disease is, on the whole, relatively easy to avoid and is far less common than other killers like cancer and heart disease, it causes so much fear because it is inevitably fatal and because, to date, no known cure has been found.

According to the Surgeon General, AIDS cannot be transmitted through normal everyday contact at work. An employee cannot acquire it from saliva, sweat, tears, urine or bowel movements, a kiss, clothes, a telephone, or a toilet seat. AIDS is transmitted through sexual contact with someone infected by the AIDS virus, by sharing drug needles and syringes with an infected person, by a mother with AIDS to her baby before or during birth, or through transfusion of infected blood. Individuals cannot acquire AIDS by giving blood, and the chance of receiving the virus through a blood transfusion has been greatly reduced.

Employers cannot require that an employee with AIDS leave the workplace while still able to work, and are required to make reasonable accommodations, if necessary. Additionally, a company faces substantial legal risk in revealing that an employee has AIDS and in testing new or current employees for AIDS.

Defamation of Character **Defamation** is the open publication of a false statement tending to harm the reputation of a person. If the statement is oral, it is called slander. If it is in writing, it is called libel. If you feel that your character has been defamed, consult an attorney to determine your rights.

"The liberty of the individual must be thus far limited; he must not make himself a nuisance to other people."

John Stuart Mill

The rights of AIDS victims to work are generally given priority over the rights of coworkers.

Truth is considered a defense in defamation charges. Most courts consider a statement protected if it is made in good faith in the discharge of a public or private duty to someone else who has a corresponding interest, right, or duty. For instance, if a security guard reported to the manager and assistant manager that an employee had attempted to steal the employer's property, the courts would most likely not consider this action defamation of character.

Smokers' Rights   Courts are tending to side with the rights of nonsmokers. At present an employer may totally forbid smoking on the job and discriminate against smokers by not hiring them. Some companies that do not totally ban smoking may identify smoking and nonsmoking areas. Often this is prompted by local ordinances that require the designation of nonsmoking and smoking areas in the workplace.

Medical Benefits   The **Health Insurance Portability and Accountability Act** (HIPAA) was passed in 1996 to provide greater portability of employee health care coverage, allowing employees leaving an employer health plan to have access to the new employer health plan without waiting periods or limitations because of preexisting conditions or health status. In addition, the **Consolidated Omnibus Budget Reconciliation Act** (COBRA) requires employers with 20 or more employees to extend healthcare coverage to employees and dependents for 18 to 36 months in situations in which they would no longer be eligible for coverage. The individual must pay 102 percent of the premium, at a minimum.

Employee files store documentation on performance and behavior on the job.

Personnel Files   Employers are compelled to protect themselves from charges of discrimination and unjust punishment or termination. Many rely on documentation in the personnel file to protect themselves in this area.

Employees can expect to find reprimands, warnings, or write-ups concerning performance or behavior in their files. Most states allow access to personnel records by employees at reasonable times. Some states allow employees to correct documents or remove erroneous materials or insert explanations of disputed materials. Employees should consult their employee handbook and state laws to determine whether access to their personnel files is allowed.

Drugs on Personal Time   Currently the courts do not give employees in private enterprise many rights in this area. Terminations of employees who test positive for drugs whether used on or off the job are upheld. Governmental employees have more rights concerning drug testing than those in private industry. Even though some drugs can stay in the system up to 72 hours after use, the courts have made no allowances for use of drugs on personal time.

Search of Work Areas   In general, employers have the right to search employee packages, files, desks, and cars in order to prevent theft and to control operations. Court restrictions on search and seizure are limited, particularly if the employer has warned employees that they are subject to search.

Employers can generally search work areas at will.

Polygraphs   The Employee Polygraph Protection Act of 1988 prohibits most private employers from using lie detector tests to screen applicants. The tests cannot be the sole reason for discharge and can only be used if a reasonable suspicion of guilt exists. Because polygraph use is limited, some employers have turned to the use of pencil and paper tests concerning honesty and substance abuse in order to screen job applicants.

"Just sign this paper agreeing to let us invade your privacy, and then empty your pockets on my desk."

Companies are concerned with employee honesty for several reasons. First, employers lose billions of dollars yearly through employee theft. Then, substance abusers cost companies billions of dollars more in higher benefit costs, lower productivity, and absenteeism. Additionally, because of the "negligent hiring theory," employers can be held liable for crimes that an employee commits on the job if they fail to screen the employee for past misdeeds or personality quirks.

Currently these tests are legal, and employers can use them to make decisions concerning hiring and firing. However, many see the tests as intrusive, subjective, and unreliable. Employers who administer these types of tests may offend potential applicants and send a message to future employees that they are not trusted.

Plant Closings The Worker Adjustment and Retraining Notification Act of 1988 requires that plants with 100 or more workers give 60 days advance notice of a shutdown affecting at least 50 workers. Layoffs of more than one-third of the work site employees for more than six months must also be announced in advance.

TECHNOLOGY CONNECTION

Technology has now made it possible for employers to monitor employees' locations in the workplace—or on the road, if the employee is, for example, driving a delivery truck—at all times. In addition, today's technology makes possible monitoring of telephone conversations, keystrokes on the computer, and Internet access.

1. Should employers have a right to monitor the activities of workers? Why or why not?

2. Why do you think an employer might feel the need to monitor employees?

3. Would you work for an employer that required you to wear a badge to track your location on the work site? Why or why not?

Dress Codes   Dress codes that are reasonably related to the business needs of the company and that are clear, consistently enforced, and communicated have generally been upheld by courts and arbitrators. Some reasonable accommodation, however, must be made if the employee asks to deviate from the dress code for religious reasons.

Blowing the Whistle on Illegal Activities   This protection is generally afforded by law only to federal and state employees. These employees cannot be terminated for reporting illegal activities within their organization.

Electronic Surveillance of Employees   Currently employers may legally survey employees electronically, particularly if they have advised the employees that surveillance may occur without the employees' knowledge and that refusal to permit it may be grounds for discipline. Some companies have employees sign waivers, others post copies of search policies. Some companies perform electronic surveillance to prevent theft and reduce unproductive time of employees not closely supervised. Employers may eavesdrop with hidden microphones and transmitters attached to lockers or telephones that pick up office conversations or spy with pinhole lenses in walls and ceilings. Some companies record the length of telephone calls, when the calls were made, and where the calls were placed. They may also monitor the content of the telephone calls.

E-mail Privacy   Currently e-mail communications are not private and can be subject to subpoena. Even e-mails that have been erased can be retrieved.

Future Rights   The future will most likely bring extensive changes in the area of miscellaneous employee rights. As technology becomes more sophisticated and inexpensive, enabling companies to perform even more thorough surveillance on employees, a push to curb this "big brother" type of activity will most likely occur. Additionally, the courts are expected to continue to move away from the employment at will doctrine, granting employees even more rights.

Employers may legally survey employees electronically to prevent theft and reduce unproductive time.

1. Have you benefited from any of the rights listed in this section? Which ones, and how did you benefit?

2. How can strong human relations skills help you avoid having problems with any of the elements covered by these rights, either as an employee or as an employer?

Summary

Various federal, state, and local laws regulate the workplace. Federal laws protect employees from discrimination based on race, religion, sex, color, age, national origin, and disability. Health and safety of workers is regulated through the Occupational Safety and Health Act. Federal laws also mandate fair labor standards, family and medical leave, retirement, disability, survivor's benefits, and unemployment compensation through the Social Security Act. State laws control compensation for employees injured or killed on the job.

Many employers offer additional benefits, such as health insurance, retirement, savings plans, or child care. These benefits, along with required benefits, can average up to 35 percent of an employee's salary.

In general, miscellaneous employee rights at work differ from those enjoyed away from the job. Public employees tend to have better-defined rights than private employees. Employees should learn what they can and cannot do in their locale.

Key Terms

discrimination
Equal Employment Opportunity
    Commission
Title VII of the Civil Rights Act
    of 1964
bona fide occupational qualification
    (BFOQ)
Pregnancy Discrimination Act
Equal Pay Act
comparable worth
Age Discrimination
    in Employment Act
sexual harassment
Americans with Disabilities Act
reasonable accommodations
Civil Rights Act of 1991
affirmative action
valuing diversity
Family Medical Leave Act
Fair Labor Standards Act
Occupational Safety and Health Act
safety
health
Occupational Safety and Health
    Administration (OSHA)
Hazard Communication Standard
Material Safety Data Sheets
Social Security Act
unemployment compensation
workers' compensation
employment at will
AIDS
defamation
Health Insurance Portability
    Accountability Act
Consolidated Omnibus Budget
    and Reconciliation Act

Review Questions

1. Which federal laws regulate discrimination in the workplace? What types of discrimination do they prohibit?
2. What is OSHA? How does it protect employees' safety and health?
3. Which major laws regulate fair labor standards? Explain them.
4. Identify three benefits that are required by law and five that may be offered voluntarily to employees.
5. What miscellaneous rights do employees have at work?

Discussion Questions

1. Review the employee rights discussed in the last section of the chapter. Do you think employees should have more rights or fewer rights?
2. Have you ever been confronted by an unsafe working condition on the job? What did you do about it?
3. Should an employer have the right to search your work area?
4. Social Security was not intended to support fully individuals who have lost income through death, disability, or retirement. Explain what other benefits companies provide to help fill the gap. Have you begun to plan for your retirement? Why or why not? If so, how?
5. Do you agree with the teenage training wage? Why or why not?
6. Does your school or place of work have designated smoking areas? Should smoking be banned altogether? Why or why not?
7. Should employers be able to tell you what to wear to work? Why might an employer care about what you wear?
8. What are your feelings about electronic surveillance in the workplace? Should employers have the right to monitor employees to see that they are working during business hours and to assess the quality of their work?

Speaking, listening, reasoning, interpreting and communicating information.

Chapter Project

Divide into two groups. Debate the following statements, one side supporting the statement and the other side opposing it.

1. Studies show that companies with diverse work forces are more productive than companies that are not diverse. Nevertheless, companies should have the right to hire and promote whom they wish.
2. An employee has no obligation to report discrimination.
3. Employees should have the right to say anything they wish at work.

Human Relations

Applications

It's Your Thing: Do What You Want To Do?

Dora had been employed at Seymour's Shop for five years. She and her supervisor, Herbert, had been at odds for months. Dora thought that he was obnoxious and disliked his ordering her around and making demands.

Dora began to complain about Herbert to others in her group. She criticized his decisions to Manuel and made fun of his clothes when talking to Chen Lee. Other workers began to pick up on this behavior and made fun of Herbert behind his back.

One evening Dora noticed Herbert in the cafe across the street from the office. A young woman was with him. The next day she reported this scene to the group, and they began to speculate concerning the woman's identity and why she and Herbert were together. Dora and the group were standing in front of the water fountain, laughing and talking, when Herbert walked up.

"Dora, I want to see you in my office right now," he said abruptly. Dora followed him in and Herbert shut the door. "Dora, I'm going to have to let you go because you are a troublemaker. Every time I turn around, you are in someone else's office gossiping and interrupting work. You are causing too much trouble."

Reasoning, responsibility, self management, sociability, exercising leadership.

1. What employer right did Herbert exercise?
2. Should Dora have been allowed freedom of speech? Was the issue really about freedom of speech? How would you have felt if you were Dora? How would you have advised Dora to behave?
3. How would you have felt if you were Herbert? What might happen to a company if employees were allowed to disrupt business and undermine authority? What are some other things Herbert might have done, even if he still ended up having to fire Dora?
4. How do you think the other members of the group will react?

Equal and Fair Are Two Different Things

"I've had it," Carmelita said as she sat down next to Emilio. "That Elvin is a real monster. He yells at me, returns my work, and makes me do it over. He's always telling me that I'm stupid when I make mistakes. He makes me so nervous that I can't think straight. I'm tempted to go to the EEOC and file charges on him. I don't think he likes Hispanics."

"I know what you mean," Emilio said. "He chewed me out in front of the whole office. I was so embarrassed that I felt like hiding."

Just then Jan walked up and joined the conversation.

Problem solving, visualizing, reasoning.

"You can try EEOC if you want," Jan said. "But he treats everyone that way. I was in Alice's office yesterday when Elvin told her what a simpleton she was because she had incorrectly added some figures. He threw the report on her desk, yelled 'Do it right or else!' and stormed out. Alice is white and she gets that treatment. I guess he treats everybody equally!"

1. What discriminatory treatment do federal laws prohibit? Would they be applicable to Carmelita and Emilio?
2. Does being treated equally mean that you will be treated fairly or as you would like to be treated?
3. How do you think Carmelita and Emilio might handle the situation?
4. Do any governmental regulations dictate the type of treatment to be received by employees?

Additional Readings and Resources

Bureau of National Affairs. *Bulletin to Management*. April 1999, Vol. 5, No. 13, p. 98.

Bureau of National Affairs. *Human Resources Library on CD*. February 1999.

DeBare, Ilana. "Living-Wage Wildfire; Cities Ponder Laws to Raise Workers' Pay." *The San Francisco Chronicle*, Business, p. 1B.

Dutton, Wayne N., Robert J. Rabin, and Lisa R. Lipman. *The Rights of Employees and Union Members*. Southern Illinois University Press, 1994.

"Ergonomics Proposal Prompts Flurry of Action." *HR News*. April 1999, p. 4.

Esty, Katharine; Richard Griffin, and Marcie Schorr Hirsch. *Workplace Diversity*. Holbrook: Adams Media Corporation, 1995.

Fick, Barbara J. *The ABA Guide to Workplace Law*. Time Books, 1997.

"HR Issues Overshadowed by Data Privacy Concerns." *HR News*. March 1999, p. 1.

http://www.dol.gov/ Web site of the U.S. Department of Labor

http://www.eeoc.gov Web site of the U.S. Equal Employment Opportunity Commission

http://www.osha.gov Web site of the Occupational Safety & Health Administration

Lash, Steve. "High Court Won't Hear Reinstatement Appeal on Affirmative Action." *Houston Chronicle*, March 30, 1999, 2A.

Lewin, Joel G. *Every Employee's Guide to the Law*. Pantheon Books, 1997.

McCladrey & Pullen, LLP. *Mandated Benefits 1998 Compliance Guide*. New York: Panel Publishers, 1998.

Maintaining Balance:

Wellness and Achievement

focus

Dr. John Dunlap, an Overland Park, Kansas, general internist, has noted a remarkable increase in patients seeking help for fatigue, headaches, gastrointestinal distress, and other complaints that can't be linked to an identifiable medical illness. Dr. Dunlap has concluded that it's a manifestation of stress and that much of it relates to the job.

The Kansas City Star, **January 31, 1999**

Should companies try to do something about employee stress? Is the problem of job stress getting worse?

After studying this chapter, you should be able to:

1. *Define a wellness program and describe the benefits to both employer and employee.*

2. *Identify some of the physical and mental effects of stress and learn ways to minimize these effects.*

3. *Describe several methods of effective time management.*

4. *Discuss the importance of maintaining proper health practices.*

In This Chapter

A **wellness program** is a total approach to health care and well-being that addresses the emotional and physical health of individuals or groups. Individuals who pursue health tend to be happier, are more productive, suffer less illness, and have a lower risk of developing serious disease.

Organizations are becoming increasingly interested in the wellness of their employees, not only because it increases productivity but also because it reduces insurance costs. Dr. Roy J. Shephard of the University of Toronto notes that the cumulative benefit of wellness programs has been estimated at between $500 to $700 per worker per year, enough to cover the cost of a modest wellness program. Additionally, it has been shown that an exercising worker is generally a happier and certainly a healthier worker. For these reasons both individuals and organizations are interested in programs that address total health.

Of course, these days people are becoming increasingly aware that a complete wellness plan includes an understanding of stress. The United Nations International Labor Organization estimates that U.S. employers lose $200 billion a year in increased absenteeism, decreased productivity, and higher health insurance costs because of stress alone. Additionally, this UN group estimates that stress is behind an estimated 15 percent of workers' compensation claims.

Companies operate a variety of programs to encourage wellness. These programs fall into the broad categories of health education, employee assistance (discussed in detail in Chapter 13), early disease detection programs, and fitness programs.

Health education programs are designed to educate employees about various health issues such as smoking, nutrition, back injuries, weight management, cancer prevention, diabetes, seat belt safety, and exercise. For instance, F&M Bank and Trust in Tulsa, Oklahoma, has a "Heart at Work Program" to inform employees how to prevent heart problems and to learn the signs of a heart attack. Other companies spread information through health fairs, seminars, or printed materials such as newsletters or brochures.

Early disease detection programs provide employees with free or reduced-cost screening for health problems such as breast cancer, diabetes, high blood pressure, and high cholesterol. Frequently, companies bring these tests to the job site in order to increase employee participation.

CASE STUDIES IN THE NEWS

The National Institute for Occupational Safety and Health (NIOSH) reports that work stress is enormously costly, both in terms of workers' well-being and corporate profitability. For this reason, NIOSH recommends combining organizational change and stress management to achieve the most effective results. Currently 50 percent of large companies in the United States provide some kind of stress management training for their employees.

Some companies provide fitness centers with a variety of exercise equipment or have other facilities that encourage physical activity, such as outdoor walking tracks. Offering reduced price memberships to community fitness centers is another method of encouraging physical activity. Also, many companies sponsor employee bowling, golf, or softball leagues and walking clubs. In addition to being fitter, employees who exercise may be avoiding serious illness. For example, statistics show that active people have a lower risk of cancer than their inactive counterparts.

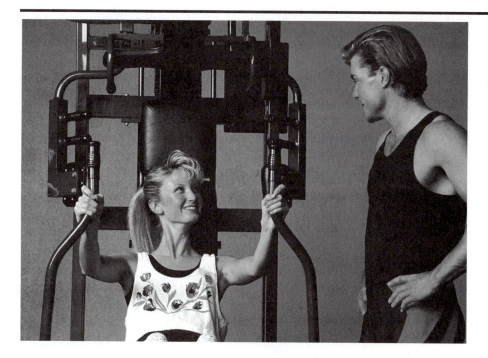

Exercise is encouraged in corporate wellness programs.

A total wellness program can help employees deal with stress and other health-related matters.

"In this stress test, we're going to hook you up to a fax machine, voice-mail unit, and a 56K modem."

Experts report that it is difficult to get workers to participate in work site wellness programs.

1. Why do you think workers do not participate?

2. What do you think companies could do to encourage workers to participate?

3. Would you participate? Why or why not?

What Is Stress?

Stress is a physical response to environmental pressures. Basically any challenge, physical or psychological, triggers a stress reaction. The body reacts the same to both physical and psychological challenges—the mind actually prepares the body for some activity in response to the external stimuli. Stress is an unavoidable effect of living. Indeed, we could not live without stress. However, if stress is too powerful, or our defenses are inadequate, physical or mental disorders may result. Generally, today, the problem is that, with the rapid pace of daily life and the pressures that seem to be ever present, we are constantly under stress, and have no time to re-energize.

Learning
Objective 2

Identify some of the physical and mental effects of stress and learn ways to minimize these effects.

ORIGINS OF STRESS

Stress is not a new phenomenon, though the term "stress" was only applied relatively recently to humans. The reaction now called stress was first recognized on the battlefield in the Civil War. Nervous and anxious reactions in the form of heart palpitations were so common among fearful soldiers that they became known as "soldier's heart." Stress was called "shell shock" during World War I and "battle fatigue" during World War II.

These reactions, in fact, existed in prehistoric times. When faced with possible danger, the autonomic nervous system responded by preparing early humans to face the situation with additional strength, energy, and endurance. Stored sugar and fat poured into the bloodstream to provide fuel for quick energy, breathing speeded up to provide more oxygen, and blood-clotting mechanisms were activated to protect against injury. Muscles tensed for action, digestion slowed to allow blood to be directed to the muscles and brain, pupils dilated to allow more light to enter the eye, and hormone production increased to prepare them either to fight or to run for safety. This response to anxiety is commonly known as the "fight or flight response."

Modern humans respond similarly to the pressures and demands of daily events. For example, you may worry or feel anxious about juggling family and job responsibilities, the local school board election, a career-limiting mistake you made at work, or a wreck you nearly had on the freeway. In each of these instances, your body reacts in much the same way early humans reacted to a wild animal or attacking enemy. A series of biochemical changes occurs, and the body's system is thrown out of balance.

Physiological reactions occur in stressful situations.

In today's society you can seldom fight or flee in these situations. The physiological responses get turned on without being used for the intended

purpose. The body is unable to release its stored energy because aggressive behavior would not be appropriate in most social situations. Repeated or chronic preparation for action without the action following can lead to stress-related diseases and disorders.

STRESS OVERLOAD

Stress can be caused by either good or bad events. Holidays, weddings, births, and moving into a new house are examples of pleasant events for most people that are usually very stressful as well. The death of a loved one,

TECHNOLOGY CONNECTION

E-mail is the communication work horse of the twenty-first century, allowing instant communication around the world. Junk e-mail and unnecessary messages are quickly becoming a problem, swamping workers and wasting precious time. Also, address lists that copy everyone on every message quickly clog electronic mail boxes. With so many other things to do, e-mail ceases to look like a convenience and starts to be an additional source of stress.

1. *What can individuals do to control the volume of junk e-mail?*

2. *Should companies regulate e-mail? Why or why not?*

Human Relations

divorce, being fired from work, or just experiencing trouble on the job are negative events that cause stress. Since stress is, by definition, a challenge, then challenges such as exams, sports competitions, or anything that includes competition can induce a stress response. Even simple daily stressors have an effect on your body. Fights with the kids, a missed bus, a flat tire, traffic, a rush job at work—all these small stressors add up. And those are just the emotional stressors. Physical stressors, which can range from poor nutrition to allergies to illness, add to the load. Chemical stressors, too—such as too much caffeine, cigarette smoke, or any other substances that affect the body's response systems—can also contribute to becoming "stressed out."

Are You Suffering from Symptoms of Job Stress?

If you are suffering from these symptoms, you may be suffering from job stress that could pose a threat to your health.

- Increased absenteeism
- Reduced civility
- Physical ailments
- Sleep dysfunction
- Reduced human interaction

quick wit

Tips for relieving stress

- Pop some popcorn without putting the lid on the pan.
- Make a list of things to do that you have already done.
- Fill out your tax form using Roman numerals.
- Drive to work in reverse.
- Read the dictionary upside down and look for secret messages.
- Write a short story using alphabet soup.

PHILIPPINE ROTARY, The Philippines. Quoted in *The Rotarian*, April 1999, p. 19.

Some experiences are obviously more stressful than others. Often, the same type of experience will be more stressful to one person than to another. Regardless of the varying intensities of the experience, each person has a limit, or a stress threshold, to the amount of stress that can be handled physically and psychologically.

As stress builds up, people will experience an overload, which results in negative symptoms or behaviors. Overeating, loss of appetite, overindulging in alcohol, ulcers, temper tantrums, headaches, hypertension, and heart disease are common results of stress overloads. Additionally, a decrease in the ability to concentrate, memory problems, insomnia, anxiety, depression, and other personality changes may accompany stress overloads. In fact, estimates are that as any of 75 percent of all medical complaints are stress-related illnesses.

Learning to deal with stress, then, can literally be a matter of life or death. A total wellness program can help you deal with stress and other health-related matters. It should include effective time management, proper diet, no smoking, exercise, relaxation, and other leisure activities. It also involves changing stressful thoughts, attitudes, and behaviors.

*Fast*Chat

Stress seems to be a way of life in today's society.

1. Do you believe modern technology has increased stress on the job? Why or why not?

2. Do you expect stress at work to continue to increase or to begin to decrease?

3. Can companies lower stress and still be competitive?

How Can You Manage Time?

Time is a precious commodity. Every individual is given the same amount of time each day to be wasted or well spent. How we choose to use our time makes the difference in whether or not we achieve our goals. Effective **time management** is simply maximizing the time that we have to our greatest advantage. When we are in control of our time, we perform better, feel better about ourselves, and suffer fewer stress-related illnesses. We can develop better time management by assessing how we use time, identifying how we waste it, and planning to use it better.

Learning
Objective 3

Describe several methods of effective time management.

ASSESSING HOW YOU SPEND YOUR TIME

The first step in assessing whether you are managing your time wisely is to determine if you are suffering any of the negative symptoms of poor time management. These negative symptoms are:

Symptoms of Poor Time Management

1. *Indecision*. You have so much to do that you cannot decide what to do first. You end up doing nothing and getting nowhere.

2. *White rabbit habit*. "I'm late, I'm late, for a very important date" accurately describes your life. Like the rabbit in Lewis Carroll's *Alice's Adventures in Wonderland*, you are always in a hurry, running late, and missing appointments and deadlines.

3. *Stress illnesses*. Responses to the pressures of poor time management include headaches, backaches, insomnia, and hives.

4. *Irritability and anger*. You stay angry and upset and have a tendency to take your frustration out on others.

Negative symptoms may make you look "out of control" and keep you from getting results. Good time management tends to be reflected in a confident and controlled approach to activities.

Another valuable step in assessing your time usage is to keep a time log, as illustrated in the Sample Time Log on page 557. Use a log for at least a one-week period. Logging your daily activities for this length of time will allow you to identify your major time-wasters. You may be surprised at the

Assess the effects of poor time management and then correct it.

amount of time you spend on innocent activities that rob you of using your precious commodity more productively.

IDENTIFYING TIME WASTERS

Lack of planning, drop-in visitors, telephone games, procrastination, meetings, over commitment, fighting brush fires, personal disorganization, the inability to say "no," and television are among the most frequent time-wasters. You may recognize some of them as being at the top of your list. Methods of handling some of the biggest time-wasters are described below.

Lack of Planning   An old adage appropriate to this situation states, "If you fail to plan, you plan to fail." Planning a course of action is crucial in accomplishing your goals. One of the easiest methods of planning is to make a list of tasks to be accomplished. Ideally, you will have a daily list of five to ten major actions in order of importance. Limiting your list to five to ten items enables you to add unexpected or forgotten items while keeping the list manageable. The important point is to stick to your list and not overcommit. Carry over any unfinished tasks to the next day and integrate them into that day's priority list. An effective way of handling your priority list is to keep it on a calendar throughout the year. This practice also provides you with an excellent record of your activities.

Time	Planned Work	Telephone	Interruption	Meeting	Unplanned/New	Reports	Other	Subject	Originator (Person)	Priority A	B	C	Other	Comments
7:30														
7:45														
8:00														
8:15														
8:30														
8:45														
9:00														
9:15														
9:30														
9:45														
10:00														
10:15														
10:30														
10:45														
11:00														
11:15														
11:30														
11:45														
12:00														
12:15														
12:30														
12:45														
1:00														
1:15														
1:30														
1:45														
2:00														
2:15														
2:30														
2:45														
3:00														
3:15														
3:30														
3:45														
4:00														
4:15														
4:30														
4:45														
5:00														

Priority Definitions:
A-Very important; high priority item
B-Important; have more time to complete
C-Less important; could be delegated or rescheduled for later time
Other-Could "not do;" wasted time

DIAGNOSTIC TEST: YOU AND TIME

	OFTEN	SOME-TIMES	RARELY
1. Do you handle each piece of paperwork only once?	❏	❏	❏
2. Do you begin and finish projects on time?	❏	❏	❏
3. Do people know the best time to reach you?	❏	❏	❏
4. Do you do something everyday that moves you closer to your long-range goals?	❏	❏	❏
5. When you are interrupted, can you return to work without losing momentum?	❏	❏	❏
6. Do you deal effectively with long-winded callers?	❏	❏	❏
7. Do you focus on preventing problems before they arise rather than solving them after they happen?	❏	❏	❏
8. Do you meet deadlines with time to spare?	❏	❏	❏
9. Are you on time to work, to meetings, and to events?	❏	❏	❏
10. Do you delegate well?	❏	❏	❏
11. Do you write daily to-do lists?	❏	❏	❏
12. Do you finish all the items on your to-do lists?	❏	❏	❏
13. Do you update in writing your professional and personal goals?	❏	❏	❏
14. Is your desk clean and organized?	❏	❏	❏
15. Can you easily find items in your files?	❏	❏	❏
Subtotal	_____	_____	_____
	×4	×2	×0
Total	══════	══════	══════

What the Test Says About You

Give yourself 4 points for every *often* you checked. Give yourself 2 points for every *sometimes*. Give youself 0 points for every *rarely*.

Add your points together and place youself in the proper group.

49–60   You manage your time well. You are in control of most days and most situations.

37–48   You manage your time well some of the time. However, you need to be more consistent with time-saving strategies. Adding new techniques is allowed!

25–36   Yor are all too often a victim of time. Don't let each day manage you. Apply the techniques you learn here right away.

13–24   You are close to losing control and probably too disorganized to enjoy quality time. A new priority-powered time plan is needed now!

0–12   You are overwhelmed, scattered, frustrated, and probably under a lot of stress. Put the techniques in this book into practice. Star chapters —for special study—that treat your problem areas.

Another useful method of planning is to use your "peak times" for tough tasks. You may be a morning person or a night person. Our body clocks, or biological rhythms, do tick strongest at different times of the day for each person. Recognizing your peak performance time may assist you in planning your more difficult tasks for that time to maximize your effectiveness. For instance, if you are a morning person, you will want to complete a difficult report early in the morning rather than waiting until late afternoon when you are not as alert.

Another time-saving tip is to plan certain activities for their nonpeak times. For example, banking on Friday afternoons will most certainly cost you more time than a midweek visit. Attempting postal business during your lunch break will find you in long lines with other individuals who had the same idea. A mid-morning or afternoon visit to the post office will probably save you time.

Drop-in or Casual Visitors Friends and colleagues may unwittingly rob you of precious time needed to meet personal or professional commitments. That drop-in visit from the coworker down the hall to discuss the Monday night football game may disrupt your concentration on an important report due by noon to your boss or throw your daily schedule completely off track. To control such intrusions, close your office door if you have one. If this signal is not successful, use your body language to show that you are busy or stand up and start toward the door. Additionally, the following phrases can be useful in controlling the length of visits:

GLOBAL CONNECTION

Americans perceive time as linear, with a past, present, and future. Because of this Americans are future oriented and prepare for it by saving, wasting, making up, or spending time. On the other hand, many other cultures treat time as a limitless pool in which certain things happen and then pass. Things come and go, as do the seasons.

1. **How can these differing views cause problems in the global workplace?**

2. **Have you ever been exposed to a different culture's concept of time? If so, what happened?**

"I appreciate your stopping by, but. . ."

"I have a tight schedule; could we talk about this on. . ." (and set a time and date)

"I have about 10 minutes before I have to go. . ." "How can I help you today?"

Telephone Games   You may have been involved in a game of "telephone tag" or applied evasive tactics with "Gabby Gerty. " The game of telephone tag—two people calling numerous times, leaving messages but never reaching each other—can take hours of unproductive time. This "game" can be avoided in several ways. Leave a message specifying what you want or leave instructions concerning required actions. If someone you need does not return your call, you might try leaving a message such as, "Unless I hear from you by close of business today, I plan . . . " This warning will normally prompt action by the other party. If all else fails, try to get your information elsewhere.

An encounter with "Gabby Gerty" involves receiving a call from someone who wants to discuss everything but the important purpose of the call. The following phrases may help control the length of time you spend on these calls:

"I appreciate your call, but. . ."

"I'm working on a term paper due this week. Can we visit later when I am not so pressed for time?"

"Could you call back when we might have more time?"

Procrastination   One of the most difficult time-wasters to control is your own procrastination. **Procrastination** is defined as putting off or intentionally delaying activities that need to be done. Once you understand the problem, you can develop methods of overcoming it. Chapter 10 and the box entitled Major Causes of Procrastination present some of the reasons we procrastinate and describe when delaying is appropriate or inappropriate.

We often have hidden meanings in what we say.

We occasionally find ourselves saying and meaning two different things:

Saying:		Meaning:	
	I really should . . .		I don't really want to . . .
	I can't do . . .		I won't do . . .
	I might . . .		I won't . . .
	I'll try to . . .		I won't . . .
	Could we discuss this some other time?		I really don't *ever* want to talk about it.

Major Causes of Procrastination

Inappropriate Causes	Appropriate Causes

Inappropriate Causes

- *Perfectionism*: You put off tasks until you can do them exactly right, the very best you can. You fear they won't be right or good enough.

- *Abdication*: You wait for things to "happen" rather than *make* them happen; you make panic decisions; you let someone else make the decision; you do nothing at all.

- *Overwhelmed*: Job/task appears too big to handle. It seems threatening.

- *Uncertainty*: You are unsure how to do the task.

Appropriate Causes

- *Stressed/exhausted*: You are too tired to think through the problem effectively. You might make a poor or wrong decision. You tend to use bad judgment and may wind up doing it over again.

- *Impulsive/emotional*: You might make snap judgments or might do things in a fit of anger and regret them.

- *Lack of Information*: You need more facts to make a good decision.

- *Feel cautious/concerned*: You heed a subconscious message that you should not do that activity.

Quick Tip

Try tackling procrastination by using the following suggestions:

1. Tackle tough problems at your body's peak performance times.
2. Break large tasks into smaller segments, so they will not seem overwhelming.
3. Use daily "to do" lists and set specific goals.
4. Fight perfectionism.
5. Seek help if needed.
6. Let go of low priority tasks in order to focus and concentrate on high priority ones.
7. Schedule appropriate blocks of times to do specific tasks.
8. Establish a reward system for positive reinforcement.

MANAGING YOUR TIME AT MEETINGS

Quick Tip . . . .

Try these guidelines for running an effective meeting:

1. Provide advance agendas reflecting timed subjects.
2. Invite only those people who are needed.
3. Start on time.
4. Set clear goals/purposes for the meeting.
5. Set time limits on the meeting and discussion topics.
6. Strictly adhere to your agenda.
7. Record and assign action items during the meeting.
8. Distribute meeting minutes within 48 hours.
9. Schedule an action-item follow-up.

. . . .

Hidden agendas can waste your meeting time.

A **planned agenda** is an outline or list of what is to be discussed or accomplished during the meeting. The agenda is a valuable tool for controlling your meeting. Ideally, an agenda should be distributed several days prior to the meeting time. People will be able to schedule their time to support the meeting and prepare information that may be needed. The agenda will serve as your guideline for a smooth transition from topic to topic and prevent the introduction of hidden agendas. A **hidden agenda** consists of topics that attendees wish to discuss that have no relevance to the purpose of your meeting. A hidden agenda can be disruptive:

Quick Tip . . . .

"Selling is like chopping wood. You must do many things to get ready to chop wood. Buy only the actual chopping really counts. You must prepare the workplace, walk to the woodpile, select a log, return to the workplace, position the log, raise the axe, split the wood, pick up the pieces; then return to the woodpile to repeat the cycle. Which action is truly significant? Splitting the wood, of course. If you don't split the wood, there's no point in the rest. If you can figure a way to split the wood without the other activities, you still have the achievement."

—Mehdi Fakarzadah

. . . .

Human Relations

As the meeting leader, you have the responsibility for adhering to the planned agenda. A successful meeting should move quickly, sufficiently cover all scheduled topics in the shortest possible time, and accomplish the planned meeting objectives.

To manage time outside of meetings, you may want to develop some definite action plans. The Sample Time Management Action Plan below provides you with a format and brief example of an action plan.

Change Required:	*Quit watching excessive TV*
Desired Result:	*Be more productive; read more, watch less*
Target Date:	*Within a week*
Actions Required:	*Unplug TV*
Key People Involved:	*Family—they won't like it*
Evaluate/modify:	*Did I achieve desired results? If not, try another approach*

Sample time management action plan

Read the Quick Tip by Mehdi Fakarzadah. Often we spend time "efficiently" but are not "effective."

1. What is the difference between *efficient* and *effective*?

2. Do you take time to determine what really matters and concentrate on that activity? Why or why not?

What Practices Will Help You Maintain Your Health?

Learning
Objective 4

Discuss the importance of maintaining proper health practices.

Your eating patterns affect your mental and physical condition.

Sound health practices are vital to a successful career. You can take responsibility for your own health by eating a balanced diet, maintaining an appropriate weight, limiting alcohol consumption, not smoking, and developing a mindset that allows you to relax and enjoy leisure time while limiting stressful thoughts, attitudes, and behaviors.

A Balanced Diet   The United States Department of Agriculture (USDA) recommends that we eat a balanced variety of foods to get the nutrients we need and at the same time the right amount of calories to maintain healthy weight. Their suggestions can be found in The Food Guide Pyramid.

Weight Management   Overweight and obesity have been associated with increased risk of developing such conditions as high blood pressure, Type 2 diabetes, and coronary artery disease. To determine whether you are at risk because of your weight, determine your Body Mass Index (BMI) by using the chart below. Then, using your BMI and waist size, determine your health risk relative to normal weight.

The Food Guide Pyramid

U.S. Department of Agriculture http://www.nal. usda.gov:8001/py/ pmap.htm

A Guide to Daily Food Choices

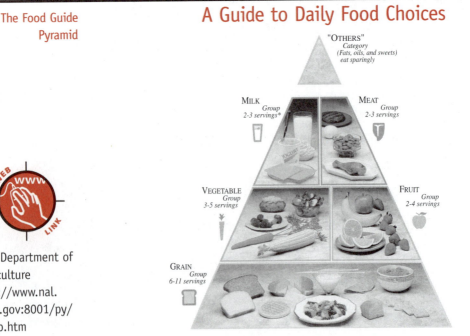

"OTHERS"
Category
(Fats, oils, and sweets)
eat sparingly

MILK
Group
2-3 servings*

MEAT
Group
2-3 servings

VEGETABLE
Group
3-5 servings

FRUIT
Group
2-4 servings

GRAIN
Group
6-11 servings

Find your height in the left-hand column. Move across that row to your weight. The number at the top of the column is the BMI for that height and weight.

BMI (kg/m²)	19	20	21	22	23	24	25	26	27	28	29	30	35	40
Height (in.)	Weight (lb.)													
58	91	96	100	105	110	115	119	124	129	134	138	143	167	191
59	94	99	104	109	114	119	124	128	133	138	143	148	173	198
60	97	102	107	112	118	123	128	133	138	143	148	153	179	204
61	100	106	111	118	122	127	132	137	143	148	153	158	185	211
62	104	109	115	120	126	131	136	142	147	153	158	164	191	218
63	107	113	118	124	130	135	141	146	152	158	163	169	197	225
64	110	116	122	128	134	140	145	151	157	163	169	174	204	232
65	114	120	126	132	138	144	150	158	162	168	174	180	210	240
66	118	124	130	136	142	148	155	161	167	173	179	186	216	247
67	121	127	134	140	146	153	159	166	172	178	185	191	223	255
68	125	131	138	144	151	158	164	171	177	184	190	197	230	262
69	128	135	142	149	155	162	169	176	182	189	196	203	236	270
70	132	139	146	153	160	167	174	181	188	195	202	207	243	278
71	136	143	150	157	165	172	179	186	193	200	208	215	250	286
72	140	147	154	162	169	177	184	191	199	206	213	221	258	294
73	144	151	159	166	174	182	189	197	204	212	219	227	265	302
74	148	155	163	171	179	186	194	202	210	218	225	233	272	311
75	152	160	168	176	184	192	200	208	216	224	232	240	279	319
76	158	164	172	180	189	197	205	213	221	230	238	246	287	328

Body weight in pounds according to height and body mass index

Risk of Associated Disease According to BMI and Waist Size			
BMI		Waist less than or equal to 40 in. (men) or 35 in. (women)	Waist greater than 40 in. (men) or 35 in. (women)
18.5 or less	Underweight		N/A
18.5–24.9	Normal		N/A
25.0–29.9	Overweight	Increased	High
30.0–34.9	Obese	High	Very high
35.0–39.9	Obese	Very High	Very High
40 or greater	Extremely Obese	Extremely High	Extremely High

BMI calculators and other nutrition resources can be found on-line at http://wvda.org, www.healthstatus.com, and www.ftc.gov/bcp/conline/pubs/health/setgoals.htm

Put a pot of chili on the stove to simmer.

Let it simmer. Meanwhile, broil a good steak.

Eat the steak. Let the chili simmer. Ignore it.

Recipe for chili from Allan Shivers, former governor of Texas

Limiting the Consumption of Alcohol Alcohol abuse leads to health risks such as suicide and alcohol-related fatalities and accidents, fetal alcohol syndrome, liver damage, and other physical impairments. These health risks were more fully detailed in Chapter 17. Elimination of or at least moderation in the consumption of alcohol is an important part of any wellness program.

Smoking Cigarette smoking is the single most important preventable cause of death in our society. Cancers of the lung, larynx, oral cavity, esophagus, pancreas, and bladder; heart and blood vessel disease; chronic bronchitis; and emphysema have all been linked to smoking. Additionally, involuntary or passive inhalation of cigarette smoke can cause or worsen symptoms of asthma, cardiovascular and respiratory diseases, pneumonia, and bronchitis. Smoking during pregnancy has been associated with premature births, small or underweight babies, and respiratory and cardiovascular problems in infants. Besides these physical implications, smoking is also a major contributor to death and injury from fires and other accidents.

In an effort to curb smoking-related problems, most states have passed legislation limiting or forbidding smoking in enclosed public places. Smoking has been banned on domestic air flights, and more nonsmokers today are demanding and obtaining smokefree environments at work and in public areas. Asking someone not to smoke around you should be done tactfully.

Giving up the smoking habit takes determination. Smoking often serves as an outlet for nervousness. The habit of smoking can become psychologically addictive. Nicotine, a key ingredient in cigarette smoke, is physiologically addictive, making it even more difficult to stop. Many programs designed to help people stop smoking are available. They are often provided in total wellness programs, and many are covered by medical insurance.

Exercise can play a key role in relieving stress and controlling weight.

Exercise Exercise is one of the most effective methods known for reducing stress. Although it is not a cure-all, exercise releases the stored energies of the "fight or flight" response. Moderate running, swimming, biking, racquetball, and basketball are all good forms of exercise for reducing stress. Regardless of which exercise form you choose, fitness experts recommend a minimum of 20 minutes of continuous exercise, three or four times a week.

However, lighter forms of exercise can be equally effective stress reducers. Working in the garden, mowing the yard, playing ping pong or pool, or taking a brisk walk can disengage you from the sources of stress. These exercises provide a "mental break."

Exercise need not be dull or seem like a chore. Its benefits, such as relieving tension, helping control weight, and lowering cholesterol, can be obtained through small changes in your personal routine. You do not have to be an accomplished athlete or a physical fitness expert to achieve desired results through exercise. In addition to establishing a regular exercise program at home or at a gym, you might consider changing simple daily habits. The following small changes in your lifestyle can increase your physical activity:

1. Use the stairs rather than the elevator.
2. Park your car at the back of the parking lot and walk to the store.
3. Put more vigor into everyday activities.
4. Take a walk each day at lunchtime or after work, and keep walking shoes in your car for these occasions.
5. Go dancing or join a square dance club.
6. Use the restroom on a different floor at work and take the stairs.

Before starting any exercise program, however, you should consult a physician to determine what is appropriate for your age and physical condition.

Relaxation   Learning the art of relaxation is crucial to controlling stress. Headaches, backaches, and nervousness can be reduced or eliminated by using progressive relaxation techniques. Nervousness wastes energy, making us more fatigued and less alert.

To relax, spend 20 to 30 minutes twice a day applying some of the various relaxation techniques. All that is necessary is a quiet place where you will not be disturbed. Mini-relaxation breaks of five minutes each throughout the day can also be invaluable in reducing stress. Only a comfortable chair or sofa is necessary. One of these techniques is described below:

Loosen any tight clothing. Close your eyes and concentrate on breathing slowly and deeply into the lower part of your chest. As you exhale, imagine the tenseness leaving you. Begin to concentrate on your toes and feet, telling yourself that they are relaxing. Think slowly and deliberately. Concentrate on relaxing and breathing until your toes and feet feel thoroughly relaxed. Gradually progress to other parts of your body until you are completely relaxed.

After you are fully relaxed, you may wish to practice visual imagery, seeing yourself relaxing on a beach or gently swinging on a hammock. Your local library or bookstore can provide you with further exercises on relaxation. Additionally, audio and visual relaxation tapes and recordings of peaceful sounds are available. And simply looking at beautiful pictures of forests, meadows, or other peaceful, green settings has been shown to elicit the relaxation response quickly and refreshingly.

Spend time during the day mentally scanning your body. Are your muscles tense? Is your stomach in knots? Do you have a tension headache or a case of indigestion? If so, you may choose to spend a few minutes breathing deeply, concentrating on relaxation, and applying some of the stress and tension-relieving exercises. With practice, you can quickly bring yourself into a peaceful state.

Enjoying leisure time is an essential part of reducing stress.

Leisure   Leisure time is important. It allows us a chance to relax and get away from daily stresses, permitting us to return refreshed and ready to work. Unfortunately, obtaining that time seems to be difficult at best. Although we live in what is often called the "short-cut society," we still have less time to enjoy stress-free activities. With the advent of fast foods, virtual offices, fax machines, cell phones and pagers, lap-top computers, microwaves, satellites, and robotics designed to make our lives easier, the pace of life has simply increased, and we are part of the frenzy.

This inability to make time for leisure activity is part of the pattern of workaholism. **Workaholics** are individuals who are consumed by their jobs and derive little pleasure from other activities. These people are likely candidates for heart attacks, depression, hypertension, insomnia, and other physical ailments. They often view their lives as one long, continuous workday reaching well into the night and are rarely able to enjoy even the thought of leisure time. They are known to carry a briefcase full of work along anywhere they go and phone into the office frequently for messages that often add pressures. For workaholics, even vacations are seldom restful because they take thoughts and worries of their jobs with them, compounding the stress.

Personality traits can also contribute to stress conditions. Two well-known personality types have been identified by extensive psychological research on behavior patterns. **Type A personalities** tend to be highly competitive, aggressive, achievement-oriented, and impatient. They typically appear pressured, rushed or hurried, and volatile and dislike waiting in lines or for traffic lights to turn green. **Type B personalities** exhibit an opposite behavior pattern. They appear more relaxed, easy-going, and even-paced in their approach to life in general. The Type B individual seldom overcommits, can say no without feeling guilty, and takes time to smell the roses along the way.

Type A individuals are more likely to experience high stress levels and exhibit stress symptoms than Type B individuals. Type A personalities are twice as prone to cardiovascular heart diseases, such as heart attacks and clogged arteries, as Type B personalities. An important step in your personal wellness program may be to identify these patterns in your personality and strive to reduce any Type A tendencies you may have.

Tips for Leaving Stress at the Office

1. Try to end the day as smoothly as possible. Start unwinding about one-half hour before you leave. Save easier jobs for last to assist you in unwinding.

2. To cut down worry about unfinished items, make a list of what needs to be done, imagine successfully completing these items, and leave them until the next morning.

3. Maintain a perspective. Remember that today's disasters are not the end of the world and will be of little importance in the future.

4. Use your commute to unwind. Listen to soothing music, read a good book, or enjoy a picturesque magazine if you are not driving.

5. Arrange with your family to be allowed a small bit of quiet time. This will help ease the transition between work and home.

6. Do not make dinner an ordeal with fancy meals. Turn off the television and limit interruptions. Limit work-related conversations at meal time.

7. Do not overschedule your leisure hours. Do not bring work home on a routine basis, and discourage colleagues from calling in the evenings with work-related questions.

In addition to making the most of our leisure time, we should choose activities carefully. For highly competitive individuals, sports, such as softball and tennis, can be as stressful as work.

Reducing stressful thoughts, attitudes, and behavior Setting realistic goals, learning to take risks, raising self-esteem, practicing positive self-talk, using communication skills, understanding the grieving process, and developing assertive behavior have been discussed in Chapters 2, 9, and 15. All of these skills can assist you in changing stressful thoughts, attitudes, and behaviors.

Another important skill that reduces stress is the ability to be self-focused. Harriet Goldhor Lerner in her book, *The Dance of Intimacy*, states that individuals who are not self-focused see others as the problem and believe the solution is for the other person to change. These individuals are unable to achieve intimacy with those around them, which increases stress. The best idea is to focus on our own problems and work on resolving them rather than trying to change the behavior of others.

Lerner also suggests avoiding what she calls "triangles." A triangle occurs when one person brings you into a problem that he or she is having with a third. Refusing to be drawn into a problem between others is a healthy behavior to learn.

Changing stressful thoughts, attitudes, and behaviors takes time and practice.

You can cultivate other healthy attitudes and behaviors:

1. Do not try to change others; accept them as they are.
2. Do not expect actions from others. Thoughts such as "they should" and "they must" can cause anger and frustration.
3. Clarify what you want and firmly state your wants in an assertive manner.
4. Recognize situations in which you have no control. A traffic jam will unclog at the same time whether you remain angry at the inconvenience or attempt to relax and spend the time productively.
5. View situations realistically. What will failure in this situation mean next month, next year, in ten years?
6. Recognize that you do have options and control of many situations. Review Chapter 3 on how to seek alternative ways of meeting wants and needs.
7. Develop a support system of friends and relatives with whom you can discuss stressful events and situations.
8. When choosing a relationship, ask whether it will be good for you or whether it will increase your stress.
9. Take coffee and lunch breaks away from the office.
10. Schedule some quiet time to be alone, during which you may dream, relax, or think.

Accepting and applying some of these attitudes and behaviors will ease feelings of stress that complicate your daily routine.

*Fast*Chat

Many individuals consciously participate in activities that are potentially harmful to their health.

1. Should companies have the right to refuse to hire individuals who smoke, even if they do not smoke at work? If not, what alternatives might companies have to keep insurance rates lower for others?

2. Should companies have the right to refuse to hire those who are overweight? Who participate in dangerous activities such as sky diving and mountain climbing?

Summary

A wellness program addresses emotional and physical health. Organizations show interest in these programs because they result in higher productivity and decreased medical and insurance costs. A good wellness plan will include an understanding of stress and of skills to control it. Today, many organizations are encouraging wellness by health education, employee assistance plans, early disease detection programs, and fitness programs.

Stress is the physical state of the body in response to environmental pressures that produce emotional discomfort. Stress can result from good or bad causes. When the body reaches its stress threshold, certain physical and mental reactions occur. Overindulging, hypertension, insomnia, anxiety, depression, heart attacks, and mental disorders are only a few of the symptoms of stress illnesses. A well-rounded wellness program helps people learn to manage stress and prevent other diseases through time management, proper diet, nonsmoking, exercise, relaxation, other leisure activities, and changing stressful thoughts, attitudes, and behaviors.

Key Terms

wellness program
stress
time management
procrastination
planned agenda
hidden agenda
workaholics
Type A personalities
Type B personalities

Review Questions

1. What is a wellness program? Why is it good for both employer and employee?
2. What are companies doing to promote employee wellness?
3. What are the physical and mental results of stress overload?
4. What are the most effective methods of time management?
5. What is the importance of proper diet in minimizing stress effects?
6. How do exercise and relaxation help in achieving wellness?
7. How can you change stressful thoughts, attitudes, and behaviors?

Discussion Questions

1. Does your organization have a wellness program for employees? If so, what are the obvious benefits of the program?
2. What symptoms of stress do you feel? What do you believe are the major causes? What do you do to reduce the stress?
3. What method of time management do you use? What benefits do you realize from your method? How might you improve your method?
4. Do you procrastinate? Why? How might you overcome your procrastination?
5. Do you have a problem finding leisure time in your daily schedule? Do you exhibit symptoms of being a workaholic? How might you better plan for leisure time?
6. Which of your thoughts, beliefs, or behaviors contribute to your feelings of stress? How might you reduce these sources of stress?

Reading; speaking; allocating time and following schedules; acquiring and evaluating information; interpreting and communicating information.

Chapter Project

Visit the U.S. Consumer Gateway on the Internet at *http://www.consumer.gov* or your local library. Find an article about health. Prepare and deliver a five minute oral presentation to your class members on a health or wellness subject discussed in this chapter

Applications

In small groups, analyze the following:

Alice in Wonderful Land

Alice had just been awarded a contract to provide a training seminar on supervisory skills to a group of new first-line supervisors at a major oil company in Dallas. This opportunity could establish her as a leader in the training field, and with the right exposure she could receive more contracts with other companies. She already had a comfortable amount of business that pushed her busy schedule, but this job could really boost her practice into high gear. Alice smiled with satisfaction at the prospects.

The only problem was the amount of time and effort required in putting a new seminar together. "How can I crowd all this new preparation into my schedule?" she wondered out loud. "I already work 14, 16, . . . sometimes even 20 hours a day just keeping up with my current contract load." The day did not seem to have enough hours to do all that needed to be done. She was also teaching a class two nights a week at the local college and had just agreed to collaborate on a project for her community that was a full year's commitment of time and effort. Her work with the youth group at the church might have to be cut back if this wonderful opportunity really got off the ground.

"With a little luck, I'll be able to pull this off and get over the hump this time. If only I don't get those awful headaches I had last week. They certainly put a damper on my productivity."

Visualizing, reasoning, knowing how to learn, and problem solving.

1. What symptoms of stress is Alice exhibiting?
2. Do you believe that Alice is an effective time manager? How might she solve her problem?
3. Should Alice accept the new contract? Why or why not?

Watch Out from Behind!

Carey had planned for weeks in advance to make this meeting successful. He had carefully selected the attendees, reserved the conference room well in advance, and prepared his briefing materials in plenty of time to go over them and make the necessary changes for clarity. He had even sent a well-organized agenda a week ago to all attendees so that they could be prepared to discuss the topics outlined. Everything would go smoothly, and they would be finished before noon.

Visualizing, reasoning, and problem solving.

Carey started the meeting promptly at 10 A.M. and moved swiftly through the first several items with good decisions made and all action items appropriately assigned. The next topic generated a great deal of conversation. Almost everyone was commenting on the plans he had outlined in his briefing. Suddenly Frank from the engineering division put a new proposal on the table for discussion. Everyone was surprised that Frank had thought out this approach so thoroughly, but they were clearly interested. Some people began adding their ideas to Frank's, and before Carey knew it, they were completely off the primary subjects of his meeting. Somehow he had lost control of his meeting and wasn't sure how he would meet the noon deadline for getting the decisions and results he needed from this fiasco.

1. What caused Carey's meeting to get off track?
2. How might Carey have prevented this problem?
3. How would you have handled Frank's action?

Addtional Readings and Resources

Alexander, Roy. *Commonsense Time Management*. New York: American Management Association, 1992.

"Cyber Chain Letter Victimizes Computer Users Across Country." *The Houston Chronicle*, March 27, 1999, Section A, page 33.

Davis, Martha, Elizabeth Robbins Eshelman, Matthew McKay, and Mat McKay. *Relaxation and Stress Reduction Workbook*. New Harbinger Publishing, 1998.

Dreyfuss, Ira. "Wellness, Exercise Progams May Save Companies Some Money." *The Desert News* (Salt Lake City, UT), February 22, 1999, Business; pg.WEB.

Golisek, Andrew. *60 Second Stress Management*. New Horizon Press, 1992.

Harris, Philip R. and Robert T. Moran. *Managing Cultural Differences*. Houston: Gulf Publishing Company, 1991.

http://www.nal.usda.gov:8001/py/pmap.htm The Food Guide Pyramid

http://www.ftc.gov/bcp/conline/pub/briefs/fitnsbrf.htm FTC Briefs The Muscle Hustle: Test Your Exercise I.Q.

http://www.ftc.gov/bcp/conline/publ/health/diets.htm Skinny on Dieting

http://www.demon.co.uk/mindtool/smundstr.html Mind Tools—Helping You to Think Your Way to an Excellent Life! Understanding Stress

http://www.fda.gov/opacom/lowlit/weightls.html Losing Weight Safely

http://warp.nal.usda.gov/fnic/publ/bibs/topics/weight/consumer.html Weight Control and Obesity, A Bibliography

Loiselle, Beth. *The Healing Power of Whole Foods*. Healthway Nutrition, 1993.

Stafford, Diane. "A Growing Workplace Threat: New Report Sees Stress as Health Hazard for Employees Sensing a Lack of Control." *The Kansas City Star*, January 31, 1999, National/World; pg. A1.

VanDerWall, Stacy. "NIOSH Report: Job Stress a 'Threat' to Workers' Health." *HR News Online*. Society for Human Resource Management, January 15, 1999.

Meeting the Future:

Global Challenges and Personal Growth

focus

When steam engines first appeared in eighteenth-century Britain, no one dreamed that the curious contraptions were part of a sweeping historical transformation now known as the Industrial Revolution. But we today have little doubt that computers and telecommunications of all forms have brought a new revolution and that this new transformation will affect human life even more profoundly than its predecessor.

We are at the start of a revolution in information, genetics, materials, the environment, and many other areas. Whole new fields—microbiotics, satellite-based communications, and urban underground automated distribution, to name a few—are wide open for those who will think intelligently about the future. As we identify the possibilities of the cyber future, we can act to make them happen or prevent them from happening. Most importantly, we can acquire useful insights into the enormous opportunities and challenges that lie ahead in this Information Age.

—**Edward Cornish,** *The Cyber Future,* **June 1999**

How do you think these new areas of development may affect you? Are you currently involved in, or planning to become involved in, any of the fields listed above? How would you see human relations skills being of benefit in an age that relies so heavily on technology? What factors in the U.S. put this country at the leading edge of the Information Age?

After studying this chapter, you should be able to:

1. *Discuss the changing demographics of the United States.*

2. *Discuss the major forces shaping our economy.*

3. *Explain what the country must do to meet the challenges of a changing work force and the new economic realities.*

4. *Explain what skills will be in demand in the twenty-first century.*

5. *Discuss what you can do to prepare yourself to enter this changing work force.*

In This Chapter

20.1 How Will Society Change?

Learning
O b j e c t i v e   1

Discuss the changing demographics of the United States.

quick wit

"Demographics are the single most important factor that nobody pays attention to, and when they do pay attention, they usually miss the point."

Peter Drucker

Demographics in the United States are shifting.

What will life be like in 50 years? Will we lead lives of leisure, with computers and robotics performing all of our work? Will our life expectancies dramatically increase based on biogenetic engineering? Will we work at home? Will all money transactions be done electronically?

All of these scenarios have been predicted by various groups and individuals, but no one knows the answers. However, experts can tell us some of what to expect as we enter the twenty-first century. Current trends in business, economics, and society will forever change the way we work and live. Innovations in technology have made our world smaller, ushering in a fast-paced, global economy that calls for drastic changes in the way companies do business. In addition, the changing nature of our work force will require ongoing assessment and modification of the way companies operate if they wish to remain competitive. Understanding this quiet revolution in the makeup of our society is important if you are to succeed.

Demographics are statistics showing population characteristics about a region or group, such as education, income, age, marital status, ethnic makeup, and other factors. Such information is necessary in preparing for the future. For example, the milestone publication by the Hudson Institute, *Workforce 2020—Work and Workers for the Twenty-First Century*, forecasts who will be working, what they will be doing, which occupations will grow most rapidly, which groups of workers will increase in the work force, and which will decline.

Currently, our society is experiencing several major shifts in its demographic makeup including the areas of work force environment, the aging population, increased cultural diversity, and changes in work force skills and education levels. Let us look at these shifts and others along with their probable impact. Unless otherwise noted, the statistical and demographic information in the remainder of this chapter is derived from *Workforce 2020*.

CHANGING WORK FORCE ENVIRONMENTS

As noted in Chapter 13, numerous changes are occurring in the work force. Technological innovations and globalization are affecting who is doing the work and where it is being done. Many changes are occurring in the work force in response to rapid economic shifts. The economy and the Internet are fostering new kinds of organizations with new kinds of practices and operating rules.

The makeup of the work force is only part of the changing environment. Alternatives are being explored in areas as diverse as how offices are laid out, how the company hierarchy is structured and how that structure is demonstrated, and even whether or not traditional offices are used. Businesses are operating internationally, while at the same time, telecommuting has made it possible for some workers to stay at home.

MORE WOMEN IN THE WORK FORCE

When we were a nation of men doing heavy-duty farm and factory jobs, women's jobs were typically those of homemakers, nurses, and teachers. The playing ground has been leveled by the Information Age. The shift from manufacturing to service industries helps by providing many jobs that are not gender-specific. In today's knowledge-based fields, people can earn their livings by what they know rather than through physical labor.

Women now constitute 49 percent of the total work force. Women have increased their numbers in management ranks and represent a significant number of business owners. While women's salaries still lag behind those of men, the gap is closing. As demographic changes reduce the pool of educated men, talented and well-prepared women are in stronger bargaining positions.

CASE STUDIES IN THE NEWS

If you are a 29-year-old college-educated woman, you are on average earning $34,000 a year. Your male counterpart with the same credentials earns $44,350 annually. Over your working lifetime, this wage gap will add up to $990,000. This gap will close as women better prepare themselves for professional careers in the Information Age.

Jilian Mincer, *Knight Ridder Tribune*

What do you think were some of the original reasons that women generally earned less than men? In what ways do you think women's roles have changed? How has this contributed to closing the gap between men's and women's wages?

CORBIS/R. W. Jones

More working mothers are in the work force than ever before. Approximately 64 percent of all married women with children under six years of age are working, which is having an impact on the types of benefits and working conditions desired by this segment of the work force. For example, many employers are providing excellent family leave policies, flexible work hours, and telecommuting as a means of accommodating families with small children. These changing conditions will be more fully explored later in this chapter.

THE AGING POPULATION

Baby boomers are those Americans born between 1945 and 1965, during the "baby boom" that followed World War II. For decades, whatever "boomers" were doing became the most significant factor in demographic studies of U.S. trends. Today, what the "boomers" are doing is getting older. The first of 76 million baby boomers turn 55 in 2001. By 2020, nearly 20 percent of our population will have reached retirement age. This means that the U.S. will have as many retirement-aged people as workers in the 20 to 35 age group. In addition, the younger generations are having fewer babies, so the percentages will continue to be weighted toward the older end of the spectrum. The following table provides a graphic depiction of the growing numbers of older people in the work force and the diminishing numbers of younger workers to replace them.

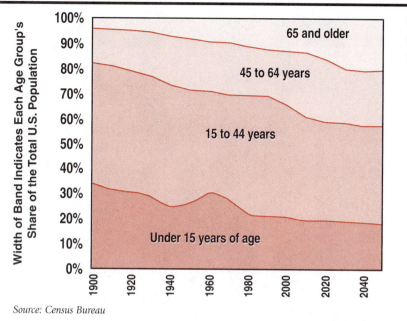

Width of Band Indicates Each Age Group's Share of the Total U.S. Population

65 and older

45 to 64 years

15 to 44 years

Under 15 years of age

Source: Census Bureau

One of the effects anticipated from these changes has to do with governmental entitlements—Social Security and Medicare. The demographics indicate that large numbers of aging baby boomers will soon be eligible to draw on these sources to supplement their pensions or retirement incomes, while smaller numbers of young workers will be replenishing the funds that support these entitlements. Not only are boomers reaching retirement age, but downsizing is often forcing people to accept early retirement.

This situation is causing government officials to consider methods to prevent the drain on Social Security and Medicare. Some of the methods include extending the retirement age, reducing the amount of benefits, and increasing tax contributions to these funds. Because it would be unfair to reduce benefits to individuals who have paid into Social Security their entire lives, and undesirable to increase taxes on the already heavily taxed U.S. worker, allowing workers to remain longer in their jobs seems the best alternative, both for the system and for the workers. The Social Security mandatory retirement age is already scheduled to increase to 67 by 2027, though an earlier implementation date may be needed. Some projections see the mandatory retirement age being eventually pushed beyond 70.

Many retirement age workers will choose to remain in the work force longer.

Quick Tip . . . .

"Given the current life expectancies, the proper retirement age will be 79 by 2010."

—Peter Drucker

But even without a change in mandatory retirement age, will these baby boomers really leave the work force in droves? They are considered to be the healthiest and most educated generation in history. It is unlikely that they will want to retire to the porch swing in their 50s. As the individual life expectancy rate moves upward toward the 80s and even 90s, many of these workers will want to remain in the work force longer. The *Washington Post* reported on March 25, 1999, that the oldest U.S. worker is F. William Sunderman, the editor of a scientific journal. He is 100 years old and still puts in a full eight-hour workday.

Research studies performed by the World Future Society indicate that many boomers may retire but use their experience and contacts to go into business for themselves, exercising their entrepreneurial spirits. These retirees are expected to move into the growth fields of providing goods and services to the Generation Xers who follow in their footsteps.

A study of perceptions of employees about workers age 50 and up, reported by Cyril Brickfield in *Manage*, found that business and industry employers have a strongly positive view of that age group. Managers interviewed in the study believed that older workers' strengths are experience, skills, and knowledge and that they have a strong commitment to quality, are emotionally stable, and are dependable in a crisis. Management perceived the weaknesses to include resistance to new techniques, physical limitations, low ambition, and less capability to learn new skills quickly

However, 83 percent of the survey participants believed that older workers have special problem-solving skills based on knowledge and experience. Brickfield concludes that productivity does not decline with age, older managers make capable decision makers, and older workers change jobs less frequently and have a greater commitment to the job, with attendance as good as or better than other age groups. He adds that perceived weaknesses of older workers can be overcome by training, job redesign, and effective

Older people make good workers.

CASE STUDIES IN THE NEWS

John Challenger is Executive Vice President of Challenger, Gray & Christmas, an outsourcing firm that follows employment trends. Challenger notes, "It is likely that, rather than stay at home, a large number of the baby boomer retirees will start up their own businesses. They may hire other retirees to work for them, thus establishing "gray businesses" made up of older workers." Years of experience and extensive business contacts will make these older workers highly competitive.

Jeff Minerd, *World Trends & Forecasts*, July 1999

In what ways does experience make these employees valuable? What do you feel will be lost as they leave the corporate world? Why is it beneficial to both boomers and the rest of society that these "gray businesses" are established?

management. Also important to remember is that they are perceptions, and not always realities. In fact, the fastest growing segment of the computer-buying public is over 50, so not everyone in the aging population is resistant to what's new.

Another effect anticipated due to the so-called "graying of America" will be the increased need for elder care capabilities. The Generation Xers will soon reach the "sandwich years," sandwiched between taking care of their children and their aging parents. By 2020, the U.S. will have one individual over 65 for every four working-age adults. Some companies will begin to offer on-site elder care facilities, just as they are offering day care for children today. It will be a means of attracting and keeping talented employees, increasing productivity, and reducing absenteeism—all of which contribute to a company's bottom profit line.

INCREASED CULTURAL DIVERSITY

The general population is making mild transitions in almost all ethnic groups. According to the Census Bureau's projections, by the year 2020 the white population will number only 64.3 percent of the total population. The African American population has grown slightly and will continue to do so, reaching 12.9 percent by the year 2020. The Census Bureau is projecting that the Asian population will reach 6.5 percent in the same time period. However, Hispanics comprise the most rapidly growing minority group in America. In 1990, Hispanics represented 9 percent of the total population, while current projections for 2020 have this group representing 16 percent.

The state of California will host an impressive 42 percent Hispanic population. Eighteen percent of the population will be Asian. The remaining one-third of California's population will be white. California sets the tone for the nation's diversification, reflecting a regional trend in the western states. As the makeup of the general population changes, the makeup of the work force will change, reflecting both the greater diversity of the population and the more global character of business.

The graph on the next page illustrates the gradual changes that have occurred in the work force since 1995 and the projected figures for 2020. While the Hispanic work force population will increase from 9 to 14 percent, the most substantial growth will be in the Asian representation, which is expected to double from 3 to 6 percent. As you can see, the work force composition very nearly follows the general population percentages. Both of these representations indicate the increasing diversification of America.

A 1998 statistic issued by the U.S. Department of Labor projected that almost one-third of the 25 million individuals entering the work force dur-

Human Relations

**COMPOSITION OF THE AMERICAN WORKFORCE,
BY ETHNIC GROUP, PERCENT, 1995-2020 (PROJECTED)**

Composition of the
American work force
by ethnic group

Percent of Total Labor Force

Year	White	Black	Hispanic	Asian
1995	76%	11%	9%	4%
2000	74%	11%	10%	5%
2005	73%	11%	11%	5%
2010	72%	11%	12%	5%
2015	70%	11%	13%	6%
2020	68%	11%	14%	6%

Legend: ☐ Asian ☐ Hispanic ☐ Black ■ White

Source: Bureau of Labor Statistics

ing the next several years will be minorities. We see evidence of this as companies place a premium on diversity training and recruiting.

Chip Carlisle, President of Wells Fargo Bank in Texas, mentions that decision quality is best when teams are well diversified and that Chief Executive Officers and top managers must be committed to making diversity a business objective. He also emphasizes that a company must follow through on its purpose. He believes that, "A company that understands and respects the many dimensions of diversity will appeal to the broadest of populations." (See the case study on page 584.)

CORBIS

Diversity is a strong
advantage for any
company operating
in the global work
world.

CASE STUDIES IN THE NEWS

Work force demographics for the United States indicate that managing diversity will be a top agenda item for effective corporate leaders for years to come. The whole point of managing diversity is paying attention to the market and customers while drawing on the uniqueness of each employee. Ortho Pharmaceuticals believes that diversity training and recruiting of minorities pays off in the bottom line. The company has calculated a cost savings of $500,000 from lower turnover among minorities and women. Other companies are also realizing the benefits.

Avon Corp. used cultural diversity to turn around low profitability in its inner-city markets. Avon made personnel changes to give African-American and Hispanic managers substantial authority over these markets. Hoechst Celanese saw productivity at plants surge after it undertook a major effort to recruit minorities and women. Among nearly 2000 retail branches of Wells Fargo Bank in a 10-state territory, eight of the top best-performing branches were led by minority or female managers.

—Chip Carlisle, President, Wells Fargo Bank (Texas) August 1998

Why do you think there is less turnover among women and minorities? What other benefits might a company realize from hiring women and minorities? What might companies need to do to help integrate these new employees into the work force?

An indicator that diversity is becoming an integral part of the work force is the recent publication by *Fortune* magazine of its list, "The 50 Best Companies for Asians, Blacks, and Hispanics" in the July 1999 issue. To be competitive in the global markets, companies will draw from talent pools representing all peoples in the U.S. and around the world. The article stated that "minority-friendly companies tend to be superior performers." Its

CASE STUDIES IN THE NEWS

One company that carries the banner for diversity is US Robotics. The company is best known for the Sportster modem and for introducing a conference call product called Conference Link. They also produce a 900 megahertz portable phone and plan to expand by entering imaging product lines. Russ Nykaza, staffing manager for the company's Personal Communications Division, is proud of the company's rapid growth and commitment to diversity. In 1998, US Robotics tripled its entry-level jobs as it continued expansion into international markets.

The range of operations spans from Illinois, Utah, and California in the states to Paris, Amsterdam, and Munich in Europe, as well as cities in Latin America. Nykaza says, "I have an incredible group of people on my staff with one member from Japan and others from Yugoslavia, Haiti, Puerto Rico and Jamaica. They all speak several languages, and each makes many contributions to the dynamics of our team." US Robotics has a "college relations task force" that targets hiring a wide representation of minorities. This successful company grew in only three years from 500 employees to 6,500, and continues its aggressive approach toward recruiting minorities.

What human relations skills would be most important when working with such a diverse group? What challenges might these groups face?

www.diversity.com, October 1999

proof of that statement comes from these companies outperforming the S&P 500 over the past three to five years.

One other ethnic group that is seldom mentioned is American Indians. Tom Smith, CEO of a $15 million plastics molding company in Ohio, is a Cherokee and president of an advocacy group called the Native American Business Alliance (NABA). As such, he is an active change agent for Indian affairs. The NABA is slowly but effectively calling for major companies to

GLOBAL CONNECTION

Rich McGinn, CEO of Lucent Technologies, believes that, "Diversity is a competitive advantage. Different people approach similar problems in different ways and diverse groups make better decisions." He believes diversity is not just about ethnicities but also about nationalities. "A group with eight passports represented will be stronger than a group with one or two." All of the company executives consider diversity a strong advantage for any company operating in the global work world.

—Geoffrey Colvin, *Fortune*, July 1999

How would having a culturally diverse work force give a company an edge in the global marketplace?

CASE STUDIES IN THE NEWS

At Lucent Technologies, around 250 American Indian employees are members of Luna, an affinity group that holds monthly conference calls connecting employees from across the country, hosts an annual meeting on an Indian reservation, provides updates on job openings, and helps address career concerns. Luna members regularly advise Lucent recruiters on seeking applicants in Native American strongholds like New Mexico. The company also draws talent from the American Indian Scientific and Engineering society in Albuquerque.

—Edward Robinson, *Fortune*, September 1999

How does this differ from traditional types of networking and mentoring? How is it similar?

"recognize and embrace the talents among all minorities." Smith says, "We have become more vocal in telling corporations that it's time to bring us into the mainstream." Some companies are listening.

CHANGES IN WORK FORCE SKILLS AND EDUCATION LEVELS

The Department of Education estimates that more than 27 million Americans over the age of 17 cannot read or write well enough to function in everyday life. Another 45 million are barely competent in these basic skills. These figures mean that one out of every three adults may not have the necessary skills to perform jobs that require reading and writing. This trend is particularly alarming when you consider that most materials written for business are geared to a twelfth-grade reading level.

Federal officials report that this number is growing by 2 million people annually. Ronni Sandroff in *Working Woman* reports that one out of eight 17-year-olds in the United States leaves school functionally illiterate.

Employers are also experiencing difficulties in finding job applicants with skills necessary to perform the available jobs. Karen DeVenuta reports in *The Wall Street Journal* that 20 to 40 percent of job applicants fail an entry-level examination requiring seventh- to ninth-grade English and fifth- to seventh-grade math.

In addition, recent studies reveal that students in the United States lag behind those of other nations in math and science achievement. *The Wall Street Journal*, in reporting the findings of an international study of 13-year-olds, pointed out that U.S. students ranked last in math proficiency. South Korean students ranked first. We also lag behind other countries in the study of foreign languages. For example, the same article reports that 100 percent of Japanese high school students have had at least six years of English, and only two-tenths of 1 percent of U.S. students have studied Japanese. If English becomes the universal language of money and world business, this foreign language deficit will put Americans at a disadvantage in the international marketplace.

This educational lag, unless reversed, will cause even more difficulties in our economy. Horror stories already abound about costly errors caused by illiteracy. A steelworker misordered $1 million in parts because he could not read well. An assembly line worker nearly killed several of his coworkers because he did not properly assemble a heavy piece of equipment. He was unable to read the assembly instructions. These costly errors will become even more numerous if the U.S. basic skills level is left unaddressed.

In addition to affecting the economy as a whole, this education lag will also affect the lives of the individual workers. The following illustration

Better educated workers earn better.

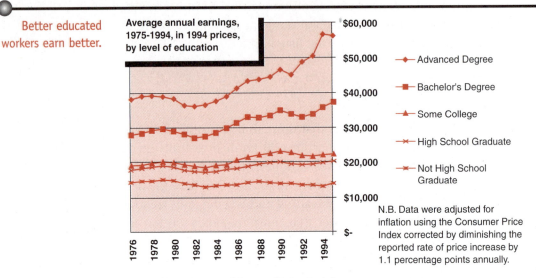

Average annual earnings, 1975-1994, in 1994 prices, by level of education

- ◆— Advanced Degree
- ■— Bachelor's Degree
- ▲— Some College
- ✕— High School Graduate
- ✱— Not High School Graduate

$60,000
$50,000
$40,000
$30,000
$20,000
$10,000
$-

N.B. Data were adjusted for inflation using the Consumer Price Index corrected by diminishing the reported rate of price increase by 1.1 percentage points annually.

1976 1978 1980 1982 1984 1986 1988 1990 1992 1994

Source: Census Bureau and Bureau of Labor Statistics.

The growing illiteracy of the work force threatens our economy.

provides a clear indication of the impact education has on income levels. As you can see, drop outs fail to keep up with inflation and high school graduates barely rise above poverty levels. College graduates continue to increase their income levels, raising their standards of living.

The disparity of income levels is expected to continue well into the twenty-first century. Our economy is producing many high-paying jobs and fewer college-degreed applicants to fill them. At the opposite end, we have more poorly-educated job seekers and fewer of those jobs in the market.

So education is vital for improving earning potential; a carefully planned education will help position you for career opportunities.

Individuals with degrees in the engineering and science fields (health, computer, and physical) tend to fare better than those with degrees in the humanities, education, and the arts. However, it is the learning that is important, and learning how to learn. You cannot stop learning when you leave school. Learning will continue throughout your career. A college degree offers great advantages, but don't assume that having a college degree will guarantee you a smooth road. Personal discipline, intelligence, desire, and persistence may bring about the same results as a degree. The thing that is valuable is knowledge, and school is generally the surest and most widely accepted way to gain knowledge.

Although Joe Liemandt, as discussed in the case study, has been very successful, even he had to spend a lot of years studying before he started his software firm. This kind of success takes hard work, skill, and knowledge, plus a creative mind to come up with a marketable product. Not everyone

Human Relations

CASE STUDIES IN THE NEWS

Joe Liemandt, 30, founded Trilogy in 1989, after dropping out of Stanford University only a few months before graduation. Trilogy Software Inc. is a small, rapidly growing software firm based in Austin, Texas. It is on the cutting edge of sales-and-marketing software. To finance the startup of his own company, Liemandt charged up 22 credit cards and had the confidence that he could make it work. If Trilogy were to go public today, analysts say, it would be valued at more than $1 billion. Four years ago, Trilogy had only 100 employees—today, it has 1,000 and plans to add another 1,000 before the summer of 1999.

Robert B. Reich, *FastCompany*, November 1998

What combination of skills do you think would contribute to being able to start your own business? What might make you confident of success? Though Liemandt didn't wait to get his diploma, do you think that the years he spent at Stanford contributed to his success?

has a gift for creating opportunities like this, but everyone can prepare for the opportunities that come along. Anyone who desires to have a career that is interesting and rewarding would do well to carefully plan an education. Job opportunities in the twenty-first century that require some level of knowledge and expertise are growing rapidly and pay well, and those with the education to fill those jobs will enjoy the rewards.

OTHER DEMOGRAPHICS

The areas of demographics described in this section are the major pieces of the puzzle, representing the biggest and most rapid changes in today's work force. However, there are other related demographics which, though they affect fewer people or are changing at a slower rate, are still significant parts of the picture. Factors as different as health issues, increasing consumer debt, giant corporations versus self-employment, faltering faith in the leadership, and desire for self-actualization will all contribute to the changing work scene.

One unpleasant demographic is the increase in the income gap. While America is still the land of opportunity, and more than 80 percent of the country's millionaires made the money themselves, not everyone is enjoying prosperity. In the past, rising incomes and standards of living decreased the gap between those people who have enough money to live satisfactorily and those who do not. This trend was reversed in the early 1980s and the gap between rich and poor began widening once again.

Several factors led to this reversal. One cause is the stagnation of our economic productivity and decrease in higher-paying manufacturing jobs, due either to automation or the relocation of these functions overseas. Another is the increase in the number of single-parent families. As discussed above, the decline in education and skill levels has a serious impact on earning power. Attitudes toward work have changed. Also, the influx of new immigrants has had an impact on the number of entry-level jobs available.

Rapid technological advances are eliminating or minimizing the numbers of jobs required at lower income levels. Conversely, the same rapid advances are creating increased needs for workers with the education and skill levels required to use those technologies.

Fewer jobs are found in the middle range of incomes. Corporate downsizing and flattening of hierarchies have forced many who were once in middle management to accept positions where they are under-employed. Also, as companies have moved to the suburbs—to escape high taxes, high costs, and/or crime—the number of jobs in the cities have declined, contributing to a rise in urban poverty.

The impact of this widening gap is expected to be felt in a number of ways. One, of course, will be in the additional cost to taxpayers for public support. Another is the increased frustration of those without, which may make itself felt in ways from how they vote to an increase in crime.

The changing work force will bring with it new wants and needs, as discussed in earlier chapters. Priorities will be different. To assure that employees remain productive, organizations will be required to address new issues. These issues, combined with forces that are shaping the economy, will revolutionize the work force of the future.

FastChat

1. How will older workers be beneficial in our future work force?

2. How do you think the issues discussed in this section will change the work force of the future?

What Forces Will Shape The Economy?

Four trends will reshape jobs and industries in the United States during the 21st century. These include a shift from goods to services, advanced technology, workplace adaptations, and further globalization expansions.

SHIFT FROM GOODS TO SERVICES

Service industries create economic value without creating a tangible product, unlike manufacturing, agriculture, and other goods-producing industries. Services such as transportation and retailing add value to manufactured goods by making them more available or useful to consumers. Services such as education and health care create value without being directly related to goods. This shift in production will affect the rate of growth of our economy, the distribution of income, and the location and organization of work.

At the beginning of the twentieth century, 63 percent of American workers produced goods and 37 percent produced services. By 1990, 22 percent of the nation produced goods and 78 percent produced services. These trends are expected to continue the decisive turn toward services with the Bureau of Economic Analysis estimating that 83 percent of the American work force will be in the service sector by 2025.

Several factors contribute to this trend. Manufacturing has become increasingly automated or has been relocated overseas, which has reduced the number of U.S. jobs involved in producing goods. More people want a wider range of goods, which calls for increased transportation and retail options. An aging population has necessitated an increase in health care, while growing children need education. The influx of immigrants requires services aimed at assisting assimilation, teaching English, and meeting other needs. Even the tight job market has created a wide range of new service jobs, from outplacement advisers to temporary agencies to job consultants.

As the baby boomers begin to retire and the Gen-Xer's settle in their high-paying jobs, vacation and world travel are expected to be a growth area. Service industries will cater to those who have more time and money on their hands, providing whatever goods and services they require. Leisure activities have become more and more important to the economy. Nearly 50 percent of the Gross National Product (GNP) has something to do with

Learning
Objective   2

Discuss the major forces shaping the economy.

Four forces are shaping our economy.

leisure, recreation, and entertainment. New jobs will arise in these service industries to replace those lost in other areas. The technology explosion, too, has created numerous service opportunities, from training to support, while also altering the way we communicate and do business.

ADVANCED TECHNOLOGIES

The 20th century experienced enormous technological change and accompanying social upheavals that few could have predicted. The 21st century is expected to hold even more rapid growth in technology and the way it influences our lives. This revolution will not take decades to unfold—the technology is changing faster than attitudes can adjust and skills can be developed.

Fax machines, e-mail, inexpensive long-distance, cell phones, and computers are all relatively recent developments. From 1990 to 1994, the number of cellular telephone subscribers increased more than 600 percent from 2.7 million to 19.3 million. Personal computers did not exist until the 1980s.

The Internet is expected to revolutionize the ways we do business.

The Internet, already growing daily in importance, will probably have an increasing impact on our lives. It is expected to revolutionize the way we buy and sell goods and services. Banking and investing processes will take a dramatic turn toward the use of technologies for transactions. Shopping and general consumerism will change dramatically. Predictions for retailing tell us that anyone with a computer and a credit card will become a global shopper. Books and printed materials will go on-line. Audio, video, and interactive capabilities will accompany printed publications, significantly changing the publishing industries.

Businesses are realizing that the Internet is essential to their operations. Individuals are rapidly learning computer usage not just for work applications, but for use in their everyday lives. In a June 1999 issue of *Fortune* magazine, Andrew Kupfer tells how rapidly use of the Internet has grown. "At the end of 1997, about 41 million American adults used the World Wide Web. That figure is expected to be at least 92 million users by 2002."

Technology industries are struggling to keep up with the demand for increased capacity. Larger cable highways, optical fiber pipes, and laser technology are all developing initiatives financed by telecommunication ventures to improve Web use in offices and homes alike. Home users will benefit through increased access to information and improved means of downloading video and audio programs. Libraries, grocery stores, gas stations, and vacation and travel arrangements all require computer-related transactions. Computers and the Internet are an integral part of our lives.

A computer can remember billions, even trillions, of facts. A computer can search a database with billions of records in a fraction of a second to help us solve complex problems. *USA Today* reported in October 1998 that IBM had developed the world's fastest computer. Developed for the Energy Department, this supercomputer could perform 3.9 trillion operations a second. Obviously, computers will take over more and more of our computational tasks just as machines took over most heavy physical labor in the past.

Don't worry, computers are not going to replace humans. No matter how sophisticated they become, they are still incapable of most human intellectual activity, from impossible-to-quantify elements like creativity and intuition to surprisingly complex tasks like driving a car. They cannot gather information or decide which figures need to be calculated and why. Some people expect them to be as intelligent as humans, but too many elements of human intelligence go beyond mere memory and computation. Plus, humans don't usually freeze or crash in the middle of a conversation or lose their memories because of a power surge. Computers are important tools, and will be increasingly important in our lives, but we must remember that they are just tools.

All this information technology has the potential of widening the division between the "haves" and the "have nots." Technology is expected to increase wealth but not to distribute it equally. As noted earlier, knowledge and skills will mean better income. If technical training is not widespread,

TECHNOLOGY CONNECTION

Futurists tell us that communication between all electronic components will be wireless. Most text will be created using continuous speech recognition. Most routine business transactions (purchases, travel reservations) will take place between a human and a virtual personality—an animated visual presence that looks like a human face. Although traditional classrooms will still exist, intelligent courseware will be the more common means of learning.

Ray Kurzweil, *Across the Board*, August 1999

The benefits seem obvious, but what do you think the disadvantages or drawbacks would be of relying so much on computers? How might we compensate or overcome these problems?

The "digital divide" is affecting economic and social change in America.

quick wit
. . . .

"Reverence for the past is important, but so is regard for the future."

. . . .
Brad Herzog

people could slip into poverty if they lose their jobs because of advancing technologies.

Another effect of technology is what sociologists call the "digital divide." Just as technology affects economic standing, it also creates social change in very subtle ways. Those with access to computers and those with good computer skills will have the advantage in an economy that rewards the cyber-educated and punishes the cyber-phobic. National policy makers, business leaders, social leaders, and concerned citizens everywhere are working tirelessly to bridge this gap.

Special efforts are being made to bring computers into communities, teach basic computer literacy, and provide Internet access to disadvantaged individuals in hopes of making them more employable. Avram Miller, in a *FastCompany* article dated July 7, 1999, says, "Closing the digital divide is the way to give each American a chance to sit at the table of opportunity created by the Information Revolution."

Computers, increasingly complex, are being programmed to mimic human intelligence. This process is called **artificial intelligence**. The B-2 Stealth bomber, one of the most complex mechanical systems ever conceived, was engineered and produced totally on the computer. Not a shred of paper was used.

TECHNOLOGY CONNECTION

Home computers are becoming more common each year. In 1996, only 40 percent of American households owned computers. By 2000 the percentage will exceed 60 percent. By 2010 Americans will experience much improved services. Computers, televisions, wireless phones, and other telecommunication devices will be integrated and supplied by a large number of competing providers. Almost 90 percent of households will own computers by 2010.

US News & World Report, October 27, 1997

Do you own a computer? If so, what do you use it for? What computer functions do you think might be useful to you in the future?

Technological innovations will continue to displace millions of employees but provide better products at lower prices. Overall, the numbers of jobs will not diminish. As some occupations disappear, new ones will be created. For example, while many manufacturing jobs are being taken by robotic replacements, the number of jobs in export-related manufacturing work has increased. Many of the manufacturing jobs lost to developing countries represented low-productivity, low-paying jobs. The demand for more specialized, high-paying jobs has increased as America produces goods for sale in ever expanding global markets.

WORKPLACE ADAPTATIONS

The pace of technological change will continue to increase. Skills and knowledge will become obsolete faster than ever before. Employers will look for workers with leading-edge skills, but the leading edge can quickly become the lagging-edge if skills aren't updated. The life of an engineer's knowledge today is, in some fields, as little as three years. Constant retraining will become essential to keep people from becoming increasingly less qualified for their jobs.

Businesses will seek to upgrade employee skills as quickly as possible. Companies have a vested interest in keeping valued employees up-to-date, and in-house training programs are on the rise. Most major corporations

Skills and knowledge will become obsolete faster than ever before.

Continuing education in the workplace will be a necessity.

TECHNOLOGY CONNECTION

"Plugged In" is a community technology-access center that is closing the gap between technological "haves" and "have nots" one bus pass at a time. Bart Decrem, a graduate of Stanford University's Law School, has brought computers and other electronic gadgets to an economically disadvantaged neighborhood in Silicon Valley. Next door to a liquor store, a car wash, and a wig shop, the run-down building is unassuming. Decrem says, "We try to expose residents to technologies in a non-threatening way."

Walk in the front door and there is a photocopy machine, a wire stand holding copies of a free local newspaper and a part-time bilingual staff person ready to sell a discount bus pass or help customers use the computers that fill the back of the room. Plugged In operates with the belief that information technology has to become part of a community. It has been so successful that most of its operational budget is provided by nearby Silicon Valley giants Sun Microsystems, Cisco Systems, Hewlett-Packard, Oracle, and Intel. Decrem understands that the real power of the Information Revolution is not the technology itself—but in teaching people to grab hold of that technology as a tool to help them build better lives.

Sara Terry, *FastCompany*, August 1999

How would you advise someone who isn't comfortable with the computer to gain some skill and confidence? To what places (such as libraries, schools, community centers) might you take them to help them gain experience? How do you find out technical information when you need it?

either have personnel on staff or bring in outside experts to make sure important skills are learned and kept sharp. This trend should increase.

For-profit and not-for-profit organizations designed to keep people's technical skills sharp are increasing in number as well. The changing technologies will result in the necessity for constant learning and adaptation by workers, but the availability of information and trainers is increasing to meet that need. Never before have we had more places or more ways to gain technical skills and knowledge.

Quick Tip . . . .

"For all workers, the premium on education, flexibility, and vision
has never been as important as in the years to come."

—Ken Blanchard

. . . .

The cyber-society will put a high premium on such entrepreneurship.
Imaginative and energetic self-starters who can recognize emerging needs
and create ways to fill them will be in high demand. One example is the
Nebraska newspaper that has begun using a software program developed by
one of the paper's new employees. The program can, in effect, write sports
stories—once the computer is fed a few facts, the program fills in the rest of
the words to make a breathless report of any sporting event.

CASE STUDIES IN THE NEWS

Martin Carnoy, professor of education and economics at Stanford University, has done extensive research on widening wage gaps. "There
has always been a big gap between the lifetime wages of those who
graduate from high school and those who graduate from college. But the
gap is bigger now than ever before." A college graduate will often earn as much
as 58 percent more than a high school graduate.

Finis Welch, professor of economics at Texas A&M says, "It's not a very good
time to be uneducated and young." He reports that employers see a high school
diploma today much like employers saw an eighth-grade education in times
past. As more and more people go to college, the people who don't are at a
growing disadvantage. He also mentions that even today's factory worker has at
least some college and the average secretary at A&M has a bachelor's degree
and some even hold master's degrees.

—L. M. Sixel, *Houston Chronicle*, January 1995

*Faced with these facts, what can you do to ensure that you are ready for the
future? How can you prepare, and how might you keep up with change?*

As discussed earlier, Americans are getting older, and another adaptation that will likely occur in the work place will be catering to the growing numbers of older workers. Whether these adaptations take the form of retraining, making accommodations for physical limitations, providing elder care for parents of workers, or some combination of these will depend on both demands of individual industries and regional demographics.

Further Globalization

Globalization is making goods and services available worldwide with no trade barriers or boundaries.

Globalization is a crucial piece of the changes we face in the twenty-first century. Container ships, jets, satellite communications, and the Internet have created an international market. Manufacturing is relocating overseas, and workers now move around the world with increasing ease. The cost of transporting goods and communicating globally has dropped so dramatically that distance is no longer an issue. Buyers in Dallas are able to transact daily business needs with sellers in South Africa.

This trend toward making goods and services worldwide in scope with no national boundaries or trade barriers on where they are sold or where they are produced is called **globalization**.

The globalization of manufacturing means that a metal bolt produced in Malaysia must precisely fit a nut made in Thailand and hold together parts made in Brazil and Chile. Electronic components may be bought from Japan, assembled in Mexico, and sold in the United States. Gone will be the days of "Made in Japan" or "Made in the U.S." as true identifiers of product origins.

Even cuisine has become more international, as those who do not travel expect greater variety at home (though what is exotic is defined by where you live—in the U.S., you may seek out Indian food; in Ecuador, Pizza Hut may win your heart). Meanwhile travelers from Asia, Europe, and the Americas hope to find the "comforts of home" when they travel, whether it takes the form of a sushi bar in Paris or a McDonald's in Moscow. The world's people and businesses share more in common every day.

Quick Tip

"He who is not courageous enough to take risks will accomplish nothing in life."

—Muhammed Ali

Nations will become more specialized economically. In this intensely competitive global market, nations will seek to discover which products

McDonald's still serves the Quarter Pounder with fries under the golden arches in Moscow.

they can produce most economically and to greatest advantage. The U.S. will begin to specialize in those markets most likely to make it competitive, so that it remains a formidable force in the world economy.

Of course, there is the danger that we will become too homogenized, that we will lose all the differences that make life good. Countering this is another trend—organizations and individuals who are trying to hang on to regional differences, biodiversity, the good things of each individual culture.

Evidence of these shifts in our economy is revealed in the growing numbers of companies with world-wide holdings. More than 100,000 firms are engaged in some type of international venture, with a combined value of more than $1 trillion. Ann Vincola, senior vice president of Work/Life Benefits in Boston, reports that, "One of every five American workers is employed at a company with a global presence and the number is

The global market will continue to affect our nations in many ways and require a constant adjustment to changing environments.

CASE STUDIES IN THE NEWS

As homogenous fast-food outlets proliferate, Slow Food is trying to raise awareness of the benefits of biodiversity. The organization's founder, Carlo Petrini, notes, "McDonald's, or any other of the big fast-food purveyors, want to make their hamburgers everywhere. We instead want to encourage respect for the culture and cooking of every region." Petrini and colleagues wrote a manifesto urging Italians not to lose sight of their cultural patrimony. Paul Bartolotta, executive chef at Chicago's Spiaggia restaurant, adds, "The Slow Food movement is one of the very few tools we have to defend ourselves from being enslaved by the speed in which the world is working."

Susanne Fowler, *The Chicago Tribune*, November 1998

This article addresses concerns over the loss of regional differences in cuisine, but what other differences do you think might be lost with increasing globalization? How do you think important traditions can be preserved while still gaining the benefits of operating in a world market?

increasing daily." In fact, many of today's fast-track employees are expected to do a job rotation abroad as part of their road to success. This involvement in the cultures of other nations has caused a unique set of problems in preparing individuals for working in countries far from home.

FastChat

1. Which technologies have affected your life, and in what ways?

2. Do you use the Internet at home, office, or school? How is it beneficial to you?

3. How would you feel about being sent overseas on a job assignment? Why do you think this is beneficial to employers and employees?

What Must Our Country Do?

All these changes challenge us to do business in new ways. Already some innovative organizations are moving to meet these challenges. However, much more must be done by private and public sectors as well as by individuals to ensure that the United States remains a strong force in the world economy.

ACCEPTING THE NEW NATURE OF WORK

As a nation we must pay more attention to the growth of economics throughout the world. We must not simply watch the trends, but adapt to them and discover the best way to utilize the benefits while minimizing the disadvantages.

In the new economy, U.S. companies will need to attract and keep the best people in order to remain competitive in an increasingly tight market. To do this, they must begin to create environments that meet more of the needs of workers. A recent report by the Center for Work & Family at Boston College reports that, "work and family issues have become an important part of attracting new and keeping experienced employees."

U.S. businesses are beginning to address the need to help employees balance work and family commitments. Work/life issues taken into consideration, usually at time of hiring, include child care benefits, maternity/parental leave rights, health care, career breaks or sabbaticals, alternative work options (flextime), and telecommuting. Work/life benefits are gaining acceptance largely because companies see the link between high morale and outstanding performance.

A 1998 study by *Fortune* magazine found that 73 percent of those companies that made the list of "100 Best Places to Work in America" reported much higher than average annual returns on their investments after improving work/life benefits. Work/life programs are definitely on the rise and represent the realities of leading a company in the new global marketplace.

Job candidates are letting employers know that they do not want their work to be their life and that they want a job with reasonable hours and benefits. What happens when people work fewer hours, at different times,

Learning
Objective   3

Explain what the country must do to meet the challenges of a changing work force and new economic realities.

quick wit

"The future ain't what it used to be."

Yogi Berra

Work/life issues are becoming an important part of the work place.

CASE STUDIES IN THE NEWS

A 1998 survey by Bethesda, Maryland-based Watson Wyatt Worldwide, reports that flex options, job sharing and other scheduling alternatives are moving into the corporate mainstream. Half of all large U.S. companies surveyed, and nearly a third of mid-sized companies, are making non-traditional arrangements commonplace. As corporate boundaries extend worldwide, an organization's work/life programs must look at issues from a global perspective. Motivating and supporting today's global work force means addressing the diverse needs and desires of all employees.

—Ann Vincola, *Global Workforce*, July 1998

How do you think the trends facing the U.S. business might compare to trends in other countries?

What do you think a company could do to accommodate an international workforce?

Integration is a method employers use for offering a full array of worklife options for selection by employees

and sometimes in places other than an office? According to a worldwide poll taken by *U.S. News & World Report*, 62 percent of the managers said shorter hours give employees an incentive to be more productive on the job. European economists have reported a rise in productivity when employees are allowed choices in work/life arrangements. Many industries have still not adopted these ideas, and downsizing has meant that many employees are spending longer hours than ever before at work, but things are beginning to change.

The Spring 1999 issue of *Future Times* said, "Sabbaticals will become standard in many professions. More workers will take a break to raise a family, start a business, take care of elder family members, or simply recharge themselves for their next stage of life." With all the technology now available, many companies are allowing employees to choose their place of work. Sue Shellenbarger, in a 1998 *Wall Street Journal* article, reports, "With the PC, cordless phones, car phones, pagers, the fax, e-mail, voice mail, etc., it may be best to let employees set their own hours and places of work. If your objectives are clear, you don't have to be in a cubicle to accomplish them."

CASE STUDIES IN THE NEWS

New grads who join the company Synopsys will find an environment that allows even hard-working technical folks to have a life outside of the company. Synopsys embraces the idea of balancing work and family. Says a company spokesman, "We understand that a lot of our people have young children and have to leave at day's end to pick them up from day care."

Besides the ability to go home on time, Synopsys employees get other work/life help from the company. The Feeling Better program provides temporary child care for employees, children with minor illnesses that keep them out of school or day care. Feeling Better is free to employees and available on short notice. Other flexibility comes from the ability to pool vacation and sick time to accommodate individual needs.

Synopsys Company Web Page, June 1998

Do you think that only people with children need help balancing work and life? What other measures might a company take to help employees achieve balance—while still remaining competitive and profitable?

In that same article, Shellenbarger coins the newest buzzword in family friendliness: integration. **Integration** is the blending of work and family to create a more satisfying whole. Employers will increasingly offer a full array of work/life options in their efforts to attract and keep top performing workers as integration becomes an increasingly important issue. The convergence of work and home life is one of the top ten trends of the next decade.

Telecommuting, when employees do their work at home on a computer that is linked to their office, is one of the many options increasingly being offered. Trend trackers all agree that much of the next century's work will be decentralized, done at home or in satellite offices on a schedule tailored to fit workers' lives and the needs of their families. The State of Oregon's Office of Energy promotes telecommuting for environmental reasons—fewer people on the roads means less pollution.

Offering employees alternatives, both in hours and in location, will become increasingly common.

Charlie Grantham, director of the Institute for the Study of Distributed Work in Windsor, California, reports that, "Between 1990 and 1998, telecommuting doubled from about 3 percent to 6 percent of the working population—or about 8.2 million people." These numbers are expected to double again in the very near future. As much as 12 percent of the population is expected to be telecommuting by the year 2005.

At the heart of all these changes is the fact that we have finally begun to separate the idea of work from the place where we do it. Acceptance will require some culture changes among supervisors, who must learn to trust employees to do their jobs. Accepting these changes will make blending—integrating—work and family a lot easier for many people.

High performance practices are encouraged among employees.

Most employers will also find it beneficial to encourage high performance practices among its employees. Of 39 high-performance practices that researchers examined, team building and self-managed work teams appeared to be the top predictors of employee empowerment and positive business outcomes, as reported in "Global High-Performance Work Practices." The outcomes most affected by these methods were product quality, customer service, worker satisfaction, and productivity.

Some companies have reported experiencing more than a 50 percent increase in productivity through high-performance practices. These companies are located in Australia, the Pacific Rim, France, South Africa, and the U.S. No matter which high-performance practices were employed, companies in all regions experienced improved results.

Managing employees in the Knowledge Era requires different methods of dealing with the creative talents. Managers should not try to gain control—they should surrender it. One way that companies are accomplishing this is by encouraging the internal formation of **Communities of Practice (COPS)**. COPS are highly-synergistic peer groups working on projects or problems of shared interest. These are small groups working toward a common purpose, the members of which need or want to know what the others in the group know. This type of group is similar to those introduced in Chapter 6.

Quick Tip

"Companies that embrace the emergent use of COPS can tap the logic of knowledge work and the spirit of community. Those that don't will be left behind.

—Gil Amelio

Human Relations

The members of a COPS group may be performing the same job (like technical reps), collaborating on a shared task (software development), or working on product development (engineers, manufacturers, specialists). This band of colleagues, held together by friendships and loyalties formed from working on one project, will often rejoin to tackle another problem simply out of mutual interest, forming an informal, inquisitive group—very dynamic, intense, and fun! These informal groups can often create and develop new ideas in much shorter time than they would by going through traditional, formal channels or waiting for a formal team to be appointed.

INCREASING PRODUCTIVITY AND QUALITY

As the economy becomes more service-oriented, we must increase worker output in health care, education, retailing, government, and other services. To stimulate the economy, the government must privatize many of its services and invest in technologies that enhance productivity in services, particularly education and health care.

To remain competitive, corporations must increase quality and productivity.

The quality of products and services must become the concern of all people involved, from the CEO to the shop floor employee, because firms will increasingly buy from those who offer high quality, low cost products.

Productivity is as much a concern as quality. Although we lead the world in innovative ideas, we often take too long to get products into the marketplace, according to Ronni Sandroff in *Working Woman*. For example, Japan takes only 40 months to move a new car from design concept through manufacturing into the market. Our system requires approximately 60 months. The United Kingdom produces new drug products in approximately 2 months, but we take 5 months. Of course, much of this is due to Federal regulations, which maintain higher safety standards than much of the rest of the world, but also slows down productivity. We need to explore how we can maintain our exceptional innovation and high safety standards and still get products to the market more quickly.

These types of problems require restructuring our management approaches. Reshaping worker attitudes and using new technology in manufacturing will help increase productivity and reduce costs. Many companies are now using progressive leadership and motivational techniques to help improve quality and productivity.

EDUCATING AND TRAINING OUR WORK FORCE

We must make sure that our work force does not lose its adaptability, flexibility, and willingness to learn. National policies that promote corporate

Continuing education is a key to economic success.

and personal willingness to retrain must be developed. We must support them with changes in tax codes to encourage lifelong learning.

As technology outpaces skill levels and skill requirements change rapidly, more companies are offering continuing education to their employees as a means to remain productive. Computer literacy heads the list of types of training offered to employees, followed closely by basic math skills. Employers provide training not only in occupational skills but also in basic skills such as reading, arithmetic, and logical reasoning. Estimates on annual spending by employers on formal and informal training of employees far exceed $200 billion. Continuing education has become a permanent fixture in corporations.

Most community colleges in the country have partnerships with businesses and industries to help train local employees, either at the company site or on campus. The training covers a variety of topics, including updated technical skills, such as new computer software; human relations and supervisory training for new supervisors; and training in new processes and procedures for employees ranging from secretaries to chemical process operators.

MEETING THE NEEDS OF THE CHANGING WORK FORCE

Today's workers bring a new set of expectations into the work force. Greater responsibility and increased involvement in decision making, recognition and appreciation for a job well done, interesting and challenging work, and more leisure time are priorities. The chapter on motivation (Chapter 3) addresses ways in which corporations are changing management styles to try to satisfy these needs.

The desire for **entrepreneurship**—organizing, managing, and assuming the risks of a business enterprise—is stronger in today's worker. Michael Kiernan points out that 70 percent of recent graduates from the Harvard Business School want to own and manage their own businesses within the

Human Relations

next five to ten years. They desire the challenge, variety, and personal satisfaction of being fully responsible for the outcome of their actions.

Companies are responding to this desire by developing what is called intrapreneurship. **Intrapreneurship** is the conscious effort of organizations to identify and support employees who wish to pursue an entrepreneurial idea for a new service or product. IBM used this process successfully to develop the personal computer.

Some companies are experimenting with motivating employees through profit sharing, which allows employees to take home in bonuses what they help earn in profits for the company. These options have been highly effective with new startup companies who offer stock options and later go public or are bought out by larger companies. Piecework or incentive pay arrangements are also being explored, with minimal hourly rates set and additional dollars earned for extra work performed.

Companies are also offering "cafeteria-style" benefit packages. Employees can select from a variety of options for medical and dental plans, short- and long-term insurance plans, and other programs for retirement benefits or other work/life options. This approach is more appealing to workers than being limited to a single plan that was selected with an economic advantage for the company. The opportunities for employees to take an active role in their working environments has never been more diverse and encouraged.

*Fast*Chat

1. What work/life issues would be important to you? How would this affect your selection of an employer?

2. How have high-performance practices affected you either at work or in school? Have you participated in any of these groups? How effective do you think they were?

3. Why do you think telecommuting has become such a prominent trend in today's work force?

4. What steps are you taking to assure that your skills and education will help in determining your desired earnings level?

Learning
Objectives 4 and 5

Explain what skills will be in demand in the twenty-first century.
Discuss what you can do to prepare yourself to enter this changing work force.

If you want to thrive in this new work world, you will need a personal strategy to navigate the exciting and turbulent times ahead. Education—and learning how to learn—will be vital. Communication and human relations skills need to be honed. Recognizing job trends and preparing for transitions into these jobs will be important to your success in the work place. You will need to be able to adjust to the new work environments and remain flexible in adapting to changes. You will have challenges, but you will have even more opportunities, and if you're prepared, your options will be almost unlimited.

PURSUE SKILL AND KNOWLEDGE

Education will become *more* important as technology provides more information because machines can't tell bad data from good, valuable information from useless, accurate information from inaccurate. Employees who can not only work with computers but who can also filter the incoming information, discern, make decisions, and address problems will be in great demand.

Do not wait for your employer to train you. Realize that you must take control of your own career and personal development and take advantage of courses at your community college. Get a degree or certificate. Learn a foreign language. Sign up for any optional training offered by your employer. Learn a new software application. Read about the cultures of countries where your company does business.

Educate yourself by reading and watching educational television programs. The more you understand about how business operates and what is going on in the world, the more effective you will be as an employee. Include information that will not become obsolete—topics that deal with life and human nature or that sharpen your problem-solving skills (most CEOs love reading mysteries, for example)—as well as keeping up with business topics and changing trends.

Acquire and practice effective communication skills (discussed in Chapter 9). As the workplace becomes more complex and fast-paced, these skills will become even more important. Good communication and human relation skills can make you more valuable as an employee and can help reduce stress, both yours and that of those around you.

RECOGNIZING JOB TRENDS

Many new jobs are surfacing as our technologies advance and the shift to services influences the work place. For example, the market gained a net of 9.4 million net new jobs between 1989 and 1996. In such a competitive and rapidly changing economy, old skills become outdated and new skills are needed. Because most people after the age of 25 change occupations three times and jobs six times, you must be prepared to recognize job shifting and learn new skills that will prepare you to make moves to your best advantage. The table on page 610 lists the twenty-five occupations projected to grow most rapidly between 1994 and 2005 as reported by the Bureau of Labor Statistics.

As technology moves into more areas of work and life, being skilled in computers becomes crucial. The more comfortable you are with computers, the better. Plan to become skilled in computer applications useful to your business and employer. These technological marvels are here to stay, and many future jobs will be tied to their use. Computers in many forms will affect both your business and your personal life. Even your recreational activities may require some use or understanding of computer applications.

Here is a sampling of jobs that are likely to provide growing opportunities in the years ahead, jobs that are likely to vanish, and jobs that will be altered by communications and information technologies. These were categorized by Thomas Henderson in a new Futurists publication, *Outlook 2000*, and placed in the three groupings shown below.

Recognizing the trends of what's in and what's out can help you tailor your career for long life rather than obsolescence. Be aware that other jobs exist. Some of them may be good opportunities for you and can help you avoid dead ends.

Future Jobs

Accelerating	Evaporating	Cybernating
Entrepreneurs, personal counselors, personal home organizers, retirement planners, aromatherapists, genetic engineers, private community guards, software engineers, construction managers, Web site designers, financial services managers, computer artists and animators	Traditional travel agents, soldiers, blue collar workers, telephone linemen, computer data entry workers, library researchers, bank tellers, and telephone operators	Storytellers for virtual-reality games, online travel agents, doctors using e-mail and video conferencing for tele-medicine practices, military planners, funeral managers

The 25 Fastest *Growing* Occupations, 1994–2005

Occupation (Only occupations with at least 100,000 employees in 1994 are included.)	Employment 1994	Employment 2005	Net job growth (thous.)	Percent change in employment
Personal & home care aides	179	391	212	118%
Home health aides	420	848	428	102%
Systems analysts	483	928	445	92%
Computer engineers	195	372	177	91%
All other computer scientists	149	283	134	90%
Physical therapists	102	183	81	79%
Residential counselors	165	290	125	76%
Human services workers	168	293	125	74%
Medical assistants	206	327	121	59%
Paralegals	110	175	65	59%
Teachers, special education	388	593	205	53%
Amusement and recreations attendants	267	406	139	52%
Corrections officers	310	468	158	51%
Guards	867	1,282	415	48%
All other health service workers	157	224	67	43%
Dental hygienists	127	180	53	42%
Dental assistants	190	269	79	42%
Adjustment clerks	373	521	148	40%
Sales workers in securities and financial services	246	335	89	36%
Bill and account collectors	250	342	92	37%
Emergency medical technicians	138	187	49	36%
Management analysts	231	312	81	35%
Bakers, bread and pastry	170	230	60	35%
Instructors and coaches, sports and physical training	283	381	98	35%
Food services and lodging managers	579	771	192	33%
All 25 occupations	**6,753**	**10,591**	**3,838**	**57%**

Source: Bureau of Labor Statistics

Technological advances have become a part of everyday life.

The table on page 612 provides a list from the Bureau of Labor Statistics of 25 occupations that are already shrinking and which will continue to fade in the 21st century. Many of these jobs will be eliminated because of advancing information technologies. New methods of performing work will enable machines to take the place of humans in some job categories. Improved software applications and smarter computer systems will replace some computer operator jobs. As you can see, the banking, accounting, and garment industries are highly affected by the shifts in occupations. New developments will affect different industries, so stay up to date on trends.

ADJUSTING TO NEW WORK ENVIRONMENTS

Quick Tip

"People will have access to information and be able to do things with it that they never thought possible."

—Cathy Lyons

Technological progress in the next decade will probably not focus on the desktop computer. Instead, it will center on bringing greater simplicity and

The 25 Fastest *Shrinking* Occupations, 1994–2005

Occupation (Only occupations with at least 100,000 employees in 1994 are included.)	Employment 1994	Employment 2005	Net job growth (thous.)	Percent change in employment
Computer operators	259	162	−97	−37%
Machine tool cutting operators	119	85	−34	−29%
Bank tellers	559	407	−152	−27%
Sewing machine operators, garment	531	391	−140	−26%
File clerks	278	236	−42	−15%
Electrical and electronic assemblers	212	182	−30	−14%
Machine-forming operators	171	151	−20	−12%
Electrical and electronic assemblers, precision	144	127	−17	−12%
Communication, transportation, and utilities operations managers	154	135	−19	−12%
Tool and die makers	142	127	−15	−11%
Service station attendants	167	148	−19	−11%
Mail clerks, except-mail-machine operators and postal service	127	116	−11	−9%
Sewing machine operators	129	117	−12	−9%
Machine feeders and offbearers	262	242	−20	−8%
Bookkeeping & accounting clerks	2181	2003	−178	−8%
Payroll and timekeeping clerks	157	144	−13	−8%
Bartenders	373	347	−26	−7%
Industrial production managers	206	191	−15	−7%
Data entry keyers, except composing	395	370	−25	−6%
Insurance policy processing clerks	179	168	−11	−6%
Telephone and cable TV line installers and repairers	191	181	−10	−5%
Machinists	369	349	−20	−5%
Stenographers	105	102	−3	−3%
All other clerical workers	721	698	−23	−3%
Wholesale and retail buyers	180	178	−2	−1%
All 25 occupations		**7,357**	**2954**	**211%**

Source: Bureau of Labor Statistics

TECHNOLOGY CONNECTION

Manufacturers of digital imaging systems, printers, scanners, and faxes will continue their momentum in providing technology-oriented products that enable workers to better manage and process information. Software applications will monitor systems and help make the knowledge worker more productive in using new technologies. Future office products will operate transparently. Intelligent data management systems will receive data and automatically put it in specific, pre-determined places. The Internet, wireless and infrared technologies will allow much greater connectivity than ever before. The challenge will be to find ways to manage the information overload.

—Jill Brown, *OfficeSystems99*, June 1999

What types of data do you think these systems will handle? What strategies can people use to avoid information overload?

wider access to the Internet. We will be cruising down the Information Highway well into the future. Many experts advise that future workers will face problems concerning the amount of information they will receive and have to process. Intelligent data management, voice-recognition activation devices or yet-to-be-developed tools will prove essential to electronic knowledge workers.

Two major trends are having a negative effect on workers today. They warrant attention so that individuals can more effectively manage them in both their personal and work life. With the information overload, individuals are feeling a greater level of stress than ever before. Through mergers, downsizing, and streamlining, companies have drastically reduced the number of employees in some areas. However, few of these companies are cutting the workload. Juliet Schoor, in her book *The Overworked American*, reveals that, "The average American worker is working one week more per year than 10 years ago and feeling a good deal more stress." Particular attention must be given to the methods of dealing with stress and managing information overload. These problems are covered elsewhere in this text, but seeking more information on these topics may give you an advantage over workers who can't cope.

"The world is progressing rapidly and resources are abundant. I'd rather go into a grocery store today than to a king's banquet a hundred years ago."

. . . .

Bill Gates

Even more changes in our work environments are projected to occur in the not-so-distant future. The office as we know it today is expected to experience a dramatic transformation. In a global environment, companies will hire the best people to do the job no matter where they live or when they prefer to work. Today, a typical office allocates about 80 percent of the space to offices and cubicles, with the rest given to formal meeting rooms, but for some companies, this will change. In the Technology Connection below, Gil Gordon, a consultant based in New Jersey, offers insight into the office of 2020.

David Meckley, senior interior designer with RMW Architecture and Design in San Francisco, predicts that "Personal belongings will be in mobile carts or lockers, and employees will be able to choose where and with whom they will work that day." Everyone will be able to plug into the network, have the equipment with them that they need, and choose a spot that suits the needs of the day or week. Meckley predicts the death of the dreaded cubicle, and his predictions are upheld by other giants in office furniture and design industries. Steelcase and Herman Miller sell more than $5 billion worth of office furniture a year and are currently designing their furniture to this new set of rules.

Several companies in Silicon Valley have already incorporated the "virtual office" concepts in their buildings. KPMG Peat Marwick's employees

TECHNOLOGY CONNECTION

"Offices will become a place for focused work that requires true collaboration and occasional socializing to cement business relationships. Eventually, only 20 percent of floor space will be devoted to individual work stations, and 40 percent will host 'touch-down spaces' to land in but not to move into. We will temporarily occupy a space to access data or check e-mail. The remaining 40 percent of space will be devoted to sites used by teams and groups for interaction and decision making practices."

—Gil Gordon, *Working Mother*, June 1999

What effect do you think this type of office would have on the work? On the employees? In what businesses do you think this would be most likely to work? Least likely?

TECHNOLOGY CONNECTION

The KPMG building has a simple, logical layout from floor to floor so workers can become quickly oriented. The furniture to be used is in flexible configurations with big obvious wheels on it. Electrical and data outlets are plentiful and easy to locate. Included are high-tech presentation facilities, display work walls, and completely integrated network and telephone technology. Everything has wheels on it and is wireless. Employees are able to take their work wherever they want to go.

The reception area features a touch screen monitor that allows visitors and staff to check the location of daily events, find a KPMG employee, and even check personal schedules. Corners of the floors are dedicated to group work areas, rather than executive office space. Touch-down areas are located throughout the building and provide private spaces where workers can make confidential telephone calls or work undisturbed when a totally isolated area is required.

—Grace M. Rodriquez, Design Consultant to KPMG

What would be some of the difficulties of trying to set up an office like this for companies that cannot afford new buildings? The majority of this company's employees are normally in the field. Do you think these ideas would work as well with a company where most people are normally in the office?

spend most of their time out in the field, and the company chose to design their new building to accommodate the new office ideas.

Many other industry-leading companies have moved to the idea of the virtual office. Hewlett-Packard, Lotus Development, and IBM have all recently joined the trend for compelling business reasons. Economic advantages are realized through reduced real estate expenses, increased productivity, higher profits, global competition, and improved customer service. For example, with 20,000 mobile employees, IBM reduced real estate costs 40 to 60 percent per site for annual savings of $35 million. IBM also reported productivity increases of 15 percent or more. Reports from other companies cite productivity increases ranging from 15 to 40 percent through employee and customer satisfaction.

GLOBAL CONNECTION

To Swedes, accustomed to offices with open spaces with windows that let in fresh air and natural light, cubicles are part of an artificial, hermetically sealed environment that Americans have carried to a point of absurdity. Germans, likewise accustomed to fresh air and open-space work environments, also dislike cubes. Even more distasteful to them is the windowless meeting room. *Ein schwarzes Loch*, the black hole, they call it. To the Japanese, accustomed to working in open offices packed with a crowd of busy co-workers, cubicles are scorned as a hindrance to effective communication.

—David Stamps, *Training*, November 1996

What cultural differences between these countries and America might account for some of the differences in what they feel is an appropriate work environment? Why do you think Americans have generally been uncomfortable with the crowds and noise of an open office?

With telecommuting becoming so prevalent in our society, one other adaptation is worth mentioning. Approximately 21 million U.S. households have more than one PC today, and that number is expected to jump to 31 million or more by 2003. Today's 37 million home offices are expected to balloon to over 50 million in that same time period. To accommodate this transition, many home builders, telephone companies, and cable companies are offering Internet connections as part of their service packages.

IBM and Bell Atlantic have plans to work together on wiring 15,000 homes on the east coast (Maine to Virginia) for home networking over their telephone lines. Cisco has teamed with AT&T to provide home networking capability to its subscribers. Intel, Microsoft, Compaq, Hewlett-Packard, and most other big technology companies are expected to join this trend. The beauty of this will be the simplification of the processes involved in connecting your at-home computers to the Internet. You will be able to have full computing capability from your kitchen, home office, or game room.

CORBIS/Roger Ressmeyer

Our homes are being wired for total communications and Internet capabilities.

REMAINING FLEXIBLE FOR THE FUTURE

The nature of work is changing, and the employees who will be most likely to get ahead are those with the flexibility to adapt to the new nature of the work force and the global economy. Strong human relations skills will help these individuals move comfortably through a work force that is nearly half female and increasingly culturally diverse, and an ability to adapt will help them adjust to anything from a new office layout to an assignment overseas.

Education is the real key to flexibility. If you know how to learn and keep your skills sharp, you will be able to keep up with changes. Knowing the things that don't change, such as human nature and the need to communicate effectively, will give you the freedom to be flexible in the areas that do change. Learning how to discover what you need to know is a valuable skill. With solid skills and on-going education as a basis for your flexibility, you will be ready to embrace change. And if nothing else is certain, you can be certain that things will continue to change.

One change that is taking place is the rise of the free agent. This growing work-world phenomenon will likely touch all our lives in some way. **Free agents** are individuals who represent themselves and are responsible for managing themselves like a business. In the middle of the Digital Age, with the availability of telecommuting, you may possibly become a free agent someday.

There's a new movement in the land—as fast-growing as it is invisible. From coast to coast, in communities large and small, citizens are declaring their independence. There are some 25 million residents of Free Agent, USA. If we add up the self-employed, the independent contractors, the temporary hires—a working definition of the population of Free Agent Nation—we end up with more than 16 percent of the American work force as free agents. Free agents in the U.S. are people who move from project to project and who work on their own, sometimes for months, sometimes for days.

—Daniel H. Pink, *FastCompany*, January 1998

Given some of the trends you've noticed occurring in business, why do you think more and more people are becoming self-employed, or otherwise working as free agents? What are some of the potential disadvantages of being a free agent? The advantages?

Perhaps the increasing number of free agents results from all the corporate downsizing and mergers leaving people adrift and reluctant to put their trust and loyalty back in the corporate arena. Some say it is because the economy is "de-integrating," work is more often being outsourced, and business has migrated to the level of the individual. Perhaps it is simply further evidence of the emerging entrepreneurial nature of today's workers. One thing for certain, free agents are out there and doing well. The success of this movement is witnessed by the growth of supporting infrastructures, such as Kinko's and Staples, who are the satellite offices for many free agents.

Making way for the Millennials will be a survival technique for the 21st century. **Millennials** are members of the generation born between 1979 and 1995. The U.S. Census Bureau reports that we have 70.2 million Millennials. This is the next group of people to influence our lives in a major way—a larger population than their parents, the Baby Boomers. They are young, aggressive, and very plugged in. They are extremely comfortable with the computer, the Internet, and all the other e-commerce items.

Having grown up seeing their parents "downsized," they realize they have to make their own opportunities and believe in their own abilities. The entrepreneurial spirit runs deep, and free agents will be strongly represented. This generation is shaping our world as we move into the 21st century.

One last reminder: the key to surviving in a knowledge-based economy is learning. Maintain a hunger for learning. Get a solid basic education. Work for companies where you will be given a chance to continually learn new processes. Associate with super-charged experts or stimulating conversationalists so you can learn from one another. Continue your education at any level to keep the momentum.

Read voraciously. Read books, magazines, newsletters, newspapers, and on-line articles in areas of interest. Watch meaningful TV features. Research interesting topics on science, technology, and professional interests. Life-long learning will be a way of life for anyone who wishes to succeed, in business or in life, in the 21st century.

CASE STUDIES IN THE NEWS

Chris Meyer is director of the Center for Business Innovation at Ernst & Young. Meyer recruits people who want to learn from one another. He says, "People are attracted to the company because working here helps them become better than they could be otherwise. Through cutting-edge innovations, the Center offers its people a window onto the future.

Meyer says, "Working in the knowledge economy requires the ability to recognize patterns, to share ideas with people inside and outside your organization, to maintain relationships with people who have common interests and to pull value out of those relationships." He believes learning how to master those skills may be the most important kind of learning there is.

—Robert Reich, Secretary of Labor, 1998

Do you think you'd enjoy working for a company that focuses on learning? How do you think it could help you? What are some ways you might be able to gain this same "edge" on your own?

Advances in technology, global communication, and lifelong learning will be the frontier of the twenty-first century.

1. What skills do you think will be most helpful to you in this new millennium?

2. What might you do to become a free agent? Would that option appeal to you and why?

3. How are you preparing yourself for success in the knowledge era?

Summary

The composition of the work force and the dynamics of the economy will dramatically change in the next century. The work force will continue to diversify, with women, minorities, and older individuals making up an increasingly greater percentage of workers. In addition, illiteracy is a tremendous problem. Concerns are that future workers will not have the educational levels necessary to perform the jobs available.

The economy faces several challenges, among them a switch from manufacturing to service, advanced technology, adapting to the changing work place, and globalization. To meet these challenges, companies must address the needs of the diverse work force, increase quality and productivity, educate and train the work force, and promote diversity.

The new jobs of the 21st century will require more skills. To meet the challenges that the future holds, you must recognize trends in the job markets, adjust to the new work environment, remain flexible for the future, and make life long learning a permanent part of your life.

Key Terms

demographics
baby boomers
artificial intelligence
globalization
integration
telecommuting
Communities of Practice
entrepreneurship
intrapreneurship
free agents
Millennials

Review Questions

1. What are the emerging demographics of this country?
2. What are the major forces shaping our economy? Explain their effects.
3. What must this country do to meet the challenges of a changing work force and new economic realities?
4. Which skills will be in demand in the 21st century?
5. What can you do to prepare yourself to enter the work force of 2020?

Discussion Questions

Working in teams, acquiring useful information, understanding social, organizational, and technological systems, designing systems, listening, speaking, thinking creatively, making decisions, solving problems, seeing things in the mind's eye, and reasoning.

1. Imagine yourself in the year 2010. What job do you expect to be performing? From what age and ethnic groups do you expect your coworkers to be? What types of equipment do you expect to be using?
2. What do you think will happen to the economy if the literacy level of the work force continues to drop?
3. What skills do you need to develop to be a part of the work force of 2020?
4. Are you fluent in another language? Why or why not? What would be the advantages of learning another language?
5. Which of the major forces shaping the economy do you think is the most important? Why?
6. What do you think will happen if the gap between the haves and the have nots continues to widen?

Chapter Project

Working in small groups, brainstorm the workplace of the future. You may bring outside source materials in for reference, check web sites for additional materials, or rely on the diverse ideas of the group members. Design an office setting of the future. You are encouraged to take pictures, draw graphic illustrations, or present items in real-time. What kind of furniture will be there? What computer connectivities, if any, will be required? Present your design to the class with a verbal briefing on what is represented and why. Describe how it will work and who will be in it. Fully develop and present your ideal workplace of the future.

Applications

In small groups analyze the following situations.

R.I.P. Manufacturing

Ian, the production manager, wandered down the silent hall of the R. I. P. Manufacturing Company. He and Wilma, the personnel manager, were the last employees left. Everyone else had been laid off, and they would be leaving and locking the doors for the final time this afternoon. He stopped by Wilma's office one last time.

"I just don't understand what happened, Wilma," Ian said thoughtfully. "I thought those new precision machines would help us improve our quality. We just couldn't compete with the Germans, though. I could never get the product cost down as low as they could. And the quality just wasn't there. You know, I can't blame our customers for buying foreign."

"I know, Ian," Wilma sighed. "I just couldn't find employees who care about quality. You know, some of those folks simply had no skills. Then, when we finally got them up to speed on the equipment, they would leave. That made keeping the plant running at peak capacity impossible."

1. To what forces did R.I.P. fall victim?
2. What changes would have been necessary to save the company? Is the company responsible? Society? Both?
3. Do you foresee this same fate for other U.S. businesses today? Why or why not?

Working in teams, negotiating, interpreting and communicating, reading, speaking and listening, reasoning and thinking creatively, making decisions, and solving problems.

Diversity Does It!

Bob Johnson, the head research scientist at Alchemy Laboratories, drummed his fingers on the desk impatiently. "Well, I still like Jasper best for the job. I think he'll make a top-flight researcher for our team."

"Oh, come off it, Bob," replied Homero, the human resources manager. "You just don't want to consider Mai because she's a woman and she's Vietnamese. You know that she has more education and experience than Jasper. She's the best qualified candidate."

"Well, Homero," Bob replied, "you know I served in Viet Nam during the war. I still have nightmares about the whole affair."

"It's your decision, Bob, but just remember this," Homero said curtly as he rose to leave. "Your department is in real trouble. You haven't come up with a new idea in two years. Jasper won't help you get there. He's not capable. Besides, if you fail to hire Mai, you'll have the EEOC on your back."

Working in teams, negotiating, interpreting, communicating, and reading, speaking and listening, reasoning and thinking creatively, making decisions and solving problems.

1. Why does Bob not want to hire Mai?
2. What are the possible financial outcomes for Alchemy Laboratories if Bob fails to hire Mai?
3. What types of problems might occur at the lab if she is hired?
4. What can the company do to make cultural diversity a workable reality?

Additional Readings and Resources

www.att.com/telecommuting. Web site where AT&T offers ideas, advice and services for companies interested in telecommuting.

www.aflcio.org/women/equalpay.htm Web site provides information on women in the workforce.

www.dol.gov Web site for the U.S. Department of Labor provides labor statistics.

Check these publications on-line:

www.wsj.com *The Wall Street Journal*

www.pathfinder.com *Time and Fortune*

www.nytimes.com *The New York Times*

www.businessweek.com *Business Week*

Pink, Daniel H. "Free Agent Nation—There's a Movement in the Land." *FastCompany*, December 1997.

Notes

Chapter 1

Adams, Alice. "Soft skills are hard to beat." *Houston Chronicle*. December 6, 1998, Focus on Engineering, 5.

Andrews, Edmund. L. "Layoffs, Step by Step." *The New York Times*. February 13, 1996, C1.

Bell, Chip. *Managers as Mentors*. Cited in *Houston Chronicle*. December 13, 1996, 34.

Carnegie, Dale. How to Win Friends and Influence People. Cited in *Fundamentals of Human Relations* by Ralph D. Wray et al, Cincinnati: South-Western Publishing, 1996.

Davenport, Thomas H. *Process Innovation: Reengineering Work through Information Technology*. Boston: Harvard Business School Press, 1993.

Directory World, Many/June 1998. Cited in *Marketing Contract Training*. September 1998, Vol. 5, No. 8, 2.

Fayol, Henri. *General and Industrial Management*. Trans. Constance Storrf. London: Sir Isaac Pitman and Sons, Ltd., 1949.

Grey, Bernadette. "The Fearless Factor." *Working Woman*, July/August 1999, 6.

Hallett, Jeffrey. *Worklife Visions*. Alexandria, VA: American Society for Personnel Administrators, 1987.

Information Week, March 1998, p. 23, and April 1998, 5.

Krantz, Gene. Presentation at San Jacinto College, Pasadena, TX, November 16, 1998.

Marchant, Valerie. "Listen Up!" *Time*, June 28, 1999.

Martin, James. *Cybercorp*. New York: Amacom, 1996.

Maxon, Terry. "New chief giving American a new personality." *Houston Chronicle*, November 29, 1998, 5D.

Mayo, Elton. *The Human Problems of an Industrial Civilization*. New York: Macmillan Publishing Company, 1934.

Patton, Carrie. "Say the Magic Words." *Working Woman*, July/August 1999, 72.

Peters, Thomas J., and Robert H. Waterman, Jr. *In Search of Excellence*. New York: Warner Books, Inc., 1982.

Pybus, Kenneth R. "Jewel out of the rough." *Houston Business Journal*, November 6, 1998, 37A.

Raskin, Andrew. "Packing It In." *Inc. Technology*, 1999, No. 2, 47.

The State of Small Business—A Report of the President. Transmitted to the Congress 1989. Washington, DC: U.S. Government Printing Office, 1989.

Taub, Eric A. "Lost on the Web?" *Parade Magazine.* November 29, 1998, 8.

Taylor, Frederick W. *Principles of Management.* New York: Harper and Brothers, 1911.

"Top 50 woman-owned businesses take a bow." *Small Business Monthly (A Supplement of Houston Business Journal)*, September 1998, 3–23.

Udall, Sheila, and Jean M. Hiltrop. *The Accidental Manager.* Paramus, NJ: Prentice Hall.

Chapter 2

Baltus, Rita K. *Personal Psychology for Life and Work.* New York: McGraw-Hill, 1983.

"Beyond Positive Thinking." *Success.* December 1988, 31–38.

Burns, David D. Feeling Good: *The New Mood Therapy.* New York: William Morrow and Company, 1980.

Chapman, Elwood N. *Attitude Your Most Priceless Possession.* Menlo Park: Crisp Publications, Inc., 1995.

Gottesfeld, Harry. *Abnormal Psychology, A Community Mental Health Perspective.* Chicago: Science Research Associates, 1979.

"In the Mind's Eye." *Readings from Scientific American.* New York: Scientific American, Inc., 1986.

Kubler-Ross, Elisabeth. *Academic American On-Line Encyclopedia.* New York: Grolier, 1988.

Luft, Joseph. *Group Processes: An Introduction to Group Dynamics.* Mountain View, CA: Mayfield Publishing, 1984.

Luft, Joseph. *The Johari Window: A Graphic Model of Awareness in Relations.* Palo Alto, CA: National Press Books, 1970.

"Managing Your Boss." *Government Executive.* April 1989, 34–37.

St. John, Walter D. "Successful Communications between Supervisors and Employees." *Personnel Journal.* January 1983, 71–77.

Sargent, Alice G. *Androgynous Manager.* New York: AMACOM, Division of American Management Association, 1983.

Strasser, Stephen. *Working It Out—Sanity & Success in the Workplace.* Englewood Cliffs, NJ: Prentice-Hall, Inc., 1989.

Chapter 3

Applegate, Gary. *Happiness, It's Your Choice.* Sherman Oaks, CA: Berringer Publishing, 1985.

Bernstein, Albert J., and Sydney Craft Rozen. "How to Re-Energize Your Staff." *Working Woman.* April 1989, 45–46.

Bittel, Lester R. and J. E. Ramsey. *Handbook for Professional Managers.* New York: McGraw-Hill, 1985.

Blanchard, Kenneth, and Spencer Johnson. *The One Minute Manager*. New York: William Morrow and Company, 1982.

Burke, Natalie. "Gen X Entrepreneurs Embrace Self-Reliance." *Nevada Outpost*, June 1, 1997.

Coates, Claudia. "Money Doesn't Buy Loyalty—Titles Do." *Associated Press*, July 19, 1998.

Drucker, Peter. *The Practice of Management*. New York: Harper & Row, 1954.

Drucker, Peter. *Management: Tasks, Responsibilities, Practices*. New York: Harper & Row, 1974.

Fuller, John. *Behavior Genetics*. New York: John Wiley & Sons, 1964.

Gellerman, Saul W. *Motivation and Productivity*. New York: American Management Association, Inc., 1963.

Herzberg, Frederick. *Work and the Nature of Man*. World Publishing Company, 1966.

Herzberg, Frederick. "One More Time: How Do You Motivate Employees?" *Harvard Business Review Classic*. September/October 1987, Reprint 87507, 112.

Maslow, Abraham H. *Motivation and Personality*. Harper & Row, 1954.

McClelland, David C. *Studies in Motivation*. New York: Appleton-Century Crofts, 1955.

McClelland, David C., and David H. Burnham. "Power Is the Great Motivator." January-February 1995, pp. 123–139.

McGregor, Douglas. *The Human Side of Enterprise*. New York: McGraw-Hill, 1960.

Sixel, L. M., "Oldies Station Has Fresh Ideas." *Houston Chronicle*, November 13, 1998.

Vroom, Victor H. *Work and Motivation*. New York: John Wiley & Sons, 1964.

Wittenberg, Peter. "Baby Boomers See Their Jobs Mainly as a Way to Pay Bills." *The Houston Post*. September 4, 1989, A-1.

Chapter 4

Barlow, Jim. "Nine steps toward a great workplace." *Houston Chronicle*, April 11, 1999.

Calano, Jimmy, and Jeff Salzman. "Ten Ways to Fire Up Your Creativity." *Working Woman*. July 1989, 94–95.

"Computers not the real reason for rage on job?" *Houston Chronicle*, March 26, 1999, 5G.

Dessler, Gary. "Management: Leading People and Organizations in the 21st Century." http://www.phlip.marist.edu/dessler/news/mlpo1117.htm

"Earned Value—Just Fun." http://nnh.com/ev/quotes2.html

Feinberg, Mortimer R. "Manager's Tipsheet—The Special Art of Managing Creative People." *Working Woman*. April 1989, 40. (Reprinted from

"Management Letter," 1988, by the Bureau of Business Practice, Inc., Waterford, CT.)

Hamel, Gary, and C.K. Prahalad. *Competing for the Future.* 1994 Soundview Executive Book Summaries, 16–24.

"How to Harness Creativity." *Personal Report for the Executive.* New York: National Institute of Business Management, July 1, 1989.

Hunter, Mark. "Work, Work, Work." *Modern Maturity*, May–June 1999, 37.

Jones, Gladys Montgomery. "Framing the Future: How Johnson and Johnson Executives Keep in Touch with a Changing Marketplace—and One Another." *Continental*, March 1999, 39–41.

Kanter, Rosabeth Moss. "How to be an Entrepreneur without Leaving Your Company." *Working Woman.* November 1988, 44, 46, 48.

Kossen, Stan. *The Human Side of Organizations.* New York: Harper & Row, 1983.

Maslow, Abraham H. "The Scientific Study of Inventive Talent." *A Source Book for Creative Thinking.* Edited by S. J. Parnes and H. F. Harding. New York: Scribner, 1962.

McFarling, Usha Lee. "Funny how humor study hit its mark." *Houston Chronicle*, April 1, 1999, 8A.

Pape, William R. "Virtual Manager. Size Matters." *Inc. Tech*, 1999, 31.

Raudsepp, Eugene. "How Creative Are You?" *Nation's Business.* June 1985, 25–26.

Schadewald, Bill. "There's a buzzword born every minute." *Houston Business Journal*, January 22–28, 1999, 24A.

Shattuck, Harry. "Humor is open to interpretation." *Houston Chronicle*, December 27, 1998, 3G.

Simmons, Kathy. "Managing Generation X." *The Rotarian*, September 1999, 8.

Sussman, Lyle, and Samuel D. Deep. *COMEX: The Communication Experience in Human Relations.* Cincinnati: South-Western Publishing Company, Inc., 1984.

Wren, Daniel. *Management Innovators: The People and Ideas that Have Shaped Modern Business.* New York: Oxford University Press, 1998.

Chapter 5

Aldag, Ramon J., and Timothy M. Stearns. *Management.* Cincinnati: South-Western Publishing, 1987.

Bittel, Lester R. *What Every Supervisor Should Know.* New York: McGraw-Hill, 1985.

Burke, Ronald S., and Lester R. Bittel. *Introduction to Management Practice.* New York: McGraw-Hill, 1981.

Carr, David K. Henry Johansson (Contributor). *Best Practices in Reengineering.* New York: McGraw Hill, 1995.

Champy, James. *Reengineering Management.* New York: Harper Business, 1995.

Davis, Brian L., Lowell W. Hellervik, Carol J. Skube, Susan H. Gebelein, and James L. Sheard. *Successful Manager's Handbook*. Minneapolis: Personnel Decisions International, 1996.

Douglas, John, and Joseph L. Massie. *Managing—A Contemporary Introduction*. Englewood Cliffs, NJ: Prentice-Hall, 1985.

Drucker, Peter F. *Management: Tasks, Responsibilities, Practices*. New York: Harper & Row, 1974.

Fishman, Charles. "Engines of Democracy." *FastCompany*. October, 1999, 174–202.

Halloran, Jack, and Douglas Benton. *Applied Human Relations*. Englewood Cliffs, NJ: Prentice-Hall, 1987.

Hammer, Michael, and James Champy. *Reengineering the Corporation*. New York: Harper Business, 1994.

Harragan, Betty Lehan. *Games Mother Never Taught You—Corporate Gamesmanship for Women*. New York: Warner Books, 1977.

http://sol.brunel.ac.uk/~jarvis/bola/competence/index.html Business Open Learning Archive Web site

http://www.semitechglobal.com Corporate Web site for Semi-Tech (Global)

Latner, Alexis Glynn. "Virtual Reality and Tangible Vision." *Collegium*. Fall '98 Winter '98, 24–26.

Pendleton, Jennifer. "Valley Business; Telecommuting Falls Short of Expections, Experts Say." *Los Angles Times*, December 8, 1998, Metro; Part B; Page 6; Zones Desk.

Peters, Tom. *The Circle of Innovation*. New York: Knopf, 1997.

Massie, Joseph L., and John Douglas. *Managing—A Contemporary Introduction*. Englewood Cliffs, NJ: Prentice-Hall, 1985.

Reece, Barry L., and Rhonda Brandt. *Effective Human Relations in Organizations*. Boston: Houghton Mifflin, 1987.

Chapter 6

Aldag, Ramon J., and Timothy M. Stearns. *Management*. Cincinnati: South-Western Publishing Company, 1987.

Berkman, Harold W., and Linda L. Neider. *The Human Relations of Organizations*. Boston: Kent Publishing Company, 1987.

Janis, Irving. *Victims of Groupthink*. Boston: Houghton Mifflin Company, 1992.

Leavitt, H. "Suppose We Took Groups Seriously . . ." in *Man and Work in Society*, edited by E. L. Cass and F. G. Zimmer. New York: Van Nostrand Reinhold, 1975.

Likert, R. "The Nature of Highly Effective Groups." in *New Patterns of Management*. New York: McGraw-Hill, 1961.

Roethlisberger, F. J., and W. J. Dickson. *Management and the Worker*. Cambridge: Harvard University Press, 1939.

Schien, E. H. *Organizational Psychology*, 3rd ed. Englewood Cliffs, NJ: Prentice-Hall, 1980.

Shaw, Marvin E. Group Dynamics: *The Psychology of Small Group Behavior*, 5th ed. New York: McGraw-Hill, 1996.

Chapter 7

"Creative Use of Workspaces Helps Companies Build on Productivity." *The Columbus Dispatch*, Sept. 27, 1999, Business Today, 8.

Dillon, Pat. "Conspiracy of Change." *Fast Company.* October 1998, 183–195.

McGregor, Douglas. *The Human Side of Enterprise*. New York: McGraw Hill, 1962.

Naisbitt, John. *Megatrends*. New York: Warner Books, 1982.

Solomon, Charlene Marner. "Building Teams Across Borders." *Global Workforce*. November 1998, 12–17.

Webster's Ninth New Collegiate Dictionary. Springfield, MA: Merriam-Webster Inc., 1985.

Chapter 8

Bachman, S. L., "Young Workers in Mexico's Economy—NAFTA Aims at Curbing Child Labor." *U.S. News and World Report*. September 1, 1997.

Chartrand, Sabra, "Unions Try to Secure a Place In The Changing Work World." The *New York Times*; www.nytimes.com/library/jobmarket/022397sabra.html.

Church, George J., "Labor Unions Arise—With New Tricks." *Time*. June 13, 1994, Volume 143, No 24.

Dillon, Sam, "Migration of GM Jobs Focus of Strikes." *New York Times*. 1998.

Fox, Justin, "Now the Doctors Want a Union?" *Fortune*. December 8, 1997.

Fox, Justin, "Big Labor Flexes Its Muscle." *Fortune*. June 1998, on line at www.pathfinder.com/fortune/magazine/1998.

Galvin, Kevin, "Child Care Workers Consider Organizing." *Associated Press*. September 13, 1997. 3D.

Grossman, Robert J., "Trying To Heal the Wounds." *HR Magazine*. September 1998, www.shrm.org/hrmagazine/articles/0998cov.htm.

Nissen, Todd, "Tentative Accord Reached at GM." *Reuters News Service*. July 29, 1998.

Ross, Wendy S., "Clinton Announces Agreement to End Aparel Sweatshops." White House Press Release, April 14, 1997.

Sixel, L.M., "Many Still Need Strength of Union." *Houston Chronicle*. September 4, 1998, Labor in Review, C.

Walt, Vivienne, "Labor's Big Bet." *U.S. News and World Report*. February 9, 1998.

Time, August 18, 1997, "The Perils of Ron Carey" Vol. 150, No. 7.

Chapter 9

"99 Ways to Power Up Your New Year" *Success*, January 1999, 70–71

Body Language for Business Success. New York: National Institute of Business Management, Inc., n.d.

Cook, William J. "American Innovators" *U.S. News & World Report*. December 28, 1998, 40–42.

Hagen, Cheryl M. "Coping at Work—Exactly What Do You Mean?" December 29, 1998, America Online.

Klinkenberg, Hilka. *At Ease . . . Professionally*. New York: Bonus Books, 1992.

Lett, Cynthia. Cited in "99 Ways to Power Up Your New Year." *Success*, January 1999, 70–71.

Mehrabian, A., and S. R. Ferris. "Inferences of Attitudes from Nonverbal Communication in Two Channels." In *Nonverbal Communication*, edited by S. Weitz. New York: Oxford University Press, 1974.

Mandell, Barrett J., and Judith Yellen. "Mastering the Memo." *Working Woman*. September 1989, D-1.

McCoy, Doris Lee. *Megatraits—12 Traits of Successful People*. Plano, TX: Wordware Publishing, Inc., 1988.

Seglin, Jeffrey L. "Diss Connection." *Inc. Tech*. 1999, No. 1, 31–32.

"Telecommuting—What Would You Do?" *Home Office Computing*. September 1999, 99–100.

Chapter 10

Austin, Nancy K. "Just Do It—The New Job Strategy." *Working Woman*. April 1990, 78–80, 126.

Bittel, Lester. *What Every Supervisor Should Know*. New York: McGraw-Hill, 1985.

Burdick, Thomas E., and Charlene A. Mitchell. "Executives Face Freeze on Fast Track." *The Houston Post*. April 4, 1988, C-1.

"Check Your 'Progress Pulse' to Measure Career Success." *The Secretary*. March 1986, 25.

Covey, Stephen R. *The 7 Habits of Highly Effective People*. New York: Fireside, 1989.

Drucker, Peter F. *Management: Tasks, Responsibilities, Practices*. New York: Harper & Row, 1974.

The George Odiorne Letter, XIV, no. 20, October 19, 1984.

John-Roger and Peter McWilliams. *The Portable Life 101*. Los Angeles: Prelude Press, 1992.

Kriegel, Robert, and Marilyn Harris Kriegel. "How to Reach Peak Performance—Naturally." *The Secretary*. March 1986, 22–24.

Laabs, Jennifer. "Has Downsizing Missed Its Mark?" *Workforce*. April 1999, 31–38.

"Lonely-at-Top Execs Want for Guidance." *The Houston Post*. September 25, 1988, G-14.

McClelland, David C. "Business Drive and National Achievement." *Harvard Business Review*. 40, 1962, 99–112.

Mitchell, Charlene, and Thomas Burdick. "Make Yourself Indispensable." *The Houston Post*. September 26, 1988, C-1.

Perror, C. "The Analysis of Goals in Complex Organizations." *American Sociological Review* 26, 1961, 854–866.

Chapter 11

Bakker, Jim. "The End of the Big Bad Boss." *Working Woman*. March 1990, 79.

Bennis, Warren. "How to Be the Leader They'll Follow." *Working Woman*. March 1990, 75–78.

Bennis, Warren. *On Becoming a Leader*. Reading, MA: Addison-Wesley Publishing Company, 1989.

Bittel, Lester R., and John W. Newstrom. *What Every Supervisor Should Know*. New York: McGraw-Hill, Inc., 1990.

Blake, Robert, and Jane Srygley Mouton. *The Managerial Grid—The Key to Leadership Excellence*. Houston, TX: Gulf Publishing Company, 1985.

Fiedler, Fred E. *A Theory of Leadership Effectiveness*. New York: McGraw-Hill, 1967.

Ghiselli, Edwin E. "Managerial Talent." *American Psychologist* 18, October 1963, 74–77.

Hersey, Paul. *The Situational Leader*. New York: Warner Books, 1985, 63.

Hersey, Paul, and Kenneth H. Blanchard. *Management of Organizational Behavior: Utilizing Human Resources*. Englewood Cliffs, NJ: Prentice-Hall, 1982.

Holland, Dutch. *Leadership . . . in Three Parts. The Management Edge*. Summer 1999.

Kotter, John P. *The Leadership Factor*. New York: The Free Press, 1966.

Massie, Joseph L., and John Douglas. *Managing: A Contemporary Introduction*. Englewood Cliffs, NJ: Prentice-Hall, 1985, 38.

McGregor, Douglas. *The Human Side of Enterprise*. New York: McGraw-Hill, 1960.

Naisbitt, John, and Patricia Aburdene. *Megatrends2000—Ten New Directions for the 1990s*. New York: William Morrow and Company, Inc., 1990.

Naisbitt, John, and Patricia Aburdene. *Re-inventing the Corporation*. New York: Warner Books, Inc., 1985.

Roberts, Wess. *Leadership Secrets of Attila the Hun*. New York: Warner Books, 1987.

Smith, Hedrick. Management Video Programs, Films for the Humanities and Sciences. 1998–1999.

Stoner, James A. F., and R. Edward Freeman. *Management*. Englewood Cliffs, NJ: Prentice-Hall, 1989.

Waterman, Robert W., Jr. *Adhocracy—The Power to Change*. Knoxville, TN: Whittle Direct Books, 1990.

Chapter 12

Birnbaum, Jeffrey H. "The Power 25: The Influence Merchants." *Fortune*, December 1998.

Blanchard, Kenneth, John P. Carlos, and Alan Randolph. *The 3 Keys to Empowerment: Release the Power Within People for Astonishing Results*. Berrett-Koehler Publishers Inc., 1999.

Book, Esther Wachs. "The Style of Power." *Fortune*. November 1996.

DuBrin, *Andrew J. Winning at Office Politics*. New York: Van Nostrand Reinhold, 1978.

French, J. R. P., and B. Raven. "The Bases of Social Power." In D. Cartwright and A. F. Zander, eds., *Group Dynamics*. 3rd ed. New York: Harper & Row, 1968.

Greene, Robert. "The Lock Jaw Law: How to Impress Friends and Influence People." *Success*. October 1998.

Klienfield, N. R. "Tall Executives Say Height Gives Them Sizable Help in Business." *The Houston Post*. March 15, 1987, Section 5, 18.

Kotter, John Phillip. *Power and Influence: Beyond Formal Authority*. New York: Free Press, 1985.

Korda, Michael. *Power! How To Get It, How To Use It*. New York: Random House, 1975.

Kruger, Pamela. "A Leader's Journey." *Fast Company*. June 1999.

Meier, Robert. "Power—Do You Lust for It?" *Success*. May 1984.

Robbins, Anthony. *Unlimited Power*. New York: Simon and Schuster, 1986.

Robbins, Anthony. *Awaken the Giant Within*. New York: Simon and Schuster, 1998

Robinson, Edward A. "You Are What You Drive." *Fortune*. November 1996.

Stewart, Thomas A. and Rajiv M. Rao. "Get With the New Power Game." *Fortune*. January, 1997.

Chapter 13

Armentrout, Bryan W. "Have Your Plans for Change Had a Change of Plan?" *HRFocus*. January 1996, 19.

Austin, Mary Ruth. "Managing Change." *Manage*, August 1997.

Becker, Franklin. "Workplace By Design." Cornell University Press, March 1998.

Bennet, Rita and Heidi O'Gorman. "Benchmark with the Best." *HRMagazine Focus*, April 1998.

Bryson, John M. "Extending Strategic Planning beyond Management." Government Executive, January 1990, 46.

Drucker, Peter. *The New Realities*. New York: Harper & Row. 1989.

Fuller, Mark B. "Business as War." *Fast Company*. November 1993.

Greenberg, Jack M., "McDonald's CEO Orders Up Changes." *Houston Chronicle*, September 1998. 4D.

http://www.diversity careers.com/diversity/coll/winter-spring 1999. . . . Starting Out At Ford.

http://www.diversity careers-spring 1999 . . . SEI Makes a Commitment to New Grads.

http://www.euen.co.uk. . . .Welcome to the EU Employers' Network.

Lewin, Kurt. "Frontiers in Group Dynamics: Concept, Method and Reality in Social Science, Social Equilibria and Social Change." *Human Relations*. June 1947, 5–41.

Longenecker, Clinton O. and Gary Pinkel. "Coaching to Win at Work." *Manage*, February 1997. 16–18

Martin, Justin. "Tomorrow's CEO's." *Fortune*. June 24, 1996, 57–62.

Naisbitt, John. *Re-inventing the Corporation*. New York: Warner Books, 1985.

Shoop, Tom. "Fighting a Hostile Takeover." *Government Executive*. March 1996.

Wolfraim, Peter, "Creating Order from Chaos." *Management Review*. March 1998, p. 48.

Wuensche, Robert, "Shanghaied In Vermont." *Houston Chronicle*. February 1999, C1.

Chapter 14

Bolles, Richard Nelson. *What Color Is Your Parachute*? Berkeley, CA: Ten Speed Press, 1998.

"Don't Call Us: Tales from the Recruiting Front." *Workforce*. June 1999, p. 42.

Fishman, Charles. "The War For Talent." *Fast Company*. August 1998, 104–108.

Green, Susan D. and Melanie C. L. Martel. *The Ultimate Job Hunter's Guidebook*. New York: Houghton Mifflin Company, 1998.

http://www.eeoc.gov Web site of the Equal Employment Opportunity Commission.

http://www.stats.bls.gov/news.release/tenure.nws.htm "Job Tenure Summary," January 30, 1997.

Imperato, Gina. "35 Ways to Land a Job Online." *Fast Company*. August 1998, 192–198.

Jackson, Tom. *Guerrilla Tactics in the Job Market*. New York: Bantam Books, 1978.

Jandt, Fred E. and Mary B. Nemnich. *Using the Interest and World Wide Web in Your Job Search*. Indianapolis: JIST Works, Inc., 1997.

Krannich, Ronald L., and William J. Banis. *High Impact Résumés and Letters How to Communicate your Qualifications to Employers*. Manassas Park, Va.: Impact Publications, 1998.

Levitt, Julie Griffin. *Your Career: How To Make It Happen*. Cincinnati, OH: South-Western Educational Publishing, 2000.

Medley, H. Anthony. *Sweaty Palms—The Neglected Art of Being Interviewed*. Berkeley, CA: Ten Speed Press, 1993.

Pollack, Ellen Joan. "Sir: Your Application for a Job is Rejected; Sincerely, Hal 9000". *Wall Street Journal*. July 30, 1998, 1, A12.

Simmons, William T. "Ten Commandments of Keeping Your Job." *Texas Business Today (Second and Third Quarters, 1998)* 1.

Chapter 15

Brown, Ed. "Etiquette Training for Geeks." *Fortune Techno file*. June 22, 1998.

Claridge, Laurann. "A Manner of Fact." *Houston Chronicle*. August 14, 1998.

Costin, Glynis. "The New Intimacy." *Buzz Magazine. The Talk of Los Angeles*, May 1997.

Cronkleton, Robert A. "Beep Impact." *Knight Ridder Tribune*. May 30, 1999.

Curry, Sheree. "Stop the E-Mail Madness!" *Fortune. Smart Managing*. May 26, 1997.

Fisher, Anne. "Overseas, U.S. Businesswomen May Have the Edge." *Fortune. Smart Managing*. September 28, 1998.

Hymowitz, Carol. "Sometimes Meetings Become Gender Games." *Wall Street Journal*. December 20, 1998.

Limbaugh, Rush. "Charming." *The Limbaugh Letter*. December 1996.

Martin, Judith. "Miss Manners on Office Etiquette." *Fortune*. November 6, 1989, p. 155, 158.

Molloy, John T. "The Key To Good Clothing Policy." *Houston Chronicle*. August 20, 1998.

Pacific Bell Wireless. "Wireless Manners Needed More Than Ever: Etiquette Expert Offers Common-Sense Tips." *Bell Network News Center*. May 3, 1999.

UPDATE: Telephone Manners—A Guide for Using the Telephone. Southwestern Bell Telephone Company, n.d.

Webster's New Collegiate Dictionary. Springfield, MA: G. & C. Merriam Company, 1976.

Chapter 16

Amend, Pat. "The Right Way to Deal with Ethical Dilemmas." *Working Woman*. December 1988, 19.

Barrett, Todd. "Business Ethics for Sale." *Newsweek*. May 9, 1988, 56.

Batsell, Jake. "Corporate Ethics: The Great Divide?" *Seattle Times*, April 6, 1998.

"Be Cool! Cultivating a Cool Culture Gives HR a Staffing Boost." *Workforce*. April 1998, Vol. 77, No. 4, pp. 50–61.

Berenbeim, Ronald. *Corporate Ethics*. New York: The Conference Board, 1987, 13.

Blanchard, Kenneth, and Norman Vincent Peale. *The Power of Ethical Management*. New York: William Morrow and Company, Inc., 1988.

Business Conduct Guidelines. The Boeing Company. August 1987.

Broadwell, Martin M. "A New Look at Ethics in Supervision." *Training*. September 1988, 40–42.

Byrne, John A. "Businesses Are Signing Up for Ethics 101." *Business Week*. February 15, 1988, 56–57.

Center for Business Ethics, Bentley College. "Are Corporations Institutionalizing Ethics?" *Journal of Business Ethics* 5, May 1986, 86.

Digh, Patricia. "Doing the Right Think Just Got Harder." *Mosiacs*, (Society for Human Resource Management), January/February, 1999, Vol. 5, No. 1, pp. 1, 4, and 5.

Driscoll, Dawn Marie, W. Michael Hoffman, and Edward Perry. *The Ethical Edge; Tales of Organizations That Have Faced Moral Crises*. Media Masters, 1995.

Drucker, Peter. *Managing in Turbulent Times*. New York: Harper & Row, 1980.

Flynn, Gillian. "Make Employee Ethics Your Business." *Personnel Journal*, June 1995, Vol. 74, No. 6, pp. 30–41.

Gray, Robert T. "Making Ethics Come Alive." *Nation's Business*. June 1988, 17–18.

Grove, Andrew S. "What's the Right Thing? Everyday Ethical Dilemmas." *Working Woman*. June 1990, 16–21.

Leo, John. "An Apology to Japanese Americans." *Time*. May 2, 1988, 70.

Morris, William, Ed. *The American Heritage Dictionary*. Boston: Houghton Mifflin Company, 1975.

Odiorne, George S. "Ethics for the Nineties." *Manage*. April 1988,: 8–33.

Pardue, Howard M. Ph.D., SPHR. "Ethics: A Human Resource Perspective." SHRM White Paper, December, 1998.

Perry, James M. "Report Reflects a Shift in Attitude on Ethics." *The Wall Street Journal*. April 18, 1989, A17.

Powell, Bill, and Carolyn Friday. "The Feds Finger the King of Junk." *Newsweek*. September 19, 1988, 42–44.

Riclefs, Roger. "Ethics in America." *The Wall Street Journal*. October 31/November 3, 1988.

Sandroff, Ronni. "How Ethical Is American Business?" *Working Woman*. September 1990, 113–116. (Questionnaire in February 1990 issue, pages 61–62.)

Silk, Leonard. "Does Morality Have a Place in the Boardroom?" *Business Month*. October 1989: 11–13.

Solomon, Charlene Marmer. "Put Your Ethics to a Global Test." *Personnel Journal*. January 1996, Vol 75. No. 1, pp. 66–74.

Solomon, Jolie. "How You Play the Game Says Whether You Win." *The Wall Street Journal*. April 1 18, 1989): B-1.

Stoner, James A. F., and R. Edward Freeman. *Management*. Englewood Cliffs, NJ: Prentice-Hall, 1989.

Thompson, Roger. "No Easy Answers." *Nation's Business*. July 1989, 19–39.

Toffler, Barbara Ley. *Tough Choices: Managers Talk Ethics*. New York: John Wiley & Sons, 1988.

"Whistleblower Protection." SHRM White Paper. Excerpted from "Small Business Handbook: Laws, Regulations, and Technical Assistance Services," U.S. Department of Labor, 1993.

Chapter 17

"Alcohol at Work." Weymouth, MA: Life Skills Education, Inc., 1986.

"Background Information: Workplace Substance Abuse." U.S. Department of Labor. (www.dol.gov/dol/asp/public/programs/drugs/backgrnd.htm)

Baird, Jane. "To Test or Not to Test." *The Houston Post*. September 4, 1989, E1, E8.

Bahls, Jane Easter. "Dealing With Drugs: Keep it Legal." *HRM Magazine*. March 1998, 106–116.

Bahls, Jane Easter. "Drugs in the Workplace." *HRM Magazine*. February 1998, 81–87.

Barbou, John A. "Cracking Down: What You Must Know about Dangerous Drugs." Series in *The Houston Post*. 1986.

Bechner, George, and Alfred Freedman. *Teen Drug Use*. Lexington, MA: Lexington Books, 1986.

Berger, Gilda, and Franklin Watts. *Crack—The New Drug Epidemic*. New York: Impact, 1987.

"Body Invaders." *The Nation*. January 8/15, 1990, 39–40.

Braiker, Harriet B. "What All Career Women Need to Know about Drinking." *Working Woman*. August 1989, 72.

Cohn, Sidney. *The Substance Abuse Problem*. New York: Haworth Press, 1981.

Decrese, Robert P., et al. *Drug Testing in the Workplace*. Washington, DC: Bureau of National Affairs, 1989.

Deming, Janet. "Drug-Free Workplace Is Good Business." *HRMagazine*. April 1990, 61–62.

"Drug Use Among U.S. Workers." *Drug Abuse Prevention Network* newsletter. Volume 2, Issue 4, Winter, 1997, p. 2–4.

Fear Itself: A Legal and Personal Analysis of Drug Testing, AIDS, Secondary Smoke, VDTs. Alexandria, VA: ASPA Foundation, 1987.

Haverland, Larry R. *Drug Information Guide.* Brooklyn, NY: Promotional Slide Guide Corporation, 1980.

Horgan, John. "Test Negative." *Scientific American.* March, 1990,: 18, 22.

Hyde, Margaret O. *Addictions: Gambling, Smoking, Cocaine Use and Others.* New York: McGraw-Hill, 1978.

Kupfer, Andrew. "Is Drug Testing Good or Bad?" *Fortune.* December 19, 1988, 133–139.

Langley, Dorothy A. *Drug Testing: The Right to Privacy vs. the Right to Test.* Dayton: Pamphlet Publications, Inc., 1988.

Maddux, Robert B., and Lynda Voorhees. *Job Performance and Chemical Dependency.* Los Altos, CA: Crisp Publications, 1987.

Marijuana Research Update. Salt Lake City: University of Utah School of Drug and Alcohol Abuse, 1985.

McGladrey & Pullen, LLP. *Mandated Benefits 1998 Compliance Guide.* New York: Panel Publishers, 1998.

Chapter 18

Ahern, Eileen, et al. *Federal Policies and Worker Status since the Thirties.* Madison, Wl: Industrial Relations Research Association, 1976.

Bittel, Lester. *What Every Supervisor Should Know.* New York: McGraw-Hill, 1985.

Bureau of National Affairs publications: *OSHA Reporter*

Bureau of National Affairs. *Bulletin to Management.* April 1999, Vol. 5, No. 13, p. 98.

Bureau of National Affairs. *Human Resources Library on CD.* February 1999.

Policy and Practice Series, Wages and Hours Reporter Chemical Hazard Communication. Washington, DC: U.S. Department of Labor/OSHA, 1987.

Commerce Clearing House publications: *EEO Manual Human Resource Management, Employee Relations*

Conrad, Pamela J., and Robert B. Maddux. *Guide to Affirmative Action: A Primer for Supervisors and Managers.* Los Altos, CA: Crisp Publications, 1988.

Dantico, John A. "Wage-Hour Law Clarifies Exempt/Nonexempt." *HRNews* (January 1990):3.

DeBare, Ilana. "Living-Wage Wildfire; Cities Ponder Laws to Raise Workers' Pay." *The San Francisco Chronicle*, Business, p. 1B.

"Employment-at-Will Erodes, Union Membership Shrinks." *Resource* (December 1989): 10.

Employment Practices Decisions. Chicago: Commerce Clearing House, Inc., 1987, volume 43, f 37,016.

Equal Employment Opportunity Commission publications: *Facts about National Origin Discrimination Facts about Pregnancy Discrimination Facts about Religious Discrimination Facts about Sexual Harassment*.

"Ergonomics Proposal Prompts Flurry of Action." *HR News*. April 1999, p. 4.

Esty, Katharine; Richard Griffin, and Marcie Schorr Hirsch. *Workplace Diversity*. Holbrook: Adams Media Corporation, 1995.

Fundamentals of Employee Benefit Programs. Washington, DC: Employee Benefit Research Institute, 1987.

"HR Issues Overshadowed by Data Privacy Concerns." *HR News*. March 1999, p. 1.

Immigration Reform and Control Act of 1986 {IRCA): Your Job and Your Rights. Washington, DC: U.S. Department of Justice, 1988.

Klinberg, Christine. "Violations of Child Labor Laws Up 250 Percent." *HRNews* (March 1990): 9.

Lash, Steve. "High Court Won't Hear Reinstatement Appeal on Affirmative Action." *Houston Chronicle*, March 30, 1999, 2A.

Lorber, Lawrence A., and J. Robert Kirk. *Fear Itself: A Legal and Personal Analysis of Drug Testing, AIDS, Secondary Smoke, and VDTs*. Alexandria, VA: The ASPA Foundation, 1987.

May, Bruce D. "Law Puts Immigration Control in Employers' Hands." *Personnel Journal* (March 1987): 106–111.

McGladrey & Pullen, LLP. *Mandated Benefits 1998 Compliance Guide*. New York: Panel Publishers, 1998.

McWhirter, Darien. *Your Rights at Work*. New York: John Wiley and Sons, 1989.

Meisinger, Susan. "House Passes Americans with Disabilities Act." *HRNews*. June 1990, 3.

Nackley, Jeffrey V. *Primer on Workers' Compensation*. Washington, DC: Bureau of National Affairs, 1987.

Novit, Mitchell S. *Essentials of Personnel Management*, 2nd ed. Engelwood Cliffs, NJ: Prentice-Hall, 1986.

Overman, Stephenie. "New Civil Rights Bill Expands Title Vll." *HRNews*. March 1990, 1.

Overman, Stephanie. "Mandated Health Insurance Reality in Some States." *HRNews*. August 1990, 9.

Scheuch, Richard. *Laborin the American Economy*. New York: Harper & Row, 1981.

Social Security Administration publications: *Retirement Survivors Disability*.

Sherman, Arthur W., Jr., George W. Bohlander, and Herbert J. Chruden. *Managing Human Resources*. Cincinnati: South-Western Publishing Company, 1988.

Thornburg, Linda. "Bush Signs Disabilities Act." *HRNews.* August 1990, 1.

Twomey, David P. *A Concise Guide to Employment Law: EEOC and OSHA.* Cincinnati: South-Western Publishing Company, 1986.

Twomey, David P. *Labor and Employment Law: Text and Cases.* Cincinnati: South-Western Publishing Company, 1989.

Understanding AIDS. Rockville, MD: U.S. Department of Health and Human Services Publication no. (CDC) HHS-58-8404, 1988.

Chapter 19

Abramson, Leonard. "Boost to Bottom Line." *Personnel Administrator.* July 1988, 36–39.

Alexander, Roy. *Commonsense Time Management.* New York: American Management Association, 1992.

Carroll, Lewis. *Alice's Adventures in Wonderland.* New York: Simon and Shuster, 1986.

Caudron, Shari, and Michael Rozek. "The Wellness Payoff." *Personnel Journal.* July 1990, 55–62.

Cavanagh, Michael E. "What You Don't Know about Stress." *Personnel Journal.* July 1988, 53–59.

Charlesworth, Edward A., and Ronald G. Nathan. *Stress Management: A Comprehensive Guide to Wellness.* New York: Atheneum, 1984.

"Cyber Chain Letter Victimizes Computer Users Across Country." *The Houston Chronicle.* March 27, 1999, Section A, page 33.

Dreyfuss, Ira. "Wellness, Exercise Programs May Save Companies Some Money." *The Desert News* (Salt Lake City, UT), February 22, 1999, Business; pg.WEB.

Hallett, Jeffrey. "The Value of Wellness: It's All in the Mind." *Personnel Administrator.* July 1988, 28–30.

Harris, Philip R. and Robert T. Moran. *Managing Cultural Differences.* Houston: Gulf Publishing Company, 1991.

http://www.nal.usda.gov:8001/py/pmap.htm The Food Guide Pyramid

Jay, Leslie. "Fax Yourself This Message: You Can Leave Stress at Work." *The Houston Post.* April 9, 1989, F1, F12.

Kolson, Ann. "Leisure Time: Is There Really Less of It?" *Houston Chronicle.* November 5, 1989, H6.

Lerner, Harriet Goldhor. *The Dance of Intimacy.* New York: Harper & Row, 1989.

Public Health Service, U.S. Department of Health and Human Services. *The 1990 Health Objectives for the Nation: A Midcourse Review.* Washington, DC: U.S. Government Printing Office, 1986.

Stafford, Diane. "A Growing Workplace Threat: New Report Sees Stress as Health Hazard for Employees Sensing a Lack of Control." *The Kansas City Star.* January 31, 1999, National/World; pg. A1.

Stokes, Stewart L., Jr. *It's About Time*. Boston: CBI Publishing Co., Inc., 1982.

The Surgeon General's Report on Nutrition and Health—Summary and Recommendations. Washington, D.C.: U.S. Government Printing Office, 1988.

United States Department of Agriculture, Human Nutrition Information Service. "Dietary Guidelines for Americans Maintain Desirable Weight." *Home and Garden Bulletins* 232-1-232-3. Washington, DC: U.S. Government Printing Office, 1986.

VanDerWall, Stacy. "NIOSH Report: Job Stress a 'Threat' to Workers' Health." *HR News Online*. Society for Human Resource Management, January 15, 1999.

Wallis, Claudia. "Stress: Can We Cope?" *Time*. June 6, 1983, 48–54.

Chapter 20

Brickfield, Cyril F. "Managing an Older Work Force." *Manage*. February 1988.

Buechner, Maryanne Murray. "Superconnected." *Time*. March 22, 1999.

Carlisle, Chip. "Diversity Training, Recruiting Pay Off for Companies." *The Houston Chronicle*. August 31, 1998.

Colvin, Geoffrey. "The 50 Best Companies for Asians, Blacks, and Hispanics." *Fortune*. July 1999.

Cornish, Edward. *Exploring Your Future*. Bethesda, MD: World Future Society, 1999.

Davy, Jo Ann. "The Office of the Future." *OfficeSystems99*. June 1999.

DeVenuta, Karen. "The Education Gap." *The Wall Street Journal*. February 9, 1990.

Fishman, Charles. "We've Seen the Future of Work." *FastCompany*. August 1996.

Gates, Bill. *Business @ The Speed of Thought: Using a Digital Nervous System*. Warner Books, USA, 1999.

Glanton, Eileen. "Top-Ranking Women See a Gap in Pay." *The Houston Chronicle*. November 10, 1998.

Grenier, Ray and George Metes. *Going Virtual*. New Jersey: Prentice Hall, 1995.

Henderson, Gary. *Outlook 1999*. San Fransisco: Bass-Hinds Publishers, 1999.

http://www.diversity.com Provides site list of articles on diversity.

http://www.divesitycareers.com Provides sources for careers with companies sensitive to diversity.

Hunter, Mark. "Work, Work, Work, It's Taking Over Our Lives." *Modern Maturity*. June 1999.

Kanter, Rosabeth Moss. "Restoring People to the Heart of the Organization." In Frances Hesselbein, Marshall Goldsmith & Richard Beckhard, Eds. *The Organization of the Future*. San Francisco: Jossey Bass, 1997.

Kupfer, Andrew. "Four Forces That Will Shape The Internet." *Fortune*. July 1998.

Kurzweil, Ray. "The Next Hundred Years." *Across the Conference Board*. August 1999.

Large, Elizabeth. "Millennials Represent Influential Force of the Future." *Baltimore Sun*. January 13, 1999.

McGinn, Daniel and John McCormick. "Your Next Job." *Newsweek*. February 1, 1999

McKay, Gretchen. "The Future Office and Me." *Pittsburgh Post*. November 1998.

Minerd, Jeff. "A Gray Wave of Entrepreneurs." *The Futurist*. July 1999

Miniter, Richard. "Bringing Work Home." *Reader's Digest*. February 1999.

Nathan, Sara. "New Computer for the Future." *USA Today*. October 29, 1998.

O'Connell, Sandra E. "The Virtual Work Place Moves at Warp Speed." *HR*. January 1999.

Paynter, Susan. "Work Place 2020." *Working Mother*. June 1999.

Perelman, Lewis. "Anything, Anywhere, Anytime, Any Questions?" *FastCompany*. April 1997.

Pink, Daniel and Michael Warshaw. "Free-Agent FAQS." *FastCompany*. December 1998.

Reich, Robert B. "The Company of the Future." *Fortune*. November 1998.

Roberts, Paul. "Kinko's—The Free Agent's Home Office." *FastCompany*. December 1997.

Saltzman, Amy. "When Less is More." *U.S. News & World Report*. October 1997.

Shellenbarger, Sue. "Rooms with a View and Flexible Hours Draw Talent to WRQ." *Wall Street Journal*. August 13, 1997.

Schlender, Brent. "The Edison of the Internet." *Fortune*. February 1999.

Sixel, L.M. "The Gap in Wages Widens Between the Haves and the Have Nots." *The Houston Chronicle*. January 1995.

Solomon, Jolie. "Firms Address Workers' Cultural Variety." *The Wall Street Journal*. February 10, 1989.

Solomon, Jolie. "Managing." *The Wall Street Journal*. September 22, 1989.

Stamps, David. "Welcome to America—Watch Out For Culture Shock." *Training*. November 1996.

Stipp, David. "Live a Lot Longer." *Fortune*. July 5, 1999.

Terry, Sara. "Across the Great Divide." *FastCompany*. August 1999.

Vincola, Ann. "Taking Your Work/Life Policy Abroad." *Global Workforce*. July 1998.

Webber, Alan. "The Future of the Company." *FastCompany*. November 1998.

Glossary

The following definitions are for terms as they are used in this book and as they apply to business and human relations.

ABC analysis Concentration of decisions where the potential for payoff is greater

Accountability perspective View that businesses are accountable for their actions, with a responsibility to individuals and the general public to be fair and considerate

Accounting function Sector of the company that keeps track of the money coming in and leaving the organization

Active listening A conscious effort to listen to both the verbal and non-verbal components of what someone is saying, without prejudging

Ad hoc committee A committee that has a limited life and serves only a one-time purpose

Affirmative action A practice designed to right past discrimination against minorities and women in the workplace by setting goals for hiring and upward mobility

AFL-CIO A combined union of members from the AFL craft unions and the CIO industrial unions that merged in 1955 as a show of strength to improve union bargaining power

Age Discrimination in Employment Act Federal legislation that prohibits discrimination against individuals age 40 and over in the workplace

Agency shop An agreement that requires workers to pay union membership dues whether or not they choose to join the union

Aggressive behavior Valuing ourselves above others and saying what we feel or think but at the expense of others; attempting to dominate or humiliate; using threats and accusations or trying to show up others; choosing for others; speaking with an air of superiority and in a voice that is demanding and rude

AIDS Acquired immunodeficiency syndrome. Rights on the job have been extended to those with AIDS.

Alcohol The most commonly abused drug in the country. Alcohol is a depressant that slows the activity of the brain and spinal cord.

American Federation of Labor (AFL) A craft union formed in 1886, led by Samuel L. Gompers

Americans with Disabilities Act Federal legislation which prohibits discrimination against individuals who are disabled

Amphetamines Synthetic nervous system stimulants

Anthropology Academic discipline that focuses on the origins and development of various cultures

Arbitration A method used to reach a final decision or ruling in labor-management disputes that enlists the services of an arbitrator whose decision is legally binding to both parties

Arbitrator A professional person whose services are requested by both the union and management to conduct a formal hearing and develop a final decision in a dispute over contract interpretation; the decision is considered legally binding to both parties

Artificial intelligence   A process whereby computers are programmed to mimic human intelligence

Assertive behavior   Using correct etiquette; feeling equal to others; making our own choices; using "I" phrases and other effective communication techniques; appearing calm and confident; having positive self-esteem and being respected by others

Autocratic leadership   Leadership style that is task-oriented and highly directive and involves close supervision and little delegation

Avoidance   Conflict resolution by totally refraining from confronting the conflict

Baby boomers   Those Americans born between 1945 and 1965, during the "baby boom" that followed World War II

Bargaining unit   The group of employees whom the union may represent in collective bargaining with management

BARS (Behaviorally anchored rating system)   An appraisal system where the behavior an employee most often exhibits is measured against a scale developed for his or her position

Behavioral school of management Study of management that focused on techniques to motivate workers

Behavioral science approach   Part of the behavioral school of management that began in the late 1950s and used controlled experiments and other scientific methods to view human behavior in the workplace

Benchmarking   A method of organizational change that involves comparing the company's practices, among internal divisions and/or against those of competitors, to determine which are best

Blacklist   A list that identified persons whom management perceived as potential troublemakers and that was exchanged among company managers to assure that union organizers were denied employment. Names of labor agitators and any other persons known to be sympathetic to unionizing efforts were placed on this list.

Bona fide occupational qualification (BFOQ)   Legitimate restrictions necessitated by the nature of an occupation. Employers must show a legitimate business reason for eliminating certain groups of individuals from a job.

Brainstorming   Group problem-solving technique that involves the spontaneous contribution of ideas from all members of the group

Business agent   A union official who helps run the affairs of the union, such as negotiating and administering the agreement, collecting dues, and recruiting new members

Centralized management   Distribution of power so all major decisions are made by those high up in the organization

Chain of command   The direction in which authority is exercised and policies and other information are communicated to lower levels

Change agent   Person who diagnoses problems, provides feedback, assists in developing strategies, or recommends interventions to benefit the organization as a whole. Also known as an Organization Development practitioner or an OD consultant.

Checklist   An appraisal instrument that offers a list of statements about performance and characteristics which supervisors can check off in order to rate an employee

Checkoff   A union agreement provision that allows unions to receive dues directly from a worker's paycheck if authorized by the employee's signature on a routinely used form

Chronological résumé   Résumé that lists experience in reverse chronological order, listing the most recent employment first. This format is beneficial when an individual has a continuous work history with progressively responsible positions.

Civil Rights Act of 1991   Federal legislation passed to improve federal civil rights laws and provide for damages in cases of intentional employment discrimination

Classical organization theory Approach begun by Fayol that focuses on management of the organization as a whole. It is part of the classical school of management.

Classical perspective   Holds that businesses need not feel responsible for social issues and should concentrate on being profitable

Classical school of management Study of management that focused on the technical efficiency of work as a way to maximize production

Closed shop   A method used by unions to assure union membership that required persons to belong to a bargaining unit prior to being hired and to lose their jobs if they were expelled from the union; abolished

by the Taft-Hartley Act

Coaching   A method of employee development that closely resembles on-the-job training where a senior experienced and skilled employee helps develop or train a junior employee

Cocaine   Stimulant derived from the coca leaf or synthesized

Code of ethics   List that requires or prohibits specific practices by employees in a particular organization or by all members of a professional group

Coercive power   Power based on fear and punishment

Cohesiveness   Degree to which group members are of one mind and act as one body

Collective bargaining   A process of negotiations between union representatives and company management representatives to establish a mutual agreement on hours, wages, and working conditions. Both parties are expected to bargain in good faith to reach a mutually acceptable agreement.

Committee   Type of task group

Common market   A group of countries that share trade policies that affect agricultural product limitations, the transportation of goods, tax laws, and import/export quotas

Communication   Process by which we exchange information through a common system of symbols, signs, or behavior

Communication breakdown   The result when a situation exceeds a person's capacity to receive and transmit messages and communication deteriorates or fails

Communities of Practice (COPS) Highly-synergistic peer groups working on projects or problems of shared interest; informal small groups working toward a common purpose

Comparable worth The issue that concerns the differences in salaries paid in traditionally female occupations versus traditionally male occupations

Compensation A defense mechanism by which individuals attempt to relieve feelings of inadequacy or frustration by excelling in other areas

Competition A healthy struggle toward goal accomplishment without interference, even when the goals are incompatible

Compromising A method of conflict resolution that addresses the issue but seldom resolves it to the complete satisfaction of both parties

Conceptual skills Administrative or big picture skills; ability to think abstractly and to analyze problems

Conflict Disagreement between individuals or groups about goal accomplishment

Conflict resolution The active management of conflict through defining and solving issues between individuals, groups, or organizations

Confrontation Conflict resolution by openly exchanging information and actively working through the differences to reach agreement

Congress of Industrial Organizations (CIO) An industrial union formed in 1936, led by John L. Lewis

Consensus A solution that all members of the group involved can support

Consolidated Omnibus Budget Reconciliation Act (COBRA) Federal legislation that requires employers to extend medical benefit coverage to employees and dependents in situations where they would no longer be eligible for coverage; individuals must pay premiums for these extended benefits

Context Conditions in which something occurs, which can throw light on its meaning

Contract A mutually acceptable written agreement signed by both the union and company representatives that is legally binding and outlines the various terms and conditions of employment agreed upon through collective bargaining

Cooperative counseling method A mutual problem-solving effort involving both parties in exploring and solving issues

Cost-benefit analysis Examination of the pros and cons of each proposed solution

Counseling A discussion technique used to assist employees with problems affecting performance on the job

Counselor A person, usually a trained professional or a supervisor, capable of dealing with a wide variety of employee problems

Craft union A union representing skilled workers primarily concerned with training apprentices to be masters of their craft

Creativity Thinking process that solves a problem or achieves a goal in an original and useful way; the ability to come up with new and unique solutions to problems

Critical incident technique An appraisal technique in which supervisors record in writing actual incidents of behavior that they observe in employees

Critical norms Norms considered essential to the survival and effectiveness of the group as a whole

Critical Path Method (CPM) The critical path is the sequence of activities requiring the longest time for completion. It will show the minimum time to complete the project.

Decentralized management Distribution of power so that important decisions are made at a lower level

Decision tree Graphic depiction of how alternative solutions lead to various possibilities

Defamation Open publication of a false statement tending to harm the reputation of a person

Deflation A fall in costs and a rise in the value of money

Delegated method Giving employees the responsibility and authority to effect change

Delegation Assigning tasks to subordinates and following up to ensure proper and timely completion

Democratic leadership Leadership style, also described as participative, that is usually preferred by modern management and involves showing concern for followers, sharing authority with them, and involving them in decision making and organizational planning

Demographics Statistics showing population characteristics about a region or group, such as education, income, age, marital status, or ethinic makeup

Denial A defense mechanism by which a person refuses to believe something that creates anxiety or frustration

Derivative power Power obtained from close association with a powerful person

Deviance Not conforming to group norms

Directive counseling A method of counseling that involves the counselor's listening to the employee's problem, allowing emotional release, determining an action plan, and advising the employee on what needs to be done

Discrimination A difference in treatment based on a factor other than individual merit

Displacement A defense mechanism by which an individual acts out anger toward a person who does not deserve it but who is a "safe" target

Downward communication Communication that begins at higher levels of the organization and flows downward

E-mail Communication medium that uses a computer, keyboard, and service provider to create messages and send them through electronic networks; also called electronic mail

Emergent leader An informal leader who emerges without formal appointment and can exert as much or more power than the formal leader

Employee assistance program (EAP) A formal company program designed to aid employees with personal problems, such as substance abuse or psychological problems, that affect their job performance

Employee association A group or association of workers from the white-collar and professional sectors of the work force, such as teachers, nurses, public sector employees, business professionals, doctors, lawyers, and clerical workers; seldom engage in collective bargaining activities; historically denied the right to strike

Employment at will   A philosophy that states the employee serves at the discretion of an employer and can be terminated at any time and for any reason, even if the employee is performing well

Empowerment   Allowing others to make decisions and have influence on desired outcomes

Enabling   Covering up for or making excuses for the behavior and performance of individuals who are abusing substances, allowing them to continue their disruptive conduct

Enlightened self-interest   Belief that organizations' and people's best interests are served by being genuinely concerned for others

Entrepreneurship   Organizing, managing, and assuming the risks of a business enterprise

Equal Employment Opportunity Commission (EEOC)   Federal agency responsible for enforcing laws related to employment discrimination

Equal Pay Act   Federal law that requires males and females be paid the same salary provided they perform the same job and have the same experience and education

Essay appraisal   An appraisal instrument on which the supervisor writes a paragraph or more concerning employee performance

Esteem needs   Level of Maslow's hierarchy that includes the need for respect from self and others and that can be met by increased responsibility, recognition for work well done, and merit increases and awards

Ethical dilemmas   Conflicts of values that arise when our sense of values or social responsibility is questioned internally or challenged externally

Ethics   "The study of the general nature of morals and of the specific moral choices to be made by individuals in their relationships with others; a set of moral principles or values" (*American Heritage Dictionary*)

Etiquette   "The forms required by good breeding or prescribed by authority to be observed in social or official life" (*Webster's*); i.e., acting appropriately in social and business situations

Executive Order 12564   Executive order that establishes a drug-free federal workplace and a drug testing program for federal employees

Expected interval testing   The process of giving drug tests at specific, preannounced times

Expert power   Power based on having specialized skills, knowledge, or expertise

Fair Labor Standards Act   Federal legislation that sets the minimum wage, equal pay, overtime, and child labor standards

Family Medical Leave Act (FMLA)   Federal legislation that provides eligible employees with up to 12 weeks of job-protected family or medical leave; absence for treatment of substance abuse qualifies for FMLA leave

Federal Drug-Free Workplace Act   Act that requires federal contractors and grantees who receive more than $25,000 in government business to certify that they will maintain a drug-free workplace

Federal Mediation and Conciliation Service   A federal agency that maintains a list of mediators to assist in resolving labor-management disputes

Feedback   Information given back to a sender that evaluates a message and states what the receiver understood

Finance function   Sector of the company that helps make decisions about how businesses should be financed

Follower-readiness   A worker's desire to achieve, willingness to accept responsibility, ability and experience with the tasks, and confidence

"For cause" testing   Drug testing of employees only when they are suspected of being under the influence of drugs or alcohol

Force field analysis   A technique used to analyze the complexities of a change and identify the forces that must be altered

Forced distribution   An approach to comparative appraisal where ratings of performances of employees are distributed over a bell-shaped curve

Forcing   Results when two persons or groups reach an impasse and allow an authoritative figure to choose one preference rather than work toward a mutually agreeable solution

Foreign Corrupt Policy Act   Law requiring companies to operate ethically in their business dealings in other cultures

Formal communication   Communication that flows up or down the formal organizational structure along the chain of command

Formal group   A group designated by the organization to fulfill specific tasks or accomplish certain organizational objectives

Formal leader   An individual who is officially given certain rights or authority over other group members and who has a degree of legitimacy granted by the formal group or organization

4 C's of communication   Reminders to improve writing; complete, concise, correct, and conversational/clear

Free agents   Individuals who represent themselves and are responsible for managing themselves like a business

Free rein leadership   Leadership style, also called laissez-faire or integrative, that allows followers to lead themselves, provides advice or information only when requested, and makes little or no effort to increase productivity or nurture or develop followers

Free rider   A person who does not pay union dues but is afforded the same benefits afforded dues-paying members because he or she is a part of the bargaining unit represented by the union

Functional authority   Authority given to staff personnel to make decisions in their area of expertise and to overrule line decisions

Functional group   Groups made up of managers and subordinates assigned to certain positions in the organizational hierarchy

Functional résumé   Résumé that emphasizes special skills that can be transferred to other areas. This resume is useful for individuals reentering the job market or wanting to change careers.

Globalization   Making goods and services available worldwide with no national boundaries or trade barriers on where they are sold or where they are produced

Goal Objective, target, or end result expected from the completion of tasks, activities, or programs

Grapevine An informal person-to-person means of circulating information or gossip

Graphic rating scale An appraisal instrument that outlines categories on which the employee is rated; the scale for each category can range from unacceptable to superior

Great man theory A theory of leadership based on the belief that certain people are born to become leaders and will emerge in that role when their time comes

Grievance A dispute between labor and management over contract interpretation

Grievance procedure A specifically defined procedure written into the contract outlining the formal steps for resolving contract disputes

Group Two or more persons who are aware of one another, interact with one another, and perceive themselves to be a group

Group norms Shared values about the kinds of behaviors that are acceptable or unacceptable to the group

Groupthink Process of deriving negative results from group decision-making efforts as a result of in-group pressures

Hallucinogens Drugs that produce chemically induced hallucinations

Halo effect A process by which an individual assumes that another's traits are all positive because one trait is positive

Hawthorne effect The idea that the human element is more important to productivity that the technical or physical aspects of the job. The effect was identified through experiments conducted by Mayo.

Hazard Communication Standard (HCS) Regulation that companies give employees access to information about the physical and health hazards of chemical substances produced, imported, or used in the workplace

Health The role of the working environment in the development of diseases such as cancer and black lung

Health Insurance Portability and Accountability Act (HIPAA) Federal legislation that allows employees leaving an employer health plan to have access to the new employer health plan without waiting periods or limitations due to preexisting conditions or health status

Hear To perceive sound with our ears

Herzberg's two-factor theory of motivation A popular theory of motivation that says two sets of factors or conditions influence the behavior of individuals at work: one set to satisfy and the other to movitate

Hidden agenda Topics that meeting attendees wish to discuss that have no relevance to the purpose of the current meeting

Horizontal communication Communication that occurs between individuals at the same level in an organization

Human relations Study of relationships among people

Human relations approach Part of the behavioral school of management that emphasized the human effect of productivity

Human relations skills   Ability to deal effectively with people through communicating, listening, being empathetic, inspiring and motivating, being perceptive, and using fair judgment

Human resources function   Sector of the company responsible for hiring, training, setting salaries and benefits, and monitoring employees in the organization

Hybrid résumé   Résumé that combines the format of functional and chronological résumés

Hygiene factors   Factors identified by Herzberg that are necessary to maintain a reasonable level of satisfaction, such as working conditions, job security, quality of supervision, and interpersonal relationships on the job

Incubation   Stage of the creative process that is mysterious and below the surface and involves reviewing ideas and information

Industrial union   A union representing primarily unskilled or semi-skilled industrial workers

Inflation   A rise in the costs of goods and services with a fall in the value of a country's currency

Influence   Ability to change the attitude or behavior of an individual or group

Informal communication   Communication that does not follow the chain of command

Informal group   A group created to satisfy the needs of individual members that are not satisfied by formal groups

Informal leader   A person within the group who is able to influence other group members because of age, knowledge, technical skills, social skills, personality, or physical strength

Information Age   The current economic era, characterized by increasingly large and complex organizations, advanced technology, and the computer

Information overload   An inability to continue processing and remembering information because of the great amount coming at us at one time

Inhalants   Hydrocarbon-containing substances that are inhaled for their intoxicating effects

Innovation   The end product of creative activity

Inspiration   The "aha" stage of the creative process; when solutions break through to conscious thought

Integration   The blending of work and family to create a more satisfying whole. Employers will increasingly offer a full array of work/life options in order to attract and keep top performing workers, as integration becomes an increasingly important issue.

Integrity   Strict adherence to a code of behavior

Interview   Process by which the prospective employer learns more about you and evaluates whether you are the best qualified candidate for the position

Intrapreneurship   The conscious effort of organizations to identify and support employees who wish to pursue a entrepreneurial idea for a new product or service

Job enlargement   Increasing the complexity of a job by adding similar tasks to those already being performed

Job enrichment Building greater responsibility and interest into task assignments

Job redesign A method of bringing about change within the organization aimed directly at the tasks performed by individuals

Job rotation Shifting employees from one job to another in hopes of reducing boredom and stimulating renewed interest in job performance

Job-seeking skills Skills that assist us in finding employment

Johari Window Model that helps us understand our relationships with others; panes represent parts of us known or not known to ourselves and others

Labor agitator Influential person capable of rallying workers toward unionizing

Laissez-faire leadership Leadership style, also called free rein or integrative, that allows followers to lead themselves, provides advice or information only when requested, and makes little or no effort to increase productivity or nurture or develop followers

Landrum-Griffin Act A federal law enacted in 1959 that requires unions to disclose the sources and disbursements of their funds, hold regularly scheduled elections by secret ballot, and restricts union officials from using union funds for personal means; intended as a means of control over possible corruption in union activities and misuse of union funds

Leadership The process of influencing the activities of individuals or organized groups so that they follow and do willingly what the leader wants them to do

Leadership style Pattern of behavior exhibited by a leader

Legitimate power Power derived from formal rank or position within an organizational hierarchy

Life cycles Stages of a business, consisting of start-up, expansion and growth, stability, decline, and phase-out or revitalization

Line and staff structure A complex organization structure in which the line (production employees) are given support by staff in such areas as law and safety

Listen To make a conscious effort to hear something and to interpret it using reason and understanding

Lockout An anti-union technique used by company management whereby the company locks the doors and shut down factory operations to avoid worker demands for improved conditions

Management Use of resources to accomplish a goal; may be nonbehavioral

Management by Objectives (MBO) A method and philosophy of management that emphasizes self-determination and allows employees to participate in setting their own goals

Management science school of management Branch of management that began after World War II and was used to solve complex management problems. The computer has played an important part in this school.

Managerial Grid® Leadership theory developed by Blake and Mouton that uses a grid to plot the degree to which leaders show concern for people and concern for production

Marijuana Drug derived from the dried leaves and flowering tops of the pistillate hemp plant

Marketing and sales function Sector of the company responsible for determining consumer needs and selling the company's products or services to the consumer

Maslow's hierarchy of needs Motivation theory that recognizes five levels of needs. Individuals are motivated by the needs within each specific level. When these needs are met, individuals are no longer motivated by that level and move upward.

Material Safety Data Sheets (MSDS) Documents which describe chemicals used in the workplace along with proper first aid treatment for exposure to or contact with the chemicals

Matrix structure A complex organization structure that uses groups of people with expertise in their individual areas who are temporarily assigned full or part time to a project from other parts of the organization

McClelland's acquired needs theory A motivational theory that states that through upbringing individuals acquire a strong desire for one of three primary needs—achievement, affiliation, and power

Mediation A method of resolving a deadlocked dispute that enlists the services of a mediator

Mediator A person viewed as an unbiased third party whose services are requested to assist in resolving difficult or deadlocked labor-management disputes

Medium The form in which a message is communicated

Mentor An experienced person who will give you objective career advice. A senior-level manager or retired professional with political savvy and an interest in helping employees achieve both career goals and the objectives of the organization

Mentoring A popular form of coaching on a personal level with the emphasis on helping employees develop to their fullest potential

Message The content of the communication sent or received; may be verbal, nonverbal, or written

Millennials Members of the generation born between 1979 and 1995

Motivation Needs or drives within individuals that energize behaviors

Motivational factors Factors identified by Herzberg that build high levels of motivation, such as achievement, advancement, recognition, responsibility, and the work itself

Motivational source fields Forces that motivate; can be outside, inside, or early

Multinational corporation A company that has goods and services based in several countries and requires business planning and marketing strategies to fit global operations rather than narrow domestic ones

Narcotics Drugs that are derivatives of the opium poppy

National Labor Relations Board (NLRB) A government agency responsible for enforcing the provisions of the Wagner Act, established in 1935

Negotiation Discussion that leads to a decision acceptable to all involved

Networking (1) Process whereby you give and receive moral support, career guidance and important information by developing contacts with people in your place of employment and in professional organizations. (2) Method of finding employment that involves telling all individuals you know that you are seeking a job and asking them to contact you if they hear of any openings.

Nondirective counseling   A method of counseling viewed as a mutual problem-solving effort involving both parties in exploring and solving issues

Nonverbal communication   Meaning conveyed through the body, the voice, or position

Norris-LaGuardia Act   A federal law enacted in 1932 to abolish the use of yellow-dog contracts by companies as an anti-union technique

Occupational Safety and Health Act Federal legislation that sets safety and health standards and ensures that they are observed in the workpalce

Occupational Safety and Health Administration (OSHA)   Federal agency that regulates safety and health in the workplace

"Offer and refusal technique"   Suggestion that men continue to offer manners they were taught while women accept those they consider proper and decline those they would rather not have

Official goals   Formally stated, abstract goals that are developed by upper management

Ongoing committee   A committee that is relatively permanent, addressing organizational issues on a standing or continuous basis

One-way communication   Communication that takes place with no feedback from the receiver

Operational goals   Concrete and close-ended goals that are the

responsibility of first-line supervisors and employees

Operative goals   Goals that are developed by middle management and are more specific than official goals

Optimists   Persons who always look on the positive side of situations

Organizational culture   A mix of the beliefs and values of society at large, the individuals who work in the organization, and the organization's leaders and founders

Organizational development   A holistic approach to organizational change involving the entire organization—its people, structures, culture, policies and procedures, and purpose

Overachiever   Individual who takes on unattainable goals

Participative method   A method of implementing organizational change that uses employee groups in the problem-solving and decision-making processes preceding the actual change

Passive behavior   The valuing of ourselves below others; lack of self-confidence while speaking; wanting to be liked and trying to please others; and avoiding unpleasant situations and confrontation

Passive power   Power source that stems from a display of helplessness

Perception   (1) Way in which we interpret, or give meaning to, sensations or messages; (2) The first stage in the creative process requiring that we view objects or situations differently

Perceptual defense mechanisms Mechanisms individuals use to handle anxiety

Performance appraisal   A measurement of how well an employee is doing on the job

Peripheral norms   Norms that, if violated, are not perceived as damaging to the group and its members

PERT chart   Graphic technique for planning projects in which a great number of tasks must be coordinated (Program Evaluation and Review Technique)

Pessimists   Persons who always look on the negative side of situations

Physiological needs   A level of Marlow's hierarchy of needs that includes the desire for food, sleep, water, shelter, and other physiological drives

Planned agenda   An outline or list of what topics are to be discussed or what is to be accomplished during a meeting

Planning   An attempt to prepare for and predict the future; it involves goals, programs, policies, rules, and procedures

PODSCORB   An acronym for the functional abilities required of leaders—planning, organizing, directing, staffing, coordinating, reporting, and budgeting

Power   The ability to influence others to do what we want them to do even if we are not a formal leader

Power-compulsive   Power personality with a lust for power; seldom satisfied with the amount of power achieved

Power politics   Developing opportunities for success

Power positioning   Conscientious use of techniques designed to position an individual for maximum personal growth and gain in an effort to develop power

Power-positive   Power personality that genuinely enjoys responsibility and thrives on the use of power

Power-shy   Power personality that tends to avoid being placed in position that require overt use of power

Power symbols   Physical traits, personality characteristics, and external physical factors that are associated with those who are perceived to be powerful

Pregnancy Discrimination Act   Federal law that prohibits discrimination against pregnant women in the workplace

Primary groups   Groups made up of family members and close friends

Primary needs   Basic needs required to sustain life comfortably, such as food, water, air, sleep, and shelter

Proactive management   Management that is characterized by looking ahead, anticipating problems, and determining solutions to potential problems before they develop

Problem   Disturbance or unsettled matter that requires a solution if the organization or person is to function effectively

Problem-solving teams   Groups of 5 to 12 volunteers from different areas of a department who meet once or twice a week to discuss ways of improving quality, efficiency, or work conditions

Process innovation   A method of enhancing productivity that blends information technology and human resource management

Procrastination   The intentional putting off or delaying of activities that need to be done

Production function   The sector of an organization that actually produces goods or performs services

Program Evaluation and Review Techniques (PERT) A model used by managers to plan and control work

Projection A defense mechanism whereby individuals attribute unacceptable thoughts or feelings about themselves to others

Protocol Business, diplomatic, or military etiquette

Psychology Academic discipline that focuses on the behavior of individuals

Public perspective View that links businesses with the government and other groups to actively solve social and environmental problems

Pyramidal hierarchy Triangular shape of an organization with the single head of the organization at the top. Smaller pyramids appear within the larger.

Quality circle Committee of 6 to 15 employees who meet regularly to examine and suggest solutions to common problems of quality

Random interval testing The process of giving drug tests to employees at varying and unannounced times

Ranking An approach to employee appraisal that involves comparing employees' performances, listing them from highest to lowest

Rationalization (1) A defense mechanism by which a person explains away a problem; (2) A planning process used by organizations for buying supplies from countries that produce them at the lowest prices and then selling the finished product wherever the highest price can be obtained

Reactive management Management characterized by being caught off guard and moving from one crisis to the next

Realistic achiever Individual who sets challenging but attainable goals

Reasonable accommodation Any action that assists a disabled employee without imposing undue hardship on the company

Receiver One to whom a message is transmitted; one who receives the message

Reengineering A change process designed to make an organization more competitive; it generally involves the fundamental rethinking and redesign of business processes to achieve dramatic improvements

Reference Individual who can vouch for your performance and character

Referent power Power based on respect or admiration

Regression A defense mechanism whereby a person retreats to an earlier behavior pattern

Relationship behavior Leader behavior with people; the extent to which the leader is supportive of followers and engages in two-way communication with them

Repression A defense mechanism by which an individual cannot remember an unpleasant event

Résumé Sales tool designed to assist in obtaining an interview

Reverse halo effect A process by which an individual assumes that another's traits are all negative because one trait is negative

Reward power Power based on the ability to give something of material or personal value to others

Right-to-work law   A provision of the Taft-Hartley Act that allows states to prohibit both the closed and the union shop contract agreements, thereby giving the worker the choice of union membership

Role ambiguity   Confusion that occurs when individuals are uncertain about what role they are to fill or what is expected of them

Roles   Differing parts that individuals play in their lives

Safety   Absence of or protection from hazards which could result in a direct injury

Safety and security needs   A level of Maslow's hierarchy of needs that reflects the desire for physical, economic, and emotional security, such as safe working conditions, job security, and periodic salary increases

Sanctions   Actions taken to force compliance with established norms

Scapegoating   A defense mechanism that relieves anxiety by blaming other persons or groups for problems

Scientific management theory   Approach begun by Taylor and enhanced by the Gilbreths that focuses on the work itself. It is part of the classical school of management.

Secondary groups   Groups made up of fellow workers or social acquaintances

Secondary needs   Needs that include security, affiliation or love, respect, and autonomy; developed as a result of an individual's values and beliefs

Sedatives   Depressants that can cause drowsiness, agitation, intellectual confusion, and impairment

Self-actualization needs   A level of Maslow's hierarchy that includes the need for personal growth, freedom of creative expression, and using one's abilities to the full extent

Self-disclosure   Revealing information to others about yourself

Self-esteem   Feelings about yourself that can be high or low

Self-managing teams   Groups of 5 to 15 employees who produce an entire product in a truly entrepreneurial sense

Self-talk   Making positive statements to ourselves

Semantics   the study of the meanings and the changing meanings of words

Sender   Person who transmits, or sends, the message

Service industries   Industries that create economic value without creating a tangible product, as opposed to manufacturing, agriculture, and other goods-producing industries

Sexual harassment   Unwelcome sexual advances, requests for sexual favors, or verbal or physical conduct of a sexual nature found in the workplace

Situational leadership   Leadership theory developed by Hersey that says leadership style must be adapted to the situation and the readiness of subordinates

Smoothing   Conflict resolution by playing down strong issues, concentrating on mutual interests, and seldom discussing negative issues

Social needs   A level of Maslow's hierarchy that centers around the desire for meaningful affiliation with others, such as love, affection, and acceptance

Social responsibility   Obligation we have to make choices or decisions that are beneficial to the whole of society; involves issues such as environmental pollution and welfare

Social Security Act   Federal legislation that mandates retirement, survivors', disability, and Medicare benefits

Sociology   Academic discipline that focuses on the interaction of two or more individuals and their relationships in group settings

Span of control   Number of people that an individual supervises

Special-purpose teams   Groups of worker and union representatives collaborating to improve quality and productivity

Statistical models   Mathematical models that assist managers with planning and controlling factors such as inventory, product mixes, and sales forecasts

Strategic planning   The systematic setting of organizational goals, defining strategies and policies to achieve them, and developing detailed plans to ensure that the strategies are implemented

Stress   The physical state of the body in response to environmental pressures that produce emotional discomfort

Strike   The majority of the union membership's refusal to work under the current conditions until some agreement can be reached toward the desired improvement

Sublimation   A defense mechanism by which an individual finds a socially acceptable way to act out feelings

Substance abuse   The misuse of alcohol, illegal drugs, and prescription drugs

Synergism   Interaction of two or more independent parts, the effects of which are greater than they would attain separately

Taft-Hartley Act   A series of amendments to the Wagner Act that imposes controls on unions' organizing activities and methods used in collective bargaining attempts

Task behavior   The extent to which a leader directs and supervises a task

Task group   A group formed for a specific reason with members drawn from various parts of an organization to accomplish a specific purpose

Team   A number of persons associated together in work or activity; representatives from a variety of different disciplines, departments, or different lines of business coming together to achieve common goals and objectives

Teambuilding   A series of activities designed to help work groups solve problems, accomplish work goals, and more effectively function through teamwork

Teamwork   The combined effort of several disciplines for maximum effectiveness in achieving common goals

Technical skills   Skills required to perform a particular task

Telecommuters   Term coined to describe people, frequently based at home, who use technology networks to send and receive work and information to and from different locations, locations (such as offices) to which they would once have needed to commute

Theory X and Y   Two sets of assumptions that leaders hold about followers, as outlined by Douglas McGregor: Theory X is a pessimistic view and Theory Y an optimistic view

Time management Using the time available to the greatest advantage

Title VII of the Civil Rights Act of 1964 Federal law that prohibits discrimination based on race, color, religion, sex, or national origin in the workplace. This law also prohibits sexual harassment.

Total person approach Human relations trend which takes into account needs and goals of the employee and acknowledges that a whole person, not just skills, is being hired

Tranquilizers Depressants that can cause drowsiness, agitation, intellectual confusion, and impairment

Transactional leadership Leadership in which leaders determine what followers need to achieve their own and organizational goals, classify those needs, and help followers gain confidence that they can reach their objectives

Transformational leadership Leadership that motivates followers to do more than they originally expected to do by raising the perceived value of the tasks, by getting them to transcend self-interest for the sake of the group goal, and by raising their need level to self-actualization

Treatment follow-up testing Drug testing used to monitor an employee's success in remaining drug free after being allowed to complete a substance abuse treatment program rather than be terminated

Triangle Situation in which a person having a problem with a third person places the responsibility for solving the problem on you

Two-way communication Communication in which feedback is received

Type A personalities Persons who tend to be highly competitive, aggressive, achievement-oriented, and impatient and typically appear pressured, hurried, and volatile

Type B personalities Persons who tend to be relaxed, easygoing, and even-paced in their approach to life

"Understanding strategy" Suggestion that once people know someone's preferences regarding business protocol, they will comply with them

Underachiever Individual who sets goals that are lower than abilities in order to protect himself from risk and anxiety

Unemployment compensation Benefits paid to those who have become unemployed involuntarily

Unilateral method A method of implementing organizational change that allows supervisors to dictate change with little or no input from the employees

Union A group or association of workers who collectively bargain with employers for improved working conditions and protection from unfair or arbitrary treatment by management

Union shop A method used by unions to assure union membership that required an employee to join the union within a specified time after being hired, usually within 60 to 90 days

Union steward A union official who represents union members' interests and protects their rights while on the job; acts as a go-between representing the union member to the company supervisor in settling disagreements

Upward communication Communication that begins in the lower levels of the organization and goes to higher levels

Upward management Process by which individuals manage their bosses

Values Principles, standards, or qualities considered worthwhile or desirable

Valuing diversity A trend which encourages the appreciation of employee differences and the value they add to the company

Verbal communication Any message sent or received through the use of words, oral or written

Verification Last stage of the creative process; testing, evaluating, revising, retesting, and reevaluating an idea

Virtual office Computer and information networks that link people in different ("remote") locations, so that they can interact and share work as if they were located in one office building

Visualization A thought process by which you view yourself as being successful

Voice mail System that extends a telephone's capabilities, receiving and storing incoming messages like an answering machine, but with the added options of responding to messages or transmitting messages to the voice mails of others

Vroom's expectancy theory A theory that views motivation as a process of choices and says people behave in certain ways based on their expectation of results

Wagner Act A federal law enacted in 1935 that ordered management to stop interfering with union organizing efforts and defined what constituted unfair labor practices; established the right of employees to form unions and collectively bargain with management on employment issues; established the National Labor Relations Board

Wellness program A total approach to employee health and well-being that addresses emotional and physical health

Whistleblowing Opposing decisions, policies, or practices within the organization if they are considered detrimental or illegal; can include publicizing such behavior outside the organization

Win-win situation The result when negotiation is handled in such a way that both sides of an issue feel they have won

Workaholics Persons who are consumed by their jobs and derive little pleasure from other activities

Workers' compensation Compensation to those who have been physically or mentally injured on the job

Yellow-dog contract Contract requiring would-be employees to sign a statement that they will not join a union

Index